*Plate I  1  White Attic lekythus*
*2  Red-figured lekythus*

GEDDES & GROSSET

# ANCIENT GREECE

## Myth & History

### H.B. Cotterill

First published 1913 by George Harrap & Company
Written by H.B. Cotterill
This edition revised and published 2004 by Geddes & Grosset,
David Dale House, New Lanark, ML11 9DJ, Scotland

This edition © 2004 Geddes & Grosset
Index compiled by and © Gerard M-F Hill, 2003

ISBN 1 84205 185 7

Printed and bound in Poland, OZGraf S.A.

# Cotterill's Preface

When the attempt is made in a book of this size to give a continuous account of the external history of Greece, and into this framework to fit a number of sketches descriptive of its art, literature, and philosophy, as well as other matters, it is of course necessary to omit many details and to rely on whatever skill one may happen to possess in selection and combination. In regard to antiquities and literature, I have drawn attention chiefly to what is extant and of general interest, and have trusted to description, illustration, and quotation rather than to disquisition and criticism. The Sections appended to each chapter treat subjects that are closely connected with the period covered by the chapter. Any of these Sections can be omitted without seriously interrupting continuity. Temples, Dress, Coins, and Vases have been relegated to Notes at the end of the volume, seeing that they are not specially connected with any one period.

The letters B.C. (but not A.D.) have been generally omitted, as unnecessary in a book on Ancient Greece.

To name in full all the books that one has to use in such work is unnecessary, but, since space did not always allow of exact reference on occasions when I annexed a fact or a sentiment, it is right that I should here acknowledge my obligations to the following modern writers: Baikie, Bérard, Bergk, Bernoulli, Buchholz, Burrows, Bury, Busolt, Butcher, Archer Butler, Chamberlain (*Grundlagen*), Christ, Dawkins, Deussen, Diehl, Donaldson, Dörpfeld, Dussaud, Sir A.J. Evans, Frazer (*Pausanias*), Furtwängler, E. Gardner, P. Gardner, Gomperz, Grote, Hall, Miss Harrison, Head, Hill, Hogarth, Holm, Hommel (*Chronology*), A. Lang, W. Leaf, Löwy, Mahaffy, Meltzer, Mover, Mosso, A.S. Murray, G. Murray, F.A. Paley, Petrie, Sir H. Rawlinson, Canon Rawlinson, Ridgeway, Ritter

5

and Preller, Schlegel, Schliemann, Schuchhardt, A.H. Smith, G. Smith, W. Smith, Tsountas, H.B. Walters, Wilamowitz, Wood (*Ephesus*), Zeller, Zimmermann.

Also, in regard to the illustrations, my thanks are due to Mr. Hasluck, of the British School in Athens, and (especially in regard to vases) to Professor H. Thiersch, of Freiburg, as well as to many others whose names are mentioned in the List. Some of the illustrations supplied by F. Bruckmann and Co. are from their fine series of *Greek and Roman Portraits*; others are from Bernoulli's *Griechische Ikonographie*. The autotypes of coins in Plates I–VI are reproductions which I was permitted by the courtesy of the Director of the British Museum to make from Mr. Head's official *Guide to the Coins of the Ancients*.

In quoting Herodotus I have, with the permission of Mr. John Murray, frequently made use of Canon Rawlinson's version, and in translating Thucydides I sometimes accepted the guidance of Dale. For the compilation of the index I am indebted to Mr. C.C. Wood.

H.B.C. Freiburg im Breisgau,
March 1913

# *Note to the Second Edition*

In this edition I have corrected misprints and other such inaccuracies and have made a few additions. As two reviewers have expressed their surprise that although Pythagoras and Plato are given a considerable number of pages, Aristotle is dismissed in a few lines, it seems advisable to point out again, what is plainly intimated on pp. 434 and 442, that the main subject of the book does not extend beyond the year 334, and that Aristotle, whose chief works were written after 335, is only mentioned in a slight forecast of a period which will be fully treated in another volume.

H.B.C. Viareggio,
September 1915

# Contents

# List of Illustrations

*In the following list the names of those to whom the author is indebted for permission to use copyright photographs, &c., are given in italic below the title of the subject.*

## Maps

## Plates

*Photo Mansell & Co.* The larger, a white Attic *lekythus* (funeral oil-vase) with polychrome painting of early, severe style (*c.* 460). The smaller, a red-figured *lekythus* of the earlier and still somewhat restrained 'beautiful style,' which afterwards became fanciful and fantastic; date *c.* 450. In British Museum.

*Photo Mansell & Co.* One has the polypus decoration; the other is an example of the characteristic Mycenaean false-necked amphora ('Bügel-kanne'). In the latter vessel the neck, to which the handles are attached, has no aperture. The spout is set in the shoulder of the vessel, and in the picture it stands in front of the 'false neck' and hides it. In British Museum.

III. An Attic Hydria of the Middle Black-figured Period (*c.* 550)     242
*Photo Mansell & Co.* Found at Vulci. Maidens fetching water from a fountain. Similar vases are inscribed with the names of the fountains Kallikrene or Kallirrhoë. This vase has the names of some of the maidens with the adjective *kalē* ('beautiful') appended, as frequently occurs in vase-paintings. On the lower part of the vase is depicted Heracles strangling the Nemean lion. In British Museum.

IV. A Late Black-figured Hydria (*c.* 510) from Vulci
*Photo Mansell & Co.* Harnessing chariot-horses. The driver in long white robe (*cf.* Fig. 74). Below, a boar-hunt. In British Museum.

V. An Apulian Funeral Amphora with Volute Handles
*Photo Mansell & Co.* Date *c.* 300. Scenes from the 'Sack of Troy' (*Iliou Persis*). Above, the death of Priam and of Hecuba; below, Ajax and Cassandra. In British Museum.

## Coin Plates

*Plates I–VI consist of reproductions from the British Museum 'Guide to the Coins of the Ancients.' Plate VII is from photographs by F. Bruckmann.*

## General Illustrations

*From the Rev. James Baikie's 'Sea Kings of Crete' (Messrs. A. & C. Black).* Since this photo was taken the site has been further excavated. See, for instance, Dr. W. Leaf's new book on Troy. There can be very little doubt that these are the actual walls from a tower of which Andromache (if Homer's story is true) saw Hector being dragged round the city behind the chariot of Achilles (*Il.* xxii. 460 *sq.*).

*Photo English Photographic Co.*

gems. Instead of the usual bull we find here large antelopes like African elands.

*From Dussaud's 'Civilisations préhelléniques' (Geuthner, Paris).* Perhaps represent transformations in masked ritual dance, or perhaps worn as charms against evil spirits.

*From Miss J.E. Harrison's 'Prolegomena' (Cambridge University Press).* Vase at Oxford. Like the Anodos of Kore, but here the maiden is Pandora (generally the Greek Eve, but here probably the 'All-giver,' Earth-goddess). Zeus, Hermes, and Epimetheus welcome her return. Compare the northern myth of Holda, the goddess of spring.

*Photo Maraghiannis.*

Top left jug and two small cups are of the exceedingly fine Kamáres ware; found in Kamáres cave, Mount Ida, Crete. Date *c.* 2000.

Two other jugs on left, one with sunflower and papyrus (?), the other with octopus, are later Minoan, *c.* 1500–1400. The former is in what is called 'Cnossus Palace style.'

Top right-hand jug, probably from an island tomb; date *c.* 2500. Black with incised lines filled with white substance.

Two-necked jug of 'Hissarlik' (Trojan) type. Date *c.* 1800.

Lowest to right: Mycenaean ware, but found in Cyprus. Date *c.* 1300.

*Photo Mansell & Co.* Two sides of same vase. Date about 850 or earlier. British Museum.

*Photo Mansell & Co.*

Upper row, three Dipylon vessels; ancient animal decoration (bird, two horses at manger) combined with the revived geometric and maeander style. See Note D. Date *c.* 800.

Lowest to left: 'Phaleron ware.' About fifty of such one-handled jugs discovered. Named after first, found on the road to Phaleron. Very different from preceding, and far more artistic. Oriental influence? Date *c.*700.

Samian two-handled jug, found in the cemetery Fikellura, Rhodes. Date *c.* 600.

Old Corinthian; easily recognized by rather heavy but finely balanced shape, colours (rich browns and yellows) and style of animals, with spaces filled with flowers, &c. Corinth was anciently a great emporium, especially for trade with the far West. Date, about Periander's age, *c.* 600.

*Photo Simiriottis, Athens.* See under Fig. 49 in this list.

*From Gardner's 'Handbook of Greek Sculpture' (Macmillan & Co. Ltd.).* One of the so-called 'Tanten' ('Aunts') excavated on the Athenian Acropolis.

*Photo Graphische Gesellschaft.*

*Photo Alinari.* In the Etruscan Museum, Florence. Perhaps the oldest inscribed Greek vase. Found by M. François at Chiusi (Clusium, the city of Lars Porsena, where great numbers of tombs, &c., have been discovered). It was in about fifty fragments, but was nearly complete. In 1900, however, an insane *employé* of the museum overthrew it, and while it lay shattered on the floor numerous shards were stolen, so that many important portions (as seen in the picture) are wanting. For questions of ancient Greek dress, weapons, chariots, vases, &c., it is invaluable. See Index and Note B. Many of the figures in the numerous scenes are named, and we learn the names of the painter and maker by the words *Klitias m'egrapsen Ergotimos m'epoiēsen,* 'Klitias painted me, Ergotimos made me'. Date perhaps about 650. Greek work imported into Etruria.

*From 'Aus dem klass. Süden,' by permission of Herr Ch. Coleman, Lübeck.*

*Photo Brogi.* To left a part of the 'Basilica.' Note the greater bulge (*entasis*) of the columns. See Note A.

*Photo Simiriottis, Athens.* See Note A.

*Photo Simiriottis, Athens.* Looking south. The rock of the ancient citadel Acrocorinth is some 1900 feet high. A village existed on the old site till 1858, when it was destroyed by an earthquake, and New Corinth was then founded on the sea-shore.

*Photo Frith.* They all represent Ramses II (*c.* 1300, the Pharaoh of Moses' youth). The Greek inscription is on the legs of the headless colossus. It is signed by 'Archon and Pelekos,' who had 'travelled with King Psamtik to Elephantiné, and as far as the river permits.' Date 594.

In middle: Attic amphora. Birth of Athene (springing from the head of Zeus).

Left lower: Ancient Corinthian crater (mixing bowl). Return of Hephaestus to Olympus, mounted on mule and accompanied by Dionysus and satyrs. A not infrequent comic subject.

From Daphnae, Egypt. Such water-jars (about thirty) only found at Daphnae (and perhaps Clazomenae). Decoration all of same type: above, Sphinxes; below, geese; in middle, procession of women. Black-figured style with white women's faces. Date *c.* 560 (age of Solon, Croesus, and Amasis).

*From Gardner's 'Handbook of Greek Sculpture' (Macmillan & Co. Ltd.).*
*Photo Mansell & Co.* Copy of the shield of the Pheidian Athene Parthenos, in British Museum. The figure that half covers its face with its arm is said to be that of Pericles, and the "bald-headed but vigorous" man on his right side to be Pheidias himself.
*Photo by Dr. Walter Leaf, Hellenic Society.*
*Photo English Photographic Co.*
*Photo Mansell & Co.* British Museum.
*Photo Alinari.*
*Photo Simiriottis, Athens.* See Note A.
*Photo Mansell & Co.*
Reconstructed by Karl Schwerzek, Ritter des kaiserl. Franz-Joseph Ordens. The work was specially favoured by the late Empress of Austria and the Imperial family. It is regarded as a very successful attempt, founded on a most careful study of all the remains. My thanks are due to the artist for kind permission to reproduce the pictures of his models given in his *Erläuterungen*, published by himself in Vienna.
*Photo R. Tamme, Dresden; reproduced by permission of the Director of the Albertinum.* A very fine head at Bologna was found by Professor Furtwängler to fit exactly a headless Athene at Dresden, which evidently belonged to the Pheidian school of sculpture. Our picture represents this body furnished with a cast of the Bologna head, and according to Professor Furtwängler, whose authority few would care to question, we have in the complete statue a fine copy of the celebrated Lemnian Athene of Pheidias. Another similar, but much mutilated, statue in the Dresden Museum has been restored on the same lines. The face of the Lemnia is cited by Lucian in a famous passage (*Imag.* vi.) as of ideal beauty and nobility, and Himerius says, probably in reference to this statue, that

19

Pheidias sometimes 'decked the virgin goddess with a blush instead of a helmet.'

88. Probable Copy of Myron's Athene                                                    336

*Photo supplied and permission for reproduction given by Dr. Swarzenski, Director of the Städtische Gallerie, Frankfurt-a.-M.* The rather repellent Marsyas of Myron is well known from a coin, a painted and a sculptured vase, and from the statue in the Lateran Museum and a small bronze in the British Museum. The Marsyas belonged to a group in which Athene, who had invented flutes and had cast them away (because they disfigured her face when she played), was represented looking disdainfully at the satyr, who 'while advancing to pick up the discarded flutes is suddenly confronted by the goddess' and starts back in dismay. The Athene was supposed to be hopelessly lost; but about 1882 this statue of Parian marble was dug up in Rome, and after lying for twenty years in a shed was recognized as probably the lost Myron, and transferred by some rich German Hellenists to the Frankfurt Gallery. It is a beautiful statue, and, if it is Myron's, must give us an idea of him as artist very different from what we gain from the Marsyas or the *Discobolos*.

Three possible Copies of the Pheidian Athene:

89. Head of a Statue in Rome                                                           340

*From Professor E. Löwy's 'Griechische Plastik' (Klinkhardt and Biermann, Leipzig).* By Antiochos, a sculptor otherwise unknown. Museo Nazionale delle Terme. The dress and helm are not like those of the Athene Parthenos, but the face is believed to be the best extant copy of that of the Pheidian goddess, and is very much the finest of the three here given.

90. A Statuette found at Athens, near the Varvakeion                                   340

*Photo English Photographic Co.* Supposed by some to be a model, by a Roman artist, of the Pheidian Athene. But it is quite incredible that it should be an exact representation. The general pose may be reproduced (as it is also in another half-finished statuette found by M. Lenormant near the Pnyx), but it is impossible to accept the face, or the exceedingly ugly device of the column supporting the right hand – though it may have been added to the original statue at some later time to prevent collapse.

91. A Red Jasper Intaglio inscribed with the name Aspasios                             340

*From Brunn-Bruckmann's 'Denkmäler der griech, und röm. Sculptur.'* At Vienna. Evidently a copy of the Pheidian Athene.

92. The 'Meidias Vase'                                                                 351

*Photo Mansell & Co.* Hydria signed with name 'Meidias.' Winckelmann esteemed it "above all others known to him" for beauty of drawing. Date *c.* 430, but, though rich, still very pure and unaffected by the 'fine style.' Below, Heracles in the Garden of the Hesperides; above, the Leucippidae carried off by Castor and Pollux.

# *Introduction*

'The battle of Marathon, even as an event in English history, is more important than the battle of Hastings. If the issue that day had been different, the Britons and the Saxons might still have been wandering in the woods.'

When John Stuart Mill wrote these words in the mid-nineteenth century he was expressing a view with which many of his contemporaries would have agreed. As they saw it, the victory of the Greeks over the Persians on that day was what ultimately enabled the Western world to breathe the air of freedom that was essentially the same as that of fifth-century Athens. It is no coincidence that it was in the years following parliamentary reform in Britain that the study of Greek history took wing, most famously with George Grote's twelve-volume narrative history. Grote gave up his seat in parliament, where he had campaigned for electoral reform, the abolition of slavery in the British Empire, and other issues on the 'philosophical radical' agenda, to concentrate on his hugely influential *magnum opus*.

When H.B. Cotterill came to write this single-volume history of Greece some six decades later, he had a solid tradition of scholarship to draw on, and also a rather different perspective from that of his Victorian predecessors who saw Athenian democracy as Greece's crowning glory. Cotterill was concerned to portray the 'inner life' of ancient Greece – the spirit that gave us the scientific and critical histories of Herodotus and Thucydides, the unblinking and sometimes frightening insights into the human condition of the Greek tragic playwrights, the mature and dignified works of the sculptors and architects of classical Greece. The 'external history', through which he leads the reader in confident and masterly style, is the framework in which we are to place and understand these inspirational works of Western culture.

Cotterill's enthusiasm for his subject and his skill as an educator – he had taught at Haileybury and Harrow – make him an ideal guide. His particular admiration for certain aspects of Greek culture – classical art, Herodotus, Socrates, for example – infuse these subjects with fresh life. On the other hand, he is not an uncritical admirer of everything in this world, and he does not gloss over the 'cold-blooded inhumanity' with which Athens, the so-called educator of Greece, was capable of treating fellow-Greeks. In 1913, the year of the book's first publication, blood was again being spilled on Greek soil in the Balkan Wars. From the vantage point of 1913, the ferocious fighting of ancient Greek wars did not seem so very unique or impressive, but the futility and human cost appeared no less horrible, and the immediacy and horror of these ancient conflicts still strikes the reader of Cotterill's text.

Cotterill was of course writing at a time when the great discoveries of archaeology and the finds of papyrus texts and inscriptions promised to open up a series of fresh and exciting perspectives on Greek history and culture. Most of the really significant finds had been made, but their evaluation and – in the case of papyri and inscriptions – publication were to continue throughout the twentieth century and into the twenty-first. Cotterill's very proper caution in the face of newly emerging evidence and his insistence on placing that evidence clearly before his readers without indulging in unnecessary theorizing and speculation make his early chapters still highly readable and informative.

Henry Bernard Cotterill was a well-travelled man and a connoisseur of the art and literature of several nations besides Greece. While a young man he joined an expedition to Africa to work against the slave trade in the tradition begun by David Livingstone. He had been presented by the boys and masters of Harrow with a large steel boat, and he had it carried in sections overland and launched it on Lake Nyasa. He navigated the lake and explored the slave routes, and he and his companions were the first white men to explore the country between Nyasa and Zanzibar. On his return to Europe, he taught in Germany for a while. He published editions and translations of various works of German and Italian classical literature, and also wrote on medieval Italy and art history.

In 1915, at the time of the publication of the second edition of this book, new advertisements appeared on the sides of London buses, carrying quotations from the funeral oration Pericles had spoken in 431 B.C. over the bodies of those who had fallen in the first year of the Peloponnesian War. The exhortation to the Athenians to stand firm against Sparta apparently needed no scholarly commentary for the population of London, after their country's first year of a war with Germany that looked as though it would be a long and bloody conflict. To that generation the identification of their freedom-loving, sea-trading nation with fifth-century Athens came naturally. It is a mark of the lasting value of Cotterill's work that he refuses to idealize the Athenian political system but takes a clear-sighted view of its virtues and flaws. His presentation of the enduring achievements of Greek art, literature and philosophy in their historical context will enthuse and inform a new generation.

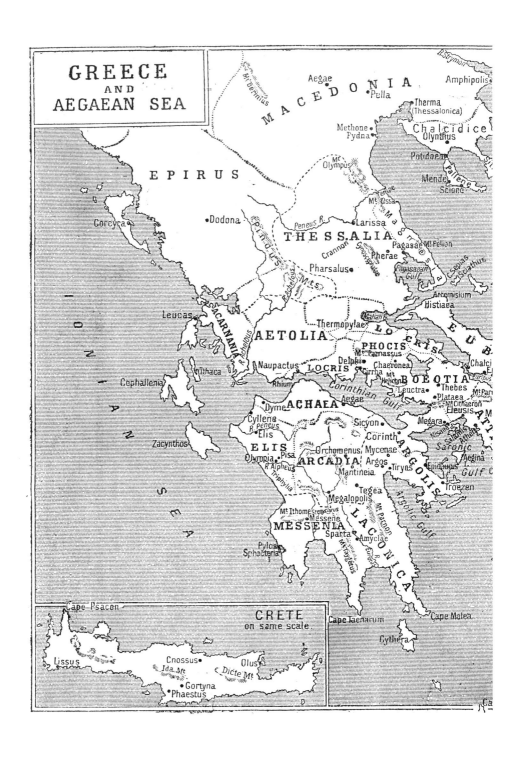

GREECE
AND
AEGAEAN SEA

English Miles

0  10  20  30  40  50  60

# Chapter 1

# The Aegean Civilization: the Achaean Supremacy (down to c. 1100)

SECTIONS – A: LANGUAGE AND WRITING – B: THE OLD RELIGION –
C: THE 'HOMERIC AGE' AND HOMER – D: CHRONOLOGY OF AEGEAN
AND OTHER CONTEMPORARY CIVILIZATIONS

Until the latter part of the nineteenth century the history of Greece (such history as is founded on the evidence of contemporary inscriptions and similar relics) was held to begin about the traditional date of the first Olympiad – namely, 776. It is true that for some two thousand years a chronology of the 'prehistoric' or 'mythical' age of Greece was accepted with more or less diffidence, and has been handed down to our times. This chronology, based on the calculations of ancient writers[1] and drawn up finally (c. 220) by the keeper of the great Alexandrian library, Eratosthenes, takes us back to the foundation of Thebes by Cadmus in 1313, a date of modest pretensions compared with those given by some old writers, who by calculating the generations of ancient dynasties and hero-families lead us back beyond Deucalion, the Greek Noah and father of all Hellenes, to Pelasgus, the ancestor of all Pelasgians, and his ancestor Inachus, the first king of Argos, who is said to have lived about 1986.

All this chronology and all the traditions of the so-called mythical age were rejected as of no historical value by almost every nineteenth-century

---

[1] See Hdt. vii. 204, where, according to the accepted genealogy of the Spartan kings, Leonidas is shown to have been the twenty-first from Heracles, whose traditional date is 1261–1209. *Cf.* Hdt. viii. 131. Some assert that Eratosthenes went back only to the Fall of Troy (1184). Thucydides fixes the Dorian invasion (return of Heracleidae) at eighty years after the Fall of Troy. Some of these dates come curiously near to those accepted by modern archaeology.

31

writer on Greece – as valueless as the legends of Brute the Trojan and the Cornish giants and early kings of Britain, which Geoffrey of Monmouth gives as serious history, and which even Milton in his history of England is half inclined to accept on the ground that 'never any to have been real persons, or done in their lives at least some part of what so long hath been remember'd, cannot be thought without too strict an incredulity.'

That in this 'mythical age' of Greece, long before the Fall of Troy, great wars had been waged[1] and great empires had existed was not denied; but even such statements as those of Thucydides and Herodotus about the sea-empire of Minos the Cretan were relegated to the realm of fable – the realm of demigods and monsters.

Nor was it denied that from certain points of view fables and traditions are of supreme interest and value. Plato himself pointed out[2] the great ethical value of poetic fiction and the uselessness and folly of attempting to unweave the rainbows of old fables – of decomposing them into allegories or sun-myths; and in this he was followed by perhaps the greatest nineteenth-century historian of Greece, Grote, who devoted the first of his twelve volumes almost entirely to the consideration of the Greek myths as wonderful products of Greek imagination, and carefully weighed their influence on the Greek mind and on the course of Greek history.

But Grote also agreed with Plato in believing it to be useless and foolish to analyse these ancient myths for the purpose of discovering any deposit of historical fact. 'The hope,' he says, 'that we may, by carrying our researches up the stream of time, exhaust the limits of fiction and land ultimately upon some points of solid truth appears to me no less illusory than the northward journey in quest of the Hyperborean Elysium' – the Earthly Paradise of the ancients, the Land beyond the North Wind.

In the later nineteenth century this point of view was gradually abandoned, even by the most sceptical. However disdainfully historians still spoke of such 'fables' as those of Pelops and Lycurgus (whom, borrowing a phrase from Herodotus, they describe as 'not men, but only gods'), none ventured to deny that there were 'points of solid truth' in legends that indicated the former existence of a great ancient Mycenaean civilization, or a

---

[1] *Vixere fortes ante Agamemnona Multi. . . .*('Many brave men lived before Agamemenon')
– Horace.

[2] In the *Phaedrus*.

still greater and more ancient civilization in Crete; for there had emerged indisputable evidence that such civilizations existed, and that in many an old legend there was at least a germ of truth.

And so I propose to relate, or mention, those myths which appear to have some connection with historical facts, or with such reconstructions as may be reasonably built up on the relics of prehistoric times.

The first part of my subject is the so-called Aegean civilization, which was brought to light in the 1870s and 1880s. Enough was discovered by excavation and research to assure us that a once undreamt-of civilization of very considerable importance did actually exist in Aegean lands long before the first Olympiad, or the invasion of the Dorians, or even the first coming of those Achaeans by whom Troy is said to have been sacked – a civilization which in all probability was already in existence at a period as far anterior to the age of Pericles as that age is anterior to our own.

At what stage in the history of humanity the first wave of Indo-Iranian migration reached Central Europe we have no means of knowing, but it is indubitable that the people whom we call the ancient Greeks, and who called themselves Hellenes, were mainly[1] of this Indo-Germanic race, and that when their northern ancestors first pushed southward into Greece they found there a race of quite a different kind – a dark-haired, lithe-limbed race, which in that age under various names seems to have inhabited most of the European lands bordering on the Mediterranean. The Northmen probably came in small bands at first, and, like the Normans of later days in Southern Europe, established themselves as chieftains among the less warlike Southerners. In time they would be followed by successive waves of invaders, many of whom would settle in the country, appropriate the land and the women and enslave the men, or drive them forth to take refuge in more barren or mountainous districts, such as Attica and Arcadia.[2]

---

[1] This is perhaps too strong. Possibly the intermixture of the northern (Achaean and Dorian) invaders with the aborigines was in time somewhat such as that of the Normans with the Anglo-Saxon and Celtic population in Britain, and the strangely rapid development and perfection of classical Greek art may have been due to the revival of art-feeling that had existed in the race before the advent of the northern invaders, just as the supremacy of Tuscan art in the fourteenth and fifteenth centuries was possibly due to the old Etruscan element.

[2] In this connection the celebrated opening chapters of Thucydides' history should be read. The discoveries of archaeology have added greatly to their interest.

Now the evidence supplied by excavation and research points to the fact that in Greece, at a period not much anterior to the age of the fair-haired Achaean princes described by Homer, this dark-haired, lithe-limbed Mediterranean race was still in possession; and similar evidence makes it clear that in Crete a people probably belonging to the same race, and of a like civilization, existed from a very early time, and possessed a powerful empire until the advent of the northern conquerors. It is this so-called Minoan and Mycenaean civilization which archaeology has revealed to us.

## The Trojan Cities

In the year 1870 the first beginning was made, by Dr. Schliemann, of the excavations that led to this result. Long before that date the ancient history of Egypt and of Mesopotamia had been to a large extent reconstructed by the discoveries of monuments and the deciphering of hieroglyphic and cuneiform inscriptions, but of the first ages of Greece what few relics were known, such as old 'Pelasgic' walls and a few ancient sepulchres and remnants of primeval pottery, were regarded with hopeless wonderment as the survivals of a civilization which had passed away into eternal oblivion. Much incredulity and some ridicule met the enthusiasm of Dr. Schliemann, therefore, when he announced his intention first to excavate ancient Troy and then to discover the tomb of Agamemnon (described by Pausanias) at Mycenae. The site of Homeric Troy he believed, in spite of the contrary opinion of scholars, to be that of the later Roman city Novum Ilium, now the Hill of Hissarlik. On this site he and his successors discovered the remains of no less than seven – possibly nine – towns. Traces of the rough-stone walls of the earliest of these towns are still visible, and within them were discovered fragments of primitive black pottery and stone implements – among which is an axe-head of white jade (nephrite), a stone said to be found in its natural state only in China. The second town had great ramparts with towers and a fortified gate, all of sun-baked brick, with a paved ramp and stone foundations. The relics were pottery (still hand-made) and stone and copper implements. Bronze seems to have been still rare, but near to the great gate, within a kind of acropolis, was discovered a very considerable treasure of gold and silver vessels and ornaments, together with copper weapons and a hideous leaden idol of some ancient female deity. The great ramparts and the wealth and art evidenced by these finely wrought gold and silver ornaments made Schliemann conclude that this was the Homeric city, and that he had discovered the Treasure of King Priam. But, almost incredible as it seemed before the discoveries of similar treasures and other works of art in Crete and at Mycenae, it is now believed that this *second* city of Troy existed at least a thousand years before the days of Priam and Agamemnon, and that the ruins of the *sixth* stratum are in all probability those of the Homeric city. These ruins consist of great and well-built walls of wrought stone (Fig. 1), far better built than so-called 'Pelasgic' walls, and enclosing a very considerable area, with remains of a high-terraced acropolis, on the summit of which was doubtless, as at Mycenae and Tiryns, the regal palace. Of the four city gates the two greatest, those to the south and the east, were guarded by strong towers, and one of these might be the famous 'Scaean Gate' of the *Iliad* except for the fact that Homer's 'Scaean Gate' seems to have looked towards the Grecian camp and the sea – evidently to the northwest, in which part the old walls were demolished (50 B.C.) in order to fortify Sigeion (Sigeum).

In this sixth city bronze[1] weapons were found, and many fragments of what is called 'Mycenaean' pottery – a glazed and painted wheel-made ware which denotes the later period of Mycenaean civilization (*c.* 1400–1200), and which has been found not only in Aegean lands, but in Spain, Italy, Egypt, Cyprus, and Asia Minor. From these and other evidences it seems highly probable that Homeric Troy was built at the time when (*c.* 1350) the northern Achaean race was still pouring down through Thessaly into Lower Greece; that the builders were a northern Indo-Iranian (Danubian) people related to the fair-haired Achaeans, namely, the Bhryges, or Phrygians; and that this sixth city[2] was afterwards burnt by foreign enemies, whom we may most reasonably suppose to have been the Achaean princes of Greece and their followers (a mixed host of Achaeans, Argives, and Aegeans) described by Homer.

The Bhryges, or Phrygians, were apparently a tribe of the same great Indo-Iranian race (originally from Northern India, but long inhabiting Central Europe) to which the Mysians and perhaps also the Lydians and

---

[1] But only one specimen of *iron* – a knife, which Schliemann believed to have slipped down from a higher stratum.

[2] Possibly also the fifth, for tradition tells us of a former sack of Troy by Telamon and Heracles.

*Fig. 1  Wall of the sixth city of Troy*

Lycians and other peoples of Asia Minor belonged,[1] as well as the Achaeans of Greece. They seem to have come over from Thrace in successive waves during several centuries. The second city of Troy was probably founded by earlier Phrygian or northern invaders, and it was possibly to later invasions of the same northern race that the destruction and refounding of the third, fourth, and fifth cities were due, on which occasions the earlier comers (Lycians and others) were driven further south. Or possibly these Indo-Iranian invaders for several centuries, before they made themselves masters of these north-western parts of Asia Minor, had been obliged to fight for existence against the older inhabitants. Who these older inhabitants were is not known for certain, but it is believed that in this age the great Empire of the Biblical Hittites, whose chief city was Carchemish, extended over much of Asia Minor. This seems proved by numerous inscriptions in Hittite script, a syllabic writing, deciphered in 1915 and found to be Indo-European.[2] Tablets, too, have been found with correspondence, in official Babylonian script, between the Hittite kings and subject states, and a treaty, in cuneiform script but Hittite language, between the Hittite king Chetasor and Ramses II of Egypt.

We hear also of a great nation of Cappadocians (possibly different from the Hittites), whose chief city was Pteria. These nations blocked the western expansion of Babylon and Assyria, and of eastern art and cuneiform writing.

The Homeric Trojans were evidently a mixed people composed of northern and aboriginal elements (Queen Hecabe, for instance, was a Phrygian), speaking a language closely akin to that of the Achaeans, and worshipping similar northern deities.[3] The chivalrous respect with which, in Homer's poem, the Achaean princes regard their foes doubtless existed in reality between the northern conquerors on both sides of the Aegean, and, in spite of all arguments about pure Achaean blood and fair hair (which the Phrygian chieftains may also have had), we can feel assured that the

---

[1] The original inhabitants of Lydia may have been non-Indo-Iranian, but they were conquered by and amalgamated with the Phrygians. These mixed peoples are called *Maeonians* (*Mēiones*) by Homer, who does not mention Lydians. The Lycians I believe to have been of Indo-Iranian stock, but not the Carians, whom Homer describes as 'speaking a strange tongue.' The Pamphylians are believed to have belonged to the later Dorian race of invaders, of whom three tribes are often mentioned: Hylleis, Pamphyli, Dymanes.

[2] See Section A, 'Writing.'

[3] See Section B, 'The Old Religion.'

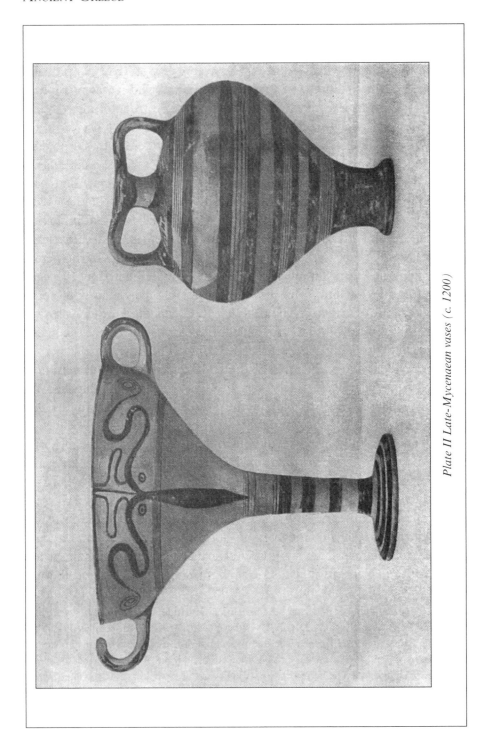

*Plate II Late-Mycenaean vases (c. 1200)*

traditions that make Pelops, the son of the Phrygian king Tantalus, give his name to the Peloponnese and found the royal house of the Pelopidae, to which Agamemnon and Menelaus belonged, as well as the traditions (repeated by the sane-minded Thucydides) which derived the great wealth of 'golden Mycenae' from Phrygian mines and the gold-sands of the Pactolus, have some historical basis.

That the founder of a royal Peloponnesian dynasty came from Phrygia, as tradition avers, we have no good reason to doubt, but the question is, I think, whether this was not long *before* the advent of the Achaeans in the Peloponnese or the Phrygians in Asia Minor. If it were so, then the older Pelopid monarchs of Pisa, Mycenae, and Sparta may well have been of Aegean or even Hittite race, and have ruled over an aboriginal Aegean population, and the tombs of which we shall soon hear may be those of these older monarchs, into whose family the Achaeans may have married when they conquered the land.

Schliemann had proved conclusively that a great Trojan city had existed, and that it had been burnt about the time of the traditional date of the Fall of Troy (1184). He had shown that there is a very solid historical basis in Homer's great poem; and further research has enabled us to reconstruct and repeople this Homeric age. But excavation was to open up vistas into far more distant ages.

## Mycenae

Dr. Schliemann had announced his intention of discovering the tomb of Agamemnon at Mycenae; and if he did not find, as he firmly believed he had done, the tomb and the very body of the great Achaean king, he found something perhaps still more wonderful.

Homer's 'golden, wide-wayed Mycenae,' the home of Agamemnon, was evidently one of the principal cities of Achaean Greece, larger than Argos, Tiryns, Corinth, or Sparta. In later days its importance declined so much that it could supply only eighty men for Thermopylae and two hundred for Plataea. Soon afterwards (462) it was destroyed by the Argives and the inhabitants were expelled, and the ingenuity of Thucydides finds some difficulty in explaining away the apparent insignificance of its ruins.

Some of these ruins were the massive ramparts and the well-known Lion Gate, which still exist; and it was within these walls of the ancient Mycenaean acropolis that the Greek traveller and writer Pausanias (to whose descriptions we owe much of our knowledge of Greek antiquities) saw the tombs, or what were then (*c.* A.D. 160) believed to be the tombs, of Atreus and Agamemnon. 'Some remnants of the encircling wall,' says Pausanias, 'are still visible, and also a gate which has lions over it. These, as they say, were built by the Cyclopes. . . . There is the tomb of Atreus and of the men whom Aegisthus slew at the banquet when they returned from Troy . . . and the tomb of Agamemnon. But Clytaemnestra and Aegisthus were buried a short distance outside the walls, for they were deemed unworthy to lie within, where Agamemnon was interred and those who fell with him.'

Trusting in this description, Dr. Schliemann, in 1876, sank a pit, some 40 yards square, within the walls of the acropolis, not far from the Lion Gate. He first came upon stone slabs, vertical and horizontal, forming what he thought to be the seats of an *agora* (place of council). Below these he found an altar and some tombstones (stelae), and under these again, some 25 feet below the surface, six square tombs hewn vertically in the solid rock. These had originally been covered with great slabs of stone. The slabs had given way, and the tombs (which are from 10 to 15 feet deep and of various sizes) were filled with earth and stones, amidst which lay embedded no less than seventeen human bodies. On excavating these tombs a great amount of treasure was discovered – rings and sword-hilts and bracelets and pins and brooches and necklaces and hundreds of other ornaments, all of pure gold, more than seven hundred golden plaques (probably once attached to the women's dresses), diadems of gold on the heads of the women and masks of gold covering the faces of some of the men, besides many other costly objects, in silver, bronze, amber, and ivory. 'Au seul point de vue de la valeur vénale,' says Diehl, 'les bijoux représentent plus de 100,000 francs d'or; au point de vue artistique et scientifique, leur prix est inestimable.' It was scarcely strange that Dr. Schliemann in his hour of triumph dispatched a telegram to the King of Greece announcing that he had discovered the tombs that Pausanias describes, and probably the tombs of those Achaean princes of 'golden Mycenae' of whom Homer sang. But are these the tombs which Pausanias saw? And are they the tombs of the Achaean princes? Before venturing to answer this question let us hear more.

Besides the six shaft-graves on the acropolis there exist (partly known before excavation by Schliemann and others) nine great vaulted sepulchres, of which the so-called Treasury of Atreus is the largest. It is a lofty

Fig. 2  The Lion Gate, Mycenae    Fig. 4  Men worshipping a snake    Fig. 3  Amenhotep III

41

'beehive' chamber, about 50 feet high, sunk into the side of a hill, and approached by a deep passage about 40 yards in length. The façade was once richly decorated. The portal, which has a lintel nearly 30 feet long and weighing some 120 tons, was flanked by alabaster columns with zigzag and spiral ornament.[1] Above the lintel was a large triangle of red porphyry, the architectural device being evidently copied from the Lion Gate. In these great sepulchres no treasure was found. They had been plundered and stripped even of their bronze decorations. Nor were any bodies discovered. But what few evidences came to light made it clear that these tombs were of a later age than the shaft-tombs of the acropolis.

Some less pretentious square tombs with slanting roofs were also discovered cut out of the rock on a lower level – probably the site of the town of Mycenae; and the remains of a palace, probably of the Achaean age, were found on the summit of the hill.

Now let us, with the aid of our illustrations, consider towards what conclusion the evidence points. I believe it will be found to point towards this conclusion: that the shaft-graves of the acropolis are the tombs of princes (possibly Pelopidae) who ruled over an 'Aegean' people before the advent of the Achaean invaders. And I believe that the great vaulted sepulchres of later date are most probably the tombs of the Achaean princes,[2] and that the palace was built by them.

(1) Firstly, the human remains were skulls and bones 'on which were remnants of flesh and skin.' They had evidently not been burnt. (Ashes were found, but probably these were the ashes of sacrificed victims – possibly also human.) Now the Achaeans, if we are to believe Homer, burnt their dead, sometimes burying the ashes under a great mound. Embalming or 'drying' a body is once mentioned, but the slain Homeric heroes (Achilles, Hector, Patroclus, Elpenor) are all burnt on a funeral pyre, and the graphic account of the process given by the ghost of

---

[1] Portions of these columns are in the British Museum. Another similar tomb, and nearly as large, is known as the Tomb of Clytaemnestra. It was mostly excavated by Mrs. Schliemann. In order to avoid perplexing the reader with details I do not describe the further excavations at Tiryns, Orchomenus, and other places, where interesting evidences of the Aegean civilization were found, but nothing at all comparable with the tombs of Mycenae.

[2] This is of course inconsistent with the assertion of Pausanias given above. He *may* have seen the acropolis tombs, but it is very remarkable that if they were known in his day they should have remained unrifled.

Odysseus' mother (*Od.* xi.) surely shows that burning was customary among the Achaeans.[1]

(2) Secondly, the dress and arms of the portrayed Mycenaean warriors are not at all what one associates with the Homeric Achaeans. In a siege-scene depicted on a fragment of a silver vessel (Fig. 5) most of the defenders of the fort are armed with slings and bows, and are stark naked, while two in the rear rank are enveloped in great hide (or bark?) shields, apparently suspended by a baldrick of thongs or cords, for the men are not holding them. Such shields are found, often in a figure-of-eight form, on other Aegean (Mycenaean and Cretan) gems and seals. This great man-covering, ox-hide shield ('as great as a tower') is, indeed, not unknown to Homer, but as a rule the Homeric shield seems to have been circular and smaller and carried by a handle,[2] and the armour (helm, greaves, and breastplate) of the Homeric warriors was of bronze. Now the warriors on the Mycenaean 'Warrior Vase' (Fig. 8) do certainly seem to carry a round, or rather a crescent-shaped, light shield, with perhaps a rim (*antyx*) of metal, but the rest of their equipment is surely not Homeric. Allowance may be made for the artlessness of the painter, but surely these fighters are not the well-greaved, bronze-clad and bronze-helmed Achaeans.

On an old painted tombstone found in the lower town of Mycenae there is depicted underneath a row of warriors a row of horses. Moreover, on old Aegean pottery (see Fig. 33) and in paintings found at Tiryns and on gems one finds horses, and also warriors in primitive two-horsed chariots with wicker breastwork. Does this, it may be asked, point to an age after the Achaean invasion? I think not. It is evident that the horse was introduced into Greece before the coming of the Achaeans, and probably the ancient myths that describe the wars between Thessalian Lapithae and the Centaurs are a reminiscence of a very early appearance of horsemen from

---

[1] Burial and burning often existed side by side, as was certainly the case in the 'classical' age of Greece. A curious inconsistency occurs to me. The skeleton of the Achaean Orestes, Herodotus tells us (i. 68), was found at Tegea in a coffin over ten feet long; but Sophocles brings on to the stage, in the *Electra*, the (supposed) ashes of Orestes enclosed in an urn. The supposed bones of Theseus, who belonged to the Aegean age, were found by Cimon in Scyros, whence they were transported to Athens.

[2] This is a point much disputed. Some argue from the apparent inconsistencies that the *Iliad* is a poem of mixed authorship and diverse ages. The small shield was invented by the Carians, according to Herodotus (i. 171). The huge shield of Ajax in Homer has seven layers of ox-hide, and must have been of enormous weight.

Fig. 6 Cretan statue

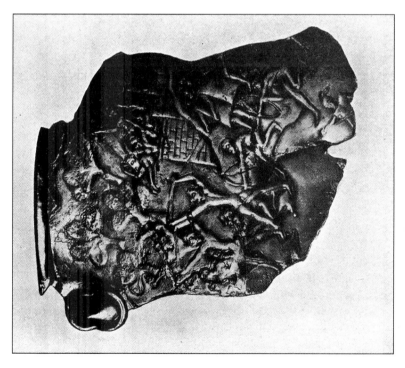

Fig. 5 Siege scene on fragment of silver vase, Mycenae

*Fig. 7  Scene from a Mycenaean gold ring*

the north. The myth of Pegasus, too (connected with Perseus and the Medusa), presupposes a knowledge of the horse.

[It may be remarked in passing that the horse is said not to be found in early Egyptian art. Possibly it was introduced by the Shepherd Kings, about 1800. It is first mentioned in the Bible in connection with Joseph and Jacob, who died in Egypt (see Gen. xlvii. 17 and l. 9). Joseph's chariot is also mentioned in Gen. xlvi. 29. Joseph probably lived under the last of the Shepherd Kings. Abraham, who visited Egypt about the year 2000, was given sheep and asses and camels by Pharaoh, but no horses are mentioned.]

But to return to the subject of Mycenaean dress. In the 'siege-scene' there are women standing on the very solidly and regularly built rampart. They seem to be applauding their defenders and deriding the foe. Their dress is not easy to discern; but on the gold ring (Figs. 7 and 28) one sees distinctly what the dress of the Mycenaean ladies of this age was like. It apparently very much resembled that of fashionable ladies of the early twentieth century, except that the whole bust seems to have been often uncovered.

Now in Homer the dress of the women is entirely different. Instead of rich-embroidered jackets or blouses (very *décolletées* sometimes, or conspicuous for their absence) and heavily flounced skirts and lofty coiffures of hair, the Achaean ladies wore a thin[1] *chitōn* (tunic, chemise) and an ample over-garment (*peplos* or *pharos*) of lighter or thicker stuff, according to the season, confined round the waist by a zone, and fastened over the shoulders and down the side by brooches. (The *peplos* given to Penelope by a suitor had twelve of such brooches; and it is remarkable that scarcely one has been found among all the Mycenaean treasures.) Over the head they wore a coif of soft, glistening tissue (*Od.* i. 354), and above this sometimes a large veil (*Od.* v. 232). The men, moreover, when not in armour were not content with the bathing-drawers sort of garment which we often find as the only article of dress in Aegean portraiture, but even such people as swineherds wore the tunic (*chitōn*) and a mantle or cloak (*chlaina, pharos*). The tunic was fastened round the waist by a belt (*zōstēr*). Thus the dress, both of men and of women, of these Mycenaeans, as far as we can judge from the evidence supplied by excavation, was very different from that of the Homeric Achaeans.

(3) The remains of various palaces and other buildings discovered at Mycenae, Tiryns, and other places where the relics (such as pottery) make us suspect a similar 'Mycenaean' civilization are in some respects like the Homeric palaces, and a decorative material mentioned by Homer (*cyan*, or blue glass-paste) has been found. These buildings, however, are possibly not Aegean, but Achaean.

(4) Among the weapons discovered at Mycenae are two daggers (Figs. 10 and 11) the blades of which are most skilfully inlaid with gold and silver and a dark substance on a ground of enamelled bronze. It is true that we find something similar in Homer, whose 'Shield of Achilles' and 'Brooch of Odysseus' and 'Belt of Heracles,' as well as his descriptions of the process of inlaying, testify to high skill in the art. But here again we have the loin-cloths and the figure-of-eight shield (in the lion-hunt), and a scene which reminds one much more of Egypt or Crete than of Homer, namely, a representation of cats, or ichneumons, hunting ducks amidst the papyrus on the banks of a river that may be meant for the Nile. There was discovered at Thebes in Egypt a very similar wall-painting; but the art of the Mycenae dagger is distinctly not Egyptian: it is evidently native work, and is a striking evidence of the high development which the art of the metal-worker had already reached among the pre-Achaean Greeks.

---

[1] Even the *chitōn* of Odysseus was as soft and glossy as the inner skin of an onion. See Note B, 'Dress.'

*Fig. 8 The 'warrior vase'*

*Fig. 9 Golden mask from Mycenae*

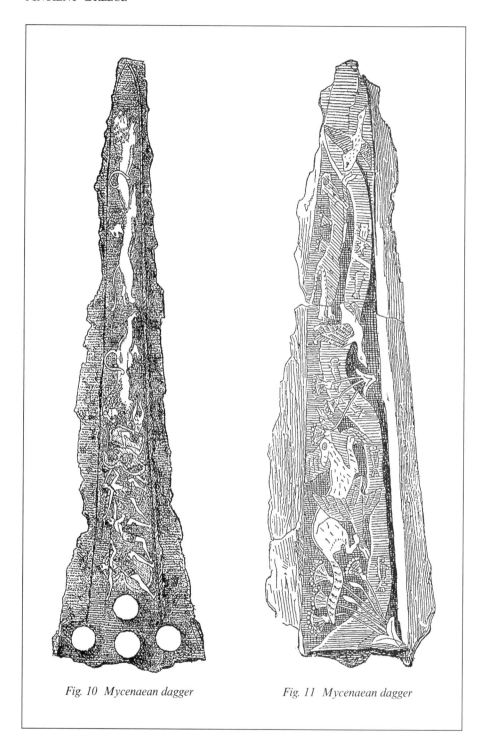

Fig. 10 Mycenaean dagger          Fig. 11 Mycenaean dagger

(5) But still more striking as works of art are two golden cups (Fig. 13) which were found, not at Mycenae, but at Vaphio,[1] near the ancient capital of Laconia, Amyclae. The skill, both in design and execution, with which the scene (perhaps the capture of wild bulls) is wrought is astonishing. 'We see here, as in the Mycenae daggers, the highest attainments of a mature art, not the promising attempts of one that is yet in its infancy. . . . They in no way resemble the often successful but always tentative experiments of an archaic Greek artist.'[2]

How are we to explain the existence of such art at such an epoch in Greece? There are, I think, only two possible explanations: either these folk of golden Mycenae, whose warriors were, when clad at all, clad and armed so differently from the Homeric Achaeans, and whose women-folk were bedizened like the ladies of *fin de siècle* Europe, not only possessed wealth and an abundance of gold (which assuredly was not produced by the Peloponnese, or any other part of Greece) and were in a high state of material civilization, but also must have been the heirs of an age of art – for such works as these Vaphio cups presume a long artistic training;[3] or else these cups are not a native product, but were imported from some land where art had flourished for a long period. This land could not have been Assyria or Phoenicia or Egypt, for there is no trace whatever of the special characteristics of Oriental or Egyptian art in this splendid *repoussé* work, which is like some *chef-d'œuvre* of Benvenuto Cellini rather than a relic of antiquity. 'The design,' says Professor E. Gardner, 'which is all round the outside of the cups, is beaten up from behind into bold relief and finished with a chisel in front; the *repoussé* plates are backed with others which are turned over at the back, so as to hold in the reliefs.' If not native Mycenaean work, and if not Assyrian, Phoenician, or Egyptian, whence could these cups have come?

## Crete

There can be only one answer. They must have come from Crete, or must have been the product of Cretan workmanship. Long before – perhaps for

[1] In a great vaulted tomb that had been brought to light by a landslip – perhaps the tomb of some Pelopid lord of Laconia.

[2] Gardner's *Handbook of Greek Sculpture*.

[3] If Dr. Flinders Petrie is right in tracing the periodical rise and decline of art by means of sculpture and in assigning about 2000 years to such periods, it would seem that the Vaphio cups were the product of an art at least 1000 years old.

Fig. 12  Golden discs and shrine

Fig. 13  Golden cups from Vaphio

a thousand years before – the days of those ancient pre-Achaean kings whose bones were unearthed at Mycenae there had existed in Crete a civilization which was only brought to light in the early twentieth century, and which we now know to have produced artistic work of a quality no less admirable than that of the Vaphio cups and to have passed its highest development before the era of 'Mycenaean' civilization – which civilization seems to have been at its highest and to have extended over a great part of the Aegean islands and over parts of Northern Greece, and to Cyprus and Rhodes, about 1500 to 1200. This far more ancient Cretan civilization, evidences of which, discovered from 1900 onwards, take us back to the Stone Age (say 3000 B.C. at the very least), is only indirectly connected with the history of the Hellenic race (if one uses the word history in its ordinary sense), but it is of very great interest and importance in regard to artistic and religious matters. I shall therefore devote a short space to its consideration.

The excavations in Crete that opened up for us a vista into so vast a realm of the past – very much more distant than that revealed by the Mycenaean and the Trojan researches of Schliemann and his successors – were first seriously begun in 1900 by Sir Arthur Evans, who went to Crete primarily in the hope of discovering further evidence of an ancient written language, his curiosity having been awakened at Athens by Cretan seals engraved with unknown hieroglyphic and linear characters. After many difficulties he was enabled to make extensive excavations on the site of the ancient city of Cnossus (or Knosos), which Homer mentions as the chief of ninety (or a hundred) towns of Crete, and where the famous artist and inventor Daedalus built the Labyrinth for King Minos, and a beautiful dancing-ground for the princess, fair-haired Ariadne. Before long the excavators unearthed the foundations of a very large palace, and a vast complex of buildings which are believed by some to have formed the celebrated Labyrinth. Store-rooms were found with rows of enormous jars, and shrines with idols and other sacred objects, and a great hall, and remains of frescoes, still bright with colour, and a handsome stone seat which has been dignified with the title 'The Throne of Minos,' and finely worked vessels of syenite and marble and alabaster and steatite (soapstone), and a great quantity of tablets covered with inscriptions and, of course, a great deal of pottery, some of it dating probably from at least 3000 – indeed, some of the ancient black pottery (like Etruscan *bucchero*) found among the Stone

*Fig. 14  Acropolis, Mycenae*

*Fig. 15  Excavations of Palace, Cnossus*

Age deposits[1] on the hill of Cephala, near Cnossus, may date from very much earlier times, possibly from 8000.

Let us briefly consider the present evidence, and then see what conclusions may reasonably be drawn from it. Our illustrations will give us a fair conception of some of the relics.

The walls of the palace (especially in the great Hall of the Double Axes[2]) show evident signs of a great conflagration. Possibly the palace and city were sacked twice during the long era of this so-called Minoan civilization, and almost everything portable that was worth carrying off (such as precious metals) has disappeared. Of what remains probably the thousands of inscribed tablets will ultimately prove the most valuable to the historian.[3] Perhaps the most interesting images from Cnossus are the pictures of these Minoan people. In the 'Cup-bearer' (Fig. 16) we have a very striking portrait (perhaps some 3500 years old) of one of these Minoan Cretans – for the features are most certainly not Oriental or Egyptian. 'The flesh-tint,' says Sir Arthur Evans, 'is of a deep reddish brown; the limbs are finely moulded, though the waist, as usual in Mycenaean fashions, is tightly drawn in by a silver-mounted girdle. . . . The profile is almost classically Greek, and the physiognomy has certainly no Semitic cast. There was something very impressive in this vision of brilliant youth and of male beauty recalled after so long an interval to the upper air from what had been, till yesterday, a forgotten world.' The youth is bearing, says Mr. Baikie, a 'gold-mounted silver cup. His loin-cloth is decorated with a beautiful quatrefoil pattern; he wears a silver ear-ornament, silver rings on the neck and upper arm, and on the wrist a bracelet with an agate gem.' Other frescoes contain similar youths, a lady (perhaps a queen) in a magnificent dress, and many other figures, as well as scenes from bull-fights. In these scenes (found also on seals), athletes, generally boys and girls, are depicted as awaiting the charge of the infuriated animal or catching it by the horns and turning a somersault, or vaulting, over its back. The bull figures largely

---

[1] These deposits (beneath the first stratum of the Bronze Age, which began about 3000) are about 20 feet deep, which gives, according to the usual calculations of archaeologists, a period of at least six thousand years.

[2] For the 'Labrys' see Section B.

[3] *Editor's note.* The inscriptions were later classified as Linear A and Linear B. The scripts of both are related, but the language of Linear A has so far eluded detection. Linear B is a later form of the script and the language of these tablets was found to be Greek. The subject of the inscriptions is administrative in nature, records of people and produce.

*Fig. 16  The cup-bearer, Cnossus*

*Fig. 17  Acrobats and elands*

in Minoan art. As will be seen later, the animal was intimately connected with the old Cretan religion, a fact which forms a 'solid point of truth' in the legends of Theseus and the Minotaur. The connection between Mycenaean and Cretan art and religious practices is, moreover, graphically confirmed by a fresco found at Tiryns, near Mycenae, and by various gems or seals where similar scenes are depicted. It is just possible, too, that the Vaphio cups may represent a scene of 'bull-grappling' (*taurokathapsia*) by athletes.

The Minoan ladies are pictured (as we find also in Egyptian art and on early Greek vases) with a skin of chalky whiteness. They are dressed in the same way as the Mycenaean women already described – with towering coiffures, tight bodices, often covering but little of the bust, richly embroidered heavily pleated and flounced skirts, and often with almost incredible wasp-waists. Such figures are found both in colour and also incised on seals (see Figs. 7 and 28).

Besides frescoes there were found figures and other objects in terracotta, faïence, ivory, and other material, and brightly coloured reliefs in plaster, one of which is a life-sized bull's head (perhaps once a part of a complete bull). It is very finely modelled and coloured, and testifies to as highly developed art as do the Vaphio cups. Also many of the Minoan vessels are of artistic workmanship. One of the steatite vessels, once probably covered with gold-leaf, represents a boxing match, another a company of soldiers with their officers (most interesting as a contrast to the Mycenae 'Warrior Vase'), and another (Fig. 24) a band of people in procession carrying what

55

may be palm-branches and preceded by a huge figure in a curious plaited costume. It is generally called a procession of harvesters, but the presence of a man with a *sistrum* (metal rattle) seems rather to point, I think, to some religious ceremony – possibly a procession of Cretan Curetes, the priests of the Cretan Zeus.

The painted stone sarcophagus found at Hagia Triada (Fig. 25) is not a specimen of good Minoan art (possibly it dates after the collapse of Cretan power and art, about 1400), but is intensely interesting as an illustration of religious rites. I shall speak of it again later, together with various idols, seals with pictures of demons (genii), and other objects.

The only other relic that I shall here describe is a very beautiful table (Fig. 19), which is believed to have been the board on which some game like draughts (mentioned in Homer) used to be played. Its framework was of gold-plated ivory, and it was richly set with crystals, blue *cyan*, gold, and silver, and decorated with reliefs of flowers and shells of great beauty.

Besides such relics we have in the vast ruins a most impressive testimony to the greatness of Crete in this so-called Minoan age. Whether or not the excavators have brought once more to the light of day the veritable Labyrinth of Cnossus or the actual dancing-ground made by Daedalus for fair-haired Ariadne, they have, at any rate, proved that the ancient traditions about the great naval power of the Cretans are not merely empty myths, and they have shown it to be highly probably that even the Minotaur fable is an imaginative version of facts, doubtless some of them of terribly tragic nature, connected with Cretan bull-worship and the bull-grappling spectacles, in which the boy and girl athletes must have often lost their lives.

Thus it is clear that in Crete a civilized and at one time powerful nation existed from at least 3000 (possibly from much earlier) down to about 1350, when some great calamity befell it, from which it never recovered.

Now both Thucydides and Herodotus speak of the ancient naval supremacy of Crete under a king Minos. Old myths tell of two Cretan kings of this name. One was the son of Zeus, a great lawgiver, who after his earthly life was made a judge (as Homer describes him) in the nether world.

The other Minos was said to be his grandson. He was the husband of Pasiphaë, and in his reign Daedalus built the Labyrinth for the Minotaur, whom the Athenian hero Theseus slew. Homer also speaks of this later Minos. He calls him the father of Ariadne and Deucalion and the grandfather of the Cretan hero Idomeneus, who fought at Troy, and says that he

Fig. 18 'Throne of Minos'

Fig. 19 Minoan game-board

conversed as a familiar friend with Zeus, and reigned 'for a space of nine years.'

Now it is almost certain that 'Minos' was, like 'Pharaoh,' a royal title, and that these kings of Crete or Cnossus were believed to be descended from the great Cretan god, the Dictaean Zeus, and it is thought that the king, as High-priest of Zeus, went up once every nine years to 'converse' with the deity in the Dictaean cave and to receive his laws (like Moses on Sinai). Moreover, research and excavation have made it clear that the old Cretan religion was closely associated with the bull, as is intimated by the myths of Europa[1] and Pasiphaë. Bulls were doubtless sacrificed to Zeus, and the king-priest seems to have performed ceremonies in the disguise of a bull-headed monster – a fact that is probably the real explanation of the Minotaur and Pasiphaë myths. By some it is believed that the priest-king, when he entered the Dictaean cave at the end of his nine-years reign, was walled up there, or slain,[2] and it is evident that at the bull-grappling spectacles given in honour of the Bull-god many human victims were done to death, mostly youths and maidens (as in the case of the sacrifices of first-born children to Moloch). It seems, therefore, that behind these old myths of the 'Bull of Minos' and Theseus and the Athenian youths and maidens sent every nine years (as Plutarch tells us) to be given over as victims to this Minotaur, there is a good deal of fact, and when Thucydides (who strongly condemns 'careless investigation of truth') tells us that Minos of Crete was the first monarch to acquire a navy and that he 'made himself master of the greater part' of the Aegean and 'swept piracy from the sea,' we need no longer doubt his accuracy nor the possibility of trustworthy traditions of the great Minoan Empire having reached the age of Pericles. That it was an empire founded on naval supremacy is remarkably confirmed by the fact that Cnossus possessed no fortifications. Moreover, the existence of numerous settlements named Minoa on the Mediterranean shores seems to prove it. One of these was on the island off Megara. In the Theseus myth Minos lays even Athens under tribute.

But before we draw conclusions in regard to this Minoan race and its connection with the early history of the Hellenic nation there is

---

[1] Europa, according to the myth, was carried off by Zeus, in the form of a bull, from Phoenicia, and it was formerly assumed that the bull-headed Cretan deity was the Phoenician Baal or Moloch. Doubtless both the Minotaur and the Talos myth do seem to point to the bull-headed Moloch and human burnt sacrifice.

[2] As happened to the Pharaoh-priest at the 'Sed' festival in Egypt.

another group of evidence to be considered, namely, that which Egypt[1] supplies.

## Egypt and Crete

The earliest evidences of what is called Minoan civilization in Crete are perhaps a little later than the age (*c.* 3500) in which King Mena is said to have founded the first of the Egyptian dynasties,[2] and the final fall of the Minoan Empire, about 1350, corresponds with the end of the XVIIIth Dynasty. In the age of the first two dynasties there was doubtless some intercourse between Egypt and Crete, but the only possible evidence of it consists in fragments of *bucchero* (black pottery) which have been found in very ancient Egyptian tombs. This pottery is believed to have come from Crete. On the other hand, very ancient vessels of syenite, some of which have been found at Cnossus, are believed to have come from Egypt. From the era of Cheops and other Pyramid-builders (IIIrd to XIth Dynasties) there is considerably more evidence of a similar nature; but it was not till about 2000, during the XIIth Dynasty, that the Cretan ware, especially the beautiful 'Kamáres' porcelain, seems to have been largely imported into Egypt. Indubitable specimens of this polychrome Minoan ware have been discovered in Egyptian tombs of this period, together with cylinders inscribed with the name of Amenemhat III, the last of the dynasty. It was this great king who built the Labyrinth near Lake Moeris in Egypt which very possibly was imitated at Cnossus by King Minos – unless indeed the Egyptian Labyrinth was suggested by the Cretan.[3]

Then follows the Dark Age of Egyptian history (XIIIth to XVIIth Dynasties), during which for some five centuries the Hyksos (a Canaanite or African nomad race) were the lords of Egypt. Of these so-called 'Shepherd Kings' the only one at all known is Khyan ('Embracer of

---

[1] There is only the very faintest evidence, if indeed it can be accepted as evidence, of any intercourse in these ages between Crete (or any other Aegean land) and Babylonia or Assyria, and (what seems strange considering the great antiquity of Sidon) very much less Phoenician influence than was formerly believed to have existed.

[2] Others put this back some two thousand years to 5500.

[3] This Egyptian Labyrinth, with its 4500 rooms, was seen by Herodotus, who describes (ii. 148) the enormous complex as the most wonderful building on earth, 'surpassing the Pyramids.' Evidently this Labyrinth was very much larger than anything discovered in Crete.

Lands'). His cartouche, carved on a lion, has been found even at Bagdad, and at Cnossus the lid of an alabaster box has been discovered bearing his name. After the Dark Age and the domination of the Hyksos (broken by the Wars of Independence) we have the famous XVIIIth Dynasty, founded by Aahmes in 1580. To this dynasty belonged the great monarchs Queen Hatshepsut, King Tutmes, and Amenhotep III (Fig. 3), who extended Egyptian trade and influence into distant countries. In the numerous inscribed and painted Egyptian records of this era there figure many foreign races, and among these is one, that of the Kephtiu, which formerly used to be regarded as Phoenician, but which is evidently Cretan. In feature, in dress, and in the high coiffure with long down-hanging tresses, these painted Kephtiu bear a most striking resemblance to the type that we have in the 'Cup-bearer' (Fig. 16), and the name Kephtiu, which is said to mean 'the men from beyond' (*i.e.* from beyond the sea), is one that well suits the Cretans. Also the fact that these Kephtiu are depicted carrying, as tribute or gifts, gold and silver vessels very similar to the Vaphio cups confirms one's belief that they are Cretans, all the more when one remembers that the era of this XVIIIth Dynasty corresponds to that of the great Palace at Cnossus, with its wonderful frescoes and other signs of an advanced civilization. Moreover, the evidence from pottery is here very strong, great quantities of Cretan ware of this period and of the succeeding centuries having been found in Egypt.

It is very striking that about 1400, the era of the sack of Cnossus and the fall of the Minoan Empire, the Kephtiu suddenly disappear from Egyptian records, and that some 100 years later, about the time of the Biblical Exodus, the names of a number of strange northern tribes are found, among whom are the 'Aqayuasha' – very possibly the Achaeans.

Not much later, again (*c.* 1200 – just about the time of the Trojan War), a great host of 'people of the sea,' leagued with the Hittites, threatened Egypt from the north-east, but they were defeated and dispersed by Ramses III. Among these invaders are mentioned Danauna (possibly Danai, *i.e.* Argives) and Pulosathu, who were probably Cretan refugees and identical with the Kephtiu – perhaps the Biblical Philistines of Kaphtor.[1]

[1] See Jer. xlvii. 4 and Gen. x. 14. After their defeat by Ramses these Pulosathu (Pelasgians? Philistines?) seem to have settled in Palestine, and it is remarkable that Cretan pottery is said to have been discovered at their chief town, Gath. Perhaps Goliath was a Cretan, and perhaps, after all, the Philistines were of a people that for some reasons may claim to be children of Light no less than the Israelites – artistically anyhow.

## Egypt and Mycenae

During the later period of Minoan civilization (say 1700–1400) the Mycenaean civilization was probably at its highest,[1] and to this period may belong the shaft-tombs on the acropolis of Mycenae. Amongst the relics there discovered we have already noted an evident Nile scene on an inlaid dagger-blade. But besides this the cartouche of the Egyptian Amenhotep III (Fig. 3), the great king of the XVIIIth Dynasty, was found in one of the later vaulted tombs, as well as several pieces of porcelain inscribed with his name. Amenhotep reigned from 1414 to 1380, so it seems likely that these later Mycenaean tombs were built about 1400. The old Aegean (Pelopid?) kings of the earlier tombs were probably supreme at Mycenae, and in the rest of the Peloponnese, until about this date, when Mycenae seems to have been conquered by some foreign enemy. Shortly afterwards the same enemy seems to have sacked Cnossus.

## General Conclusions

The question now naturally arises, *who* were these invaders? And this question leads us to a still larger one, namely, what conclusions can we from all this evidence reasonably draw in regard to the early inhabitants of Greece, and those migrations and invasions and heroes and dynasties of which Greek myths tell so much, but which used to be generally regarded as quite worthless fables?

Firstly, then, who were these invaders who seem to have conquered Mycenae and some years later to have sacked Cnossus?

The old tradition, handed down to us by Herodotus, says that when Daedalus made himself wings and thus escaped to Southern Italy and Sicily he was pursued by Minos, and that, Minos having come to a tragic end in Sicily, a great host of Cretans set forth in ships to avenge his death; but they failed in their object and lost their fleet in a tempest and founded Hyria in Southern Italy, where they changed their name to Messapian Iapygians. Herodotus also learnt from the inhabitants of Praesos, in Crete,

---

[1] Not only are traces of 'Mycenaean' civilization found in Aegean lands and islands, as well as in Northern Greece, and even in Sicily and Spain, but it seems that there were Mycenaean kings in Cyprus about 1450. And yet Mycenae was evidently not a great naval power.

61

that after this national disaster 'men of various nations flocked to Crete, destitute as it now was of inhabitants; but none came in such numbers as the Greeks.' He places the death of this King Minos three generations before the Trojan War, say in 1330.

What truth there may be in this tale of a Cretan-Sicilian expedition one cannot say. Possibly it represents the general exodus of Cretans *after* the advent of 'men of various nations' from over the sea. Of these invaders, according to Herodotus, the Greeks (Hellenes) were the most numerous, and among the various nations which inhabited Crete in a somewhat later, post-Dorian, age the first that Homer mentions are the Achaeans,[1] which looks as if then they were still the paramount race.

All our evidence, I think, points to the Achaeans as the conquerors of the Mycenaeans and other Aegean peoples, and as the sackers of Cnossus, and points to the period 1400–1200 as that during which these northern invaders (of whom we have already heard much in connection with the Homeric age and the sixth city of Troy) extended their conquests over Greece and as far as Crete. That these Achaeans (perhaps the 'Aqayuasha' of Egyptian records, of whom we have heard) made themselves lords not only of mainland Greece but also of the Aegean, and perhaps Crete, seems probable also from Homer's statement (quoted by Thucydides) that Agamemnon, the great Achaean king, ruled not only over all Argos but over 'many islands.'

The second and larger question which we must endeavour to answer is, what conclusions we may reasonably accept in regard to the races which inhabited Greece before the advent of the Achaeans. We have already seen that they were probably a dark-haired, lithe-limbed people, such as we find the ancient Cretans to be depicted, and we have spoken of them as the 'Aegean' race. Let us now hear what old Greek tradition says about these early inhabitants of Greece, and their conquerors, the Achaeans.

At the beginning of his history Thucydides, after speaking of the continual migrations of the tribes of ancient Greece, mentions the 'Pelasgian' name as that which was most widely applied to these tribes. Long before the time of Thucydides these Pelasgians had been frequently mentioned by Homer, who speaks of them in Thessaly, Boeotia, Attica, and even in the Peloponnese, and also in Asia Minor (possibly aboriginal Phrygians,

---

[1] *Od.* xix. 175. He mentions also aboriginal Cretans, Cydonians, Pelasgians, and the (evidently later) Dorians.

fighting on the side of the Trojans) and in Crete. He gives the epithet 'divine' (heaven-descended? aboriginal?) to these Pelasgians. Moreover, he applies the epithet 'Pelasgian' to the northern (Thessalian) Argos, and to the Zeus whose oracle was at Dodona, in Epirus.

Herodotus also tells us of Pelasgians who built the old walls of the Athenian Acropolis, and it seems certain that the original lords of what was later the Athenian Acropolis were those Pelasgi or Cecropes whom later 'autochthonous' families of Athens claimed as their ancestors.

It seems not impossible that these ancient Pelasgians were of the same race as the Etruscans or Tyrrhenians, called Tyrseni (perhaps 'Tower Men') by the Greeks.[1] It is also not impossible that the Pulosathu of Crete (the Philistines?), of whom we have already heard, were Pelasgians; and, lastly, it is quite possible that the Turusha, one of the oversea tribes mentioned as having invaded Egypt about 1300 together with the Aqayuasha (Achaeans?), were these Tyrseni or Etruscans.

However this may be, it is not surprising that formerly all writers on Greece accepted the word 'Pelasgian' as the most satisfactory name to cover the unknown tribes inhabiting Greece at the time of the Achaean invasions. But of late years this name has met with disfavour, for it is evident that the newly discovered 'Aegean' race was not identical with the Pelasgic, and it is our knowledge of this so-called Aegean race that now allows us to reconstruct and repeople to some extent that obscure 'mythical' age formerly regarded as unworthy of the attention of the historian.

The only satisfactory answer, therefore, that we can give in regard to the pre-Achaean inhabitants of Greece is this: there were doubtless also other peoples (such as these Pelasgians), but in the southern parts of Greece the main race, and the only race that we really know anything about for certain, was this Mycenaean, or Aegean, race, to which probably the Cretans were closely related. They were a dark-haired, long-headed people, not of Semitic origin, but possibly with some affinity to the Egyptians. They lived

---

[1] Hesiod (*c.* 750), or some early imitator, mentions the Tyrseni of Italy and possibly even King Latinus! The Etruscans called themselves 'Rasena.' Some three centuries later Herodotus asserts that the Tyrseni of Italy came from Lydia, and also that Pelasgians were expelled from Athens and settled in Lemnos. Now other traditions say that there were people called Tyrsenes in Lemnos, who were believed to be Tyrrhenians, and an inscription found in Lemnos is said to show similarities to old Etruscan. According to Pliny and Varro, there was a great Labyrinth, like the Cretan, connected with the tomb of Lars Porsena at Clusium, in Etruria. *Cf.* Thuc. iv. 109.

in Greece in what is called the Bronze Age – that is, before iron came into general use – and perhaps before bronze was invented, which could not have been until *tin* was brought from western lands (from Spain, and perhaps even from Britain). Before tin was procurable to mix with their copper, which they obtained in abundance from Cyprus and also from Chalcis, in Euboea, they were obliged to make their weapons and tools of copper, or of stone or obsidian. In early times possibly some of these Aegean folk (*e.g.* at Orchomenus, Tiryns, and other marshy places) dwelt in lake-villages, like the Stone Age inhabitants of other parts of Europe. The northern invaders, the Achaeans, seem to have introduced the more general use of bronze for weapons and armour. Then, about 1250, iron, which hitherto had been among Aegean peoples a rare material for rings and small ornaments, began to be used for sharp-edged tools (as we find it in Homer), and gradually won its way into general use.[1] Possibly the arts of smelting and of forging iron (graphically described in the *Odyssey*, ix. 391) may have been introduced by the Achaeans; but the metal may have been found less commonly by them in Greece, which may account for its comparatively rare mention by Homer.

During this Bronze Age (that is, before the advent of the northern invaders) there were in Greece doubtless other important cities, besides Mycenae and Tiryns and Amyclae and Orchomenus, inhabited by Aegeans or Pelasgians or whatever else we may call these early races, but, except in a few cases, their memorials have utterly perished. Of Athens, however, and of Thebes we have some remarkable traditions.

### Athens in Pre-Dorian Times

On account of the poverty of its soil, as Thucydides tells us, and also perhaps on account of the more warlike character of its inhabitants, Attica seems never to have been permanently conquered by invaders. It apparently remained (as also Arcadia in the Peloponnese) finally unoccupied by the Achaeans,[2] and the ancient Pelasgian race was the main stock from which the later Athenians sprang, though much else was grafted upon it. Of these

---

[1] See Hesiod's *Erga* for these various Ages. *Cf.* p. 133.

[2] This evidently accounts for the fact that Athens is almost entirely ignored by Homer, the glorifier of the Achaeans. (In later times the Athenians perhaps inserted certain lines in their own honour.)

old Pelasgian aborigines a relic may still be seen, namely, a few blocks of bluish limestone which formed a part of the rampart built round their citadel. This old wall was by the later Athenians called the 'Pelasgic' or 'Pelargic' wall, and to the north-west of the Acropolis was an open space called the 'Pelasgion,' on which it was forbidden to build, until at the beginning of the Peloponnesian War (431), when thousands were flocking from the country into the city, the old law was allowed to lapse.[1] Herodotus tells of old Pelasgian kings of Attica, Cecrops and Erechtheus, regarded, of course, later as divine[2] and associated with the ancient snake-worship so common in the cult of the dead. According to one old legend, Cecrops came from Egypt – which, indeed, possibly was the cradle of the Aegean and Pelasgian people. He is said to have introduced a higher form of religion and to have abolished bloody (human?) sacrifice. On the old Cecropian citadel was built by his son Erechtheus a temple, first dedicated to Poseidon, but afterwards (as we see from Homer, *Od.* vii. 82) given over to the new tutelary deity, Athene;[3] or perhaps they shared it until the first Parthenon was built. Aegeus, grandson of Erechtheus, is said to have been the father of Theseus, and if (as we have seen to be possible) the myth of Theseus and King Minos refers to facts that occurred in the last era of Minoan civilization – *i.e.* about 1350 – it will follow that Cecrops might have lived (granting that tradition is fairly correct) about 1450. Thus the era of the ancient traditional Pelasgian kings of Athens would correspond with the highest period of Mycenaean civilization, and the tradition which tells us that Theseus was driven from his throne[4] may very possibly be founded on the fact that the Achaeans, though they did not retain possession, captured Athens. And the strange story of the fierce battle, in the very midst of the city, in which Theseus conquered the Amazons may point to

---

[1] Thuc. ii. 17.

[2] The ancient Erechtheion, or 'house of Erechtheus,' preceded the temple of Athene. Some writers assert that Cecrops (as also many another old hero, such as Odysseus, or even the lawgiver Lycurgus) was originally 'only a god.' Surely the reverse process is more credible.

[3] The contest between Poseidon and Athene for the tutelage of the city was the subject of the west pediment of the later Parthenon (see Fig. 86). Codrus is said to have decided it. Others say that it was decided by the votes of the Athenian women, who beat the men by one vote – and were immediately disfranchised!

[4] He retired to the island Scyros, where he was murdered. Some nine hundred years later what were supposed to be his bones were brought to Athens by Cimon and consigned to the Theseion (Theseum) – perhaps not what is now so called.

some disturbance caused by the pressure from the north of the Achaean invaders.

## Thebes in Pre-Dorian Times

Another ancient city of Greece was seven-gated Thebes, which has left us many remarkable legends, but very few ruins, and almost no relics of its early existence – as is the case with most places that have been continuously inhabited. Homer speaks of Amphion (Niobe's husband) and Zethus as its founders, and perhaps this is the oldest tradition, and points to a dynasty (possibly from Phrygia, the home of Niobe and her brother Pelops) before that of Cadmus, who is generally said to have founded Thebes. Cadmus, according to Herodotus, was a Phoenician,[1] and 'introduced the art of writing, whereof the Greeks till then had been ignorant.' Fourth in descent from Cadmus was Oedipus, whose tragic fate is related by Sophocles. One of the sons of Oedipus, according to the old legend, expelled by his brother fled to the Peloponnese and incited the famous and disastrous expedition of the Seven against Thebes, in which six of the seven heroes perished; but later their descendants (Epigoni) made a second expedition and razed Thebes to the ground.

This well-known myth doubtless rests on traditions of real facts, and these facts were probably of this nature. When the successive waves of northern invaders – whom we may conveniently call by the collective name of Achaeans – rolled southward through Upper Greece, the seven-portal'd stronghold of Thebes, with its mighty ramparts and towers (see *Od.* xi. 264) and its Cadmeia, the acropolis built by Cadmus, at first proved impregnable; but after the invaders had firmly planted themselves in southern Argos they sent an army across the Isthmus or the Gulf of Corinth and succeeded in capturing the city. With this theory the traditional date of Cadmus (1313) and that of the expedition of the Seven against Thebes (1213) fit in very fairly, and the theory that these attacks on Thebes were made by an elder generation of the Homeric 'Achaeans' and 'Argives' is in agreement with what Homer and Hesiod and others relate.

But let us hear further what is known, or what may be reasonably

---

[1] The name may possibly mean 'the Oriental'; *cf.* Hebrew *qedem*, the East. Some, however, assert that what few relics have been discovered of Thebes are purely *Minoan* in character.

inferred, about these invaders who, doubtless in many successive waves and under many different names, poured into Greece, evidently from the north, during perhaps two centuries (1400–1200).

It is said[1] that parts of Central Europe during these ages were peopled by a race which in many points resembled the Achaeans described by Homer. In the Austrian Alps not far from Salzburg there is a place named Hallstatt, where about a thousand graves have been examined. The relics point to a transition between the ages of bronze and iron. Armour and shields (round metal shields very unlike the huge Aegean shield) and swords of both metals were found, and a great number of brooches (*fibulae*, Greek *peronai*), such as those with which, as we have already seen, the Homeric woman's *peplos* and the man's *chlaina* were fastened. Not much silver was found, but many ornaments of amber (from northern seas), and gold and a blue vitreous substance like the Homeric *cyan*. Both burial and cremation seem to have been practised. Whether there is any evidence of horses and chariots I do not know.

It seems possible that bands of this northern, fair-haired, broad-headed Indo-Iranian race made their way from time to time down into Epirus and Thessaly, and established themselves in the district of Pelasgic Argos, also called Phthiotis, the home of the Homeric Achilles. Here they probably collected a large army of the native Argives, and at the head of this Argive host pressed southward, crossed the Corinthian Gulf, overran the Peloponnese (except perhaps Arcadia), and founded that southern Argos of which Agamemnon was afterwards king,[2] and which before the advent of the Achaeans and their Argives was probably called Larisa (one of the very numerous 'Larisas,' or forts, in Greece and Asia Minor) and was a mere outpost of royal Mycenae.

Now in Thessaly, perhaps before the advent of the Achaeans (unless they accompanied or followed them from the north), lived a people called Hellenes. They were evidently of Indo-Iranian, not Pelasgic, race. Tradition makes Hellen, their ancestor, son of the Greek Noah, Deucalion, and asserts that he reigned over Thessalian Phthiotis, or Phthia, as Homer

---

[1] See especially Professor Ridgeway's *Early Age of Greece*. Others regard this 'Hallstatt civilization' as dating only from about 700.

[2] In Homer Diomede seems to be prince of the city Argos, probably under the suzerainty of Agamemnon, who lived at Mycenae. The theory has already been mentioned that Agamemnon and his Achaeans and Argives were only transported from Thessaly to the Peloponnese by a poet's imagination.

calls it, which was the home of Achilles. The district inhabited by these Hellenes – the original Hellas – seems to have been the valley of the river Spercheios (now called Ellada), which runs into the sea not far north of Thermopylae. Some of these Hellenes seem to have joined in the southward march, and to have been merged in the larger host of Argives and Achaeans – for in Homer the Hellenes, and the pan-Hellenes, are still the Thessalian folk who followed Achilles, and Hellas is still only a district in Thessaly. It was not till much later, as Thucydides says, that the names Hellas and Hellenes won their broader meanings, and denoted the land and the peoples of what we call the Greek race not only in Greece proper but in Asia Minor, Africa, Sicily, and Italy.[1]

These invading bands of Achaeans, with their Argive and Hellene followers, seem to have settled themselves chiefly in the Peloponnese. Mycenae was evidently captured by them, but the signs of conflagration which are found both at Mycenae and at Tiryns are very likely due to the later Dorians, of whom we shall soon hear. The Achaeans were probably not such a refined and artistically civilized people as the Mycenaeans whom they had conquered, but they were not, as the Dorians seem to have been, what Homer calls 'savages wanton and wild, despisers of justice,' and they seem to have assimilated much that was valuable in the old Aegean civilization. Indeed, the pictures that Homer gives us of these Achaean princes are those of men warlike and haughty, and sometimes terribly cruel and crafty, but endowed with deep feelings of affection and reverence and with a keen sensitiveness to all that is gracious and beautiful. To their possession of such qualities may be due the otherwise inexplicable fact that the tombs of the Mycenaean monarchs were discovered intact after the lapse of more than 3000 years. How these could have escaped the Dorians and later marauders is puzzling enough, but that they were not at once

---

[1] It is curious also how the word 'Greek' won its way from an equally obscure origin. Aristotle indeed asserts that near Dodona, in Epirus, there lived in early ages a people 'then called Greeks, but now Hellenes'; and Sophocles perhaps used the name; but it is generally supposed that it was the Romans who first gave the name to the Hellenes whom they met in Southern Italy (Magna Graecia). It has been pointed out that a band of Graians from Boeotia joined the Euboeans in founding Cyme (Cumae) in Italy, and that their name was applied by the Romans to all Hellenic people. Nations are sometimes named from apparently small causes (*e.g.* Americans, Swiss), and are often known to foreigners by non-native names, *e.g.* Germans, Allemands, Tedeschi, Dutch, Kafirs, Etruscans (Rasena), Lycians (Termilae).

plundered by the Achaeans seems explainable by assuming (as I assumed before) that these Achaeans did not ravage and enslave, but, like the Norman adventurers in later ages, constituted themselves the lords of the native population, and probably married princesses of the native dynasties. On this assumption Atreus and Agamemnon, though mainly of Achaean blood, might have regarded the old Pelopidae as their ancestors, and in this case would have carefully kept intact their tombs on the acropolis. Later, perhaps, the effects of some conflagration may have concealed them from the invader.

Having thus given a sketch of what is known about the early – so-called Aegean – age of Greece, and having shown the connection between this Aegean civilization and that of Crete, Egypt, and Troy, and having discussed some of the more important traditions in their possible relation to certain great occurrences in Greece proper down to the final establishment of the Achaeans in Southern Greece (say about 1200), I shall now, before continuing the account of historical, or quasi-historical, events, treat in the following three sections three subjects connected with what has been already written – namely, the questions of 'Language and Writing', 'The Old Religion', 'The "Homeric Age" and Homer'. The fourth section will contain a chronological table (with, of course, many somewhat audaciously hazarded dates) which will give a bird's-eye view of the era that we have been considering. These and other such sections may be regarded as supplementary monographs, not as integral parts of the main subject of the book.

## SECTION A: LANGUAGE AND WRITING

A chapter on the old Aegean and Pelasgic languages necessarily exhibits some similarity to the celebrated chapter on the snakes of Ireland.[1] Of ancient Cretan, which was perhaps related to the Mycenaean and other Aegean languages, we do, indeed, possess some thousands of inscriptions, but not one single symbol or letter of all these inscriptions has yet been satisfactorily deciphered, far less has any certain meaning been extracted. It is uncertain whether Pelasgic was of the same family as the Aegean and Cretan, and whether all these languages, or any one of them, belonged to

---

[1] *Editor's note.* The chapter 'Concerning Snakes' in *The Natural History of Ireland* reads simply: 'There are no snakes to be met with throughout the whole island.'

the Indo-Iranian stock or to the Semitic, or to some other entirely unknown stock, from which perhaps also the Hittite language was derived.

Herodotus tells us that, to judge from various Pelasgian tribes of his day (some in Macedonia, others on the Hellespont) and from cities 'which have dropped the name, but are in fact Pelasgian,' their language was certainly 'barbarous'; but of course this is no proof of its having been a non-Indo-European language, and tells us no more than Homer does when he calls the Carians 'barbarous-tongued.' As we have already seen, there is a possibility of the Pelasgic being closely related to the Etruscan, and we have also seen that this same language may possibly have been spoken by Goliath and his fellow-Philistines. But to speak of the Pelasgic as the principal language or dialect of ancient Greece, and to assume that it may have been the same as the Mycenaean, and related to the Cretan, is, of course, mere guesswork. All we can be fairly certain about is that the pre-Hellenic language, or languages, left behind names of places and other words which were adopted by the northern invaders, and which are evidently from no Greek source. 'Larisa' is a name that survived both in Thessaly and in Asia Minor. It seems to mean 'a fortress.' 'Olympos' and 'Parnassos' are others. Words with the termination -*inth*(*os*) are thought to be Pelasgic or Aegean – *e.g.* Corinthos, Tiryn(th)s, Olynthos, Zacynthos, Rhadaminthys, Hyacinthos, and Labyrinthos. As far as we can tell, these and other such words, supposed to be relics of the old Pelasgic or Aegean, have no affinity to any Indo-European or to any Semitic language.

Writing was well known in the second millennium B.C. not only in Egypt and Babylonia, and perhaps in a great part of Asia Minor, but also in Crete, and, as ancient seals and other inscribed objects prove, it had existed there ever since at least 2000 – long before the advent of the Phoenician alphabet. This Minoan script – of which there are various forms – was probably a Cretan[1] invention, although in its oldest form it seems to have some affinity to Egyptian hieroglyphics, in its most ancient form being pictographic. It consisted of rude pictures or symbols denoting objects themselves. Later it became hieroglyphic, in which system the symbol denoted the *name* of an object, *i.e.* a word. Finally it became linear, with different types of signs, one class of which denoted *syllables* (not mere *sounds*, as in the alphabetic system). Thousands of tablets with this linear script were discovered. It went through various changes, and after the great catastrophe of *c.* 1400

---

[1] Similar script has been found in some of the islands – *e.g.* Thera and Melos.

*Fig. 20  Cretan jars for oil or corn*

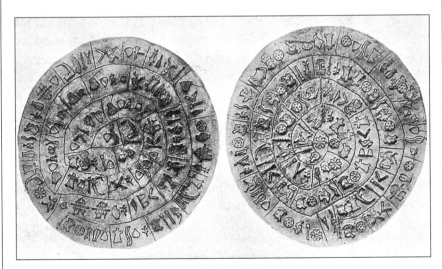

*Fig. 21  Clay disc of Phaestus*

*Fig. 22  Tablets with Cretan linear script*

developed a more systematic method of representing words and sentences, and a cursive character which seems to presume the knowledge of pen and ink. In the later form the Minoan script stands on a level very much higher than Egyptian hieroglyphics or Babylonian cuneiform.

Perhaps the most remarkable of all inscriptions found in Crete is that on both faces of the so-called disc of Phaestus (Fig. 21), a circular clay tablet about 7 inches in diameter. The date is perhaps about 1800. It is evidently not merely pictographic, and is divided into periods, which may represent words, or sentences. The regularity of these divisions and the repetition of certain symbols, such as the crested or horse-maned warrior[1] and the circle with seven dots (can they be the sky and seven planets?), have made some believe that it is a poem – possibly a hymn to the Cretan Zeus or the Great Mother. However, even its place of origin and its relation to Minoan scripts are uncertain.

In later times, after Greek influence had established itself in Crete, there was a considerable district at the eastern end of the island inhabited by the descendants of the old Cretan race (Eteocretes, or true-Cretans, as Homer

---

[1] Reminding one of Egyptian pictures of the Pulosathu (Philistines), and still more of the description by Herodotus of Libyans in the army of Xerxes who wore on the head 'the scalps of horses with the ears and mane standing upright as a crest.'

calls them). Among them an old Cretan language survived, as the Erse in Ireland and the Basque in Spain. But the old script was apparently forgotten, and an inscription in this language written in Greek letters has been discovered. Unfortunately, although we can read it, we cannot extract any meaning from it.

The earliest mention of writing in Greek literature is probably to be found in Homer's *Iliad* (vi. 168), where King Proetus of Argos sends Bellerophon to Lycia with 'direful signs' written on a 'closed tablet,' in order that the Lycian king should kill him on his arrival. These 'direful signs' may have been pictorial, or (as Proetus had lived in Lycia) they may have been in Lycian writing,[1] or in such a script as the Hittites employed – hieroglyphic or the so-called Cypriot syllabarium – which seems to have been widely used in Asia Minor, for imitations of it are said to have been found among the ornamental devices on ancient Trojan pottery.

Although not related in very ancient Greek literature, the fable of Philomela (daughter of the old Athenian king Pandion) may be mentioned as implying knowledge of writing, for she wove words into a *peplos* to communicate with her sister Procne. The Apple of Discord was, moreover, inscribed.

The invention, or anyhow the introduction into Europe, of the alphabet is due to the Phoenicians. The Phoenician script consisted (like other Semitic scripts) solely of consonants and breathings. The Greeks seem to have adopted about fourteen consonants from the Phoenicians and to have used the Phoenician breathings (aspirates) to represent the four vowel sounds A, E, I, O. Then from the East probably came the Greek *upsilon* (Y), which at first was a consonant (*i.e.* the *digamma*, pronounced like V or F), and the *ēta* (H), which in classical Greek is ē, but at first was an aspirate, as later in Latin. It is found as aspirate on old Greek vases. Later it was cut in half vertically, and the halves were used as the hard and soft breathings. The H as aspirate can be seen on Hiero's helmet (Fig. 77) and on Tataia's oil-flask (Fig. 23). Other consonants, *e.g.* Ψ = PS, *psi*, Ξ = X, *xi*, and the long vowel Ω = Ō, *omega*, were invented later – probably in Ionia, or perhaps Sicily. The ancient Ϙ (*koppa*; Hebr. *Koph*) was introduced very

---

[1] The ancient Lycian alphabet is said to have had more vowels than consonants, so that it was probably non-Semitic, but it differed entirely from the Greek, although Greece and Lycia seem to have been from early times closely connected. Indeed, the word 'Lycian' is wholly Greek. The people called themselves 'Termilae,' as Herodotus says, and as is proved by inscriptions.

early into Corinth, and is found on Corinthian vases down to Roman times. An old form of the Σ = S, *sigma* was undulatory or written with three strokes, as in Fig. 23. At Corinth we find the sibilant written ᛖ. This is found also on coins of Paestum. Euripides (in a fragment) describes all the letters of the name ΘΗΣΕΥΣ (THESEUS), and hence we see that in Attica about 440 the H was the ē and the Σ was already written with four strokes.

As we have seen, the art of writing is said by old authors to have been brought to Greece by Cadmus of Thebes. It is perhaps more probable that it was first introduced from the East into Asiatic Hellas, and thence to Athens. But several variations of Hellenic script existed, and the 'Cadmean' or some other may have preceded the Ionian in Greece proper. The full alphabet of twenty-four letters (called the Simonidean, after the Cean poet) seems first to have been used in Samos, and not to have reached Athens until after the Peloponnesian War (403). At first the Greeks often wrote from right to left (see Fig. 23), as was done in Phoenician and other Semitic languages. Then they sometimes wrote alternate lines in different directions, 'turning the oxen,' as they expressed it, at the end of each line (*boustrophēdon*), or else they placed the words in a column (*kionēdon*), as in some Oriental languages.

We may regard 1000–900 (*i.e.* about the age of Solomon and Hiram of Tyre) as the period in which the art of writing became known to the Greeks through the same Phoenicians who helped Solomon to build his Temple. Although doubtless it was long before it came into anything like general use, it was most probably used for private, if not public, purposes[1] during one or two centuries before an Attic jar, now in the Museum at Athens, was incised with what is believed to be the earliest Greek inscription extant. The inscription, scratched on the shoulder of the jar in primitive Greek letters, is to this effect: 'He who of all the dancers the most gaily skips, His shall be this vase.' The date of this jar and of the inscription (which seems to have been incised in the still soft clay) is supposed to be about 700. Above is shown another very interesting inscription, perhaps nearly as old, scratched by a child (or for a child) on her *lekythos* – a clay bottle for oil or scented water. Do not the letters seem to build a fairy bridge across the gulf of all these 2500 years? The signature of the artists Ergotimus and Clitias,

---

[1] The name of Lycurgus is said to have been inscribed on the ancient discus of Iphitus which was preserved at Olympia. The entire absence of all relics of Greek inscriptions of this age is remarkable.

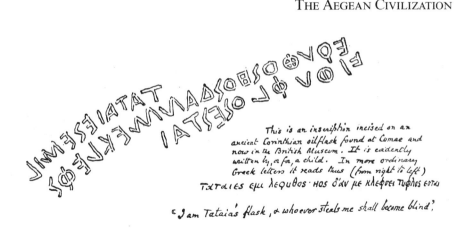

This is an inscription incised on an ancient Corinthian oilflask found at Cumae and now in the British Museum. It is evidently written by, or for, a child. In more ordinary Greek letters it reads thus (from right to left)

ΤΑΤΑΙΕΣ ΕΜΙ ΛΕΟυΘΟΣ · ΗΟΣ ΔΑΝ ΜΕ ΚΛΕΦΣΕΙ ΤΥΦΛΟΣ ΕΣΤΑΙ

'I am Tataia's flask, & whoever steals me shall become blind.'

*Fig. 23  Inscription on Tataia's Flask*

who made and painted the François Vase (Fig. 39), may be not very much later. The Greek inscriptions on the Abu Simbel colossus (Fig. 44) are of about 594.

### SECTION B: THE OLD RELIGION

When we speak of the old religion of the Greeks as distinguished from the later worship of the Olympian deities it must not be forgotten that the feeling of awe and the sense of mystery which were the sources of that earlier religion are inexhaustible in human nature, and that side by side with the worship of Zeus and Athene there continued to exist all through the so-called classical age many old rites and esoteric creeds and secret practices, such as we hear of in connection with the Eleusinian and other mysteries, and with the Dionysiac (Bacchic) orgies, and the occult and doubtless sometimes noble teachings of the Orphic theology. Indeed, this old mysticism long survived, as it was bound to do, what has been called the short-lived puppet-show of the Olympian hierarchy, and one of the last things that we know of the Athenians is that many centuries after they had lost what little belief they ever had in the deities of their pantheon they had reverted to that 'wonder' which is said to be the fountain-head of all religion, and were standing once more in doubt and awe before the altar of a nameless god.

It would be futile to divide the ages of Greek history into certain periods and assign to each its peculiar form of religion. But there are certain underlying principles and many external characteristics which distinguish the

75

pre-Hellenic and the Homeric forms of religion; and even the external form of a nation's religion is of interest and helps one to understand that nation. I shall, therefore, first consider some of the distinguishing principles and then some of the very striking differences in the kind of deities and the kind of worship that we find in the two religions.

What chiefly distinguishes the old religion from the later is that it was based mainly, if not entirely, on the dread of evil spirits (*deisidaimonia*). It was a religion of atonement, propitiation, exorcism, purification, riddance – the turning aside of evil influence (*apotropē*). Sacrifices and offerings were made on the principle *do ut abeas* – *i.e.* 'I give in order that thou depart.'

As it is still with many a barbarous people, so also in Greece in early times, before the Hellenic imagination had personified in human shape the powers of nature, every not quite usual manifestation of natural force and every unusual natural object was suspected of harbouring powers hostile to man. 'The earth is full of evil things, and full the sea,' says Hesiod. Pests and plagues and deadly 'snatchers' and winged disease were lurking and swarming and flitting about on all sides, and the evil eye was ever on the watch. Ghosts and ghoulish things haunted the darkness of night and of the grave.

The souls of the dead manifested themselves not seldom in the form of snakes, to which propitiatory offerings were made, and the powers of the nether world, hungering for blood, were doubtless at times appeased by human sacrifice – of which many evidences survived to a later age in cere-monies of substitution or other curious rites whose meaning had long been lost.[1] And in later times, as we shall see, there were many other survivals of old chthonic ritual, as it is called, connected with the worship of the powers of the earth, especially with that of the Earth-Mother, Demeter, and of Dionysus.

This religion of dread and exorcism gave place – probably somewhat rapidly and not permanently – to a religion which was not only wholly dif-ferent in its external forms of worship, but was founded on an entirely dif-ferent basis, namely, that of *service* (*therapeia*), the principle of which was *do ut des* – *i.e.* 'I give that thou mayst give.' The offering was no longer made in order to propitiate some dreaded demonic power, but given to a deity

---

[1] The stories of Isaac and of Iphigeneia denote the substitution of animals for the human victim. Aelian tells of a curious rite where a baby calf was dressed up and furnished with boots (*cothurni*) and thus sacrificed.

endowed with human feelings and human reason – one who would surely grant some favour in return for the service. The gloomy chthonic rites and the horrors of human sacrifice and the orgies of Dionysus Zagreus, in which the victim was torn to pieces and devoured raw (with some idea of 'eating the god'), and all the 'spook' and mystery and monstrosity and barbarity and sacerdotalism[1] that is connected with such religion, disappeared apparently in a short time after the coming of the Achaeans – for in all Homer there is scarce a trace of such things.[2] It is true that we cannot infer from Homer's picture (even if it is a true picture of a certain class) that the bulk of the Greek nation in the so-called heroic age had renounced the old faith and adopted the new. Possibly behind the dazzling scene of the Achaean and Argive hosts and behind all the brilliant 'puppet show' of the Olympian hierarchy there was still a dark background in Greece itself where the old monstrous beliefs and the old ritual still lurked, like the Python of Delphi before it was slain by Apollo.

But for a time at least this new and brighter religion was destined to prevail – to become the recognized national religion of Greece – and before returning to consider some of the ancient pre-Hellenic deities and their 'supersession' (as it has been called) by the gods of the northern invaders, we should note well how the Hellenic imagination transformed all the ghouls and pests and other evil and monstrous things into Fates and Harpies and Sirens and Gorgons, depriving them thus of the vague, gruesome horror of their mysterious *un*-human nature. Apollo comes with his bright shafts, and Heracles, the god of health,[3] the conqueror of Death itself and the husband of ever-blooming Hebe – and they put to flight the swarming hordes of evil things, and the mountain glades re-echo to the laughter of dryads and nymphs, and the sands of the sea-shore become the dancing-grounds of ocean nereids. Even the terrible Furies themselves – though in a

---

[1] The immense number of priests, prophets, hierophants, and other such mediums connected with the Orphic and similar mystic systems is often mentioned. Priestly office connected with the mysteries was the hereditary right of certain great families, such as the Eumolpidae. What such things can develop into may be seen from the history of the Persian Magi.

[2] There certainly is the slaughter of Trojan captives by Achilles at the funeral of Patroclus; but that was scarcely human sacrifice.

[3] Miss Harrison reproduces pictures in one of which Heracles is beating to death with his club a little winged pest (*kēr*) – perhaps a prehistoric bacillus – and in another an emaciated bald-headed thing – perhaps the bacillus of old age.

later age still worshipped with mystical chthonic rites as denizens of Hell – seem to have won for themselves a worship of service, and almost of affectionate veneration, as the August and Kindly Goddesses. Instead of hideous and savage rites and human sacrifice and wild orgies where live victims are torn to pieces and their bleeding flesh devoured by the worshippers in their mystical yearning to 'eat the god' and thus participate in the divine, we have Homeric prayer and sacrifice and libation, by which the gods are invoked as beings endowed with human affections, in the full assurance (scarce ever deceived) of help and favour;[1] we have joyous sacrificial feasts at which the gods themselves sometimes are present in visible shape. 'Ever till now,' says King Alcinous (who, though no Achaean, is of orthodox Olympian creed), 'ever till now have the gods appeared to us in manifest form whenever we offered glorious hecatombs, and they feast with us, sitting at our side where we are seated. Ay, and if any lonely wayfarer meet them, they nowise conceal themselves – for we are nigh [akin] unto the gods.' The common form of invocation to the supreme deity as 'Father Zeus,' the father both of men and of gods, whose thunder is often a sign of favour, and who 'follows with his protecting care' even the stranger and the beggar, is in itself a striking evidence of the new religious spirit, reminding one much more of the northern All-Vater, Woden, than the Bull-god of Crete or the monstrous and horrid Dionysus Zagreus.

In Homer all is intensely human. There is none of that 'spook' and that childish dread of the supernatural which often make folklore lose its human interest. We find very few monstrous shapes (such as the huge octopus-like Scylla, and the vague terror of the 'Gorgon head' in *Od.* xi. 634), no bull-headed or serpent-tailed men (Proteus is no permanent monster, and the sirens and sea-nymphs are purely human in form), no owl-headed Athene or cow-headed Hera, although the old epithets of these goddesses point to the monstrosities of an earlier creed. Even the winged Pegasus is omitted in the story of Bellerophon as told by Homer. It is true that we have Circe ('Hawk-goddess') with her wand and her baleful drugs – but how intensely human she is! How this 'dread goddess,' this hawk-headed Eastern witch, is transformed into a human being with womanly affections of love and pity! In the Homeric Hades, too, one feels, it is true, the presence of the supernatural. But could anything be more pathetically human than the meeting of Odysseus with his mother, or with Elpenor, or

---

[1] Unfulfilled prayer we find occasionally; *e.g. Od.* ix. 553.

with Agamemnon – or with Ajax? Here and there in the *Odyssey* charms and drugs are mentioned – but never with superstitious awe. The plant 'moly' which Hermes gives Odysseus as a charm – 'black at the root, but the flower is like unto milk in its whiteness' – excites in us a sense of delight, not of dread or mystery; and when the sons of Autolycus bind for Odysseus the wound that the boar of Parnassus had ripped in his leg, and 'staunch the dark red blood with a song of enchantment,' we notice it merely as we should notice some old superstitious habit of the present day. The Cyclops himself is nothing but an enormous human being; and he too prays to Poseidon as his father, although he speaks contemptuously of the gods as his inferiors in strength. And how the touch of nature makes us akin to the divine when Hermes complains of his weary flight across the boundless expanses of ocean, afar from the cities of men where he might have obtained a little refreshment at some sacrificial feast! And how touching is the motherly pride and joy of Leto while she watches her daughter Artemis among her attendant nymphs! The Homeric gods are as intensely human as the Pheidian gods that on the Parthenon frieze await the approaching procession of their worshippers. And they are the gods of all 'bread-eating races of mortals' – universal deities, not mere local or ancestral divinities.

This different conception of the supernatural was doubtless introduced by the northern invaders, whom we may perhaps speak of under the collective name of Achaeans. The character of these northmen evidently differed much from that of the southern peoples whom they conquered. They had the vigour, the courage, the open, if somewhat overbearing and inartistic, nature of northern folk; they had the contempt for all craven dread of supernatural powers and monstrous things which tends to characterize the Indo-Iranian people. They looked up to the heights of the sunlit dome of heaven and to the vast expanses of cloudland and imagined *there* the home of the gods – not in the gloom of a nether world haunted by forms of horror. They did not hide their dead in shaft-tombs, but sent them heavenwards in the flames that leaped upward from the funeral pyre.

Let us now consider some of the ancient deities and rites as contrasted with those of the later 'heroic' age. Out of a vast and confused congeries of fact and theory I shall choose just a few of the most intelligible.

As in the case of pre-Hellenic races and pre-Hellenic civilization, we have to turn to Crete and Mycenae for most of our evidence in regard to pre-Hellenic religion. The evidence supplied by Crete is, of course, only indirectly applicable, but it seems to confirm and supplement what little is

*Fig. 24 'Harvester Vase'*

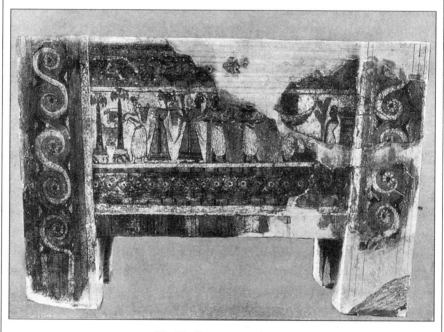

*Fig. 25 Cretan sarcophagus*

known about the religion of the Mycenaean and other Aegean and Pelasgic peoples, if we may use these words to denote the early inhabitants of what we mean by 'Greece' and some of its adjacent islands.

In the earliest age of which we have evidence no temples seem to have existed. Probably groves and caverns were first used, such as the cave at Delphi, or the Dictaean cave in Crete, the fabled birthplace of the Cretan Zeus, where an ancient altar and a table of libation have been found, as well as the ashes of victims and votive offerings, among which are numerous bronzed models of the double axe, the symbol of divinity.

In Crete no remains have been discovered of large temples, but in the palaces as well as in ordinary houses small rooms seem to have been set apart for worship, and in one case, at Gournia, what seems to have been a little much-frequented shrine (for it was approached by a well-worn paved path) stood in the midst of the town.

In Greece itself, among the Aegean and Pelasgic peoples, if we may draw conclusions from the evidence of later days, the first objects of religious worship were stocks and stones – possibly sometimes such meteorites as the images of the Tauric and Ephesian Artemis, which 'fell from heaven.' These were at first formless and unhoused. Later they were shaped into some rough resemblance to the human form, though generally legless, as we see from old descriptions of archaic wooden Greek idols (*xoana*), and from many ancient images in earth-ware which have been dug up.

In Crete, besides such ancient legless and armless idols, have been discovered many representations or models of (1) sacred symbolic objects, (2) divinities.

The symbolic objects evidently signified the presence of divinity in what is called *an-iconic* ritual (*i.e.* a ritual without actual idols; such as was used in the Mysteries, where certain sacred objects were believed to possess a supernatural influence). Of these symbols the *horns of consecration* and the *double axe* (see the Cretan Sarcophagus, Fig. 25) are the commonest. The horns (reminding one of the horns of the Jewish altar, and evidently connected with the worship of a Bull-god – possibly Moloch) are depicted frequently in frescoes and on seals when any religious scene is represented. They have also been found at Mycenae. The double axe also occurs on seals and in frescoes, often in combination with the horns, and is, moreover, found impressed on stucco or cut on stonework.

In the great Palace of Cnossus this *Labrys*, or double axe, is to be seen on many a pillar or block, and it can scarcely be doubted that *Labyrinth*

*Fig. 26  Griffins and pillar*

means 'the house [or place] of the double axe.' The word *Labrys* is said to be Carian. It occurs in the title *Labraunda*, given to the Carian Zeus. The termination *-nth* we have already noted as probably Aegean. What was symbolized by the Cretan Labrys, or double axe, is not known, but it has been supposed that it may have intimated the combined godhead of Sun and Moon, or of the ancient Cretan Earth-goddess and the Cretan Zeus. The symbol is not confined to Crete. It may be seen on Carian and other coins (Coin Plates I. 5 and V. 2, pp. 490, 497).

Besides the horns and the axe we find the pillar – evidently also a symbol of divine presence, as was probably the pillar set up by Jacob at Bethel. In the picture of the Lion Gate at Mycenae (Fig. 2) and in the figure with griffins it will be seen that between the animals stands a pillar, whereas in the next illustration we have the same motive, but the goddess herself has taken the place of the pillar.

Another symbol, or sacred object, is a tree that reminds one somewhat of the ancient Babylonian and Biblical Tree of Life or of Knowledge. It occurs on gems and seals and in paintings (see Figs. 7 and 28). Sometimes it is being watered by grotesque genii, or is being uprooted by a priest, or it bears great bunches of fruit like dates, which in one case are being gathered by a diminutive female.

Another very interesting sacred object – for such it seems to be, as it was found in a shrine – is a cross of grey and yellow marble, which is exactly

*Fig. 27  Earth-goddess and lions*

*Fig. 28  Ritual dance and uprooting of sacred tree*

like a Christian cross 'of orthodox Greek shape,' as Sir Arthur Evans says. A model of this cross may be seen in the British Museum.

Many rude idols have been found – mostly legless and armless – merely grotesque attempts to represent the supernatural. Remarkable evidences of demon and bogy worship are given by numerous seals and gems (see Fig. 31), where we find hideous and monstrous combinations of bird, beast, and human being. Perhaps they were used as charms.[1]

---

[1] Some hold these monstrous forms to be priests or priestesses in disguise, perhaps performing a kind of transformation dance.

*Fig. 29  Genii (priests?) watering sacred tree*

But the most important fact of this nature that has been brought to light by excavation is that the most ancient Cretan deity was a goddess whom we meet in Greek mythology under various names – for doubtless Ge (Earth), Cybele[1] or Rhea (daughter of Earth and the Great Mother of the gods), Demeter (Mother Earth), and the ancient pre-Hellenic or Asiatic Hecate or Artemis (triform and many-breasted) are all closely related to this ancient Cretan goddess. We find her, pictured amidst all kinds of wild animals, as the goddess of nature, the 'Lady of Wild Creatures' (*potnia thērōn*), as was the later Artemis. Frequently, as we have already seen, she is attended by lions, or by serpents which coil themselves around her. Possibly as goddess of the air she is given doves and other birds, as goddess of earth she is attended by lions, and as goddess of the nether world she has the serpent, thus resembling the triform Hecate – who was moon-goddess Selene in heaven, the huntress Artemis on earth, and identical with Persephone in Hades.

According to the *Theogony* of Hesiod the first of all things that sprang from Chaos was Gaia, or Ge (Earth), who by Uranus (Heaven) was the mother of the Titan-god Cronos (Time?). The sister and wife of this old god Cronos was Rhea (Rheia), or Cybele, and their children were the elder Olympian gods, Demeter, Hera, Hades, Poseidon, and Zeus (who seems to have been not the eldest, though the King of Olympus). Now Cronos had the habit of swallowing his offspring, but Rhea fled to Crete and gave birth to Zeus in a cavern on Mount Ida or Mount Dicte; or, according to Hesiod,

---

[1] Semele (mother of Dionysus) may also mean 'Earth-goddess' and be another form of Cybele. Both Cybele and Dionysus are attended by lions. Cybele (also Cybele and perhaps Cybebe) seems to have been the Phrygian name of Rhea.

*Fig. 30 The 'Lady of Wild Creatures'*

she gave over the child to 'mighty Gaia in broad Crete to nurse and rear,' and Gaia hid it 'in an inaccessible cavern under the divine earth on the Aegean[1] mount' – probably the cave of Eileithyia mentioned by Homer (*Od.* xix. 188).

It seems therefore, I think, very probable that the ancient Nature-goddess whose effigies have been found in Crete is this 'mighty Gaia' of Hesiod – though doubtless she was assimilated to her daughter Rhea, who, as the mother of Zeus Cretagenes, is called the Idaean or Dictaean, or the Mountain Mother (*Idaia, Diktynna, Mētēr oreiē*).

We have seen how Greek mythology brings the northern god Zeus to Crete. His worship there was not grafted on to the old religion till the advent of northern invaders, who made their supreme Sky-god the son of the ancient Cretan Earth-Mother.[2] On old Cretan seals and gems there appears associated with the great goddess what seems to be an inferior male deity. He sometimes stands in a reverential attitude before her (as perhaps in Fig. 27), and is also depicted as floating in the sky and apparently beating

---

[1] Aegean (Aigaios) seems to come from some Pelasgic or Aegean word of unknown meaning. The name of this Cretan mountain may have given rise to the myth that Zeus was suckled in the Dictaean cave by the goat Amalthea (Grk. *aigeios* = 'of a goat'). Later writers derive 'Aegean' from Aegeus, the father of Theseus.

[2] On coins of Phaestus Zeus is represented as quite young.

*Fig. 31  Cretan seals (from Zakro)*

his figure-of-eight shield with his spear (Fig. 7). This possibly is meant to represent a sky-god producing thunder, but he cannot well be Zeus, for these relics date from an age far anterior to the introduction of the northern god. This inferior male deity was perhaps fused into the person of Zeus Cretagenes.

There were other localities that claimed to be the birth-place of Zeus, among them Thebes and Ithome, and also the Trojan Ida, but the claims of Crete were generally recognized.

A curious ancient legend relates that Zeus – weary perhaps of sovereignty – retired to Crete and died there. His tomb was said to be on Mount Juktas, near Cnossus. Doubtless this legend inspired the wondrous description by Dante of the gigantic image (like that of Daniel's dream) of Time, or the World's Ages, standing within the Cretan Ida. The claim of the Cretans to possess the tomb of the king of the gods is said to have caused, or increased, their reputation as liars; but if the verse quoted by St. Paul was written by Epimenides (*c.* 600) they seem to have had the reputation considerably before what one would consider the probable date of the decease of Zeus.

There seem to be also evidences of a younger Cretan goddess, the daughter of the Earth-Mother, whose presence some suspect in the stories of Britomartis, Europa, and Ariadne. In later times she seems sometimes to have been identified with Aphrodite (Astarte), but her true representative in the Olympian family is doubtless Koré (*i.e.* the Maiden), the daughter of Demeter, or Ge-meter, the Earth-Mother. This Maiden, it is fabled, was carried off by Hades to his realm of darkness while she was gathering flowers, and under the name of Persephone was made the Queen of the Underworld, but was allowed every year to return to her mother Earth – an allegory of the yearly return of spring (see Fig. 32).

Besides these ancient Cretan deities there are, as we have seen, many evidences of a monstrous bull-headed deity – whether of native origin or derived from some tauriform Oriental deity, such as Moloch, or from the bull-Dionysus of Thrace, of whose orgies I have already spoken, it is impossible to feel certain. 'Of the ritual of the Bull-god in Crete,' says Miss Harrison, 'we know that it consisted in part of the tearing and eating of a bull; and behind is the dreadful suspicion of human sacrifice.' As we have already seen, Minos was probably the high-priest, and was possibly even regarded as the incarnation, of this monstrous deity, and may have himself been sacrificed in the Dictaean cave at the end of his nine years of

*Fig. 32  The return of the Earth-maiden (here Pandora)*

sovereignty. The later legend makes Zeus the original Phoenician-Cretan Bull-god, and Minos his son, but it seems more likely that the monstrous deity existed in Crete long before the advent of Zeus or of the Phoenicians, and that behind the horrid story of Pasiphaë and the Minotaur 'there lurks some mystical ceremony of ritual wedlock [of the Cretan queen] with a primitive bull-headed divinity.'

How far this ancient Cretan religion was similar to the religion of pre-Hellenic Greece it is impossible to say. The day may soon come when a sudden shaft of light will be let into what is still a very dark corner of history. At present we can only point to the fact that numerous signs of connection have been discovered. The bull is found in Mycenaean art; the horns of consecration, the double axe, and the sacred tree occur on (perhaps native) gems and plaques and rings, and in many ancient tombs in Greece and the Aegean islands small rude idols of stone, bronze, lead, and gold have been found which seem to represent a Nature-goddess (sometimes attended by birds) similar to, if not identical with, the Cretan Gaia.

This is, in the main, all that is known of the religion of Greece before the coming of the Achaeans and the Olympian gods, and, except what we are told by Homer and Hesiod, and the still more doubtful evidence that we gather from what was related afterwards by Herodotus and other Greek writers, almost all our knowledge of the Olympian gods and ritual begins after the Dark Age of some three centuries which followed the next invasion of northmen, that of the Dorians.

A few facts, however, seem to emerge here and there, and these we will consider in combination with what we are told by Homer. But it must be remembered that Homer wrote perhaps three centuries after the Achaean, or heroic, age, and may have indulged in a good deal of imaginative reconstruction.

In Homer we find the regime of the new gods already well established. Each has his or her special functions and appointed place in the Olympian family, and instead of a Mighty Mother we have a well-marked *patria potestas* (patriarchal authority). There are, indeed, signs that the worship of these new gods had already lasted a considerable time, for familiarity had already bred contempt, and the behaviour of some of the deities as described in the poems was such as to excite indignation in the mind of even such a philosopher as Plato.

Of most of these Olympians it is difficult to trace the lineage. In some cases they are doubtless grand and beautiful re-creations, the prime elements of which were deities of the older religions, Northern, Aegean, Pelasgian, and also sometimes Oriental. But Zeus is apparently almost purely northern – the Indo-Iranian Dyaus-piter, the Day-Father or Sky-god, and the Papas or Bronton (Father or Thunderer) of the Phrygians. He was evidently introduced in a very early age into the mountainous country in North-western Greece (Epirus, or 'Mainland,' as it was called by the islanders), which, as well as parts of Thessaly, was then inhabited by Achaeans, or others of the same race, before they made their great descent on Southern Greece.[1] Even before the coming of the Achaeans there existed in Epirus the far-famed sanctuary and oracle of Dodona, where some Pelasgian Earth-Mother gave responses through her priestesses by the murmuring of her doves. This sanctuary was, it seems, annexed by the northern Zeus, who (as Homer tells us) adopted the name of the 'Dodonaean' or 'Pelasgic' Zeus. As god of the air he gave his oracles through the voices of winds moaning and rustling in his sacred oak-grove

---

[1] The Achaeans were apparently driven finally from Epirus about the time of the Dorian invasion of Greece (*c.* 1100) by a barbaric northern tribe, the Illyrians. Epirus and Aetolia thenceforth were regarded as mainly barbarian (non-Hellenic) lands.

Fig. 33  Minoan, Mycenaean, and Trojan ware, c. 2000–1300
(See List of Illustrations and Note D)

amidst the murmur of falling waters and the clangor of bronzen vessels struck by wind-moved hammers. Later he was brought to other Pelasgic and Aegean lands, and given the kingship of the new Olympian hierarchy. Apollo was also doubtless of northern origin, but his many diverse attributes (as Sender of Pestilence, Sun-god, Harp-god, etc.) show that he was a re-creation out of various deities. There was later a Dorian Apollo with special attributes (see Pindar, *Pyth.* v.), of whom many old statues[1] seem to be representations, but by the Achaeans, if we may believe Homer, Apollo was worshipped as Phoebus, 'the bright sun-god' and sender of sudden death. Hermes, the Messenger, was probably a native Aegean (Arcadian) god. The Hermes statues of later art seem to be a survival of old legless and armless idols. Demeter, as we have already seen, was originally a native Earth-Mother. Leto and Semele and Dionysus,[2] Artemis and others were probably old deities, but they received many new features and were transformed from grotesque and monstrous shapes into things of beauty and grandeur.

Such wondrous transmutation or re-creation one finds in all great art, but perhaps nowhere as in Homer. When we think of some ghoulish Aegean idol or some many-breasted Cybele and then turn to the majestic Zeus of Homer, or to Hermes the Messenger, or to Artemis, the virgin huntress amidst her forest-nymphs, and when we mark the loving reverence and trustfulness with which Homer's men and women address the deities and speak of their justice and their affection, we realize the enormous and seemingly impassable gulf that separates the two conceptions of deity – conceptions which were not separated by any wide gulf of time, but probably existed for a period side by side. Of course, Homer did not live in the age that he describes, and his poetic instinct may have eliminated much of the grotesque and monstrous which still survived in that age, and may have lent it some features that belonged to his own; but, however that may be, the Homeric gods stand already on the same level as the Olympian Zeus and the Lemnian Athene of Pheidias, or even the still more humanly beautiful, if less divinely majestic, Cnidian Aphrodite of Praxiteles. Indeed, Pheidias confessed that he found in Homer alone the ideal that he realized in his Olympian Zeus.

---

[1] For these 'Apollos' see p. 249–500

[2] Homer says but little of Dionysus, possibly avoiding him as associated with horrors. He associates him (*Od.* xi.) with Crete and probably with the Bull-god, as well as with the East (Nysa) and Thrace (*Il.* vi.). It was left for later Greek art to transform him into the joyous, boisterous wine-god.

It is this transforming and creative power which makes Greek art and literature by far the most precious legacy of past ages. Antiquarian and historical research gives us what is mere erudition when it is not touched to life by a love and admiration for the creations of Greek imagination and the revelations of Greek thought. All these excavations and discoveries in Crete and Mycenae and Troy and elsewhere, as well as all research and higher criticism in such subjects as the Homeric question or the Athenian Constitution, derive their only real value and interest from the fact that they lead us towards a better understanding and a fuller appreciation of the art and literature and philosophy of Greece, and of the character of her greatest men.

### SECTION C: THE 'HOMERIC AGE' AND HOMER

Homer and the 'Homeric age' do not really belong to the same period, for the Homeric poems – even the earliest parts of them – were not written in the age that they describe, as is evident from the fact that the poet frequently speaks of the men of his own age as far inferior to the heroes who fought at Troy, although these were again inferior to the greater heroes of an earlier age, such as Heracles (*Il.* v. 304; *Od.* viii. 223, etc.). But it is necessary to treat the two subjects together, for these poems are the only evidence of this Achaean or Homeric age. The Mycenaean shaft-graves have indeed supplied evidence of an age of unsuspected civilization, but, as we have seen, great differences are apparent in regard to dress, armour, disposal of the dead, and probably religion, between the Mycenaean civilization and that world which Homer describes. These differences and the necessary supposition of an almost incredibly rapid and complete development of another state of things, and of another entirely different conception of deity, coupled with the fact that we have practically no evidence whatever of this 'Homeric age' except what we are told by the Homeric poems, have made some writers assert that these poems give merely an imaginative picture of a world that never existed, and that, except a small 'nucleus' (some ancient ballad describing the 'wrath' of a sea-god, Achilles, against a land-god, Agamemnon, both of whom had their habitat somewhere in Thessaly, whence they were transported by later Homeric bards to the Peloponnese), the *Iliad* is a farrago compounded by several generations of rhapsodists, a kind of epical romance in which the fiction of some long-past mythical age was depicted and from which

almost all anachronisms[1] were carefully eliminated by the bards themselves and their critical auditors. The *Odyssey*, according to such critics, is
of much later date than the older parts of the *Iliad*, and was compiled by
similar bards, or perhaps by a single highly gifted bard, from old stories of
adventures in the Euxine, which were transferred to western seas.[2]
Moreover, Odysseus was 'only a god,' and Penelope only a goddess.

There certainly is much vagueness in the geography of the *Odyssey*, and
evident confusion of the far East with the far West. Circe's original home
was Colchis, and her island Aeaea is said to have been near the sunrise. (She
and her brother Aeëtes were both, perhaps, originally bird-headed Eastern
deities.) Moreover, the original home of the Cimmerians was evidently the
Crimea. Altogether there can, I think, be no doubt that the poems, especially the *Iliad*, underwent in the course of centuries of public recitation a
certain amount of pruning and reshaping, that ancient Aeolic words may
have been modernized into the later Ionian dialect, and that lines glorify-
ing certain families or places may have been inserted, and possibly also
some episodes. Moreover, it is possible that when the poems were arranged
into books and canonized in the age of Peisistratus (about 520) some read-
justment and welding took place. But any long disquisition on these much-
vexed questions would be here out of place, and I shall merely state my own
slowly formed conviction that both these poems owe their main structure
and most of their details to one great poet, that the age which he depicted
was no mere fiction, and that he lived near enough to that age to paint, by
the help of traditions and ballads, its main features with very considerable
exactitude. It is a saying of Socrates that 'about flute-playing musicians

[1] Such writers point gleefully to numerous cases where 'good old Homer is caught napping'
(to use Horace's expression) – various inconsistencies and slips of memory, such as occur
in the best of poets. They also assert that he sometimes describes shields as man-covering
and as huge 'as a tower,' and at other times gives the warriors the small round Carian shield
and breast-plates, etc. – as if different kinds of shield and armour might not have been in
use! Also they point at the mention of *iron* (*Od.* xix. 13) as 'attracting [to bloodshed],'
whereas iron is elsewhere in the poems used only for knives and axes – not for weapons.
But the 'Iron Age' had already begun, and it was doubtless used already for weapons,
though 'bronze' was the usual term in poetry. How plentiful iron already was is plain from
*Od.* i. 184, where a whole cargo of it is brought from Temesa (in Italy?).

[2] A French writer, Bérard, has endeavoured to prove that the *Odyssey* is founded on the log-
books of Phoenicians (who certainly as early as the time of Solomon visited Spain, and
perhaps South Africa), and discovers Calypso's island on the African coast not far from
Gibraltar.

judge best, and about poetry poets.' When the poet Goethe first read the celebrated *Prolegomena* of the German scholar Wolf, the originator of modern Homer-scepticism, he was puzzled and half convinced. But he very wisely determined to re-read Homer, and ended by recanting his half assent to the 'subjective stuff and nonsense,' declaring that 'behind these poems there stands a splendid unity – a single, lofty, creative mind.' It was doubtless a similar poetic instinct, innate in the Greek race, which preserved the true Homer in the midst of a mass of inferior ballad-epics (those of the so-called Cyclic poets), many of which had appropriated his name, and finally sifted out the true ore and cast aside the rubbish.

The old Boeotian poet Hesiod, whose date and works have been subjected to a similar critical process, and who probably lived *c.* 700, gives testimony, of course rejected by the critics in question, that an age of heroes preceded his own age (the age of iron). In this heroic age, he says, took place the expedition of the Seven against seven-gated Thebes, and that against Troy for the sake of fair-haired Helen. Herodotus, whose testimony is however of a much later date (about 480–430), tells us that he believed Homer and Hesiod to have both lived 400 years before his time.[1]

Seven cities claimed to have been the birthplace of Homer. The presence of Aeolic forms in his Ionic Greek seems to prove that he lived in Southern Aeolis, perhaps in Chios, or in Cyme or in its daughter-city old Smyrna, which was then Aeolian. (It was afterwards moved a few miles south over the Ionian frontier.) Some, indeed, imagine that the oldest strata of the Homeric poems were written entirely in 'ancient Aeolic' (a dialect related to the later 'Lesbian' of Sappho and Alcaeus), and afterwards worked over into Ionic (an early dialect of the Ionic used some four centuries later by Herodotus), Aeolian forms being left when the scansion did not allow of change. This is, of course, pure guesswork, as is also the theory that the old Achaeans of Thessaly invented the hexameter rhythm, and that their ancient ballads about their local feuds formed the basis of the Trojan fiction; but until this is proved I think we may reasonably believe that Homer belonged to one of the early 'Ionian' colonial families who began to come over about 1040, some 150 years after the fall of Troy had first attracted Achaeans and other Greeks to settle in Aeolis. Who these 'Ionians' were I shall discuss in the following chapter. Possibly Homer,

---

[1] *Editor's note.* It is generally now accepted that Hesiod lived *c.* 700 and that the Homeric poems were composed around 750–725.

though himself Ionian, lived across the Aeolian (Achaean) border, and thus came across the old Aeolic (Achaean) ballads (possibly in hexameter rhythm) and thence formed his great epic, finding eager auditors amongst the descendants of those Achaeans who had sacked Troy and opened up the country to Greek colonization. Whether Homer himself emigrated from Greece, or whether he ever visited Greece, it is impossible to say. Hesiod uses words which have been made to mean that he met Homer at Chalcis, in Euboea, and conquered him in a poetical contest; indeed, an alternative reading of these words (*Erga* 657) asserts this; but it is very improbable. Homer however knew Greece well, though he may never have seen it. The local colour of his poems is that of the mother-country, and not of Asia Minor. His gods and his Muses dwell evidently on the Thessalian Olympus. Achaea, Pylos, Mycenae, Argos, Phthia, and all other Greek places, are spoken of with a kind of *Heimweh*; and how often do the expressions 'homewards,' 'fatherland,' 'land of his fathers' occur! On the other hand, Asia Minor is for Homer a wild un-Greek country. Of Phrygia, Maeonia, Lycia, and of islands such as Lesbos and Chios we hear (*Od.* iii. 170), but no word of Aeolis or of Ionia as Greek colonies. Miletus is mentioned as ruled by the 'Carians of barbarous tongue.'

It would be out of place here to retell the oft-told tale of Troy and the Wanderings of Odysseus, but for those who do not reject the world of Homer as a fiction it is intensely interesting to examine his evidence – the only evidence we possess – in regard to this age of Achaean supremacy. I will therefore note a few points.

In the *Iliad* we find the Achaeans and their Argive soldiery under the abnormal (though perhaps for them not uncommon) conditions of war and camp-life in a foreign land, and although we learn less of the state of civilization than we might have learnt had the scene of the epic been laid at Sparta or Mycenae, we learn much else. In the *Odyssey*, on the other hand, we have descriptions of home life: of palaces, of farmsteads and orchards and agriculture, of the cottages and work of herdsmen, of townsfolk and their town, of meetings of the citizens, of busy wharves and arsenals and shipping, of masters and mistresses amid their servants and thralls; and, besides these Ithacan and Phaeacian pictures, we are given particulars of a chariot journey (evidently on a tolerably good road) across a part of the Peloponnese and a very distinct picture of the home of Menelaus and Helen at Sparta, and also a glimpse of the Mycenaean palace of Agamemnon. By means of all these various pictures, and by fitting together the almost innumerable details that we find in both poems, we are able to form a fairly complete conception of the Achaean world in peace[1] and in war.

Pictures of religious rites, of sacrifices and libations and funeral ceremonies are frequent, and sometimes we are reminded of the old religion. Thus in the visit to Hades (*Od.* xi.) we have a threefold libation to the ghosts of the dead – of honey-milk, of wine, and of water – reminding us of an ancient Cretan libation table with three basins found in the Dictaean cave. Moreover, on the same occasion Odysseus fills a hole that he had dug in the ground with the blood of victims, and the ghosts come flocking round it in their longing to drink – a picture that recalls the 'feeding holes' for blood libation which have been found on the summit of Mycenaean tombs. Again, many instances occur of sanctuaries and altars in the open air, under oaks and plane-trees and palms (*Od.* vi. 162), and there is frequent mention of sacred groves and sacred precincts. But we also have a few definite references to temples – such as the 'house of Erechtheus' at Athens (possibly a late accretion) and the 'temples of the gods' and the 'shrine of Poseidon' (evidently not a grove) in the Phaeacian city (*Od.* vi. 10 and 266), and in the sixth book of the *Iliad* there is given with a few touches a fine sketch of the temple of Athene in Troy and the seated statue of the goddess, on whose knees (1. 273) Hecabe lays a *peplos*, just as was still done by the Athenians of the age of Pericles at the Panathenaic festival – a scene depicted on the frieze of the Parthenon. There are also descriptions of funeral ceremonies, such as the celebrated picture of the funeral of Patroclus in the twenty-third book of the *Iliad*, and the exquisitely beautiful, though possibly not Homeric,[2] scene of the mourning for Achilles (*Od.* xxiv.), and the *cortège* round his funeral pyre, and the pathetic lines which tell us how Odysseus

---

[1] In the following very incomplete list every word conjures up some picture or series of pictures for any one who knows the *Odyssey*: Spinning, weaving, dress, beds, tables, chairs, metal-work, inlaying, forging, goblets, brooches, hunting, fishing, vineyards, gardening, bathing, swimming, horses, mules, goats, cattle, swine, geese, dogs, lions, eagles, palaces, house-building, ship-building, raft-building, sailing, rowing, feasting, athletic games, boxing, draughts, ball-playing, acrobats, dancing, music, law-courts, funerals, sacrifices, beggars, clothes-washing, wagons, chariots.

[2] The so-called *Nekyia deutera* (second visit to the dead), if not by Homer himself, is worthy of him. It is like a figure by Praxiteles added to an unfinished group by Pheidias. Some affirm that the *first* descent (Book XI) was inserted (and composed?) by some Orphic teacher, perhaps Onomacritus, when the Homeric poems were collected and arranged in the time of Peisistratus. This I prefer not to believe.

and his men felled trees and built a pyre and burnt the body of their comrade Elpenor, and how they then piled a mound above his buried ashes and erected on the top of the mound the oar 'with which in life he had rowed amidst his mates,' as his ghost in Hades had implored them to do. Achaean funerals, as we have already seen, were generally of this character – cremation and burial of ashes. There is, however, one word (*tarchyein*) thrice used in the *Iliad* which seems to point to some older custom, such as was prevalent in Egypt, for the word means to 'dry' (like smoked fish).

Among the Homeric Achaeans the kingship was hereditary, although it seems as if the family prerogative had to be confirmed by Zeus, probably through oracular response or omens, for Telemachus allows this (*Od.* i. 386 *ff.*) and speaks of the possibility of some other of the Ithacan princes (whom he also calls 'kings' – *basilees*) being elected instead of himself. In the *Iliad* Agamemnon is the over-lord of all the Achaean princes and the head of the army; in the *Odyssey* Odysseus is the over-lord of all the Ithacan chieftains and nobles and possesses large estates and many flocks and herds and the rights of pasture on the mainland and in Ithaca. The king has a privy council (*boulē*) formed of elders and nobles, and there is also a public assembly (Agora), which in the *Iliad* naturally consists of all the fighting men – perhaps of others too, for one can hardly conceive Thersites as a fighter. In the *Odyssey* we have descriptions of both Ithacan and Phaeacian assemblies, consisting evidently of all the free men of the state. They seem, as a rule, to have been summoned merely to hear the decisions of the king and his *boulē*; but sometimes they certainly took their own course, breaking up in disorder, some following one leader and some another (*e.g. Od.* iii. 137 *ff.*).

The land seems to have belonged mainly to the Achaean noble families, who probably held their hereditary title from the king and *boulē*. There seem also to have been 'common lands' (*Il.* xii. 422), and even thralls, such as the swineherd Eumaeus, could receive in tenant-right a 'lot' (*klēros*) from his lord, and those who were not landowners (*aklēroi*) could engage farm-labourers and evidently hire land for cultivation (*Od.* xi. 490), but the family *klēroi* (allotments) probably took up most of the good soil and pasturage. These allotments could be divided among members of a family (in Crete anyhow, as we see from *Od.* xiv. 209), but, being held in feu-right from a liege lord, could not be sold. Hesiod, however, speaks of the gods granting the blessing of 'buying your neighbour's allotment instead of his buying yours.' But that was later, and in Boeotia.

The Homeric palace, or large house, stood often in a palisaded or walled courtyard. It consisted of a portico and a raised 'stoep,' where guests slept, and a great *megaron* (hall) which was used for meals and also as a sleeping-place; but there were also frequently (*e.g.* in Odysseus' palace) workrooms and bedrooms in the back part of the house, those for the women upstairs. Descriptions are given, more or less full, of the palaces of Odysseus, Alcinous, Menelaus, Circe, and what I have called glimpses of Agamemnon's Mycenaean palace and of the quarters of Achilles in the Greek camp. Circe's palace had a flat roof where guests could sleep. The palace of Alcinous had a frieze, or coping, of blue glass-paste (*cyan*) such as has been found in a palace at Tiryns. Its walls were bronzen (doubtless plated with bronze, as in the 'Treasury of Atreus' at Mycenae), and its doors and door-handle were of gold; the door-posts and lintel were of silver and the threshold was of bronze. The palace of Menelaus is described as gleaming with bronze, gold, amber, silver, and ivory.

Art treasures, Achaean and Sidonian, are frequently described: metal-work, embroidery, fine-woven cloths, carved woodwork, and other artistic objects. The 'Shield of Achilles' testifies to a high proficiency in the art of metal inlay, though we must perhaps allow something for imagination. The art of writing has already been mentioned.

Exceedingly beautiful are the relations between those who are bound by ties of affection and kinship. Nowhere in literature is to be found anything more touching and beautiful than the love of Achilles for Patroclus, of Andromache and of old Priam for Hector, of Hector for his wife and child, of Telemachus for his mother, of Penelope and of Anticleia for Odysseus; and even such love is equalled by the tender affection of the old nurse Eurycleia and the swineherd Eumaeus and the old Dolius (all of them slaves) for their masters and their mistress. When the good old swine-herd saw Telemachus once more, whom he feared the suitors had mur-dered,

. . . to welcome his master he hastened,
Kissed him on both of his cheeks, on his beautiful eyes and his forehead,
Kissed him on both of his hands, while big tears fell from his eyelids.

And in the same way all the maids who had remained faithful to Odysseus, when they recognized him after the slaughter of the suitors, crowded round him,

Lovingly kissing his head and his shoulders in token of welcome,
Grasping and kissing his hands.

In Homer there is not much of that high-wrought sentiment which plays
such a large part in modern romance. Indeed, there is a good deal that
would offend the delicate sensibilities of the writer and reader of such
romance. An hour or so after Odysseus' rather unconventional interrup-
tion of their ball-playing on the river-bank, Nausicaä (who was a lady if
ever there was one) confesses openly and without the slightest touch of sentiment to her maidens that she would be delighted to have him as a
husband.

Passionate love seems in Homer to be regarded as somewhat contemptible as well as dangerous. The names of Briseis, Calypso, and Circe
do not awaken very pleasant associations. Helen bitterly bewails, even
before Priam, the madness of passionate love sent her by Aphrodite, and
although the greybeards of Troy seem to condone it on account of her irresistible charms, and although – what is still more strange – Menelaus
himself condones it, and lives contentedly with her after her ten years' infidelity, the general verdict seems to agree with her self-accusation of 'dog-
faced' shamelessness and with her self-contempt. Clytaemnestra affords
another example. She is described by Nestor as good by nature; but illicit
love maddened her and led her to murder her husband. With the deities
passion cannot, of course, lead to crime, for they are above law, but in their
case such emotions are represented as even more contemptible and ridiculous than in the case of a mortal; and when Hephaestus, as an injured
husband, demands compensation of Ares (*Od.* vii.) the satire reaches its
climax.

Nothing, indeed, is more remarkable than the way in which the gods –
who are generally treated with great respect, and even veneration – are satirized in this matter. The Homeric Zeus is a majestic figure, and inspires
deep reverence in mortal hearts, but he does not escape ridicule. Although
he sends Hermes to warn Aegisthus against his design of seducing
Clytaemnestra, the Father of the Gods himself earns an unenviable notoriety in matters of love, and at such moments stands on a much lower moral
level than mortals such as Hector or Odysseus; for though Odysseus was
not faultless, the relations between him and Penelope are very much more
edifying and very much more beautiful than are frequently the relations
between the King and Queen of Heaven. Indeed, family life on earth is

pictured as being on the whole happier than it is in heaven. In spite of the fact that a wife was often practically bought by the suitor who could offer the largest 'bride-gift' to the parents, married life in that age, if we may accept Homer's descriptions, was often a life of the deepest affection and of unbounded confidence – such a life as Odysseus himself pictured to Nausicaä:

So shall the gods all blessings bestow that thy soul desireth –
Husband and home; and oneness of heart may heaven vouchsafe thee,
Blessing supreme – since nought can be wished that is greater and better
While united in heart and in mind are dwelling together
Husband and wife. 'Tis a sight brings sorrow to wishers of evil,
Joy to the wishers of good. But the joy in their hearts is the loudest.

As a description of a work of art – of an art derived from the old Mycenaean and Cretan artists – the 'Shield of Achilles' (*Il.* xviii.) is of great interest to the antiquarian, but its chief value, of course, consists in the fact that it is magnificent poetry and that it gives such wondrously vivid, and in their main features doubtless accurate, pictures of the life of this age – the age of Achaean supremacy. The fivefold shield was wrought by Hephaestus of 'unyielding bronze and tin and costly gold and silver.' In the centre he fashioned 'earth and sky and sea and the unwearied sun and the full moon and all the constellations with which heaven is crowned, the Pleiades and Hyades and Orion and the Bear, who alone hath no share in the baths of Ocean.' Round the outer rim flowed the 'mighty strength of the river of Ocean,' and in the middle space were city scenes and scenes of country life. First we have scenes of peace within a city – a bridal procession, a court of law; then we see a city beleaguered, and warriors, led by Ares and Athene, arming for a sortie and an ambuscade; then cattle-lifting and a general fray. Next come pictures of rural life: a field being ploughed by many plough-men, and as each one reaches the limit of the field he receives a cup of sweet wine, and turns refreshed, eager to reach again the end of his furrow, 'and behind him it grew black, and looked like ploughed earth, though wrought in gold.' Then we have a reaping scene, the heavy crop falling in swaths at the sweep of the sickles, and being bound into sheaves, while the king looks on in silence with exultant heart, and beneath a great oak a banquet is being prepared. Then comes a vintage scene – the luscious fruit borne in woven baskets amid music and dancing. Then herdsmen drive their cattle forth to pasture, and nigh to the watering-place and the waving reed-bed two lions attack and drag off a bull, while the men vainly urge on their dogs, who bark furiously but keep aloof. Then in a beautiful valley we see a great flock of white sheep and the sheepfolds and the shepherds' huts. Lastly, there is a dancing-ground 'like to that which once Daedalus made in broad Cnossus for fair Ariadne,' and here maidens and youths are dancing, those crowned with fair garlands and these with golden swords hanging from silver baldricks, and two acrobats are turning somersaults amidst the surrounding crowd while a minstrel makes music with his harp.

Very interesting, too, is the description of the dress and the golden brooch of Odysseus. The passage occurs in the fictitious account (*Od.* xix.) that he gives Penelope of how once in Cretan Cnossus he met and hospitably entertained – himself!

Purple and thick was the cloak that was worn by the godlike Odysseus,
Twofold, knit by a brooch that was fashioned of gold and was furnished
Doubly with sockets for pins; and the front was embossed with a picture:
Here was a hound that was holding a dappled fawn with his forefeet,
Watching it struggle; and all that beheld were greatly astonished
How, though golden, the hound kept watching the fawn as he choked it,
While in the longing to win an escape with the legs it was writhing.
Further, I noticed the tunic he wore: 'twas of linen that glister'd
Like to the delicate skin that is peeled from a shrivelling onion;
Such was the softness thereof; and it gleamed as the sun in his glory.

# SECTION D: APPROXIMATE CHRONOLOGY OF 'AEGEAN' AND OTHER CONTEMPORARY CIVILIZATIONS

| CRETE, MYCENAE, AND ISLANDS | EGYPT | ELSEWHERE |
|---|---|---|
| 8000(?)–3000<br>Later Stone Age (Neolithic)<br>Black burnished pottery (*bucchero*) with linear scratches. Idols, seals, copper daggers. Still 20 feet unexplored deposit of this age near Cnossus. Bronze begins. Tin brought from far West ? | [Pre-dynastic black ware ; also pictures of ships. Already evident intercourse with Crete. Obsidian brought from Aegaean.]<br><br>Dynasty I–II (3500–3000)<br>Mena first king.<br>Diorite and syenite vessels (also in Crete). | Troy I (3500)<br>Stone implements, earth-ware (white jade !). Inscriptions of old Babylonian Empire (Sumir and Accad) begin, c. 3000. |
| 3000–2000. Bronze Age (till c. 1250)<br><br>Early Minoan Period<br>Stone vessels and idols, great jars. Hand-made unglazed ware and spiral painted ornament. (Also in Melos, Amorgos, &c.) Pictorial writing. Early palaces at Cnossus and Phaestus. | Dynasty III–XI (3000–2000)<br>Cheops and other Pyramid-builders. | Northern tribes (Mysians, Phrygians, Lycians ?) begin to pass over from Thrace to N.W. Asia Minor.<br>Troy 2 and 3 (2500–?)<br>Stone and copper implements. Leaden idols. Gold treasure. Bronze rare.<br>Sidon founded (2500 ? or much earlier ?)<br>Tyre, 'daughter of Sidon,' founded (2000). |
| 2000–1600<br>Middle Minoan Period<br>First great Palace and Labyrinth at Cnossus. Wheel-made glazed pottery with curved lines. Polychrome Kamáres ware.<br>Then figure decoration : marine animals and others. Khyan's cartouche at Cnossus.<br>Hieroglyphic writing (phonetic).<br>The Phaestus disc.<br>Warriors with great shields (crescent or figure-of-eight).<br>Women's dress : bodice and flounced skirt. Men's : often only drawers and leg-gear.<br>First great Palace at Cnossus burnt (c. 1850) and Later Palace begun.<br>Linear (syllabic) writing begins (c. 1800) in Crete.<br><br>Oldest Shaft-graves at Mycenae<br>Gold ornaments, glazed Mycenaean ware (also in Thera, &c.), silver raised work, gems, seals, iron rings (rare) | Dynasty XII–XVII (2000–1580)<br>Amenemhat III builds the great Labyrinth near Lake Moeris.<br>*Abraham and Sarah* in Egypt (1850 ?).<br>Dark Age. Hyksos (Shepher Kings), of whom Khyan ('Land Embracer') the best known. Horses and wagons introduced by Hyksos ?<br>*Joseph* perhaps under last Hyksos king (Apepi ?). | Troy 4 (2000 ?)<br>Assyrian kings begin (c. 1850)<br>Khyan's cartouche also at Bagdad. |

1600–1400
Late Minoan Period
Cretan frescoes, bronze-work, plaster reliefs, Later Palace at Cnossus finished. Great splendour. Bull-fights.
Hagia Triada vases and sarcophagus.
The palaces at Mycenae and Tiryns built?
Cartouche of Amenhotep III at Mycenae.
The Vaphio cups (or earlier?).
Mycenaean civilization at its highest.

1400–1200. Achaeans at Mycenae. Sack of Cnossus and Phaestus (by Achaeans? or by Mycenaeans driven south by Achaeans?).
Temporary reoccupation, and then decline and fall of Minoan Empire.
Olympian gods begin to be superimposed on old religion.

Iron Age begins (c. 1250)
1200–1100
Homeric (Heroic) Age
Achaeans supreme in most of S. Greece, and perhaps in Crete.
Trojan War.
The vaulted tombs of Mycenae?
Homeric dress and armour: smaller round shield, greaves, &c., introduced.
Pottery again with geometric decoration, as also in later 'Dipylon' ware

1100–1000
Crete conquered by Dorians.
Codrus king of Athens (traditional date of death 1044.)
Introduction of Greek alphabet.

---

1580. Aahmes conquers Hyksos and founds Dynasty XVIII (1580–1350)

1500. Tutmes III invades Mesopotamia.

Pictures of Kephtiu (Cretans?) offering Mycenaean ware to Tutmes.

1414. Amenhotep III

Dynasty XIX (1350–1200)
Name Kephtiu (Philistines from Kaphtor, Jer. xlvii. 4?) disappears.

Ramses II [*Moses*]

Merenptah [*Exodus*], 1300

Dynasty XX (Ramses III–XIV, 1200–1100)
'Peoples of the Sea,' perhaps driven south by Achaeans, invade Egypt, but are defeated by Ramses III (c. 1180).
Odysseus and Menelaus in Egypt?

Dynasty XXI (priestly: 1100–950)
Period of decline.

---

Troy 5 (1600)

'Mycenaean' kings in Cyprus.
Cuneiform tablets written by them to kings of Egypt (1450).
Cecrops of Athens (1450?)
Nineveh becomes a great city (1400).

Successive Achaean invasions from Central Europe (c. 1400–1200). They conquer 'Mycenaeans' and Peloponnese.

Troy 6 built (c. 1350)
[Cadmus founds Thebes, traditional date 1313.]
Hittite Empire in Asia Minor.
Treaty between Ramses II and the Hittite king Chetasor (1250).
[Argonauts, traditional date 1225.
'Seven against Thebes,' traditional date 1213.]

Aeolian colonization begins
'Pulosathu' among the 'People of the Sea' defeated by Ramses III, possibly the Philistines (Pelasgi? Cretans? Kephtiu?). They settle in Canaan. (Cretan pottery found at Gath.)

Troy 6 burnt (traditional date 1184)
1120. Tiglath-pileser.
Philistines conquer Israel and Sidon. Samson.

Ionian colonization begins
New Greek colonies in Cyprus (Salamis).
Dorian invaders from N. Greece conquer Crete, some Aegean islands (and Pamphylia?).
Others settle in S.E. Peloponnese.
Saul, David (c. 1000).
Sidon subject to her 'daughter' Tyre.

*Chapter 2*

# *The Dark Age ( c. 1100 to 776 )*

## *The Dorians – The Colonization of Aeolis,*
## *Ionia, and Doris*

SECTIONS – A: DIPYLON ANTIQUITIES – B: HESIOD – C: THE
PHOENICIANS AND SOME OTHER NATIONS DURING THE DARK AGE

Of the age that we have been considering, that of the Achaean supremacy, we have in Homer's poems a wonderfully distinct, though perhaps somewhat imaginative, picture. These Homeric men and women and the world in which they lived, although we have no memorials of them but words, seem very near to us – nearer by far than many nations of whom we have abundant relics, such as the Babylonians, Assyrians, and Egyptians – nearer, too, than many a people of an age not far removed from our own. Without its venerable poet this Achaean age would doubtless be as much of a blank as the three centuries which followed it – an epoch which is indeed fairly rich in myths, but about which we know for certain much less than we do about the far earlier Minoan and Egyptian civilizations. One fact, however, is indubitable. It was an epoch of great invasions or 'migrations,' which rapidly changed the character of the population and the civilization in many parts of Greece and extended the Hellenic name to large tracts of country on the other side of the Aegean Sea.

First, let us see what the myths say.

### Mythical Accounts of the Migrations

Hellen, king of Phthia, in Thessaly, and son of Deucalion (the Greek Noah), was the mythical ancestor of all the Hellenes. Aeolus and Dorus were his sons, Achaeus and Ion his grandsons through another son. From these 'eponymous' heroes were descended the Aeolians, Dorians, Achaeans, and Ionians. The Aeolians lived in Thessaly and the Dorians in Doris, a small district in central North Greece. The Ionians settled in the country afterwards called Achaea, and the Achaeans conquered the whole of the Peloponnese except this district of the Ionians and the mountain strongholds of the Arcadians.

Now in the Peloponnese there had been before the coming of the Achaeans two great reigning dynasties – the descendants of Perseus (who is said to have founded Tiryns and Mycenae) and the Pelopid princes of Pisa, Olympia, and Amyclae, with whom, as we have already seen, the northern Achaean invaders probably intermarried and identified themselves. The last of the Perseid dynasty had been Eurystheus (the king of Argos who enslaved Heracles). He was succeeded by the Pelopid Atreus. On the death of Heracles (traditional date 1209) his children were exiled from Argos. They endeavoured to return and recover their possessions, but after Hyllus, the son of Heracles, had been killed in single combat they promised to renounce all further attempts for a hundred years. At the end of this time (1104) they put themselves at the head of a great army of Dorians,[1] who espoused their cause, and who were finding the little district of Doris between Oeta and Parnassus too narrow for their needs. This Dorian host, helped by the Aetolians and Locrians, built a fleet at a port thereafter known as Naupactus ('Place of Shipbuilding'), and overran most of the Peloponnese, which was divided among the Heracleidae and their Dorian allies. The most powerful of the Peloponnesian monarchs was the Pelopid-Achaean Tisamenus, son of Orestes (and, therefore, grandson of Agamemnon). He was either slain or else compelled to retire with his Achaeans to the northern district of the Peloponnese, which was, as already stated, inhabited by Ionians. These Ionians were driven out by the Achaeans, and took refuge in Attica.

Now the king of Athens about this time was Codrus, of the race of Nestor, whose descendants had been driven out of Pylos by the Dorians. When the Dorians also attacked Attica Codrus devoted himself to death,

---

[1] Plato gives a very different story, namely, that the Achaeans who returned from Troy were not received by the people at home, and, being expelled, put themselves under the leadership of a chief named Dorieus and changed their name to Dorians. They then allied themselves with the Heracleidae and recaptured the Peloponnese. This is worth mentioning if only to show the very great variations in such old myths.

and thus (in accordance with an oracle) saved his country. His sons quarrelled, and when the oracle gave its verdict for one of them the other went off with a 'mixed multitude' consisting to a great extent of the Ionian refugees, and, making his way from island to island across the Aegean, founded colonies on the coast of Asia Minor, which ultimately developed into Ionia with its twelve great cities.

The story of the 'Aeolic migration' is thus narrated by old writers: on the 'Return of the Heracleidae' – *i.e.* invasion of the Peloponnese by the Dorians – those of the Achaeans who did not remain with Tisamenus in Achaea crossed the Isthmus and made their way to Boeotia and thence through Thessaly and Thrace to the Hellespont; or else they reached the port of Aulis, the very place where Agamemnon had been delayed by winds and had started with his assembled fleet for Troy, and thence, accompanied by many Euboeans and others, they sailed across the Aegean by the chain of islands that stretches from Euboea to the Troad. They made settlements in Lesbos and the adjacent mainland, capturing or founding twelve cities, of which Cyme, named after a town in Euboea, was the first – the mother-city of Smyrna, and mother, or perhaps sister, to the more famous Cyme in Italy, the Cumae of the Romans.

Other forms of the legend, one of which is given by Pindar, make this Aeolian migration take place some twenty years *before* the 'Return of the Heracleidae' (*i.e.* in 1124), and affirm that Orestes himself led the emigrants. According to the Augustan writer Strabo, Orestes started with them, but died in Arcadia – a version which agrees with the story of Herodotus that the bones of Orestes were discovered some five and a half centuries later at Tegea, in Arcadia.

Now under these various myths about the Dorian invasion and the Aeolic and Ionic migrations there is doubtless a basis of historical facts, and probably these facts are somewhat as follows.

### Aeolic Migration

Possibly even before the siege of Troy there had been a considerable stream of migration across the Northern Aegean by way of the islands that form a chain between the Pagasaean Gulf in Thessaly and the Troad. Pagasae is celebrated in mythology as the port where Jason built the *Argo*, and whence the Argonauts set forth on their voyage to unknown eastern lands, and the legend evidently gives poetic form to some such early adventures. From

Thessaly, which was in early days the home of the Achaeans and the 'Aeolian Boeotians,' it is quite possible that bands of sea-rovers, who either called themselves or were called by their Mysian and Phrygian foes Aeolians (possibly a corruption of the word Achaeans), made their way across to Lesbos and the Troad, and that it was the hostility between these Greek adventurers and the natives (also of northern Indo-Iranian race) which ultimately brought about the Trojan War and the expedition of Agamemnon and his allies and the fall of the great Phrygian stronghold.

Even if we accept Homer's account, which gives no hint of Aeolian or any other Greek settlements in Asia Minor, it is not unlikely that the fall of Troy may have at once opened up the south of the Troad and Lesbos and the adjacent mainland to emigrants from Greece, Achaean and other, who probably assembled at Pagasae, or Aulis, or some such point of departure and crossed the Aegean by the islands. This theory seems to fit in fairly well with the version of the myth which makes Orestes head the first band of emigrants not so very long after the Trojan War and some time before the invasion of the Dorian Northmen. Doubtless the pressure of this invasion caused a large increase of emigration to the Aeolian settlements, as well as to the country to the south of Aeolis, which had been till then only sparsely occupied, if occupied at all, by another section of the Greek race – the Ionians, or Iavones, as they called themselves.

## Ionic Migration

According to the myths, as we have seen, the Ionians originally inhabited the north of the Peloponnese, and when pressed by the refugee Achaeans withdrew to Attica, and thence, under leaders of the Pylian house of Codrus, passed over to Asia Minor. This would make the Ionic migration a direct result of the Dorian invasion of the Peloponnese; and doubtless, as already remarked, this invasion did cause a great exodus of the conquered peoples, many of whom made their way to the islands and to Crete, as well as to the mainland on the further side of the Aegean.

As Ionia plays such an important part in Greek history, it is a question of deep interest who these Iavones, or Ionians, were. They are only once mentioned by Homer. He gives them the epithet 'chiton-trailing' – a strange epithet for warriors, and never used by any other Greek writer. They take part in defending the ships against the attack of Hector, and are apparently closely associated, if not identified, with the Athenians. All tradition agrees with Homer in such association or identification. If not actually Athenians, these Iavones, or Ionians, were certainly non-Achaean settlers in Argolis and Attica, and probably of the same Aegean or Pelasgic race as the Athenians themselves. For it seems fairly certain that the Athenians, who always boasted of their old Pelasgic origin, remained to a large extent as a race unaffected both by Achaean and by Dorian influence. They were, as Herodotus asserts, Hellenized Pelasgians and Aegeans rather than true Hellenes. In speech and religion they were Hellenic, just as much as the Achaeans, but in their deeper instincts there were elements which were derived from the old pre-Hellenic race and which very possibly accounted for many of their characteristics and proved the main cause of that rapid and wonderful aesthetic and intellectual development which took place later among the Ionic section of the Greek race.

In the case of the Asiatic Ionians probably these aesthetic instincts were less modified by vigorous Northern influences than was the case with the Athenians, and doubtless also in time the enervating climate (though highly praised by Herodotus, whose native clime it was), as well as the enervating influences of the wealthy Lydians and the semi-Oriental Carians and other peoples of Asia Minor, contributed to produce that Ionian luxury and voluptuousness which were in such sharp contrast to the *sōphrosynē*, the self-restraint, of all that is greatest in Athenian art and character. For some centuries, however, Ionia, like the Greek colonies in Sicily and Italy, seems to have far outstripped the mother-country not only in the size and magnificence of its cities – some of which were probably never surpassed by Athens itself – but also in most civilized arts. For instance, as we have seen, Ionia probably knew and practised the art of writing for some time before it was much used in Greece.

The colonists were by no means only Ionians. Herodotus calls them a mixed multitude composed of many diverse tribes from North and South Greece. Moreover, he states that they brought no wives with them and intermarried largely with the Carians. They founded, or captured and refounded, in course of time the twelve important cities which later formed the Ionic Amphictiony, Phocaea being the northernmost and the southernmost Miletus (formerly a Carian city, according to Homer), which, together with Myus and Priene, lay on the magnificent Bay of Latmus, now changed into a vast swampy plain by the deposits of the river Maeander. These twelve cities afterwards had a common place of assembly and of worship, sacred to Poseidon, on the northern slope of Mount Mycale. Here they met at the pan-Ionic festival, as the pan-Hellenic world met at Olympia.

But this is anticipating. For the present it suffices to have pointed out the probability of this Ionian migration having begun before the advent of the Dorians in the Peloponnese, and to have shown the likelihood that many of these 'Ionian' emigrants were of non-Hellenic (that is, of Aegean rather than Achaean) race. The fact that in Ionia – indeed, on all the coast of Western Asia Minor – very few traces of 'Mycenaean' civilization have as yet been discovered need not disturb us, for these Ionians of, say, 1100 were by no means the Aegeans of the 'Mycenaean' age, and the fact that the great Ionian cities were, with the exception of Miletus, continuously inhabited down to a late age makes it unlikely that relics of early times have survived. Moreover, what few relics have been discovered – especially by Mr. Hogarth in his excavation of the earliest temple of Artemis at Ephesus – seem at least to have a strong affinity to the relics of Aegean and Cretan civilization. Among these are many figurines of Artemis as Earth-Mother and golden plaques and the double-axe decoration.

## Doric Invasions (1100–900)

Though the colonization of Aeolis and Ionia evidently began before the great pressure of the Dorian invasion (c. 1100), it was doubtless owing to that invasion that such multitudes found their way across the Aegean. We have already heard the mythical account of these Dorians and of the 'Return of the Heracleidae.' These myths probably arose from the fact that the descendants of these Dorian conquerors tried to make out some hereditary claim to the countries which their ancestors had invaded; but it is, of course, possible that invasion may have been incited by exiles, a thing that has happened many times in history. More probably, however, the Dorians moved southward because they were hard pressed by other northern tribes.

Northern Greece had been from early ages the scene of constant invasions and of constant migrations. We have already heard of a great nation of northern barbarians, the Illyrians, who poured into Epirus and swept the Achaeans eastward across the Pindus range into the country north of the Peneios. Hither from the north came the Petthaloi, or Thessaloi, and drove the Achaeans southward to Phthia. For some time these Thessalians held North Thessaly and reduced the original natives to serfdom. Then they attacked the Boeotians, who were, it is said, an Aeolian people at that time inhabiting the fertile valley of the Peneios in Central Thessaly. The Boeotians, forced southward, occupied the country known henceforth as Boeotia; and it is likely that this invasion may have caused the Dorians to cross over into the Peloponnese. These Dorians were apparently just at that time encamped in the basin between Mount Oeta and Mount Parnassus (to the north-west of Delphi). The small area of this district of 'Doris' seems to preclude the possibility that a great host of warriors, such as the Dorians certainly were, could have made it their settled home for any length of time. Probably they had made their way down from the far north, following the great central range of Pindus, and had for the time occupied what was afterwards known as Doris and regarded as the original home of the Dorian race. During their sojourn here or on their moves southward (which probably went on for years) they seem to have possessed themselves of the Delphic shrine and oracle, for we find at a later period ancient Dorian families at Delphi possessing prerogatives as Apollo's priests.

Doubtless these Dorians were of the same Indo-Iranian stock as the Achaeans. They seem to have worshipped the same, or similar, deities, and to have accepted the Olympian religion as they found it in Greece, possibly adding a few features, such as the cult of the Doric Apollo – possibly that god of the sun who with his bright arrows slew the Python of Delphi and banished the old snake-worship. But in many points they were evidently very different. Instead of assimilating the civilization of the conquered peoples they seem to have swept it almost out of existence. But possibly the 'darkness' of this age is due mainly to our ignorance. Although no evidence is forthcoming of anything in the way of art and refinement in the countries overrun by these early Dorians during several centuries, it is just possible that their advent did not cause such devastation as has been supposed. Still, judging from the Spartans, who were the only pure Dorians of later times, one may reasonably believe that their early ancestors, fresh from the north, were barbarians such as the Gauls or Huns, and it seems a very natural conclusion that the Aegean-Achaean civilization was for a long time almost annihilated in Greece, except in Attica, which preserved its independence and helped also to foster civilization in the colonies of Asia Minor.

The Dorians seem to have been armed with iron, the commoner use of which metal may have given them a great superiority in war. They bore round metal shields, and wore a square woollen cloak, fastened over the shoulders with brooches (safety-pins).

We have seen that they built a number of ships at Naupactus. In these ships many of them evidently crossed over to the Peloponnese, landing at various points. They conquered all the south-western parts, driving out the Achaean or Aegean lords of Amyclae, near which they founded Sparta – destined, though without wall or citadel, to become the mistress not only of Laconia, but for a time of nearly the whole of Hellas. But it seems probable that a considerable force of these Dorians set forth at once in their new-built ships for more distant conquests. They captured and occupied the islands of Thera and Melos, and made a descent on Crete, where they swept away the last remnants of Minoan civilization and introduced Dorian customs and laws.[1] The similarity of the name of one of the three Dorian clans (Pamphyli) to that of the people of Pamphylia has induced some writers to assert that these adventurers even reached and gave their name and language to that land.

In the Peloponnese the Dorians eventually extended their conquests to Argolis, and it was doubtless their devastating fire which, about 950, left its marks on the ruins of Mycenae and Tiryns. Argos now was made the chief city of the Argive plain, and the Dorian occupation lasted apparently for some centuries; but afterwards, although traces of Dorian government remained, Argos became a great adversary of Sparta. The lofty citadel of Corinth, the Acrocorinthus, was also seized by a Dorian adventurer, Aletes ('Wanderer'), and the city, under the sovereignty of the Dorian Argive kings, became, doubtless by virtue of its two seas, a place of maritime importance. Even Megara was seized and became a thoroughly Dorian town; and later (perhaps about 800) the island of Aegina was also occupied, and for nearly four centuries proved a Dorian thorn in the side of Athens, until the Athenians were forced to clear the country of its older population and settle it anew with loyal colonists.

It was probably after thus extending and consolidating their conquests in the Peloponnese that the Dorian chiefs led bands of emigrants across the Aegean, evidently by way of the Doric islands of Thera and Melos, to

---

[1] The similarity of Spartan and Cretan laws and constitution is noticed by old writers. Homer speaks of Dorians as one of many diverse races in Crete – the only time he mentions the name – and possibly calls them 'three-tribed.' If these are the Dorians of 1100 or so the mention is an anachronism, but it only proves that Homer did not write before that date. 'Pamphyli' really means 'of mixed races.'

Crete and thence to Rhodes, where they founded, or annexed, the three cities of Lindus, Ialysus, and Cameirus.[1] Then the island Cos was occupied by them, and two cities, Cnidus and Halicarnassus, were founded on the mainland. These six settlements formed the Hexapolis of the new oversea Doris – nominally a Dorian colony, but to a large extent really Carian; for, especially in Halicarnassus, which was by far the most important of these cities, the native Carian element was preponderant, and 'Carian dynasts' (among whom we shall later find Queen Artemisia I and Mausolus) seem to have established their rule from an early period.

Thus during this so-called Dark Age very great and important movements and changes evidently took place. The Aegean, from which (if Thucydides is right) in an earlier age the Minoan fleets had swept the pirates and expelled the Carians, became during this period a Grecian sea, fringed on all sides, except the extreme north, with Grecian colonies – which extended, as we shall see later, even to Cyprus. Nor were the changes in social and political matters less important, for even in the twilight of the archaic period, before we emerge into the full light of history, we can discern the fact that the old monarchical system has already begun to give way, that to a considerable extent constituted law has taken the place of absolute government and those unwritten traditional ordinances (*themistes*) of which we hear in Homer, and that the city, with its larger and more systematized community and its function as political centre of a district, has succeeded to migratory life and loosely grouped village communities clustered (as in Mycenae) around the stronghold of some chieftain. Moreover, the sites of towns were affected by the new state of things, as Thucydides tells us in his celebrated opening chapters. 'When there were now greater facilities for navigation,' he says, 'cities were built with walls on the sea-shore, and they began to occupy isthmuses, with a view to commerce and security, whereas the older cities, owing to the long continuance of piracy, were built farther off the sea.' Of the cities especially affected by the disappearance of piracy and the more settled state of things was Corinth, which took advantage of its position on the Isthmus, and in early

---

[1] Mentioned in the 'Catalogue of the Ships' (*Iliad*, ii.). The Rhodians also in this passage are described as divided into three (Dorian) clans. But the 'Catalogue' is admittedly full of late intercalations. Thera, Melos, and Rhodes were colonized by Aegeans long before the coming of the Dorians. A 'Mycenaean' cemetery at Ialysus has given many evidences of this. In Thera a volcanic disturbance buried a Mycenaean town, which has been partially excavated, and in Melos a citadel has been discovered dating from about 2000.

days became a great emporium and the first naval power in Greece, so that we may well credit the assertion of Thucydides that the first triremes were built there[1] – war-galleys of 170 oars with three banks of oarsmen – and that the first Greek naval battle was between the Corinthians and their own colonists, the Corcyraeans.

Of other cities in Greece during this Dark Age we have a few dim myths and a few relics, such as the contents of the so-called Dipylon cemetery at Athens (see Section A) and various objects found at Argos and Sparta. But when the veil rises and Greek history begins we find some of these cities, or rather states (for they had already begun to develop into organized communities), furnished with constitutions and in possession of much else that necessarily presumes a considerable period of stable government and prosperity. It will therefore be well to consider here some of the more important facts connected with two cities which will later occupy much of our attention, namely, Athens and Sparta, and see how far these facts, as they meet our view at the dawn of history (say about 700), may be traced to their sources in this Dark Age (say between 1000 and 700), although in doing this we shall be forestalling to some extent. It is, of course, quite incredible that these three or four centuries between the Dorian invasion and the beginning of certified history should in Greece itself have been a total blank, but almost the only proof that it was not so resides in facts that really belong to the next age – facts which it may not be too audacious to try to trace to their origin with the help of more or less mythical accounts given by ancient writers.

## Athens

Of Athens and its ancient mythical history we have already heard something, namely, how it was perhaps captured, but not permanently held, by the Achaeans, how it repelled the Dorians and retained its independence, and how the last of its kings, Codrus, for his country's sake devoted himself to death (c. 1044).

Now so great, it is said, was the admiration of the Athenians for this heroic act of Codrus that they determined to allow no one else the royal

---

[1] This was not until c. 700, when they were perhaps introduced by the Phoenicians. The trireme does not seem to have superseded the old fifty-oared biremes in other parts of Greece till shortly before the Persian wars (c. 500). In later times warships had often five banks. Alexander and the Ptolemies built vessels which, it is asserted, had *forty* banks!

prerogatives, and elected Medon, the son of the king,[1] as their chief magistrate for life, giving him the title *archōn* ('ruler'). Such is the possibly mythical version of the fact that early in the Dark Age the absolute monarch in Athens was superseded by a constitutional and accountable magistracy – perhaps elected by the nobles out of their own body. This magistracy consisted probably from the first of three archons, such as existed (though combined later with 'lawgivers') down to the time of the Roman Emperors. They were the chief civil magistrate (called later *eponymos*, because he gave his name to the year), the chief military commander (polemarch), and the King Archon (*basileus*). The King Archon may at first have belonged to the royal house, but he held the merest shadow of kingly power, being allowed to retain little but the pontifical functions of royalty (as the Rex Sacrificulus at Rome after the expulsion of the kings and the election of praetors and consuls). This seems to have been in many of the states of Hellas the first stage in the evolution of the later republics. On account of the great increase of ordinary citizens, traders, agriculturists, and so on, the military element gradually lost its exclusive political influence, and the king, as head of the army, lost his political supremacy. Some powerful clique or family of nobles then assumed this supremacy, electing perhaps one of their number as polemarch, or war-leader, and others as permanent, or annual, civil magistrates. This state of things – that of a close aristocracy or oligarchy – we find in early days at Corinth, where the Bacchiad family for a considerable time held the reins of government. And as it happened at Corinth, so it also happened in many other cases that some specially strong-minded and ambitious noble overthrew the aristocracy (sometimes by coming forward as a demagogue and obtaining the support of the people) and constituted himself 'tyrant' or despot. He differed from a hereditary monarch by basing his claims on force rather than on divine right, and generally surrounded himself with a strong bodyguard, but not unfrequently he proved a beneficent ruler, and one that forwarded the material prosperity of the people far more than was often done by republican governments. The last stage of evolution was, as we shall see later, the establishment of a constitutional democracy on the expulsion of the *tyrannos*.

---

[1] His younger brother, Neleus, led the emigrants to Ionia (see p. 107). The archonship was at first a life-office and perhaps limited to the Medontid family. About 750 its term was reduced to ten years, in 683 it was made an annual office, and finally the nine chief magistrates were all called archons.

It was either during the reigns of the early Athenian kings (tradition attributes it to the reign of Theseus) or shortly after the institution of the archonship that Athens became the capital of the whole of Attica – an event which was of the very greatest moment, giving her in time a position as political centre of an united state which was possessed by no other city in Greece. In spite of the poverty of its soil Attica had received many foreign immigrants, such as the Achaean and the Ionian refugees. We hear of twelve Attic 'kingships' in the age of Cecrops. These petty chieftains in course of time, either by compulsion or willingly, became subject to the growing Athenian power, which extended its dominion first over the plain of the Cephisus and then over the country east of Mount Hymettus and north of Pentelicus from Cape Sunion to Marathon. To the west, over Eleusis and its plain, the new Athenian state did not for the present extend its sovereignty, but the whole of the *Actē* (or 'coastland') – from which word is probably derived the name 'Attica' – formed now a single community.[1] This community was divided into four tribes, which received old Ionian names,[2] the meanings of which are obscure. Tradition attributes the formation and naming of these four 'Ionian' tribes of Attica to the mythical King Ion, ancestor of all Ionians. Some modern writers assert that the names were derived from Miletus, where similar tribes existed. But it seems more reasonable to suppose that they were names in use among Ionian settlers in Attica, who probably were divided into four tribes as the Dorians were into three. Each tribe had its tribe-king, and contained three *phratriai* (brotherhoods) and numerous clans and families.[3] The families of each clan recognized, and perhaps worshipped, a common ancestor, or a special deity, and were bound together by various social ties. They had a special burial-place, and perhaps community in land property.

But besides this it seems probable that from the first these four 'Ionian' tribes were divided into the *trittyes* (thirds) and *naucraria* (shipownings) of which we hear so much in later days. These divisions were perhaps local (like the original demes, or townships, into which Theseus is said to have portioned out Attica), but they were evidently made for purposes of

---

[1] This *synoikia*, or Union of Attica, was commemorated even in the days of Plutarch by a festival in which offerings were made to the goddess Eirene (Peace).

[2] Geleontes, Argades, Aegicores, and Hopletes.

[3] In later writers the calculation was 1 tribe = 30 *phratriai* = 90 clans = 2700 families, thus giving 10,800 families in all.

military and naval finance, the *naucraria* each probably supplying, as later in Solon's constitution, the equipment of one ship.[1]

During this period of about three centuries (*i.e.* from the abolition of monarchy until the first Olympiad), during which Athens gradually became the political centre of Attica, the Athenian state was doubtless, as we find it still in the seventh century, an aristocracy with democratic tendencies. This seems plain not only from the political constitution which we have been considering, but also from what little we know of the social order. The whole people was divided into three classes, the Eupatridae ('Well-born'), the Georgi ('Land-workers'), and the Demiurgi ('Public Workers'). The nobles were large landowners. Many of them had removed into the city from their country estates, which they worked by means of labourers, who retained a sixth of the produce. The Demiurgi were craftsmen of all kinds, such as those who made and painted those 'Dipylon' vases which are the sole relics of this age. Some of the workers probably had a limited franchise, but there seems to have been a large number even of the free population who had not the rights of citizenship.

This is about all we know, or can venture to guess, about Athens in the Dark Age, except what we may infer from what is called 'Dipylon civilization,' which I shall consider later.


## Sparta

Let us now turn to Sparta, which offers a very interesting contrast.

After the Dorians had established themselves in the western and southern part of the Peloponnese some of them seem to have put themselves at the head of bands of those fighting men and adventurers who had doubtless accompanied them in great numbers from the north and to have set forth in quest of new conquests in lands over the sea. Other Dorian chiefs in course of time, as we have seen, also doubtless at the head of armies largely composed of non-Dorians, made themselves masters of Mycenae, Argos, Corinth, and even Aegina. But the main body of the true-born Dorians – a body of probably only some six or eight thousand warriors – seem to have chosen Sparta, or Lacedaemon, the ancient residence of the

---

[1] Until lately this has been doubted, and the word *naucraria* has been derived from other sources, because it was assumed that Athens *had no fleet* before the time of Solon. We shall see that this assumption was wrong. See Section A.

Achaean princes (in Homer it is the residence of Menelaus), as their permanent abode. It was evidently at this time a place consisting of several
(afterwards five) villages, which even in a later age were not closely united
in one community, and remained unwalled and without a fortified acropolis almost down to the time of the Romans; for the Dorians despised fortifications[1] and relied solely on their superiority in open battle. They were a
comparatively small number in the midst of a hostile population, and it
was evidently with no small difficulty that they held their own, for even at
the beginning of the so-called historical age of Greece (c. 776) they were in
possession of little more than the valley of the Eurotas, on which their city
lay, and tradition asserts that it was not for over 200 years – i.e. not until
the reign of the Spartan king Teleclus (c. 850) – that they succeeded in dis-
lodging a remnant of the Achaeans from the ancient town of Amyclae,
about half a dozen miles distant from Sparta. The aborigines, Aegeans,
Achaeans, Cynurians, or whatever else they may have been, were either
reduced to serfdom and called Helots (probably 'Captives'), or were
allowed to form free municipalities in the neighbourhood of Sparta[2]
without being granted civic rights. These latter, treated, perhaps, more
leniently because they had offered less resistance, were called Perioeci
('Dwellers round about'), and formed the mercantile class, the Spartiatae,
or true Dorian Spartans, not deigning to engage in such occupations or to
acquire wealth.

The Helots were not slaves. They were in some ways no worse off than
the mediaeval villein or Russian serf, and could even acquire property,
which was more than the Roman slave was allowed, for even his *peculium*
belonged by law to his master. But the original Helots had been masters of
the country, and their descendants, conscious of this, and being doubtless
often equal to the Spartiates in civilized instincts, bitterly resented their lot,
and the constant danger of insurrection was one of the main reasons why
Sparta lived under martial law. A very striking specimen of the measures
adopted by the Spartans to meet this danger was the Crypteia, or secret
society of young Spartiates, who were empowered by law to kill at once any

---

[1] Their want of practice in siege operations caused them often great trouble in wars against
the Messenians, and during the Persian and Peloponnesian wars they had frequently to
rely on the assistance of their allies in such matters.

[2] Later in the whole of Laconia, where there were a hundred such townships; but they
formed no organic state like the Attic towns – indeed, they were a constant source of
danger to Sparta.

Helot whom they might suspect as dangerous. To cover such glaring injustice by a show of law it was the custom for certain magistrates (the ephors) every year, when assuming office, to *declare war* formally against the Helots!

The whole of the political power lay in the hands of the Spartiatae, who formed a military caste of no great size.[1] As might be expected, kingship was the inherent and permanent form of rule. The Spartan kings, who claimed an unbroken lineage from Hercules (extending back a century beyond the advent of the Dorians), retained the regal office and title, if with diminished rights, for nearly a thousand years, while almost every other city of Hellas passed through various phases of government. Possibly the fact that two kings held power at the same time, though it sounds a dangerous state of things, may have limited the abuse of regal power and helped to preserve kingship from its usual fate. This dual kingship is said by old writers to have arisen from the difficulty caused by the fact that the king of the Dorian invaders, Aristodemus, left twins as heirs to his throne. Modern writers try to explain it by a possible coalition of two tribes, each of which insisted on retaining its king; but the old explanation seems quite as probable. However that may be, the state of things was evidently not such as would seem likely to result in a very satisfactory dispensation of justice, far less in any form of settled government and constituted law. So it is not surprising that Herodotus (i. 65) is of the opinion that in early times the Lacedaemonians were 'the very worst governed people in Greece.' But Sparta at some period during the Dark Age received a very complete and rigid, if not a very highly organized, constitution. It was not such a constitution as is gradually evolved to meet the higher needs of a people. It has all the marks of construction, and the main structure was doubtless conceived and framed by some one lawgiver. This lawgiver, according to old tradition, was Lycurgus. He was regent for his young nephew, King Labotas, or Charilaus, and either during this regency or after a period of voluntary exile and of travel in distant lands, being encouraged by the Delphic oracle and having gained the support of the chief men of the city, he procured the introduction of his new constitution. Then, after having extracted a promise from the people to keep his laws until his return, he

---

[1] After Thermopylae (according to Herodotus) Xerxes was told by Demaratus that Sparta contained about 8000 full-grown men. After Leuctra (371) the Spartans with full citizenship numbered only about 1500.

quitted Sparta forever. It has been said that 'Lycurgus was not a man; he was only a god';[1] that his name means 'protector against wolves,' and that he may have been identical with the ancient Arcadian wolf-repelling deity who was called by the Greeks Zeus Lykaios. All this is possible; but it seems to some minds more natural that one should begin by being a hero, or a great lawgiver, and end in being a god. Anyhow, to save time and space for more important matters, let us accept Lycurgus, whether a man or only a god, as the great lawgiver who, when the 'very worst governed people in Greece' found things becoming intolerable, was begged, or allowed, to draw up a constitution of a very rigid and drastic nature – such a constitution as should be fitting for a military camp where martial law was to prevail and where the one end of all law and all social order was to turn out the best soldiers and the best soldiers' wives.

The following are, shortly stated, some of the chief features of this constitution as it existed about 700 to 600. It is impossible to say for certain which portions of the structure are the most ancient, but there is no reason to doubt that the greater part had existed, as Thucydides asserts, at least from about 800, and that many of these 'Dorian ordinances,' as Pindar calls them, were derived from very early times, if not, as he believed, from the days of the mythical Dorian hero Aegimius.

The functions of the two kings were military and religious. They had supreme command and dictatorial power in war, and were high-priests of the Spartan Zeus and Apollo. The kingship was hereditary, but the son succeeded who was eldest born after his father's accession. In later times (for instance, during the Persian wars) only one king held military command. The kings had a council, like the Homeric Boule, called the Gerusia (Council of Elders). It consisted only of nobles, but they were elected by the people. There was also a public assembly, like the Homeric Agora, called the Apella. To this every citizen of thirty years belonged. In early days it was summoned by the kings, later by the ephors. The vote of the public assembly was given by acclamation.

Although Sparta never reached democracy pure and simple, things had

---

[1] The phrase seems to be borrowed from Herodotus: 'Whether Zalmoxis was really a man, or nothing but a native god of the Getae, I now bid him farewell' (iv. 96). Herodotus (i. 65) tells us that Lycurgus 'introduced from Crete the system of laws still observed by the Spartans.' This is also asserted by Aristotle. The resemblances in the Cretan and Spartan constitutions seem to be limited to a few features such as the *syssitia* (messes), and are probably due to Doric influences in Crete.

with them, as everywhere else, a tendency towards democracy, of which the creation of the ephors (possibly not till about 760) was a proof. The ephors ('overseers' or 'guardians') were representatives of the people, like the tribunes in Roman history, elected after long contests between the military caste and the working classes, which seem to have included many who had been degraded from the ranks of the Spartiatae as well as the Laconian Perioeci. Every month the ephors and the kings exchanged vows to abide by the laws and to support one another's authority. There were five ephors – one evidently for each of the five villages, or demes, of which, as we have seen, Sparta was composed. They had much of the judicial power in their hands, and could even indict the kings. Two of them accompanied the army in war.

Thus at Sparta we find a striking example of that mixed constitution which, when a carefully balanced construction, has proved elsewhere (as, for instance, in England) more durable than any other form of government, possessing something of the stability of the triangle of forces and of a universe of three dimensions.

More characteristic even than this political machinery was the social constitution of Sparta, which was regarded with intense admiration (at a distance) by many other Greek citizens, and which Plato, struck perhaps by its artistic symmetry, like that of some great Doric temple, took as the type after which he constructed the framework of his Ideal State – although his ideal ruler and ideal citizen had nothing in common with those of the Spartan lawgiver.[1]

Many of the details of this 'Spartan discipline' and many stories connected therewith are well known. I shall therefore merely touch on a few points.

One of the main points was that the Spartiat warrior-citizen should be wholly free from the degrading necessity of working to provide for himself and his family. He possessed landed patrimony which could not be sold or broken up, and this land was tilled by serfs, who had to supply the lord of the manor with corn, wine, and fruit. The serfs (Helots) of the Spartan noble were not his property. They belonged to the state, which alone could emancipate them; and this was sometimes done as a reward for valour in war. Hence arose a class like the Roman *libertini* (freedmen).

---

[1] For a very full discussion of Lycurgus and his 'Laws and Discipline' see Grote, Part II, chap. vi.

Every new-born child was inspected by the tribal authorities, and if deemed too feeble or unhealthy it was taken to Mount Taygetus and left there to die. At seven years the boy was taken from home and was kept in a great military school until the age of twenty, when he entered the army and was allowed to marry, but was still obliged to live apart from his wife in barracks. At thirty he was considered a man and received the rights of a citizen.

Every Spartan male citizen was obliged to take his meals at a public 'mess' (*syssition*) under the management of the War Minister – such messes as More imagined in his Utopia, except that in Utopia messing in the public halls was not compulsory, and women were also admitted.

The education of the Spartan had an aim very different from that of the Athenian – anyhow the Athenian of the higher type in classical times, whose ideal was a truly cultured, perfectly balanced, harmonious character, not the production of a highly trained fighter nor professional or mercantile success. Money-making and luxury were indeed, theoretically, despised by the Spartiat, though he seems to have been more open to a bribe than other Hellenes.[1] But his contempt for such things did not spring from any hunger for angels' food, as Dante calls it. The Spartan youth – as also the Spartan girl – doubtless received a splendid physical training, and did full credit to the scientific breeding of muscular and athletic citizens, but they were, even in the age of Demosthenes,[2] for the most part not taught to read, and, according to Plato, many of the Spartans 'could not do the simplest sum in arithmetic, nor did they care a jot for science, or logic, or any such things.' Thus the governing classes in Sparta were probably more illiterate than the mercantile Perioeci, or even the Helots, and had to depend (as was also often the case among the Romans) on slaves or hired amanuenses.

The love of the Spartans for brevity in speech – which accounts for the meaning of the word 'laconic' – is well illustrated by the following story, told by Herodotus. Some Samians came to Sparta to ask for aid against the tyrant Polycrates, and 'had audience of the magistrates, before whom they made a long speech, as was natural with persons greatly in need of

---

[1] To substantiate this I would refer the reader to Hdt. iii. 148, v. 51, vi. 72; Thuc. i. 129 and 131, ii. 21, viii. 50. What use the gold would be to them *in Sparta*, where only iron money was allowed until the time of Alexander the Great, it is difficult to see.

[2] See Grote, ii. 307, and Plato's *Hippias Major*.

help. Now after this speech was ended the Spartans replied that they had forgotten the first half of it and could make nothing of the remainder. So the Samians had another audience, whereat they simply said, showing a bag that they had brought with them, *The bag needs flour*. The Spartans answered that they did not need to have said *The bag*.' In the speeches attributed by Thucydides to Lacedaemonians during the Peloponnesian War they seem to be quite as fond of long-winded argument as other speakers. But the pitilessly curt question by which, Thucydides says, they decided the fate of the Plataeans certainly savoured of Spartan brevity.

A curious Spartan custom (scarcely traceable to their northern origin) was that of not only allowing, even in regard to female dress, a free exposure of the person, but also of insisting on nudity, in the case of both sexes, on certain public occasions, such as displays of gymnastic exercises. What many might regard as a survival of barbarism was regarded not only by the Spartans, but in course of time (as Thucydides seems to intimate) by all Hellenes, as a proof of higher civilization – though only as far as male nudity was concerned. How different the feeling in the rest of Greece was in regard to female nudity can be seen from the fact that, though nude male statues in early times are the rule, undraped female statues are extremely rare until about 400.

The Dorian race, like some other northern races, seems to have possessed very little art instinct; but, as has happened in other cases, the intermingling of the vigorous northern with the softer and more imaginative southern nature produced a very fine type of artistic character. Many of the Dorian or half-Dorian cities of Hellas, such as Argos, Sicyon, Syracuse, Halicarnassus, and Acragas, were distinguished for art – for their sculpture, their coins, their magnificent temples – while Sparta, or the dominant class in Sparta, remained to a wonderful degree purely Dorian, and inartistic. Some writers have suggested that before the introduction of their military discipline the tastes of the Spartans were somewhat more cultured than they were in historical times. However that may be, a certain amount of art feeling seems to have survived even that discipline, for although, as Professor Gardner says, 'the traditional notion of the Spartan character is hardly such as to lead us to expect that Sparta was in early times a centre of artistic work and influence,' nevertheless we do find that the art of sculpture, probably introduced from Crete, flourished in Sparta in the seventh century, and we hear of Sparta being visited by the great Lesbian musician,

Terpander (676), and by the Lydian lyric poet, Alcman,[1] who is said to have made it his home (*c.* 650).

Terpander is said to have instituted at Sparta a musical contest at the great festival in honour of the Carneian Apollo. He was the musician who added three strings to the tetrachord of the lyre. It may seem strange that the conservative Spartans gave him such a friendly reception, for on a later occasion, when Timotheus of Miletus, who had added four strings to the heptachord, visited Sparta, the ephors, says Cicero, ordered his extra strings to be broken before he was allowed to compete.

By the way, Terpander seems to have got credit for what he was not the first to invent, seeing that on a Cretan sarcophagus (Fig. 25) of a date at least eight centuries before Terpander a musician is depicted with a lyre of seven strings.

We know, of course, very little about Greek music of this age, but it seems that the native Dorian music not only differed from the Lydian, Aeolian, Phrygian, and Iastian (Ionian) in 'mode' – whether that means scale or pitch – but also in rhythm and time, being used generally as accompaniment to processionals and martial strains rather than to bardic and lyric poetry. The Homeric *kitharis* (cithara), or phorminx, was perhaps originally the harp or lute of the northern races, and probably this instrument rather than the *lyra* or *chelys* (tortoise-shell) – *i.e.* the Aegean and Egyptian lyre – was popular at Sparta, and what delighted the soul of the Spartiat was doubtless the old martial ballad or war-song, such as we shall hear of when we come to Tyrtaeus.

We have wandered somewhat from the Dark Age while following up things which had their first origins in that era Before passing on to what until lately, before the discovery of the Minoan and Mycenaean civilizations, was regarded as the beginning of Greek history, I shall in the following sections briefly discuss two subjects, namely, 'Dipylon' antiquities and Hesiod's poems, the consideration of which may throw faint shafts of light into the obscurity of the two centuries preceding the first Olympiad. In the third section I shall offer a few remarks about the contemporary history of certain nations closely connected with the history of Greece. Of these the somewhat mysterious Phoenician people specially interests us, for in early times it came into closer contact with the Hellenic world than did the great Oriental empires or Egypt, and the desperate conflict of this

---

[1] Fragments of songs by Alcman composed for choirs of Spartan girls are still extant.

Semitic race with the Sicilian Greeks and later with the Romans lends additional interest to the subject.

## SECTION A: DIPYLON ANTIQUITIES

The expression 'Dipylon antiquities' is used rather loosely to cover all Greek relics of the age to which belong many of the objects found in an ancient cemetery excavated near the ruins of the Dipylon – that is, the 'Double Gate' of Athens, a great city gate with an inner and an outer portal, probably built in Periclean times not far from the more ancient and smaller Sacred Gate, through which the Sacred Way led to Eleusis, passing through the Outer Cerameicus (Potters' Quarter). The Cerameicus was used as the cemetery of Athens, and many beautiful monuments (stelae) of a later age are still to be seen there, in the 'Street of Tombs.' The ancient cemetery near the Dipylon was to a great extent covered by later tombs, under and amidst which have been excavated some hundreds of ancient graves. Some of these are said to date from the ninth century or even earlier. In many of the graves of the 'Dipylon age' (say 1000 to 800 B.C.) the dead had been buried unburnt; in some their ashes were found. The most valuable relics were very numerous fragments of pottery, as well as entire vases, some of which, of large size, were standing upright on the top of shaft-graves or tile-built tombs. The oldest of this pottery, which is of red clay painted with lustrous black on a yellowish surface, is *geometric* in its style, showing that there had been a curious relapse from the much earlier Mycenaean style, in which we have already found sea animals and even human beings depicted. These early Dipylon vases (see Fig. 35) show a fine decorative sense, but at first offer nothing but geometric patterns. Then they begin to introduce animals, and more generally birds, of an amusingly primitive type. Then they give other animals, such as horses; then human figures; and finally we have large compositions (found, however, only on *Athenian* Dipylon vases) showing an ambitious style of painting not far removed from that of the first black-figured Attic vases, such as the François Vase (Fig. 39). These pictures give by far the most clear and intelligible information that we possess concerning the 'Dipylon age.' Almost all else besides pottery seems to have entirely disappeared, except some old foundations and a vast quantity of bronze and terracotta objects, most of which tell us next to nothing.

First to be noticed are the ships. They are biremes, with forty or fifty

*Fig. 34  Dipylon vase (See List of Ilustrations)*

125

oarsmen in two ranks, and this proves that the Athenians already possessed the beginnings of a fleet and a considerable skill in shipbuilding and naval matters. The ships seem even already to be furnished with rams at the bows. But it also seems to show that these pictures date before the introduction of the trireme, which was known to the Corinthians by about 700, as we have already seen; indeed, the picture of an Athenian bireme given in Fig. 34 may be of a date two centuries before 700, and is an exceedingly interesting and valuable confirmation of what we have heard on the subject of the Athenian *naucraria* (see pp 115–16).

Then we have numerous pictures of horses and of chariots: first two-horsed chariots, with very primitive horses and with men whose wasp-waists remind one of Minoan and Mycenaean art; and in some cases much of the human figure is concealed by the great Mycenaean or Minoan figure-of-eight shield, while in others the smaller round shield is held by the handle. Then we find – what are not found in Homer – four-horsed chariots, and also even horsemen. Finally we have scenes – sea-fights, processions, funeral ceremonies, etc. Some of the funeral scenes intimate an ostentation and magnificence quite astonishing in this Dark Age – although not unknown to us in Homer – the bier being attended by a great number of chariots or ships.

The general appearance of the Athenians (and doubtless of other Greek peoples) in the 'Dipylon' age is depicted graphically, though perhaps not flatteringly, on these vases. Both men and women have impossibly narrow waists, and the legs, when in view, are often enormously thick. Much of this is, of course, due to want of skill and exaggeration, but the main features of the dress are doubtless true. The women are dressed much in the same fashion as the Minoan and Mycenaean women, in tight bodices and bell-shaped skirts – such as Hesiod also describes (p. 134). It is evident that the Achaean *peplos* of Homer's women, if it ever became fashionable at Athens in early days, had in the period 1000–800 given way again to the earlier Mycenaean style of dress, while the square Doric dress, with a flap over the shoulder needing a long pin or *fibula* (brooch, safety-pin), such as one sees on the François Vase (Fig. 39), had not yet been adopted at Athens, although the immense number of very long metal pins and of large *fibulae* found with *later* 'Dipylon' vases in Boeotia and at Argos (not to mention Sparta) shows that fashion changed rapidly, as it is wont to do.[1]

---

[1] For more on the subject of dress see Note B.

*Fig. 35 Dipylon, Phaleron, Samian, and Corinthian ware, c. 800–600 (See List of Illustrations and Note D)*

Everything seems to point to a civilization at Athens in the Dark Age something like the old Mycenaean, and not much changed either by the Achaean (Homeric) or the later Doric influence – at all events, in its earlier stages.

Pottery of the same kind as the Athenian, but not with large painted scenes, has been excavated from the temple of Apollo on Mount Ptoön, in Boeotia, and also at Tanagra and Thebes – mostly *geometric* in style, but some of it evidently dating from late Mycenaean times, notably an earthenware box discovered at Thebes, on which we find the Earth-Mother with her animals.

In the great Doric temple of Aphaia and the shrine of Aphrodite in Aegina much pottery has been excavated, some of it Mycenaean and some imported or native 'Dipylon' ware and early Corinthian. This pottery supplements the evidence from Athens.

In the temple of Hera at Argos, excavated by the American School at Athens, have been found, besides many bronzes and long dress-pins (used in the Doric female dress), a number of fragments of vases with pictures of horses and chariots like those discovered at Athens, and of the same 'Dipylon' period.

On the island Thera 'Dipylon' ware and other relics of this age have been found, and what are possibly some of the first known Greek inscriptions cut on rock.

At Delphi and at Olympia thousands of bronzes dating from this age have been excavated, all testifying to no mean civilization and to an enormous cult of certain deities. At Tiryns, besides much else, we have various representations of the female dress of the Dark Age, and again we find a tight-fitting frock, evidently more like the Mycenaean bodice and skirt than the square Doric *chitōn* fastened at the shoulder with pins.

Contemporary with this 'Dipylon' ware, found in all these places and testifying to a civilization very different from the Spartan, we have the wonderfully beautiful proto-Corinthian ware, which shows a very advanced state of artistic skill, but gives us no such pictures of contemporary life as the Athenian vases. This is unfortunate, for Corinth in this age was a great trade emporium and a naval power, and it would be most interesting to discover some evidences of this Corinthian civilization.

Now, if we turn to Sparta we find something quite different. Excavations made by the British School of Athens have brought to light what seems to be the base of the great altar of Artemis Orthia. This goddess and her altar are mentioned by Xenophon and by Plutarch.[1] Spartan youths were flogged at the altar in order to test their endurance, and sometimes died under the ordeal. In or near this old altar and the neighbouring temple of Artemis Orthia (which existed from early days down to about 600) a vast number of lead and terracotta votive figures of the goddess, as well as bronzes and fragments of pottery, were found. The early pottery is *geometric* and something like the 'Dipylon,' but the other relics seem to point to quite a different (Doric) civilization. There are many grotesque winged figures and evident Earth-Mothers, and also many nude female figures, which are attributed to Oriental influence (as being un-Greek), but which surely seem to point towards the curious Spartan ideas on this subject already mentioned.

SECTION B: HESIOD

The personality of Hesiod has not been questioned like that of Homer. It is perhaps too frequently and strongly affirmed by Hesiod himself, who names himself and gives us a good deal about his father and his brother Perses, and a great deal about his own philosophy of life, whereas nowhere in the *Iliad* or the *Odyssey* is there any personal note, such as we have in Milton's great epic, nor any suggestion of the poet's existence, except in the opening addresses to the Muse – unless, indeed, we are to recognize Homer in his blind bard, Demodocus, as we recognize Shakespeare in Prospero.

Hesiod's date, however, and Hesiod's poems afford rich material for the sceptic.

Herodotus, as we have already seen, places both Hesiod and Homer at about 850 or 900, and he mentions Hesiod before Homer, as do several other writers. But internal evidence seems to show that the Homeric poems are older than the *Erga* and the *Theogonia*, and such modern criticism as delights in 'bringing low the strong and diminishing the illustrious,' as Hesiod expresses it, has brought low and diminished his date little by little until we find him flourishing about 700, seventy years and more after the first Olympiad.

---

[1] In Hdt. iv. 87 we find an Artemis Orthosia at Byzantium, and we hear of her also in Lemnos. Also the form Orthasia has been discovered at Sparta. The word Orthia means 'straight' or 'loud-voiced' in Greek. It may refer to the yells of the priests trying to drown the cries of human victims – for this ceremony of bloody flogging may have been substitutory. But perhaps it is some northern word in disguise.

To discuss the question in detail is here impossible. As in the case of Homer, I can only state my belief. Much evidence seems to me to point to about 850 as the date of Hesiod's poems, and this belief is confirmed by something besides, and perhaps better than, philological and archaeological arguments.

About two centuries after Hesiod's age we shall meet with what is sometimes called the first exact date in Greek history. It is the date April 6, 648, on which day, astronomers tell us, a total solar eclipse took place. Now Hesiod tells us something about the star Arcturus which, although it certainly does not allow us to make such an exact deduction, does supply us with very interesting information. He says that Arcturus had its sunset-rising sixty days after the winter solstice *i.e.* about February 19. But Arcturus *now* rises at sunset in Greece about March 30, and one can calculate from this difference (caused by the precession of equinoxes) that Hesiod probably lived about 2780 years ago. This gives his date at about 870. He had, of course, no means of observing very accurately such risings and settings of the stars, and he may have got his information from some older observer, so that the evidence cannot be regarded as quite exact, but within fifty years or so it seems to be trustworthy.

Hesiod tells us that his father came from Cyme in Aeolis, whither perhaps the family had migrated from Aeolian Boeotia (Thessaly), and had settled at Ascra, on the northern slopes of Mount Helicon – a place 'bad in winter, wretched in summer, and never pleasant.' Possibly Hesiod was born at Cyme, and he may have had memories of the softer climate of Asia Minor, as also of the Aeolic dialect, which he sometimes uses; but he seems to have passed his early years at Ascra, shepherding his father's flocks or working on the farm, and doubtless often wandering alone on Mount Helicon and neglecting his work; and against the theory of his Asiatic birth stands the fact that, as he tells us, he was only once on the sea, namely, when he crossed the Euripus Strait, from Aulis to Euboea, in order to take part in a poetical contest – at which he won a tripod. Legend, as we have already seen, asserts that he won that tripod in a contest against Homer himself. On the death of his father his brother Perses succeeded in ousting him from his share of the farm by bribing the judges – 'gift-devouring kings,' as he calls them.

The poems attributed to Hesiod, and cited as his by Pindar, Aristophanes, Plato, and other ancient writers, are the *Works and Days* (*Erga kai Hēmerai, i.e.* 'Farming Operations and Lucky and Unlucky

Days') and the *Theogonia* ('The Genealogy of the Gods'). Another poem, *The Shield of Heracles*, is generally printed with his works, but is evidently of later date. The two former poems contain, no doubt, many interpolations made by rhapsodes and later 'Hesiodic poets,' but there is much that is undoubtedly authentic and valuable to the historian. Moreover, what is of more importance, across the homespun warp of rules and maxims there runs many a bright thread of Horatian wit and wisdom and of deep and true feeling, and at times there comes a golden flash of true poetry, as in the description of the Five Ages in the *Erga* and the celebrated meeting of Hesiod with the Muses on Mount Helicon which forms the opening of the *Theogonia*.

As a creative poet and a master of language Homer is incomparably the greater, but Hesiod touches at times chords of far deeper import, giving voice to his own human nature and that of the common people.

The *Erga* ('Works and Days') is addressed to his brother, 'most foolish Perses,' to whom he gives many a sharp reproof and much sage advice, in order to save him from being ruined by his thriftless and dishonest ways and his love of lounging and gossip. The poem offers us a very graphic picture of Boeotian country life in the 'Dipylon' age. Hesiod's love of the country and of animals and of the stars, his interest in farming and in ships and boats (in spite of his dislike of the 'churlish sea'), his reverence for Zeus and his laws, his belief in prayer and in good guardian spirits (line 122), his conviction that work is the happiest lot for a mortal, 'whatever he may be in fortune'; that often 'the half is more than the whole'; that wealth should not be 'clutched at' nor won by guile of tongue, but accepted as the gift of heaven; that home-life is far better than gadding about and gossiping – all this testifies to a state of mind by no means entirely miserable and discontented among the country folk of Boeotia. The very epithets and names that he gives to animals show his delight in them and his keen observation. The ox is described as if he were, like the Irishman's pig, a member of the family; the snail is the 'house-carrier,' the ant is 'the knowing one,' the cuttle-fish is 'the boneless one,' wild beasts are 'forest-sleepers,' the swallow is 'early-wailing,' the spider is 'high-hovering.' Bees, drones, hawks, ravens, nightingales, dogs, mules, are all mentioned with knowledge and sympathy. The horse (if we exclude Pegasus) is referred to once only, and that in a line of doubtful authenticity. As regards Hesiod's keen observation of nature, what could be more Wordsworthian than his likening of a certain kind of tree-leaf as it unfolds in spring to the 'foot of an alighting raven'?

*Fig. 36  Foundations of Apollo's Temple, West Delphi*

But there is a dark side to his picture. He inveighs with great bitterness against the avarice and injustice of this age of iron in which fate has set him – this age in which 'money is the life of wretched mortals,' and which will go from bad to worse until, 'veiling their fair faces in white mantles, Honour and Righteous Indignation shall leave mankind and flee away from the broad-wayed earth to Olympus, to the race of the immortal gods.' He denounces people for their jealousies and strife and scandal-mongering and eternal lawsuits. 'Potter quarrels with potter and carpenter with carpenter; beggar envies beggar and minstrel minstrel.' And his bitterness is especially intense against the heartlessness and greed and injustice that he sees in those around him – intensest, perhaps, against his own brother and the unrighteous judges who have deprived him of his heritage. He calls upon Zeus to smite with his thunderbolt, and to send again to earth his daughter, Justice,[1] who has been dragged with insults through the streets by mortals and expelled from her own tribunals – that goddess who alone can bring back peace and golden prosperity to a land ruined by tyranny and the idleness of wealth.

We have thus a picture of aristocratic oppression such as we found also intimated at Athens, and of an unhappy state of things among the working classes. Laws and law-courts and law-court holidays are mentioned, but it is evident that the power of 'deciding questions of ancient right [*themistes*] by straight judgments,' of which Hesiod speaks, too often lay in the hands of 'gift-devouring kings.' Hesiod's cry for justice and for equality before the law is the earliest in European literature. So, too, he is the first to assert the nobility of work rather than that of rank and wealth, and to claim for poetry a function higher than that of recounting pretty fictions in the halls of the nobility.[2]

Hesiod touches at times on questions of the deepest import. His maxims

---

[1] The word *Dikē* (Justice), or some word derived from it, occurs fourteen times in thirty lines. Homer's description of the blessings brought by a good king offers a striking contrast (*Od.* xix. 109).

[2] 'Field-abiding shepherds, shameless ones, mere belly-gods,' exclaim the Muses who bring to Hesiod the staff of laurel, 'we know to tell of many things resembling what is real, but we know also to sing, whene'er we wish, of what is true.' Doubtless he refers here once more to lounging and scandal-mongering, such as was connected with recitations of old ballads. It by no means follows that he considered 'didactic' poetry higher than such poetry as that of Homer. He was too good a poet for that; but he believed, as Aristophanes did, that the poet was the 'teacher of men' in the highest sense.

are, however, not always such as we approve. Thus he tells us that 'easy and smooth is the way to evil and toilsome the way to virtue, steep and rough at first; but when one reaches the height then it becomes easier, though ever difficult' – which reads like a combined quotation from the Bible and from Dante. But he also tells us to 'love those who love us,' to 'give to him that giveth, but not to him that giveth not,' and to ask a next-door neighbour to dinner because he may prove useful in some future village squabble. Again, 'Give good measure,' he says, 'yes, an over-measure if you can, so that you may find a sure supply when you need it.'

Another of his maxims shows a dry humour and a worldly wisdom, doubtless learnt by bitter experience. 'Even in the case of a brother,' he says, 'insist on having a witness – but do it with a laugh.'

In the *Erga* there are evident signs of that superstitious dread of the supernatural which we noticed in the older Greek religion, but which is scarcely perceptible in Homer. Hesiod speaks with gloomy apprehension of all the curses, the swarming diseases and things of dread, that have been brought on the earth by the theft of Prometheus and the creation of the first woman, Pandora. 'The land,' he exclaims, 'is full of evil things and full the sea.' And he gives numerous rules for the avoidance of evil results: 'Not at a feast of the gods to cut the dry from the quick on the five-branched thing [the hand]'; 'not, when men are drinking, to lay the wineladle over the wine-bowl – for 'tis a most fatal thing to do.' Then he gives a long list of lucky and unlucky days, reminding one forcibly of Old Moore's Almanack.

Lastly, dress is sometimes mentioned. In his description of the effects of cold weather (which he evidently hated) Hesiod advises one to get as a 'protection for one's flesh' a thick-woven soft *chlaina* (mantle) and a *chitōn* (tunic) reaching down to the feet, and ox-hide sandals lined with felt. This male attire is thoroughly Homeric; but the dress of the fashionable lady among these Boeotian country folk seems to have been rather of the Mycenaean style, such as we found in contemporary Dipylon vase-paintings. Doubtless the lady in question wore a dress of the latest Athenian fashion, with tight bodice and flounced skirt and well-padded protrusions. Hesiod is giving advice to a young farmer, such as his brother: 'Don't let yourself be taken in,' he says, 'by any fashionably dressed woman who comes trying with wheedling flatteries to making herself mistress of your farm' – and the real meaning of the epithet he applies to her is 'furnished with a big bustle behind.'

The *Theogonia* is more Homeric in its language than the *Erga*, and of a

Fig. 37 Archaic statue, excavated on the Acropolis (See List of Illustrations)

quite different tone. It is chiefly taken up with a long account of the genesis of the Universe from Chaos and with a genealogy of the gods. The presence of Love as the formative and creative principle in this Hesiodic Genesis is very remarkable. It forestalls some of the wisest guesses of later Greek sages. The poem does not throw so much light as the *Erga* on life in the Dark Age, but it shows that a very complex and complete mythology had already grown up around the hierarchy formed by the superimposition of the northern on the old Aegean or Pelasgian deities. The opening lines of the *Theogonia*, describing the visit of the Muses to Hesiod on Mount Helicon, are of very high merit as poetry, and, together with not a few other passages in his poems, entirely justify the honour conferred by these daughters of Memory on one whom a modern writer has called a 'gifted rustic.'

## SECTION C: THE PHOENICIANS AND SOME OTHER NATIONS DURING THE DARK AGE

Since the discovery of the Minoan and Mycenaean civilizations the Phoenicians have lost the credit of having introduced art into Crete and Greece. But they had most of the Aegean and Mediterranean sea-trade in their hands for some centuries – probably from the decline of the Minoan naval supremacy until the rise of Corinthian and Athenian sea-power (about 1400 to 750). Indeed, in still earlier times they seem to have been a nation of merchant princes, such as Isaiah describes them (xxiii. 1–8). They probably introduced the Egyptian decimal coinage into Babylon as well as the 'ell.' They are said to have brought the vine and the olive to Crete. In old Egyptian monuments the tribute of the Phoenicians includes the products of many distant lands. In the time of Moses (*c.* 1350) they possessed the colony of Tartessus, or Tarshish, in Spain, and had perhaps already reached Britain and the Baltic, as well as the west coast of Africa (where later they had three hundred factories) and the Euxine. Gades (Cadiz) was founded probably about the time of the Trojan War, and Utica about 1100. In the time of Solomon (960) they had fleets also on the Red Sea, which brought gold from India or South Africa. Indeed, perhaps these were the oldest fleets possessed by the Phoenicians, for the men of Tyre and Sidon are said to have come originally from the Red Sea, or Persian Gulf – perhaps from the 'land of Punt,' as Abyssinia or Somaliland is called in an Egyptian inscription of the Vth Dynasty (*c.* 3000). Possibly, too, the Greek name Phoenix, which was believed to mean 'the red man,' or 'the man of the red land' (land of the sun, or sun-god?), may have originally meant 'the man of Punt' (*cf.* Latin Punicus, Poenus).

When Herodotus visited new Tyre (*c.* 450) he was told by the priests of Melcarth, the Phoenician Heracles, that ancient Tyre was founded about 2750. If Tyre was the 'daughter of Sidon,' as we are told in the Bible, Sidon must have existed from at least 3000, and it was the chief city of Phoenicia until about 1120, when it was conquered by the Philistines. A century or so later, in the days of Solomon and King Hiram, Tyre took the lead. Both Jezebel, Ahab's wife, and Queen Dido were members of the same dynasty as Hiram. At this era Assyria became very powerful under Shalmanezer II, and Tyre was captured by the Assyrians. Perhaps on account of this Assyrian oppression a large body of Phoenicians, led, as tradition says, by the Princess Elissa (Dido), made a new home (*c.* 825) on the coast of Africa, not far from the older colony Utica. This new city was Carthage.

The fact that the Phoenicians had settlements in all quarters of the Mediterranean even in the fourteenth century, and that they doubtless took with them the worship of the bull-headed Phoenician sun-god Baal, or Moloch, to whom human sacrifices were made, has very naturally caused many to believe that the Cretan bull-worship and the Minotaur and Talos legends were originally derived from this source, and that the myths of Theseus and Iphigeneia are reminiscences of the abolition of Phoenician human sacrifice by Greek influence. However that may be, it is evident that the Phoenicians had little or nothing to do with Aegean and Cretan art or with ancient Minoan writing. But they introduced, as we have seen, the alphabet into Hellas, and they also (*pace* some modern writers) possessed no mean craft as 'cunning workers,' as the Bible and also Homer tell us. Thus a silver wine-bowl described by Homer was 'more beautiful than all others on earth, since it was wrought by those cunning workers the Sidonians.' Another such *kratēr* was given to Menelaus by the king of the Sidonians, and a beautiful *peplos* worked by Sidonian women is mentioned. But it must be allowed that the *Odyssey* usually gives us a picture of the Phoenician not as craftsman but as trader and artful huckster of gauds and trinkets – such a despicable creature as the Phaeacian Euryalus describes when pouring contempt on Odysseus:

Nay, O stranger, and truly I liken thee not to a mortal
Practised in any of all of the contests known to the nations;
Rather to one that frequents with his well-benched vessel the harbours,

Skipper, methinks, of a folk of the sea who traffic as chapmen,
Mindful of nought but the bales and careful of nought but the cargo,
Ay and the grab and the gain.

No large settlements were made by the Phoenicians on Aegean shores, except perhaps Cameirus, in Rhodes, but they had numerous marts and purple-factories – one perhaps on the Isthmus of Corinth and another near the Peiraeus. The struggle between the Semitic and Japhetic races – a struggle which, no less than the Persian wars, was to decide the destiny of Europe – took place, not in the Aegean, but in Sicily, where by the eighth century the Phoenicians, Uticans, and Carthaginians possessed many trade-stations, and whither during the eighth century, as we shall see, a large stream of Greek colonists began to find its way. This struggle (with which the battles of Himera and Crimisus and the Punic wars are connected) lasted for six centuries, till the total demolition of Carthage by the Romans in 146.

Of Crete during the Dark Age very little is known. We have seen that in the heroic age, if we may accept Homer's account, it possessed, some two centuries after the sack of Cnossus, ninety or a hundred towns and was inhabited by many different races, among whom Dorians are mentioned. The great Dorian invasion a century or so later evidently subjected the whole island to that race, and for some centuries it was probably under Dorian kings and had a constitution not unlike the Spartan, except that there seem to have been no Perioeci, but only serfs and nobles. Later we find the kingly office abolished and an aristocracy in power, and the executive in the hands of ten magistrates called *kosmoi*.

Of Cyprus we had some notice during the age of Aegean civilization. Mycenaean kings are said to have ruled there in the fifteenth century. Aegean pottery of this era, together with Egyptian scarabs and ornaments of the XVIIIth Dynasty (Queen Ti and Amenhotep III), have been discovered in a tomb at Enkomi, near Salamis, and clay tablets have been found in Egypt inscribed with cuneiform missives to the Pharaohs from these Mycenaean Cypriot kings. The island was in early ages sometimes subject to Egypt, and on account of its valuable copper-mines was also evidently occupied by Phoenicians, but the latest researches (by Ohnefalsch Richter) seem to prove that Hellenic civilization and the Olympian gods (Athene, Heracles, Aphrodite, and others) preceded the Phoenician supremacy, and that the Phoenician kings destroyed Greek temples and razed Greek inscriptions.[1] If this be so, the Paphian Aphrodite was not derived from the Eastern Astarte, but Astarte was superimposed on the Cyprian-Greek divinity, who seems to have been a kind of Earth-goddess, or a Spring-goddess (like Kore), with such titles as 'The Idaean Mother' and 'She who spreadeth abroad the roses.' The Greeks who introduced these deities were, of course, not the Mycenaeans, but Hellenes, and it seems likely that the old tradition (see Hor. *Carm.* I, vii., and Virg. *Aen.* i. 619) about Teucer, brother of Ajax, having been expelled from Salamis on his return from Troy and having founded a new Salamis in Cyprus has for its basis a historical fact; for about the time when the colonization of Ionia was at its height (*c.* 1050) a considerable body of Greeks, probably Achaeans with Arcadian and other followers who were pressed by Dorian invaders, are said to have left Greece and to have made their way to the old Aegean colonies in Cyprus. The chief Greek towns in Cyprus were Paphos, Lapathus, Marion, Curion, Salamis, and later Soli; but in some of these there was also a large Phoenician element. During the next two centuries and more Cyprus seems to have been ruled by the 'kings' of the numerous cities, for about 720 the Assyrian monarch Sargon (who carried Israel away into captivity) conquered the island, and we find in the inscription on the stele which he set up there (now in Berlin) seven Yatman (Cyprian) kings mentioned, and in an inscription of Assarhaddon, the son of Sennacherib (Fig. 38), ten Cypriot kings are described as his subjects.

Of Egypt during this age the notices are scanty. In the period 1120–950 (from the time of Samson and the Philistine supremacy in Palestine until the days of Solomon) it was ruled by the inglorious priestly Tanite Dynasty (the XXIst). Then Sheshenk, or Shishak, of the XXIInd Dynasty, carried war into Palestine and captured Jerusalem, as we learn from an inscription at Karnak (*cf.* 2 Chron. xii.). After this Egypt was evidently overrun by the Aethiopian hosts of whom we read in 2 Chron. xiv., and the XXVth Dynasty was one of Aethiopian kings. Then, about 674, Egypt is conquered by the great Assyrian monarch Assarhaddon. The liberation of Egypt (*c.* 665) from the Assyrian yoke by Psamtik I with the aid of Ionian 'men of bronze' opened, as we shall see later, a new epoch, and brought Egypt into closer relations with Greece.

The great empires of the East, Babylonia and Assyria, have hitherto

---

[1] It seems strange that in these Greek (or Cypriot?) inscriptions neither Zeus nor Kore nor Dionysus is mentioned.

*Fig. 38  Assarhaddon with captive Egyptian and Aethiopian*

come into no direct contact with Greece, nor even with the Greek colonies, except, perhaps, in the case of Sargon's conquest of Cyprus, which has been mentioned. It is enough to note here that Assyria during the Dark Age was in constant war with Babylonia, and in the ninth century, under its great kings Assurnasirpal and Shalmanezer II, conquered Phoenicia and made head against the Syrian kings of Damascus.

After the expulsion of the Assyrians from Egypt, and the rise of the Median power under Cyaxares, these Oriental peoples will occupy more of our attention; for one of the striking traits which especially distinguish the history of Greece is the fact that we are so often brought into contact with other great ancient civilizations, and it is of deep import that, although subjected to such influences, Hellenic art and literature and philosophy retained an almost perfectly independent character, and have remained till our own day not only supreme in beauty of form, but also incomparable for originality, if we accept that word in its true sense.

# Chapter 3

# From the First Olympiad to Peisistratus (776 to 560)

*An Age of Colonization – The Euxine – Sicily – South Italy – The Homeland – Argos – Sparta – Tyrants and Sages – Athens*

SECTIONS – A: EGYPT AND CYRENE – B: LYDIA AND EASTERN KINGS – C: THE GAMES – D: THE POETS

Although when we speak of Greek art and literature and philosophy (the three priceless legacies that Greece has left us) we instinctively think of Greece itself and especially of Athens, which in the so-called classic era was the 'eye of Hellas,' the fact is that Greece owes much of its fame to its colonies.[1] Of colonial origin were Homer, Archilochus, Terpander, Arion, Alcaeus, Sappho, Stesichorus, Simonides, Anacreon, the younger Simonides, Theocritus, and other Greek poets. The historian Herodotus was born at Halicarnassus. All the great early philosophers were Ionians. Thales, Anaximander, and Anaximenes were of Miletus, Heracleitus of Ephesus, Pythagoras of Samos, Xenophanes of Colophon. Of the seven sages four were colonials, and among celebrated colonial artists may be mentioned Paeonius, Pythagoras, Scopas, Polygnotus, Parrhasius, Apelles, Zeuxis. The arts of working in marble and of bronze-casting came, it is said, from Chios and Lesbos; sculpture came from Crete. The coins, too, of many of the cities of Greater Hellas, such as the beautiful Syracusan coins, were finer than any produced in the mother-country; and, lastly, many of the magnificent temples in Ionia, Sicily, and Southern Italy, of which some are still standing, were built long before the Parthenon.

[1] See dates of the foundation of early Greek colonies, p. 512.

142

It is, indeed, a striking view that the Hellenic world offers about the end of the seventh century. Greece itself, with no very large population and in no very highly advanced state of civilization or art, is already the mother of cities, which extend from Sicily and Italy, and even the south of Gaul, to the further shores of the Euxine. The Aeolian and Ionian and Cyprian Greek cities date, as we have seen, from much earlier times. Doubtless emigration went on continuously during the interval, but it is not till about the date of the first Olympiad that we hear for certain of the first Hellenic colonies in the West and on the Propontis and Euxine.

The question arises, what were the reasons of this very large emigration from the old country? Greece is not a fertile land. 'Want hath ever been a foster-sister to Hellas,' said the Spartan Demaratus to King Xerxes. But doubtless also a land-grabbing aristocracy (who were glad to get rid of discontents), as well as the wretched state of things that we have seen described by Hesiod, aggravated much the condition of the peasant and the artisan, so that without any great surplus of population[1] there was a natural impulse among the working classes to get away to freer lands; and many of the leisured classes would also be attracted by the love of adventure. The vast numbers of emigrants may thus be partly explained, and the huge population of some of these colonial cities was, of course, partly due to a large native element.

Although in early days serious conflicts took place between some of the colonies and their mother-cities, such as the naval war (c. 664) between Corinth and Corcyra already mentioned, the general result of the expansion of Greece was to strengthen immensely Hellenic patriotism, if one may use these words to express the sense of the oneness of the whole Hellenic race – or rather of the whole people of Greece, including all its diverse races, and all its progeny in other lands – in contradistinction to the outer world of barbarians. The Greek colonies were, as a rule, more Greek than Greece itself. They looked on the mother-country with the deepest affection and reverence. No colony was founded without consulting the great Greek oracle at Delphi and procuring an 'oekist' (founder appointed by some Greek mother-city); and a flame from the sacred fire that burnt in the town-hall (*prytaneion*) at home was carried abroad in order to light the

---

[1] Even two and a half centuries later (430) Athens had only 80,000 inhabitants, half of whom were slaves. At Marathon (490) the Athenian army only numbered about 9000.

public hearth in the new city. They took with them also the religion of their Grecian home. They sent frequent deputations to the festivals of the metropolis, and received with reverence its envoys. The founder who had been supplied by the city in Greece was often worshipped after his death as a divinity; and no new colony was sent forth from a Greek colony without obtaining a founder from the mother-city.

And for Greece itself the existence of her colonies – of this great Hellenic community extending over so much of the then known world – was of great moment. 'The influence of Greater Greece,' says the late Professor Butcher, 'is the determining fact in the history of the Hellenic people.' Not only, as was the case in our Elizabethan age, did the opening up of new worlds stir the imagination and enlarge the vision of Greek poets and deepen the insight of Greek thinkers, but the existence of Greater Hellas had much influence in developing, for good or for evil, the imperial policy of Athens in the days of her power, and in determining her fate.

## The Euxine

Although they were, perhaps, not so ancient as some of the colonies in the far West, Greek settlements on the Euxine and the Propontis were founded in very early times.[1] Doubtless there was trade between the Euxine shores and the Greek cities of Asia Minor from early days of the first colonization of Aeolis and Ionia. Indeed, as we have seen, the old fable of the Argonauts points to the beginnings of intercourse between Greece itself and the Euxine even before the Aeolian migration. The Greek town of Sinope, on the south shore of the Euxine, claimed to have been founded by Miletus about the middle of the eighth century. It was, old writers say, destroyed by the Cimmerians, and was refounded about 630. Another Milesian colony, Trapezus (now Trebizond), lay some 400 miles more to the east, not far from Colchis, the country of Medea and the mythical Golden Fleece. Probably even in these early days there were Grecian marts and halting-places along the coasts of the Propontis and Euxine. On not a few of these sites regular settlements were in course of time founded by various Greek cities. Little Megara especially distinguished itself by founding (*c.* 685) Calchedon, or Chalcedon, on the Bosporus, and some thirty years later occupied the opposite shore, where, on account of the magnificent site

---

[1] The plates of coins should be referred to, and the explanations in Note C.

*Fig. 39  The 'François Vase' (See List of Illustrations)*

145

that it enjoyed, the city of Byzantium rose rapidly to importance, and in later times became one of the most famous cities in the world. Sestos and Lampsacus (once Phoenician) were settled by Aeolians, Abydos and Cyzicus by Milesians. These Hellespontine towns owed their prosperity to the ever-increasing commerce between the Euxine and the Aegean and Grecian ports. The trade in iron and silver and flax and other products from Colchis and the country of the Chalybes and other lands on the South Euxine was in course of time supplemented by trade with its northern shores, where numerous Greek settlements were made, such as Odessus and Olbia, on the Dnieper mouth, and Panticapaeum in the Tauric Chersonese (Crimea), while at the mouth of the river Phasis – where the Argonauts reached the home of Medea – the Greek town of Phasis arose, and another, Dioscurias, still closer to the great range of the Caucasus. On the North Aegean, too, various cities were now founded, of which Potidaea, a colony of Corinth, and Methone, a Euboean settlement, are of the most importance historically.

## Cyme in Italy

The western waters of the Mediterranean were navigated by Phoenician traders in very early times, and some of their settlements preceded the first Greek settlements in these parts by at least 500 years. By about 1350, as we have seen, Tarshish, or Tartessus, the Phoenician port in Spain, was well known, and Gades was founded about 1200. Doubtless these navigators spread the worship of their gods, Melcarth (the Phoenician Heracles) and the bull-headed sun-god Baal or Moloch, and hence we have the old Greek legends of Heracles erecting pillars at the straits near Tarshish and capturing the cattle of the monster Geryon, and of the sacred cattle of the sun-god Eëlios, which, as Homer tells us, the companions of Odysseus slew in Sicily.[1] Tradition, indeed, intimates that a hundred years and more before the days of Odysseus a Greek city, Cyme (Cumae), existed in Italy, close to what was afterwards known as Lake Avernus, nor far from the frontier of the great Etrurian or Tyrrhenian nation – those Tyrseni of whom we heard in connection with the Pelasgians, and whom we shall meet again in the

---

[1] *Od.* xii. The seven herds probably have reference to the seven planets. Can the name Eëlios be connected with El, the primitive Semitic name of God – probably the sun-god?

time of Hiero.[1] The tradition about this ancient Greek city is repeated by Virgil; Daedalus, he says, after flying from Crete to escape Minos, alighted at Cumae, and hung up his wings there in Apollo's temple. The date of this – that is, the flight of Daedalus and the death of Minos – would be, according to Herodotus (viii. 171), some three generations before the Trojan war.

Perhaps, however, the first important colonization of Cyme by the Greeks took place about 800. The colonists were mainly from Cyme in Aeolis, the home of Hesiod's father, and from Cyme in Euboea, the mother-city. Chalcidians and other Euboeans joined, and it is just possible that a small contingent of Graioi from Boeotia gave to the Italians in the neighbourhood of Cumae the name which the natives of Italy first applied to the Hellene race, and by which we now generally designate it.

## Sicily

The Chalcidians of Euboea and the Cymaeans also founded (735) the first Greek city in Sicily, Naxos (destroyed in later times by Dionysius), and not long afterwards Catane (now Catania), Leontini, Zancle (the 'sickle-harbour,' like Drepanon; afterwards renamed as Messene), and Himera on the north coast (celebrated later for the great victory of Greeks over Carthaginians in 480, perhaps on the same day as the victory of Salamis; finally razed to the ground by the Carthaginians in 409).

Before the coming of the Greeks the eastern half of Sicily was held by the Sicels, who had probably crossed from Italy and driven the older inhabitants, the Sicans, towards the western parts of the island. Besides these there were the Elymi, whose chief city was Egesta, and whom tradition asserted to be descendants of Trojans left there by Aeneas on his voyage to Latium. On the Sicilian coasts there were also numerous Phoenician stations, but no large settlements. It was not until after the rise of the naval and military power of Carthage, about 550, that Sicily became the arena of the great struggle between the Semitic and Hellenic races.

Some[2] of the most famous of the Greek cities of Sicily were founded by Dorians, mostly in the south-eastern corner of the island. Of these cities Syracuse, a colony of Corinth, was the oldest, and in the same year (734)

---

[1] Hesiod (if the passage is authentic) speaks not only of Etruria, but of the Latins and King Latinus. His connection with Aeolian Cyme may explain his knowledge.

[2] Our main authority is here Thucydides (Book VI).

Corcyra (Corfu) was also colonized by the Corinthians.[1] The small state of Megara, which showed such vigour on the Euxine, placed a Hyblaean Megara on the coast north of Syracuse, and a century later this settlement, with the aid of the mother-city, founded on the south-western coast the city of Selinus, famed for its majestic temples, all built in the two centuries of its existence before its utter destruction by the Carthaginian Hannibal at the same time as Himera (409). The remains of these temples and of the acropolis form probably the greatest mass of ruins in Europe, and the metopes of the temples afford some of the oldest and most interesting specimens of Greek sculpture (see Fig. 60). The name of Selinus is probably of Phoenician origin, but the word *selinon* means 'wild celery' in Greek, and that the Selinuntines accepted this meaning is proved by their coins, on which the plant is depicted (see Plate IV, 5). Possibly Homer's description of Calypso's isle with its 'meadows of violets and celery' may have favoured the interpretation.

About 688 Gela, a Sicel town overlooking the southern sea, was occupied by Greek Rhodians and Cretans. It became later a city of importance, and is famous as the home of the great Syracusan princes Gelo and Hiero, and as the death-place of Aeschylus. In 581 Gela founded, with an oekist from Rhodes, the city of Acragas (Agrigentum, and now Girgenti), about fifty miles distant towards the west, on a lofty site not far from the sea. Acragas, the city of the notorious tyrant Phalaris and of Thero, who shared with Gelo the victory of Himera, became a city of vast population and wealth, as was testified by the line of magnificent temples on its southern front, some of which are still standing (see Fig. 76). The greatest of these, the Olympieion, now a wilderness of ruin, was the vastest of all Greek temples.

The Greeks did not try to colonize the west of Sicily.[2] Here Egesta (or Segesta), the city of the Elymi, held sway in alliance with Phoenicians, whose settlements at Panormus (Palermo) and on the island Motya gradually developed into important towns. The people of Motya were afterwards (397) transferred by the Carthaginians to the great Punic city of

---

[1] Both sites had already been occupied by Euboeans, who were expelled. Corcyra never became of much importance, and after the Peloponnesian War dwindled to almost nothing, while Syracuse at its prime occupied a larger space than Rome under the Empire. Its walls were about fifteen miles in length, those of Rome about twelve. But Rome's population was greater by far.

[2] But see Greek temple, Fig. 57.

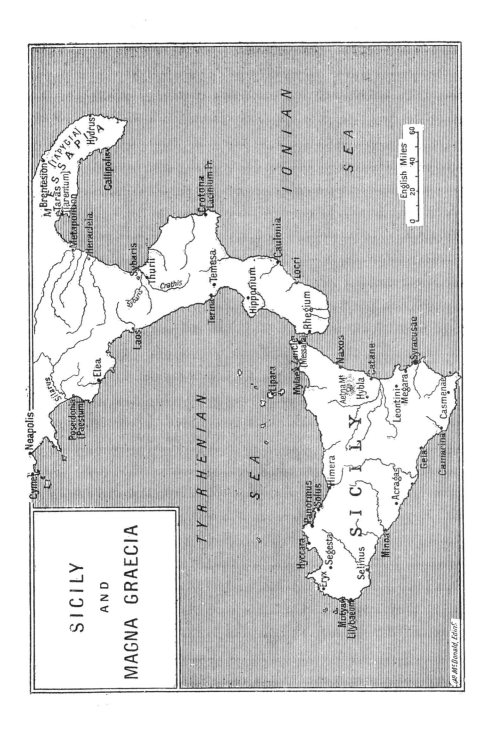

SICILY
AND
MAGNA GRAECIA

149

Lilybaeum, on the neighbouring mainland. At the north-west corner of Sicily, on Mount Eryx, overlooking the sea, stood a famous temple dedicated to a goddess, called Aphrodite by the Greeks and Venus Erycina by the Romans – evidently either a Phoenician Astarte or some Elymian (Phrygian?) Nature-goddess.

## Magna Graecia ('Greater Greece')

We must now return to Italy. Here by the middle of the seventh century we find some fifteen flourishing Greek cities occupying almost the whole of the line of the southern coasts from Brundisium to Cumae; and by about 550 their number will have increased to twenty or more, some of them greater than any city in the mother-country. The earliest of these was founded in 721 by Achaeans from the Peloponnese, who seem to have found their harbourless and rugged country, with its twelve obscure townships, both unattractive and overpopulated, and to have made settlements first in the island Zacynthus, and then to have made their way across to Italy, as the south-western extremity of the Hesperian peninsula was already called.

Here, just within the great gulf, they founded Sybaris, on an alluvial plain between the rivers Sybaris and Crathis, and some eighteen years later they planted Croton on a fine harbour, near to the Lacinian promontory, where still stands a solitary column of the great temple of Hera which for ages greeted the Greek as he came from the motherland to Greater Hellas, and where he was wont to sacrifice and offer gifts before he sailed further (see Fig. 40). Both of these settlements became at an early era very great and powerful cities and the mothers of many other Greek towns. Sybaris is said to have possessed twenty-five such dependencies and to have ruled over four of the native peoples. It became a great trade emporium, and in order to extend its commerce by land-routes to Etruria and the far West it founded on the Tyrrhene Sea the cities of Laos and Scidros and that of Poseidonia (Paestum), whose magnificent Doric temples are still standing almost intact (Fig. 41). The wealth and luxury of Sybaris are proverbial. Its army is said to have numbered 300,000 (perhaps mainly native troops), and the circuit of its walls to have rivalled that of Syracuse. But even in the days of Herodotus Sybaris was only a memory, for in 510 it was utterly destroyed by its rival Croton, as we shall see later when we come to the life of Pythagoras. On the western coast also Croton planted various towns, of which Terina was one (see coin 13 on Plate III). Another was on the site of

*Fig. 40  Lacinian cape and column*

*Fig. 41  Poseidon's Temple, Paestum*

the old Ausonian port Temesa (or Tempsa), perhaps mentioned in the *Odyssey* as an export-mart for bronze.[1]

Another great Greek city was Taras, or Tarentum, situated in Iapygian territory at the head of the great gulf which still bears its name. It is said to have been originally a Cretan settlement, but about 708 it was occupied by Spartans. Taras was the only colony ever founded by Sparta, and tradition accounts for its foundation by a strange story, perhaps invented to explain the word Partheniae ('The Maidens' Children'), who are said to have been its first settlers, for it was related that on their return from a very long campaign against the Messenians the Spartans found a large number of illegitimate youths, and that these, after an attempted rebellion, were dispatched to the far West under the leadership of a certain Phalanthus. This Phalanthus was afterwards worshipped as the son of Poseidon, and was represented on Tarentine coins astride a dolphin (see Plate II, 3). Taras became renowned for its industrial products – its wool and pottery and dyes – but is historically connected more with Rome than Greece, although for a long period, after the fall of Sybaris, it was perhaps the most powerful and wealthy of all the cities of Greater Hellas.

Two other Greek cities, Metapontion and Siris, stood on the shores of the Gulf of Tarentum, between Tarentum and Sybaris. The former was founded by Sybaris with the aid of the Peloponnesian Achaeans, Siris by the Ionian city Colophon.[2] No other city of Ionia attempted to found a colony during this age in the West; but the Aeolians were more venturesome, for Phocaea, which had already the important settlement of Lampsacus on the Propontis, about 600 planted a colony at Massalia (Marseille), near the delta of the Rhone – the westernmost of all Greek cities, except its own later settlements in Spain. The Phocaeans also had settlements in Corsica, where about 565 (according to Herodotus) they founded a city called Alalia. Some twenty years later, as we shall see, in order to escape from the Persians, almost the whole population of Phocaea took ship for Alalia, but being expelled from Corsica by the Carthaginians and Etruscans they fled to Rhegium and thence founded Elea (Velia), on the west Italian coast, to the south of Poseidonia. It is possible that Xenophanes of Colophon may have fled to Siris from Asia to escape the Persians, and may have joined the Phocaean fugitives at Rhegium and have

---

[1] If so, this (*Od.* i. 184) is the earliest mention of any Italian town.
[2] The poet Archilochus (*c.* 650) writes of Siris as if it were known to him.

been among the first colonists of the city, whose name owes its survival mainly to the fame of the school of philosophy that he founded there.

Among the more important Greek colonies of this age must be mentioned Cyrene, in North Africa; but as its foundation (*c.* 630) is connected with the opening up of Egypt to Greek commerce it will be described later when we consider that subject.

## The Homeland: Corinth

The Greeks calculated all their dates from the victory of Coroebus in the foot-race at the Olympic Games (revived, it is said, by Lycurgus and Iphitus) in the year that we call 776 B.C. They regarded this as the beginning of the historical period; but there is very little known for certain about Greece – less, perhaps, than we know about the Greek colonies – during the first century of this epoch.

It is evident that about the eighth century Corinth was a great mercantile and maritime power. With her newly invented triremes and her great trading vessels she dominated two seas. She had founded Syracuse and colonized Corcyra, which colony had become strong enough by 664 to oppose her mother-city in the first sea-fight known to Thucydides.

## Argos

In the Peloponnese, while Sparta was engaged in long warfare with the Messenians and at times holding her own with difficulty, Argos seems to have been a leading state. In 668 the Argives, it is said, defeated the Spartans at Hysiae. They captured Mycenae and Tiryns, overran Aegina, and, perhaps, held for some time all the eastern coast of Laconia and even the island of Cythera (see Hdt. i. 82). Corinth, too, is said to have fallen for a time into their hands. The successes of Argos at this era are attributed to the famous Argive king Pheidon, who (as we shall see later) reinstated the people of Pisa in the management of the Olympic Games and instituted himself as president, claiming the right through his ancestor Heracles. His date is, however, very uncertain.[1] To him is also attributed the introduction

---

[1] Alexander the Great, to prove his right to compete at Olympia, claimed descent from Pheidon. Pausanias (A.D. 160) asserts that Pheidon presided at the eighth Olympiad (748), but Herodotus says that Pheidon's son was a suitor for Agarista, which would make *his* date about 620, and his father's about 660.

of systematic weights and measures, as standards for which he deposited bars of metal in the great temple of Argive Hera. The first homeland Greek coins were struck in Aegina, probably in Pheidon's reign and after Pheidonian standards.

The Argive hegemony in the Peloponnese seems to have declined rapidly after the reign of Pheidon, a fact evidently due to the rise of the Spartan power. According to tradition, Pheidon's interference at Olympia roused the wrath of the Spartans, who reinstated the Eleans and expelled the Argives.

### Sparta

Sparta during the first century of the historical period, as we have seen, took but little share in colonization, and her one colony, Taras, is said to have originated from her political difficulties. During these years she was mainly engaged in fighting the Messenians – those western neighbours of hers who, after a hundred years of warfare, submitted (those who remained in Messenia) to be treated almost as slaves for two centuries, and then, having rebelled, were ejected (in 464) from their homeland, and finally, a century later, were restored by Epameinondas, never again to be conquered by their old enemies, but to become the subjects of Rome.

These Messenians inhabited the south-western corner of the Peloponnese,[1] cut off from the Spartan valley of the Eurotas by the great range of Mount Taygetus. Their land consisted of the fertile plain of Stenyclarus, through which the river Pamisus flows; and to the west is a mountainous district in which the strong fortress of Ithome was built, overlooking the plain across which Homer describes Telemachus driving on his journey from Pylos to Pherae and Sparta.

The first Dorian chiefs, who, in order to justify their overlordship, claimed descent from Heracles, seem to have resided at Stenyclarus, on the northern stream of the Pamisus, and never to have conquered the southern district of Pylos. The number of these Dorians was evidently small, and in course of time the dominant race may have been very considerably merged in the native Messenian people. This may partly explain the treatment these rebellious half-castes received – as severe as that accorded to revolted Helots – at the hands of the pure-bred Dorian Spartiates.

---

[1] Homer mentions Messene, the district of Pherae, and its ruler Orsilochus. The city of Messene was first built by Epameinondas.

Of the origin and the events of the first Messenian war (traditional date 743–724) many picturesque legends survive, handed down by writers who lived much later, but who may have collected the traditions from the Messenians restored to their country by Epameinondas (370). These legends tell of a Messenian hero, Aristodemus, who determined to sacrifice his own daughter to save his country, then slew her in anger, and slew himself afterwards on her tomb. They tell of a Spartan king, Theopompus, who, after many battles, in the twentieth year of the war captured and razed Ithome and reduced all the Messenians who did not leave their country to the same level of serfdom as that of the Helots.

After about forty years the Messenians again rebelled, and a second war of nearly equal length took place (traditional date 685–668). In the first war some of the other Peloponnesian states had taken a part, and on the outbreak of hostilities Corinth again sent aid to Sparta, while on the side of the Messenians were the Argives, Arcadians, Sicyonians, and the people of Pisa. The hero of this war was Aristomenes, under whose leadership the Messenians inflicted such defeats on the Spartans that they sent to the Delphic oracle for advice. This bade them apply to Athens for a leader. The Athenians, it is said, sent them in disdain a lame schoolmaster, Tyrtaeus, and this man by his martial songs so aroused the courage of the Spartans that, although they were defeated in a great battle by the Boar's Grave, on the plain of Stenyclarus, they again renewed the contest, and besieged the Messenians, it is said, for eleven years in their new mountain stronghold, Eira. During this siege Aristomenes performed many prodigies of valour, and was several times taken prisoner; but he always managed to escape – once, it is said, even from the great pit Caiadas in Sparta, into which the Spartans used to cast their criminals. This feat he performed by grasping the tail of a fox, which, struggling to get free, showed him the underground aperture by which it had entered. But no heroism could save the Messenians. Eira was captured. Many escaped to Arcadia or to Rhegium and other places over the sea; the rest were again enslaved. Aristomenes is said to have gone to Rhodes, and to have died there.

Fragments of the songs of Tyrtaeus exist, and I shall speak of them later. They mention some of the events of this second Messenian war; but they do not name Aristomenes. The songs were, says Athenaeus, chanted by a single voice to the accompaniment of the flute. They consisted in spirited appeals to the Spartans to show courage in battle and to maintain law and order (*eunomia*) at home. It should perhaps be added that some modern writers regard Tyrtaeus as a Spartan and the story of his origin as an Athenian invention.

### Tyrants (Ionia: Corinth: Megara: Sicyon)

While Sparta was thus laying the foundations of her future supremacy very important changes had been taking place in other cities of Greece. We have already seen how the old hereditary monarchies of Homeric days had in many cases given place to constitutions which were aristocracies in form but which contained within them a strong tendency towards democracy – a tendency that even under the permanent monarchical system of the Spartan state manifested itself in the creation of the popular magistracy of the ephors. We have also noticed the growing demand for constituted law and the adoption by Sparta of a code possibly founded to some extent on the laws of Crete and other ancient nations. Besides the half-mythical Lycurgus we hear of the shepherd Zaleucus, who (about 664) was authorized by the Delphic oracle to devise a constitution for the Italian Locrians, and slew himself for having unwittingly transgressed one of his own laws; and of Charondas, who gave a code to Sicilian Catane; and we shall soon hear of the Athenian lawgivers Dracon and Solon. The cry for justice – for equality before the law – uttered by Hesiod was making itself heard. And the great increase of the trading and labouring classes began to give them a consciousness of power and the desire for self-government. Moreover, the introduction of a new method in warfare helped greatly towards these ends. Instead of a Homeric Achilles or a Messenian Aristomenes we have serried ranks of mailed hoplites, and it is on these infantry-spearmen, drawn from the poorer classes, rather than on the high-born *hippeis* (knights), that the hope of victory now depends.

But the struggle of the people for self-government was long and difficult. In not a few cases it led to nothing but frequent and violent changes of constitution, which proved perhaps more disastrous than a permanent absolutism would have been. In others its first result was a relapse – or perhaps we may regard it as an advance towards democracy through a necessary phase. Aristocracy was exchanged for tyranny. The process has already been described. Feuds (such as arose in mediaeval Florence) disunited the aristocratic party, and some ambitious noble would invoke the aid of the people against his rivals and succeed in establishing himself as 'tyrant' – that is, as an unconstitutional despot.[1] Greek 'tyrannies' seem to have first arisen in Ionia. About 620 we hear of a tyrant of Ephesus marrying the daughter of Alyattes, the king of Lydia, and about the same time Miletus flourished exceedingly under the tyrant Thrasybulus.

Lesbos, on the other hand, evidently suffered long and severely from its aristocrats and despots, being oppressed first by the oligarchy of the Penthelids and then by tyrants. The last tyrant seems to have been expelled from Mytilene by the people under the leadership of Pittacus and the brothers of the poet Alcaeus, of both of whom we shall learn more when we turn to the poets and sages of this era. Pittacus had distinguished himself in war against Athens, and had won the confidence of the people. He was elected absolute dictator (*aisymnētēs*) of Mytilene for ten years, during which time he governed with such wisdom as to render possible the return of the exiled nobles, among whom was the poet Alcaeus himself.

Of the wealth and splendour of the Ionian cities during this age of despots, both on the mainland of Asia and on the Aegean islands, there is evidence enough, although we know almost nothing about their history. In the so-called Homeric *Hymn to Apollo* (perhaps dating from about 600) a fine description is given of the magnificence of the great festival on the island Delos, which was the religious centre of the Ionic world until the Asiatic Ionians instituted their festivals at the temple of Ephesus.

Indeed, at this time Ionia was apparently far in advance of the homeland in many civilized arts, and during the age of Solon and Peisistratus Athens adopted largely Ionian luxury and Ionian dress – that soft linen raiment and those golden cicalas, worn even by men as hair ornaments, of which Thucydides speaks somewhat contemptuously. And probably surpassing Athens itself in Ionian splendour were the Euboean cities of Eretria and Chalcis, of which we have already heard as the mothers of colonies. But they exhausted themselves in a conflict for the possession of the fertile Lelantine plain. So long and embittered was this war that, if we believe Thucydides, almost all Greece (as well as Miletus and Samos) took part in it. These Euboean cities declined rapidly in importance. Chalcis was

---

[1] The word *tyrannos* (possibly a Doric form of *koiranos*, a ruler, and connected with the common word *kyrios*, lord, or perhaps an Asiatic word) had no moral significance. It merely signified that the ruler had no hereditary or constitutional claim. It was perhaps first used by the Greeks with reference to the Lydian kings (see Archilochus, frag. 21). The king of Persia was always *Basileus*.

crushed by Athens, and the Eretrians were carried away to Persia by Darius.

In the homeland several important cities during this era (660–560) fell under tyrannies. Those of Corinth, Megara, and Sicyon are of special interest.

At Corinth the monarchy of the Heracleid kings had long ago, as we have already seen, given way to the oligarchy of the noble, or royal, family of the Bacchiadae. This oligarchy was overthrown (*c.* 655) by Cypselus, about whose birth Herodotus relates a curious old story. The mother, it was said, belonged to the Bacchiad family, but she was lame, and was given in marriage to Aëtion, who was poor but of the noble house of the Lapithae. An oracle had declared that their son would prove a rock to fall on Corinth and crush lawless power, and the oligarchs sent men to murder the child; but (as in the 'Babes in the Wood') the murderers were overcome by pity, and while they hesitated the mother, Labda, hid her infant in a *kypselē* – either a corn-bin or a great jar (*pithos*), such as the one depicted in Fig. 20 – and thus saved him. So he very naturally received the name Cypselus. The story is, perhaps, scarcely worth repeating except as an example of the kind of myth that higher criticism rejects as being evolved in explanation of a name; but it is also interesting because this chest or jar connects itself, as we shall see later, with the celebrated 'chest of Cypselus' – perhaps the earliest Greek work of art (besides the Shield of Achilles and that of Heracles!) of which we have a detailed description.

It was probably before, possibly during, the reign of Cypselus that the naval battle between Corinth and Corcyra took place which has been mentioned. Corinth evidently gained the victory, for while Cypselus and his son Periander held power this city seems to have developed on the north-western coast of Greece a considerable colonial empire, including Anactorium, Ambracia, Apollonia, and Leucas – which in the Homeric age was a peninsula (Nericon, the kingdom of Laertes), but was now converted into an island by a channel cut through its isthmus. It was also evidently at this time that Corcyra, with an oekist of Heracleid descent from the mother-city, Corinth, founded that city of Epidamnus which, according to Thucydides, was the first cause of open hostilities in the Peloponnesian War.

The son of Cypselus, Periander, could claim at least the shadow of hereditary right, but he seems to have found it necessary to protect himself by means of a strong bodyguard of mercenaries and by forcibly ridding himself of troublesome nobles. In this connection Herodotus tells almost

*Fig. 42 Apollo's Temple, Corinth*

*Fig. 43 Site of Corinth and the Acrocorinthus*

exactly the same story that is told by Livy about Tarquin. Periander sent for advice to Thrasybulus, tyrant of Miletus, who said nothing to the messenger, but led him through a field of corn and 'broke off and threw away, as he went, all such ears of corn as overtopped the rest.' Aristotle and other writers confirm the description of Periander given by Herodotus. Together with Thrasybulus, he is said to have drawn up a regular code of 'sanguinary maxims,' as Grote calls them, of a Machiavellian nature. He is described by Herodotus as at first 'milder than his father,' but afterwards a blood-thirsty despot; and revolting stories are recounted of his private life (including the murder of his wife, Melissa, and his quarrel with his son, whom he outlawed and banished to Corcyra). So hated was the tyrant by all that when, in old age, he proposed that his son should return and take his place at Corinth, and that he himself should come to Corcyra, the Corcyraeans, in their terror at the prospect, put the son to death – for which deed Periander took on them a terrible vengeance.[1]

This is one view. Others laud Periander as a wise and just though a severe ruler, and explain away the alleged acts of cruelty and oppression as wholesome sumptuary legislation. His wisdom was, indeed, so famed in some quarters that his name is found in some lists of the Seven Sages. That Corinth rose to great prosperity under his rule is undeniable, and it is more than possible that the immense increase of wealth and luxury made repressive measures necessary. Of wealth and magnificence an evident proof is what we hear of a colossal golden statue of Zeus and the famous chest of Cypselus, two of many splendid offerings made to Olympia by the Cypselid family. At Delphi, too, the treasure-house of the Corinthians was built, it is said, by Cypselus; and there still exists at Corinth a relic of the age, perhaps of the reign, of Periander – seven great columns of what was once a mighty Doric temple sacred to Apollo (Fig. 42). Like others of the Greek tyrants, Periander seems to have been a patron not only of sculpture and architecture, but also of music and poetry, for Arion, the Jonah-like story of whose escape (on the back of a dolphin) when cast into the sea seems to belong to the region of myths, was doubtless a minstrel at the Corinthian court.[2] Corinth, with its two seas, had fleets on both sides of

---

[1] See Hdt. iii. 48–53, v. 92. The story of the 300 Corcyraean youths whom Periander seized and attempted to send to Alyattes of Lydia is told with great detail by Herodotus and bears the stamp of truth.

[2] For Arion see Index.

the Isthmus, and was in touch not only with the Adriatic, Great Hellas, Sicily, and the far West, not only with the Euxine and with Miletus and Rhodes and Cyprus, but also with the newly founded Cyrene and with Egypt, in this age first opened up to Greek trade. The reign of Periander (625–585) was contemporary with the last years of Psamtik I, who liberated Egypt from Assyria, and the reigns of the famous Pharaoh Necho and his son Psamtik II. It is an interesting proof of the tyrant's close connection with Egypt that the nephew who succeeded him bore the name Psammetichus.

Megara, of whose adventurous spirit and maritime power we have already had remarkable evidence in the foundation of Byzantium and Selinus, seems to have suffered as much as any Greek city from a despotic aristocracy. At last, possibly with the help of the Corinthian Cypselus, a certain Theagenes established himself as tyrant (*c.* 630) by adopting the usual method of obtaining permission to form a bodyguard and then exterminating political rivals. After a reign of about twenty years his power was overthrown, and Megara became for a long time the arena of fierce conflicts between the popular and aristocratic parties, of which what little is known reminds one by its intensely bitter personal feeling of the old Florentine feuds rather than of political and social upheavals such as the Secession of the Plebs. Again and again the nobles were expelled and the popular party sated their lust for vengeance by confiscating property, cancelling the debts of the poor, and demanding even repayment of the interest; again and again the nobles returned, and finally established themselves firmly in power. It is of these troubled times that the poet Theognis sings. I shall speak of his poems later.

Sicyon, whose small territory lay not far to the west of Corinth and was under Dorian oligarchs in early times, seems to have been ruled by tyrants of Ionian blood from the days of the second Messenian war. Of these only Cleisthenes is known to history, and that mainly on account of his connection with Athens; for his daughter Agarista, of whose wooing and wedding Herodotus (vi. 126 *ff.*) gives us such a graphic and humorous account, was the wife of Megacles, and mother of the Athenian reformer Cleisthenes. The Sicyonian tyrant, it is said, in his hatred of all things Dorian and Argive, forbade at Sicyon the recitation of Homer, who glorifies Argos and the Argives, and changed the names of the three Doric tribes in Sicyon into names meaning swine, asses, and pigs.

## The Sages

In the later period of the age which we are considering is found the first distinct evidence of that philosophical thought, that earnest search after truth, which is one of the noblest characteristics of Greek civilization. Before the days of Socrates Greek thought was directed more towards the solution of physical than metaphysical problems. The so-called Ionic philosophers propounded theories of wonderful boldness and penetration on the origin and constitution of the material universe, which formed as it were stepping-stones to doctrines on the nature of the soul and of deity. But even before these Ionic philosophers and others, whom I shall consider at the end of the age of Peisistratus, we find signs of deep reflection on ethical questions, on questions of right and wrong, on the moral sense as a guide to action, on virtue and vice, justice and injustice.

Many such reflections, revealing the deep, fundamental beliefs of the human heart, we find in Homer – though not stated didactically – and, as we have seen, the cry for justice is loud in Hesiod. Of course these beliefs exist in every age; but it is not till towards the end of the seventh century that we find them expressed by Greek thinkers and men of action, and the form of expression is either the sententious and passionate verse of the so-called gnomic poets (among whom Solon and Theognis and the older Simonides are reckoned), or moralizing stories in prose, such as the Fables of Aesop, or else short, pithy, wise sayings, such as those which are attributed to the Seven Sages.

Some of these Seven, all of whom flourished in the period 600–550, and whom the next age reverenced for their wisdom, were men pre-eminent as rulers or lawgivers, and one was renowned as the first and perhaps the greatest of the Ionic philosophers. Most of them doubtless wrote, and some of their writings were probably well known to the ancients, but hardly anything remains except fragments of Solon's verse, of which I shall speak later.

According to Plato the Seven Sages were Thales of Miletus, Solon of Athens, Pittacus of Mytilene, Bias of Priene, Cleobulus of Lindus (Rhodes), Myson of Chenae, and Chilon of Sparta. Others, strangely enough, insert Periander of Corinth in the place of Myson. Opinions seem to have differed much as to the authentic list. Not only do the names of the last three vary considerably, but we have lists of ten, and even of seventeen. In later times each of the Sages was credited with one distinctive maxim, and some of these maxims, such as 'Know thyself,' 'Nothing too much,' 'Know thy opportunity,' were inscribed on Apollo's temple at Delphi. Cleobulus and his daughter seem to have made a reputation by their riddles, and the poet Simonides speaks of this Sage as a 'foolish mortal.' Periander, as we have seen, may have suffered much from calumny, but if his wisdom, as is likely, was such as is found in Machiavelli's *Principe*, we cannot wonder that Plato omits him.

## Athens, 776–560

In a former chapter we obtained glimpses of Athens in the Dark Age, and saw that she too, like most of the Greek cities, was at that time under the rule of aristocracies. This continued during the seventh century. The government was carried on by archons, whose term of office had been (*c.* 750) reduced to ten years. Then, in 683, three annual archons were instituted. From this time onward a list seems to have been kept of the archons, the chief of whom gave his name to the year, and was therefore called the *archōn eponymos*. As deliberative and legislative council, like the Homeric *boulē*, the archons had the Areopagus, consisting of past archons and fifty-one special judges (*ephetai*) and other nobles (Eupatridae).

The Areopagus, one of the most ancient institutions of Athens, was originally a court of justice for cases of murder and homicide, evidently established, like the English 'blood-wite,' in order to regulate private vengeance. According to the legend adopted by the Greek dramatists, it was before this divinely instituted court, and by the votes of the gods themselves, that Orestes was acquitted when, chased by the Furies for the murder of his mother, he sought sanctuary at Athene's shrine in Athens. As Aeschylus intimates, the court was closely connected with the worship of the Furies as avengers of blood, and it is likely that the name Areopagus, which was conferred to distinguish this court from Solon's *boulē*, and was in later ages believed to mean 'The Hill of Mars' (*Areios pagos*), really means 'The Hill of the Arai' (Avengers) – as the Semnai, or 'Awful Goddesses,' are called by Aeschylus himself. The court was gradually empowered to interfere in matters of religion and morals, and then in political affairs; but after serving as the supreme council of the aristocracy it lost much of its power under the reforms of Solon and Cleisthenes, and finally (in the age of Demosthenes) was allowed to retain no authority except in trivial questions of ritual, gymnastics, public parks, and the like.

The Athenian Ecclesia, the great popular assembly lineally descended from the Homeric Agora, probably began to gain more political influence after the institution of annual archons and of the tribal guilds. There are many evidences of a considerable advance towards democracy about the opening of the seventh century. On account of the great increase of trade and the invention of money, wealth began to abound and to determine social and political status. As in the later Servian constitution at Rome, the people (formerly, as we have seen, divided into nobles, land-workers, and public workers) were now, or perhaps in Solon's time, for political purposes classed according to income. Five hundred measures of corn and oil (or the equivalent) put a man in the highest class, to which the chief magistracies were confined; three hundred gave him the title of knight, and two hundred that of *zeugitēs*, which meant that he belonged to the rank of the well-to-do peasant, the owner of a span of oxen. Another sign of advance was the annual election (about 650) of six legislators (*thesmothetai*), who, like the Roman *decemviri*, or perhaps more like the Roman tribunes of the people, represented a growing determination to acquire equal rights before the law. These six *thesmothetai*, whose office was to examine laws and supervise justice, were associated with the three supreme magistrates, so that henceforth we hear of nine archons.

While matters were in this state an event took place which, perhaps because it is so graphically described by Thucydides, as well as by Herodotus and by Plutarch, seems to stand out as the first distinct picture in the history of Athens.

Among the Athenian noble families (Eupatridae) one of the most distinguished was that of the Alcmaeonidae, a branch of the Neleid family, which claimed descent from the kings of Pylos. Now in the year 632, when the Alcmaeonid Megacles was archon, an attempt was made by an Athenian noble, Cylon by name, who had distinguished himself as winner of the foot-race at Olympia, to establish himself as tyrant at Athens. He had married the daughter of Theagenes of Megara, and, incited by this tyrant's success, and by an oracle which he misinterpreted, with a band of young Athenians and Megarian soldiery he seized the Acropolis, trusting in popular discontent. He was not supported, and, after being blockaded for some time, he is said by Thucydides (not, however, by Herodotus) to have made his escape. His comrades were forced to capitulate. They sought sanctuary at the 'altar of the Acropolis' – evidently that of Athene Polias. 'And those of the Athenians who had been commissioned to keep guard, when they saw them dying of famine in the temple raised them up, promising to do them no harm; but they led them away and killed them. Others were cut down as they tried to seat themselves in front of the altars of the Awful Goddesses.'

Plutarch adds a graphic touch – one that recalls other examples of the virtue of divine protection being transmitted by contact. He says that the besieged, when under promise of quarter they left Athene's temple, *fastened themselves with a rope* to the statue of the goddess and were making their way down from the Acropolis, when the rope broke,[1] and they fled to the sanctuary of the Furies, which happened to be near, but were all cut down.

Cylon's unsuccessful raid is historically of importance, for the belief that a curse had been incurred by Megacles and by the Alcmaeonidae in this double act of sacrilege influenced the course of events on more than one occasion. The taint, as Grote says, 'was supposed to be transmitted to the descendants of Megacles, and we shall find the wound reopened not only in the second and third generation, but also two centuries after the original event.' (See Index and Hdt. v. 71, Thuc. i. 126.) For a long time public feeling seems to have been deeply affected by exasperation mingled with superstitious dread. At length – perhaps about 625, or perhaps later (for Solon is said by some to have suggested it) – the Alcmaeonidae were tried before a special court of 300 nobles and were banished, those who had already died being disinterred and cast forth as an 'accursed thing' beyond the borders of Attica. But religious excitement and despondent gloom still dominated. Pestilence appeared, and neither sacrifice nor purification was of any avail. The Delphic oracle was consulted, and bade the Athenians seek some healer from a distant land.

It will be remembered that in Hesiod, as well as elsewhere, there are many evidences of the persistence of the superstitious dread of the supernatural and of the belief in the efficacy of propitiatory rites and charms which were such striking characteristics of the ancient Greek religion, but which seem to have crept away for a time into obscure hiding-places at the advent of the Olympian gods. In a later age we shall find these superstitions revived in the Mysteries and the Orphic religion, and it is interesting to notice that also at the period which we are now considering such vague terrors and beliefs prevailed very generally. We read of many magicians and healers, such as the Hyperborean Abaris, and Aristeas of Metapontion, and Thaletas the Cretan, who was summoned to Sparta to stay a pestilence, and in connection with this ineradicable tendency towards *deisidaimonia* may

---

[1] This, according to Plutarch, was urged by the Alcmaeonidae as a defence against the charge of sacrilege. For other cases of a belief in the efficacy of attachment see Hdt. i. 26 (where Ephesus, when besieged, is connected by a cord with the temple of Artemis outside the walls), and Thuc. iii. 104 (where Rheneia is connected with Delos by a chain).

be named the philosopher Pythagoras and the Sicilian Empedocles, both of whom were regarded as more than human.

The healer whom the Athenians sent for (perhaps about 625, perhaps considerably later) was the Cretan Epimenides, about whom wondrous tales are told. He is said to have fallen asleep in a cave and to have slept (like Rip Van Winkle) for more than half a century, and to have lived 150 or even 300 years. By his contemporaries, as also by Plato and Cicero, he was regarded as divinely inspired, and even Aristotle himself speaks of him as something not quite canny. Besides being a prophet and a healer, he was a prolific poet, and possibly one very celebrated line of his, on the subject of the Cretans, has been preserved by St. Paul. As for his visit to Athens, I will quote what is said by Grote, who does not dismiss this very possible case of faith-healing, which is of great interest both psychologically and historically, with the curt contempt shown by some other writers. 'Epimenides is said to have turned out some white and black sheep on the Areopagus, directing attendants to follow and watch them, and to erect new altars to the appropriate local deities on the spots where the animals lay down. He founded new chapels and established various lustral ceremonies; and more especially he regulated the worship paid by the women in such a manner as to calm the violent impulses which had before agitated them. . . . The general fact of his visit and the salutary effects produced in removing the religious despondency which oppressed the Athenians are well attested.'

The pestilence very probably departed in the wake of the religious despondency, but in this disturbed state of public feeling doubtless political animosities were intensified and lawlessness grew rampant.

As a drastic remedy the Athenians commissioned Dracon, the archon of the year 621, to reform the laws and publish a written code. Dracon's laws were 'written in blood,' as an orator of later days expressed it. His reforms seem to have consisted largely in terrorism. He increased penalties to such an extent that petty theft was punishable by death,[1] and debt exposed a man to the danger of slavery. Such relapse to barbarism may have had an

---

[1] See Hor. *Sat.* I, iii. 115 *ff.*, where the allusion is evidently to Dracon. Aristotle intimates that even idleness was thus punishable. An Egyptian law of King Amasis punished with death a man who would not work to support his family. Dracon's laws have perhaps been misrepresented. He may have merely codified old and severe laws, some already lapsed. He seems to have instituted some carefully framed legal forms, such as trials for various cases of homicide. Even inanimate objects charged with homicide, if condemned, were solemnly cast forth beyond the frontier. Also the fifty-one *ephetai* (special judges) may have been his creation.

effect for a time, but could not permanently satisfy either rich or poor. The fact that the laws were now fixed in writing was an immense advantage, but their publication doubtless made the poorer classes realize all the more keenly the intolerable state of bondage and misery into which they had been brought by debt and mortgage and the insolent exactions of the rich, by which many had been reduced to actual slavery or to the necessity of selling their own children as slaves to pitiless creditors.

At this crisis a great and wise man arose who refounded the state on the basis of true democracy, as some two and a half centuries later the celebrated Rogations of Licinius set upon its true basis the Roman republic.

I do not intend to give any detailed account of Solon's constitution. It is a subject that requires full and special treatment, and such it has received from writers who regard the political history of Greece as of great importance. To me it seems that we have little to learn from Greece in politics – as little, perhaps, as from her perpetual internal feuds. I shall, therefore, while giving a sketch of Solon's personality, touch very briefly on his reforms.

Solon was born about 638, some seventeen years before the archonship of Dracon. He claimed descent from Codrus, and from Poseidon through the Pylian Nestor, and his mother was a cousin of Peisistratus. But his patrimony had been wasted, and he took to trade and visited many distant lands, where he gained not only riches but a knowledge of the world and of human character and of letters which placed him on a level probably much higher than that of most Athenians of his day. It was natural that under such circumstances he should express his opinions and feelings in a written form; and that this form should be verse was almost inevitable, for (as we shall see in a subsequent section) there was as yet no prose literature. His high birth and the great reputation that his knowledge brought him, and perhaps also his newly acquired wealth, led to his election, in 594, as archon with unlimited legislative powers, in order that he should discover some *modus vivendi* between the people and the rapacious aristocracy. Doubtless his life had brought him much in contact with the working classes, and at the same time he was closely connected with the nobility, so that great hopes were placed in his mediation.

His first move must have startled both parties. On entering office he should have made the usual public declaration that he would 'preserve undiminished all private property.' Instead of this, he published an ordinance named the *Seisachtheia* (the 'Shaking off of Burdens'), which cancelled all obligations that pledged the liberty of the debtor and set free

167

all debtor-slaves. Then he repealed all Dracon's laws except those that dealt with homicide, and having thus cleared the ground, and having deprived the oligarchic Areopagus of some important functions, he laid the foundation of the future Athenian democracy by extending the franchise to the Thetes (lit. hirelings), the lowest of the four classes, by instituting the Heliaea, or popular courts of justice, in which every citizen in turn could take his place among the dicasts (judges or jurymen), and by introducing election by lot.[1] Moreover, he formed a new council (*boulē*) of 400 members chosen from the whole people except the Thetes, and transferred to this council from the Areopagus the work of preparing measures to be submitted to the Ecclesia. In addition to these constitutional reforms he limited private land-owning and forbade exportation of Attic products, except oil. Solon's laws were written, or inscribed, on tablets or pillars (*axones, kyrbeis*), which revolved on a pivot, and were first kept in the Acropolis, but later, by the advice of Ephialtes, were placed in the Agora.

Whether it was before, during, or even long after his archonship is quite uncertain, but the conquest of Salamis by Athens is said to have been due to Solon's influence. Eleusis had been annexed long before, but Salamis, lying close in front of the Peiraeus, was still in the possession of Megara, and so often had the Athenians vainly tried to conquer it that, it is said, they forbade under penalty of death any proposal to renew the attempt. Pretending to be in a divinely inspired frenzy, Solon recited in public some verses in which he passionately denounced the cowardice of 'Salamis-abandoners,' and called on the Athenians to 'cast aside their disgrace' and once more to 'fight for the lovely island.' The result of this appeal was another attack on Salamis, which ended, perhaps by the arbitrage of Sparta, in the island being separated permanently from Megara and divided among Athenian cleruchs (lot-holders). It seems possible that Peisistratus acted as general in this war, and succeeded in occupying Nisaea, the port of Megara – a military success that perhaps made effective the Athenians' claim that Salamis had originally belonged to them.[2]

---

[1] Lot was used for selecting the nine archons out of forty candidates proposed by the tribes. The Heliaea soon deprived the archons of all judicial power and became the final court of justice.

[2] Both sides appealed to the mode of burial in the ancient tombs of Salamis. The Athenians cited the (perhaps interpolated) line in the Homeric 'Catalogue of Ships' in which Ajax, who brought twelve ships from Salamis, is said to have 'drawn them up where the Athenian hosts were encamped.'

Herodotus tells us that the Athenians swore to obey Solon's laws for ten (Plutarch says a hundred) years, and that during these ten years he visited Egypt and Cyprus[1] and other distant lands. If this took place soon after his archonship he must have returned to Athens about 582, and as he did not die till about 558 there is an interval of over twenty years which we must suppose him to have passed at Athens, possibly making voyages from time to time across the Aegean. But even if his visit to Egypt and Cyprus took place much later (Herodotus says he was in Egypt in the reign of Amasis, who came to the throne in 570), and if he did not return to Athens until about 562, there is no reason why between 560 and his death in 558 he may not have visited King Croesus, as Herodotus asserts – although this was denied even in Plutarch's day as chronologically impossible, and is denied by some modern writers. The well-known story of this visit, so beautifully narrated by Herodotus, will be given later.

It was probably during the absence of Solon (c. 568) that the unsuccessful attack on Aegina was made by the Athenians which, according to Herodotus (v. 87), had such a dramatic ending and caused a revolution in the dress fashions of Athenian women, on account of their having stabbed to death with their long stiletto dress-pins the sole survivor of the ill-fated expedition (see Note B on Dress). This attack was repelled with Argive help; and for some time to come we shall find Athens and Argos on anything but friendly terms.

Fierce dissensions had again broken out in Athens – so fierce that for two years no archons were elected. The party of the Plain, composed of rich landowners, was headed by Lycurgus; that of the Coast, formed mainly of the industrial and working classes, was led by that Megacles who had married Agarista of Sicyon – a grandson of the Megacles whose sacrilege in the matter of Cylon had caused a temporary banishment of the Alcmaeonid family. At last, taking advantage of these dissensions, a friend and relative of Solon, a man who had distinguished himself in the war against Megara and had won great favour among the extreme democrats and other discontents, created a third party, that of the Hills – so called because it comprised many of the peasants of the Attic highlands. This man was Peisistratus, the rise and fall of whose tyranny will be the subject of the next chapter.

Solon is said to have detected and denounced, but in vain, the ambitious

---

[1] In Cyprus he is said to have persuaded a prince to found the city Soli.

projects of Peisistratus. He died about two years after the establishment of the tyranny. His ashes, it is said, were by his orders strewn over the soil of Salamis.

## SECTION A: EGYPT AND CYRENE (*c.* 670–570)

In Section C, Chapter 2, I sketched the history of Egypt, as far as it touches that of Greece, down to its conquest (*c.* 674) by the Assyrian monarch Assarhaddon. Some five years later this great king of Nineveh and Babylon abdicated (weary of power, like Charles V), and was succeeded by the unwarlike and literary Assurbanipal, known to the Greeks as Sardanapalos.

Now of the twelve vassal-kings who still governed Egypt under the suzerainty of Assyria, one named Psamtik (Psammetichus), of Libyan descent, who reigned at Saïs, in the Delta, is said by Herodotus to have been dethroned by his fellow-rulers and to have fled to the marshes. Having sent to inquire of the famous Egyptian oracle of Leto, he was told that 'vengeance would come from the sea, when bronzen men should appear.' Not long afterwards some bronze-clad Carian and Ionian warriors were driven by storms to the Egyptian shore (some scholars believe they were purposely sent by the king of Lydia), and by their help Psamtik brought the whole land under his sway, founding thus the dynasty of the four Saïtic kings, and defeated Assurbanipal (*c.* 664) and finally drove the Assyrians out of Egypt. He naturally showed great favour to the Ionians and other Greeks, who now for the first time were allowed to settle freely in Egypt. About 660 the Milesians founded the trade-settlement Naucratis, the ruins of which have lately been discovered on the west bank of the Canopus Nile, not far from Saïs.[1] Greek mercenaries formed the right wing of the army, and also the garrison in the new and least remote Egyptian stronghold, Defenneh (called by the Greeks 'Daphnae,' *i.e.* Laurels), which Psamtik had built as a defence against his eastern foes. These favours are said to have so incensed the native Egyptian soldiery, who had to garrison the distant Aethiopian and Libyan frontiers, that they revolted, and 240,000 of them marched south and settled in Aethiopia (perhaps Abyssinia), four

---

[1] No large temples but numerous small ones have been found – evidently the 'chapels' of the various Hellenic settlers. Later a great fortified brick enclosure, the Helleneion, with large stone storehouses, was built, probably by leave of King Amasis.

months' journey beyond Syene (Assouan) and two beyond Meroë (Khartum).

Psamtik reigned for forty-seven years, and extended his dominions to the boundaries of Syria, but there he was stopped by the Scythians, who at this period swept over the east of Asia Minor and were only induced by a large bribe not to attack Egypt itself. Of Necho, his successor, we have already heard. He also favoured the Greeks, and they helped him to build his triremes and merchant fleets. In his ships Phoenicians circumnavigated Africa. He cut a canal from the Nile to the Red Sea, and prolonged the Suez Canal, begun in the fourteenth century B.C. by King Seti and finished by de Lesseps in the nineteenth century A.D. He defeated and slew King Josiah at Megiddo, and advanced as far as the Euphrates, but was defeated at Carchemish (601) by Nebucadnezar, the young king of the new Babylonian Empire – for Nineveh and the Assyrian Empire had fallen in the year 606.

His son, Psammis (Psamtik II), made an expedition against the Aethiopians, or possibly the Deserters[1] who had settled in Aethiopia. In his army were many Greek mercenaries, and one can yet see at Abu Simbel, on the Upper Nile, some forty miles before reaching Wady Halfa, Greek names and inscriptions on the legs of a colossus (Fig. 44) cut by some of these soldiers.

Psamtik II was succeeded by his son Apries (the Hophra of the Bible), who gave refuge to a 'remnant' of Jews after Judah had been carried away to Babylon by Nebucadnezar in 587. Among these Jews was Jeremiah, who had been set free by Nebucadnezar and had in vain tried to dissuade his countrymen from leaving their native land, but had accompanied them to Tahpanhes (Defenneh, or Daphnae), where they were allowed to settle, pro-tected by the Greek garrison of the frontier fortress.[2] It will be remembered how Jeremiah (xliii. 10) buried great stones in clay at the entry of 'Pharaoh's house' at Daphnae and prophesied that Nebucadnezar would come and set up his throne and his royal pavilion above these stones. Nebucadnezar did come (c. 572), as both Jeremiah and Ezekiel had prophesied, and overran Egypt right up to Syene (Assouan); and at Daphnae archaeologists found not only Greek pottery in abundance, but the relics of the burnt palace of Hophra, and also a square pavement which may possibly be the very stones

---

[1] Called also 'Left-wing men' ('Asmachs' = Abyssinians?) because deprived of the place of honour on the right wing; whence their discontent and rebellion.

[2] 2 Kings xxv. 26; Jer. xl.–xliii. (perhaps partly by the 'Deutero-Jeremiah').

'hid in the clay' by Jeremiah, above which the king of Babylon set up his throne and pavilion. Nebucadnezar and his Babylonians did not remain long, and an unsuccessful expedition by the Egyptian native army against Cyrene caused disturbances amidst which Hophra (Apries), although supported by his Greek troops, was dethroned by Aahmes, known in Greek history as Amasis, in whose reign, as we shall see later, there was much friendly intercourse between Egypt and Hellas; for although Greek mercenaries had fought against him he was wise enough to forget it.

The unsuccessful expedition of the Egyptian army against Cyrene was possibly made against the wishes of Apries, and none of his Greek soldiers took part in it – as was but natural, for Cyrene (some 200 miles to the west of Egypt) was a Greek colony. It was founded (c. 630) by aborigines of the small volcanic island Thera, who had quarrelled with Dorian settlers. After several failures[1] a site was found in the hills about eight miles from the coast and about 1800 feet above the sea, near to a fine spring and in a part of Libya where, according to Herodotus, there were three different climates, allowing harvest during eight months of the year, and such abundant rains that the natives described the place as one in which 'the sky leaks.' Here Aristoteles of Thera founded Cyrene and adopted the native name Battus ('King'), and for eight generations the Battiadae held kingly power. About 560 Cyrene founded Barca, which soon rivalled its mother-city. In its earlier days (c. 580) Cyrene gained literary fame from its poet Eugammon, who, like other Cyclic poets, tried to finish the stories of the *Iliad* and *Odyssey*. He wrote the *Telegoneia*, the story of the son of Odysseus and Circe, and (as Virgil did for the Romans) connected the legend of Troy with the history of his countrymen. At a later period Cyrene was the home of several renowned philosophers and literary men, and Cyrenaica, with its five prosperous cities, became a very rich province of the Ptolemies, and afterwards of Rome. The wealth of Cyrene was largely due to the now extinct plant *silphion*, which was used for food and also for physic (see Coin Plate VI, 6, page 498).

SECTION B: LYDIA AND EASTERN KINGS (776–560)

Except Cyrene there was no point of antagonism between Hellas and Egypt, and the conflict between the Hellenic and Semitic races in Sicily was

---

[1] Herodotus (iv. 145 *ff.*) gives a very long story of these Therans and of misinterpreted oracles, etc. See also iv. 199.

yet to come, but in Asia Minor the Greek colonies had a vast hinterland of Oriental or semi-Oriental nations – the wild Pisidian tribes, the Lycians, Carians, Mysians, Phrygians, Lydians – some of them of Indo-Iranian blood largely intermixed with that of the old Cappadocian and Hittite aborigines. And behind all these again loomed during the earlier ages the mighty empires of old Babylonia, of Assyria, and of the Babylon of Nebucadnezar, soon to be replaced by the still more dangerous empire of the Medes and Persians.

Perhaps it is not too much to say that the destiny of modern Europe was decided by the battles of Salamis and Himera – which took place, if we may believe tradition, on the self-same day. Anyhow, it was decided by the result of the conflict of Hellas with the non-Hellenic world, especially with Persia and Carthage. It is therefore advisable, without distracting our attention too much, to keep the chief of these nations in view.

Down to the conquest of Lydia by Cyrus (546) the great empires of the far East had not come into direct contact with the Hellenic world, except that Greeks in Cyprus had become subjects of the Assyrian kings Sargon and Assarhaddon, and Greek mercenaries had fought against Nebucadnezar in Egypt. In Ionia and Greece itself much had doubtless been heard of the vast cities and armies of Assyria and Babylonia, and something of the learning of the East, such as the Chaldean astronomy and their system of weights, had been introduced; but during the age that we are considering (776–560) Phrygia and Lydia formed a buffer between Asiatic Hellas and the far East, and what at present concerns us is the history of these nearer Oriental countries and their relation to Ionia.

In Phrygia, which enclosed Lydia on the east, the dominant race (as we saw in Chapter 1) was of Northern (Indo-Iranian) stock, and therefore was akin to the Greek. Phrygians evidently settled also in Lydia and are the 'Maeonians' mentioned by Homer (who knows nothing of 'Lydians'). They founded what some writers have even called a 'Heracleid' (Greek) dynasty of Lydian kings, who, as also the Phrygian kings (named alternately Gordias and Midas), lived on friendly terms with the Ionian and Aeolian Greeks. The wealth and civilization of both nations were evidently considerable. They seem to have introduced the alphabet at an early age, and their music and decorative art had influence on the Greeks. One King Midas (perhaps the one to whom the fable gives donkey's ears) made the gift of his royal throne to the temple at Delphi – the first offering, says Herodotus, made by a 'barbarian.'

173

But it is of Lydia that we hear most. Its capital, Sardis, was built on a precipitous spur of Mount Tmolus, whence flowed into the Hermus the gold-bearing stream Pactolus – one of the sources of Lydian wealth. The 'Heracleid' kings seem to have brought the country to a high state of prosperity. Herodotus even relates that these early Lydians colonized Umbria, in Italy, and founded the Tyrrhenian (Etruscan) nation; and he tells us that they invented 'all the games that are common to them and the Greeks,' and also the use of gold-and-silver (*elektron*) coinage.

The last of the 'Heracleid' kings was Candaules.[1] He was slain (*c.* 716) by Gyges, who established the dynasty of the native Lydian Mermnadae, to which Croesus belonged. Gyges extended the Lydian power over Mysia and endeavoured to conquer the Greek seaboard of the Aegean, but about 680 Lydia itself was attacked from the north and east by the innumerable hordes of a wild northern people called the Cimmerians.

The Cimmerians (doubtless the originals of Homer's fabulous Cimmerians on the further shore of the river Ocean) were probably driven south from their country (Cimmeria, *i.e.* the Crimea) by the pressure of other northern tribes. Whether they came by way of the Danube delta or the Caucasus is unknown, but they captured the Greek city Sinope and made it their chief camp, whence they ravaged almost the whole of Asia Minor, and even attacked the great Assyrian king, Assarhaddon. At first Gyges was successful, and he sent many Cimmerian captives in chains to Nineveh – the first act of Lydian homage to Assyria, if such it was, that we hear of. But two years later the Cimmerians again poured down from the north, slew Gyges, plundered Sardis, and pressed southwards, where they destroyed Magnesia and burnt the great temple of Artemis that stood outside the city walls of Ephesus. Of these hordes of ravaging northern barbarians the Ephesian poet Callinus speaks (as we shall see in Section D), and a vivid picture of them is given on a sarcophagus of Clazomenae (Fig. 45).

Between Gyges and Croesus three kings reigned, Ardys (678–629), Sadyattes (629–617), and Alyattes (617–560). During this period we hear of various invasions of West Asia Minor by Cimmerians, while in the far East the Scythians, another wild northern people, totally defeated the king

---

[1] An Indo-European name meaning 'dog-throttler,' corresponding to *kynankēs*, an epithet given by Hipponax to the god Hermes: 'O dog-throttler Hermes, by the Maeonians called Candaules.' War-dogs were used by the Cimmerians and other barbarians. For the dramatic story of Candaules and Gyges see Hdt. i. 7. Coinage was probably first introduced by Gyges. See Note C.

Fig. 44  Colossi of Abu Simbel

Fig. 45  Cimmerians on the sarcophagus of Clazomenae

of Media, Cyaxares, and for twenty-eight years (640–612) were dominant even as far south as the Philistine city of Ascalon, which they sacked. Indeed, it was only by bribes that Psamtik I saved Egypt from them.

In spite of these recurring Cimmerian invasions Ardys and Sadyattes seem to have attacked Ionia. Priene and perhaps other cities were taken, and Miletus was much harassed by them. Alyattes finally expelled the Cimmerians. He then turned his arms against the Greeks, wishing doubtless to acquire a seaboard for Lydia. He took and utterly destroyed (c. 590) new Smyrna,[1] which now almost disappears from the history of ancient Greece, but after warring for eleven years against Miletus (now under the tyranny of Thrasybulus, Periander's friend) he made peace, probably because Lydia was assailed by a new foe, namely, the Medes, who under Cyaxares (the conqueror of Babylon) and his son Astyages were extending the new Median empire towards the Aegean. In the sixth year this war between Lydia and the Medes was ended by a strange occurrence. In the midst of a battle the sun was darkened, and the combatants were so alarmed that they ceased fighting and concluded a peace. This solar eclipse, the date of which was May 28, 585, is of interest not only because it gives us (like the eclipse of 648 recorded by Archilochus) an exact date, but because it was foretold, more or less accurately, by the philosopher Thales. This was perhaps the first eclipse predicted by a European. Thales gained his knowledge of the lunar cycle (of about seventeen years) and the astronomical data for calculating eclipses from the Egyptians, who themselves, it is likely, were indebted to the Chaldeans of Babylon.[2] But whatever may have been the source of his knowledge, the prediction of Thales was a momentous event, for it was, as far as we know, the very first attempt made in Europe to lay the foundation of inductive science. It marks, as Grote says, the beginning in the Hellenic world of scientific prediction as distinguished from the prophecies of soothsayers, oracles, and omens.

To seal the peace with Media King Alyattes gave his daughter in marriage to Astyages, and for the next forty years Lydia enjoyed, under Alyattes and his son Croesus, brilliant prosperity, until Cyrus the Persian overthrew the Median Astyages, and twelve years later (546) attacked and overthrew the Lydian Croesus also, as we shall see in the next chapter.

---

[1] See p. 94. But Pindar afterwards mentions Smyrna as a 'bright city.'

[2] Ptolemy, the great geographer and astronomer, although he lived in Egypt, cites the Chaldean calculations for eclipses as the earliest (i.e. from 721). Egyptian astronomical knowledge, however, dates at least from the time of the Pyramids (c. 3000).

## EASTERN KINGS OF PERIOD 776–538

| EGYPT | ASSYRIA | MEDIA | LYDIA |
|---|---|---|---|
| XXVth Dynasty (Aethiopian kings). | Tiglath-pileser II, 745–727. | | Candaules. |
| Tirhaka (in Bible). | Shalmanezer IV, 727–722. | | Gyges, 716–678. |
| | Sargon, 722–705. | | Ardys, 678–629. |
| | Sennacherib, 705–682. | Deioces founds Media, c. 700. | |
| Conquered by Assarhaddon, 672. | Assarhaddon, 682–669. | | |
| Psamtik I, 664–617. | Assurbanipal (Sardanapalos), 669–626. | Phraortes, c. 650–625. | Sadyattes, 629–617. |
| Necho, 617–601 | [Three unimportant kings.] | Cyaxares, c. 625–595. | Alyattes, 617–560. |
| | 606. Nineveh destroyed by Cyaxares of Media and Nabopolassar of Babylonia. | | |
| | **NEW BABYLONIA** | | |
| Psamtik II, 601–595 | Nebucadnezar, 604–562. | Astyages, 595–559. | Croesus, 560–546. |
| Apries (Hophra), 595–570. | Evil-Merodach, 562–560. | ¹Cyaxares II (?) 559–. Probably dethroned by Cyrus (c. 549). | 546 (549?) Croesus dethroned by Cyrus. |
| Amasis, 570–526. | [Two others.] | | |
| | Nabonid (Labynetus²), to 538. | | |

538. Cyrus takes Babylon and founds the PERSIAN EMPIRE.

¹ Unknown to Herodotus, but given by Xenophon. Probably the 'Darius the Median' of Daniel v. 31.

² Labynetus is probably a title. Herodotus calls both Nebucadnezar and Nabonid by this name. He is the Belshazzar of Daniel, or perhaps his father.

177

SECTION C: THE GAMES

It is a trite remark that Greece was never a nation; and it is true that Hellas, and even the Hellenic homeland, had no political coherence. Very rarely, as Thucydides says, did the Greek states take any combined action, and even against the Persians the combination was by no means complete. Greek patriotism was not based on the idea of political union, far less on that of any central imperial power. All imperialism, all hegemony of Greek over Greek, was as odious as tyranny to the deeper instincts of the race, and although such temporary structures as the Athenian Empire and the Spartan and Theban supremacies arose from time to time, they were maintained by forces foreign to true Hellenic genius. But though not united politically, often torn asunder by internecine feuds, the Hellenic world was united in heart by sentiments perhaps nobler than those of ordinary patriotism – by the proud consciousness of kinship not only in blood but in the deepest sympathies of human nature, such as find expression in religion and art and literature.

This fact is finely stated in the message sent by the Athenians to Sparta before the capture of Athens by Mardonius the Persian: 'Not all the gold that the earth contains would bribe us to take part with the Medes and help them to enslave our countrymen. . . . There is our common brotherhood, our common language, the altars and the sacrifices of which we all partake, and the common character which we bear. Did the Athenians betray all this, of a truth it would not be well.'

This consciousness, which more and more counteracted the old antipathies between Doric, Ionian, and other sections of the race, and inspired all Hellas with a feeling of boundless superiority over the nations that surrounded it on all sides – though some of these 'barbarians' could boast of a civilization far more ancient and a sense of truth and honour[1] far keener than that of the Greeks – was fostered by the great religious festivals held by the mother-cities, to which the colonies of the Hellenic world sent solemn embassies (*theōriai*) vying with each other in the magnificence of their offerings.

Also for the Greeks of the colonies there were meeting-places where great festivals were held, such as the Lacinian promontory in South Italy,

---

[1] See later remarks on the Persian character. The traitor was never far to seek among the Greeks, but was scarcely known among the Persians.

*Fig. 46  Site of Olympia and Vale of the Alpheios*

*Fig. 47  Heraion, Olympia*

179

and the island of Delos. This island, lying in the midst of the Cyclades, which offer easy transit between Greece and Ionia, was in early times an important entrepôt. It was also the religious centre of the Ionian world, famed as the birthplace of Artemis and Apollo and for the most ancient oracle of the god.[1] Every fifth year the birth of the twin deities was celebrated with magnificence, amidst a great concourse, vividly described in the ancient *Hymn to Apollo*: 'Hither gather the long-robed Ionians with their children and chaste wives. They wrestle, they dance, they sing in memory of the god. He who saw them would say they were immortal and ageless, so much grace and charm would he find in viewing the men, the fair-girdled women, the swift ships, and riches of every kind.' (See also Thuc. iii. 104.) These festivals seem to have been accompanied by contests in music and poetry. The temple, with its priceless treasure of offerings, was not touched by the Persians, who plundered most of the other islands, but the Delian festivals seem to have ceased during the Persian supremacy. They were revived with great ostentation by the Athenians of the Empire, who used to send splendid *theōriai* in the sacred Delian galley (*Salaminia*); but this revival was of short duration, for Delos had lost its special sanctity in rivalry with Delphi, and the centre of religious life for the Ionians had been long since transferred to the great temple of Artemis at Ephesus, as that of their political life was transferred to the pan-Ionian assembly on Mount Mycale.

By far the most famous, if not the most ancient, pan-Hellenic assembly was that held at Olympia, where Heracles is said to have consecrated (*c.* 1200) a sanctuary to Zeus, and to have founded games after his victory over Augeas, king of Elis. Others even attribute the foundation to Pelops (*c.* 1280). Tradition asserts that the games, which had fallen into disuse, were reinstituted by Lycurgus of Sparta and Iphitus, king of Elis;[2] to prove which was shown at Olympia the discus of Iphitus inscribed with the name of Lycurgus. Perhaps it was on this occasion that the Eleans, supported by Sparta, usurped the presidency at the games, held till then by the people of

---

[1] Homer speaks only of Apollo's altar in Delos. Excavation has revealed a sanctuary with small temples of Artemis, Apollo, Leto, and Aphrodite – perhaps built on the site of the great ancient temple. Statues, possibly of Artemis, have been discovered (see Fig. 50). The original Delian statue of Apollo was said to have been brought thither by Theseus from Crete.

[2] Traditional date 884. Others give 776, *i.e.* the year of the victory of Coroebus, from which the Olympiads are dated.

Pisa, in whose territory Olympia lay, and to whom, as we have already seen, King Pheidon of Argos (*c.* 680) for a time restored their rights. During the seventh century all the victors were Spartans, Messenians, and Eleans, so that it seems as if the games were confined to these peoples. After the Messenian wars (*c.* 600) we find competitors from other Greek states, and later many of the most celebrated victors came from South Italy, Sicily, and other parts of Hellas. None but pure Hellenes were allowed to compete. Foreigners might be spectators, but no slave nor any woman was allowed to be present.[1]

From 776 to 724 the games consisted merely of a foot-race of about three hundred yards. Longer races were then introduced, and the *pentathlon* (a fivefold contest in running, leaping, wrestling, discus- and spear-throwing) and chariot-races, and lastly the *pancration* (combined boxing and wrestling). The competitors had to undergo a training of ten months and special practice for a month at Olympia under supervision, and to make sacrifices and to vow that they would compete fairly. There were official trainers besides the judges (*hellanodikai*), who awarded the prizes – wreaths cut with a golden knife from the sacred olive-tree, which, it was said, Heracles had planted.

Marvellous stories were told of the feats of some of the victors. The distances (fifty feet or so) covered by them in leaping seem incredible, but how they used the *haltēres* – *i.e.* 'leaping weights' held in the hands while jumping – is a matter for debate. Of activity and endurance we have a striking example in the victor of the nine-mile race, who is said to have continued running after passing the goal, and to have reached Argos, some fifty miles distant, on the same evening.

The festival took place every fourth year. At first it was limited to a single day (probably that of the first full moon after the summer solstice). After the Persian wars it was extended to five days. The vast multitudes who camped on the slopes of the Mount of Cronos and the sandy hillocks between the beds of the Alpheus and the Cladeus, and who for five days stood in dense throngs around the racecourse and *palaestra*, must have suffered greatly from heat and drought – for the river-water was scanty and bad, and it was not till a late age that a reservoir of pure water was made

---

[1] Perhaps no married women; and possibly exceptions were made with Spartan women. A story is told of a woman being detected in male attire, but as her son was victor she was forgiven.

by the wealthy Roman, Herodes Atticus. No wonder that special sacrifices were offered to Zeus the Averter of Flies!

A 'holy truce' was proclaimed for the whole month, during which all warfare was forbidden and the land of Elis was considered sacred.

The *temenos*, or sacred precinct, at Olympia was called the Altis.[1] Within it stood in early days the ancient temple of Zeus, on the site of which was probably afterwards built the wonderful structure for which Pheidias made his famous statue, and where the equally famous chest of Cypselus was kept. Another temple contained the tomb of Pelops, and very ancient stone foundations have been excavated which are believed to have belonged to the temple of Hera and Zeus – an edifice of sun-baked brick with wooden Doric columns dating from perhaps 1000 (see Fig. 47). In an open space of the Altis stood the great altar of Zeus, and outside the walls was the Stadion, a racecourse about two hundred yards in length. Such was Olympia in the age of Lycurgus, and also of Pheidon; but in time the old buildings were replaced by marble temples, and many other magnificent structures arose within and without the Altis – halls and porticoes and trea-sure-houses. More than eighty altars erected to the various deities testified to the vast numbers of the worshippers, who came from all parts of Hellas;[2] the avenues were lined with the statues of victorious athletes, and both within and without the temples were erected the masterpieces of renowned sculptors, such as the Olympian Zeus of Pheidias, the Victory of Paeonius, and the Hermes of Praxiteles.[3]

Even in the sixth century, as we shall see, men like Xenophanes the philosopher spoke disdainfully of the glorification of the athlete. Euripides, too, in the fragment that survives of his *Autolycus*, calls athletes the worst of all the ills of Hellas, and Socrates, one of the hardiest and bravest of sol-diers, spoke of such men with contempt, as did also Epameinondas.

In a still later age – when chryselephantine statues of royal Macedonians stood in the Philippeion at Olympia – the games degenerated into mere professional contests, and Alexander the Great himself is said to have

---

[1] Probably the Elean form of *alsos*, a sacred grove. The Altis was a square of about two hundred yards each way, enclosed by great walls.

[2] As one might infer from its site on the western shores of Greece, Olympia was frequented far more by the Greeks of Western Hellas than by those of Ionia. Out of the twelve trea-sure-houses five were erected by Greeks of Sicily and South Italy, one by Epidamnus, one by Cyrene, and one by Byzantium.

[3] See Figs. 93, 112, and coin 10, Coin Plate III.

despised 'athleticism.' Under the earlier Roman emperors the Olympic Games were celebrated with great magnificence, but were abolished in A.D. 394 by Theodosius I. His grandson, Theodosius II, had all the temples burnt. But many a splendid ruin still remained, and afforded material to Christian church-builders, as well as to Goths, Slavs, and Turks. At last the great columns and pediments of the temple of Zeus were overthrown by an earthquake. Excavations made by the Germans about 1876 brought to light not only old foundations and many fragments of architectural sculpture, but also the two statues already mentioned, the Hermes and the Victory – both of them original masterpieces by great Greek artists. Of these and of the sculptures of the Zeus temple I shall speak again later.

Pan-Hellenic festivals with athletic and sometimes musical and poetical contests were held also at Delphi, at Nemea, and on the Isthmus. For all of them great antiquity was claimed. The Isthmian Games were said to date from the age of Theseus and Sisyphus, the Nemean from that of the Seven against Thebes, while Apollo himself was said to have founded the Pythian Games at Delphi. But very little is known of them until they were refounded – the Isthmian festival, in honour of Poseidon, possibly by Periander of Corinth, and the Nemean, in honour of Zeus, by the Argives. These festivals were biennial. At the same time as they were reinstituted (c. 580) the Pythian Games were revived. At the original Pythian festival there were probably only contests in music and poetry. The great temple stood, as the Homeric *Hymn to Apollo* says, 'in a hollow, rugged glen beneath the overhanging crags of snowy Parnassus' – a site very unsuitable for athletic gatherings and horse-races. Nor did the god himself seem to favour such things, for in the same *Hymn* the poet protests in the deity's name against the clatter of chariots and horses around his temple, and the 'drinking of mules at the sacred fountains.' But when an arena was found at sufficient distance, so that the tumult of games should not disturb the sanctity of his oracle, Apollo was content and vouchsafed his favour. This arena was the plain of Cirrha, or Crissa, lying between Delphi and the sea. The people of Crissa, to whom belonged the port at which pilgrims landed, levied heavy dues and otherwise annoyed the people of Delphi, who had control of the Delphic shrine. These appealed to the Amphictiony[1] – a religious league of North Grecian states

---

[1] *Amphictiones* means 'dwellers around.' The league was probably begun by the neighbours of a shrine of Demeter near Thermopylae, and gradually grew until the Amphictionic Council had great influence. See *Dict. Ant.*

*Fig. 48  Vale of Tempe and mouth of River Peneios*

*Fig. 49  Site of Delphi, before the old village of Kastri had been cleared away*

– which espoused their cause, and with the help of Cleisthenes of Sicyon, after a struggle of about ten years (the first Sacred War), succeeded in capturing Crissa (590). They razed it to the ground and dedicated the Crissaean plain to the service of the Delphian god; and on this plain was held the Pythian festival, which for its musical, poetical, and artistic contests, as well as for its chariot-races, became scarcely less famed than that of Olympia itself. French excavators have brought to light the remains of the great temple and of about six others, as well as a theatre, stadium, and gymnasium, not far from the Castalian Fount, and the paved Sacred Way which winds up the huge stone terraces on which Apollo's temple stood. This Sacred Way was lined by treasure-houses erected by many of the chief cities of Greece, and was once filled with priceless works of art, almost all of which have naturally disappeared, for Delphi was the prey of plunderers during many ages. Fine architectural sculptures have, however, been recovered, especially some that belonged to the Athenian, Sicyonian, and Cnidian treasuries, and also numerous statues, offerings to the Delphic god. Of these the most remarkable are a colossal Sphinx dedicated by the people of Naxos, and the bronze charioteer (Fig. 74) which was probably erected as a thank-offering for victory in a chariot-race by Polyzalus, the brother of Hiero.

## SECTION D: THE POETS (776–560)

We have seen how by the time of Hesiod the old monarchical and feudal feeling had largely given way to the natural yearnings for personal liberty and independent thought, and how such yearnings, thwarted by the rich and high-born oppressor, found vent in bitter lament and the cry for justice and equality. The true poet – who ever interprets his age – no longer deigned to sing the praises of heaven-descended princes. The epic bard, or rhapsode, indeed, still existed, and the Cyclic writers (so called because they attempted to finish the whole cycle of the legend of Troy) supplied him with material such as the *Sack of Ilion*, the *Cypria*, the *Little Iliad*, and the *Telegoneia*, and sometimes, for a change, with mock-heroic parodies of the Homeric epic such as the *Margites*, the story of a booby-hero who 'knew many professions but knew all badly,' or the *Batrachomyomachia*, the 'Battle of the Frogs and Mice.' And there were (as there are in most ages) poets who wrote religious verse – hymns for festivals of the gods, some of them, such as the 'Homeric' hymns to Apollo and Demeter, of great dignity and beauty. But all this was a survival. The spirit of the age was another, and poetry demanded new forms in which to sing of freedom and fatherland, love and friendship, wisdom and virtue, life and death.

The first of these new forms was elegiac verse, which in its original home, Caria and Lydia, was of a dirge-like character and was accompanied by mournful flute-music. But the metre, a couplet consisting of the epic hexameter and a similar but shorter and more energetic verse with two emphatic monosyllables, was adopted by the Greeks for their war-songs, and also for exhortatory poetry (*hypothēkai*) and sententious maxims (*gnōmai*), and for the expression of personal feelings and opinions on all subjects affecting human life. Among the elegiac poets of this age the chief were Callinus, Tyrtaeus, Mimnermus, and Solon.

The second form was iambic verse, generally of a satiric character, the chief writers of which were Semonides of Amorgos and Archilochus.

The third form was lyrical verse. These early lyrical poets stand on a level immeasurably higher than that of the elegiac and iambic writers. The best known, though, alas! by repute rather than from what has survived of their poetry, are Sappho and Alcaeus, with whom one may perhaps venture to associate Alcman, Arion, and Stesichorus.

The following brief accounts of these poets and of some of their surviving works may prove interesting. Further biographical details will be found in classical dictionaries.

(1) Callinus of Ephesus was perhaps the inventor of the elegiac couplet. His seems to have been mostly war-poetry. Among the few verses of his that are extant he calls upon his countrymen to rouse themselves: 'How long will ye lie idle, while war fills all the world? . . . 'Tis honourable and glorious for a man to fight for his fatherland, his children, and the wife of his youth. . . . It is not possible to escape one's destined death. . . . Many a man has fled battle and the clash of arms only to return to his home and find there the doom of death.' In a verse preserved by Strabo Callinus exclaims: 'Now is coming the host of the Cimmerians, those doers of terrible deeds!' It is therefore probable that by his war-songs he roused the Ephesians against these savages, who (*c.* 678) had captured Sardis and killed the Lydian king Gyges, and soon afterwards burnt the temple of Artemis, just outside the walls of Ephesus.

(2) Of Tyrtaeus (*c.* 660) we have already heard. Whether he was really an Athenian, or whether his birthplace, Aphidna in Laconia, was confused with Aphidna in Attica, is unknown. Fragments survive of 'Tyrtaean' marching songs in anapaestic measure and about eighty elegiac couplets,

some of which have a splendid swing. The language is almost pure Ionic, not Doric; which is strange if he was really Spartan. Moreover, his poetry (if it is his) contains numerous lines almost identical with lines of Callinus, so that some hold that it was written in Ionia by some Milesian poet and attributed to Tyrtaeus. Among Tyrtaean elegiac exhortations (*hypothēkai*) are some fine verses encouraging young warriors not to desert their elders in battle. 'What a foul sight,' the poet exclaims, 'is a white-headed warrior lying dead in the front ranks! But in the youth everything is seemly; he is handsome alive and handsome also when fallen in the van of the battle.' Besides, he adds, bravery is the best policy; the bold survive, while all the herd of cowards perishes. Of his elegy *Eunomia* ('Good Order') about thirty lines are extant. In it the poet calls on the citizens to avoid dissension and to respect the Pythian oracle as the source of law and order. He mentions the 'god-honoured kings' of Sparta, especially Theopompus, under whose command, after nineteen years, 'we conquered Messenia, good to plough and good to plant.' Another fragment (possibly genuine) depicts vividly a well-known characteristic of the Spartans: 'The love of money and naught else shall ruin Sparta. . . . Thus hath golden-haired Apollo prophesied from his rich shrine.'

(3) The poetry of Mimnermus (*c.* 630) is of a more personal character. Some of it is addressed to Nanno, a flute-girl. 'What is life,' he exclaims, 'without golden Aphrodite?' Old age is a terrible thing; its doom (*kēr*) is worse than that of death, destroying both eyes and mind.[1] Like Horace he sings of the joys of youth, and bids one gather them *donec virenti canities abest* ('while grey hairs are still far from youth's bloom'). Perhaps more interesting than his views on this subject are the verses in which he tells how an ancestor of his drove in rout the phalanxes of Lydian horsemen on the plain of the Hermus. This was evidently in a fight between the people of Smyrna, the poet's birthplace, and King Gyges, who failed to take the city. Three generations later (*c.* 590) Alyattes of Lydia captured and razed Smyrna (see p. 176). But Mimnermus probably did not live to see this evil day, though he seems to have survived to the manhood of Solon (*c.* 600), who answered his assertion that life was over at seventy[2] by bidding him substitute 'eighty.'

---

[1] Perhaps these *kēres* of Mimnermus are the evil spirits, or, as Miss Harrison has argued, the bacilli, of old age and death. See p. 77.

[2] Strangely enough, Solon in his *Ten Ages* gives seventy as the limit, and Herodotus makes him give the same in his conversation with Croesus.

(4) When Solon was in Egypt, says the grandfather of Critias in Plato's *Timaeus*, he heard from the priests (the same priests who told him that the Greeks were always children) the wonderful story of the isle Atlantis. 'Ay,' adds the old Critias, 'if he had not taken up poetry as a mere by-work, but had worked at it earnestly like others and had composed a poem on this story that he brought from Egypt, instead of having been obliged to neglect it on account of all the political troubles that he found here at Athens, I believe that neither Hesiod nor Homer nor any other poet would have been more famous.'

In spite of Critias, or even of Plato himself, it is not easy to believe that Solon could ever have been a great poet. But his verses are often exceedingly eloquent and forcible, and on account of his great reputation as statesman and sage they are of supreme interest. In an age when writing was still a rare accomplishment and one had to trust mainly to the living voice, those who had anything to say and who wished to impress it on the memory of their hearers chose a rhythmical form – which, after all, is the natural mode of expression for the emotions, and far less artificial than literary prose.[1] Even laws, it is said, were anciently published in rhythmical language, and not only sages such as Solon and Bias (who wrote a poem of two thousand lines), but also many of the earlier philosophers, as Parmenides, Heracleitus, Xenophanes, Empedocles, and perhaps even Thales himself, expressed their doctrines in verse – a method which, as the magnificent *De Rerum Natura* of Lucretius in a later age proved, allows the imagination its sublimest flights, but which might have its disadvantages for writers on what is nowadays called philosophy. The extant verses of Solon are (*a*) eight lines of his celebrated verses, originally a hundred, about Salamis; (*b*) *Exhortations* to the Athenians; (*c*) *Exhortations* to himself; (*d*) some trochaic and iambic verses.

The sense of his lines about Salamis is as follows: 'I came myself as a herald from lovely Salamis, having composed an order [series] of verses instead of a set-speech. . . . Would that I had been then [when we gave up Salamis] a man of Pholegandros or Sicine [little Aegean islands] rather than an Athenian, for swiftly this report might be spread abroad: *This is an Attic man – one of the Salamis-abandoners.*'

---

[1] Aesop (*c.* 570) should here be mentioned. If he wrote his Fables in verse, as is probable, they were known later only in a prose version; for Socrates, when in prison, bidden by the god to 'make his life more musical,' versified some of them.

In his *Exhortations* to the Athenians he eloquently describes the ruin brought on a city which loves injustice – how its poor are sold into slavery and not even the courtyard doors keep out disaster from a man's home. He sings of Order and Disorder, and of feuds between rich and poor. 'I stood holding before both a mighty buckler, nor did I let either win unjustly.' 'It is hard,' he says, 'to please all in great undertakings.' He speaks of the Demos, and how it best obeys its leaders when not given too loose a rein nor held in too tight; and he addresses a remark to this same Demos which shows how thoroughly he understood its nature: 'Each one of you singly treadeth in the tracks of the fox [is foxish in cunning], but when ye are all together the mind within you is a gaping gooselike thing; for ye pay regard to the tongue and the word of any wheedling flatterer and look not at all to what is being *done*.'

The *Exhortations* to himself contain many wise saws and maxims – *e.g.* 'Wealth is good, but not when ill-acquired'; 'God is a righteous judge, not quick to anger as a man.'

A very interesting fragment is his *Ten Ages*, in which he depicts with almost Shakespearean art the state of man at every seventh year of his life – from the child of seven shedding his first teeth to the septuagenarian 'ripe to receive his destined doom of death,' an expression inconsistent with his answer to Mimnermus. He probably lived eighty years himself, and one of his finest sayings was, 'I grow old ever learning many things.'

Of historical interest (if genuine) are the lines that he addressed to Philocyprus, the Cyprian prince, bidding him farewell, and wishing him long life at his new city, Soli (see p. 169).

Among the fragments of his trochaic tetrameters there is a rather amusing passage in which he pretends to quote public criticism of the fact that he followed the example of Pittacus rather than that of Periander. 'Solon,' he says, 'was a man of no deep wisdom or judgment, for when God gave him good things he would not accept them, and, having enclosed his catch, became nervous and did not haul his big net to land. If *I* had got hold of such power and boundless wealth, even if I had been tyrant of Athens for a single day, I should have been willing to be flayed to make a wine-skin and have all my family exterminated.'

In his iambics he gives a most interesting account of how he released debtors and recalled those who had been sold into foreign slavery.

(5) Horace says that 'fury armed Archilochus with his own iambus.' Doubtless iambic rhythm (which in some languages, such as English, is the

natural rhythm of emotional language) existed before.[1] It is found, for instance, in the *Margites*, sometimes attributed to Homer, and it was probably used in chants at Demeter mysteries and other religious ceremonies; whence perhaps Archilochus borrowed it, for his father was a priest of Demeter, and he himself won the prize for a hymn to the goddess. But possibly the iambic trimeter (the metre used by the great Greek dramatists) was invented by this poet of Paros, who used it with dire effect, it is said, in his scathing satires against Lycambes and his daughters. From fragments of his poems (which comprised elegiacs, iambics, trochaic tetrameters, and also combinations of various rhythms, imitated by Horace in his *Epodes*) it seems that he visited Southern Italy, for he speaks of the 'streams of the Siris, more lovely than Thasos.' Also he mentions Euboea, and describes the Euboean mode of fighting: 'not much bending of bows nor many slings, but the terrible work of the sword'; so, perhaps, he took part in the Lelantine war of Chalcis and Eretria (p. 157). He joined an expedition to Thasos made by the Parians, attracted by the gold-mines of that island and of the opposite Thracian mainland; but it seems to have been unsuccessful. He speaks of Thasos with dislike as a bare, rocky ridge 'like a donkey's back.' In a fight with Thracians he lost his shield (a fact that probably accounts for a similar story about Alcaeus, and certainly accounts for the imaginative loss of Horace's shield at Philippi). His lines on the subject may be thus rendered:

> Some Thracian's doubtless chuckling o'er an unexpected find –
> A brand-new shield, which much against my will I left behind.
> Well, anyhow, I saved my life. The shield may go to pot!
> Another and a better one can easily be got.

More important for the chronologist is the fact that, perhaps while he was in Thasos, he witnessed a solar eclipse, for this gives us the first quite certain date in Greek history, viz. April 6, 648. 'Nothing,' he says, 'is incredible and impossible any longer, since Zeus created night at noonday, hiding the light of the blazing sun; and pale dread fell upon mortals. Henceforth

---

[1] The essential difference between the hexametric and iambic rhythms consists in the fact that the spondee (or dactyl) is in equipoise, its two parts balancing each other and producing a smooth onward motion, whereas the trochee or iambus ($^-$ˇ or ˇ$^-$) causes an agitated, up-and-down movement.

all things can be believed and expected. Let none wonder even if the beasts of the forest exchange with dolphins and dwell in the briny realms, and the resounding billows become dearer to them than the dry land, while the mountains delight those others.' Possibly there is reference here to his former love for the fair Neobule, Lycambes' daughter, now changed into the bitterest disdain.

But of all that has survived of Archilochus the lines are the finest in which he addresses his own soul, as Odysseus does in the *Odyssey*. 'Soul, soul, storm-tossed by desperate cares, come forth and defend thyself breast-foremost 'gainst thy foes, and station thyself in safety anigh the ambush of the enemy. And if victorious, triumph not openly, nor, if conquered, fall on thy face in thy house and lament, but rejoice in all that is joyous and vex not thyself too much because of evil men, remembering that such is the way of mortals.' Words like these and a line such as

Gyges with all his golden wealth is naught to me,

come like a breath of fresh air across all the long ages of dusty, dreary warfare and politics that so often form the main subject of history.

(6) Semonides, called also Simonides, probably from being confused with the later poet of that name, was a Samian by birth, but migrated, perhaps as oekist of a Samian colony, to the little island of Amorgos. Like Archilochus, he used the iambic trimeter for satire; but his satire was not directed against individuals, and his only extant complete poem, in spite of some very caustic passages, is quite Horatian in its playful humour. This poem, which is of about a hundred lines, describes the creation of ten different kinds of women – the dirty from the pig, the sly from the fox, the shameless and inquisitive from the dog, the stupid from earth, the unstable from water, the obstinate from the donkey, the thievish from the cat, the coquettish from the horse, the mischievous from the monkey, and, lastly, the good and industrious from the bee. The last he describes with as much enthusiasm as Solomon himself, and a couplet of his preserved by Clement of Alexandria repeats almost word for word Hesiod's assertion that 'nothing can a man win better than a good woman, or worse than a bad one.' Some of the pictures in this poem of Semonides are exceedingly vivid – such as that of the coquette, who will take no share in household duties, but sits afar from the hearth, fearing the soot, and performs her ablutions and anointings twice or even three times daily, and 'carries on her head a

deep mane of hair all combed out and overshadowed with flowers – a pretty sight indeed for others, but to her lord and master a misfortune, unless he be some tyrant or sceptre-bearing king who delights in such things.'

(7) Alcman was born at Sardis, in Lydia, but his father was probably Greek. How he came to Sparta is unknown. Either, like Terpander, he was invited thither, or he came originally as a slave and gained his freedom and civic honours by his poetry. He is, according to the canon of the Alexandrine grammarians, the first Greek lyric poet. His language is the old Laconian dialect. He wrote hymns, love- and war-songs, and *Parthenia* (songs for Spartan maidens), all of which seem to have been true *songs* and of a far higher poetic value than the verses of Tyrtaeus. The form, too, of his poems is very different from that of the elegiac and iambic poets. They consist of short lines, mostly trochaic and dactylic, arranged in strophes and antistrophes – a system invented by him, amplified by Stesichorus and Pindar, and adopted by the Attic dramatists for their choral odes – in which also the Doric dialect is often used. He lived about 670–600, and was thus probably a contemporary of Tyrtaeus.

Of his poetry numerous fragments remain. Of these the most important was discovered (written on papyrus) in Egypt. It is a *Parthenion*, meant to be sung by virgins at the festival of Artemis Orthia (see p. 129). There are also four hexameters of great beauty, addressed in old age to the Spartan maidens. He laments that he can no longer take part in their songs and dances and wishes he were some bright-coloured sacred sea-bird 'that over the foam of the sea with dauntless heart amid the halcyons flies.' His lines descriptive of the stillness of night have all the vividness, if not the pathos, of Goethe's *Ueber allen Gipfeln ist Ruh'*.

(8) Arion (*c.* 625) was a native of Lesbos, which he left probably early, before the days of Alcaeus and Sappho. He spent most of his life at the court of Periander of Corinth, where he became famous as a minstrel and song-writer. According to Herodotus, as well as Aristotle, he was 'the first to invent the dithyramb measure.' More probably he adapted the rough measures and boisterous ribaldry of the old Cyclic, or dithyramb, chorus, sung at rustic dances in honour of Dionysus. There is nothing of Arion's poetry extant, although the historian Aelian (third century A.D.) quotes verses in which Arion himself is supposed to give an account of his rescue by the dolphin. Aelian also appeals to the inscription on the bronze statue of Arion and his dolphin erected on Cape Taenarus to prove the truth of

that account; and perhaps there is more truth in the story than we believe. Pliny tells of a dolphin (porpoise) who used to carry a boy to and from school every day across the bay of Baiae.

(9) Stesichorus (*c.* 632–556) was born at Himera, in Sicily. One tradition asserts that he was a son of Hesiod. He incurred the hostility of the notorious tyrant Phalaris and fled to Catane, where he died. His tomb gave the name to one of the city gates. This name, Stesichorus, he is said to have received in addition to his original name Tisias because he was famed as an 'arranger of choruses.' He is said to have brought the lyric art to perfection in language and rhythm, but the bulk of his writings seems to have been on epic subjects – the old Trojan and Orestean legends and the myths about Heracles. Of these poems numerous fragments survive, but they are of little interest except the first three lines (preserved for us by Plato) of the celebrated *Palinode* with which Stesichorus atoned for having slandered Helen of Troy and thus, it is said, recovered his eyesight: 'It is not true – that story. Thou didst never embark on well-benched ships nor reach the battlements of Troy.' It was not Helen herself that Paris carried off, but only a phantom – that 'double' of Helen which plays a part in Greek legend and literature and is intimated in the beautiful episode of the *Helena* in Goethe's *Faust*.

(10) Alcaeus (*c.* 645–580) belonged to a noble family of Mytilene in Lesbos. He took part against the tyrant Myrsilus, and after the defeat of the Lesbians by the Athenians at Sigeum (in defence of which stronghold he distinguished himself – and perhaps lost his shield) he, as well as his brother and many others of the aristocratic party, went into exile (*c.* 596). He seems to have been for some time in Egypt, where Apries (Hophra) was reigning and Naucratis, the Greek settlement, was already a flourishing town. Hither, too, perhaps with Alcaeus, came Charaxus, the brother of Sappho – and possibly even Sappho herself. The brother of Alcaeus took service under Nebucadnezar, and may have been at the sack of Daphnae (see p. 171), but probably he returned with the poet to Mytilene. Here Alcaeus violently opposed the democratic party, and when Pittacus (*c.* 590) was made dictator (see p. 157) he was imprisoned; but the wise Pittacus seems to have forgiven him, and probably the two became friends. A true and tender friendship existed also between Alcaeus and Sappho, who was the younger by a few years. His poetry breathes passionate emotion. He sings of gods and of men, of war and arms, of love and wine. In verses still extant he describes the ship of the state (a picture copied by Horace) tossed on the waves, rolling to and fro with sails rent and the water rising ever

higher in the hull. Two lines survive addressed to Sappho: 'O violet-weaving, holy, sweetly smiling Sappho, I wish to say something to thee, but shame prevents me.' Of all his poems (ten books of which once existed) we have but these lines and a few other fragments. Many of his odes were written in the measure (a stanza of four lines) invented by him, and named after him – a measure well known from Horace's translations and imitations of the Aeolian bard; known also to English readers from Tennyson's fine stanzas addressed to Milton.

(11) Sappho, like Alcaeus, was a Lesbian, and had her home at Mytilene; but for some years (c. 596–590) she too lived in exile, perhaps in Sicily – possibly also at Naucratis. At Mytilene her house, which she named 'The Home of the Muses,' was the gathering-place of many literary and fashionable women, and as Lesbos was at this time, it is said, rich in female writers. Most of Sappho's poems were written for solo performance, and many allude to erotic love between young women. Many stories grew up around her name in later times, including the tale of her hapless infatuation for the mythical Phaon, the ugly ferryman who was rejuvenated and beautified by Aphrodite, and her fatal leap from the Leucadian precipice.

Sappho's poetry has the exquisite natural grace and the delicate but distinct outlines of the finest Greek sculpture – such sculpture as we see on the frieze of the Parthenon or on some beautiful Athenian stele. Both in thought and in language it offers the very greatest contrast imaginable to what is often regarded as the true poetical method of expressing deep emotion. It affects one not by the display of vehement passion, but by impressing on one's mind a picture which haunts the memory and ever afterwards has the power of stirring one's feelings as if it were a real experience.

Even the fragments that remain of her nine books of poems allow us to accept without hesitation the judgment of ancient critics, who were unanimous in their almost reverential admiration. Among these surviving fragments are three probably complete odes in her favourite measure, invented by her (or some say by Alcaeus) and known as the Sapphic.[1]

No translation can give any hint of the beauty and power of her language, but even a rough prose version of some of these relics of her poetry may be more useful and interesting than biographical details and critical comments. First let us take the ode to Aphrodite:

---

[1] Horace used the Sapphic metre twenty-six times and the Alcaic thirty-seven times. Probably the best example of the metre in English is Canning's 'Needy Knife-grinder.'

'Immortal Aphrodite on thy throne of many colours, daughter of Zeus, weaver of wiles, I implore thee, break not my heart, O Lady, with excess of love and of anguish, but come hither, if ever before thou heardest from afar my cries and, leaving the golden mansion of thy father, didst yoke thy car and come; and swiftly thy winsome sparrows brought thee over the dark earth, eddying their rapid wings, from heaven through the midmost aether; and quickly they arrived, and thou, O blessed one, smiling with thy divine countenance, didst ask what ailed me now again, and why again I called on thee, and what in my maddened heart I wished. *Whom dost thou desire that Persuasion should bring to thy friendship? Who doeth thee wrong, O Sappho? E'en if she fleeth, she shall soon pursue thee; and if she accepteth not gifts, yet shall she give them; and if she loveth not, soon shall she love – yea, even against her will.* Come to me also now, and set me free from grievous cares, and all that my heart longs to be fulfilled do thou fulfil, and be once more my helper!'

The second is an ode that was discovered among the papyrus manuscripts found at Oxyrhynchus, in Egypt. It was addressed by Sappho to her brother Charaxus, at Naucratis, where he is said to have disgraced himself with his relations by falling in love with the notorious Rhodopis, who was a slave-girl (a fellow-slave, says Herodotus, of Aesop the fable-writer), and was redeemed by Charaxus at a great expense – for which he was 'often lashed by Sappho in her poetry':

'I implore you, Sea-nymphs, grant that my brother return hither in safety, and that all things which in his heart he may desire be fulfilled, and that he may atone for all the errors of the past and become a joy to his friends and a sorrow to his enemies; and to us may he never prove of no account. And may he wish to make his sister share in his good name, and may he forget the grievous pain of what in days past made him mourn and break his heart, as he heard at some festival of the citizens a wounding word that cut right deep into the quick and, though ceasing for a time, ere long returned again.'

The third ode, also in Sapphic measure, gives us, without any attempt at direct description, a picture of a beautiful maiden beloved by Sappho:

'Like unto the gods seemeth to me that man who sits in thy presence and nigh unto thee listens to thy sweet voice and laughter, which ever sets a-throbbing the heart within my bosom. For when I look e'en for a moment on thee, no voice comes any more, but my tongue fails utterly and a soft glow at once spreads o'er my face, and I see no more with my eyes, and my ears are filled with sounds, and the sweat pours down and trembling seizeth all my body, and I am more pallid than grass and am so distraught that I seem nigh unto death itself.'

Another short poem, in a different metre, intimates by a different poetical process, and again without any direct description, the loveliness of Sappho's friend Atthis, who had married a Lydian and had gone with him to Sardis:

'Now amidst Lydian women she shineth in her beauty as, whene'er the sun is set, the rosy moon, having round her all the stars, spreads abroad her light o'er the briny sea alike and o'er the flowery fields; and the dew lies there, beautiful, and roses revive and bloom, and fragile chervil and rich-blossoming melilot.'

A very different woman is pictured in another fragment:

'When thou art dead thou shalt lie there, and never shall there be any remembrance of thee nor any longing for thee in days to come, for thou hast no share in the roses of Pieria [poetry and music], but when thy soul has flown forth, also in the mansion of Hades unnoticed thou shalt flit about with the dim inglorious dead.'

Many other beautiful fragments of Sappho's poetry survive. Well-known lines of Byron were evidently inspired by her address to the evening star:

'O Hesperus that bringest back all things which the gleaming dawn dispersed, thou bringest the sheep, thou bringest the goat, thou bringest the boy back to his mother.'

A graphic picture of autumn is given in a few words: 'All round it pipeth chill amidst the orchard boughs; the leaves are quivering and the foliage falls.' Another touch of autumn, recalling Coleridge's 'one red leaf on the topmost twig,' is given in what may be the fragment of some marriage-song: 'As a sweet apple blusheth on the tip of the branch, on the topmost tip, and the apple-pickers have forgotten it – nay, have not forgotten it, but have been unable to reach it.'

Chapter 4

# The Age of Peisistratus and the Rise of Persia (560–500)

SECTIONS – A: POETS AND PHILOSOPHERS – B: THE ORDERS OF GREEK
ARCHITECTURE – C: SCULPTURE, DOWN TO THE PERSIAN WARS

To the student of comparative politics the history of Athens from 560 to
500 is especially attractive, for during this period, while the democratic constitution framed by Solon still continued to exist, as Thucydides says, in its
essential features, the state was for many years under the absolute control
of a single man and his heirs, who, although the power was seized by the
usual methods, may be regarded rather as constitutional rulers than as
despots. That Athens for a time lost her liberty and emerged from the trial
stronger and better prepared to face the foe of Hellas cannot but be of deep
interest, but the phenomena of political evolution form by no means the
main subject of Greek history. Such phenomena are due to ever-recurring
influences working on average human nature, and they may be traced under
various conditions in the stories of many another nation;[1] but genius has
ever something new to tell us, and from Greek genius we may learn what
we cannot learn from any other source. I shall therefore content myself
with giving a brief account of the reign, or tyranny, of Peisistratus and his
sons and of the reforms of Cleisthenes, and shall reserve more of the space
at my disposal for matters of greater importance.

When Solon returned to Athens (c. 562) dissension was at its height, and
it is quite possible that, finding his influence of no avail, he again left for
the East and visited Croesus, who ascended the throne of Lydia in 560. In

---

[1] By a strange coincidence the same year (510) saw the banishment of the Tarquins from
Rome and of the Peisistratidae from Athens.

*Fig. 50 'Artemis of Delos'*        *Fig. 51 Stele of Aristion*

199

this same year Peisistratus, the cousin of Solon, and the leader, as we have seen, of the so-called party of the Hills, consisting mainly of peasants and ultra-democrats, persuaded the people by means of a stratagem[1] to allow him a bodyguard, and seized the Acropolis. Hereupon his political opponents left Athens, and he seems to have quietly assumed the reins of government and to have remained in power for about five years. Solon, when again in Athens, is said to have appealed to the people to 'pluck the tyrant up by the roots,' but in vain. Some relate that he returned to his friend the king of Soli, in Cyprus, but from his verses to Mimnermus (if they are his) it seems likely that he remained at Athens and lived till c. 558, and found life at eighty not unenjoyable, even under a despot.

Two or three years later Peisistratus was driven out by the united parties of the Coast and the Plain, but they quarrelled, and by the aid of Megacles he returned (c. 550). The stratagem by which this was effected would be incredible if we did not know how ineradicable proved the old *deisidaimonia* – that eerie dread of the supernatural which was so universal in an earlier age, and to which the Athenians seem to have been especially susceptible. The story is that Peisistratus entered Athens in a chariot on which there stood by his side a stalwart peasant woman arrayed as Athene, and that the mob accepted the apparition as genuine and reinstated him in power. Peisistratus had promised to marry the daughter of Megacles (who was the head of the Alcmaeonid nobles), and he did so, but he refused to treat her as his wife, for he had a family by a former wife and was unwilling to connect himself with descendants of Cylon, who were regarded as accursed. This led to his second banishment, which lasted for ten years, until about 540, when, with mercenaries from Argos and Naxos, he crossed from Euboea to Marathon, surprised or won over the Athenian troops and entered the city, where he re-established himself as absolute ruler, sending the children of his adversaries as hostages to his friend Lygdamis, tyrant of Naxos, and expelling the Alcmaeonidae.

The rule of Peisistratus during the next thirteen years is said to have been wise and beneficial. He feued much of the land to peasants, encouraged agriculture, extended Athenian power and commerce abroad, recapturing Sigeum from the Lesbians and promoting Greek influence on the shores of

---

[1] By displaying self-inflicted wounds. We have a similar story connected with Sextus Tarquin, and with Odysseus (*Od.* iv. 244). The grant of a bodyguard was proposed to the Ecclesia by Aristion, whose portrait we probably have in Fig. 51.

the Hellespont, where the Thracian Chersonese was now governed by an Athenian – the half-uncle of the famous Miltiades.

About this elder Miltiades a picturesque story is told. He was, says Herodotus, a victor in the Olympian chariot-race and a man of high distinction, but an adversary of Peisistratus. One day (*c.* 558) as he sat in the porch of his house, probably brooding over the success of his rival, some wayfarers 'in outlandish garments and armed with lances' approached. He offered them entertainment, and after the banquet was over they told him that the Delphic oracle had bidden them take back with them to their country, the Thracian Chersonese, the first man who offered them hospitality, for he would help them against their enemies. Miltiades, perhaps glad to leave Athens, acceded to their entreaties and became 'king' of the Chersonese and a friend of Croesus. He was succeeded in his office as Thracian prince and Athenian governor of the Greek settlements on the Hellespont by a nephew, who was (*c.* 520) succeeded by the younger and more celebrated Miltiades.

Under Peisistratus Athens seems to have begun to assert that hegemony in the Ionic world which she afterwards attained. The lord of the Ionian mother-city took upon himself, as Thucydides says, to 'purify' Delos by removing all the tombs within sight of the temple. He also ordered that the Homeric poems, recited at the Delian and other festivals, should be collected and arranged and written out in the Attic script and divided into books. Possibly on this occasion lines may have been inserted in order to connect Athens with the great Ionian epic – for, whatever the reason may be, Homer had said but little about the Athenians and their legends. This revision of Homer was undertaken by Peisistratus and his son Hipparchus in order to regulate the hitherto arbitrary and disconnected recitations of the poem at the great festival of Athene, which had been lately founded. At this festival took place the musical and athletic contests and the stately procession of which we have such precious records in the so-called Panathenaic prize-vases and in the frieze of the Parthenon (see Figs. 55 and 85).

Besides the Panathenaic festival Peisistratus revived or amplified the rustic festival, which had been held from early ages in honour of Dionysus (the Lenaia, or 'Festival of the Wine-vat'), such as we have already heard of in connection with Arion at Corinth. At this new festival, which was called the Great Dionysia, the old dances and songs performed originally by peasants dressed up as satyrs were in course of time combined with

201

dialogue and with representations of old legends, and this 'goat-song' performance (*tragōidia*) developed little by little into the Attic drama. The chief composer and director of these Dionysiac performances in the age of Peisistratus was Thespis, who is often spoken of as the father of Attic tragedy. He is said to have first introduced dialogue and to have himself taken the part of the actor who, in various disguises and with a stained or masked face, conversed with the chorus of dancers. The first representation of this kind at the New Dionysia is said to have taken place in 535.

During the rule of Peisistratus and his sons the huge temple of Olympian Zeus was begun and many fine buildings were erected. Some of these will be described later. One of his most useful works was a system of pipes by which Athens was supplied with water, possibly from the Upper Ilissus, or more probably from Kallirrhoë ('Fair-stream'), a natural source near the Ilissus and the Olympieion, to the south-east of the Acropolis.

Peisistratus died in 527 and left the government to his eldest son, Hippias, while the second, Hipparchus (like a King Archon), had, perhaps together with a younger brother Thessalus, the control of religious festivals, literary and musical contests, and the like.[1]

For thirteen years Athens seems to have enjoyed an uneventful prosperity under the Peisistratidae. We know really next to nothing of this period, except that Hippias and his brother were, like the Medici of Florence, patrons of art, and that Anacreon and Simonides of Ceos visited their court. Herodotus speaks of them as oppressive tyrants, while Thucydides, who was related to the Peisistratidae, but whose judgment was not likely to have been warped by prejudice, asserts that they 'cultivated virtue and intellect.' He allows, however, that 'their tyranny proved galling at last,' and that Hippias ultimately proved not only a tyrant but a traitor to his country.

In 514 Hipparchus was assassinated by Harmodius and Aristogeiton. He had conceived an infatuation for the young Harmodius, and having been repelled he insulted the sister of the youth, refusing her as a 'basket-carrier' in the Panathenaic procession.[2] So the two friends planned to kill Hipparchus and his brother; 'but, having suspected,' says Thucydides, 'that

---

[1] See Thuc. i. 20 and vi. 54 *ff.*, and Hdt. v. 55. Also the pseudo-Plato in his *Hipparchus* says that this prince 'first introduced Homer into Greece.' The writer, whether Plato or not, evidently regarded Hipparchus as the chief ruler – a belief stigmatized by Thucydides.

[2] According to Herodotus the Gephyraean family to which Harmodius belonged was originally Phoenician, and was 'excluded at Athens from a number of privileges.' Perhaps this was a legal ground for the rejection of the girl.

information had been given to Hippias by their accomplices, they abstained from attacking him, as being forewarned, and as they wished to do something at all hazards, having fallen in with Hipparchus, who was arranging the Panathenaic procession, they slew him.'

Possibly at first no great enthusiasm was excited by the act – or else it was suppressed by dread – but not many years later, after the expulsion of Hippias, statues were erected to the Tyrannicides, and popular songs, such as the well-known drinking-song (*skolion*) composed by the otherwise unknown Callistratus, 'I'll wreathe my sword in myrtle bough,' prove how the Athenians had learnt to detest the name of the Peisistratidae. This hatred was much intensified by the tyrannical conduct of Hippias after the murder of his brother. 'Being now in greater apprehension,' says Thucydides, 'he put to death many citizens, and also kept his eye on foreign states in whatever quarter he had a prospect of safe retreat in case of revolution.' Doubtless among these foreign states was Persia.

After four years the revolution came. The exiled Alcmaeonidae, who longed to return to Athens, had at length succeeded in obtaining the aid of Sparta in the following way. The great temple at Delphi had been burnt down, and a public subscription through the whole of Greece had enabled the Delphic treasury to contract for its reconstruction. The Alcmaeonidae undertook the contract, and, using marble instead of the specified *poros*, rebuilt the temple with such magnificence and so won the favour of the Pythian priests that whenever the Spartans came to consult the oracle the invariable answer was, 'First liberate Athens!' Sparta, by the conquest of Tegea and the defeat of Argos, had made herself the head of a Peloponnesian league, and was strong enough to interfere in Northern Greece. The first raid into Attica was defeated by cavalry sent from Thessaly to aid Hippias, but the Spartan king Cleomenes then led a strong force against Athens, and Hippias, blockaded in the 'Pelasgic fortress' (*i.e.* the Acropolis), and hearing of the capture of his children, capitulated (510). He was allowed to leave Attica 'under treaty,' together with his children, and went, says Thucydides, 'first to Sigeum, then to Lampsacus, and thence to the court of King Darius.'

Now the head of the Alcmaeonidae who had been thus restored to Athens was Cleisthenes. He was the grandson of Cleisthenes the tyrant of Sicyon, whose daughter married the Athenian Megacles. Of this Megacles we have already heard much. It was his daughter (and therefore the sister of Cleisthenes) whom Peisistratus married and rejected.

On the expulsion of Hippias, whose absolute rule had kept open feuds in abeyance, political discussion once more began. Cleisthenes, the personal foe of the Peisistratidae, was naturally opposed to the old regime, and, as Herodotus expresses it, 'called to his aid the common people.' He was opposed by Isagoras and the aristocratical party. Isagoras, being worsted, appealed to Sparta, and the Spartans sent a peremptory order (as they did again seventy-seven years later, in reference to Pericles) that the Athenians should 'cast out the accursed thing' – the 'pollution of the goddess' – namely, the Alcmaeonidae.[1]

Cleisthenes was forced to leave Athens. This, however, did not content Isagoras and his party. They invited the Spartans; whereupon King Cleomenes came and expelled 700 Athenian families. But on his trying to dissolve the Ecclesia and establish an oligarchy the Athenians rose. The Spartans were blockaded for two days in the Acropolis, and then accepted terms, purchasing their lives by handing over their mercenaries to the tender mercies of the Athenians, who put them all to death, among them a Delphian who, as pancratiast, had won three victories at the Pythian and two at the Olympic Games, and whose statue by the celebrated Argive sculptor Ageladas (the master of Pheidias, Myron, and Polycleitus) was seen nearly 700 years later at Olympia by the traveller Pausanias.

Cleisthenes and the 700 families were then recalled. Cleomenes endeavoured to invade Attica again, and although the attempt failed (the Spartan kings having quarrelled), the Athenians were so alarmed, if we are to believe Herodotus, that they actually sent ambassadors to Sardis to sue for the alliance of Darius; but they were told that the friendship of the Great King was only to be bought by earth and water, tokens of vassalage. Possibly it was not in alarm that they did this, but in arrogance, for we find them soon afterwards inflicting crushing defeats on the Boeotians and the Chalcidians (of Euboea), who had joined the Spartans in their last invasion of Attica. The rich Lelantine plain (see p.157) was allotted to Athenian settlers, and many Chalcidian prisoners were kept fettered at Athens until they were ransomed at two *minae* apiece (perhaps equivalent to about 200 days' wages for a skilled worker). 'The chains wherewith they were fettered,' says Herodotus, 'were hung up by the Athenians in their Acropolis, where they were still to be seen in my day, hanging against a wall scorched by the Median flames.' From a tenth of the ransom-money a

---

[1] See about Cylon p. 164; also Thuc. i. 126, and Hdt. v. 70.

magnificent bronze quadriga was set up to the left of the old gate of the Acropolis.[1] Moreover, in a *stoa* (portico) at Delphi the Athenians dedicated (as we learn from an inscription discovered there) arms and beaks of ships captured in this war.

The people of Aegina had made common cause with the Boeotians against their old enemy, Athens. In Solon's time, as we have seen, the Athenians had attacked Aegina, not long after their conquest of Salamis, but had been driven out of the island by the Argives.[2] Since that time hostility had smouldered, but it now broke out openly, and the Aeginetans carried on a chronic 'unheralded' war with Athens right down to the time of the Persian war, making constant descents on the coast of Attica and on the Athenian port Phaleron. Such was their embitterment that shortly before the battle of Salamis the Spartans had to interfere and send Aeginetans as hostages to Athens in order to prevent Aegina aiding the Persians; nor did Aegina cease to be a thorn in the side of Athens till (in 431) the inhabitants were expelled and the island was incorporated in the Attic state.

Thus Athens began to unfold her powers – a fact that Herodotus justly attributes to her regained political freedom. 'These things show,' he says, 'that while undergoing oppression they let themselves be beaten, since they worked for a master; but as soon as they got their liberty each man was eager to do the best he could.'

Had this rewon liberty retained the basis of the old Solonian constitution the old political feuds would have assuredly reappeared and led even again to some form of enslavement, but fortune willed it that Cleisthenes should discover a method by which all the local and clan influences which had made party feeling so rancorous and dangerous should be eliminated, and the good of the state should become the one object of political activity. Having abolished the four old Ionic tribes, which were founded on locality, profession, and wealth, he formed ten tribes solely for political purposes. Each of these new political tribes consisted of three *trittyes* (thirds) taken from three different regions of Attica, so that the tribal vote was not prejudiced by local influences. Each tribe had to supply a contingent of hoplites,

---

[1] Pericles perhaps set up another on the right hand (*c.* 446), and when the new Propylaea were built (*c.* 437) they were probably put on new bases. One of these bases with traces of the inscription quoted by Herodotus (v. 77) has been found.

[2] See Hdt. v. 82 *ff.*, and Note B, Dress.

some cavalry,[1] and one of the ten generals of the Athenian army. Fifty men from every tribe, chosen by lot from a selected number, formed the new council (*boulē*) of 500. This council, in conjunction with the archons and other magistrates, managed all internal affairs and initiated laws to be sanctioned by the great Assembly (Ecclesia). But for the dispatch of business the *boulē* had a permanent committee. Each of its ten groups of councillors took it in turn to act as this committee for thirty-six days (the tenth of the year of 360 days, which was rectified by intercalating a month every five years). While they sat on committee these deputies were called *prytaneis* (presidents), and their tribe was the 'presiding tribe' during this space of thirty-six days (which was called a *prytaneia*). The people's Assembly (Ecclesia) probably met, as it did in later times, every nine days – or it may have been summoned only on special occasions to sanction a law by plebiscite or to dispose of some referendum. Of the Areopagus we hear little at this period. It probably existed with only an empty show of authority.

Ostracism may have been an invention of Cleisthenes, though it seems to have been used first in 488. It was a useful method of getting rid for a time of a dangerous citizen. The council and Assembly first decided (and could only do it during the sixth *prytaneia*) that an *ostrakismos* was advisable. On a fixed day barricades were erected in the Agora and every voter of the ten tribes gave his vote by casting into an urn an *ostrakon* (potsherd) on which he had inscribed the name of any citizen whom he held to be especially dangerous. The man against whom most votes were given, should his *ostraka* number at least 6000 – *i.e.* about a fifth of the number of the voters – was exiled for ten (later for five) years, but lost neither his citizenship nor his property.

## The Rise of Persia

We must now turn from the affairs of the refounded democracy of the little Attic state to note the rise of a mighty empire which before long will threaten to annihilate the whole of the eastern while Carthage is endeavouring to annihilate the western world of Hellas.

---

[1] The tribal regiment was called a 'tribe' (*phylē*). The subdivisions were *taxeis* and *lochoi*. See Hdt. vi. 111. In Solon's time Athens could muster barely a hundred horsemen, and even at the beginning of the Peloponnesian War only about a thousand.

It would take us too far afield to follow Herodotus in his investigations of the origins of the feud between Greece and the Asiatic 'barbarian,' nor will it be possible to repeat many of the countless stories that he tells in connection with the Lydian, Median, and Persian kings, stories with which he allures the reader to Egypt and Scythia and many another strange land and people before he launches out into the subject of the Graeco-Persian war.

I have already traced the history of Assyria and Babylon down to the death of King Nebucadnezar in 562, that of Lydia to the accession of Croesus in 560, and that of Media to the death of Astyages in 559, and we have seen that the great kings of Nineveh and Babylon had never (except in the case of Cyprus) come into collision with the Greeks. But the early Lydian kings had attacked and subjugated several of the Ionian and Aeolian cities, and Croesus, as soon as he was firmly seated on the Lydian throne, made himself master of all the Greek cities on the mainland of Asia Minor except Miletus, and even made preparations to invade the islands, but was, says Herodotus, deterred by a witty remark of the sage Bias.[1] Ephesus was the first city he attacked – 'The Ephesians, when he laid siege to the place, made an offering of their city to Artemis by stretching a rope[2] from the town wall to the temple of the goddess, which was distant from the ancient city by a space of seven furlongs.' This was evidently the new temple of the Ephesian Artemis, which was still being built to replace the old temple burnt by the Cimmerians in 677. After capturing Ephesus, Croesus presented to this temple, says Herodotus, 'golden heifers and most of the columns.' The sculptured drum of one of these columns is now in the British Museum (Fig. 120). On it were found the Greek letters BA . . . . KP . . . . . . AN . . . . . EN, which have been (doubtless rightly) restored to ΒΑΣΙΛΕΥΣ ΚΡΟΙΣΟΣ ΑΝΑΘΗΚΕΝ, (BASILEUS KROISOS ANATHĒKEN) i.e. 'King Croesus dedicated.'

The wealth[3] of Croesus, as that of his ancestor Gyges and the Phrygian Midas, was proverbial. Although the conqueror of the Greek cities of Aeolis and Ionia, he was a great admirer of Hellenic civilization, and his court at Sardis was frequented by many Greeks of distinction. He made,

---

[1] Herodotus says: 'Within my own knowledge Croesus was the first to inflict injury on the Greeks'; but Alyattes, Sadyattes, and perhaps Ardys attacked the Greek cities.

[2] See p. 165, footnote.

[3] See Hdt. i. 50 and 92. For the Lydian coinage see Note C, Coins.

*Fig. 52  The Croesus column*

moreover, many splendid offerings to Greek temples, of which Herodotus gives a description that may well excite wonder, if not incredulity.

Shortly after the accession of Croesus, perhaps in 560–559, Solon not improbably, as we have seen, visited Sardis. Croesus, a young man of thirty-five in the first flush of kingly pride, bade the sage tell him whom of all men he had ever met he deemed the most happy. Solon cited an Athenian, Tellos by name, who had been blessed with domestic happiness and had died a soldier's death in defence of his country, and as second happiest he cited the Spartan youths Cleobis and Bito, who, when the oxen failed to come, yoked themselves to a car and drew their aged mother five-and-forty furlongs to the festival of Hera at Argos, and died in the temple; and when Croesus asked him in astonishment how he ventured to put the happiness of such people on a level with *his*, Solon replied that no wealth could give good fortune, and that even a fortunate man cannot for certain be called 'happy' until he is dead, for 'in every matter it behoveth us to mark well the end.'

Soon afterwards Croesus learnt that all his gold could not save him from the grief of losing his favourite son, and some ten years later he was taught the wisdom of marking well the end. His kingdom had extended itself eastward over all Phrygia, Mysia, and Paphlygonia, as far as the river Halys, and hearing of the presumptuous doings of Cyrus and his Persians and Medes, he got together a great army of Lydians and Greeks and crossed over into Cappadocia to challenge the new foe – not before having consulted the oracle at Delphi. The Delphic god, though he received gifts of almost indescribable magnificence from Croesus, played him a rather disingenuous trick, bidding him (as Ahab was bidden) go up, for he would destroy a mighty empire. So vast had the power of Croesus become that doubtless he had visions of making himself the king of Media in the place of this usurper who had dethroned the old Astyages. But the empire that he should destroy was his own, as the oracle afterwards explained. After an indecisive battle near the ancient capital of Cappadocia, Pteria, he retreated to Sardis, which was soon afterwards stormed by Cyrus. Croesus was condemned to die. He was placed, with twice seven noble Lydian youths, on a great funeral pyre. The pyre was lighted, and as the flames shot upward he was heard to call aloud three times on the name of Solon. Cyrus demanded the reason, and when he learnt it he bade the fire be quenched. But it was too late; the flames were not to be mastered. Then Croesus called on Apollo, and a sudden deluge of rain extinguished the fire. Cyrus, deeply moved by the miracle, made Croesus his counsellor and constant companion.

Cyrus captured Sardis probably in 546. Thirteen years earlier he had (according to Herodotus) dethroned the Median king Astyages. His father, Cambyses, a descendant of a noble chieftain named Achaemenes, was prince of the Persians, a race of bold and hardy mountaineers, closely akin to the Medes, living in the highlands between Media and the Persian Gulf. This Cambyses married a daughter of the Median king, and their son, the young Cyrus, putting himself at the head of a body of Persians, succeeded (in 559) in conquering his grandfather and establishing the Medo-Persian Empire. This Medo-Persian Empire, when first Cyrus mounted the throne,[1] occupied, roughly speaking, the lands between the Caspian, the Persian Gulf, the Indus, and the valley of the Tigris. Its chief cities were Pasargadae, Persepolis, Ecbatana, and Susa. The general name given to this vast country by its inhabitants was Iran, and these inhabitants are therefore generally said to have belonged to the Iranian branch of the Indo-Iranian race. In religion they were followers of Zoroaster and worshipped Mithras, the sun-god. According to Herodotus they had neither images of gods nor temples nor altars, 'accounting the use of such things a folly.' As fire-worshippers they probably had no idols, and there seems to be no trace of ancient *Persian* (though of course of Chaldean) temples, but huge stone altars on open-air terraces have been discovered which were apparently used for sacrifice to the sun-god. Probably the Persians had a purer form of Zoroastrian fire-worship than the other Iranian peoples, such as the Chaldeans and Medes, regarding Light and Darkness as symbols of the powers of good and evil, also symbolized by the deities Ormuzd and Ahriman. The priests and religious teachers, called *Magi*, formed a very select and influential caste. Of the character and the customs of the Persians graphic and full descriptions are given by Herodotus (i. 131 *ff.* and elsewhere) and by Xenophon and

---

[1] Herodotus gives a story about the infancy of Cyrus and his childhood at the court of Astyages which has great similarity to the Roman legend of Romulus and Remus and King Numitor (Hdt. i. 107 *ff.*). It should be mentioned that Xenophon, who wrote later but knew personally the younger Cyrus, and Ctesias, who was surgeon to that prince's brother (Artaxerxes II), give versions very different from that of Herodotus. Xenophon states in his *Cyropaedeia*, where he describes the bringing up of Cyrus the Great, that Cyrus never rebelled against his grandfather, but acted as his general and the general of his son, Cyaxares II (unknown to Herodotus), and that he even took Babylon (538) as the general of this Cyaxares II (perhaps the 'Darius the Median' of Daniel v. 31), whom he later dethroned. Ctesias asserts that Cyrus and Astyages were in no way related. According to Herodotus, Cyrus was a great-nephew of Croesus, who married a sister of Astyages.

other writers. Many acts of magnanimity are related of the Persian kings,[1] and their contempt for the huckstering and rhetorical arts and deceits of the Greek Agora, as well as for the venality and treachery not only of the ordinary Greek but even of Greek leaders, was frequently and openly expressed. 'The most disgraceful thing in the world, in their opinion,' says Herodotus, 'is to tell a lie'; and when he remarks that 'the Persians look upon themselves as very greatly superior in all respects to the rest of mankind,' we cannot but concede that in *some* respects at least they do offer a very striking contrast to the less admirable sides of the Greek character. Thus one cannot help contrasting such facts as the treatment by Darius of the Eretrian captives and the terrible decree passed by the Athenians against Mytilene. It is true that in this case intense excitement may be pleaded and the decree was ultimately reversed – so that the process somewhat reminds one of what Herodotus says about the Persians: 'It is their practice to deliberate upon affairs of importance when they are drunk, and then on the morrow, when they are sober, to reconsider it.'[2]

After his conquest of Lydia Cyrus returned to the far East, leaving his general Harpagus to reduce the Greek Asiatic cities, all of which, with the exception of powerful Miletus, had aided their liege-lord Croesus. Harpagus had no very difficult task, for these cities, in constant feud, were ever a prey to the invader. Had they but formed a confederation, as the sage Thales, it is said, advised,[3] Ionia and Aeolis might perhaps have offered a successful resistance to the advance of Persia; but the consciousness of disunion in the face of such overwhelming odds paralysed them, and we are scarcely surprised when we hear that another sage, Bias of Priene, advised the Ionians to migrate *en masse* to Sardinia, and that the people of Phocaea, when besieged, embarked on their ships and sailed away (most of them) to Corsica,[4] while the people of Teos made for Thrace, where they founded Abdera.

---

[1] See Hdt. vi. 41 and 119, vii. 136, etc. Even the mad Cambyses was capable of generous impulses. Doubtless such qualities coexisted with terrible callousness towards human suffering. As for the painful subject of the ever-present Greek traitor, one need only think of Eretria and Thermopylae and Marathon and Aegina and Thebes and Pausanias and Themistocles and Miltiades and many other names.

[2] Sometimes, he adds, they reversed the process. See Tacitus, *Germ.* xxii.

[3] Thales is said to have persuaded the Milesians not to aid Croesus. But Miletus was in alliance with Lydia, and we hear of Thales himself aiding Croesus by damming up the river Halys in order to allow him to pass over.

[4] See p. 152 as to the Phocaeans at Alalia and Elea.

Cyrus meantime had attacked Babylonia. The great Nebucadnezar had died in 562, and had been succeeded by several Babylonian kings, the fourth of whom, Nabonid (whose regal title seems to have been Labynetus), ruled in great state at Babylon, where the Jews with Daniel were still in captivity. He had made alliance with Amasis of Egypt, Croesus of Lydia, and Polycrates of Samos against the usurper Cyrus. The conquest of Babylonia by Cyrus seems to have lasted about ten years. In 538 he succeeded in capturing Babylon by diverting the Euphrates.[1] Not content with the mighty empire that he had now under his rule, he made an expedition into what is now Russian Turkestan against a Scythian tribe, the Massagetae. In this remote land, near the Aral lake, he fell in battle (529). The queen of the Massagetae is said to have placed his head in a bowl of blood and bade it drink its fill.[2] Cambyses, his son, increased the Persian Empire by the conquest of Egypt.

During the first thirty-four years of the period we are considering in this chapter (560–500) Egypt had enjoyed independence and prosperity under King Aahmes (Amasis), whose friendship with the Greeks has already been mentioned. He had conquered Cyprus and had formed an alliance with Polycrates, the powerful despot of Samos, who, with a strong fleet of fifty-oared ships of war, had defied Cyrus and Harpagus. All that Polycrates undertook seemed to prosper. His court, at which the poets Ibycus and Anacreon lived, and which Amasis possibly honoured with his presence, rivalled the fame of that of Periander or Peisistratus, and under his rule the city of Samos was furnished with its splendid harbour and the great temple of Hera and many other magnificent buildings, as well as with the celebrated Samian aqueduct, with its tunnel of seven furlongs. But the envy of the gods was aroused, and Amasis, foreseeing the ruin of the Samian tyrant (as all readers of Schiller's fine ballad know), renounced his friendship. Perhaps the fact lying beneath the story of the Ring is that the kings quarrelled; for we hear that Polycrates sent forty of his penteconters (which mutinied and never arrived) to aid Cambyses in his attack on Egypt. Not long afterwards (523), having apparently broken again with Cambyses, he fell into an ambuscade laid by the satrap of Sardis, who crucified him. Before Cambyses reached Egypt King Amasis had died (525). His son,

[1] Hdt. i. 191. The Belshazzar of Daniel is either Nabonid himself or (as inscriptions seem to prove) his son, who was acting as governor of Babylon.
[2] See note at end of this chapter.

Psamtik III, was defeated near Pelusium, and Memphis was then captured and the whole of Egypt and Cyrene submitted to the Persians. But, incensed at his failure to conquer Aethiopia, Cambyses vented his fury in acts of sacrilege (such as mutilating the corpse of Amasis and stabbing the sacred bull Apis) and in other deeds so indescribably cruel and foolish that one is forced to believe that he was insane. One assassination, that of his brother Bardyia, or Smerdis, who was regent of some of the eastern provinces of the empire, caused the fall of the tyrant; for a false Smerdis, one of the Magi, named Gaumata, pretending to be the murdered prince, proclaimed himself king, and Cambyses hastened homeward, and somewhere in Syria either met his death by an accident, as related by Herodotus, or committed suicide, as is stated by the Darius inscription at Behistun.

The false Smerdis, keeping himself out of sight in his palace to avoid detection, held power for eight months so firmly that, according to the Darius inscription, 'no Persian or Mede had the courage to oppose him.' But seven nobles, who, by means of one of the women of the royal harem, Herodotus says, discovered that he possessed no ears and was a Mede and a Magian whom Cambyses had thus punished for some offence, slew the pretender and a great number of the Magi. One of these nobles, Darius, the son of the satrap Hystaspes, was elected king. Herodotus gives a graphic description of how it was arranged that the man should be king whose horse neighed first, and how the groom of Darius won the royal crown for his master. Some scholars, however, reject the story as childish, and assert that Hystaspes[1] was the legitimate heir of Cyrus. The probability is that the false Smerdis was a pretender put forward by the party of the Medes and Magi (who, although Persian priests, were of Median extraction), and that his overthrow meant the triumph of the Persian royal house of the Achaemenidae, to which Darius (as Xerxes asserts in Hdt. vii. 11) unquestionably belonged; and Darius strengthened the tie by marrying Atossa, a daughter of Cyrus, who had been Cambyses' queen.

Darius began to reign in 521, and reigned for thirty-six years. After suppressing revolts that broke out more than once in Media and Babylonia and forced him to capture Babylon twice, he confirmed the Persian sovereignty in his western empire by placing Phrygia, Lydia, and Ionia under satraps, to whom the tyrants of the Greek cities of the mainland paid tribute and

---

[1] Hystaspes was, according to Herodotus, 'governor of Persia' (iii. 70). In the Behistun inscription he is called a general of his son Darius (!) and a satrap of Parthia.

furnished troops and ships as vassals of the Great King. Samos, too, which under Polycrates had defied Darius, was conquered and 'netted' and given over to the brother of Polycrates, who had won the friendship of the young Darius when he was in Egypt with Cambyses.[1]

But it was not only in war that the empire of Darius was great. It attained a wealth and a magnificence of Oriental civilization which in ancient times were probably never equalled.[2] The gold *staters* of King Darius, known as 'Darics' (probably the 'dram' of Ezra and Nehemiah), circulated throughout Hellas. The chief cities were connected by carefully kept roads, and there was a system of royal mails carried by relays of horses and couriers (*angareia*). The 'royal road' between Sardis and Susa, some 1500 miles in length and with about a hundred stations, was traversed by pedestrians in about ninety days, and by a post or courier, of course, in far less time. (Herodotus, who describes it fully, probably travelled by this route.)

After he had reigned about eight years Darius, it is said, conceived a desire to punish the Scythians for their invasion of Media, which had taken place about a century before (see pp. 174, 176). Whether this was his real object or whether his purpose was the conquest of Thrace and the acquisition of the gold-mines of this country and of Dacia is questioned. Herodotus had far better opportunities than we have of learning the truth, and there can be little doubt that the professed object was what he asserts it to have been, but there is no less doubt that what he describes as a disastrous failure resulted in the establishment of Persian supremacy in Thrace, and even in Macedonia, for the next fifteen years or so.

As for the story that Herodotus gives us of this Scythian expedition, it certainly contains a good deal that sounds impossible, especially in regard to the distances traversed in a comparatively short time; but the chronicler himself had visited Scythia (he had been, for instance, four days' journey up the river Bug, and evidently knew the Dnieper and its sturgeon), and had collected an immense amount of information about the country, as well as reports, more or less founded on facts, about the nations further north, and what he relates has a deep interest for everyone except the purely scientific historian. He tells us that Darius collected an army of 700,000

[1] For this story see Hdt. iii. 139; and for the process of 'driving' or 'netting' a hostile country see Hdt. iii. 149, vi. 31.

[2] See Hdt. iii. 89 *ff.* for an account of the revenues of Darius from his immense empire of twenty satrapies.

men and a fleet of 600 Greek ships. The ships, or some of them, he sent up the Danube, and ordered a bridge to be thrown across the river above the delta. His army crossed the Bosporus by another bridge, constructed by the Samian Mandrocles (who afterwards gave to the Heraion at Samos a picture of the passage of the troops, with Darius seated on his throne in the foreground), and two marble pillars with inscriptions in Greek and Assyrian were erected. One of these Herodotus seems to have seen later at Byzantium.

Having reached the Danube, Darius left the Ionian Greeks in charge of the bridge, and, giving them a leathern thong in which sixty knots had been tied, he bade them untie one every day, and if he had not returned when the last had been untied they were to sail home. He then set out 'with all speed,' and, following the retreating Scythians, marched as far as the Maeotic lake (Sea of Azov) and the Don, and even perhaps the Volga! But the Scythians doubled and re-entered their own country, and baffled and harassed the returning Persians; and some of them, stealing ahead, reached the Danube and urged the Greeks to destroy the bridge. This proposal was strongly seconded by Miltiades, who was now, as we have seen, the Greek 'tyrant' of the Chersonese, and had been obliged to join the expedition. But when Histiaeus of Miletus opposed it, saying that their existence as tyrants depended wholly on Persia, the Greek leaders decided (to the great disdain of the Scythians, who called them the 'faithfullest of slaves') only to break the bridge for a distance of a bow-shot from the Scythian side, and to await the return of Darius, though the sixtieth knot had long ago been untied. At length the Persians arrived. 'It was night, and their terror when they found the bridge broken was great. . . . But there was in the army of Darius an Egyptian, who had a louder voice than any other man in the world. He was bid by Darius to stand at the water's edge and call Histiaeus the Milesian, who, hearing him at the very first summons, brought across the fleet. . . . Thus the Persians escaped from Scythia.' And Darius, having reached Sestos, took the bulk of his army across the Hellespont and returned to Sardis. But, although Herodotus seems to regard the return of the king as a flight rather than a dignified withdrawal after a successful campaign, 80,000 men were left behind in Europe under the command of Megabazus, who 'subdued to the dominion of the king all the towns and all the nations of these parts.' For some time the whole of Thrace and the islands of the North Aegean remained in the possession of Persia, and tribute was probably exacted from the

Macedonian king.[1] After the revolt of Ionia in 499 the Thracians (whom Herodotus calls 'the most powerful people in the world, except, of course, the Indians') threw off the Persian yoke, and were forthwith invaded by the Scythians, who succeeded even in driving Miltiades out of the Chersonese.

The fourth book of Herodotus consists mainly of his account of Scythia and the Scythians. Whatever may be its value from the standpoint of the historical critic, it is very fascinating. Much that he recounts is founded on his own experiences and may be accepted as trustworthy, and as for the stories that he retails about the fabled lands beyond the Tanaïs (Don) – about the one-eyed Arimaspi and the treasure of sacred gold guarded by griffins (recalling the Rheingold and the dragons of the Siegfried legend), and about the Hyperboreans and the 'Perpherees,' those maiden-messengers who brought (possibly from Britain) gifts packed in wheat-straw to the shrine of Artemis in Delos, and died there, and were honoured as deities with the hair-offerings of Delian youths and maidens[2] – all such things he merely repeats on hearsay for whatever human interest they may possess, and he especially warns us that much of it was derived from a very weird person, namely, a poet and traveller named Aristeas, a kind of 'spectreman,' as Herodotus calls him, who was said to have vanished on several occasions and to have reappeared after the lapse of years – once, indeed, after the lapse of over three centuries; having recounted which fact, Herodotus uses his favourite formula and allows that 'enough has been said concerning Aristeas.'

The geography of Herodotus is a subject too large to discuss fully here. I must content myself with one or two of his remarks. 'I cannot but laugh,' he says, 'when I see numbers of persons drawing maps of the world . . . and making the ocean-stream running all round the earth, and the earth itself an exact circle, as if described with a pair of compasses, with Europe and Asia of just the same size.' Doubtless here he is making a thrust at Hecataeus, his predecessor in history-writing, who composed a text to the map that Anaximander made of the world (see p. 229). He then proceeds to give his own ideas as to the shape and relative size of the three continents, and asserts that Europe is by far the largest – so much larger that he 'cannot conceive why three different names, and women's names especially,

---

[1] For the fate of one Persian embassy demanding tribute see Hdt. v. 17.

[2] Hdt. iv. 33. It reads like the legend of some St. Walpurga. Herodotus himself saw their graves 'on the left as one enters the precinct of Artemis.'

Fig. 53  Tomb of Cyrus

Fig. 54  The Olympieion, Athens

should have been given to what is really only one continent.' In one point at least he was right. 'As for Libya,' he says, 'we know it to be washed on all sides by the sea, except where it is attached to Asia.' He gives as proof the circumnavigation of Africa by Pharaoh Necho's Phoenician sailors,[1] but he rejects just the one bit of evidence that for us is conclusive. 'On their return,' he says, 'they declared (and I for my part do not believe this, though perhaps others may) that in sailing round Libya they had the sun upon their right hand' – *i.e.* on looking towards the noonday sun the east was to their right. Another attempt to circumnavigate Africa was made, says Herodotus, by a nephew of Darius, who was condemned to death for some crime, but respited on condition that he should 'sail round Libya.' He seems to have got as far as the Guinea coast, where he discovered a 'dwarfish race,' but his ships 'refused to go any further' (perhaps on account of the south trade-winds), and he returned and (like Walter Raleigh) was put to death in execution of the former sentence.

### Note on the Tombs of Cyrus and Darius

(See Figs. 53 and 73)

The story related by Herodotus about the death of Cyrus seems inconsistent with the fact that his tomb (a cenotaph?) was to be seen at Pasargadae, where Alexander the Great visited it – and punished severely those who had pillaged it. There still exists at Pasargadae (if the ruins in the valley of the Murghab are really the remains of the ancient capital of the Achaemenid princes) a square building on an eminence amidst desolate scenery which may be this celebrated tomb of Cyrus, once surrounded by luxuriant parks. It is now called the 'Tomb of Solomon's Mother.' Here there have been discovered many stones inscribed with the name of Cyrus, and also a relief of a four-winged figure surmounted by a curious structure like an Egyptian headdress – possibly a portrait of Cyrus set up by Cambyses. Darius abandoned Pasargadae and built, sixty miles further down the valley, the magnificent city of Persepolis, called by the Greeks 'the richest city under the sun' – until Alexander plundered its treasury, where he found 120,000 talents of gold. On the site of Persepolis enormous ruins still exist of the architectural works and sculptures of Darius and Xerxes. There is a huge pylon or portal with winged bulls, and some of the hundred columns of the

---

[1] See p. 171.

immense Hall of Xerxes, and the great flight of steps that led up to his palace, which, it is said, Alexander set on fire, incited by the notorious Athenian courtesan Thaïs. On the side of the Royal Mount near Persepolis are the tombs of Darius and of some of the later Persian kings, as well as many monuments of the Sassanidae, who ruled Persia during the Roman Empire and until Persia fell into the hands of the Mahometans. The tomb of Darius is cut out of the solid rock in the middle of a perpendicular precipice (Fig. 73). At Behistun in Media, between Babylon and Ecbatana, on the face of the rock in a precipitous gully there may still be seen the sculptured relief that records, with inscriptions in three Oriental languages, the victories over revolted provinces which Darius gained in the first three years of his reign.

SECTION A: POETS AND PHILOSOPHERS (560–500)

How far the political state of a country influences art is a question difficult to answer. Perhaps it might be possible to discover some apparent connection between the events related in the last chapter and the fact that in the Hellenic world during this period, although many magnificent temples were erected and sculpture was beginning to show signs of the coming glory, as far as we can judge from surviving fragments no really great poetry was written – nothing at all comparable with that of Sappho or Alcaeus – while during the next century or so more great poetry, as well as great sculpture and architecture and oratory and philosophy, was produced by one single city of Greece than we can perhaps find in any other century of the world's history.

**The Poets**

At Athens, as we have seen, the first beginnings of the Attic drama were made, during the rule of the Peisistratidae, by Thespis, who introduced dialogue into the rude choruses of vintage festivals. He was followed by Choerilus and Phrynichus and Pratinas and others, by whom these Dionysiac performances were developed into drama. All these three must have written plays of no mean value, for they contended not unsuccessfully with Aeschylus himself in his younger days. Of their works we know scarcely anything. Choerilus wrote something like 150 pieces. Phrynichus gained a tragic victory in 511, and some eighteen years later had the misfortune to write a drama representing the capture of Miletus by the

Persians (494), which so painfully affected the Athenians that he was fined 1000 drachmae. Sixteen years later (478) he gained the prize with the *Phoenissae*. In this play he gave a description of the battle of Salamis which Aeschylus is said to have imitated in his *Persae*.[1] But we are here encroaching on what belongs to the next century.

Of other Greek poets, or verse-writers, of the period 560–500 the most notable are Theognis, Xenophanes, Ibycus, Anacreon, and Simonides of Ceos.

It may be remembered that one of the cities which fell under the rule of a tyrant was Megara. About the year 640 Theagenes overthrew the aristocratic party and held power for some time; but he was ejected, and for the next century the state suffered from endless conflicts between the nobles and the people, in the midst of which troubles the Athenians, at Solon's instigation, wrested Salamis from Megara, and even for a time occupied her port, Nisaea. Among the nobles banished during a temporary supremacy of the democratic party was Theognis. He seems to have spent many years in exile in Sicily and Euboea (*c.* 550), but to have returned and lived at Megara until the Persian peril was imminent; for in his poem he prays Apollo to 'keep far from this city the savage host of the Medes.' Of the 1368 lines in elegiac metre which are attributed to Theognis (collected about 400 B.C.), about half – those addressed to a young nobleman, Cyrnus – are perhaps authentic. They pour the bitterest contempt on the 'bad' and 'cowardly' (*kakoi, deiloi*) – cant terms among the aristocrats for the working classes – and call upon the 'good' and 'brave' (*agathoi, esthloi*) to trample on the neck of their hated inferiors and to keep themselves from the contamination of the common herd. Theognis laments that Megara is still the same but her people are all changed, that for the sake of gold the noble deigns to wed the daughter of the vile plebeian, and that those who once were the good are now base and vile. Historically all this is of interest. It seems also to have been thought valuable educationally, for it was much used by schoolmasters and by lecturing Sophists; but regarded as poetry it is very poor stuff, about on a level with Tupper's *Proverbial Philosophy*, or even below it, being tainted with virulence and a maudlin pessimism.[2]

---

[1] See p. 339. In Aristophanes' *Frogs* (1296) this charge seems rebutted.

[2] He steals, and spoils in stealing, the well-known saying, which King Midas learnt from the god Silenus, and which Sophocles used with such pathetic effect, that 'The happiest lot is never to have been born – or to return as soon as possible thither whence we came.'

Of a very different character are the verses of Xenophanes. He is, as we shall see, more important as a thinker than as a poet, but the vigorous lines in which he expressed some of his convictions are very notable not only for their thoughts but also for their form. In his chief poem (*Peri Physeōs*, 'On Nature'), of which fragments survive, he inveighs against the popular anthropomorphic conception of Deity, and especially against Homer and Hesiod for attributing human weaknesses and follies to the gods. 'God,' he says, 'is wholly Sight and wholly Thought and wholly Hearing, and with no effort He rules all things by the working of His mind. . . . There is one God, supreme among divinities and men, like unto mortals neither in body nor in thought.' The Aethiop, he says, makes his gods black, the Thracian makes his blue-eyed and blond, and if horses and oxen and lions had hands and could write and do handiwork as men, they would have formed conceptions and made images of gods in their own likeness. We possess also fragments of his elegiacs, in which are found many wise and manly sayings about self-restraint and the true enjoyment of life, and a fine passage in which he contrasts the glory won by Olympic victors with that which wisdom confers on a man. 'If anyone should win by swiftness of foot, or in the pentathlon, there where is the precinct of Zeus by the streams of the Pisa, or else by wrestling, or by being skilled in painful boxing, or that formidable contest that they call the pancratium, he would be granted a conspicuous front seat at the games, and food would be given him by the city from public funds and a gift such as to be an heirloom for ever; or e'en if he won the victory by means of his horses, and not by his own strength, he would gain all these things . . . but he would not deserve them as I do; for better than the strength of man or of horses is our [human] wisdom.' Xenophanes was born at the Ionian city Colophon, but left it (some say, banished on account of his heretical poem) at the age of twenty-five. In the fragment which tells us this he says that he is already ninety-two years old, having 'tossed about through Hellenic lands' for sixty-seven years In another fragment he asks himself: 'How old wast thou when the Mede arrived?' It seems probable, therefore, that he left Colophon on account of the Persian invasion under Harpagus (*c.* 545), when the Phocaeans abandoned their city and sailed to Corsica. We have already seen (see p. 152) that he possibly joined these Phocaeans in founding Elea, where he is said to have lived in very modest circumstances to about his hundredth year. We shall hear more of him as a philosopher.

At the semi-Oriental court of Samos we find the poets Ibycus and

Anacreon (c. 550–522). Ibycus, a native of Rhegium, is said to have been tutor to Polycrates. From the few lines that we possess of his voluptuously imaginative poetry, and from the fact that he is called by Suidas the 'maddest of all love-poets,' one may infer what was his influence on the youthful prince. But it should be remarked that, as far as one can judge from a few lines, there was in Ibycus (as also in the genuine Anacreon) intense passion without any of that effeminate sentimentality which is found in later Greek love-poetry. His conception of Eros is that of a strong and terrible deity, 'like the Thracian Boreas blazing with lightning,' or of an insidious and mighty wizard: 'From under dark eyebrows shooting forth ravishing glances with enchantments of every kind, he casteth me into the immeasurable toils of the Cyprian goddess.' He is said also to have composed epic poems similar to those of the Cyclic writers. The story of his death at the hands of robbers and of the detection of the crime has become well known through Schiller's fine ballad, *The Cranes of Ibycus*.[1]

Anacreon was a native of Teos, in Ionia. When the city was taken by Harpagus (544) he migrated to Abdera, in Thrace. Thence he came to Samos, and lived there until the crucifixion of Polycrates in 523, when Hipparchus is said to have sent a trireme to bring him to Athens. Here he spent some years, but probably returned to Abdera or Teos. He died two years after the battle of Salamis, at the age of eighty-five, choked by a grape-stone. The Athenians erected a statue of him (seen by Pausanias) in the characteristic guise of a drunken old man. Much that passed under the name of Anacreon is evidently the product of 'Anacreontic' poets of later times. Some of these Anacreontic odes are exceedingly clever and pretty, such, for instance, as the *Address to a Painter*, which was adduced by Lessing, in his *Laocoön*, as an example of the kind of pictorial description that poetry should *not* attempt. It is nevertheless very charming, and ends in a most ingenious conceit. 'Come, good painter,' exclaims the poet, 'paint my absent mistress as I bid thee.' He then gives exact details – the soft black locks, the ivory brow, the milk and roses of the cheeks, the marble neck and bust; but, as if feeling the uselessness of all such word-painting, he bids the painter stop, and, turning to the picture created by his own imagination, he calls upon it to speak and answer him. It is exceedingly clever and pretty. But this is not how Homer and Shakespeare make us realize the beauty of

---

[1] Schiller imagines him journeying from Rhegium to Corinth to take part in the Isthmian Games.

Helen and Juliet. Probably, however, we form quite a wrong idea of
Anacreon's poetry when we associate him with such delicately worded
trifles, for in fragments of what is undoubtedly his work we find a very different style and some quite different conceptions. Thus, like Ibycus, he gives
us a picture of Love (Eros) which offers a very striking contrast to the
winged, roguish, rose-fettered urchin of the Anacreontics. 'Like a smith,
with mighty hammer,' he says, 'Eros smote me and plunged me in a wintry
torrent.' This is the Eros of the older poets and sculptors, the first-born of
the gods of whom Hesiod sings, the strong-limbed, manly Eros of
Praxiteles, not the chubby little Cupid with his toy bow and quiver whom
we meet so often in Hellenistic and Roman art.

One generally associates Simonides of Ceos (556–467) with Marathon
and Thermopylae. But while he was a boy Croesus was still reigning, and
he was already nearly thirty years of age when Peisistratus died. About 525
he was invited by Hipparchus to leave his home on the island of Ceos and
to come to Athens, where Anacreon was then living. When Hipparchus was
murdered by Harmodius and Aristogeiton he went to Thessaly, probably
to the court of the Aleuadae, the princes of Larissa, whose submission to
the Persians probably occasioned his return to Athens. Here he became
intimate with Themistocles and was held in great honour for his learning
and poetical genius. Four years after the battle of Salamis, when he was
eighty years old, he gained the prize at the Great Dionysia – the fifty-sixth
public prize for poetry, as he tells us, that he had won. Soon afterwards,
together with his nephew, the poet Bacchylides, he went to Syracuse, where,
at the court of Hiero, he met Aeschylus and Pindar. He died at Syracuse,
aged eighty-nine, in 467. Thus his life extended almost from the age of
Solon to that of Pericles, and he was a contemporary for a few years of
both Thales and Socrates. In considering him one is therefore obliged either
to anticipate or to defer considerably. He seems to have produced a great
amount of poetry in his long life – hymns to the gods, funeral eulogies and
elegies, triumphal odes, dithyrambs, and odes in honour of victors at the
games. In such odes he, as also his nephew Bacchylides, had a powerful
rival in Pindar, by whose sublimity of imagination and majesty of language, it is said, they were both eclipsed. Nevertheless some of the fragments of his poetry that survive are as fine as almost anything in Pindar,
and the subject is certainly sometimes on a far higher level than that of the
ordinary Pindaric ode. In an encomium on those who fell with Leonidas
he says: 'Splendid was the fortune of those who died at Thermopylae and

glorious their fate. Their tomb is an altar; instead of wails there is remembrance, and lamentation is changed into praise; such a shroud neither decay shall e'er destroy, nor time, that conquereth all. This resting-place of brave men hath received to dwell within it the glory of Hellas.' The metres of these odes are probably such as had been used from an early age in musical compositions. They seem to be conditioned by various musical rhythms (Doric, Aeolic, Lydian, etc.), and to be, as Horace says with reference to Pindar, free from all law,[1] except that the poem has certain divisions (strophes, antistrophes, epodes, etc.). Simonides is remembered chiefly on account of the famous lines, quoted by Herodotus, that were engraved on the monuments at Thermopylae.[2] Herodotus does not mention Simonides as their author, but Cicero and other writers do. Another couplet, on the Athenians who fought at Marathon, is attributed to Simonides by the rhetorician Aristides, and some lines of his beginning 'I am the bravest of beasts' may have been composed as the inscription for the stone lion which, as Herodotus tells us, was set up at Thermopylae in memory of Leonidas. Earlier in life (c. 506) he wrote, it is said, an epitaph for the Athenians who fell in the Chalcidian war. Simonides is said to have invented, or introduced, the letters eta, omega, xi, upsilon: ē, ō, x, u.

## The Philosophers

Some of the older Greek philosophers, such as Xenophanes, Parmenides, and Empedocles, may be classed also among the poets, and others, such as Thales and Pythagoras, would perhaps be conceded a like honour if their writings had survived. The incomparable insight into the life of things which distinguishes Greek thought from what often usurps the name of philosophy was due mainly to the poetical spirit that animated it. As Plato tells us, the truths which are the object of the 'lover of wisdom' cannot be

---

[1] Of the forty-four extant odes of Pindar only two have any decided metrical similarity, and these two are addressed to the same person and probably form one consecutive piece.

[2] Thus translated by Rawlinson:

> Here did four thousand men from Pelops' land
> Against three hundred myriads bravely stand;

and

> Go, stranger, and to Lacedaemon tell
> That here, obeying her behests, we fell.

learnt in the same way as scientific facts, but only by the help of our imaginative faculties and by contemplation; and his statement is confirmed by Aristotle himself, who says that 'poetry is more philosophical and more worthy of serious regard than history.'

In the Greek thinkers of the period that we are examining there are noticeable three distinct methods of regarding the universe. The Ionic philosophers, fixing their gaze on the visible order of things, endeavoured to discover the prime element or self-created and self-moving elementary substance to which the material universe owes its origin and existence. The Eleatic school, of which Xenophanes was the founder, sought the one true existence behind appearances, denying the reality, or even the very existence, of the material world. Pythagoras taught that the life of things – that which alone gives them any true existence – is the relation that they bear to the one life of all (as numbers to unity), and that their nature and their reality as objects of the sensible universe depend on the relation that they bear (like numbers) to one another. Thus, all things being bound together into a cosmos by proportion, the universe is of the nature of harmony. To give any full and systematic account of the theories of these early Greek thinkers is here impossible, but if the essential characteristics of the three schools are kept in mind the following facts will perhaps fall into place and offer a fairly intelligible picture.

Thales of Miletus (c. 636–546) was the first of the Ionic 'Physicists,' and is regarded as the father of Greek philosophy, as well as the chief of the Seven Sages. Herodotus asserts that he was of Phoenician origin, and possibly the Semitic strain may account for genius in his case, as it has done in others. When Thales was still a young man, Miletus, then 'a rich and powerful city' and the mother of many colonies, fell under the rule of the tyrant Thrasybulus (see p. 160), the friend and Machiavellian adviser of Periander; and it remained under his rule for more than forty years. Thales is said to have visited Egypt and to have acquired there the knowledge of geometry and astronomical calculation which enabled him to foretell the eclipse[1] that put an end to the battle between Astyages of Media and the Lydian king Alyattes (585). Possibly he also learnt in Egypt a certain

---

[1] The Chaldeans, from whom possibly (but not probably) the Egyptians learnt their astronomy, are said to have registered, or calculated, eclipses from about 720. They are said to have believed the world to have existed for 172,000 years. But the Indian sages claim an antiquity of two million years for their astronomical tables, and doubtless the most ancient names of the constellations are of Indian origin.

amount of geology – enough to make him a 'sedimentarist' and a believer in water as the prime element – for Herodotus, who also was in Egypt, gives us a long description of the formation of the country by alluvial deposit, which he held to have been going on for some 12,000 years. Miletus was harassed a good deal by Alyattes, but under Croesus the Milesians (almost alone of the Ionian Greeks) retained their independence, and Thales is said to have advised his fellow-citizens not to aid the Lydian king against Cyrus – advice which probably saved the city from being taken by Harpagus. But the anxiety caused by the advance of Persia is shown by the fact that Thales tried to persuade the Ionians to form a 'confederation,' with Teos as capital. It must have been soon after this that he died.

Whether Thales wrote anything is not known. What we know of his doctrines we learn from Plato, Aristotle, and other writers. The fact that he chose water as the prime substance should be connected closely with the fact that he conceived such prime substance to be in perpetual motion, and mind, or intelligence, to be present wherever there was motion;[1] and, as motion exists everywhere in the universe, he asserted that 'all is full of gods,' and that even the kinetic power of the magnet and of amber proved their possession of what he called a 'soulless soul' (or 'lifeless vitality'). Cicero, indeed, says that Thales spoke of the 'Mind of the Universe' as being equivalent to 'God,' but it is probable that his theories were unconnected with religious ideas – that is, that they were entirely materialistic and without any assumption of a spiritual or intellectual 'first cause,' such as was proclaimed later by Anaxagoras. Consequently, in order to account for movement he was obliged to conceive his prime substance as self-moving, and, indeed, self-created, and was thus driven to face the same difficulties that all materialists are forced to encounter. Some writer has remarked that 'a lake formed by the Maeander now covers the native city of the man who taught that everything comes from and returns to water.' The story of his falling down a well into his favourite element while stargazing is perhaps a playful invention.

In connection with Thales it may be interesting to raise the question how far, if at all, Greek philosophy was indebted to the philosophy of the East. It is indubitable that Thales and Pythagoras, and perhaps other early Greek philosophers, visited Egypt, and perhaps other Eastern lands, and it seems possible that, as far as their external form is concerned, some of the

---

[1] *Cf.* 'And the Spirit of God moved upon the face of the waters.' The theory of Thales is like that of the modern Monist.

doctrines of Greek thinkers, such as that of 'transmigration,' had an Oriental or Egyptian origin,[1] and that the belief in the immortality of the soul, which we find so strongly asserted by Socrates, was not evolved by Greek thought, but introduced from Eastern sources; moreover, in Vedanta philosophy there are doctrines of 'abstraction' and of the triune nature of the Deity (as Intelligence, Matter, and Multitude) which have a singular resemblance to the Socratic doctrine of the 'release and purification of the body' and to the Monad and Triad doctrine of Pythagoras, and others that closely resemble the Eleatic denial of the reality of the sensible world; but it is surely not impossible that the human mind is so constructed that it may (perhaps must) arrive at similar formulae; or, if it be true that Greece accepted certain forms of Eastern thought, it is no less true that Hellenic genius reinspired these forms with a new life so that they are as truly original creations as *Hamlet* or *Faust*.

The human mind seems generally to find no insuperable difficulty in forming a vague conception of an inert prime element (more or less immaterial) existing from all eternity; but for the conception of a cosmos, an ordered, differentiated universe, or even of 'matter' itself, it is necessary to account for the ordering force, and one instinctively rejects the 'self-moved' material prime element of Thales and the 'self-moved' atoms of Democritus, of which we shall hear later. This difficulty accounts for the creative Love (Eros) of Hesiod, the 'love and hate of the atoms' of Empedocles, the *Nous* (Mind) of Anaxagoras, and all other such attempts to visualize and personify the mysterious power which manifests itself in motion and life, and it is not surprising that Anaximander (*c.* 610–545), a contemporary and fellow-citizen, perhaps a disciple, of Thales, should have attempted to go a little further toward the realm of the Immaterial in his search for a first cause of motion. He is said to have been the first Greek philosopher who wrote a prose work. Of this work (entitled, as usual, *About Nature*) nothing but a few quotations survive, but they prove that the author proclaimed as the prime element, or rather the first 'principle' (for he was the first to use the word *archē*), what he called 'the infinite' or 'unconditioned' (*to apeiron*), by which he probably meant matter not exactly in a chaotic state, but with its elements (*stoicheia*) not yet differentiated.[2] But

---

[1] Herodotus asserts this (ii. 123), but no proof has been found of it in Egyptian monuments.

[2] See Cicero, *De Nat. Deor.* i. Plato uses *to apeiron* for primal 'matter' regarded merely as a passive, potential, formless existence – and this seems practically what Anaximander meant.

*Fig. 55  Black-figured vases, c. 700–500 (See List of Illustrations and Note D)*

his *archē* is really quite as materialistic as that of Thales, and is less conceivable. Instead of 'self-movement' he has to imagine 'counteracting forces,' such as heat and cold, dryness and moisture, in order to produce a cosmos. His theory that living things were evolved out of damp matter and that men as well as all other animals were at first fish-like has affinity to modern morphological doctrines. He is said to have invented the sun-dial (though Herodotus credits the Babylonians with the invention) and to have made a map of the world and an astronomical globe. The map is said to have been engraved on a brass tablet, and was perhaps the very one which (*c.* 499) Aristagoras of Miletus took over to show the Spartans the extent of the Persian Empire, and for which Hecataeus wrote a text. A third Milesian, Anaximenes, proclaimed as the *archē* an illimitable element of the nature of air – the life-breath, as it were, of the universe. This seems a relapse; but we know too little of his doctrines to be certain. The earth he believed to float sustained in the midst of air, and he is said to have been the first (Greek?) to teach that the moon's light came from the sun. If, as it is said, he taught Anaxagoras (born in 500) and was himself a disciple of Anaximander, he must have lived to a great age.

In connection with these Physicists may be mentioned Heracleitus of Ephesus, for, although he lived somewhat later (*c.* 540–470), and although his genius was of a strikingly original, imaginative, and independent character (justifying his proud remark, 'I have gone to no teacher but myself,' and perhaps even justifying the gift of his own book to the temple of Artemis as the most precious offering he could make), nevertheless the fact that he accepted a 'prime element' makes it convenient to class him with the other Ionian philosophers.

During most of the life of Heracleitus Ephesus was under the sovereignty of Persia and the rule of Greek tyrants. But he evidently lived to see the day of liberation, for in his work *On Nature* he pours bitter disdain on the Ephesian democracy for having banished his friend Hermodorus (who, by the way, some twenty-six years later helped the Roman *decemviri* to draw up their Twelve Tables). This would seem to prove that he wrote the book after the recovery of Sestos by the Athenians and the liberation of Ionia from the Persian yoke (478).

To judge from the 136 short fragments of his writings that survive Heracleitus expressed himself in very trenchant aphorisms. The following are some of them: 'War is the father of all things' (*i.e.* all things are evolved by antagonistic forces); 'No man can wade twice in the same stream' (*i.e.* material objects are always changing); 'The wisest of men is an ape to the gods'; 'Life is the death of gods, death their life'; 'Men are mortal gods, gods immortal men'; 'A man's character is his destiny'; 'Learning teaches not wisdom.' In connection with this last aphorism he added: 'Otherwise learning would have taught Hesiod and Pythagoras and Xenophanes and Hecataeus.' Still more strongly he expressed himself about Homer and Archilochus, saying that they 'ought to be whipped.' Such language is intelligible enough, so that probably it was the abstruseness of his doctrines rather than his words that won him the title 'the Obscure.' Even Socrates confessed that there were many things in the book of Heracleitus that needed a 'Delian diver' to bring them up from their obscure depths.

Heracleitus held fire to be the prime element. Possibly he was led to the choice by Oriental (Zoroastrian) influence. But by 'fire' he meant a subtle, fiery, aetherial substance rather than flame. Of this self-kindled, ever-vibrating fiery aether he conceived the human soul and the soul of the universe, and even Deity itself, to consist.[1] Doubtless fire, or heat, was believed by him (as it is, or was until lately, believed by modern science) to be caused by, or to *be*, vibration or undulation, and it was evidently as a most striking form, or symbol, of perpetual and inconceivably rapid motion that he chose it, for all his philosophy was founded on the axiom that there is no true existence except in motion, in mutation, development, action, transition. 'All is in flux' (*panta rhei*) was his fundamental dogma. There is no such thing as a permanent state of being. Being (existence) consists in change. Nothing exists except in merging its identity in something else. Thus, 'Death is life, life is death,' and 'Sleep and waking are the same,' or (if I may slightly change his form of expression and put some of his aphorisms into the words of three great modern poets), 'There is no Death! What seems so is transition,'[2] 'To sleep is to wake,' and 'Living are the dead, and I am the apparition, I the spectre.' Such doctrines, so unintelligible to the many, probably credited him with the obscurity and melancholy which have attached themselves to his memory.

Of the life and poems of Xenophanes I have already spoken. His

[1] Anticipating by some 2400 years the assertion of the modern Monist, who tells us that the only possible God is 'the sum total of the vibrations of the Ether.' Socrates was accused by Aristophanes (of course falsely) of having enthroned 'Aetherial Vortex' in the place of Zeus.

[2] In the *Phaedo* Socrates (or Plato) speaks of transition from life to death and from death to life in reference to the immortality of the soul.

philosophy offers a very striking contrast to that of Heracleitus, and forms a part of the first rude foundation on which was reared the Ideal Theory of Plato.

Heracleitus asserted that nothing truly exists except in so far as it is in motion, mutation, transition – that is, as a link in the endless chain of cause and effect. Xenophanes, on the contrary, asserted that all motion and mutation and transition, as well as the things that they affect, are merely appearances, the multitudinous phenomena of the senses (*ta polla*), which are not existent except so far as they stand in relation to the one eternal and immutable Reality, the 'unmoved source of motion' and the only source of all being. In his poetry, as we have seen, he gives this immutable and eternal Reality the name of God. As a philosopher he calls it the One – an expression used also by Pythagoras and by Plato. But though he held that things of the senses (the Many) are non-existent in their variety and their mutations and their relation to one another, he asserted that they exist truly by virtue of their relation to the One. Thus the keystone of the Eleatic school is 'All things One' rather than 'The One *and* the Many', which was the formula of Platonic philosophy; and we should regard the creed of Xenophanes as pantheistic rather than dualistic – that is, as identifying spirit and matter rather than separating them by an impassable gulf, as Plato seems to do. But however that may be, it is clear that Xenophanes himself allowed the *practical* existence of sensible objects and of change and motion – allowed, as Socrates did, that such phenomena, although not the objects of true knowledge, could be used as 'rafts' to carry us across the sea of human life – whereas some of his successors, such as Parmenides and Zeno, insisted on the absolute non-existence of the natural world, and were thus landed in absurdities. Under Zeno the sublime philosophy of the founder degenerated into metaphysical quibbles and paradoxes and puzzles about the infinitely small and great, such as the puzzle of Achilles and the tortoise. He denied not only the absolute reality but also the practical existence of the sensible world and the possibility of motion – a doctrine refuted, it is said, by an unbeliever who rose from his seat and walked across the lecture-room, or lecture-portico, of the philosopher. Hence the expression *Solvitur ambulando* ('it is solved by walking').

The one doctrine of real importance in the philosophy of Xenophanes, and that which places it on a level quite different from that of the Ionic Physicists, is that which asserts the reality of things to depend on their relation to the one true existence – a doctrine substantially the same as that of

231

Socrates, who taught that everything exists by virtue of its *true*, not its apparent, cause, and that the only true knowledge is the knowledge of the *true* cause of things.

Pythagoras (*c.* 570–490) was a contemporary of Xenophanes and a generation earlier than Heracleitus. He and Xenophanes, living only some 120 miles distant from each other in Southern Italy, may be supposed to have met; but there was evidently not much mutual admiration, if we may judge from some very contemptuous verses of Xenophanes. 'They relate,' he says, 'that once when he [Pythagoras] was going past while a puppy was being whipped, he was touched with pity and exclaimed: "Leave off! Beat him not! for he is the soul of a friend of mine. I recognized it at once by his voice."'

Pythagoras was a Samian, but about 540, after having visited the East and Egypt,[1] he left Samos, perhaps in order to escape from the frivolous court of Polycrates, and settled in Croton. Here he seems to have gained great influence with the wealthy aristocratical party. Three hundred Crotoniats he formed into an Order, bound together by vows of allegiance and secrecy, after the fashion of Freemasons, whom they also resembled in possessing secret signs. On new members a period of probation, some say of seven years, was imposed, during which they were tested in their powers of keeping silence (like the Trappists) and in keeping their temper and in mental capacities. Only a few were initiated into the secret (esoteric) doctrines and rites, which were perhaps of an Orphic character, and seem to have been specially connected with the worship of Apollo; and it is possible that Pythagoras was identified by his followers with Apollo and that he laid claim (as Empedocles did later) to supernatural powers. The rule of the Order seems to have included strict abstinence from animal food – a practice necessarily involved in the creed of transmigration of souls.[2] Music and athletics formed an indispensable part in the system. When a member wished to leave the Order he was presented with double his original subscription and allowed to depart, but over his seat in the refectory was

---

[1] Herodotus evidently alludes (ii. 123) to him, though he declines to mention his name, when he speaks of certain Greek writers having appropriated and published as their own the Egyptian (?) doctrine of Transmigration. In iv. 95 he calls him 'not the meanest of Greek philosophers.'

[2] Beans were also taboo, if we are to take Horace's joke seriously (*Sat.* II, vi. 63), who intimates that some relative of Pythagoras had been a bean. Grote rejects Pythagorean vegetarianism as a fable because Milo *must* have had a meat diet!

erected a monument, and funeral rites were celebrated to intimate his philosophic decease. To the chief lodge (so to speak) at Croton were affiliated others in Taras, Sybaris, Metapontion, and other towns.

Perhaps it was owing to the political influence of these aristocratical Pythagorean societies that in 510 (the year when Tarquin and Hippias were expelled) Croton utterly destroyed Sybaris,[1] which had led into the field, we are told, an army of 300,000 men, against whom Milo, the celebrated Pythagorean wrestler (six times Olympic victor), did deeds like those of Samson. Soon after this the popular party, under the leadership of Cylon, gained the upper hand in Croton, and the Pythagorean societies fell under ban. Milo's house, where forty disciples were assembled, was set on fire by the mob, and all but two perished – possibly Pythagoras among them; but some say that he had fled to Taras some years previously, and thence to Metapontion, where 400 years later, Cicero tells us, his tomb was to be seen.[2] Probably Pythagoras, like Socrates and many other wise men, wrote nothing, although there is a story of his having left all his writings to his daughter Damo, with orders not to publish them – a command that she kept, although in great poverty. There are extant so-called 'Golden Verses' (seventy-one hexameters) which are attributed to him, but they are evidently a late fabrication. One of his disciples, Philolaus, who is said to have escaped from the conflagration and taken refuge in Greece, incorporated the doctrines of the school in a book (of course called *On Nature*), but only a few questionable relics of this book, as also of about ninety other works by the older Pythagoreans, survive (including some fragments ascribed to Archytas, the famous Tarentine mathematician, well known to readers of Horace). The disappearance of these old records is doubtless due to the fierce persecutions to which the sect was exposed. For the life and doctrines of Pythagoras we are almost entirely dependent on a few comments of Aristotle and on the writings of Porphyry and Iamblichus, neo-Platonists of the third century A.D., at which epoch, at Alexandria, there was a great revival of the mystical doctrines of the school and an attempt to proclaim Pythagoras as the anti-Christian Messiah.

---

[1] Sixty-seven years later, after a vain attempt to revive Croton, Thurii was founded (443) in the vicinity. Herodotus probably took part in the founding of Thurii and saw the ruins of Sybaris.

[2] In Cicero's time the revival of Pythagoreanism was beginning. In early days the Romans, when bidden by an oracle to erect a statue to the wisest of the Greeks, erected one to Pythagoras.

*Fig. 56 Ancient black-figured amphora (See List of Illustrations and Note D)*

Plato himself borrowed largely from Pythagoras. Timaeus of Locri, a Pythagorean, is said to have been Plato's teacher, and in the dialogue *Timaeus* Plato propounds views on the physical universe which are perhaps mainly Pythagorean; but it is as impossible to say how far they are Platonized as to say how far the doctrines of Socrates were Pythagorized by Plato. In the *Phaedrus* Plato uses, doubtless merely as a parable, the doctrine of Transmigration and of the ten periods of the soul as it was taught by Pythagoras, and the Platonic theory of Ideas is founded on Pythagorean and Eleatic doctrines of the One and the Many.

The main thesis of the Pythagorean system of philosophy is that the human mind recognizes within itself certain laws without which thought is impossible, and in these laws it possesses a revelation of the natural laws to which the structure of the universe is due. Now of these intellectual laws those of *number* are the most immutable and categorical, and the universe (both the sensible and the intellectual) is an 'imitation' or 'realization' of the laws of number, where Deity is the omnipresent Unit or Monad – of which all numbers consist, though it is itself no number – and prime (brute, chaotic) matter is the Duad, and the ordered Cosmos (formed by the addition of the creative Monad to the chaotic Duad) is the Triad.[1]

Now, strictly speaking, the *sensible* universe, according to this theory, is number realized in space, and when number is realized in space it is geometry. Therefore we find that with Pythagoras, as with Plato, geometry was the foundation of all true science. He himself is said to have discovered the most important fact of the equality of the square on the long side of a right-angled triangle to the sum of the squares on the shorter sides – and to have sacrificed a hundred oxen as thank-offering.[2] But in his philosophy he seems to have adopted numbers, as being more readily expressive of ratio and proportion than are lines and areas. As numbers are dependent for their individual existence on the unit, so sensible objects are dependent for their specific existence on their true cause – the One, or Deity. But the existence of natural objects as *phenomena* depends on their relation to all other such objects (nothing being of any meaning or value, or conceivable, by itself), in the same way as every intelligible number stands related, in a

---

[1] Natural objects (under three dimensions) are triads, and human nature is a triad, and the mind's conception of Deity is also a triad. Later Pythagoreans made the *Four* represent solidity, the *Five* quality (colour, etc.), the *Six* vitality, the *Seven* mind, and so on.

[2] Hardly consistent with his transmigration and vegetarian principles!

certain ratio or proportion, to every other number. Thus all things of the senses are knit together into one harmonious whole, and the natural universe is a Harmony.[1]

In passing it may be observed that many phenomena seem (though this may be merely due to the constitution of the human mind) to be the results of the vibration of some one prime element ('ether'?) at different rates, so that we have light and electricity and the octaves of sound and colour, and possibly of taste and smell, all related and standing in certain numerical ratios each to the other. But their specific existence, as light and sound and so on, is due, as Pythagoras expresses it, to their relation, not to each other, but to the Unit. Thus, when Professor Romanes asserted that with one persistent force and one prime matter he could account for the universe, Darwin answered: 'I could not disprove it if some one should assert that God had given certain attributes to force so that it develops into light, heat, electricity, and magnetism – and perhaps even into life.'

This doctrine of the harmonious system of the universe is one of the most suggestive and illuminating of all parables. But scientifically Pythagoras was, of course, on the wrong lines. He attempted to force Nature into accordance with his theories; and of this we have a striking instance in the fact that, in order to complete the mystic 'Decad,' he added a tenth to the then-known nine celestial bodies which circled round the central Fire or Watch-tower of Zeus. This tenth body he called the Antichthon ('Counter-earth'). How such a method differs from that by which Neptune was discovered need scarcely be explained.

The gulf between Physics and Ethics Pythagoras conceived to be bridged by music, which is at once a subject of intellectual research and a means of affecting the emotions. The explanation of the musical intervals and of harmony as due to proportion is attributed to him, although some accounts of his experiments are apocryphal, seeing that hammers of different weight do not produce different notes from the same anvil or bell. But he seems to have discovered the fact that a chord at the same tension vibrates in proportion to its length: that half the length produces the octave above the original note, two-thirds produces a musical fifth, three-fourths a fourth, and eight-ninths a major tone.

Thus from Physics to Ethics, from the sensible world to the world of mind

---

[1] Hence the Pythagorean 'music of the spheres,' which our ears are too dull, or from long familiarity too callous, to perceive.

and morals, we pass by the bridge of Music – climb the Beanstalk, as it were, and find ourselves in a fairyland where our dull, boorish materialism not seldom wakes to find itself 'translated' and invested with an ass's head. Even in this realm Pythagoras, or later Pythagorean philosophy, ventures to use the scale of Number and reads off vice as imperfect and virtue as perfect proportion – a virtuous life (*i.e.* virtue realized in action) as the straight line, abstract justice as the square number, and a just life as the geometric square. The soul he defines as a 'self-moving number,' or triune Monad, and thus asserts it to be of the same nature as Deity – a connection that doubtless encouraged his claim to supernatural powers. These formulae are, of course, merely little curiosities preserved for us by later writers, and are of no value except as curiosities; nor can we regard otherwise such stories as that of the recognition by Pythagoras in the temple of Hera at Argos of the shield which he had used (as Euphorbus, the Trojan) in a former life. But, however unworthy of serious regard they may appear to some minds, such a parable as that of Metempsychosis, with its gradual redemption of the human soul by purification, initiation, and intuition, until it is fit to dwell with the gods, and such an imaginative conception as the harmony of the universe and the music of the spheres, are (as Aristotle himself allows) of more value to the true thinker than much that goes by the name of scientific metaphysics. The main structure of the Pythagorean philosophy, however dimly it looms through the ages, is of impressive grandeur – a watch-tower of Zeus overlooking the infinities of space and time.

## SECTION B: THE ORDERS OF GREEK ARCHITECTURE

Something has already been said about the primitive shrines of the Mycenaean age and the temples of Homeric times, and some of the temples of the earlier historic period have been mentioned. Others will be mentioned later in connection with historical events and with sculpture, and further information will be found in Note A at the end of this book, and can be supplemented by reference to the Index and the List of Illustrations.

But without attempting to trace minutely the evolution of the Greek temple or to describe the technical details of Greek architecture (on which points full information can be found in dictionaries and textbooks) it may be well to state here the main characteristics of the different orders and to add a few facts in connection with some of the chief temples.

*Fig. 57 Temple near Segesta*

The original shrine, generally of wood or sunburnt brick, was an oblong, or rarely a round, building, like the ancient Greek house, with a porch. Sometimes this porch had side walls and perhaps a couple of wooden pillars in front, so that the whole building consisted of a hall (the shrine proper, or *naos*) and a closed forecourt (*pronaos*).[1] Then the row of pillars or columns was extended across the whole front of the building and the side walls of the porch were omitted, so that an open portico was formed.[2] Then a porch or portico was placed at both ends of the building.[3] Next, a row of columns was extended all round the building, which was said to be *peripteros – i.e.* winged, or aisled – and sometimes the portico had two rows of columns.[4] Lastly, two rows of columns were placed all round, and there were also columned porches at both ends of the building itself.[5] Such a temple was called *dipteros*, 'two-winged.' The interior sanctuary (the *naos* or *sēkos*, in which was the statue of the divinity facing east, so that the light of the rising sun should illuminate it) had side walls, but frequently had also inside them two rows of columns (as in the great Paestum temple), forming aisles and perhaps supporting the roof. These interior aisles were sometimes formed by two tiers of small columns, one on the top of the other. Whether the interior building was generally, or ever, hypaethral – *i.e.* open to the sky – is not quite certain. Certain it is that the statue was not often unprotected by a roof; and it is probable that the open space was only just enough to allow of sufficient light, as in the Pantheon at Rome.

The number of columns in the front of a temple was two, four, six, eight, or ten. The side (counting the corner columns) had generally one more than double the number of the front columns. Thus the Parthenon is $8 \times 17$, the Theseion is $6 \times 13$, as also is the temple of Zeus at Olympia; but Paestum is $6 \times 14$, and so is the splendid temple at Segesta (Fig. 57).

The three orders of Greek architecture are the Doric (especially used in Western Hellas), the Ionic (at first peculiar to Ionia), and the Corinthian. In the motherland we find all three styles, but the Doric is the most ancient.

The Corinthian, with its slender shaft and its capital ornamented with rows of acanthus leaves, need not occupy our attention now, for it was first invented about the time of the Peloponnesian War. The earliest specimen

[1] *Ex.* the Treasure-house of Megara at Delphi.
[2] *Ex.* the Erechtheion.
[3] *Ex.* the Nike temple at Athens.
[4] *Ex.* the Zeus temple at Olympia and the Parthenon.
[5] *Ex.* the Artemis temple at Ephesus.

known (*c.* 430) is said to have been a single column (now lost) inserted in the Ionic court of the Doric temple at Phigaleia (Fig. 84). Other fine examples are the monument of Lysicrates (Fig. 137), the 'Temple of the Winds,' and the splendid columns of the Olympieion at Athens (Figs. 54, 135), erected by the Emperor Hadrian.

The Doric order has a baseless, somewhat tapering column, surmounted by a capital composed of a thick slab (*abax*, or *abacus*) lying on a very flat oval moulding (the *echinus*). The columns bear a plain architrave ('main beam'), which supports the frieze and the projecting cornice.

The Ionic order has a slenderer column,[1] standing on a base, and bearing a capital whose main characteristic is two large spiral volutes (evidently an artistic modification of the ox-heads which occur in Oriental architecture, *e.g.* in the Persepolis columns). The columns carry an entablature composed, as in the Doric order, of architrave, frieze, and cornice, but the face of the architrave is cut into three planes, each projecting a little above the one below it, and the friezes of the two orders differ essentially. This difference of the friezes will be noted at once in pictures of Doric and Ionic temples. It will be seen that the Ionic frieze is one undivided space, either plain or filled with a line of figures in procession or otherwise forming a continuous series, whereas in the Doric temples the frieze consists of numerous spaces (metopes), either left plain or else filled each by a single group of figures,[2] and every metope is divided from the next by a kind of tablet of three bands sundered by flutings (triglyphs). These triglyphs are said to represent the ends of the rafters, which were visible in the old wooden temples, and the round ornaments on the mutules just above and below the frieze are supposed to represent rain-drops, or perhaps nail-heads.

Another characteristic, especially in the Doric style, is that the column not only tapers considerably but has a slight outward curve (called the *entasis*) in the middle, the object of which may have been to correct some optical error in perspective. In the Parthenon this bulge is scarcely perceptible. In the temple of Demeter at Paestum, and still more in the

---

[1] The Ionic column scarcely tapers at all. Its height is 16 to 18 semi-diameters (modules). That of the Parthenon columns is 12. In the great Paestum temple it is only 8, and in the Apollo temple at Corinth (the most ancient perhaps in Greece) it is only 7⅔. The columns of Atreus' Treasury and the Lion Gate (Mycenae) taper *downwards*.

[2] In the Parthenon the external frieze consisted of metopes and triglyphs, but the frieze of the inner building was Ionic in character, although the columns were Doric. This is the frieze, representing the Panathenaic procession, which is in the British Museum.

'Basilica,' it is disagreeably noticeable (Fig. 41). At Phigaleia it seems entirely absent.

The columns of all three orders have almost always parallel flutings. The Doric are sharp-edged, shallower, and fewer (twenty in the Parthenon), the Ionic and Corinthian generally separated by fillets, semicircular, and numbering from twenty-four up to thirty-two. Sometimes the lower part of the Ionic column was left plain, or (as at Ephesus) was used for sculptured reliefs. In later times spiral flutings were sometimes used.

In point of size, especially in regard to height, Greek temples are, of course, not comparable with our cathedrals, nor with the great temples of the East, and, as Herodotus himself remarks, 'although the temple of Ephesus is worthy of note, and also the temple of Samos, if all the great works of the Greeks could be put together in one they would not equal things that are to be seen in Egypt.' The length of the Olympieion at Acragas (Girgenti), the largest temple in the Hellenic world, but (like its Athenian namesake) never completed, was 363 feet; that of the Samian Heraion was 346, that of the (earlier) Ephesian temple was 342, and that of the Parthenon is 227 feet. St. Paul's Cathedral is 513 feet long and St. Peter's at Rome is 613 feet.

## SECTION C: SCULPTURE, DOWN TO THE PERSIAN WARS

In a former section we considered some of the main characteristics of the religion that preceded the introduction of the Olympian hierarchy, and noticed how the feelings of awe and dread for the supernatural revealed themselves in grotesque and horrible effigies, which were regarded with superstitious reverence. This fetish-worship was by no means eradicated by the new Olympian religion. Although we find little or no trace of 'spook' or superstitious awe in Homer, who seems to shrink instinctively from all that is grotesque, monstrous, and uncanny, the old *deisidaimonia* survived (as we saw in Hesiod's case) side by side with the brighter and more openly professed Olympian orthodoxy, and during the sixth century there seems to have been a great recrudescence of 'chthonian' cult, aggravated by the introduction and spread of the Orphic creed and rites and the institution, or revival, of Dionysian and Eleusinian Mysteries. This subject we shall meet again when we come to the philosophers of the fifth century. At present it will suffice to note the fact that Greek sculpture was apparently a direct evolution from the fabrication of grotesque fetish-idols, although

*Plate III An Attic hydria of the middle black-figured period (c. 550)*

it is impossible by any analysis to discover the vital force which effected this wondrous development – a development which in many cases, such as that of Egypt and of Assyria and of other Oriental nations, has scarcely taken place at all, and in no other case has been so rapid and so perfect as in Greek art. Certainly we cannot account for it by what we call civilization. In our sense of the word the Persian Empire was in the age of Aeschylus and Pheidias at a higher stage of civilization than Greece, and in the Hellenic world the advent of a more scientific learning and research and criticism was contemporary with the degeneracy, and was soon followed by the disappearance, of all true art, until its renaissance in other forms. But however inexplicable it may be, it is an incontestable fact that within less than two centuries the superstitious awe attaching to some ghoulish monstrosity or some formless stock or meteorite gave place to reverence for the images of a Pheidian Zeus or Athene – reverence paid not so much to the present deity as to the manifestation of the grand, the serene, and the beautiful.[1]

The vital power which effected this development revealed its workings not only in sculpture but also in other creations of Hellenic genius – in Greek literature, Greek thought, Greek mythology, and Greek theology, all of which bear testimony to a genius essentially formative and artistic – perhaps we may say essentially sculpturesque – a genius well described as the converse of that of the Jewish nation, and one for which the dangers of idolatry were to a great extent neutralized by poetic imagination and reverence for the ideally beautiful.

Doubtless the imaginative and allegorical pictures of the Olympian gods and the Olympian creed which we find in the art of Homer and Pheidias and the dramatists do not reveal to us the gross anthropomorphic superstitions of the populace, which were, as we have seen, as bitterly denounced by Xenophanes as was Jewish idolatry by Isaiah. Doubtless, as in every age, the religion of the thinker and the true artist was not that of the people, but in spite of all the superstitions in which it was involved (and we need only think of Socrates to realize them) this anthropomorphism of the popular theology was a result of the same formative spirit to which was due the

---

[1] The testimony of many writers to the effect produced by the Pheidian Zeus at Olympia is very striking. 'Let a man sick and weary in soul,' says one of these, 'who has passed through many distresses and sorrows, whose pillow is unvisited by kindly sleep, stand in front of this image; he will, I deem, forget all the terrors and troubles of human life.' (Quoted by Professor Bury.)

evolution of Greek sculpture from the formless or grotesque effigies of the early age of Greece.

Whether we should regard Greek plastic art as lineally descended from Aegean it is not easy to say. Aegean plastic art (as we see by the Vaphio cups) attained an astonishing proficiency, but was apparently swept out of existence by the Dorians. It may have survived and been the germ from which sprang the glories of the Periclean age, but it is foolish to refuse to recognize in Hellenic art, as in Hellenic thought, the presence of many elements derived from other sources – from Crete, Lydia, Phrygia, the East, and Egypt – and to insist on an 'autochthonous' originality in the case of Greek sculpture or Greek thought which cannot be claimed for Giotto, Dante, or Shakespeare. But whether of Aegean or other origin in regard to some of its elements, the art of classical Hellas is, of course, original in the true sense of the word, being a re-creation – and that, too, into a far higher existence.

Genuine statuary is said to have begun in Greece about 600, and the so-called 'archaic' period extends to the end of the Persian wars, say 480. Of this period I shall give a brief review, prefaced by a few remarks on the fetish-worship which preceded the attempt to represent deity, and later also the human form divine, as a thing of perfect beauty.

The ancient Greek idol was often merely a symbol of divine presence – sometimes a rude figure (such as one finds in thousands on sites of temples) of clay or wood or lead, frequently grotesque or monstrous, sometimes a formless stock,[1] or a 'heaven-fallen' stone, or a pillar, such as we hear of in the Bible and see in the Lion Gate at Mycenae and in pictures of the Earth-goddess. Real statuary assuredly existed in Greece (as, of course, in Egypt and the East) before the sixth century,[2] and rich and elaborate relief-work was produced, as we see from the descriptions of the famous Cypselus chest and the carved throne of the Apollo image at Amyclae. The former, which Pausanias saw some 800 years later in the Heraion at Olympia, was

---

[1] These old wooden idols were called *xoana* ('carved things'). See Hdt. v. 82.

[2] *E.g.* the gold and silver dogs and the golden torch-bearers of *Od.* vii. and the Apollo statue intimated by *Il.* i. 28, and the statue of Athene in *Il.* vi. 92 and 303, evidently imagined in a sitting position. A colossal gold-plated statue of Zeus was given by Cypselus or Periander (*c.* 600) to Olympia. Also we hear of an artist of Rhegium, Clearchus, who at a very early period made a bronze statue (not cast, but plated) of Zeus at Sparta. Moreover, there is a stone sculpture still existing in Greece that is far older than Homer – the Lions of Mycenae.

presented probably by Periander, and was asserted to have been the actual chest in which Cypselus was hidden by his mother (*c.* 655). In any case it is probably the most ancient specimen of artistic Greek carved work (if it was by a Greek artist) of which we have historical record. The reliefs, in cedar wood, ivory, and gold, represented mythological subjects (Pelops, Heracles, Perseus, etc.) in thirty-three panels arranged in five parallel rows. The Amyclaean throne was also decorated by about twenty-seven reliefs (probably in bronze), and was supported by figures of the Seasons, the Graces, Tritons, etc. It was the work of a Lydian (Magnesian) artist, Bathycles, who may have come to Sparta in the time of Croesus (say 550), but whose date is possibly considerably earlier. This was a work produced by a foreign artist[1] as a throne, or screen, for a Greek god. But in what form was that god represented? He was, as Pausanias tells us, a bronzen pillar, some 45 feet high, 'with head and hands and feet attached.' Such old fetishes, pillars and logs and meteorites, sometimes quite formless or else shaped into some rude resemblance to humanity or to some monstrous thing, and decked out with ornaments, were not seldom preserved reverentially in temples – hidden away like Bambini and relics and displayed only on solemn occasions – long after a splendid statue of the deity had been erected in the sanctuary. At Troy we hear of the Palladium, and at Ephesus and on the Tauric Chersonese of the heaven-fallen image of Artemis, and in the Erechtheion there was kept an old *xoanon* of Athene long after the Pheidian goddess had been erected in the Parthenon, and at Phigaleia existed (and was renewed in bronze by Onatas of Aegina) a monstrous horse-headed Demeter. Doubtless of the nature of the ancient wooden or clay idol were the 'Aeacidae' – the images of the old Aeginetan heroes Aeacus, Telamon, and Peleus of which Herodotus tells us. The Aeginetans, he says, when appealed to by the Thebans for help, 'sent them the Aeacidae,' and the Thebans, 'relying on the assistance of the Aeacidae,' ventured on war, but were beaten; whereupon they returned the Aeacidae and 'besought the Aeginetans to send them men instead.' Moreover, in spite of this experience,

---

[1] Lydia, Phrygia, and Lycia all seem to have reached an advanced stage in plastic art before Greece, and doubtless, as well as Egypt, Crete, and the East, contributed many important elements for the development of Greek sculpture. The great rock-relief of 'Niobe' (probably the Earth-Mother Cybele) on Mount Sipylus in Lydia is very ancient, and so are recently discovered tombs in Phrygia with lions like those of Mycenae. Sculptured monuments of high antiquity, probably of Hittite provenance, have lately been discovered at Pteria, the ancient capital of Cappadocia.

just before the battle of Salamis, says Herodotus, 'a ship was sent by the Athenians to Aegina to fetch Aeacus and the other Aeacidae.'

According to tradition, the first sculptors and workers in metals were superhuman beings, such as Hephaestus and the fabled tribes of Phrygian Dactyli and Cretan and Rhodian Telchines and Lemnian Cabiri and the Cyclopes. Then we hear of Daedalus. The name may be an epithet ('the artificer'), but there is no good reason to doubt that it was given to some great worker in metals and sculptor and inventor (possibly even of wings!), whom legend and Homer[1] connect with Minos, and thus also with Theseus and Athens, intimating doubtless the artistic connection between Crete and Greece in the Minoan age.

Daedalus is said to have made statues that could see and walk, and even run away if they were not chained to their pedestals! This we may accept as an imaginative way of saying that he first gave usable-looking legs to statues and opened their eyes and freed their arms.[2] But it will be seen that he and his followers, the Daedalidae, did not succeed at once in banishing the type of the old image with cone-shaped or columnar nether extremities and arms glued to its side, or with its figure swathed in massive drapery and forming a solid piece with the marble on which it is seated – as if doomed to sit there for all eternity.

After about 600 the sculptors and masterpieces mentioned by old writers become very numerous, but of many nothing survives but the name. For our object it will be enough to limit ourselves to what can be illustrated by extant monuments. Of these relics there are several well-defined types, in which we trace the evolution from the primitive idol to a statue of high artistic value.

(1) The first of these types is a figure whose lower half, though no longer a mere column or block, is columnar, with the legs undefined and entirely hidden by a stiff, shapeless skirt, below which the feet protrude side by side. The arms are attached to the sides, the drapery has no real folds or texture, but is a solid mass marked with conventional lines. The headdress is of an Egyptian or Oriental character, generally with broad flat masses of hair hanging down in front of each shoulder. This type is well illustrated by the

---

[1] Homer frequently uses cognate words (*daidaleos, daidallein,* etc.) in connection with artistic decoration, but only mentions Daedalus as the maker of a dancing-ground for Ariadne. With 'Daedalus' *cf.* the half-mythical sculptor 'Smilis' (*smile* = sculptor's chisel).

[2] Something analogous can be said of Giotto.

*Fig. 58  Statue from the Branchidae Temple*

*Fig. 59  The 'Harpy Tomb'*

247

'Naxian Artemis' (Fig. 50) discovered in Delos, where Nicandra of Naxos dedicated the image to the goddess, and by a similar, but headless, statue found near the site of the great Hera temple in Samos.

(2) Secondly, there are heavily draped seated figures which, in early examples, seem, as has been said, to form one solid piece with the block or throne on which they sit. Of this type the Branchidae statues (which are in the British Museum) offer fine examples. The specimen given in Fig. 58 is inscribed with the name 'Chares of Teichiussa,' probably some great Milesian, possibly a tyrant of Miletus long before its destruction by Darius in 494. (See Note A at the end of this book for the Branchidae temple.)

The Cretan statue given in Fig. 6 was perhaps of the same character. The lower half is wanting, but not only the flat masses of pendent (probably false) hair but also the general pose remind one forcibly of seated Egyptian statues. It is the only specimen extant of Cretan sculpture of this period, and shows perhaps the style of the followers of Daedalus, such as Dipoenus and Scyllis, who are said to have introduced statuary (*c.* 580) from Crete into the Peloponnese. This statue is perhaps considerably older than any of those from the temple of the Branchidae.

(3) Thirdly, we have winged figures, possibly an imitation[1] from Oriental art. In classical Greek art wings are rare, as being unnatural. In Oriental art we often have four or six wings, and it seems just possible that the oldest Greek Victory (Nike) extant may have had six. It is a very uncouth thing, but is highly interesting as one of the first Greek statues with unmistakable legs – legs, too, that are bent. Perhaps the goddess was represented flying. From small bronzes that repeat the type it seems probable that the figure floated, suspended by the drapery. Its wings were probably coloured. It has a rather sour archaic smile and an elaborate system of forehead curls and pendent tresses. It is also interesting because it may be the actual statue referred to by Aristophanes, who says that Achermus of Chios was the first to make a winged Nike. It was discovered in Delos, whither many statues were sent as offerings from other Aegean islands, and a pedestal was dis-covered near it on which were the names of Micciades and Achermus, the Chian sculptors, whose date is about 570. Winged figures occur also on vases and in other art-relics of this period. They are sometimes purely

---

[1] For wings in Greek sculpture I may perhaps refer to an appendix in my edition of Virgil's *Aeneid*, i. (Blackie & Son). In later sculpture Victory, Cupid, and Death are winged. See Fig. 120 and p. 441.

decorative (as perhaps on the Clazomenae sarcophagus, Fig. 45), some-times they represent a winged Artemis, sometimes Harpies, Fates (*kēres*), genii, or evil spirits. The finest example of this (of about 550) is the famous 'Harpy tomb,' a monument evidently of Greek (Ionic) work, but discov-ered in Lycia and now in the British Museum (Fig. 59). The winged bird-like figures are doubtless death-goddesses who are carrying away the souls of the dead. The central portion represents probably Hades, the king of the lower world, or else a deceased hero, receiving gifts – a motive found on many Greek tombs, the earliest examples being very ancient Spartan grave-stones.[1] These sculptures formed a part of the frieze of a massive square monument, some 30 feet high. The relief was elaborately painted, but the colours have quite disappeared. From frescoes on the internal walls of the sepulchral chamber it seems as if the monument was used in early Christian times by a 'Stylite' (a hermit who lived on the top of a column).

(4) Fourthly, we have draped figures, mostly female, in which the arms are, in later examples, no longer attached to the sides, but bent and pro-jecting forward (made of a separate piece and inserted) or crossed over the body; and the left foot is almost always advanced. In these statues the drapery is no longer massive and conventional, but treated with a skill that shows a very great advance. Of this type we have striking examples in the fourteen female statues excavated in the late 1880s on the Acropolis (see p. 253). Their date is probably about 520 to 500.

(5) Lastly, a large number of later archaic Greek statues belong to what is called the 'nude male' type.[2] They are full length, and fully developed in limb, and show great anatomical knowledge and artistic skill. They seem not seldom to represent the god Apollo[3] (thence are commonly known as 'Apollos'), but are evidently sometimes statues of athletes. Nude 'Apollos' of this type have been found in Naxos, Thera, Melos, and other places. A very striking early example, now at Munich, was found at Tenea (between Corinth and Mycenae). It has the antique Egyptian 'wig' and the archaic grimace, but the anatomy is finely treated. The finest examples, however, come from Boeotia, especially from the sanctuary of Apollo on Mount Ptoön. They are archaic in style, but give evidence of a careful study of the

---

[1] *Cf.* the (later) stele of Hegeso, Fig. 106.

[2] These various types are given by Professor E. Gardner in his *Handbook of Greek Sculpture*.

[3] A colossal nude Poseidon was found at Sunion in 1906.

human body, and are the first distinct intimations of that mastery of the Greeks in statuary which has never been approached. In connection with these 'Apollos' should be mentioned the statues of athletes. We hear of wooden statues of athletes erected at Olympia about 540, and one at Phigaleia perhaps as early as 560. The chief makers of athlete statues were the sculptors of Argos and Sicyon. Ancient writers speak of the great pre-eminence of these schools, and doubtless their statuary, which consisted at this epoch mainly of *andriantes* ('men-portraits') rather than *agalmata* or *anathēmata* (images for worship or dedication), had a very great influence on Attic art. Unfortunately – perhaps because they worked mostly in bronze, which tempted the plunderer – nothing of any importance, except a bronze statuette of a very heavily built athlete, has survived, and we must content ourselves with the facts that the Argive Ageladas[1] was the master of two of the most illustrious Athenian sculptors, Pheidias and Myron, as well as of Polycleitus (who himself was perhaps an Argive), and that Canachus of Sicyon made for the Branchidae temple a bronze Apollo which was carried off by Darius and restored by Seleucus.

The reliefs on Attic tombstones of this period may be mentioned in connection with portrait sculpture. Of these the most interesting is that of Aristion (Fig. 51), probably the same Aristion who proposed giving a bodyguard to Peisistratus (*c.* 560). Although archaic in style, it shows the very delicate modelling and finish for which the early Athenian school is so remarkable.

Thus, very faintly and discontinuously amidst all the complexities of the subject, we are able to trace the evolution of the statue of the classical period from the primitive *xoanon*. In doing this we have left unnoticed some very important facts connected with the use of statuary for architectural purposes. I shall, therefore, add a few words about, firstly, the sculptures from the ancient temple at Selinus; secondly, the archaic sculptures excavated on the Athenian Acropolis; and, thirdly, the Aeginetan marbles.

(1) On the site of the most ancient of the temples at Selinus, in Sicily (see Note A), have been discovered some metopes (reliefs on a Doric frieze) which are probably the oldest extant perfect specimens of Greek architectural sculpture. Originally they were coloured and had a dark blue

---

[1] See Hdt. v. 72 for the Olympian victor (*c.* 520) whose statue by Ageladas was seen at Olympia by Pausanias. As Ageladas also made a statue of Zeus for the Messenians at Naupactus in 459, he must have lived and worked to a great age.

*Fig. 60 Europa on the bull, metope from temple at Selinus*

background, but only faint traces of colour remain. They date from about 600, and are thus some half-century older than the Croesus column, and still older than the 'Harpy tomb' (Figs. 52, 59). Three of the earliest of them, casts of which are to be seen in the British Museum, represent Perseus cutting off the Gorgon's head, Heracles carrying the Cercopes[1] suspended like rabbits to the two ends of a pole, and a chariot with its four horses facing the spectator – a clever bit of perspective. Some of the figures are exceedingly uncouth, misproportioned, and distorted, and the faces repulsive with their goggle eyes and meaningless stare, but they are interesting as being original Greek work (Selinus having been founded by Megara), and showing no such evidence of Egyptian, Cretan, or Oriental influence as is noticeable in much of the early sculpture that we have been considering. The Selinus metope of which Fig. 60 gives a representation is from another temple, and is perhaps of somewhat later date (say about 580). It is of very much more artistic conception and execution, and has considerable dignity and vigour and delicacy in detail, although it is thoroughly archaic in its outlines and perspective. The subject – Europa being carried by the bull across the sea (intimated by a dolphin) from Phoenicia to Crete – seems to point to Cretan workmanship or influence.

(2) After the departure of the Persians, who had twice (in 480 and 479) sacked Athens and had burnt or broken down as far as they could every temple and monument, the Athenians at once set to work to rebuild on a more magnificent scale, and in order to obtain a larger area on the Acropolis they erected (on the advice of Cimon or Themistocles) strong walls on the upper slopes and filled in the spaces between these walls and the top of the hill, using for this purpose the relics of the old temples – such as the ancient temple of Athene Polias – which had stood on the summit. During the years 1882–87 these spaces were thoroughly searched, and many statues and inscriptions and architectural fragments were excavated, which have thrown a great deal of light on the question of Athenian sculpture in the sixth century. The most important of these finds are (*a*) remains of the pediments of some very ancient temples, (*b*) remains of the pediment of the temple of Athene Polias – rebuilt by Peisistratus – and (*c*) a series of fourteen female statues, more or less perfect.

(*a*) The ancient pediments (to be seen in the Acropolis Museum at Athens) are of yellow limestone (*poros*). One represents Heracles killing the

---

[1] For these mischievous little gnomes see Rawlinson's note to Hdt. vii. 216.

Hydra; in another he is wrestling with Triton, the 'old man of the sea,' while from the other corner is advancing – perhaps against Zeus, who was his great adversary – the horrid monster Typhon, with three human heads and busts (reminding one of Dante's Geryon, whose face was that of a just man), and a winged body with interwoven snakes for feet, and a long dragon tail. All these monsters were originally painted in bright reds and blues and greens, like terracottas, and set against a coloured background. They doubtless date from a time earlier than that of Peisistratus – probably from about the same period as that of the Selinus sculptures. So shocking to the modern Hellenist does their barbarous monstrosity appear – especially when imagined in their pristine glare of colour – that some suppose them to be products of the Dark Age, and to have been buried out of sight long before the advent of the Persians, as offensive to public taste. Perhaps one was the pediment of the ancient shrine of Athene Polias before it was rebuilt by Peisistratus.

(b) The pediment of the old temple of Athene was in Parian marble. Its fragments have been successfully reconstructed into a 'gigantomachia' – a battle between Athene and giants. Three she has overthrown, and is striking at one with her spear while she holds extended the *aegis* – originally gorgeously decorated with red and blue and green scales. The date of this marble pediment may be about 540. It was probably erected by Peisistratus when he turned the old shrine of Athene into a Doric temple (see Note A).

(c) Fourteen female draped statues in Parian marble (eight of them with heads) were excavated, mostly from the filled-up space between the Erechtheion and the north-western wall of the Acropolis. What they represent, whether priestesses or donors or dedicated portraits, is unknown. Perhaps they stood in or near the old temple of Athene. They are all in slightly different attitudes, but all are erect, with left foot advanced and forearm projecting horizontally, as if they held some offering in the hand (Fig. 37). The dress – evidently that which prevailed at Athens in the age of Peisistratus – consists of a long crimpled Ionic *chitōn*, fastened above the upper arm with small brooches (*peronai*, Latin *fibulae*) or buttons, and a *peplos*, doubled and fastened over the right shoulder by *fibulae*. In some cases the *peplos* is wanting; in others it is fastened, like a Doric *chitōn*, over both shoulders. The drapery, of which parts were richly decorated and coloured, is of exquisitely delicate and elaborate workmanship, though in this, as in the type of face and otherwise, there is a great difference between

253

the earlier and the later of these statues. Some have the goggle eyes and meaningless stare or grimace of archaic sculpture; in others the face shows considerable character and is very finely modelled, giving evidence of a great advance in the direction of that feminine grace and delicacy which is one of the characteristics of early Attic sculpture, and to which, when wedded to the manly vigour of the athletic Argive school, we owe the development of the highest types of Greek plastic art – those which we associate with the names of Pheidias, Myron, and Praxiteles.

Before the excavations on the Acropolis we possessed scarcely any relics of Athenian sculpture during the period preceding the Persian wars. Nor was this surprising, for the Persians were not only intensely embittered against Athens and therefore wreaked their vengeance by wholesale destruction, but they were also fire-worshippers and therefore iconoclasts. In Asia Minor the Ephesian temple was the only one spared by Xerxes, and in Attica every shrine and every image was destroyed or mutilated. This explains the total disappearance of many buildings and works of art mentioned by ancient writers. And much that was made of valuable material and was transportable was doubtless carried off to the East. This probably accounts for the disappearance of the bronze four-horse chariot which is said to have been erected on the left hand of the steps leading up to the Acropolis, as a trophy[1] of the victorious Chalcidian campaign of 506. It certainly does account for the temporary disappearance of another work of art – the bronze statues of the tyrannicides Harmodius and Aristogeiton, made by the sculptor Antenor, whose name occurs on what is believed to be the basis of the largest and best preserved of the 'Tanten' ('Aunts') – to use a name that has been given to the draped female statues lately described. These bronze tyrannicides were carried off by Xerxes, but restored to Athens by Alexander the Great, or one of his successors, and were seen by Pausanias standing in the Athenian Agora side by side with the marble statues (possibly replicas from memory) which had been erected at once (c. 477) to retrieve the loss. Now for the most part of the six centuries between the age of Xerxes and that of Pausanias these groups – one in bronze and the other in marble – were among the most familiar sights in Athens. They seem to have been spared even by the rapacious Sulla, and by Caligula and Nero himself, but possibly found their way to Constantinople with the bronzen Athene and the Olympian Zeus of Pheidias. Anyhow,

---

[1] Pericles probably set another in its place.

they disappeared. But reproductions of one of the groups on a vase and a coin and a marble chair led to the recognition of two statues in the Naples Museum (Fig. 61) as copies – it is uncertain whether of Antenor's bronzes or the marbles of Critius and Nesiotes. Probably Antenor's statues (if we may judge from the 'Tante' attributed to him) were much more archaic in style than these dramatically animated figures. It should be remarked that the figure with the *chlamys* on the left arm is that of Aristogeiton, the elder of the two tyrannicides, and that the original statue had a bearded head, for which in modern times a youthful beardless head of fourth-century work has been substituted.

The last Athenian statue that I shall mention here belongs as regards date rather to the next period, for Calamis, the sculptor with whom it has been associated, was born only some ten years before Pheidias and survived him (having, it is said, made a statue to Apollo, the Stayer of Evil, to commemorate the cessation of the great plague of 430). Calamis is classed by ancient writers among the greatest Greek sculptors, and the list of his works is long. He made many famous statues of gods, and was also celebrated for his horses. He is said to have been an Athenian, and his style was probably that of the earlier Attic school, which, as we have seen, was distinguished for its grace and delicacy rather than for athletic muscularity and vigour. There is no surviving work which can be attributed to him with certainty, but there is one possible attribution – especially as he is known to have accepted various commissions from Hiero of Syracuse and to have made him several bronze horses. The statue in question (Fig. 74) is an exceedingly fine bronze which was found at Delphi about fifteen years ago. It represents a youthful charioteer, who stood originally on a chariot at rest, to judge from fragments of the horses that have been found. The tranquil, self-possessed dignity of the figure, the careful and graceful treatment of the long charioteer robe, and the exceedingly delicate modelling of the arms, hands, and feet offer a striking contrast to the bold, Michelangelesque work of the Peloponnesian athletic schools. Upon the basis a fragmentary inscription contains the word *polyzalos* ('much-loved'), which may be a name; and possibly the group was dedicated by Polyzalus, brother to Hiero. This high-bred youth is therefore possibly Polyzalus himself or some younger member of the princely Syracusan family. It is known that Hiero won chariot-races at Olympia.

(3) The so-called Aeginetan marbles, remains of the two pediments of

Fig. 61  The tyrannicides

256

*Fig. 62  Temple of Aphaia, Aegina*

*Fig. 63  Aegina pediment*

the temple of Aphaia, were discovered in 1811. Casts are to be seen in the British Museum, but the originals are in the Glyptothek at Munich, restored and reconstructed by the Danish sculptor Thorwaldsen (Fig. 63). A more successful reconstruction (the models of which are also in the Munich Museum) was made by Professor Furtwängler, who in 1901 excavated further fragments. He divided the combatants into groups, and made the archers shoot towards the corners instead of towards the centre, where Athene stands, and filled up the two corners with two prostrate bodies. The scene of the west pediment is evidently some episode in the Trojan War in which Aeginetan heroes (Aeacidae, such as Ajax and Achilles?) took part, and the subject of the east pediment seems to be the earlier expedition against Laomedon of Troy made by Heracles and Telamon, king of Aegina. Both the figures of Athene are stiff and archaic. Possibly they are old statues belonging to the temple before the erection of the other figures – which date evidently from the years following the battle of Marathon. Some of the figures had bronze armour originally. At this epoch paint or gilt was used only for dress, ornaments, eyes, lips, and hair. The nude was mostly represented by plain or tinted marble. Its surface was very often oiled and polished and slightly coloured, both in the case of Parian and also in that of the somewhat yellower Pentelic (Attic) marble, which came into use during the fifth century. The glittering white of Carrara marble, unrelieved by any colour, as we see it in modern sculpture galleries, would have seemed repellently cold and inartistic to the Greek. The dismay that we generally feel at colour in statuary and architecture may be an evidence of very refined sensibility, but it is essentially un-Greek.

The sculptor of these pediments is not known for certain, but probably it was Onatas, the most celebrated of the Aeginetan school, which was evidently closely related to the Peloponnesian schools of athletic sculpture. Before Onatas, another famous Aeginetan sculptor, Smilis, had made the Samian Hera; and ancient writers give us to understand that Aegina in early times was famed for its sculptors, but of this we possess almost no evidence except these Aeginetan marbles; and the Aeginetan school, even if famous, was short-lived, for the existence of Aegina as an independent state was blotted out by Athens in 455. Onatas is said to have made statues for many cities both in Greece and Western Hellas, and, like Calamis, to have received commissions from Hiero for bronze horses and charioteers. He also made warrior groups for dedication at Olympia and Delphi. It is therefore very probable that the pediments of the Aegina temple were his work. They show remarkable anatomical knowledge. The modelling of the limbs is exact and firm. But the faces are those of mere fighters or athletes, entirely devoid of higher human interest, and, except perhaps technically, these specimens of Aeginetan art stand lower than many older sculptures, and very much lower than the best Attic art of the next period.

# Chapter 5

# The Persian Invasions
# (500–478)

In the last chapter the thread of the narrative was dropped at the arrival of Darius at Sardis after his Thracian and Scythian expedition of 512. He had left Megabazus with an army of 80,000 men in Thrace, the greater part of which, as well as Paeonia, to the west of the Strymon, was brought under Persian dominion and remained tributary to the Great King for some fifteen years.

When Darius left Sardis for Susa he appointed his brother Artaphernes satrap of the western province of the Persian Empire. The Greek cities on the mainland were governed by Greek tyrants who were responsible to this Persian satrap at Sardis. For some years things went on quietly. Then came the explosion known as the Ionian revolt, and this was followed by the Persian invasions of Greece: first (after an unsuccessful attempt by Mardonius) the invasion by the fleet and army of Darius under the command of Datis and Artaphernes, who were beaten at Marathon; then the far more serious invasion by Xerxes, whom the Greeks defeated at Salamis.

The story of the Ionic revolt and the Persian invasions is told by Herodotus in the last four books of his history. With an art that veils itself in seeming artlessness he leads us leisurely onward with his simple, unaffected tale, lingering ever and again over what some may deem unessential details, and making long and delightful digressions, but leaving nevertheless in the mind a far more distinct picture than that which we gain from many more scrupulously critical and correct accounts. Those who have the

260

leisure for such reading, and are not forced by a scientific conscience or by the exigencies of examination to use the more sceptical and accurate compilations of modern historians, will find in Herodotus, or in the admirable, though rather free, version of his history by Canon Rawlinson, the best and most attractive of all descriptions of this period. The same kind of sensation as one has when gliding gently and steadily over a smooth blue sea, with now and then a slight pressure of the hand on the tiller, will be experienced as the story is followed, with now and then a glance at some footnote which respectfully corrects or supplements the statements of the Father of History.

This episode of the world's history is so well known and has been related so often that I shall not attempt to give any very detailed account of it. Moreover, whatever value the story, as told by Herodotus, has for the true student – and it has much – consists in its panoramic effects and its revelation of human and national character, and this value is not increased by a too anxious reconstruction of battles and other military operations, or a too anxious scepticism as regards statistics. I shall therefore briefly state the main facts, and then add a little colour to the bare outline by quoting descriptive passages from Herodotus or other sources.[1]

It will be remembered that Histiaeus, tyrant of Miletus, who had accompanied Darius on the Scythian expedition, had persuaded his fellow-Greeks not to break down the bridge over the Danube. The king bade him name his reward. He asked for the gift of the town Myrcinus, on the river Strymon, near the site of the future Amphipolis, and at once began to fortify it and to collect troops – a procedure which so aroused the suspicions of Megabazus, the commander of the Persian army in Thrace, that he sent word to Darius. The result was that Darius, who was still at Sardis, informed Histiaeus that he could not bear his absence any longer and ordered him to come to Sardis, and thence took him to Susa, where for twelve years he led the envied life of a 'benefactor of the king' – gnawing his heart with anger and longing for an opportunity for revenge.

Now the government of Miletus had passed into the hands of Aristagoras, the son-in-law of Histiaeus. He quarrelled with a Persian commander, Megabates, with whom he had made an unsuccessful raid on Naxos, and (perhaps encouraged by a message from Histiaeus tattooed on

---

[1] Quotations in this chapter are all from Herodotus, unless otherwise stated. My versions are founded to some extent on Canon Rawlinson's translation.

the head of a slave) resolved to incite a general revolt of the Hellenic cities against Persia. Democracies were set up in place of tyrannies, and Aristagoras himself, having resigned his government, visited Sparta and vainly tried to win the aid of King Cleomenes. He then went to Athens, and 'it being easier,' says Herodotus, 'to deceive a multitude than one man, he succeeded with the Athenians, who were 30,000, though he had failed with Cleomenes. They voted that twenty ships should be sent to the aid of the Ionians . . . and these ships were the beginning of trouble between the Greeks and the barbarians.' The Eretrians joined with five triremes. With their fleet thus powerfully reinforced, the Ionians, had they followed the advice of the historian Hecataeus to fortify some island, might have held their own in the Aegean and on the coast, but, having landed near Ephesus, they marched up to Sardis 'with a great host,' and took it. The city contained many houses built of reed, and, a fire having broken out, it was burnt (497). The Greeks hastily retreated, but were overtaken and cut to pieces by Artaphernes and the Persians, and though the revolt spread to Cyprus and Caria and the Propontis, it was suppressed. Aristagoras fled to Myrcinus and met his death in Thrace, but Miletus still headed the revolt against Persia. Histiaeus, having at length persuaded Darius to let him return to the West in order to pacify his fellow-Greeks, aroused the suspicions of Artaphernes at Sardis and fled. He tried in vain to re-enter Miletus. Then he took to piracy in the Hellespont, but at last was caught and put to death by the Persian satrap, an act reprimanded by Darius, who, when the head of Histiaeus was brought to him, bade it be buried honourably 'as the head of a man who had been a great benefactor to the king and his people.'

The Persians then with a vast land force, and with 600 ships drawn from Phoenicia, Cyprus, and Egypt, prepared to lay siege to Miletus. The Greek fleet of 353 triremes assembled at the island of Lade – now a hillock in the midst of the wide swampy plain which was once the splendid Latmic bay at the mouth of the Maeander. Treason and cowardice gave the victory to the barbarians. The Samians deserted in the midst of the battle and sailed home.[1] Miletus was captured (493). 'Most of the men were killed. The women and children were made slaves. Those whose lives were spared were carried to Susa, but received no ill-treatment from Darius, who established them at Ampe, a city on the Persian Gulf near the mouth of the Tigris. The

[1] Shortly afterwards a large number of the Samians 'of the richer sort' went off to Western Hellas and occupied Zancle (Messina).

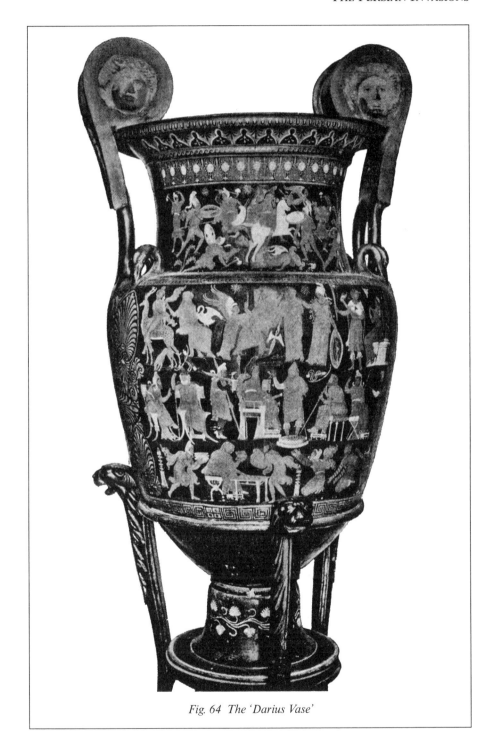

*Fig. 64  The 'Darius Vase'*

263

sanctuary [of the Branchidae] at Didyma was plundered and burnt.' (See p. 248 and Fig. 58.)

On his expulsion from Athens in 510 Hippias, the son of Peisistratus, had lived first at Sigeum. The Spartans had tried to restore him, but had been foiled by their allies. He then did his utmost to gain help from Persia, and Artaphernes had threatened Athenian envoys at Sardis that 'if they wished to remain safe, they must receive Hippias back'; but nothing had come of it. Though now an old man of seventy, Hippias himself, who was now at Susa, had doubtless urged his claims with Darius during these last dozen years or so, and had rejoiced at the anger of the Great King against the Athenians and at the subjugation of the Ionians. It was, however, not the laments of the old Hippias but the burning of Sardis that determined Darius to wipe out Athens and Eretria from existence and transport their inhabitants to the far East. In the spring of 492 he ordered Mardonius, 'a youth lately married to Artazostra, the king's daughter,' to take a great fleet from Cilicia to the Hellespont, whither a vast army was sent to meet him. (On his voyage along the Ionian coast he 'put down all the tyrants and established democracies' – a fact that Herodotus regards as 'a marvel.') He crossed the Hellespont successfully with all his land army, but his fleet was wrecked while attempting to round the dangerous promontory of Athos. 'It is said that the number of ships destroyed was nearly 300, and the men who perished were more than 20,000. The sea around Athos abounds in monsters, and some of the men were seized and devoured by these animals.' After subjugating a Thracian tribe, from whom he had suffered great losses, Mardonius withdrew to Asia, 'having failed disgracefully.'

When Darius had first heard of the burning of Sardis, 'laying aside all thought of the Ionians, who would, he was sure, pay dearly for their revolt, he had asked, *Who are these Athenians?*' – as Cyrus once had asked, *Who are these Spartans?* – 'and when he was informed, he called for his bow and placed an arrow on the string and shot into the sky, exclaiming, *Grant me, Zeus*' – he probably said *Ormuzd* – '*to revenge myself on these Athenians!* Then he bade one of his attendants every day when his dinner was served thrice to repeat these words: *Master, remember the Athenians!*' And now the failure of Mardonius had deepened his resentment and his determination. He transferred the command of the armament to the Mede Datis and to his own nephew Artaphernes, who had probably succeeded his father as satrap at Sardis. A mighty fleet was collected by the seaport towns tributary to Persia, and heralds were sent demanding earth and water from the islands and also from the cities in Greece, a large number of whom, says Herodotus, including Aegina, sent the required tokens of submission. But the heralds 'were thrown at Athens into the barathron' – an *oubliette* for criminals – 'and at Sparta[1] into a well, and bidden to take therefrom earth and water.' Then Datis and Artaphernes, 'with orders to carry the Athenians and Eretrians away captive and to bring them into the presence of Darius,' took their fleet of 600 triremes across the Aegean. They burnt the city of the Naxians and took hostages from other islands, but by the command of Darius they spared the temple and treasure of Delos,[2] on which island Datis landed and made a burnt-offering of 300 talents of frankincense. 'After his departure,' says Herodotus, 'Delos (as the Delians told me) was shaken by an earthquake – the first and last that has been felt there to this day.' In passing we may remark that Thucydides (ii. 8) says exactly the same of an earthquake that occurred at the beginning of the Peloponnesian War. The great fleet then reached Euboea. Eretria had begged Athens for help, and 4000 Athenian settlers were directed to act as auxiliaries, but these, finding the Eretrians meditating flight or treason, escaped from Euboea. After a siege of six days, two traitors, 'both citizens of good repute,' betrayed the city to the Persians. It was plundered and burnt, and most of the citizens were carried away to Susa. 'King Darius,' says Herodotus – and it is another example of Persian magnanimity – 'before they were made his captives, cherished fierce indignation against these men for having injured him unprovoked, but now that he saw them brought into his presence and subjected to him he did them no further harm, and only settled them at a place called Ardericca, 210 furlongs from Susa. . . . And here they continued till my time, and still spoke their old language.'

From Eretria, by the advice of the old Hippias, the Persians crossed over to Attica. 'And because there was no place in all Attica so convenient for their horse as Marathon, and as it lay, moreover, quite close to Eretria,

---

[1] Probably the flight of the Spartan king Demaratus to the court of Darius in 491 had incensed the Spartans. Later two Spartans voluntarily went to Susa to atone for this murder of the heralds with their lives, but were freely pardoned by Xerxes (Hdt. vi. 134–136).

[2] A still more striking example of the regard that Darius and his Persians – but not Xerxes – showed for the temples of Apollo (whom they perhaps identified with the Sun-god) is the fact that Datis, after his defeat at Marathon, having found a gilt image of Apollo that his men had looted, took it to Delos in his own ship and begged the Delians to restore it to its temple in Greece – which was not done for twenty years.

therefore Hippias conducted them thither.' Of the three Attic plains offering a favourable landing-place, the Thriasian, the Athenian, and the Marathonian, the last – about twenty-two miles from Athens – was for the Persian armament by far the most accessible; and doubtless Hippias remembered vividly how, fifty years before, he had accompanied his father, Peisistratus, in his successful expedition from Eretria, and how they had landed at Marathon and had surprised and routed the Athenian army.

'When intelligence of this reached the Athenians, they likewise marched their troops to Marathon, and there stood on the defensive, having at their head ten generals, of whom one was Miltiades.' They seem to have chosen the rather shorter and steeper path that skirts round Pentelicus to the north, for we find them 'drawn up in order of battle in the sacred precinct of Heracles,' to the north-west of the Persian encampment. 'Before they left the city, the generals had sent off to Sparta a herald, who was by profession a trained runner. . . . He reached Sparta' – some 135 miles distant – 'on the very next day. . . . The Spartans wished to help the Athenians, but were unable to come to their aid at once, being unwilling to break the established rule. They could not march out of Sparta on the ninth, when the moon had not yet reached its full. So they waited for the full of the moon.' These statements, so composedly made by Herodotus, amaze one. Why, we ask, had not the Athenians secured the aid of the Spartans and other allies long ago? Surely all that had happened in Euboea was known to them. Surely they knew that their turn would come next. And the fact that Aegina, and perhaps Thebes, and other Greek cities had sent earth and water to the barbarians ought surely to have made them still more anxious to organize resistance – if they meant to offer resistance. And how is it credible that a highly civilized Greek people, the people that prided itself on being representative Hellenes, the foremost of Greek states, the head of a powerful league of Greek cities, should have let a superstition prevent them sending help when the very existence of Greece was at stake? It would truly be incredible had we not in Greek history other similar cases, and no explanation can be found except, as Grote says, in a most astounding 'attribute of Greek character' – or perhaps we might more justly call it Spartan character. One can but cite such instances and leave them to explain themselves. Other cases, as we shall see, occurred in connection with Thermopylae and with Salamis.[1]

[1] See Hdt. vi. 106, vii. 206, ix. 7; Thuc. iv. 5, v. 54. One is reminded of the Jews refusing to fight on the Sabbath during the siege of Jerusalem by the Romans.

The battle has been described and 'reconstructed' times without number. I shall content myself with noting a few points of interest. The Athenian hoplites numbered perhaps 9000 and the gallant little Plataean contingent 1000. The total Greek loss was 192! The Persians had about 200,000 foot and 10,000 cavalry; but all this armament could not well have taken part in the fight. They lost, says Herodotus, 6400 men and seven ships. The rest of the great fleet – some 600 triremes and many transports – at once sailed south and rounded Sunion, with the evident intention of capturing Athens, possibly incited to do so by a signal, the flashing of a shield from the top of Pentelicus, a treacherous act which none has ever explained, but which was attributed (Herodotus thinks wrongly) to the Alcmaeonidae. The walls of the city had been demolished by the Peisistratidae, and it could have offered no resistance had not the Athenian army, leaving Aristides and his regiment to guard the field, hastened back (Herodotus only says 'with all possible speed,' which has sometimes been interpreted as 'on the same day'), and the Persians, seeing them and probably learning the approach of the 2000 Spartans, who had at length started, abandoned their project and sailed away. 'After the full of the moon,' says Herodotus, '2000 Spartans came to Athens. So eager had they been to arrive in time that they took only three days to reach Attica. They came too late for the battle, but as they had a strong desire to see the Medes, they continued their march to Marathon, and there viewed the slain. Then, after bestowing great praise on the Athenians for their achievement, they returned.'

Before passing on let us note a few points of interest about the personalities involved.

After the Greek wings had closed in and routed the victorious Persians in the centre and had chased them to the sea, 'they laid hold of the ships and called for fire; and it was here that Callimachus, the polemarch, after greatly distinguishing himself, was slain . . . and Cynaegeirus, the son of Euphorion, having seized on a ship by the decoration at the stern, had his hand cut off by the blow of an axe, and thus perished.' This Cynaegeirus was the brother of the poet Aeschylus, who himself, as well as another brother, Ameinias, was present at the battle[1] and probably took part in the celebrated charge of the Athenian hoplites. That Callimachus was the 'polemarch' – that is, the official commander-in-chief of the ten generals

---

[1] He doubtless also fought at Salamis – so vividly described in his *Persae* – and at Plataea, and an Ameinias, possibly this brother of his, greatly distinguished himself at Salamis.

*Fig. 65  Pythagoras*

*Fig. 66  Aeschylus*

*Fig. 67  Miltiades*

*Fig. 68  Themistocles*

(each perhaps in command of a *phylē* of 1000 men) – is allowed by Herodotus, but he states that Miltiades won over Callimachus to give his casting vote for risking the battle, and that the other nine generals, 'when their turn came to command, gave up their right to Miltiades,' who nevertheless 'waited until his own day of command came,' and then won the battle. This has been questioned, for it is asserted that daily command by rotation came into practice later; but there is no sufficient reason to doubt the account given by Herodotus, and in any case Miltiades was practically, if not officially, the victor of Marathon – as the Athenians, too, thought, for besides the ten pillars on the field of battle in memory of the fallen a monument was, it is said, erected in honour of him. It will be remembered that he had succeeded his uncle as tyrant of the Chersonese. He had incurred the resentment of Darius by voting for the destruction of the bridge over the Danube (see p. 215) and by conquering and handing over to the Athenians the islands of Lemnos and Imbros, and on the failure of the Ionic revolt he had fled to Athens. His son, Metiochus, had been captured by the Persians. ('Darius, however, when the Phoenicians brought him into his presence, was so far from doing him any hurt that he loaded him with favours, giving him a house and estates and also a Persian wife.') His popularity at Athens was partly due to the acquisition of Lemnos and Imbros and partly to his hostility to the Peisistratidae, who had assassinated his father Cimon (celebrated for having thrice won with the same mares the four-horse chariot-race at Olympia); moreover, his experience in war and his knowledge of the Persians doubtless led to his election as general.

Besides Aeschylus and Callimachus and Miltiades two famous men, afterwards great rivals, Aristides and Themistocles, took part in the battle – the former as general, the latter a young man of perhaps twenty-six.

Some thirty years later, in the great public portico near the Athenian Agora known as the Poikile Stoa (the 'Painted Portico'), the Michelangelo of antiquity, Polygnotus, depicted the battle of Marathon. He seems to have chosen three scenes: the first was the charge of the Athenians and Plataeans, the second was the slaughter of the Persians in the swamp, the third showed the attack of the Greeks on the ships. The Persian leaders, Datis and Artaphernes, and the Greek generals Callimachus and Miltiades and others were portrayed – Cynaegeirus, too, seizing the stern of the vessel.

Something should perhaps be said here about the Spartan leaders – though they were conspicuous for their absence.

We have several times already heard of the Spartan king Cleomenes. He had reigned since about 520, and had helped to eject Hippias, but had failed in a second expedition to Athens. He had resisted the appeal of the Milesians and the bribes of their envoy, Aristagoras.[1] As was often the case (an inevitable and perhaps intentional result of the curious dual system), the two Spartan kings had quarrelled. Cleomenes, who was wild and impulsive (touched, indeed, with insanity, if we are to believe Herodotus), succeeded finally, a year before Marathon, in persuading the Delphic oracle to declare his rival, King Demaratus, to be illegitimate. Demaratus fled to the court of Darius,[2] and we shall find him later as the trusted adviser of Xerxes. A year after Marathon Cleomenes was proved to have tampered with the Delphic oracle in order to dethrone his rival, and took to flight. He was allowed to return, but showed signs of insanity and was fettered and placed under the guard of a Helot, and committed suicide. Leonidas, his half-brother, succeeded, and when he died at Thermopylae Cleombrotus and then Pausanias held the regency for his son Pleistarchus. Demaratus was succeeded by Leotychidas, who reigned till 469.

The counsel given by Solon to Croesus to 'mark well the end' has a striking application in regard to many – indeed, to most – of the famous leaders and statesmen of Greek history.

The end of Miltiades is especially painful. He used his popularity to persuade the Athenians to put a fleet of seventy fully manned ships at his disposal, 'without saying what country he was going to attack, but only that it was a very wealthy land, where they might easily get as much gold as they could carry away.' In order to avenge some private wrong he attacked the island of Paros; but after besieging the town in vain, he was persuaded by a Parian prisoner, a priestess, to steal some sacred object – for this was apparently his purpose in going by night to a Parian temple. On his return he injured himself when jumping from the wall of the precinct, and he returned invalided to Athens. Here he was impeached for having deceived the Athenians. His life was spared, but he was fined fifty talents. 'Soon

---

[1] See Hdt. v. 49 *ff.* for the story of the bronzen map and the dismissal of Aristagoras for having suggested to the Spartans a three months' march up to Babylon; and how the little Gorgo, daughter of Cleomenes, and afterwards wife of her half-uncle Leonidas, saved her father from accepting the bribe.

[2] Many famous Greeks went over to the Persians. I need only mention the two 'saviours of Greece,' Themistocles and the victor of Plataea, Pausanias.

afterwards his leg gangrened and mortified; and so Miltiades died; and the fine was paid by his son Cimon.'

What was the end of Hippias is uncertain. Herodotus gives a graphic picture of the old man landing at Marathon, and 'marshalling the companies of the barbarians as they disembarked'; but we hear no more. Had he been killed in the battle we should have surely heard of it. Some assert that he retired to Lemnos, which was now for a time reoccupied by the Persians, but was reannexed by Athens after Salamis. We hear of Peisistratidae – perhaps sons of Hippias – at the court of Xerxes.

The occurrences in Greece during the interval between the battle of Marathon and that of Salamis proved of very great moment in deciding the fate of the Hellenic race. Let us first consider these, and then turn to Persia and the vast preparations of Darius and Xerxes for wreaking vengeance on Athens.

The perpetual hostility between Athens and Aegina has been frequently mentioned, and it will be remembered that the Athenians had denounced Aegina to Sparta for having sent earth and water to the Persian king. Sparta, the head of a great confederation to which even Athens belonged, had lately, by means of a rather mean ruse,[1] defeated its great rival Argos, and had almost exterminated the Argive warriors – so that the city 'was left so bare of men that the slaves managed the state and administered everything until the sons of those who were slain by Cleomenes grew up.' Sparta, therefore, felt justified in acting in a high-handed manner, and, having taken hostages from the Aeginetans, handed them over to the Athenians. After Marathon these hostages were demanded back by the Aeginetans, but the demand was refused by Athens, and continual fighting went on between the two states from about 487 until 483, when, in prospect of renewed invasion by the Persians, the Greek states assembled on the Corinthian isthmus and decided to patch up all quarrels.

Probably, as Herodotus says, 'the breaking out of this Aeginetan war was the saving of Greece; for hereby the Athenians were forced to become a maritime power.'

Even in the Dark Age, as we have seen, Athens possessed a considerable navy; but as a maritime power she was then out-rivalled by Corinth, and in later days by Corcyra and Syracuse, and had held her own with much difficulty against Aegina. The quarrel with this neighbouring island-state

---

[1] Hdt. vi. 78.

induced the Athenians now to build ships, and the man who suggested this (doubtless foreseeing Salamis) was the great statesman Themistocles.

Even before the battle of Marathon he had been archon,[1] and had carried a measure for the fortification of the Peiraeus and the preparation of docks in the three natural harbours; and the work was begun; but it was not completed until after the Persian wars. Themistocles, as we are told by Thucydides in a masterly analysis of his character (i. 138), was 'the best judge of things present with the least deliberation, and the best conjecturer of the future.' This insight and foresight made him believe that the safety of Greece and the future greatness of Athens depended on her sea-power.

Marathon had been a victory for Athenian hoplites – the conservative citizens of Athens, whose political leaders were Aristides and Xanthippus. Themistocles, though no professional party-leader or demagogue, gained the allegiance of the mercantile and naval part of the population, of that 'nautical rabble' on which Aristophanes – the praiser of good old Marathonian times – pours such contempt. The claims of the Peiraeus were beginning to make themselves heard. It was felt by some that Athens, if she was to be a great maritime power, should not be at the distance of four miles from the sea, and doubtless the transference of the city to the Peiraean peninsula would have saved her from enormous difficulties and expenses (such as those connected with her Long Walls); but the feeling against abandoning the ancestral site and the Acropolis was exceedingly strong and prevailed. The policy urged by Themistocles was that of fortifying the harbours of Athens and increasing her navy. About the year 483 fortune offered him the following opportunity. 'The Athenians, having a large sum of money in their treasury, the produce of the mines at Laurion [near Sunion], were meaning to distribute it among the full-grown citizens, who would have received ten drachmae apiece, when Themistocles persuaded them to build with the money two hundred ships' – more probably to raise their navy to this number – 'to help them in their war against the Aeginetans. . . . The new ships were not used for this purpose, but became a help to Greece in her hour of need.'

About the personality of Themistocles and his two chief rivals, Xanthippus and Aristides, a few words should be said. He was the son of

---

[1] If this was, as stated, in 493–2, and if he was born, as stated, about 514, he would have been only about twenty-one years of age. Hitherto the open beach of Phaleron had sufficed for the warships.

a middle-class Athenian, Neocles. His mother was a foreigner, a Thracian or Halicarnassian. He owed, therefore, his citizenship to the late reforms of Cleisthenes, and his early political pre-eminence under such unfavourable conditions to very unusual abilities. His meteor-like career and fall will be related in connection with historical events. Probably no one ever earned more justly the name of a saviour of his country, nor that of a traitor – although many illustrious Greeks contest with him the latter title to fame.

Xanthippus was connected through his wife, Agarista (a niece of the reformer Cleisthenes), with the celebrated Alcmaeonidae. He was a leader of the old democratic party, which held to the reforms of Cleisthenes against the more advanced radical and nautical doctrines of Themistocles. In 483, things having come to a crisis between the two parties, an appeal was made to ostracism and Xanthippus was banished (see Fig. 75). At the battle of Salamis he returned, was made admiral in place of Themistocles in 479, and fought at Mycale. He was the father of Pericles, who began to take part in public affairs about 469.

Aristides was of noble Athenian family. He was, as we have seen, one of the generals at Marathon. In the following year he was archon. He had been an intimate friend of Cleisthenes (who had evidently died about 500). His character gained him the surname 'the Just.' He took part with Xanthippus in opposing the policy of Themistocles, and like him was ostracized (483 or 482). In this connection a rather trite story should perhaps be retold. An illiterate voter appealed to a bystander to scratch on his *ostrakon* (potsherd) the name Aristides. The bystander, who happened to be Aristides himself, complied with the request, but asked the man why he wished to ostracize Aristides. 'Because,' was the answer, 'I'm so tired of hearing him called *the Just.*' Aristides, permitted to return, took part in the battle of Salamis, as we shall see, and became a great power in the state. To him and Cimon, the son of Miltiades, was chiefly due the building up of the Athenian Empire. He lived to see the ostracism of Themistocles, and died, almost in poverty, in the year 468.

Let us now turn to Persia. After the return of Datis and Artaphernes the determination of Darius to chastise Greece seems to have urged him to collect a still vaster armament. But in the midst of these preparations he died (485). His latter years had been troubled by the quarrels of his sons in regard to the succession. Artabazanes was the eldest, but was born before, whereas Xerxes was born soon after, the accession of Darius. Moreover, the mother of Xerxes was Atossa, the daughter of Cyrus and widow of Cambyses, and she was regarded as the chief wife of Darius. He therefore (influenced also, it is said, by the arguments of the exiled Spartan Demaratus, who had himself lost his kingship through a question of legitimacy) appointed Xerxes as his heir. Xerxes was a mere youth. He was at first 'coldly disposed towards a Grecian war,' and gave his attention to subduing Egypt, which had revolted, and over which he set his brother Achaemenes as satrap. (Achaemenes led the Egyptian naval contingent in the invasion of Greece, and was afterwards killed in Egypt.) After his return from Egypt Xerxes called a council and pledged himself 'not to rest till he had taken and burnt Athens.' The plan was warmly supported by Mardonius, who had constantly incited Xerxes to avenge the Persians, and had been seconded by messengers from the Aleuadae (the Thessalian princes who had espoused the cause of the Persians), and by certain Peisistratidae (perhaps sons of Hippias), as well as by an 'oracle-monger,' Onomacritus by name, who had long ago been banished by Hipparchus from Athens for having forged prophecies under the venerable name of Musaeus. This Orphic seer 'had plied Xerxes with his oracles, and the Peisistratidae and Aleuadae had not ceased to press him with their advice, till at last Xerxes had yielded.' But his uncle Artabanus was strongly opposed to the attempt, extolling the invincible bravery of the Greeks, while Mardonius sneered at them as cowards, saying, 'Though I went as far as Macedonia and came little short of reaching Athens itself, yet not a soul ventured to come out against me to battle.' Xerxes was disquieted by the advice of his uncle; but he had a vision which bade him keep to his former decision, and after the vision had twice appeared he bade Artabanus don the royal robes and lay himself on the royal bed. The vision then appeared also to him, and 'threatened him and endeavoured to burn out his eyes with red-hot irons.' So he was convinced; and, encouraged by still another vision, Xerxes sent forth orders to all the nations in the Persian Empire to collect men and horses and chariots and transports and ships of war.

Herodotus uses all the resources of his inimitable art in order to impress one with the incomparable vastness of the armament of Xerxes. Some of his statistics may perhaps be questionable, but in spite of all that it has suffered at the hands of scepticism and criticism his account of the invasion still remains by far the most worthy of perusal, for it is a work of art and not merely a bare enumeration of well-authenticated facts. As my space allows me only the choice between constructing a narrative from provable statistics and offering some of the innumerable pictures delineated by Herodotus, I shall adopt the latter course.

'In the first place, because the former fleet had met with so great a disaster at Athos, preparations were made there during three years. Detachments were sent by the various nations whereof the army was composed. These relieved each other in turn and worked at a moat beneath the lash. The people dwelling about Athos also bore a part in the labour. Athos is a great mountain stretching out far into the sea, and where it ends towards the mainland there is a neck of land some twelve furlongs wide, the whole extent of which is a level plain, broken only by a few low hills'; and the modern name of the locality (Provlaka) means 'the canal in front [of the mountain].' Distinct traces of Xerxes' canal are still visible. The isthmus is formed of deposits of sand and marl, and its highest part is only 50 feet above sea-level, so that the cutting of a canal was a comparatively easy task. 'It seems to me,' says, nevertheless, our historian, 'that Xerxes was actuated by pride, wishing to display his power and to leave a memorial to posterity, for, although it was possible with no trouble at all to have the ships drawn across the isthmus, he ordered that a canal should be made of such width as to allow two triremes to pass abreast with oars in action.'

Xerxes met the main body of his Eastern troops in Cappadocia, and spent the winter of 481 at Sardis. Meantime all the contingents of nearly fifty different nations, land and sea forces, were assembling near the Hellespont, and preparations were being made to throw a double bridge across the strait. 'Near Sestos and just opposite Abydos there is a rocky tongue of land which runs out for some distance into the sea. Towards this tongue they constructed a double bridge from Abydos, the Phoenicians making one line of it with cables of white flax, the Egyptians for the other using ropes of papyrus. But after the channel (which is seven furlongs wide) had been bridged it happened that a great storm arose and broke the whole work to pieces. Now when Xerxes heard thereof he was filled with wrath and straightway sent orders that the Hellespont should receive three hundred lashes, and that fetters should be cast into it. Nay, I have even heard it said that he bade branders take their irons and brand the Hellespont. And while the sea was thus punished by his orders, he also commanded that the overseers of the work should lose their heads.'

So a new bridge was built. Six hundred and seventy-four ships of war (triremes and penteconters) were arranged in two lines, and over each of these were stretched by means of capstans six huge cables, some of flax and

275

*A late black-figured hydria (c. 510) from Vulci*

some of papyrus (the former weighing not less than fifty-seven pounds the cubit). Transversely were laid immense planks, and a road was formed with brushwood and earth, and fenced with a high boarding, so that the animals should not see the water. Then Xerxes set forth from Sardis. 'At the moment of departure the sun suddenly quitted his seat in the heavens, though there were no clouds in sight.'[1] The omen was favourably interpreted by the Magi, and Xerxes 'proceeded on his way with great gladness of heart. . . . First of all went the baggage-carriers and the beasts of burden, and then a vast crowd of many nations . . . then in front of the king a thousand picked horsemen of the Persian race and a thousand spearmen; then ten sacred horses richly caparisoned and the holy car of Zeus [Ormuzd] drawn by eight milk-white steeds with their charioteer on foot; for no mortal may mount upon the car. Next came Xerxes himself, in a chariot drawn by Nisaean horses – but when the fancy took him he would alight and travel in a litter. Then immediately behind the king a thousand spearmen, the noblest of the Persians, and a thousand Persian horsemen; then ten thousand on foot, all picked men. And of these last one thousand carried spears with golden pomegranates at their lower ends instead of spikes,[2] and these encircled the other nine thousand, who bore on their spears pomegranates of silver; and the thousand Persians who followed after Xerxes had golden apples.'

On reaching Ilium (Troy), where the water of the Scamander,[3] naturally enough, 'failed to satisfy the thirst of men and cattle,' Xerxes (as afterwards Alexander) ascended the citadel, and 'made an offering of a thousand oxen to the Trojan Athene, while the Magi poured libations to the heroes who were slain at Troy.' Thence he arrived at Abydos, and from a white marble throne (or platform) viewed all his land forces and all his ships; and when the appointed day had come 'they burnt all kinds of spices on the bridge and strewed the way with myrtle boughs, while they anxiously waited for

---

[1] Here our chronicler seems to have made a slip, and to have transferred to this occasion an eclipse which occurred in the preceding spring – probably before the departure of Xerxes from Susa.

[2] In the monuments of Persepolis such pomegranates or apples may be recognized.

[3] The Scamander has, like many rivers in hot countries, a wide bed, but is reduced to a small brook in summer. It was now fairly early in the year; but, as in other cases where the veracity of Herodotus has been questioned, it is very easy to believe that a host of perhaps a million with innumerable beasts of burden would soon exhaust the drinkable water of such a stream.

the sun, hoping to see him as he rose. And now the sun appeared; and Xerxes took a golden goblet and poured a libation into the sea, praying the while with his face turned to the sun; and after he had prayed he cast the golden cup into the Hellespont, and with it a golden bowl and a Persian sword of the kind that they call *acinaces*. I cannot say for certain whether it was as an offering to the sun-god that he threw these things into the deep, or whether he repented of having scourged the Hellespont. . . . And as soon as Xerxes had reached the European side, he stood to contemplate his army as they crossed under the lash. And the crossing continued during seven days and seven nights, without cessation or pause.'

From Sestos the land forces marched westwards and met the fleet at Doriscus on the Thracian sea-coast, near to the river Hebrus. Here Xerxes numbered his forces. 'A body of ten thousand men was brought to a certain place and made to stand together as close as possible; then a circle was drawn round them and the men were let go; then, where the circle had been, a fence was built about the height of a man's middle, and the enclosure was filled continually with fresh troops, till the whole of the army had thus been numbered.' The sum total was 1,700,000. Herodotus takes this as the number of Asiatic foot-soldiers, and adds 80,000 horsemen, and also camel-riders and charioteers, and half a million seamen – the crews and soldiers of 1207 triremes and 3000 smaller vessels. Thus, together with some 300,000 men pressed into service in Europe,[1] he makes 2,641,610 combatants, and to these he adds the same number of non-combatants, arriving at a grand total of over five millions. Doubtless the nobles were attended by their harems and large retinues, but the Persian and Median picked troops only amounted, including the famous 10,000 'Immortals,' to about 24,000 (Hdt. vii. 40, 41) – about one-hundredth of the whole army, which was mainly a motley host of picturesquely dressed savages, many of them only armed with light javelins or flint-headed arrows (or 'staves with one end hardened in the fire'), and certainly well able to look after themselves without such slaves and attendants as, for instance, the Spartan hoplites took into battle.[2] As for the number of combatants given by Herodotus, we need not whittle it down to about a seventh, as is done by some sceptics. Six millions, it is said, took the Red Cross, and a million combatants, with a 'vast multitude' of followers, composed the host of

---

[1] Also quite half the naval force was supplied by Greeks, or nations of Greek lineage.

[2] At Plataea each Spartan hoplite was accompanied by *seven* Helots.

invaders in the First Crusade under far less favourable commissariat conditions. Doubtless the provisioning of such a vast multitude as this army of Xerxes was difficult, but immense stores had been laid up beforehand in Thrace, and the whole country, according to Herodotus, was drained of its riches by the enormous strain put upon it (Hdt. vii. 25; see also vii. 118–120, where the cost of one meal is reckoned at about £6 million, and the joke is made that 'if the order had been to provide breakfast as well as dinner, the people of Abdera must have fled, or have been entirely ruined').

The descriptions given by Herodotus of the warriors of the forty-six different nations, with their various weapons and costumes, are most graphic and interesting, but are too long to repeat. Doubtless he draws largely on his own reminiscences, for he travelled much in the East and in Africa. Some of his word-pictures are corroborated by Persian and Egyptian monuments. Among the many commanders may be noted Mardonius, the brother-in-law of Xerxes, and Achaemenes, his brother, and that other unfortunate brother of his, Masistes, whose tragic story is told by our historian (ix. 108 *ff.*), and that queen of Halicarnassus, Artemisia, who distinguished herself so highly at Salamis, and whose 'brave and manly spirit moved the special wonder' of her fellow-countryman Herodotus.

At Doriscus the king, having reviewed his land army, 'exchanged his chariot for a Sidonian vessel, and, sitting beneath a golden awning, sailed along before the prows of all his vessels,' drawn up at some distance from the shore, 'with fighting men upon the decks accoutred as for war.' Elated with pride, he turned to the exiled Spartan king Demaratus, asking whether the Greeks would dare to oppose such an armament. The answer was memorable: 'Poverty hath at all times been a fellow-dweller with us in the land, but Valour has come to us as an ally whom we have gained by wisdom and strict laws. . . . Brave are all the Greeks, but as for the Lacedaemonians they will never accept slavery. As for their numbers do not ask; for if only a thousand take the field they will meet thee in battle, so will any number, less or more.' Xerxes laughed at this and rejoined: 'Let them be five thousand and we shall have more than a thousand to each one of theirs; . . . and much more he said in contemptuous ridicule; and Demaratus answered all, and added: "Though they be free men they are not free in all respects, for law is their master. This master they fear more than thy subjects fear thee, and his commandment is always the same, forbidding them to flee whatever be the number of their foes, and requiring them to stand firm and to conquer – or else to die."'

From Doriscus the vast armament marched westward, crossed the Strymon, and arrived at Acanthus, near the Athos canal. Then, passing through Chalcidice, it reached Therma (later named Thessalonice after the sister of Alexander the Great). The fleet meanwhile sailed through the canal and rounded the promontories of Sithonia and Pallene, gathering fresh supplies of men and ships and provisions from the numerous Greek cities on the coast. During the land march – which followed the same route as that later traversed by St. Paul – 'the camels were set upon by lions which came down by night'; and Herodotus adds: 'The whole of that region is full of lions[1] and wild bulls with huge horns, which are imported into Greece.'

From Therma King Xerxes beheld in the far distance the mountains Ossa and Olympus, and embarking on a Sidonian vessel he visited the mouth of the Peneios (Penéus), which discharges its waters through the narrow vale, or ravine, of Tempe (Fig. 48). 'Wise men, truly,' he remarked, 'are they of Thessaly, and good reason they had to change their minds, for nothing more is needed but to fill up the gorge with an embankment, and lo! all Thessaly would be laid under water.' And possibly he was right, for Thessaly was once a great lake,[2] until, as Herodotus believed, the gorge of Tempe was formed by volcanic disturbance, or by erosion. The remark of Xerxes alluded to the fact that the Thessalians had begged the southern Greeks to make a stand at the pass of Tempe. Ten thousand hoplites were dispatched – the Athenian contingent under Themistocles – but the Macedonian king, Alexander I, sent to warn them of the vastness of the Persian army, and when it was discovered that there were several other practicable passes from the north (by one of which Xerxes led his army) the troops were recalled; whereupon the Thessalians, doubtless to the great satisfaction of their Aleuad princes, who had long before held treasonable correspondence with Xerxes (Hdt. vii. 6), 'warmly espoused the side of the Medes, and were of the greatest service to Xerxes during the war.'

This expedition had set out while Xerxes was at Abydos; for when the Greeks had learned for certain that the invasion would take place, they had convened an assembly, under the presidency of Sparta, at the Corinthian isthmus. It was the first time in Greek history that a congress of all the

---

[1] Aristotle confirms this. Tradition from the age of Heracles to that of the *Nibelungenlied* asserts the presence of lions in Europe. The 'wild bull' is probably the aurochs (urus). Classical writers also tell of *bonasi* (wild oxen), *alces* (elk), *bubali* (buffalo?).

[2] The Greek tradition of the Deluge is connected with Thessaly, the Greek Noah, Deucalion, having been king of Thessalian Phthia.

states of Greece had been summoned – the first time (with the exception perhaps of the Trojan War) that all Greece, indeed all the Hellenic world, was called upon to co-operate against a common enemy. Besides deciding to defend Thessaly, they agreed to put an end to all feuds among themselves, such as that between Athens and Aegina, and between Sparta and Argos. In spite of the jealousy of Athens, Sparta was given the leadership on land and on the sea. They determined also to send an appeal to Gelo, the powerful lord of Syracuse, and to Corcyra and Crete. Also they at once dispatched spies to Sardis, while Xerxes was still there. The spies were detected, but sent back unharmed by Xerxes, 'after having been taken round the Persian camp and having viewed everything to their hearts' content'; for he expected that the Greeks, when they heard of the vastness of his army, would submit and 'save him the trouble of the expedition.' The embassy to Gelo, 'whose power was said to be far greater than that of any single state in Greece,' failed because he demanded the chief command – or, anyhow, the command of the naval forces – and when this was indignantly refused he dismissed the envoys with the contemptuous remark: 'Ye have, it seems, no lack of commanders; but ye are likely to lack men to receive their orders.' The Corcyraeans made lavish promises, but failed to keep them – 'watching to see what turn the war would take.' The Cretans, warned by an oracle, refused point-blank. The Argives, when asked to lay aside their feud and aid in repelling the Persians, applied to the Delphic oracle, which, in cowardly fashion, bade them 'warily guard their own head.' They then made, like Gelo, extravagant demands, and ultimately stood aside – probably in collusion with the Persians. 'Some,' says Herodotus, 'go even so far as to say that the Argives first invited the Persians to invade Greece, because of their ill-success against Lacedaemon' – nor is this impossible, for at the outbreak of the Peloponnesian War both the Athenians and the Lacedaemonians, according to Thucydides (ii. 7), 'intended to send embassies to the Persian king and to the barbarians in other parts, whencesoever either hoped to gain assistance.'

On their return from Thessaly the Greeks once more took counsel together on the Corinthian isthmus. 'The opinion prevailed that they should guard the pass of Thermopylae, since it was narrower than the Thessalian defile, and at the same time nearer to them. Of the pathway by which the Greeks who fell at Thermopylae were circumvented they had no knowledge as yet. At the same time it was resolved that the fleet should proceed to Artemisium, in the region of Histiaeotis [in Northern Euboea].'

The Greek fleet of rather more than 300 warships, of which 200 were supplied by Athens, took up its station near Artemisium, and the Persian fleet arrived at the precipitous promontory of Magnesia, which is formed by the long ridge of Mount Pelion. They had sent forward ten swift ships, which succeeded in capturing three Greek vessels on the look-out, and when fire-signals[1] from the island Sciathos informed the Greeks of this disaster they 'quitted their anchorage at Artemisium, and, leaving scouts on the Euboean heights to watch the enemy, withdrew to Chalcis, intending to guard the Euripus' – the narrow strait between Euboea and the mainland. But the movements and sequence of events as described by Herodotus are difficult to follow. One great fact emerges – the wreck of 400 vessels of the Persian fleet, which had taken up a dangerous position off the harbourless Magnesian coast-line. 'The ships of the first row were moored to the land, while the rest swung at anchor further off. The beach extended but a very little way, so they had to anchor off the shore, row upon row, eight deep. In this manner they passed the night; but at dawn calm and stillness gave place to a raging sea and a violent storm. . . . Such as put the loss of the Persian fleet at lowest say that 400 ships were destroyed and that a countless multitude of men perished[2] and a vast amount of treasure was engulfed.' To some the fact may appear not worthy of mention, but it may help one to realize better the Greek character when we learn that the people of Delphi 'earned the everlasting gratitude of the Greeks' for cheering them with the oracle that 'the winds would do Greece good service,' and that the Athenians attributed this storm to the sacrifices and prayers that they offered to Boreas (to whom later they erected a temple on the banks of the Ilissus). It is also psychologically if not historically interesting to note that the winds were influenced also by the entreaties of the foe, for 'after the storm had lasted three days, at length the Persian Magi, by offering sacrifices to the winds and charming them with the help of conjurers, succeeded in laying the tempest; or perhaps,' adds Herodotus, 'it ceased of itself.' The loss of 400 vessels out of their immense fleet was a matter of no vital importance to the Persians. They moved round Cape Sepias to the shelter of the great Pagasaean Gulf and took up station near the port

---

[1] Evidently some code was used by the Greeks, for such news could not have been foreseen. For fire-signals see Aesch. *Agam.* 29 and 272 *ff*.; Thuc. ii. 94, iii. 22, 80; Hdt. vii. 182, ix. 2 (where a system of signals between Attica and Sardis is mentioned). The news of Plataea is said to have reached Mycale on the same day (see p. 297).

[2] As also at Salamis, for the Persians could not swim (Hdt. viii. 89).

whence Jason in the *Argo* put forth on to the high sea, called from that fact Aphetae ('the place of letting loose'). Meantime the Greeks had returned to Artemisium and managed to capture fifteen stray Persian vessels. Although terribly alarmed at the huge fleet of Xerxes, they held their post (Themistocles, it is said, having received a bribe of thirty talents from the Euboeans, and having given five to the Spartan admiral Eurybiadas), and in several engagements did considerable damage to the enemy and captured thirty more of their ships. But the Persians, determined on their part to capture the whole Greek fleet, and 'not let even a torch-bearer slip through their hands,' sent a squadron of 200 warships to circumnavigate Euboea and seize the strait of the Euripus. News of this was brought to the Greeks, it was said, by a diver – a Greek of Scione, Scyllias by name. 'I marvel much,' says Herodotus, 'if the tale commonly told be true. 'Tis said he dived into the sea at Aphetae and did not once come to the surface till he reached Artemisium, a distance of nearly eighty' – really sixty – 'furlongs. Many things are related of this man that are plainly false, but some seem to be true. For my part I think he made the passage to Artemisium in a boat.'

The 200 Persian ships never arrived at their destination. 'Heaven so contrived it that the Persian fleet might not greatly exceed the Greek, but be brought nearly to its level. The squadron was therefore entirely lost about the Hollows of Euboea.'

The Greeks had scouts on watch near Thermopylae and near Artemisium, ready to sail at any moment with news. The watches in the Maliac Gulf 'now arrived at Artemisium with the news of what had befallen Leonidas and those who were with him.' Forthwith the Greek fleet sailed off southward, through the Euripus, and the Persians captured Histiaea and overran the north of Euboea.

Themistocles had cut inscriptions on the rocks at various places on the coast, entreating the Ionians and Carians not to fight against their ancestors, and pointing out that it was through them that Greece had incurred the enmity of the Persians. Whether this had any result we are not told, and whether any of these inscriptions are extant I cannot say.

Meanwhile the battle of Thermopylae had been fought.

It was the wish of the Lacedaemonians and their Peloponnesian allies that Northern Greece should be abandoned to its fate, and that a stand should be made at the Isthmus. But they were conscious that it would be vain to hold the Isthmus if the Persians had the supremacy on the sea,[1] and that their safety depended on the fleet, two-thirds of which belonged to Athens. To please the Athenians, therefore, they sent a small body of men northwards. 'They intended presumably, when they had celebrated the Carnean festival, to hasten in full force to join the army; and the rest of their allies intended to act similarly, for it happened that the Olympic Games fell exactly at this period.[2] None of them expected that the contest at Thermopylae would be decided so speedily; therefore they were content to send forward merely an advance-guard.' Leonidas took with him 300 Spartan veterans[3] and some 3000 other Peloponnesians, and was joined by about 3000 from Northern Greece, including 400 Thebans, whom he 'made a point of demanding from Thebes, because the Thebans were strongly suspected of being well inclined to the Medes' – a suspicion which, if we can believe Herodotus, was fully confirmed by their shameful surrender in the midst of the fight at Thermopylae, where they suffered the indignity of being branded as fugitive slaves by the Persian victor (Hdt. vii. 233. But later writers know nothing of this, and perhaps Herodotus was influenced by the bitter anti-Theban feeling prevalent after the Persian wars).

The pass of Thermopylae has been much broadened by alluvial deposits. A swampy plain of about two miles now separates the waters of the Maliac Gulf from the precipices of Mount Kallidromos. Formerly the pass itself (by the hot sulphur springs) was about fifty feet wide, and there were two other places where it was still narrower, that to the east allowing only the passage of a single wagon (Herodotus however speaks of marshes between the road and the sea). At Thermopylae itself there were the remains of an ancient wall, built by the Phocians as a defence against the Thessalians. This the Greeks now repaired, and here they determined to make their stand. Xerxes took up his headquarters at Trachis, just to the west of the

---

[1] In a fine passage (vii. 139) Herodotus expresses his convictions on this point and, Doric as he was by origin, shows his impartiality. 'I cannot see,' he says, 'what possible use walls across the Isthmus could have been if the king had had the mastery on the sea. If, then, a man should say that the Athenians were the saviours of Greece, he would not exceed the truth.' With this compare the advice given to Xerxes by Demaratus (vii. 235) – viz. to send ships to attack the coasts of Laconia, and 'the Isthmus and the cities of the Peloponnese will surrender without a battle.'

[2] *Cf.* p. 2266.

[3] All fathers with sons living. Sparta only possessed 8000 full-grown Spartiats, if we are to believe Demaratus. The numbers given by Herodotus (vii. 202) do not seem to agree with the inscription that he quotes (vii. 228).

*Fig. 69  Thermopylae*

*Fig. 70  Tomb of Leonidas (?)*

285

pass, and 'after waiting four days, expecting that the Greeks would run away, he grew wroth with their impudence,' and sent Median troops, who were beaten back with great loss, and then commanded his Immortals to attack. 'They, it was thought, would soon finish the business.' But they too were repelled, and 'during these assaults, it is said, Xerxes, who was watching the battle, thrice leaped from the throne on which he was sitting, in terror for his army.' On the third day the traitor appeared. Ephialtes,[1] a man of Malis, offered to guide the Persians by a steep pathway across the mountains so as to cut off the Greeks in the rear. Xerxes sent Hydarnes with the Immortals – probably not all the Ten Thousand. They ascended the ravine of the stream Asopus, between the Trachinian cliffs and Mount Oeta (famous in connection with the legends of Heracles), and surprised at break of day and put to rout the thousand Phocians who were guarding this mountain path. Leonidas, having learnt the fact from a seer and from deserters,[2] dismissed all the Greeks except his 300 Spartans, the Thebans (whose fidelity he suspected), and 700 Thespians. It is just possible that he detached other troops – numbering perhaps about 2500 – in order to oppose the Immortals; but we hear of no collision. According to Herodotus, the devoted band of Spartans and Thespians, having retreated to a hillock, were assaulted on both sides and massacred, while the Thebans surrendered. Later and more rhetorical writers describe the battle with ridiculous exaggeration. One asserts that the Spartans not only drove back the Persians to their camp, but that Leonidas snatched the diadem from the head of Xerxes. The account given by Herodotus bears the impress of truthfulness and impartiality – except possibly in regard to the Thebans. The loss of the Persians he gives at 20,000 (probably too many) and that of the Greeks at 4000, including many Helots (*seven* of whom generally attended each Spartan). He asserts that Xerxes gave permission to the seamen of the fleet to come and view the battlefield, and buried or concealed all the Persian dead except a thousand. 'It was indeed most truly a laughable device – on the one side 1000 men lying strewn all about the field,

---

[1] It is but fair to say that Herodotus names others; but he feels so certain that he 'leaves this name on record' as that of the real perpetrator. Ephialtes, anyhow, had a price set on his head by the deputies of the Amphictionic Council, which, by the way, had its ancient meeting-place at Anthela, in the pass of Thermopylae.

[2] Both rather strange sources. The seer was Megistias, who refused to desert Leonidas and was killed and had the honour of an epitaph by Simonides (Hdt. vii. 221, 228). Who the *deserters* could have been is not easy to say.

on the other 4000 crowded together on one spot.' Two brothers of Xerxes were among the slain. The body of Leonidas was maltreated by Xerxes, who cut off the head and crucified the trunk. This act excited the wonder of Herodotus: 'for the Persians are wont to honour those who show themselves valiant in fight more than any nation I know' – a statement that is confirmed by many of his anecdotes. The sulphur springs still exist, and their water is bluish green, just as it is described by Pausanias. About a mile to the west of these springs is a round hillock which is probably the mound (*kolōnos*) on which the Spartans and Thespians made their last stand. 'The hillock,' says Herodotus, 'is at the entrance of the pass' – *i.e.* as one comes from the west – 'where the stone lion stands[1] which was set up in honour of Leonidas. . . . The slain were buried where they fell, and in their honour and for those no less who were slain before Leonidas sent away the allies an inscription was set up . . . and another for the Spartans alone.' For these inscriptions (rejected as later bombast by some scholars) (see p. 224). It will be noticed that 4000 'from Pelops' land' are mentioned. On a column at Sparta, which was seen six hundred years later by Pausanias, were engraved the names of Leonidas and his 300 Spartans – or 299, for one, being ill, or not returning when sent on a message, escaped. He was treated with great contumely, but 'wiped away all his disgrace at Plataea,' where he was slain.

The Persian army now poured into Phocis, Boeotia, and Attica. The Phocians took refuge on Mount Parnassus, and the temple of Delphi was only saved by the aid of the god, who repulsed the barbarian plunderers by lightning and by hurling down from the heights great masses of rock – seen afterwards by Herodotus. The Thespians and Plataeans, who alone of the Boeotians had not surrendered, fled to the Peloponnese, and their towns were burnt and plundered. Attica was ravaged. When Athens was reached it was found to be deserted, except for a small garrison in the Acropolis, who had 'barricaded the citadel with planks and boards,' in accordance with what they held to be the meaning of a Delphic oracle. For the Pythian god, though he defended his own treasure, gave what seems craven counsel in this hour of need. He had bidden the Argives 'warily guard their own head,' and when the Athenians sent messengers to Delphi they were consternated by the answer that all was lost – head and body, hands and feet – and that they were to depart from the sanctuary and 'o'erspread their

---

[1] This lion existed till the time of Tiberius.

hearts with woes'; and when they as suppliants implored a more comfortable response, the priestess answered that Athene could gain no more from Olympian Zeus except the promise that their 'wooden wall' should remain undestroyed. Some interpreted this literally, and demanded that the Acropolis should be fortified with wood and be strongly garrisoned, and this seems to have been done. But Themistocles (whom some accuse of having prompted the oracle) persuaded the great majority that by the 'wooden wall' was meant the fleet, and the question now to be decided was whether to 'quit Attica without lifting a hand and make a settlement in some other country' – as the Phocaeans and Samians had done – or to venture a sea-fight. In any case Athens would have to be abandoned for a time. Themistocles and his fellow-generals 'issued a proclamation that every Athenian should save his children and household as best he could. Whereupon some sent their families to Aegina, some to Salamis, but the greater number to Troezen. This removal was made with all possible haste, partly from the desire to obey the oracle, but still more for another reason.' This reason was that the huge serpent which lived in the temple of Athene Polias (or was supposed to live there, for Herodotus throws doubt on its existence) no longer consumed its honey-cake; 'so they believed that the goddess had already abandoned the Acropolis.' Xerxes therefore found and sacked a deserted city. The Persians set fire to the wooden wall of the Acropolis, and after two weeks' siege scaled the north side by a secret path, massacred the garrison, and destroyed the temples and statues. (The destruction was completed on the later occupation by Mardonius.)

Meantime the Spartans under Cleombrotus (the regent for the child-king, Pleistarchus, son of Leonidas), together with their allies – Arcadians, Corinthians, Eleans, and others – were busily fortifying the Isthmus. They blocked the Scironian Way, which led past precipitous rocks on the eastern shore, and then 'decided to build a wall right across the Isthmus. Stones, bricks, timber, baskets filled with sand, were used . . . and they laboured ceaselessly night and day.' Their policy was not only selfish but foolish, for had Themistocles carried out his threat made to the Spartan admiral Eurybiadas, to sail away with all the Athenians and refound the city of Siris in Italy, little would have availed them their Isthmian wall.

Councils were held now on both sides. The fleet of Xerxes had arrived off Phaleron, and he came aboard a ship (probably his favourite Sidonian vessel) and 'sat in a seat of honour; and the sovereigns of nations and the captains of ships were sent for, and took their seats according to the rank assigned them of the king. In the first seat sat the king of Sidon, and after him the king of Tyre, and then the rest in their order. And Xerxes sent Mardonius and questioned each whether a sea-fight should be risked or no. And all gave the same answer, advising to engage the Greeks, except only Artemisia.' The speech of Artemisia, as given by Herodotus, was audacious in its contempt for the seamanship of the king's allies and for its advice to risk no naval engagement. It was fully expected that 'her life would be forfeit.' But Xerxes took it good-naturedly and 'gave orders that the advice of the greater number should be followed, and resolved that he himself would be an eye-witness of the combat.'

The council of the Greeks was of a stormier character. The Spartan admiral Eurybiadas, seconded by the Corinthian captain Adeimantus, insisted that the fleet should retire to the Isthmus, and thus abandon Salamis, Aegina, and Megara; and fierce altercations took place between them and Themistocles, who when bidden to be silent, 'since he was a man without a city,' replied with justice that his 200 ships of war were as good as any city in Greece. Eurybiadas, conscious that the only safety for the Peloponnese lay in these ships (for of 378 warships the Athenians supplied 200), at length yielded; but Themistocles still feared the influence of the Peloponnesians, and sent a secret message to the commanders of the Persian fleet, saying that 'fear had seized the Greeks and they were meditating a hasty flight.' Forthwith the Persians 'landed troops on the islet Psyttaleia, between Salamis and the mainland, and advanced their western wing towards Salamis[1] so as to enclose the Greeks, moving forward at the same time their centre so as to fill the whole strait as far as Munychia.'

At this critical moment Herodotus brings on to the stage Aristides. He and Xanthippus and other political exiles had been recalled while Xerxes was still in Thessaly, but he seems to have delayed his return, and is now just in time to co-operate with Themistocles (to whom he offers reconciliation) and to announce to the council of sea-captains that 'he has come from Aegina and has barely escaped, for the Greek fleet is now entirely enclosed by the ships of Xerxes.' While they still doubted a Tenian trireme, which had deserted from the Persians ('and for this reason the Tenians were described on the tripod at Delphi among those who overthrew the barbarian'), arrived and confirmed the news. The battle of Salamis (September

---

[1] Diodorus, but not Herodotus, says that 200 Egyptian vessels were sent round Salamis to the south to cut off the retreat of the Greeks.

20, 480) is described graphically by Herodotus (vii. 84 *ff.*), and also by Aeschylus (*Persae*, 359 *ff.*), who was an eye-witness but as a poet perhaps may have drawn somewhat on his imagination. The main features in both descriptions are similar. Numerous reconstructions have been made, and almost every detail given by older writers has been questioned or modified. Some theorists (*e.g.* Gobineau and Chamberlain) have even doubted whether any real sea-battle took place.

The main body of the Greek fleet engaged the Phoenicians and the rest of the Persian centre in the strait between Salamis and Mount Aegaleos (at the base of which Xerxes sat on his throne viewing the conflict), 'fighting in order and keeping their line, while the barbarians were in confusion and had no plan in any of their movements, so that the result of the battle could scarce be other than it was.' The immense number of the Persian ships proved disastrous to them. While attempting to overwhelm the Greeks they crowded tumultuously into the narrow strait, and the repulse of the foremost lines threw all the vast throng of vessels into inextricable confusion (vii. 89). Then the Aeginetan ships, which formed the right wing of the Greek fleet,[1] managed to turn the left wing of the Persians (held by the Ionians) and charged the disordered centre of the enemy's fleet, while Aristides, 'taking a number of Athenian hoplites which were drawn up on the shore of Salamis, landed them on the islet of Psyttaleia and slew all the Persians by whom it was occupied.' The attack of the Aeginetans decided the battle.[2] The Persians collected their vessels at Phaleron, and the Greeks, 'expecting another attack, made preparations.' But Herodotus represents Xerxes as in a great state of panic. 'He made up his mind to fly; but, as he wished to hide his project alike from the Greeks and his own people, he set to work to carry a mound across the strait to Salamis, and at the same time began fastening a number of Phoenician merchantships together to serve at once for a bridge and a rampart.' But his brother-in-law Mardonius was not deceived, for 'long acquaintance enabled him to read all the king's thoughts,' and with the approval also of Artemisia, who reminded Xerxes that he had burnt Athens and thus had gained the purpose of his

---

[1] Either inside the strait or on the south-east coast of Salamis.

[2] They were accorded the first prize for valour (*ta aristeia*). The Corinthians were, perhaps unfairly, accused by the Athenians of having tried to desert in the midst of the battle. Aeschylus represents Xerxes as tearing his raiment and uttering shrieks when he saw the slaughter on Psyttaleia. I have omitted the well-known story of Artemisia sinking a friendly ship to save herself (Hdt. vii. 87).

*Fig. 71  Bay of Salamis*

*Fig. 72  Walls of Themistocles*

expedition, the plan was formed that the king should return to the East overland, that the fleet should at once sail to the Hellespont to guard the bridge, and that Mardonius, after escorting the king through Thessaly, should retain 300,000 men, including the 10,000 Immortals, for the purpose of completing the conquest of Greece.

If all the tales told of the return of Xerxes are true it was as disastrous as Napoleon's retreat from Moscow. Herodotus himself refuses to believe that the king 'never once loosed his girdle till he came to the city of Abdera, not feeling himself till then in safety'; but he tells us that famine and disease so thinned the ranks of his troops that he reached the Hellespont with a mere fraction of his former army. Aeschylus draws on his imagination and gives us a fine picture, scarcely less impressive than that of the disaster of Pharaoh's host in the Red Sea. He tells us how the Strymon, frozen over in a single night and unfrozen by the heat of the next day's sun, swallowed up great numbers of panic-stricken fugitives. By some Xerxes is said to have taken ship from Eïon (on the Strymon) and to have been nearly lost in a storm – during which, in order to lighten the vessel, a great number of Persian nobles, 'having made obeisance, leaped overboard.' Others say that he reached the Hellespont, but found the bridge destroyed by storms – not that this was of much consequence, for his fleet had arrived.

The Greeks had pursued the ships of the enemy only as far as Andros. Themistocles had tried to induce them to continue the pursuit and annihilate the Persian fleet, but the Peloponnesians were still afraid that the land forces of Xerxes might march against the Isthmus, and refused to set sail.[1] Then, it is said, Themistocles once more sent a messenger (the same faithful slave, Sicinnus, the tutor to his sons) and informed Xerxes that it was by his own influence that the pursuit had been abandoned. Possibly this was a fabrication of later days, after Themistocles had proved a traitor; possibly it was a result of that preternatural insight into the future with which he is credited by Thucydides. However that may be, he is said to have urged this act as a reason for expecting favour when he reached the court of Xerxes as an exile.

That the journey of Xerxes was not a flight is apparent from the fact that the troops which had accompanied him to the Hellespont not only returned

---

[1] Cleombrotus, in command at the Isthmus, had intended to follow up the retreating Persian land forces, but had been stopped by – an eclipse! This happened, they say, at 2 p.m. on October 2, 480.

to Thessaly, where they rejoined Mardonius, but also during their return march undertook, under the command of Artabazus, the reduction of the cities of Olynthus and Potidaea. Olynthus was captured and all the inhabitants were 'led out to a marsh and put to death.' Potidaea withstood a siege, and treason, for three months, and ultimately many of the besieging Persians were caught by a spring-tide or bore and, 'not being able to swim, perished immediately.' 'The Potidaeans say,' remarks Herodotus, 'that what caused this spring-tide was the profanation by these very men of a temple and image of Poseidon. And in this they seem to me to say well.'

Mardonius now sent as envoy to Athens the king of Macedonia, Alexander I, who had ties both with the Athenians and with Persia. In the name of the Great King forgiveness and friendship were offered. But the Athenians answered: 'So long as the sun keeps his present course we will never join alliance with Xerxes'; and to the Lacedaemonians, who had hastily sent an embassy to oppose Alexander, they declared: 'Not all the gold that the whole earth contains would bribe us to take part with the Medes. . . . First, there is the burning and destruction of our temples and the images of our gods. . . . Then there is our common brotherhood with the Greeks, our common language, the altars and sacrifices at which we all partake, the common character that we bear. Did the Athenians betray all these, of a truth it would not be well. While one Athenian remains alive we will never join alliance with Xerxes.' Mardonius therefore though the Thebans advised him to stay in Thessaly and send gold to the leaders of the Greeks, marched down upon Athens. 'But on his arrival he did not find the Athenians. They had again withdrawn, some to their ships, the greater number to Salamis. So he only gained possession of an empty city.' This was in July 479. The reason why the Athenians had again withdrawn was because the Spartans had refused to leave their Isthmian wall and march north to help in opposing Mardonius, alleging in excuse (as so often they had done) a religious festival – this time the 'Hyacinthia.' Mean and selfish as such conduct appears, especially in contrast to that of the Athenians, it was soon to be proved once more that when face to face with the foe they possessed a splendid courage. To them was mainly due the great victory of Plataea, which forever liberated Greece from the Persian invader.

The Athenians, dispossessed of their city, though they had for a second time rejected with disdain the proposals of Mardonius, sent word to the Spartan regent Pausanias (Cleombrotus having died soon after the eclipse) that they, and also Megara and Plataea, would be forced to surrender to the Mede unless the Lacedaemonians would help them. Hereupon 5000 Spartiats were ordered to start northwards under the command of Pausanias. They were accompanied by many Helots and Perioeci and other Peloponnesians, and joined by the Athenians under the command of Aristides, so that the whole army may have numbered 70,000 men, among whom, according to Herodotus, there were 38,700 hoplites.

Mardonius, when he heard of this army, resolved to withdraw to Thebes, as Attica was too hilly for his cavalry and there was 'no way of escape from the country except through defiles.' Before leaving Athens he completed as far as possible the destruction of the city and its temples, leaving the Acropolis a waste of ruins. His army, says Herodotus, numbered about 300,000 and perhaps 50,000 Greek auxiliaries. About six miles to the south of Thebes he built a huge fort, 'a square of about ten furlongs each way,' with ramparts and towers formed of trees that he cut down in all directions. His army he encamped along the Asopus, which flows through the plain between Thebes and the great range of Cithaeron, the boundary between Boeotia and Attica. Here, with his rear covered by the Thebans, he awaited Pausanias, who crossed into Boeotia, and, finding the enemy blocking the way, disposed his forces on the north slopes of Cithaeron. For ten days the armies faced one another. The Greeks were much harassed by the cavalry, having themselves no horse; but in the skirmishes the leader of the Persian horsemen, Masistius, a splendid warrior with golden breastplate, was slain; whereupon the Persians 'made great lamentation, shaving all the hair from their heads and cutting the manes from their war-horses and sumpter-beasts, while they vented their grief in cries so loud that all Boeotia resounded with the clamour.' Day by day the numbers of the Greeks increased, but so great was the self-confidence of the barbarians that Artabazus advised Mardonius merely to wait, as the Greeks would never venture down into the plain, and to harass them and cut off their supplies and ply the leaders with bribes. The Persian horse did indeed cut off their communications by occupying the passes in their rear, and succeeded in reaching and choking up the fountain Gargaphia on which they relied for water. But Mardonius was impatient for a battle, and decided to attack, and, according to Herodotus, the news of this decision was brought to the Greek outposts by the Macedonian king Alexander.

The battle is exceedingly difficult to 'reconstruct.' I shall not attempt to describe, far less to explain, all the false moves, the blunders, and the unobeyed orders that have complicated the question. The chief facts seem to have been that the Athenians, after accepting the proposal of Pausanias that they should oppose the Immortals and Persian picked troops, were ordered to fight the Thebans and other renegade Greeks, and that when the decisive moment came they were held in check by their opponents and were unable to take any great part in the actual rout of the barbarians. This rout was effected mainly by the Lacedaemonians and Tegeans. After falling back and being followed up by the main body of the Persians, they halted for some time – losing many men by the arrows of the foe, shot from behind the line of wicker shields, while they sacrificed and calmly waited for favourable omens – and then, the omens allowing it, they swept forward, broke through the array of wicker shields, and put the whole host of the enemy to flight. 'The barbarians many times seized hold of the Greek spears and broke them; for in boldness and warlike spirit they were nowise inferior to the Greeks, but they were without real shields, and far below their opponents in skill with weapons. . . . The fight was hardest where Mardonius, mounted on a white horse and surrounded by the bravest of the Persians, the Ten Thousand, fought. So long as he was alive these troops resisted, but when he fell,[1] and those with him, all the others took to flight.' Artabazus, seeing how the day was going, wheeled off with 40,000 men and made his way northwards. The Thebans, after fighting with desperate fury and losing 300 men, retreated to their city. Most of the routed Persian army fled for refuge to their wooden rampart, closely followed by the Spartans, who, however, being unskilled in siege operations, had to await the arrival of the Athenians before they were able to take the fortification.[2] A terrible massacre ensued. Only 3000 are said to have survived out of the immense host; but possibly many escaped and joined Artabazus, who with great difficulty reached Byzantium and crossed to Asia. The spoil was enormous,[3] and during many years afterwards the Plataeans used to find treasures of gold and silver on the battlefield. The loss of the Spartans is given by Herodotus at 91, of the Tegeans at 16, and of the Athenians at 52 (though Plutarch states the whole loss, probably including Helots, at 1360). It would therefore seem that, in spite of the fierce depreciation to

---

[1] His body was treated with respect by Pausanias, but was stolen.

[2] *Cf.* Thuc. i. 102. The Spartan city itself was without walls. The Spartans despised and hated such defences, as is seen from their bitter opposition to the building of the Athenian Long Walls.

[3] The throne and scimitar of Mardonius and the golden breastplate of Masistius were still to be seen in the Athenian Acropolis in the time of Pausanias, 600 years later.

which their conduct in the battle has been subjected by some writers, the Athenians had a certain amount of fighting. Of the Corinthians and Megarians Herodotus says that they were drawn up at some distance and *did not know* that a battle was being fought! At last they learnt the fact and rushed forward, but were cut to pieces by the Theban cavalry. The Spartans were given the chief credit for the victory. 'The Athenians,' says Herodotus, 'and the Tegeans fought well, but the prowess shown by the Lacedaemonians was beyond either.' Pindar gives Sparta the chief praise. Aeschylus, too, attributes the victory to the 'Doric spear.' A tenth of the booty was set aside for the Delphic treasury, and colossal bronze images of Zeus and Poseidon were erected at Olympia and the Isthmus respectively. At Delphi was dedicated, says Herodotus, 'the golden tripod which stands on the bronze serpent with three heads close to the altar.' On the base of the supporting pillar, formed of three serpents, were inscribed the names of the Greek states which had joined to repel the Persian invader. This base was removed by Constantine the Great to the Hippodrome at Constantinople (Istanbul).[1]

The battle of Plataea was fought probably on August 12, 479. 'On the same day,' says Herodotus, 'another defeat befell the Persians at Mycale, in Ionia.' The Greek fleet had started in the spring to aid the Ionians, who had entreated their help against the Persians. But it had got no further than Delos, for 'all beyond that seemed to the Greeks full of danger and swarming with Persian troops.' For some months it lay idle at Delos. But on the urgent appeal of the Samians the Spartan king Leotychidas, induced by favourable omens (especially by the lucky-sounding name of the Samian envoy), decided to attack the Persian fleet, which lay in the lee of Samos. When the Greeks reached the Samian coast near the great temple of Hera, the Persians, who shrank from a naval battle, dismissed all their Phoenician vessels and stranded the rest on Cape Mycale, where they had a land force of 60,000 men under the command of Tigranes. The Greeks disembarked and after a desperate fight carried the ramparts of the naval camp and burned the ships, the Athenians especially distinguishing themselves, and the victory being rendered more easy by the wholesale desertion of the Ionian auxiliaries of the enemy. According to Herodotus, the news of the

---

[1] Discovered in 1880, when Constantinople was occupied by the Western Powers. Mahommed II, on the capture of Constantinople by the Turks, smashed the jaw of one of the serpents with his battle-axe (Gibbon, ch. 68). See p. 307.

victory at Plataea, which had been gained on the very same forenoon, arrived in time to cheer the Greeks while advancing to the fight. This is, of course, rejected as a fable by many writers. Possibly fire-signals (if visible by day) may be the explanation. If not, perhaps it may have been one of those cases in which the knowledge of an event seems to have been transmitted over great distances by some unexplained agency – such as the Greeks named 'divine rumour' (*phēmē, ossa*).

The Greek fleet then sailed to the Hellespont, but when they found Xerxes' bridge destroyed the Spartans went home. The Athenians, however, laid siege to Sestos, still in the possession of the Persians, and late in the autumn of 478 they succeeded in capturing it. 'This done, they sailed back to Greece, carrying with them, besides other treasures, the shore cables from the bridge of Xerxes, which they wished to dedicate in their temples.' These are, all but a few lines, the last words of the history of Herodotus.

## SECTION A: THE GREEKS AND CARTHAGINIANS IN SICILY (500–478)

While Greece was fighting for her existence against the Persian invader the Greeks in Western Hellas were also struggling against an Asiatic race – the Phoenicians and the Phoenician colony of Carthage. It seems, indeed, probable that Carthage and Persia were acting in concert.

We have already noted the rise of the Greek colonies in Sicily and Southern Italy. During the first period of their existence the Phoenician settlements in Sicily gave them little or no trouble, but these offered a valuable base to the navies of the rapidly growing Carthaginian state, which, in alliance with the powerful and piratical princes of Etruria, began to gain supremacy in the Western Mediterranean, and almost annihilated, as we have seen, the Phocaean fleet at the battle of Alalia, off the coast of Corsica (*c.* 535). Carthage now dominated Sardinia and Corsica, and intended to dominate Sicily. Indeed, as early as about 565 a Carthaginian army, commanded by Malchus, had landed in Sicily, and seems to have won a battle against the tyrant Phalaris of Acragas. But it was not till the era of Xerxes that the Carthaginians made a serious effort to wrest the island from the Greeks. Meanwhile Hellenic civilization and power in Greater Greece, in spite of devastating internecine wars and such disasters as the annihilation of Sybaris by Croton, had reached a very high stage of development. The chief cities of Sicily had fallen into the power of despots. In the north Himera was ruled by Terillus. In the south and east Acragas (Agrigentum) and Syracuse[1] were ruled by Thero and his son-in-law Gelo, and attained very great prosperity and power under these despots. Gelo, originally a general of Hippocrates, tyrant of Gela, had succeeded to the lordship of that city, and when appealed to by the exiled Syracusan Gamori (landed nobility) had reinstated them and at the same time seized the power also in Syracuse. He gave over the tyranny of Gela to his brother Hiero, and as ruler of Syracuse adorned the city with many fine buildings and with magnificent docks and raised her to the rank of a great naval power, while he increased her wealth and her population greatly by transferring thither many of the richer inhabitants of captured Camarina and Hyblaean Megara – the poorer being sold into foreign slavery; for he 'regarded the *dēmos* ['people'],' says Herodotus, 'as a most unpleasant neighbour.' While Gelo and his brothers, Hiero, Polyzalus, and Thrasybulus, kept their magnificent court at Syracuse, the city of Acragas, though not yet adorned with its splendid temples,[2] became wealthy and powerful under the rule of Thero, whose daughter Demarete became Gelo's wife; and when Thero quarrelled with Terillus and drove him out of Himera, and Terillus appealed to the Carthaginians for aid (as Hippias appealed to the Persians), the lords of Syracuse and Acragas combined to oppose the foreign invader. It was at this moment that the envoys from Greece came to beg Gelo for assistance against Persia;[3] and it can cause no wonder that he was unable to promise it, though he possessed a 'far larger fleet and army' than any other Greek state. The Carthaginians, about 300,000 men under Hamilcar, landed at Panormus (Palermo) and besieged Thero in Himera. Gelo hastened to his relief, and by a ruse gained entrance to Hamilcar's naval camp. Then, profiting by the confusion, he assailed the land camp

---

[1] For reference the following may be useful: Syracuse founded by Dorians 734; under aristocracies and democracies till the despots Gelo (485), Hiero (478), Thrasybulus (467); then democracy; besieged by Athenians 413; democracy overthrown by Dionysius (406–367), whose son, Dionysius the Younger, was finally dethroned by Timoleon in 343. In passing it is interesting to note that Sicily for some 3000 years (perhaps for much longer) has been the arena of racial strife. One need only mention the following names to recall such conflicts: Sicals, Sicanians, Elymi, Phoenicians, Greeks, Carthaginians, Romans, Vandals, Heruli, East Goths, Byzantines, Arabs, Normans, Franks, Germans, French, Aragon princes, Bourbons.

[2] Built by slave labour after the battle of Himera. See Note A (5).

[3] See p. 281. Gelo is accused by Herodotus of having sent three ships to Delphi under the command of a certain Cadmus, who took with him 'a large sum of money and a stock of friendly words, and was to watch and see what turn the Persian war might take.'

Fig. 73  Tomb of Darius

Fig. 74  Charioteer found at Delphi

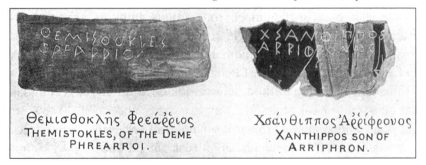

Θεμισθοκλῆς Φρεάρριος
THEMISTOKLES, OF THE DEME
PHREARROI.

Χσάνθιππος Ἀρρίφρονος
XANTHIPPOS SON OF
ARRIPHRON.

Fig. 75  Ostraka of Themistocles and Xanthippus

Fig. 76  The 'Concordia' Temple

Fig. 77  Bronze Etruscan Helmet

299

also. The struggle was fierce and long, but the victory complete. Half the Punic army was massacred; the rest were enslaved. Only one single vessel, we are told by Diodorus, reached Carthage. A fine picture is given by Herodotus, which is well worth a moment's pause, although it may not represent an historical fact; indeed, Herodotus, as often, gives the thing for what it is worth – and it is worth much from a standpoint other than that of the scientific historian.

'After the battle Hamilcar disappeared. Gelo made the strictest search, but he could not be found, dead or alive. The Carthaginians, who take probability for their guide, give the following account. Hamilcar, they say, during all the time that the battle raged, which was from dawn till evening, remained in the camp [near the shore] sacrificing and seeking favourable omens, while he burned on a huge pyre the entire bodies of victims. Here, as he poured libations on the sacrifices, he saw the rout of his army; whereupon he cast himself headlong into the flames, and so was consumed and disappeared. Whether it happened in this way or not, certain it is that the Carthaginians offer him sacrifice.' The oft-repeated assertion of old writers that the leaders of armies, both Greek and Roman, would refuse to give battle without obtaining favourable omens[1] often gives one pause. Here is the case of the commander of a Carthaginian[2] army absenting himself all day from an important battle for such purposes.

The battles of Himera and Salamis (as those of Mycale and Plataea) were believed to have been fought on the same day (September 20, 480). It is, of course, possible that this was not so; but there is little to be gained by doubting it. From the spoil a large present was made by the Syracusans to Demarete, the wife of Gelo. The silver coins, called *Demareteia*, struck on this occasion, some of which still exist, are exceedingly beautiful (see coin 6, Plate IV). At Himera exist the remains of a temple near the mouth of the river. It may have been the very temple before which Hamilcar offered sacrifice to Poseidon.

Gelo died in 478, the year of the capture of Sestos by the Athenians, the last event recorded by Herodotus. The reign of his brother Hiero therefore really belongs to our next period; but it may be better to anticipate a little

---

[1] The well-known exception of P. Claudius and the refractory chickens was followed by a crushing defeat!

[2] Hamilcar is said to have been Greek from his mother's side, and at Himera to have sacrificed, not to Phoenician deities, but to Poseidon.

for the sake of continuity. During the twelve years of his reign Syracuse was probably the most notable city of the Hellenic world, both for its power and for its patronage of the fine arts. At the court of Hiero and at that of Thero of Acragas we find Simonides, Bacchylides, Pindar, and Aeschylus. The victories of Hiero and others of the Sicilian princes at the Olympic and Pythian chariot-races were celebrated by the first poets of the day. The exact dates of some of these victories (extending from 482 to 472) have been ascertained by means of papyrus manuscripts discovered in Egypt; and at Delphi was excavated the famous bronze statue of the charioteer (Fig. 74) dedicated by Hiero's brother Polyzalus, evidently as a thanksgiving for victory. Beneath all this display there was doubtless much to disgust – much tyranny and inhumanity,[1] much insolent, if magnificent, patronage of genius. Of all this there are evidences not only in recorded acts of barbarity, but even in hints dropped by Pindar himself, in spite of his evident admiration of the feudal pomp of the Syracusan court. One feat performed by Hiero justly earned the gratitude of Hellas. The people of the Greek city of Cumae, or Cyme, in Italy (see pp. 146–7), were hard pressed by the Etruscans – the same Etruscans, or Tyrseni, whose pirate-fleet had rendered so much aid to the Carthaginians, the same people who had espoused the cause of the Tarquins and had, under their king, Lars Porsena, besieged Rome some thirty years before. Hiero sent his fleet and inflicted a crushing defeat on the Etruscans. Of this victory we possess a most interesting memorial (Fig. 77) – a bronze Etruscan helmet, found (1817) at Olympia. Its inscription says: 'Hiero and the Syracusans [dedicate] to Zeus Tyrrhenian spoil from Cyme.' In the splendid ode that Pindar wrote to celebrate, primarily, the victory which Hiero's horses gained at the Pythian Games in the same year (474) he also alludes to the victory of Cyme, and prays Zeus that 'the Phoenician and the war-cry of the Tyrseni may remain in peace at home, having seen the grievous ruin of their ships before Cyme.'

In 472 Thero of Acragas died. His son quarrelled with Hiero and was overthrown, and Acragas became a free republic. Not long after Hiero's death in 467 his brother Thrasybulus, who succeeded him, was expelled on account of his cruelty and avarice, and Syracuse also became free. Its further connection with Greece will occupy our attention when we come to the ill-fated Sicilian expedition of the Athenians and to the visits of Plato to the court of Dionysius.

---

[1] Sinister stories are told of Hiero's conduct towards Polyzalus, who had married Demarete.

SECTION B: PINDAR (522–442)

Pindar and Aeschylus were contemporaries, but the plays of Aeschylus are perhaps better considered in connection with those of the other Attic dramatists, whereas Pindar, both in feeling and in form, belongs to a different school. Although it is full of wise saws and pious sentiments, and parades with great pomp and solemnity the dogmas and legends of the popular religion, the poetry of Pindar – such at least as we possess – is for the most part a majestically magniloquent glorification of wealth and high birth and success; while Aeschylus, though for a time he enjoyed, as did Pindar, the regal patronage of the Syracusan court, moved in quite another, and a far higher, world of thought and feeling, and in his dramas pictured, in language of still more superb audacity and with a far sublimer imagination, the wrestlings of the human soul against the mysterious decrees of Fate.

Pindar was born at or near Thebes about 522. He studied at Athens, and when still a youth of sixteen composed dithyrambs for public festivals. On his return he came under the influence of the Theban poetess Corinna, some fragments of whose lyrics have been discovered in papyrus manuscripts. She advised him to introduce mythology into his poetry. The result was a hymn written for the Thebans, twelve lines of which are extant. In these twelve short lines there are twelve different proper names and sixteen epithets, mostly long made-up words. This hymn is said to have introduced every mythological character connected with Thebes. No wonder that Corinna's criticism was, 'One should sow with the hand and not with the whole sack.' He seems soon to have become noted as a poet. The earliest of his *epinikia* ('songs of victory'), all of which we probably possess, was written in 502. It was in honour of a Thessalian youth who had won the foot-race at the Pythian Games, and it extols the Aleuadae (*Pyth.* x.). But Pindar did not share the Medizing propensities of these princes. He belonged to the small minority at Thebes which sympathized strongly with the victors at Marathon and Salamis and Plataea. Indeed, it is said that (perhaps later in life) in consequence of his praises of Athens he was severely fined by his fellow-citizens, and that the Athenians made him their public guest (*proxenos*) and paid him twice the sum and erected a bronze statue to him. His poetry was greatly admired by Alexander I of Macedonia[1] – who, as we have

---

[1] As lovers of Milton's sonnets know, Pindar's house was consequently spared by Alexander the Great (as it had been already by the Spartans).

seen, submitted to Persia, but was Greek at heart – and also by Thero of Acragas and Hiero of Syracuse, for both of whom he wrote numerous *enkōmia* (panegyrics) and *epinikia*. In 473, a year after the great victory of Hiero at Cyme, Pindar went to Sicily, where he lived for about four years. Here he may have met Aeschylus (who, however, probably went there first in 468), and certainly met Simonides (who died *c.* 468) and the nephew of Simonides, the lyric poet Bacchylides, who was also employed by Hiero to celebrate his victories at the games.[1] In 468 Pindar was again in Thebes, whence he sent a fine ode (*Ol.* vi.) to Syracuse. Hiero was at this time suffering from a serious disease, and in 467 he died. In the next year Pindar wrote two of his finest odes (*Pyth.* iv. and v.) for Arcesilaus IV, king of Cyrene – a descendant of Battus (see p. 172) – and it is just possible that the poet visited Cyrene and also Rhodes. In 460 he wrote one of his *epinikia*, and another in 452, at Olympia. His last poem was a hymn to Persephone, of which three words are extant. He is said to have died at Argos, in the theatre.

There were seventeen volumes of Pindar's poems – hymns, paeans, dithyrambs, dirges, *enkōmia, epinikia*, and others. Besides about 150 fragments of other poems, we possess, probably complete, the forty-four *epinikia*, or odes of triumph, which were written in honour of victors at the games – Olympic, Pythian, Nemean, and Isthmian – and were recited at banquets or festive processions (*kōmoi*). The earliest (*Pythian* x.) has been mentioned. Another early one (*Pythian* vii.) is in honour of an Athenian, Megacles, perhaps a son of the reformer Cleisthenes, and it is interesting to note that this ode, as also the only other written for an Athenian (*Nemean* ii.), is remarkably short, and that there is a good deal said about avoiding envy. The date is that of the battle of Marathon, and Megacles had already been twice ostracized – so, what with the Medizing tendency of the Thebans and the democratic dislike of hero-worship at Athens, we cannot wonder at Pindar's brevity and sage advice. Exceedingly fine and historically the most interesting are the numerous *epinikia* composed for Thero and Hiero – 'King of Syracuse,' as the poet calls him, using a title that Hiero assumed about 478. In one of these (*Pythian* i.) Pindar celebrates the victory gained by Hiero's chariot horses (or perhaps by his

---

[1] Bacchylides was regarded by some ancient writers as a formidable rival of Pindar, but several of his poems discovered among Egyptian papyrus manuscripts seem to prove that, though he possessed elegance and taste, he was a poet of no high order.

celebrated racer Pherenikus) at the Pythian Games in 474, and alludes (as we have already seen) to the still more important victory won at Cyme in the same year, and also to the battles of Salamis and Plataea and Himera. 'I will claim a reward,' he says, 'from Salamis for the sake of the Athenians, and at Sparta I will tell of the fight before Cithaeron where the Medes with their crooked bows were smitten, and by the well-watered banks of the Himera I will pay the sons of Deinomenes [Hiero and his brothers] the hymn that is their due for deeds of valour.' Fourteen of the odes are for Sicilian victors, and not a few are in honour of Aeginetans, for whom Pindar seems to have had a special partiality. In a series of six of his 'Nemeans' he extols the Aeacidae, and contrasts the noble character of Ajax with that of Odysseus, of whom he says: 'I deem that his fame became greater than his deeds and sufferings through the sweet singer Homer.'

The metre of the Pindaric odes seems at first sight – as it seemed to Horace – to be quite arbitrary. But, although there is scarcely any resemblance between the metres of the various odes, each of them consists of parts (strophes, epodes, etc.) to which the same or a similar metre recurs. The rhythms were doubtless based on the kind of music (Doric, Aeolic, Lydian, etc.) to which the poems were set. Grandeur of expression, often rising to sublimity but sometimes sinking to magniloquence, is the striking characteristic of Pindar's poetry. Although he possesses no such sublimity of imagination[1] as Aeschylus, or Dante, or Milton, the onward rush of thought, clothed in superb language, is magnificent. He compares himself to an eagle. 'I send thee,' he says, 'this mingled draught of honey and white milk – late indeed! but amidst the birds of the air the eagle is swift: he marketh from afar, and, swooping suddenly, seizeth with his talons the tawny prey; but cackling jackdaws haunt the lower ground.' Gray, too, has pictured for us the Theban eagle as

> Sailing with supreme dominion
> Thro' the azure deep of air;

and Horace in one of his finest odes has likened Pindar to a mighty torrent, and to a wild swan winging its way through the realms of cloudland.

---

[1] The finest imaginative picture in Pindar is perhaps that of the eagle of Zeus lulled to sleep by the tones of Apollo's golden lyre (*Pythian* i.). The paraphrase by Gray in his *Progress of Poetry* does it very poor justice.

Although he accepted many strange myths for artistic purposes, Pindar protested strongly, as Xenophanes had done, against all that was derogatory of the dignity of the gods. 'It is seemly,' he says, 'for a man to speak nobly of the deities.' And although for artistic purposes he makes use of the Olympian gods, in most cases when he is expressing his own beliefs he speaks of 'God' as Xenophanes and other sages, and indeed Homer himself, had done. 'One must not strive with God,' he says, 'who now exalteth the one and now giveth great glory to others.' God, he tells us, 'o'ertakes the eagle in its flight and passeth the dolphin in the sea.' If God does not 'swiftly put forth his hand to the helm of the state, it is oft no easy task for the rulers to guide it aright.'

He is full of wise, if rather trite, saws and maxims. The best of them is perhaps preserved by Herodotus and Plato: 'Law is king of all.' Others are: 'Future days are wisest witnesses' (which reminds one of Solon); 'Silence is oft wisest for a man'; 'We all die but once.' His wisdom does not bear the impress of deep conviction; it is purely decorative – like exquisite embroidery. Not a few dark threads of melancholy and embitterment sometimes traverse the web – due perhaps to the rivalry of other poets, and to that 'envy' of which he sometimes sings – possibly also to a too close contact with regal wealth and luxury. Pythagorean and Orphic influences can perhaps be traced in some passages where he speaks of purification and initiation, and of the rewards and punishments in a future life. A fine picture of the life of spirits in Elysium is given in a fragment of one of his dirges, reminding one of similar pictures by Virgil and Dante and of passages in Plato's *Phaedo*. In another fragmentary dirge he speaks thus of death:

'By a happy destiny all travel towards a bourne where they are loosed from toil. The body, indeed, followeth almighty Death, but still alive remaineth a shadowy image of vitality, and this alone is of origin divine.'

The Orphic teachings doubtless were associated with much superstition and priestcraft, but, together with Pythagorean mysticism, they helped by their imaginative parables to keep alive in the hearts of many the beliefs that lie at the root of all true religion.

# Chapter 6

# The Rise of the Athenian Empire (478–439)

SECTIONS – A: ARCHITECTURE AND SCULPTURE – B: AESCHYLUS, HERODOTUS AND PHILOSOPHERS OF THE PERIOD

The capture of Sestos is, as we have seen, the last event recorded by Herodotus in his history of the Persian invasions; but Persia continued to hold important posts in Thrace,[1] and, although after Mycale the Ionian and Aeolian cities regained autonomy, the barbarian was still at their gates; nor was it unlikely that Xerxes would attempt to revenge himself on Greece itself. The need for combined action was therefore strongly felt. Hitherto Sparta had been regarded as leader. Although the victories of Marathon and Salamis had been due mainly to Athens, and although her ships formed the bulk of the Greek fleet, the allies had hitherto refused to submit to Athenian leadership, and the supreme command both on land and on the sea had been held by Spartans – by Eurybiadas at Salamis, by Pausanias at Plataea, and by Leotychidas at Mycale. How the command of the allied fleet was acquired by Athens, and how she made herself the head of a great anti-Persian confederacy, and how out of this leadership (*hēgemonia*) in less than twenty years she developed an empire (*archē*) which extended its victories even to Cyprus and Egyptian Memphis, has been recounted by many writers; and although this period lies between those described in detail by Herodotus and by Thucydides, enough is told by both, especially by Thucydides,[2] to render possible a fairly satisfactory reconstruction.

---

[1] Doriscus was evidently still Persian when Herodotus wrote vii. 106–107.

[2] Thuc. i. 89 *ff.* and the speech of the Athenians in i. 74. Other sources are inscriptions, Plutarch, and Nepos.

But it is not my purpose to follow closely the evolution of the Athenian Empire, nor the varying fortune of those long-protracted struggles for supremacy which often fill so many pages of Greek history with their wearisome and ever-recurring details of battles and sieges and seditions and revolts and butcheries. Such things, it is true, form the main staple of one of the greatest of histories – that of Thucydides – but they are so skilfully interwoven, now with the brilliant rhetoric and the intricate arguments of fictitious speeches, now with some subtle analysis of character or motive, now with some trenchant criticism or the vivid description of a beleaguered town or plague-stricken city or sickening butchery, that we are at times almost persuaded that these miserable squabbles and atrocities are, as he believed them to be, not only more worthy of record than what Herodotus calls 'the great and wonderful deeds of the Greeks and barbarians' in the Persian wars, but even of more consequence to posterity than all the legacies of Greek art, Greek poetry, and Greek philosophy. A 'possession for ever' doubtless his book will remain, but not by reason of its minute record of events, many of which have no longer any value except in so far as they may at times give us a fuller view of the dark side of Greek character.

The transfer of the naval command from Sparta to Athens happened thus. In the year following the capture of Sestos (in which Leotychidas and the Spartan ships had taken no part) a fleet composed mainly of Athenian and Ionian vessels was put under the command of the Spartan Pausanias, who as the victor at Plataea enjoyed great popularity in spite of his overweening arrogance.[1] He made for Cyprus and cleared the island of the Persians; then he sailed to Byzantium. Here he laid himself open to the charge of Medism. He was accused of releasing Persian prisoners, assuming Median habits and dress, and even of treasonable correspondence with the Great King,[2] and was recalled to Sparta. The Ionian allies hereupon,

---

[1] On the dedicated tripod (p. 296) he had caused only his own name to be inscribed as the conqueror of the Mede. The Spartans erased the distich and engraved the names of the cities (Thuc. i. 132). This doubtless rankled in his mind, and (as seen in Cleomenes) the peculiar temperament and training of the Spartans seem to have induced a tendency towards unbridled passion and insanity.

[2] His letter to Xerxes, proposing to marry his daughter, and the reply of Xerxes, are given by Thucydides. The fate of Pausanias may be best related here, so as to avoid discontinuity. He hired a private trireme and returned to Byzantium, where he conducted himself like a Persian magnate and was guilty of many excesses. He even got possession of Sestos, but the Athenians sent Cimon with a squadron and expelled him. Having retired to Cleonae

*Fig. 78  Group of gods, Parthenon Frieze*

*Fig. 79  The 'Strangford' Shield*

weary of arrogant despotism, begged the Athenians to assume the command of the fleet, and although another admiral (Dorkis) was sent out from Sparta, he was not recognized. The acquiescence of Sparta seems remarkable, but was probably due to the influence of the military caste of the old school, which regarded sea-power as an illusion. To this influence was also probably due a raid on Thessaly made about this time (c. 476) by the Spartans under their king Leotychidas, who landed in the Gulf of Pagasae, and might perhaps have annexed the whole of Thessaly unless he had proved as venal as many of his compatriots. He was convicted of receiving bribes from the Persian-loving Aleuadae, and only saved his life by seeking sanctuary at Tegea.

Here we may perhaps glance at the question of what Thucydides calls the entirely different character of the Spartans and the Athenians. Many of these differences have been noted by the Attic historian, who during his exile of twenty years had special opportunities for studying them, and it would be a most interesting, if exceedingly difficult, task to collect all that he has said on the subject, to compare it with what has been said by Herodotus and other ancient writers, and to see how far it is borne out by historical facts. From various passages – such as the speech of the Corinthians in i. 70, where the contrast is strongly brought out, and in i. 141, where Pericles points out the practical advantages possessed by Athens, and his great speech (iii. 39–40), where he delineates the main features of Spartan and Athenian character – one may gain a fairly clear impression of his finely drawn distinctions, but to restate that impression in any other form, especially in a still more concise form, is almost impossible. These passages should be studied. In passing I can but offer a few epithets such as may perhaps occur to the reader of Thucydides as roughly intimating his judgments. The Spartans he seems to regard as eminently

Footnote 2 *(continued)*

in the Troad, he renewed his intrigues with the Persians and was again summoned to Sparta, where, suspected of inciting a rising among the Helots, and being also convicted by a ruse (see Thuc. i. 133) of his correspondence with Persia, he fled for sanctuary into a small building in the precinct of Athene and was walled up there by the ephors and died of starvation (471). Although he was carried out of the sanctuary while still breathing, the Delphic oracle ordered atonement for the pollution; and this 'pollution' was urged as a charge by the Athenians when, at the beginning of the Peloponnesian War, they themselves were ordered by the Spartans to cast out the Alcmaeonid 'pollution' in the person of Pericles.

dilatory, enslaved to tradition and system, unimaginative, illiterate, boorish, short-sighted and narrow in policy, unenterprising, unideal, incapable of foreseeing difficulties, cold-blooded, tenacious, heroically but stupidly regardless of danger and death, and incredibly superstitious and venal. The character of the Athenians he seems to consider a rare composite of the practical and the ideal: they are at once 'most enterprising and most prudent,' 'lovers of the beautiful but also of economy, lovers of learning but also of manliness,' magnanimous but severe (alas! we might add, often inhumanly cruel), generous but exacting, sanguine, impulsive, imaginative, brilliant, versatile, restless but capable of strenuous and protracted effort, fascinating but false. The last two epithets may be exemplified by the intense affection and the intense hatred that, far more than Sparta, Athens seems to have excited under various conditions. The enthusiasm for Athens among the Ionian Greeks at the formation of the Confederacy was evidently very strong, but it was soon to be followed by a detestation as universal and still more intense, so that at the beginning of the Peloponnesian War 'the good wishes of all men made greatly for the Lacedaemonians . . . so angry were most with the Athenians, some of them from a wish to be liberated from their rule and others from a fear of being brought under it.'[1]

During the next few years we hear but little of Sparta. We have chiefly to note the foundation and rapid development of the so-called Confederacy of Delos – the work especially of Aristides and Cimon; and, secondly, the important changes effected at Athens by the influence of Themistocles.

**The Confederacy of Delos**

The allies, especially the Ionians, had begged Athens to assume the naval command. This led to the formation of a league, nominally anti-Persian, under the hegemony of Athens. The isle of Delos, the sacred ancient gathering-place of the Ionic race, was chosen as headquarters and as treasure-house. In course of time the Confederacy included about 260 towns (Aristophanes says a thousand!), situated mostly in Ionia and Aeolis and the adjacent islands and Euboea. According to its wealth each state had to contribute its share in fully equipped vessels, or the equivalent in tribute (*phoros*). Most of the smaller and some of the greater states preferred the

---

[1] Thuc. ii. 8. All quotations in this chapter are from Thucydides, if not otherwise specified. Dale's translation has been used to some extent.

latter method, and thus practically subscribed to the enlargement of the Athenian fleet, and what was at first the voluntary subscription of a confederate was soon regarded by Athens as the tribute of a subject. The work of valuation was entrusted to Aristides, and his estimates gave such general satisfaction that they remained in force for half a century. To Cimon, the son of Miltiades, was given the command of the confederate fleet. His first feat, after expelling Pausanias from Byzantium, was the capture of Eïon – stubbornly defended by the Persian Boges, who finally lit a pyre and flung his wife and children and slaves and himself into the flames. A year or two later (473) Cimon distinguished himself by capturing from pirates the illustrious isle of Scyros, and still more by discovering, as was believed, the bones of Theseus, who, tradition asserts, when expelled from Athens was murdered on this island by Lycomedes (the king at whose court Achilles lived for some time disguised as a girl). The bones were brought to Athens, and possibly the Theseion was built to receive them; but this is doubted (see Note A). Some five years later (468) the confederate fleet, after having driven the Persians from several Lycian and Carian cities, gained a brilliant victory over the Persian fleet at the mouth of the Eurymedon in Pamphylia. About 200 of the enemy's vessels were destroyed, as well as a reinforcement of 80 Phoenician ships that arrived after the battle, and the Greeks are said to have disembarked and routed the Persian land troops on the same day.

Shortly before this battle, doubtless with the full approval of Athens, though also doubtless not with the full approval of the confederate council (for Thucydides speaks of it as the 'subjugation of an allied city *contrary to agreement*'), Cimon had reduced by force the island of Naxos, which had signified its intention of withdrawing from the Confederacy. The Naxians were henceforth treated as '*subject* allies' of Athens, and this precedent was soon followed by similar cases. Thasos quarrelled with Athens about a gold-mine and 'revolted' (for thus the Athenians now described withdrawal from the league). After two years it was reduced (463), having hoped in vain for the aid of the Lacedaemonians, who were prevented from keeping their promise by an earthquake – and this time a really serious one, as we shall see later.

One after another the states of the Confederacy, discontented with Athens for using the funds and the fleet against Greeks instead of against Persians, were either reduced by force or acquiesced in being treated as tributaries of the Athenian Empire, until only Chios, Lesbos, and Samos were still autonomous and not liable to military service under Athenian

*Fig. 80  Temple on Sunion*

*Fig. 81  Theseion, or perhaps Temple of Hephaestus*

commanders, although obliged to contribute contingents to the confederate fleet; and, if we allow ourselves to look forward a few years, we may note here that in 454 the treasury was removed from Delos to Athens and the Confederacy came practically to an end, although this name still continued to be used officially instead of the word 'Empire' (*archē*) – a word odious to the democratic Hellene, except in the case of such lovers of freedom as the Athenians, who, as Goethe said, loved no freedom but their own. From its full development in 454 until its total collapse at the end of the Peloponnesian War this Athenian Empire existed just half a century. But this is anticipation, and we must now return and note what has been occurring at Athens itself.

## Themistocles and Events at Athens

In a former chapter I touched upon the personality and political tenets of the four leading Athenians during the Persian invasion, namely, Themistocles, Xanthippus, Aristides, and Cimon. To Themistocles it was mainly due that Athens had become a maritime power and had conquered at Salamis. Xanthippus had succeeded him in the command of the fleet, and had won the battle of Mycale. Aristides had distinguished himself at Marathon and at Salamis, and had commanded at Plataea, and was the chief organizer of the Confederacy. Cimon, the youngest of the four, the son of Miltiades, was actively occupied in extending the oversea empire of Athens. He and Aristides belonged to the older school of Cleisthenic republicanism, opposed to the more advanced democratic and 'Peiraean' influences of Themistocles, and were politically in sympathy with Xanthippus; but between Cimon and Xanthippus was a very strong hereditary hostility, for Xanthippus had been the chief accuser of Miltiades. Themistocles was not a professional party politician, nor was he, as the other three, of noble family. He stood, therefore, somewhat apart, but exercised great influence on the decisions of the Ecclesia. Even before the battle of Marathon, in 493, he had as archon persuaded the Athenians to begin the fortification of the Peiraeus and the formation of new docks. These operations had been stopped by the Persian invasions. On his suggestion they were now renewed, and walls round Athens itself were begun, enclosing a greater space than those demolished by Peisistratus and by the Persians. Hereupon Sparta sent envoys to propose the stoppage of the work and the demolition of all fortifications in Greece; but Themistocles, says Thucydides, went to Sparta and deluded the authorities with various excuses, while at home 'the whole population, men, women, and children, worked at the building, sparing neither private nor public edifice. . . . And the building still shows even now' – as its relics do even in our day – 'that it was executed in haste, for the foundations are laid with stones of all kinds, and many columns from tombs and sculptured blocks were inserted.' Thus Themistocles was soon able to inform the Lacedaemonians that 'Athens was already walled and capable of defending itself,' and that 'as the Athenians had abandoned their city without the leave of Sparta, so without her leave they intended to have their city walled.'

Besides the erection of city ramparts there was an immense amount of clearance and rebuilding to be done in Athens itself and on the Acropolis, where, as we have already seen, the debris of the old temples and sculptures was cast into the spaces between the new walls and the newly levelled plateau. On this plateau arose the new temples, which will be described later. The new walls of the Acropolis were probably erected, not by the advice of Themistocles, but by that of Cimon, since we hear of the southern wall being built out of the spoils of the battle of the Eurymedon (468), when Themistocles was an exile at Argos, or perhaps already a fugitive in Asia.

Whether he was suspected of Medism or of receiving bribes, or whether arrogance made him unpopular, or whether his political opponents persuaded the Ecclesia that he was a danger to the state, is not known, but that he was ostracized is certain – and the fact is illustrated, if not proved, by the potsherd bearing his name that may be seen in the British Museum (Fig. 75). This was probably in 471, the same year in which Pausanias met his fate. For some years he 'had a house at Argos and used to travel about the Peloponnese.' Then, apparently about 467, the Lacedaemonians accused him to the Athenians of having taken part in the intrigues of Pausanias. He fled, first to Corcyra, then through Thessaly (aided by the king, Admetus) to Asia, and ultimately reached Susa. Here he wrote a letter to Artaxerxes, who was now king (his father, Xerxes, having been murdered by Artabanus in 465), claiming recognition as a 'benefactor of the king' for his messages sent to Xerxes (see p. 292) and asking for a year's grace in order that he might learn the Persian language. At the end of this time he presented himself and gained such favour with the Persian king – to whom he proposed plans, never to be carried out, for the conquest of Greece – that he was made governor of Asiatic Magnesia and was supplied with

314

bread and wine by the cities of Lampsacus and Myus. Thus he lived, as a Persian magnate, till about 450. The story that he poisoned himself with bull's blood probably arose from a statue that was erected to him in Magnesia, which represented him pouring a libation while standing near a slain bull. 'His relations say that his bones were carried over to Attica and buried there without the knowledge of the Athenians.' A tomb in the rock near the Peiraeus lighthouse was for many years in modern times shown as the tomb of Themistocles.

Aristides had died[1] in the year of the battle of the Eurymedon (468), and Cimon was thus for a time without any powerful political opponent. But Xanthippus, his hereditary enemy, now dead or retired, had left behind him a son who was to attain by his splendid gifts of intellect and character an almost absolute control of the state. Nor was it long before the popularity of the victor of the Eurymedon – the generous and jovial old sailor whose plentiful lack of wit had been proverbial in his earlier days and whose preferences were still for wine-bouts and aristocratic boon companions rather than for statesmanship and philosophy – suffered total eclipse. Ostracism – the almost inevitable fate of the eminent Athenian statesman – came upon him under rather dramatic circumstances. He had always obstinately maintained that the one object of Athens should be to extend her oversea empire and harass Persia, and that she should recognize the supremacy of Sparta on land and live at peace with her – a doctrine that won him the contemptuous sobriquet of the Laconizer or Philo-Laconian. Now in 464 a very severe earthquake laid Sparta in ruins. Many Spartans perished, and the opportunity was seized by the Messenian Helots, who, after defeating the Spartans with the loss of 300 men on the plain of Stenyclarus, fortified themselves (as their forefathers had done) on Mount Ithome. For more than two years they defied the Spartans, who at last appealed for assistance to Athens – the Athenians being skilled in siege operations. Cimon, in spite of the opposition of Pericles and another newly risen anti-oligarchical politician, Ephialtes, carried the Assembly with him by his sailor eloquence. 'Consent not,' he exclaimed, 'to see Hellas lamed and our city without her yoke-fellow!' Four thousand Athenian hoplites were sent under his command to help in the siege of Ithome; but Ithome was not

---

[1] He is said to have died so poor that he was buried at public expense. Some of his descendants, fortune-tellers and beggars, were granted rations by the state. The descendants of Themistocles were wealthy and respected. One was a friend of Pausanias the traveller.

easily to be taken, and the Spartans, perhaps suspecting treason, suddenly and insultingly dismissed the Athenian troops. The indignation at Athens was intense, and Cimon was ostracized. For about two years longer Ithome defied capture. At last the Messenians capitulated on the condition that they should leave the Peloponnese; and Athens offered them a site for a new home at Naupactus, the haven on the Corinthian Gulf which, it will be remembered, was so called because it served as a ship-yard for the Dorians on their invasion of the Peloponnese. It had been lately occupied by the Athenians as a naval station, a kind of Gibraltar commanding the entrance of the gulf and the trade with Western Hellas. In a later age we shall hear again of these Messenians of Naupactus (see Figs. 93, 123, and pp. 361, 417).

Soon after the ostracism of Cimon, the friend of Pericles, Ephialtes, was assassinated – probably in revenge for his attacks on the ancient and aristocratic council of the Areopagus, which he accused of corrupt practices and caused to be deprived of the relics of its political power, leaving it nothing but jurisdiction in cases of homicide and a few religious functions.[1] Pericles now and for the next thirty years stood alone at the helm of the state, often, it is true, fiercely assailed, but only for one short period opposed by a rival of any importance.

The 'age of Pericles,' if we limit the name to these thirty years and except the outbreak of the Peloponnesian War, offers comparatively little of moment in its military and political occurrences, but much that is of supreme literary and artistic interest. It is true that the fame of Pericles himself rests mainly on his statecraft, and it was to his genius and his good fortune that Athens owed a measure of peace during the time of her greatest artistic and intellectual activity, but, putting aside the question whether a policy which resulted in the universal hatred of Athens and the acclamation of Sparta as the liberator of Greece was really a great policy, what the Periclean age has of value for us is very slightly connected with the facts of its political history. These facts I shall therefore state as concisely as possible.

461–459. After Cimon's banishment Athens breaks with Sparta and forms an entente with Argos (the *Oresteia* of Aeschylus reflects this feeling). Megara puts itself under the protectorate of Athens. Long Walls are built between Megara and its port Nisaea and garrisoned by Athenians, who

---

[1] See remarks on the *Eumenides*, p. 344.

*Fig. 82  Metopes from the Parthenon*

thus command the passes of Geraneia leading to the Isthmus. A fleet of 200 Athenian and confederate ships cross from Cyprus to Egypt to assist the Libyan king Inaros to free Egypt from the Persians. They sail up the Nile as far as the Pyramids and capture Memphis, except the 'White Citadel,' which holds out for years. (Finally, in 454, Artaxerxes sends a great army and besieges the Greeks on a Nile island, which he takes by diverting the stream. The Greeks burn their ships and capitulate and are allowed to retreat to Cyrene. A reinforcement of fifty triremes sent from Athens is annihilated by the Phoenician fleet in the Nile.)

458–450. The occupation of Megara by Athens causes war with Corinth and with Aegina. The Athenians, though many of their warships are in Egypt, capture seventy Aeginetan vessels and force Aegina to surrender the rest and to be enrolled as subject state in the Confederacy. The Lacedaemonians send troops to Northern Greece to defend their mother-country, Doris, against the Phocians, and use the opportunity to re-establish a Boeotian league, with Thebes at its head, to counteract Athens. On their return they threaten Athens and rout the Athenians at Tanagra, but soon afterwards Athens reoccupies Boeotia. At the battle of Tanagra the exiled Cimon had appeared and offered to fight as hoplite. His request was refused, but he was allowed to return to Athens. Some years later he negotiates a five-year truce between Athens and Sparta. He is reinstated as admiral of the confederate fleet, and once more renews naval operations against Persia. During the blockade of Cition in Cyprus he dies. From 458 to 455 the two Long Walls from Athens to the Peiraeus are built (see p. 322).

448. After the death of Cimon the Greeks and Persians seem to have agreed to abstain from hostilities. It is doubtful whether a formal treaty was made. Thucydides does not mention it. Some later writers assert that Callias, brother-in-law of Cimon, went to Susa to ratify it and that the Persian king promised to send no ships into the Aegean or the Propontis, nor to cross the river Halys, nor to claim the Greek Asiatic cities, except those in Cyprus, which were surrendered to the Phoenicians. A copy of this treaty, it is said, was engraved on a column at Athens. As we hear soon after (Thuc. i. 115) of a satrap of Sardis, some of these details are evidently incorrect.

447. Boeotia revolts and the Athenians suffer a severe defeat and lose many prisoners at Coroneia. Euboea revolts, but is reduced by Pericles. Even Megara, which had voluntarily put itself under Athenian protection,

finds Athenian imperialism too hard a taskmaster, or possibly is induced to revolt by the oligarchical faction, and massacres the Athenian garrison. Then a Peloponnesian army invades Attica.

446. Thirty Years' Peace is concluded. Athens agrees to surrender Megara and Achaea, and it is stipulated that neither side shall tamper with the other's allies. The terms are humiliating for Athens and for the policy of Pericles. The loss of Megara and the Long Walls of Nisaea deprives Athens of the command of the Isthmus of Corinth, and exposes her to attack from the Peloponnese.

445–431. During these fourteen years Pericles has absolute control of the state, not by virtue of any special official position (he is officially only one of the ten *stratēgoi*, or generals, re-elected yearly), but merely through strength of character and intellect. About 443 a politician named Thucydides (not the historian, but the son of Melesias), a relative of Cimon, heads a party that violently opposes the imperial policy of Pericles, asserting that even the weal of the empire should not override justice and honour. These 'little Athenians' (so to speak) sit apart in the public Assembly to show their contempt of the malodorous *dēmos* (populace) and its hero, whom they accuse (doubtless with some justice) of misappropriating the funds of the Confederacy for the purpose of adorning Athens and carrying on her wars against fellow-Greeks. Pericles argues that as long as the allies are protected satisfactorily by Athens they have no right to interfere with the finances – an argument well suited to win the approval of an imperialistic mob. Thucydides, who seems to have been an orator scarcely inferior to Pericles himself, and who evidently stood on a higher level of political morality, is said to have complained, and doubtless with much reason, that 'even when he had thrown Pericles he denied that he had fallen and talked over those who had seen him fall.' It is therefore not surprising that when Thucydides proposed a trial by ostracism he himself was banished (443). It was perhaps in the same year that after an unsuccessful attempt had been made by the Sybarites to refound their city (destroyed by Croton in 510), Pericles settled the pan-Hellenic colony of Thurii near the site of Sybaris – a fact the more interesting because both Herodotus and the orator Lysias were probably among the first colonists, and because Hippodamus (see p. 322) laid out the plan of the new city on the new method, with streets at right angles, as he did at the Peiraeus.

439. Samos, one of the three autonomous allies and the richest of them, now shared the fate of Naxos and of many others of the confederates. The

Samian oligarchy quarrelled with Miletus, and refused to accept the arbitration of Athens, which was in favour of the Milesians, some say because Aspasia, who was Milesian, influenced Pericles! Pericles himself probably went out in command of the fleet and established a democracy; but the exiles returned, and again Pericles went out, this time having as a fellow-*stratēgos* the poet Sophocles, who had lately gained great fame by his *Antigone*. After a blockade of nine months Samos surrendered her fleet and paid 1000 talents indemnity. Also Byzantium revolted, but was forced to return to allegiance. Perhaps it was at this time that Pericles visited the Euxine with a large fleet, and sailed as far as the Crimea. In his funeral speech in honour of those who fell in the Samian war his eloquence is said to have produced an extraordinary effect. He was crowned as an Olympic victor. But Cimon's sister Elpinice (who seems not to have accepted Pericles' definition of the ideal woman as one about whom least is said) reproached him publicly with having triumphed over fellow-Greeks, while her brother had triumphed only over the barbarian.

We have now arrived at events (the sedition at Epidamnus and the sea-fight of the Corcyraeans against the Corinthians) which were among the immediate causes of the outbreak of the Peloponnesian War, and it will be better to reserve them for consideration in closer connection with the war. Also whatever more there is to be said, or quoted, on the subject of the policy and character of Pericles will be more intelligible if deferred to the end of his career. In the following sections a brief account is given of some of the important artistic and literary works produced during the period that we have been considering.

SECTION A: ARCHITECTURE AND SCULPTURE (*c.* 478–431)

When the Athenians returned to their city after its second occupation by the Persians and the withdrawal of Mardonius in 479 they at once set to work, as we have seen, to clear away the ruins and to rebuild. They were also persuaded by Themistocles to surround Athens with new ramparts and to fortify also the Peiraeus, and, probably by Cimon's advice, they set aside some of the spoil taken from the Persians at the Eurymedon for the building of the great south wall of the Acropolis, and perhaps also for clearing and enlarging the plateau and either attempting to restore the old temple of Athene Polias (see Note A, 14) or laying foundations for new temples. More, however, was not accomplished until about twenty years

Fig. 83  Parthenon from the west

Fig. 84  Apollo's Temple, Phigaleia

later, when Pericles, at the zenith of his power, induced the Athenians to vote a large sum (partly their own and partly taken from the treasury of the confederates) for the erection of the Parthenon, which was built on old foundations, but after a new plan, devised by the architect Ictinus.

But before we come to the Parthenon and its sculptures a few words should be said about some works of great political, if not artistic, importance, namely, the port of the Peiraeus and the Long Walls which connected it with Athens. The fortifications of the Peiraeus, as also the first formation of docks in its three natural inlets, Munychia, Zea, and 'The Harbour,' of which Cantharus ('The Cup') was the part used by warships, were due to the influence of Themistocles, and probably the Long Walls were begun or planned before his exile; but they seem to have been finished between 458 and 455. These walls diverged considerably in order to include both the Peiraeus and the open bay of Phaleron, the beach of which, some two miles in extent, offered an easy landing-place for an invader. About 443 Pericles induced the Athenians to remedy this defect by building another long wall parallel to the northern wall, and at a distance from it of about 400 yards, thus forming a far narrower and more defensible fortified passage of about four miles between the port and the upper city. After the completion of this third wall the old Phaleron wall was no longer kept in repair, and the open beach of the Phaleron bay was deserted for the quays and marts of the new harbours. The town of Peiraeus, spreading round the great harbour and Zea, and up the slopes of Acte and Munychia, was laid out on a new plan, in rectangular blocks, by the Milesian architect Hippodamus, who also laid out the new cities of Thurii and Rhodes, and whose name was given to the chief market-place in the Peiraeus. A fine Emporion, or 'Place of Commerce,' and a spacious colonnaded 'Showplace' (Deigma) for imported merchandise were constructed, and a thousand talents spent on new docks and an arsenal.

The Peiraeus in modern times recovered its ancient name as well as its ancient prosperity. As late as 1835 it was known as Porto Leone. This name its little fishing hamlet received on account of the ancient stone lion which once stood at the entrance of the harbour, and which was carried off by the Venetians in 1687 and now stands in front of the arsenal at Venice.

Having secured their city and their port by ramparts and long walls, the Athenians were easily won over by Pericles to believe that it was their duty to show their gratitude for deliverance from the barbarian by erecting worthier shrines to the gods. They had still stored up in their treasury a great amount of Persian spoil, and the yearly tribute of their subject allies was about 600 talents – some at least of which they thought it justifiable to use in adorning the imperial city. On the Acropolis, in the place of the ancient temples burnt by Mardonius, had arisen – or perhaps had only been begun – a new shrine to receive the old wooden idol of Athene, which had doubt-less been hidden away during the barbarian invasion. And Cimon, who did not believe in fortifying the city, had built a strong portal and a south wall for the citadel. Moreover, on the plateau inside Cimon's Gate statues were again erected, among them (*c.* 460) a colossal bronze Athene by Pheidias, then about thirty-five years of age, and some ten years later perhaps his scarcely less famous Lemnian Athene (see Fig. 87 and List of Illustrations).

The greater statue – which was dedicated from Persian spoils and was sometimes called the 'Promachos,' or Champion Goddess – is said to have been, together with its pedestal, 66 feet high. In representations of the Acropolis on coins it overtops considerably the Parthenon and the Propylaea. The crest on the helmet and the gilded tip of the spear served, says Pausanias, as a landmark for sailors, like the gilt angel on the Venetian Campanile. The statue stood on the Acropolis for eight centuries, and was then probably taken to Constantinople, and was destroyed by the Latin Crusaders in A.D. 1203. The Lemnian Athene was a smaller bronze statue dedicated by the Athenian colonists of Lemnos. This island, as we have seen, was gained for Athens by Miltiades shortly before the battle of Marathon, and the colonists probably commissioned Pheidias to make the statue about 450.

But Athens possessed no longer – indeed, she never had possessed – any shrine worthy of her goddess, any temple so majestic as that of Delphi or of Olympia or Ephesus or Samos or Sicilian Acragas or Selinus, or even far-away Italian Paestum.

So keenly did Pericles feel this that in 448, having perhaps failed in getting money voted by the Athenians, he induced or allowed them to send an embassy to the other Grecian states proposing a pan-Hellenic congress in order to discuss various matters, especially the restoration of the temples burnt by the barbarians. Naturally the 'twenty elderly Athenians were rebuffed,' as Grote tells us. Sparta cared little for grand temples and such things, and doubtless regarded the proposal as a sly stroke of policy for increasing the imperial power of Athens. Perhaps this rebuff effected what the eloquence of Pericles had failed to effect.

The chief buildings erected by the Athenians in this period were the

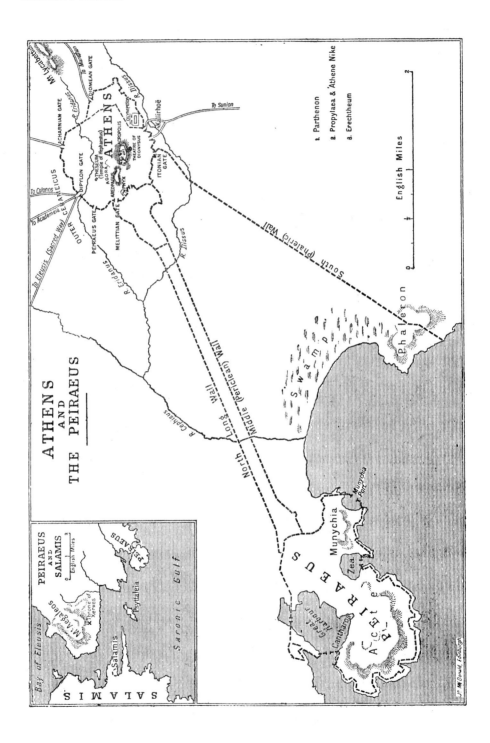

ATHENS
AND
THE PEIRAEUS

PEIRAEUS
AND
SALAMIS

1. Parthenon
2. Propylaea & Athene Nike
3. Erechtheum

English Miles

Parthenon (*c.* 445–438), the Theseion, the temple on Sunion, the Odeion, the new Propylaea (437–432), and the Hall of Mysteries at Eleusis. Besides these we may note the splendid temple of Apollo at Phigaleia, in Messenia, designed by the Athenian Ictinus, the chief architect of the Parthenon. Three of these, and also the Erechtheion, which was somewhat later, are described in Note A at the end of this volume. Of the others the following brief account may be useful.

The Propylaea (*i.e.* the Gate-porticoes) took the place of the fortress-portal built by Cimon, and were for show rather than for defence. The edifice was designed by Mnesicles and built between 437 and 432. It consisted of a massive wall in which were pierced five gateways, and on each side of the wall was a portico of six Doric columns. Through the central gateway ran the main road. The other gateways, two on each side, were on a higher basement, reached by several steps of marble and one of black Eleusinian stone. The gateways had massive doors, whose 'harsh thunder' is mentioned by Aristophanes. The inner roof of the fore-portico was supported by six Ionic columns. This central building was to be flanked by projecting wings with colonnades backed by spacious halls. The north wing, much of which, together with considerable portions of the central building, still exists, was fairly well completed, and contained a portico and a hall (Pinakotheke) in which votive paintings were hung, some of them probably by the famous painter Polygnotus. (He had probably already painted his fresco (?) of the battle of Marathon in the Stoa Poikile, near the market-place, and a picture of the Descent of Odysseus into Hades for the Lesche of the Cnidians at Delphi.) The south wing, however, was never completed, either because of the Peloponnesian War or else because the ground had already been consecrated as the site of the temples of Brauronian Artemis and Athene Nike, and the priests refused to give it up. Whatever may have been the reason, the little temple of Athene Nike was built on this projecting cliff, as is explained in Note A.

The Odeion, or Music Hall, was built soon after Pericles had got rid of his opponent Thucydides (442) and was able to indulge more freely his wish to spend public money on splendid structures. Its site was on the south-west slope of the Acropolis, not far from the theatre of Dionysus. (A far greater Odeion was built three centuries later near the Propylaea by Herodes Atticus. In passing note that the theatre of Dionysus, in which all the masterpieces of the Attic drama were first performed, was at this time only a somewhat primitive stage facing the Acropolis, on the natural slope of which the audience was accommodated with wooden benches or dug-out seats. The huge auditorium, capable of holding 15,000 spectators, was excavated and furnished with stone seats in the fourth century.)

The Hall of Mysteries at Eleusis was constructed about the same time to replace the old building destroyed by the Persians. The design was by Ictinus, and the superintending architect was Coroebus. The inner temple (Telesterion, or 'Place of Initiation') was partly built into the rock of the Eleusinian acropolis. It was afterwards (c. 310) furnished with a fine Doric colonnade. The Mysteries were celebrated here down to A.D. 396, when the building was burnt by Alaric.

The Parthenon was begun about 445, some three years before the ostracism of Thucydides. It is therefore probable that his indictment of Pericles was based mainly on the great expenses demanded for this magnificent temple.[1] The designer was Ictinus, the builder Callicrates, and to Pheidias was entrusted the decorative work. It is regarded as the purest type of Doric architecture, the characteristics of which I have explained elsewhere. Its dimensions are 228 by 101 feet; its peristyle consists of $8 \times 17$ columns of about 35 feet. At both ends there is a double portico, the inner row of columns standing on a level with the inner temple and two steps above the stylobat (basement of the outer columns). The sanctuary containing the gold and ivory statue of Athene by Pheidias, which was 38 feet high, formed the larger (eastern) part of the inner temple, and was enclosed by walls and divided lengthwise, like a church with its nave and two aisles, by two rows of small columns arranged in two tiers, one above the other. The statue stood facing the eastern portal, so as to receive the light of the rising sun, or perhaps the sunlight from the open space in the roof – if the Parthenon was a hypaethral temple. Behind this sanctuary (called the Hecatompedos, or 'Hundred-foot Shrine,' being 100 Attic feet in length) was a smaller compartment with its entrance at the west end of the temple. This was the 'Parthenon' proper. It was perhaps so named because it was (besides being the treasure-house) the dwelling of the maiden priestesses of the goddess, and it may have given its name to the whole temple. But possibly the word 'Parthenon' ('Room of the Maiden,' or 'the Maidens') was originally applied to the temple itself, although it seems that at first it

---

[1] Grote gives 3000 talents as perhaps spent at this time on public buildings. The gold on the Athene statue weighed 40 talents. In the treasury at the beginning of the Peloponnesian War were 6000 talents (Thuc. ii. 13).

retained the name of the old temple of Athene Polias. Apart from its sculptures and regarded only as a building, the Parthenon possesses, even in its present state, a beauty and dignity such as we seek in vain in other ancient ruins, however impressive. It is as impossible to analyse and define such qualities as to discover by dissection the causes of what is great and beautiful in the art of Pheidias or of Sophocles; but it is possible to note the wonderful care that in the best Greek architecture, as in the best Greek sculpture and poetry, was given to details of symmetry and proportion. Doubtless in order to render the perspective effect more perfectly harmonious and to lend a certain undefinable grace and beauty to the whole building, the use of the absolutely straight line was avoided to a great extent. The columns not only taper gently, and gently diminish the width of their flutings, but have the slight convexity in their middle parts which is known as *entasis*. They also all lean very slightly inwards, and the corner columns are slightly thicker than the others. Even the steps of the marble basement are not exactly horizontal, but have a slight convexity. By what rules, if by any, the Greeks thus attempted to eliminate the imperfections of natural perspective as presented to us by our dull senses it is impossible to say.

The Parthenon was built of Pentelic (Attic) marble, which was first used about this time, all finer architectural and statuary work having been until now done in the imported Parian marble. The Pentelic stone contains a certain amount of iron, to which is due the rich golden tint that it acquires. As has been stated elsewhere, colour was used for the decoration of Greek temples and statuary very much more freely than we are willing to believe, accustomed as we are to Greek architecture and sculptures deprived of their original colours and to the dazzling white of Carrara marble in modern statues. How far the Parthenon was decorated externally with colour is not easy to discover, but probably the columns and architraves were left uncoloured (though ornamented with wreaths, shields, etc.) or were only slightly tinted, while the mouldings and other decorations were brightly coloured, as well as the dress and other details of the pediment sculptures and the reliefs of the metopes and frieze, all of which had doubtless a background of dark red or blue. Above the architraves of the outer colonnade (as in all Doric temples) the frieze was divided by triglyphs into metopes. These metopes, ninety-two in number, were all sculptured in very high relief. As each forms a distinct picture it is easy to understand why metopes generally represent concentrated and vigorous action, every group

*Fig. 85 Portions of Parthenon Frieze*

being self-balanced and independent. In the Parthenon the metopes depict contests between Centaurs and Lapithae and between Greeks and Amazons (Fig. 82), and possibly (on the north side, where the reliefs are very weather-worn) scenes from the Trojan War. Fifteen of the best are in the British Museum. Some are exceedingly vigorous and wonderfully balanced, and were possibly the work of Pheidias or of Myron, who excelled in poise amidst violent action (as in his *Diskobolos* and his Marsyas); these have a decided likeness to the high-reliefs of the Theseion. Others again are of very inferior design and workmanship, and were probably by disciples of the 'athletic' school of Argos.

The frieze of the Parthenon (much of which is in the British Museum) was a continuous frieze, as in an Ionic temple, and ran above the inner columns of the porticoes, all round the outside of the walls of the sanctuary. It could thus be seen by those who walked, or a procession which marched, round the Parthenon, and 'the figures would seem to advance as the spectator moved' (Gardner).

Being under the colonnade and only lighted from below, the sculptures (especially the lower portions) were in very low relief, so as to avoid too deep shadows. The continuous (Ionic) frieze is, of course, well adapted for the representation of processions. The subject of the Parthenon frieze is the Panathenaic procession, the great solemnity that took place every fourth year in connection with the Panathenaic games, and in which all the richest and noblest born, all the magistrates and colonial and foreign representatives, all the youth and beauty of Athens, took an eager part. The procession consists of knights on horseback, charioteers, victims for sacrifice, musicians, maidens carrying the sacred vessels and baskets, the archons and other dignitaries; and over the main portal of the temple is seated in dignified expectation, awaiting the procession of worshippers, Athene herself with all the other Olympian divinities – a magnificent group. Nigh at hand is a priest with the sacred robe (*peplos*) which was offered to Athene on these occasions. There is a unity of design as well as a similarity of workmanship in the whole frieze from which it is fairly safe to conclude that it was mainly the work of Pheidias himself, or carried out under his direct supervision. Perhaps there is a concentration of power in a single statue which may make it a more wonderful product of creative art than any sculptured group or continuous frieze can be (the difference being somewhat analogous to that between a drama and an epic), but by reason of its incomparable grace and beauty the Parthenon frieze, even in its present state, holds something of the same place among works of sculpture that the *Odyssey* holds among works of poetic literature, while the groups of the two pediments may perhaps be likened to the *Iliad*.

The sculptures of the pediments, doubtless also designed by Pheidias and executed under his direct supervision, were still more wonderful for their masculine beauty and power than the frieze was for its beauty of delicate grace. So much we can tell from their scanty and mutilated remains – most of which may be seen in the British Museum. It is impossible for me to attempt any full description here, or to discuss the very numerous and diverse theories as to the meaning of the various figures and the way in which they were grouped. A fairly satisfactory reconstruction, or rather restoration, made by the Austrian sculptor Schwerzek, is given in Fig. 86. All such reconstructions are considerably indebted to drawings of the Parthenon that were made by a French artist, Carrey, in 1674, a few years before a German gunner of the Venetian forces besieging the Turks in the Acropolis succeeded in dropping a shell into the Turkish powder magazine, which was located in the Parthenon, with the result that a great part of the temple, until then in fair preservation, was demolished and many of the sculptures were shattered. The Venetian commander endeavoured to carry off the figure of Poseidon and the horses of Athene's chariot, but the whole group fell and was broken to pieces. In 1801 the English ambassador, Lord Elgin, procured a firman allowing him to 'remove a few blocks of stone and figures,' and removed the greater part of the metopes, frieze, and pediment sculptures – perhaps fortunately, as they were thus saved from further destruction by weather and vandalism.

The subject of the east pediment was the birth of Athene. The central figures are lost. They perhaps represented the birth as it is frequently depicted on old vases, where the goddess in the form of a small fully armed figure springs forth from the head of Zeus, which has been smitten by Hephaestus with his hammer; or more probably Pheidias chose a moment of more dignity, and represented the goddess already in full stature by the side of her father. An extant but mutilated figure is believed to represent Iris starting to take the news to mortals. In the left corner Helios (the sun) is rising from the sea in his chariot, and in the right the moon (Selene) is descending with her chariot into the waves. The other figures, sometimes called 'Theseus' (or 'Olympus'), 'The Three Fates' (or 'The Seasons'), and so on, are all of uncertain meaning. The subject of the west pediment was the contest of Poseidon and Athene for the land of Attica (see p. 65).

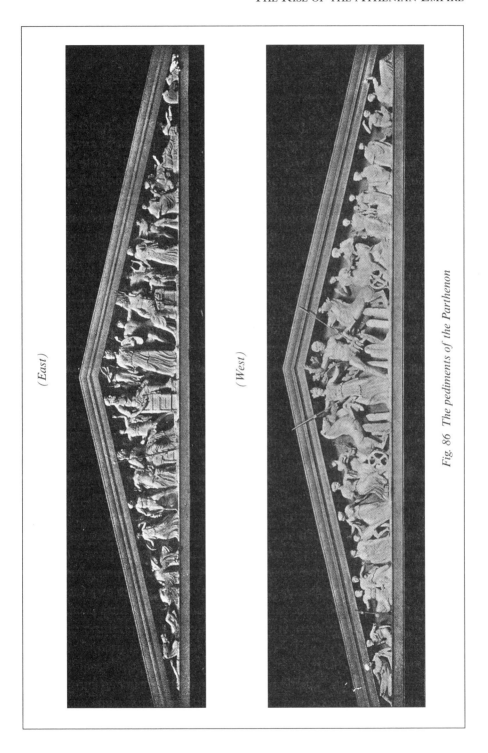

(East)

(West)

*Fig 86 The pediments of the Parthenon*

Poseidon produced, to support his claim, a spring of salt water, and Athene made an olive-tree spring forth. (Both were preserved as objects of reverence in the ancient 'house of Erechtheus,' which was replaced by the Erechtheion.) The central group of Poseidon, Athene, and the horses of Athene's chariot were destroyed as has been explained. Carrey's sketch depicts Poseidon as a huge nude figure starting backwards in amazement before Athene, much as Marsyas does in Myron's group (see Fig. 88 and explanation, see p. 334). The chariot of Poseidon, on the right, was probably drawn by sea-horses. Reclining figures that once filled the corners may perhaps have represented the streams Ilissus and Cephisus, between which Athens lay. But the relics are too few and too mutilated to serve for any certain reconstruction, and it may be safer to confine one's admiration to them as single figures and as examples of unrivalled skill in the technique of sculpture – 'marvellous translations into marble,' as they have been called, 'of flesh and of drapery.'

Pheidias was born about 490, so he must have had distinct memories of Marathon, and perhaps fought at Salamis and Plataea. Among his earliest works was a group (Miltiades amidst gods and heroes) erected at Delphi, probably by Cimon to commemorate Marathon and his father. His colossal bronze Athene has already been mentioned, and his Athene Lemnia. Of his chryselephantine Athene Parthenos we are forced to form our only conception from two most unattractive statuettes and a few gems, busts, and coins (Figs. 89, 90, 91). After the dedication of the Parthenon in 438 (though the chronology is uncertain) Pheidias seems to have spent five years at Olympia working at his great statue of Olympian Zeus, which ancient writers describe as the most majestic and impressive of all images of the gods. The throne on which Zeus was seated was probably, with its supporting pedestal (22 feet broad), the most magnificent work of decorative sculpture ever produced. Every available surface was used for reliefs or paintings. The statue itself was about 40 feet high, and the whole monument perhaps over 60 feet, so that, it was said, Zeus could not stand up without putting his head through the roof. On the extended right hand of the god stood a Victory, on his sceptre perched his eagle. Rough imitations of the monument and of the head of this Pheidian Zeus may be seen on coins (Coin Plate VI, 8, V, 5, and III, 10), and some of these heads are incomparably more satisfactory than any relic we possess of the Athene; but this is all that is extant to help us to form any conception of the greatest masterpiece of Greek sculpture. Caligula tried to remove the statue, but portents, it is said, deterred him.

It was probably after his return to Athens, about 432, that Pheidias was accused (by the enemies of Pericles) of peculation and sacrilege. He was able to refute the first charge because, by the advice of Pericles, he had made all the gold ornaments of the Athene detachable, and could thus prove that he had used the whole of the forty talents entrusted to him. The other accusation was based on the fact that he had introduced his own portrait and that of Pericles in the decorations of Athene's shield (see Fig. 79 and List of Illustrations). It is said that he – the great artist who had been lately the pride of Athens and of all Greece – was condemned on this trivial charge and thrown into prison and died there – a fact almost incredible if we had not the cases of Anaxagoras and Socrates and others to prove how fatal were the results of giving judicial powers to a bigoted and litigious populace, whose vaunted reverence for law was merely a reverence for their own verdicts, not for any principles of justice and humanity. The creation of the jury courts, that much-lauded gift (confirmed by the wise Pericles himself) to the Athenian mob, led to the pernicious influence of sophists and rhetoricians and inflammatory talk of all kinds, and the consequences were inevitable.

Contemporary with Pheidias were the sculptor Calamis, renowned for his Attic grace uninfluenced by Argive 'athleticism' and renowned for his horses (see the Delphic charioteer, Fig. 74 and p. 255), and Alcamenes, a Lesbian, and Paeonius, of Mende in Thrace. These two are said by Pausanias to have made the fine pediment sculptures for the magnificent temple of Zeus at Olympia (c. 450, some years before Pheidias was summoned to make the great statue). Many of these sculptures have been recovered – enough to allow of a fairly complete reconstruction of the two pediments, which represented the race of Pelops and Oenomaus and the fight of the Centaurs and Lapithae. Except one majestic statue with outstretched arm – perhaps an Apollo – the excavated figures have not, however, raised our esteem for these sculptors. Nor can one easily believe that such a heavy, stiff, and somewhat antiquated style could ever have been practised by a sculptor who (perhaps when an old man and influenced by the Attic grace of Pheidias) was able to produce such a miracle of delicate beauty and lightness as the 'Nike of Paeonius,' one of the two great art treasures discovered by the excavators at Olympia (Fig. 93). Another and perhaps greater contemporary of Pheidias was Myron (c. 500–410), an Attic sculptor, who seems to have studied under Ageladas at Argos, probably together with Pheidias, and to have adopted the Argive 'athletic' style.

We have fine copies of two at least of his works – the well-known *Diskobolos* ('Dicus-thrower') and the equally well-known figure of the satyr Marsyas starting back when confronted by Athene. This group is described by Pliny and others, but the second figure was supposed to have been irrecoverably lost. In the late nineteenth century there was discovered at Rome what almost certainly is a copy of the Athene, now in Frankfurt (Fig. 88). The original was in bronze, a material preferred by the Argive school and well adapted for statues representing violent motion – or, rather, that momentary poise in the midst of motion which is so conspicuous a characteristic of Myron's works and is selected by Lessing (in his *Laocoön*) as an essential characteristic of all great sculpture.

SECTION B: AESCHYLUS, HERODOTUS AND PHILOSOPHERS OF THE PERIOD

How the Attic drama originated in Doric dithyrambs and in 'goat-dances' performed at vintage festivals in honour of Dionysus, the wine-god, has been told, and we have seen how dialogue was introduced (perhaps by Thespis) between the chorus and its leader, and also how the performances were transferred from the vintage gatherings 'in the marshes' outside Athens to a primitive theatre on the south-eastern slope of the Acropolis, where later the great theatre of Dionysus was constructed.

**Aeschylus**

In the time of Aeschylus (525–456) various innovations were made, some of them doubtless by him. A second 'hypocrite' (*i.e.* 'answerer,' or speaker) was added, so that the narrative and the 'drama' (action) became much developed and more independent of the chorus, which now fell more into the background. Masks and costumes were improved and the high buskin (the cothurnus, like the Elizabethan chopin) introduced. Statues, houses and temples, curtains, painted rocks and groves and other scenery, doors for exits and entrances, and other such stage apparatus, began to take the place of the central *thymelē* (altar) round which the old dances had been performed, and, by about 430, movable platforms, wheeled or revolving on pivots, cranes, and other machinery for the descent and ascent of deities, became common. But to the end the classical Attic drama retained much of its original scenic simplicity. It was always more sculpturesque than pictorial. Sophocles introduced a third, perhaps a fourth, actor; but this number was seldom, if ever, exceeded. Spectacular effects seem to have been almost entirely disregarded, and nuances of by-play and facial expression were made impossible by the great size of the open-air theatres and by the masks of the actors. The one thing of importance – and it must have been exceedingly difficult, needing mechanical aids – was audible and effective recitation both of dialogue and of chorus, for textbooks were unknown, and the vast audiences would doubtless be eager to hear and criticize the new versions of the familiar legends that generally formed the subjects of these dramas.[1]

It has already been mentioned that Aeschylus fought at Marathon, where his brother Cynaegeirus was killed. Probably he was present also at Salamis and at Plataea, and some believe that the 'Ameinias of Pallene' who at Salamis first attacked the Persians was the youngest of his brothers.[2] He first competed for the tragic prize about 499, and first won it in 484. He is believed to have invented the 'trilogy' – a group of three connected, or unconnected, tragedies, followed usually by a semi-comic 'satyric' play. In 468 he was defeated by the young Sophocles, amidst great public excitement. Cimon in this year brought the bones of Theseus from Scyros, and he with his nine fellow-generals were asked to act as judges, and decided in favour of Sophocles. It has been said that either on this account or because he was beaten by Simonides in the composition of the Marathon epitaph (which, however, was in 489!), or else because he was accused of revealing the Eleusinian Mysteries or of impious language (perhaps in his *Prometheus*, where Zeus is blasphemed), Aeschylus withdrew to the court of Hiero at Syracuse. It seems, however, that he had already been in Syracuse (about 475–470), where he must have known Simonides and Pindar. Hiero died in 467, and the poet, who was again in Athens in 465, returned to Sicily after the production of his *Oresteia* at Athens, and died (456) at Gela – killed, it is said, by being struck on the head by a tortoise dropped by an eagle, in fulfilment of a prophecy that he should perish by a 'stroke from heaven.'

Of the seventy or more tragedies attributed to Aeschylus we possess only

---

[1] The *Persians* of Aeschylus was a striking exception. So was the *Capture of Miletus*, by Phrynichus (p. 219). The knowledge of the audience and the supposed ignorance of the characters in the play as to the approaching catastrophe allowed place to that 'dramatic irony' which is especially associated with Sophocles.

[2] Hdt. viii. 84, 91; Aesch. *Pers.* 409; also scholia of the Medici MS.

Fig. 87 Probable copy of the Pheidian
Athene Lemnia

Fig. 88 Probable copy of Myron's
Athene (Marsyas group)

(See List of Illustrations)

seven complete,[1] but these seven are more than enough to prove that in dramatic power and sublimity he is, with perhaps the one exception of Shakespeare, the greatest of poets, and in majesty and might of language unrivalled. His plots are simple, and in the earlier dramas there is a want of movement, the chorus sometimes being unduly prominent and using exceedingly obscure language; but the dramatic effect is often overpowering. 'Terror,' says Schlegel, 'is his element, and not the softer affections.[2] He holds up a Medusa's head before the petrified spectators.' His mind seems to have been deeply imbued by awe of mysterious powers – such powers as we hear of in the old religion of Greece and the Orphic and Eleusinian Mysteries.[3] There is constant reference to expiation and purification and the averting of evil, to dreams and oracles and portents and spectral apparitions and to the ancient chthonian (infernal) deities, especially to the primal Earth-Mother. In some passages, says Paley, there is scarcely a word that does not involve some mystic doctrine. In splendid contrast to this background of gloom with its sinister Fates and terrific Furies, stand the figures of the gods of Olympus, the benign sunlight deities – Zeus and Apollo and Athene. To these also Aeschylus pays reverence, but rather perhaps as personifications of Nature and agents of those supreme spiritual powers of good and evil the manifestations of whose irresistible will are intimated under such names as Fate and Destiny and Justice and Retribution, and that Infatuation that maddens a man and goads him on to insolence and impiety and tempts him to 'kick against the altar of Righteousness.'

Aeschylus is said to have belonged to the aristocratic anti-popular party

---

[1] The preservation of classical works is due mainly to the critics and writers of Alexandria, where there was a vast library (destroyed by Omar in A.D. 641), founded by the Ptolemies (c. 300 B.C.). They chose what was most popular and what best illustrated their theories of art. Sophocles wrote, it is said, 130 plays, of which only seven are extant. Of Euripides we have eighteen complete plays, and several lengthy fragments of others, found on papyrus.

[2] In the *Frogs* of Aristophanes is an amusing scene (in Hades) between Aeschylus and Euripides, where the claims of the two poets are tested by Dionysus – partly by means of a balance to weigh their verses. Aeschylus boasts that 'nobody ever accused him of describing a woman in love.' 'No,' says Euripides, 'there's nothing of Aphrodite in *you!*' 'And may there never be!' answers Aeschylus.

[3] It is notable that Aeschylus was born at Eleusis, and as a child may have received many such impressions; and this may account for the charge of 'revealing the mysteries' in his poetry. Cicero says that he was 'almost a Pythagorean,' and certainly there is much in his poetry that recalls Pythagorean doctrines.

of Aristides and Cimon, and to have opposed the innovations of Themistocles. But his glorification of the battle of Salamis seems scarcely consistent with a bigoted anti-naval policy, and his *Eumenides* is not, as is sometimes imagined, directed against the action of the party of Ephialtes (see p. 315), but is rather a recognition of the Areopagus as the supreme court for cases of homicide. His reverence for the divine rights of kingship is very perceptible, and he seems to have been much impressed by the magnificence of the Persian court. Indeed, one may perhaps trace an Oriental influence in some of his imaginings, which at times are scarcely Greek in their audacity and grotesqueness – a quality noticed by Aristophanes, who makes Euripides ridicule the 'horse-cocks' (griffins) and 'goat-stags' of Aeschylean drama.

No translation can reproduce the splendours and sublimities of the verse of Aeschylus, but some idea of the greatness of his dramatic power may be gained by reading even an unpretentious prose version, not of selected passages, but of an entire play, or, still better, of the great Trilogy – perhaps the mightiest drama in all literature. The pages of a volume on Ancient Greece could scarcely be better filled than with such a version; but I shall have to content myself with giving a brief account of the seven extant plays.

(1) The *Suppliants* is probably the earliest extant Greek tragedy. Some connect it with the alliance of Athens and Argos and the Egyptian expedition of 460–459. But from the style and the antique form of the drama, which consists mainly of chorus, it seems certain that the true date is about 488. The suppliants, who form the chorus, are the fifty Danaïdes who with their father, King Danaus, have fled from Egypt to Argos in order to escape hated nuptials with their cousins, the fifty sons of King Aegyptus. They plead for protection as descendants of Argive Io, whose wanderings (in the form of a heifer) had brought her to Egypt. Pelasgus, the Argive king, grants their prayer and repels the insolent black herald who demands their surrender. There were only two actors, as Danaus and the herald were played by the same person. The trilogy consisted of the *Egyptians*, the *Suppliants*, and the *Danaïdes*. In the last the Danaïdes were, it is believed, tried for the murder of their cousins (whom after all they had been compelled to marry), and were seemingly acquitted, although according to the well-known legend they suffered punishment in Hades. It is unlikely that Aeschylus introduced the sentimental exception of Hypermnestra, who alone, out of pity or love, is said to have disobeyed her father and spared her husband (Hor. *Carmina* III, xi.).

(2) The *Seven against Thebes* (467) was preceded in a trilogy by *Laïos* and *Oedipus*, and followed by a satyric play, the *Sphinx*. For the story of the expedition of the seven heroes see p. 66. In the *Frogs* of Aristophanes Aeschylus describes it as a play 'cram-full of Ares.' The moment chosen is that of the assault on the city. After a long and vivid report by a messenger who describes the assailing host to the chorus of Theban women and the king, Eteocles stations a Theban hero at each of the seven gates, and, goaded by the Erinys of a father's curse, in spite of the entreaties of the chorus and his own foreknowledge of inevitable death, determines to meet his brother Polyneices in mortal combat, in which both are slain. Antigone and Ismene then appear, mourning their brothers in a very beautiful and pathetic lamentation, in which the younger echoes in somewhat different form the broken utterances of the elder sister. In defiance of the proclamation of the new 'ruler of the Cadmean city' (Creon), Antigone now states her determination to bury Polyneices, her brother. Thus we are brought to the moment with which the *Antigone* of Sophocles opens; and modern criticism gravely (and perhaps not unreasonably) suspects that this last scene may have been added by some later writer in order to link the *Seven* up with the Sophoclean play.

(3) The *Persae* is the only extant Greek tragedy dealing with contemporary history. It was performed at Athens (with other plays on legendary subjects) about eight years after the battle of Salamis. Possibly it was written in Sicily for King Hiero and first performed at Syracuse. The scene is laid in Persia, in front of the tomb of Darius (see Fig. 73 and p. 210), near Persepolis,[1] where, awaiting Queen Atossa, is collected a band of twelve elders – 'Faithfuls.' They chant of the crossing of the Hellespont and of the innumerable host that has accompanied Xerxes to Greece, but express their anxiety at hearing no news. The mother-queen Atossa approaches. She too is full of anxiety about her son Xerxes, and has been disturbed by strange dreams, and will offer libations at the tomb of her deified husband. A messenger now arrives and relates the disasters of the Persians. The descriptions of the battle of Salamis and the terrified flight of Xerxes and the catastrophe at the river Strymon (see p. 292) are exceedingly fine, and most interesting as the earliest picture that we possess of any great historical event in Greek history – if

---

[1] The 'city of the Persians' (line 15) may, I think, be Persepolis; but Susa and Ecbatana are alone mentioned by name.

*Figs 89–91 Three possible copies of the Pheidian Athene (See List of Illustrations)*

we exclude the Homeric poems! The ghost of Darius now rises from the tomb, and to him Atossa recounts the disastrous story of the invasion, whereat the spirit of the Great King, full of mourning and of wrath at the folly of his son, prophesies the utter defeat of the Persians at Plataea – being able, as are the spirits in Dante's *Inferno*, to foresee the future, though ignorant of the present. After the disappearance of the ghost of Darius, Xerxes and his retinue arrive in a pitiable state of despair and terror, and the play ends amidst their heart-rending lamentations – a scene that, however unhistorical, must have highly delighted an Athenian audience.[1]

(4) *Prometheus Bound* was written perhaps a few years after the great eruption of Aetna (*c.* 478; see Thuc. iii. 116), which is mentioned prophetically (l. 375). But the highly developed form of the play, with its finely finished metrical and rhetorical language and the predominance of the dramatic over the lyrical element, and the possibility of a third actor (though Prometheus may have been an effigy), as well as the probable use of stage machinery (*e.g.* in the case of the ocean nymphs, whose advent is heralded by the flutter of wings), has induced some to give it a much later date and even needlessly to question its authenticity.

The other plays of the trilogy were the *Fire-bearing Prometheus* and the *Loosing of Prometheus*. Of the last some fragments survive, as well as a Latin version by Cicero of about thirty lines – enough to prove that we have lost a magnificent Greek drama on the same subject as Shelley's very un-Greek *Prometheus Unbound*. The fable of Prometheus (with whom Epimetheus and Pandora are sometimes associated) is of great antiquity and probably of Eastern origin. Aeschylus borrows names and the main features of his picture from Hesiod's *Theogonia*. He depicts the Titan, a divinity of the old dynasty of Cronos and the benefactor of the human race, fettered to the side of a precipice in the Caucasus, but still defying the power of Zeus and refusing to divulge the oracle of Themis which threatened the overthrow of the usurping Olympian deity. Prometheus is visited by the ocean nymphs and their father Oceanus. To him he recounts all the blessings of civilization (letters, numbers, astronomy, houses, horses, ships, etc.) that he had brought to mortals, whom he depicts as having been weak and miserable and living 'like frail ants in sunless caverns' before his gift of

---

[1] In the *Frogs* Dionysus exclaims (*à propos* of the *Persae*): 'Ay, truly, and I was delighted when news was brought of the death of Darius.' There seems some slight error here.

fire,[1] and he refuses the counsel of the sea-god to make peace with Zeus. Then Io, who has also been greatly wronged by Zeus and is now in the form of a heifer wandering through the world (from Argos to Egypt *via* the Caucasus), appears on the scene. She relates her wanderings and Prometheus foretells her future, and how her progeny (the Danaïdes) will return to Argos, and how an Argive hero (Heracles, a son of Zeus) will come to set him free, and how Zeus himself will have to appeal to him for help – power and deity have to appeal to knowledge. Hermes then visits him, but his arrogant behests are repelled with scorn, and amidst a terrific storm and earthquake the drama ends. It is interesting to note that although the real scene of the sufferings of Prometheus was, according to scholiasts, the 'European shores of the Ocean,' the spot intimated by Aeschylus (Scythia is mentioned in our play, and the Caucasus in a fragment of the *Loosing*) became so localized that Pompey the Great during the Mithridatic war undertook a long journey in order to visit it.

(5) The *Oresteia*, or 'Story of Orestes,' consisting of the *Agamemnon*, the *Choephoroe* ('Libation-carriers'), and the *Eumenides* ('Furies'), won the first prize in 458. Soon afterwards Aeschylus went for the second time to Sicily, probably in order to produce the play there also. It is the only extant Greek trilogy. The (lost) satyric play by which it was followed was *Proteus*, which probably depicted the entertaining adventure of Menelaus among the seals.[2]

The *Agamemnon* opens with the monologue of the sentinel who so long has watched at night for fire-beacons announcing the fall of Troy. Suddenly the signal flashes in the far distance, and he hurries forth to the queen. A band of Argive elders enters. In an ode of great sublimity they sing of the long, disastrous war, and of portents and of the direful curse that broods over the house of Pelops. Clytaemnestra now appears and exultingly proclaims the capture of Troy and the return of the king; but our suspicions are aroused by the gloomy chants of the elders, who forebode some

---

[1] The golden age of Cronos seems inconsistent with this. Horace and others attribute diseases and degeneration to the advent of fire and the gifts of Pandora. The fable has analogy to that of the Tree of Knowledge.

[2] *Od.* iv. The only complete satyr play extant is the *Cyclops* by Euripides. The subjects of these lighter plays were often taken from Homer; *e.g. Nausicaä, or The Washerwomen*. It is noticeable that Aeschylus wrote the *Oresteia* at an age (sixty-seven) when nowadays men are regarded as past work, especially creative work. Sophocles wrote many of his finest plays between his sixty-fifth and ninetieth years.

terrible catastrophe. A herald arrives. He describes the sack of Troy and then announces the approach of Agamemnon, who appears followed by chariots laden with spoil and by captives, among whom is Priam's daughter, the prophetess Cassandra. Clytaemnestra welcomes her husband with feigned joy and reverence, and offers friendly words to her hated rival, Cassandra. The chorus once more utters its dark forebodings, and Cassandra, foreseeing the impending terrors and her own fate, breaks forth into lamentation and describes the ghastly visions that she sees in her ecstasy. Then she rushes into the palace to meet her fate, while from behind the scenes we hear the groans of the murdered king. The palace door opens and we see Clytaemnestra standing by the body of her murdered husband and hear her proudly, insolently, confess the crime and justify it as righteous requital for the sacrifice of her daughter Iphigeneia. Here she is joined by Aegisthus, her accomplice in infidelity and murder, amidst whose fierce altercation with the elders the drama ends.

The *Choephoroe* tells the same story as the *Electra* of Sophocles and of Euripides (to which it forms a most interesting contrast) – namely, the return of Orestes (who had been sent away to Phocis when a child by his mother Clytaemnestra), the recognition of him by his sister Electra, and the slaying of the queen together with her paramour by her own son, who has brought her the false tidings of his own death. The character of Electra is wonderfully drawn, and that of Clytaemnestra is perhaps even more impressive in its defiant pride and almost majestic Lady-Macbeth-like insolence than in the *Agamemnon*. The 'libation-carriers' are the maidens who, together with Electra, have been ordered by the queen, because of an evil dream, to make offerings at the tomb of Agamemnon – probably in Mycenae. The drama ends by a vision of the Furies, beheld by Orestes, who flees in terror before them.

The opening scene of the *Eumenides* is before the great temple at Delphi. The aged Pythian priestess enters the shrine to offer prayers to the goddess Earth and other ancient deities and then to take her seat on the oracular tripod. She returns terrified and scarce able to say what she has seen: a suppliant at the central altar, his hands and sword dripping with blood, closely surrounded by a band of slumbering monstrous forms – like Gorgons or Harpies, but wingless, black, distilling filthy ooze from their eyes and snorting forth in sleep their fetid breath. She has hardly ended when Apollo comes forth leading Orestes. He promises him safe passage to Athens, entrusting him to the care of Hermes. The temple door has remained open,

343

and within we see the Furies lying asleep around the central altar – the 'navel of the earth' – above which arises a spectral form, the ghost of Clytaemnestra, which calls on the sleepers to awake and pursue. With horrid moans and groans they answer, still asleep; then, waking, they find their victim fled, and chanting their terrible song they dance wildly round the altar, till Apollo drives them forth from his temple. The scene now changes. Orestes is embracing the statue before Athene's temple on the Athenian Acropolis. The Furies arrive and claim their victim, uttering their terrible cry for vengeance in a magnificent hymn in which they chant of sin and inexorable retribution. But Athene appears in her four-horse chariot. She bids the herald summon the council of the Areopagus, 'the best of my citizens.' Perhaps the scene is supposed to be changed to the 'hill of Ares' (or rather 'of Curses' – *i.e.* of the Avenging Goddesses). Apollo appears to advocate the cause of Orestes against the accusing Furies. The judges cast their ballots into the two urns. The votes are equal. Athene gives the verdict in favour of Orestes, and the rage of the Furies against the 'younger deities' is allayed, and even their blessings are elicited, by the promise of Athene to assign them a special sanctuary 'near the house of Erechtheus' (probably in the dark cleft still existing amid the north-eastern crags of the Areopagus). Here they are to be worshipped as the 'Eumenides,' or 'Kindly Goddesses.'

## Herodotus

The passages that have been quoted from Herodotus in connection with the Persian invasions will have shown, to some extent, the character of his work. Much has been written about it, both in praise and in depreciation, but for those who care to read the book itself – of which there are good annotated translations – such criticism is mostly superfluous. Here I shall content myself with offering a few biographical data and a few general remarks.

As historian Herodotus was preceded by Hecataeus of Miletus and Hellanicus of Mytilene. The former has already been mentioned in connection with the Ionic revolt and as having written a geography (*Travels round the Earth*) for the map or globe of Anaximander. His history is mentioned several times by Herodotus, who also speaks of his having been in Egypt. The 'Attic history' of Hellanicus is mentioned by Thucydides.

Herodotus, who tells us (ii. 143) that he was not accustomed to 'boast of his family,' was born (*c.* 484) in the Dorian city of Halicarnassus in Caria, whence he withdrew, or was banished, in consequence of a revolt against the ruler, or tyrant, Lygdamis – the grandson of that Queen Artemisia whose courage at Salamis was so admired by Xerxes, and also by his historian. Probably in Samos or Lesbos he acquired the Ionic dialect in which he wrote – apparently a selection from the four forms of the ordinary Ionic combined with Attic and epic elements. His travels extended to Scythia (nearly to the Crimea), Babylon, and Elephantiné (near Assouan). He seems to have returned to Halicarnassus and aided in expelling Lygdamis. His evident admiration for Athens seems to confirm the assertion that he lived there, under the patronage of Pericles, for some time. It is even stated that the Athenians presented him with ten talents for reciting his history at the Panathenaea (c. 446). Also perhaps he recited it at Olympia; and Thucydides, then a boy, is said to have been present – and to have shed tears; but chronology makes this improbable. In 444–443 the Athenians and the cityless Sybarites founded Thurii, close to the site of ruined Sybaris, and Herodotus may have been among the first colonists. He may also have composed his history (from previous notes) at Thurii, and perhaps he died there about 426. Some say that he (as also the orator Lysias) returned to Greece, and that he died at Pella, in Macedonia. From his mention (i. 130) of a revolt of the Medes against Darius, which was thought to be the revolt of 408 against Darius II, instead of the earlier revolt against Darius Hystaspes, it has been wrongly believed that Herodotus lived until nearly the end of the Peloponnesian War. In spite of all the sins of omission and commission laid to his charge by the modern historical critic – his inaccuracies, his credulity, his reverence for prophecies and oracles, his belief in the efficacy of images and prayer and sacrifice, his tendency to seek for supernatural causes, his partiality, and so on[1] – this 'naive, uncritical, entrancing story-teller' possesses gifts that many a more scientific chronicler might well envy. By his keen powers of observation he has collected an immense amount of interesting and curious information in regard not merely to events but also to customs and character and cities and countries, and much else, and, what is of even greater importance, his human sympathies allow him an insight into the true causes of

---

[1] Sometimes he ventures to express a doubt (e.g. 'or perhaps the wind ceased of itself'), or prays gods and heroes to forgive his scepticism. He was very far removed from a credulous fool or a bigot. 'My duty,' he says, 'is to report all that is said, but I am not obliged to believe it all.'

things which Thucydides, with all his skilful analysis of secondary and superficial motives, does not possess. The great agent in shaping outward circumstances, as Professor Butcher says, is the human will. But human will is profoundly influenced by beliefs and feelings that lie very deep in human nature, and into these depths mere critical acumen has no such insight as that which is sometimes vouchsafed to the 'naive' and sympathetic spirit.

## Philosophers of the Period

The Eleatic philosophers Parmenides and Zeno have already been mentioned as followers of Xenophanes (see p. 231), and it has been shown how his doctrine of the one eternal and immutable Reality, the source and cause of all the natural universe, degenerated in course of time into a barren denial of the existence (even the temporal, practical existence) of sensible things, and of the possibility of motion. With Parmenides the sublime philosophy of his master still retained much of its elevation and aroused the reverent admiration of Socrates and of Plato, who speaks of his 'wondrous depth.' As an old man Parmenides is said to have visited Athens (c. 448), and Plato describes (possibly invents) a very interesting interview in which Socrates, then quite a young man, imparts to him his newly conceived Ideal theory and is encouraged by him to develop and apply it more boldly. Indeed, it was the Eleatic belief in the one immaterial Reality – involving the denial of the absolute reality of sensible objects – that was the foundation of the Socratic (or Platonic) belief in the divine Will as the one true cause of all things. This denial of the real existence of natural objects has ever encountered the ridicule of the uninitiated, but, 'paradoxical as it may appear, this insistence on the unreality of the sensible world is the only way in which worth and meaning can be given to it.' Misunderstood, it leads to all kinds of extravagant absurdities, as it did in the case of Zeno, who wasted his energies on endless intellectual puzzles and quibbles about the impossibility of motion and the non-existence of place and so on. He is interesting merely because the Sophists were (though they may not have acknowledged it) his lineal descendants. With them, as with him, there was no absolute truth, and consequently no absolute knowledge. Their highest object was intellectualism and rhetorical artifice – that art of Belial, 'to make the worse appear the better reason.'

Zeno is said to have accompanied Parmenides to Athens in 448, and to have been at that time about forty years of age. The only important literary relics of these two Eleatics are about a hundred hexameters by Parmenides, besides a Latin version of about fifty more. In one fragment he offers us a fine imaginative picture – a vision in which he is borne aloft, in a chariot drawn by the horses of Wisdom, out of the night of Ignorance and through the portal of the goddess Justice, up into the sunlit realm of Knowledge. In other fragments he insists again and again on the existence of the One and the non-existence of the Many, and he asserts that all sensible things are resultants produced by two counteracting principles, such as cold and heat, darkness and light, force and inertia.

Empedocles of Acragas, the last of the great colonial sages, was a man of supreme intellectual powers and of a most extraordinary character. His personality is half hidden in fable, for he claimed supernatural powers as a divinity exiled for a time from heaven, and was reverenced as such. Mounted on a chariot, clad in purple robes, and crowned with Delphic laurel and with gold, he made triumphal progress through Sicily. Many miracles of healing are attributed to him. It is even said that he raised the dead. By his art – perhaps by draining a marsh – Selinus was freed from pestilence (see coin 5, Plate IV). Some assert that he threw himself into the crater of Aetna (as happens in Matthew Arnold's poem) to solve the mystery of existence. Others say that after a banquet, when all his companions had fallen asleep, he disappeared, and, like Elijah, was borne aloft to heaven. The modern critic is more inclined to accept the statement of Timaeus, the historian of Sicily, that he took ship for the Peloponnese and died there. That he was a great poet is proved by the magnificent eulogy addressed to him by Lucretius, and also by a fragment of about 470 lines from his poem on Nature, which is grand in language and contains some highly imaginative metaphors. His philosophy seems to have combined some of the main doctrines of the Ionic, Eleatic, and Pythagorean schools. Like Xenophanes he believed in the one real existence, and denied the testimony of the senses to be absolutely true. He developed a cosmology, founded on the four elements. These elements, however, are not 'self-created' or 'self-moving,' as with the old Ionic sages; they are mere material (*hylē*) subject to the influence of immaterial forces, which he named 'love' and 'hate,' the attraction and repulsion caused by which set up an eddying motion and thus formed the natural world out of chaos. Should 'love' finally conquer, the world would relapse into a state (*apoion*) where there is no counteraction, no contradistinction, no genus or species or other differentiation, and where everything is everything else. He seems to have originated the theory of 'emanations' (adopted by Democritus, and described by Lucretius) – that is, the giving off by natural objects of minute particles that affect those elements of our sense-organs which are of the same nature. Hence the doctrine 'Like is affected by like,' which was later applied even to things immaterial – as by Plato to the relation between the intellect and its cognate Ideas.

The attribution of affections and will to elemental matter (or to prime monads, *i.e.* atoms) converted the universe, so to speak, into a living and sensitive thing, such as Virgil describes in a celebrated passage (*Aen.* vi. 723 *ff.*), but was in reality no more intelligible than the old Ionic doctrine of self-created and self-moving prime elements. The one great difficulty remained, and for the materialist still remains, viz. to account for this omnipresent Will or Energy in Nature. 'Amid the mysteries,' says Herbert Spencer, 'that become the more mysterious the more they are thought about, there will remain the one absolute certainty that we are ever in the presence of an infinite and eternal energy from which all things proceed.' To attempt to explain it as due to chemical affinity, gravity, magnetism, or any such natural force does not in the least help towards a solution. We still ask: Whence comes the force that causes these physical manifestations?

It was Anaxagoras who first gave a definite answer to this question. He held, indeed, that matter was eternal, infinite, indestructible, and uncreated (for his mind refused to believe in 'creation from nothing'), but he believed that it existed originally in a chaotic state in which 'all things were together [*homou*]' – that is, not differentiated and distinguishable – until 'Mind [*Nous*] came and arranged them into a Cosmos.' This Mind, or Intelligence, is conceived by Anaxagoras as not immanent in matter, far less as identical with matter, but as an immaterial ordering Will, self-existent (*eph' heautou*), omniscient, and 'with supreme lordship over all things.' Thus we have no longer a materialistic explanation of the universe (which, in spite of their doctrines in regard to the Deity, was still apparently held by Xenophanes and others like him), and no longer a Monistic identification of mind and matter, nor even such 'Higher Pantheism' as that described by Tennyson, but a distinct confession of a spiritual cause of the ordered universe.

Both Plato and Aristotle, however, complain that Anaxagoras (as is the case with many of us) only called in this divine Intelligence when in difficulties – so that Socrates is said (in the *Phaedo*) to have given up the study of his works because the writer had not the courage to apply his own doctrine in physical questions. But, timid guess as it was, it was apparently the first conception by a Greek thinker of a God of infinite power and goodness, such as was proclaimed by Socrates, so that we cannot be surprised at the words of Aristotle: 'When one of them said that there is in Nature an Intelligence that is the cause of the order of the universe, this man appears alone to have been sober among the wild speculations of his predecessors.'

Anaxagoras (*c.* 500–428) was a native of Clazomenae, in Ionia. Probably soon after the battle of Salamis he went to Athens, where he lived for about thirty years. He was an intimate friend of Pericles, and his teachings exercised great influence on Euripides. In 450 he was accused of impiety by the Athenian mob and the high-priests of Olympian orthodoxy, and only escaped death by the eloquent pleadings of Pericles. He retired to Lampsacus, where he died in 428.

*Chapter 7*

# The Peloponnesian War
# (431–404)

SECTIONS – A: THUCYDIDES – B: SOPHOCLES, EURIPIDES,
ARISTOPHANES – C: DEMOCRITUS, THE SOPHISTS, SOCRATES –
D: SCULPTURE

In 445 a Thirty Years' Peace had been concluded between the Athenians
and the Peloponnesians, who had been in a state of almost continuous hostility for about fifteen years. This peace had lasted only some twelve years
– those years during which the Parthenon and the third Long Wall of
Athens and the docks and marts of the Peiraeus were built – when events
occurred that led to the declaration of war by Sparta. The conflict lasted
for about twenty-seven years. After the first ten years of ineffectual
warfare, consisting mainly of such reprisals as were possible between a
maritime and a land power, a respite was given by the Peace of Nicias (421),
but the break was so short that, with Thucydides, we may regard the war
as scarcely interrupted. Hostilities were soon renewed. Had the Athenians
remained true to the policy of Pericles and renounced all ambitious
attempts to increase their oversea empire, they might have retained their
maritime supremacy; but, under the influence of such demagogues and
adventurers as Cleon and Alcibiades, they embarked on the disastrous
Sicilian expedition (415), by which, and by the revolt of almost all their
allies, their power was fatally undermined and rapidly sank, until Sparta,
which had built ships and had even stooped to solicit the powerful aid of
Persia against the 'enslaver of Greece,' crushed the Athenian fleet at the
battle of Aegospotami, captured Athens, razed her Long Walls, and put an
end to her empire (404).

The story of this Peloponnesian War (as we call it, regarding it from the

*Fig. 92 The 'Meidias Vase' (See List of Illustrations)*

351

Athenian point of view) is told very fully by Thucydides down to the year 411, and is continued by Xenophon in his *Hellenica*. Later historians have repeated, sometimes with a vast amount of comment, all the details of every little skirmish or political complication. Doubtless during these twenty-seven years many heroic deeds were done, and some memorable events took place, as well as many that every true lover of Greece would gladly forget; but there is a very great deal to be found in the hundreds of pages often devoted to this war which is for us of no importance whatever – except when we associate it with memories of Thucydides. All these miserable fightings and butcheries, all this hateful internal strife and hatred and treason and inhumanity, bulk so largely in the ordinary Greek history because they have been recounted by a writer perhaps unrivalled for graphic description, for brilliant rhetoric, and for powers of subtle analysis. I do not purpose to make any attempt to describe fully the details of the war, but shall give a concise statement of the chief events of this period and then some descriptive passages from Thucydides.

## The Peloponnesian War (431–404)

In the last chapter we followed the course of events down to the revolt and reduction of Samos in 439. Some five years later incidents occurred in connection with two Corinthian colonies, Corcyra and Potidaea, which (as Corinth was the great maritime rival of Athens) induced the Athenians to interfere, and led to remonstrance and finally an ultimatum from Sparta, as the head of the Peloponnesian league and the champion of the liberties of Greece.

The trouble began at Epidamnus (Dyrrhachium, in Illyria), a colony of Corcyra (Corfu). The Epidamnians, harassed by exiled oligarchs, appealed to Corcyra, and, obtaining no aid, with the advice of the Delphic oracle turned to Corinth, which sent them troops. The Corcyraeans forthwith blockaded Epidamnus. Corinth sent seventy-five ships against them, but the Corcyraeans had a large fleet, and, after defeating the Corinthian ships, captured Epidamnus. Then Corinth, highly indignant, resolved to collect a great navy. Both sides appealed to Athens, and Athens (though it was a hostile act against the democracy of Epidamnus) was induced by the prospect of such strong maritime support against her future Peloponnesian enemies to make an alliance with Corcyra, and sent ships. A naval battle then took place (433) off the Sybota islets, near Corcyra. The Athenian ships held aloof at first, but interfered to save the Corcyraeans from defeat. The Corinthians sailed homewards, much incensed at the breach of the Thirty Years' Peace – a charge repelled by the Athenians, who asserted that Corcyra had belonged to neither of the two great confederacies, and that Athens had a right to defend her new ally.

Another complication with Corinth arose in 'the regions Thraceward', as Thrace was known. Potidaea, on the isthmus of Pallene, was a Corinthian colony, but had become a tributary ally of Athens, and was now ordered by the Athenians to eject its Corinthian officials. It refused. Corinthian forces were sent to support its revolt, but were defeated, and Potidaea was closely besieged for two years by the Athenians.[1] Corinth now appealed to Sparta, which was itself incensed at Athens for having (on the advice of Pericles) excluded Megara from its ports and marts. An Athenian envoy was, perhaps accidentally, present at Sparta, and was allowed to answer the Megarians and Corinthians. Thucydides has taken the opportunity to give us some brilliant speeches, which, though fictitious, probably represent fairly accurately the arguments on both sides. The Peloponnesian confederates, he tells us, held two assemblies, and the Corinthians were allowed a final speech, in which they vehemently incited Sparta to overthrow the 'despot city' which was trying to enslave all Greece. In spite of the prudent advice of the king, Archidamus, the violent war-speech of an ephor carried the assembly, and, after receiving encouragement from the Delphic oracle (which did not feel ashamed of thus inciting fratricidal war), and after making various trivial demands (*e.g.* that Athens should cast out the 'pollution' in the person of Pericles), Sparta sent an ultimatum: 'The Athenians can avoid war if they restore the independence of the Hellenes.'

The speech of Pericles at this juncture was (if we accept the version given by Thucydides) a splendid example of fiery and yet dignified oratory. He advised a temperate answer and a proposal of arbitration, but a decisive refusal of all unjustifiable demands. Regarding war as inevitable, he reviewed the resources of both sides and pointed out that the Lacedaemonians, having neither ships nor money, could not carry on any protracted war. Formerly Themistocles had advised the abandonment of Athens; Pericles now advised the Athenians to trust not only to their wooden but also to their stone walls, and to abandon their open country to

---

[1] A monument now in the British Museum extols those who fell on the Athenian side.

devastation. He believed in a Fabian policy of exhaustion. War was inevitable, was indeed practically declared, but they still, says Thucydides, had intercourse without heralds, until early in the year 431, when the first act of open hostility took place – an attack by the Thebans on the town of Plataea, which, though Boeotian, had always remained faithful to Athens. The attack failed and a massacre of Theban prisoners – the precursor of many such barbarities, if that word can be applied with double intensity to the Greeks themselves – was the signal for the beginning of the long and miserable civil war.

Archidamus and his Peloponnesians forthwith invaded Attica, from which flocks and herds had been removed to Euboea and the inhabitants to Athens, where the overcrowding was terrible. Pericles, in spite of fierce opposition, prevented the Athenians from sallying forth against the foe. The fleet was sent against the Peloponnese and Peloponnesian colonies, but very little was effected. In their excitement and alarm, and perhaps in order to relieve the overcrowding of the city, the Athenians decided to expel the whole population of Aegina and to settle the island with Athenians. The Aeginetans found a home at Thyrea in Laconia, as the Messenians had at Naupactus, but a few years later were captured and enslaved by the Athenians.

To what a degree our interest in the war is purely literary is plain from the fact that for many the most memorable event of this first year is the great speech of Pericles – a funeral panegyric in honour of those who had already fallen,[1] and whose bones were now buried with great ceremony in the Cerameicus without the walls. This celebrated speech, reported by one who was himself doubtless present, must have been so impressed on the memories, and perhaps also the tablets, of many that we may feel sure that we possess in the famous eleven chapters of Thucydides much of what Pericles actually said. Indeed, all the three great orations of Pericles that Thucydides has preserved – the first in favour of war, the second in honour of the fallen, and the third, spoken shortly before his death, in self-defence against his assailants – have, in spite of many a brilliant Thucydidean antithesis, an impress of originality which we find in no other of his reported speeches.

In the second year of the war, after the annual invasion and devastation

---

[1] Fig. 104 represents Athene contemplating a stele with the names (possibly) of these same warriors.

354

of Attica, a calamity befell Athens which probably contributed more than the bloodiest defeats to her final overthrow.[1] Out of perhaps 100,000 citizens about a fifth, besides an 'indiscoverable number' of slaves, foreigners, and others, died of a terrible plague[2] which continued for two years, and after a year's intermission broke out again with great virulence. A vivid description – as vivid as anything in Boccaccio, Defoe, Virgil, or Lucretius – is given by Thucydides, who was himself struck down by the disease, but recovered. In the midst of this distress Athens made overtures of peace, but they were rejected. Pericles meanwhile had made an unsuccessful sea-raid on the Peloponnese, and on his return was vehemently assailed, and fined, and deprived of his post as *stratēgos* (general). His eloquent and dignified defence caused a revulsion of feeling and he was reinstated in his command, but many sufferings had of late fallen upon him. He had been constantly lampooned and satirized and insulted both by political and private enemies.

His friends Pheidias and Anaxagoras, the greatest artist and the greatest philosopher of the day, had been assailed by bigotry and calumny; the one had died in prison, the other was an exile. Aspasia, with whom he lived, and whose house was a centre of intellectual and artistic life, had been accused, perhaps by Cleon, of impiety and immorality. Both his sons (by a wife from whom he was separated) died of the plague, and the blow seems to have left him a broken man.[3] A year or so later he died, it is said from a low fever after an attack of the plague. As he lay dying and seemingly unconscious, his friends, says Plutarch, spoke together in praise of him, but he heard it and interrupted them saying: 'What chiefly gives me pride is that no Athenian ever put on mourning for any act of mine.' By friends and enemies alike the wonderful eloquence of Pericles is attested. Aristophanes describes him as the Olympian Zeus hurling his flaming thunderbolts, and Plato extols his 'majestic intelligence.' His character and his policy are graphically described by Thucydides (see p. 370–1), and though the

---

[1] See Note A (Phigaleia). A statue to Apollo, the 'Averter of Pestilence,' by Calamis was dedicated in Athens about 430.

[2] Perhaps some malignant form of variola, now extinct; evidently not the bubonic plague. Curiously, no account is given by the great physician Hippocrates, who lived from 460 to 356.

[3] Plutarch describes him as breaking down into uncontrollable tears and sobs at the funeral of his favourite son, Paralus. The elder, Xanthippus, was a *mauvais sujet* and caused him much trouble. His son Pericles, by Aspasia, was legitimatized before the death of his father.

partiality of the historian is apparent,[1] we may rather accept his estimate than the suggestion of Plutarch that he corrupted the people by display and by distributions of public money and by 'nursing up the city in elegant pleasures' in order to maintain his personal power, or the accusation of his assailants that he 'fanned up the war' to escape the charge of peculation. At the same time, while fully allowing his integrity and sincerity, it is possible to doubt the wisdom of a policy which, although opposed to imperialistic adventure, was in support of an empire that had been built up on a foundation of tyrannical injustice, extortion, and bloodshed, and was doomed to perish by the hatred that it inspired not only in the rest of the Hellenic world,[2] but also among its so-called allies.

While the plague was raging an armament had been sent to storm Potidaea, which still held out, but a fourth of the troops had perished by the disease and the rest returned. Early in 429, however, the town surrendered to blockade[3] after such sufferings that the garrison had fed on the bodies of the slain. Fair terms were granted, which intensely displeased the Athenian mob, who had looked forward to a great capture of slaves and a wholesale butchery to gratify their resentment. About the same time the Spartans massacred a number of prisoners captured at sea and cast their bodies out for the birds and beasts. The Athenians retaliated by murdering Spartan envoys who had fallen into their hands and by serving the bodies in like fashion. Henceforward acts like these and of still greater ferocity became common, till at Aegospotami from three to four thousand Athenian prisoners were butchered in cold blood.

The chief events of the next five years (429–424), besides the almost annual devastation of Attica, were the capture of Plataea by the Lacedaemonians, the revolt and reduction of Mytilene, the revolution and massacre at Corcyra, the capture of Spartans on Sphacteria, and the defeat of Athens at Delion. The following brief accounts of these facts will be supplemented later by descriptive passages from Thucydides.

In 429, instead of devastating Attica, Archidamus and his Peloponnesians cross the ridge of Cithaeron, and the Plataeans, on the (never

---

[1] In spite of the fact that he was related to the family of Cimon, the hereditary opponent of Xanthippus and Pericles.

[2] Thucydides, though an Athenian, tells us that at the beginning of the war public feeling through the whole of Greece was 'greatly in favour of the Lacedaemonians' as adversaries of the 'despot city.'

[3] Socrates served as Athenian hoplite in this campaign.

fulfilled) promise of aid from Athens, determine to stand a siege. The account that Thucydides has given of this siege, with all its picturesque details of vallation and countervallation, of mines, battering-rams, and so on, and of the escape of about half the garrison, who on a moonless winter night amidst a storm of wind and rain scaled the besiegers' walls and waded across the flooded moats, covered with fragile ice, and reached Athens in safety – this picture has made the siege of little Plataea, with its garrison of 400, and later only 200, Plataeans and 80 Athenians, as famous as that of Syracuse, Saguntum, or Magdeburg. Athens, either from cowardice or because of the plague, thought it best to forget its promised aid, and at last, in the summer of 427, the Plataeans surrendered at discretion. In vain they appealed to the memory of Marathon and their heroic ancestors and to the tombs of the Spartans who fell at the battle of Plataea. Commissioners sent from Sparta to decide their fate put to each man only the question whether in the present war he had done any service to the Spartans or their allies. All the 200 were slaughtered, as well as some Athenians, and Plataea was razed to the ground.

While Plataea was still being besieged (428) Mytilene, the capital of Lesbos, nominally still an autonomous ally of Athens, was induced by the oligarchical party to assert, as Samos had done, its independence. Lesbian envoys appealed to the Greeks assembled at the Olympic Games, and Lesbos was admitted into the Peloponnesian league. The Athenians, though much crippled by the plague and by want of money, dispatched forty ships under Paches and blockaded Mytilene. The Spartans also sent a fleet, but it returned without daring to attack the Athenians, and ultimately the democrats in the city forced the authorities to capitulate on the condition that its fate should be decided by the Assembly at Athens. At Athens there had come to the front a politician named Cleon. The character of Cleon as drawn by Aristophanes, who was an aristocrat in politics and his private enemy, as well as by Thucydides, who was banished by his influence, is that of a loud-voiced, brutal, overbearing demagogue, one of the most pernicious products of the jury courts and the Ecclesia; and, after making all due allowances for personal dislike and for political rancour, as well as for the exaggerations of comic caricature, this tanner or leather-seller, who has been sedulously whitewashed by some modern writers, seems to have really been something very like the picture given by his two great contemporaries. That on one occasion, as we shall see, he gained a remarkable success, and that his chauvinistic war-policy may have been more to the advantage of the Athenian Empire than that advocated by the milder-tempered Nicias, can be allowed without causing us to exchange the portrait of the man given us by Aristophanes in his *Knights* for that offered by writers who describe him as a 'great Opposition speaker,' not more unnecessarily virulent than Demosthenes, Cicero, Milton, or Chatham, and withal a discoverer and castigator of social and political scandals and a true friend of the poorer classes. This man proposed that all the grown-up men of Mytilene should be put to death, and his proposal was passed. A ship of war was forthwith sent with orders to Paches to carry out the terrible verdict. But a revulsion of feeling set in. On the next day the Assembly was again summoned, and by a small minority, in spite of Cleon's efforts, the decree was revoked. A swift vessel was dispatched to overtake the trireme, which had the start of a day and a night. Paches had already received the warrant and was preparing to execute it when the reprieve arrived. The Athenian mob was satiated with the blood of about 1000 ringleaders[1] who had been sent to Athens, and Paches, on his return, was arraigned on some charge and committed suicide in the presence of the Athenian burghers who were judging the case.

One of the most vivid scenes depicted by Thucydides is that of the horrible massacres of the Corcyraean oligarchs by their fellow-citizens which took place at this period (427–425). The episode, with all its revolting details – perhaps as revolting in their inhuman, unnatural ferocity as anything in the world's history – has been recounted by many writers.[2] The event is only indirectly connected with the Peloponnesian War, and need not be retailed anew. The last scene of this insane butchery of fellow-Greeks and fellow-citizens, as described by Thucydides, together with his reflections on moral and political feeling in Greece at this time, will be given or referred to later. Here it is only necessary to say that the trouble was begun by the fact that Corinth sent back to Corcyra the 250 high-born prisoners whom they had captured in the sea-fight off Sybota (433). The rest of the prisoners they had sold as slaves, but had kept and treated with especial lenience these nobles, with the intention of using them later for the establishment of an oligarchy in Corcyra. The occasion now presented itself, as Athens was weakened by the plague and distracted by the Lesbian

---

[1] Some would read Λ (lambda) instead of A (alpha) in Thuc. iii. 50, *i.e.* 'thirty' instead of 'a thousand.' (Greek letters also did service as numerals.)

[2] See Thuc. iii. 71 *ff.*, iv. 45 *ff.*

revolt. The return of these prisoners was the signal for a revolution, in which, after some temporary successes and many atrocities, the oligarchs were overwhelmed and driven out. They returned and entrenched themselves in a stronghold, Istone, but finally capitulated to the Athenians and the democrats and were all massacred.

Another important event of this first period of the war, also vividly described by Thucydides, is the capture of some 300 Spartans on the island of Sphacteria. An Athenian fleet had been dispatched in 425 to interfere in the affairs of the Sicilian cities and to help the democratic party at Corcyra. As they coasted round the Peloponnese the Athenians had fortified and occupied Pylos,[1] the promontory which together with Sphacteria forms the great landlocked bay famous in modern history under the name Navarino. The Spartans sent considerable forces by land and by sea to eject the Athenians, who were commanded by Demosthenes and numbered 200 with perhaps 1000 Messenians. The Athenian fleet then hastened back from Corcyra and defeated the Peloponnesian vessels, forcing them to run ashore at the north end of the bay. They then blockaded Sphacteria, on which was the main body of the picked land troops of the Spartans. The alarm was so great at Sparta that a truce was made in order that envoys should be sent to Athens to treat for peace. The stranded Spartan ships and others, sixty in all, were handed over to the Athenians on the promise that they should be restored at the expiration of the truce – a promise which, by the way, was not fulfilled. At Athens all right-thinking men were doubtless inclined for peace, and it would have been a wise decision, and one that might have affected deeply the future of the Hellenic race and of European civilization, had the Athenian people taken advantage of their good fortune to end honourably this most foolish and detestable civil war.

But the evil passions of the mob and their greed for the aggrandizement of the empire were stirred up by Cleon. Nisaea (the port of Megara), the Corinthian ports, the whole of Achaea, and Troezen was the price that Athens demanded for peace; and the demand was refused. But the blockade of Sphacteria lasted long and the mob at Athens grew impatient. 'If I were commander,' bragged Cleon before the Assembly, 'I would soon do it!' At these words Nicias, the *stratēgos*, who had been mocked by Cleon for not going off to Pylos and capturing the Spartans, rose up and offered to cede his command to the demagogue. The mob was tickled, and insisted.

---

[1] The Homeric 'sandy Pylos,' Nestor's town, was in the vicinity.

*Fig. 93 The Nike (Victory) of Paeonius*

Finally Cleon accepted, and with a band of mercenaries, refusing the offer of Athenian hoplites and promising, doubtless amid great laughter, to return within twenty days with the Spartan captives, he set out for Pylos, and, to the amazement of all and the discomfiture of many, within the stipulated twenty days he and Demosthenes returned with the Spartan prisoners – nearly 300 men. The fight had been very severe. The Spartans had been driven with heavy loss gradually back till they had taken their last stand, as at Thermopylae, on a height; but, when circumvented, as at Thermopylae, they doubtless felt no such enthusiasm for their cause as those around Leonidas had felt, and they surrendered – a course never before taken, perhaps, in Spartan warfare. Sphacteria was strongly garrisoned with Messenians from Naupactus, whose exultation at the crushing defeat of their ancient foe found, and still finds, expression in a gift that they made from the spoil to the sacred precinct at Olympia – a splendid figure of Victory floating aloft amidst trailing wind-blown drapery – the work of the sculptor Paeonius (Fig. 93).

In the next year (424) the Athenians captured the island of Cythera – a formidable base for naval operations against Sparta. Also Nisaea and its Long Walls (built by themselves *c.* 460) fell into their hands. Athens was now at the acme of her success, and might have well accepted the generous terms offered by Sparta. But some Ate, or spirit of self-destruction, seems to have goaded her onward to ruin. Elated by good fortune and incited by the ambitious militarism of the *stratēgos* Demosthenes and the harangues of Cleon, the populace determined to take revenge on Thebes for the defeat of Coroneia and the loss of Boeotia. The crushing overthrow of Delion (424) was the result. The Athenian general, Hippocrates, was slain and his army of 7000 hoplites and 20,000 light-armed troops was routed by the Thebans, who used, apparently for the first time, a formation (twenty-five deep) like that of the phalanx, to which their future victories were mainly due.

With the battle of Delion is associated the name of Socrates. He is said to have fought with great courage and to have contributed much to an orderly retreat, thus saving many lives, among them that of Alcibiades.

After the defeat at Delion (424) disaster overtook the Athenians also in Thrace. The Spartan Brasidas, who had already distinguished himself at Pylos and Megara, with a strong body of Peloponnesian hoplites, had traversed Thessaly and Macedonia, where he joined forces with Perdiccas, the Macedonian king, and invaded the Athenian possessions in Thrace, proclaiming himself as their liberator from slavery. His chivalrous and humane character seems to have favoured his success no less than his courage and the rapidity of his strategic movements. Acanthus, Stageiros, and other cities welcomed him, and by a forced march he surprised Amphipolis, which came to terms with him before the arrival of the Athenian ships from Thasos under command of Thucydides, the son of Olorus, as the historian calls himself when relating the mishap. Thucydides rescued Eïon, the port of Amphipolis at the mouth of the Strymon, but this did not save him from banishment, which, he tells us, lasted twenty years (424–404). Disheartened by the defeat at Delion and by the brilliant successes of Brasidas in Thrace, the Athenians concluded a truce, for the purpose of considering the terms of a definite peace. Two days, however, after the truce had begun the town of Scione (on Pallene, south of Potidaea) opened its gates to Brasidas and welcomed him with enthusiasm, offering him a golden crown as the liberator of Greece from Athenian slavery. At Athens the exasperation was intense, and Cleon carried a proposal that Scione should be razed and all its male inhabitants be slain – which was eventually done. Cleon himself was sent with forces to Thrace, and in a fight under the walls of Amphipolis both he and Brasidas fell. Their deaths strengthened the hands of Nicias and others who wished to put an end to the war, and in 421 the so-called Peace of Nicias was concluded for fifty years. Prisoners and places captured during the war were to be restored; but Amphipolis refused to belong again to Athens, and Athens refused to evacuate Pylos, and in spite of all the efforts of the prudent Nicias, who was thwarted by the intrigues of the brilliant and unprincipled young Alcibiades, formal peace soon relapsed into overt hostility. Sparta and Athens were nominally in alliance, but Alcibiades brought about an alliance also between Athens and Argos, which state had set itself at the head of a new Peloponnesian league, thus defying the supremacy of Sparta. Such a state of things could not last. Sparta put an army into the field, and the allied forces of the Argives, Mantineians, and Athenians suffered a severe defeat at the battle of Mantineia (418).

For two or three years no great event, we are told, took place except the capture of Scione and the massacre of all its male inhabitants, and an entirely unprovoked and unjustifiable attack by Athens on the island of Melos, which was quite independent and had taken no part in the war. On the proposal of Alcibiades it was commanded to subject itself to the Athenian Empire, and on its refusal it was besieged and reduced; all the adult males were massacred, all the women and children sold as slaves. Thucydides gives us in full the arguments used by the Melians and by the Athenians at a conference held before the perpetration of this hideous atrocity. The cold-blooded inhumanity of the Athenians, their insolent assertion of the right of the stronger and their impious appeal to the example of the gods themselves to support that claim, affect one like the prelude to some terrific catastrophe in a tragedy of Aeschylus, and prepare us for the calamity that is shortly to befall Athens and her empire.

The pitiful story of the Sicilian disaster is well known to readers of Thucydides and has been retold by many writers, who have vied with each other in depicting anew all its pathetic and harrowing incidents. What makes it so especially pitiable and horrible is the fact that this ferocious fratricidal conflict was due to nothing but the insatiable greed for dominion and supremacy on the part of that Hellenic people to whom for many reasons we owe an inestimable debt of gratitude. As the main object of this book is to draw attention to some of these reasons rather than to recount external history, and as this Sicilian episode has little or no connection with the true inner life of Greece and would be, even as framework, of little assistance to us, the following facts may suffice.

The Greek cities of Sicily and Southern Italy owed their origin, some to Dorian, others to Ionian founders, and, although their own internecine feuds and their own struggle for existence against the Carthaginians and Etruscans were for them matters of prime importance, their sympathies were doubtless enlisted on the side of their respective mother-cities in the long war that was desolating the land. But, in spite of the progress of democracy, sympathy with Sparta, increased by a growing resentment against the ambitious and tyrannical conduct of Athens, had become ever stronger, and when in 425 the Athenian fleet, sent, as has been related,[1] to support Leontini against Syracuse, at last reached Sicily it could do nothing, for at a conference of the Sicilian cities it was decided (on the proposal of the Syracusan Hermocrates) to lay aside dissension and to brook no foreign interference in Sicilian affairs. So incensed were the Athenians at this wise and most justifiable decision that they punished severely by fines and banishment the two admirals of their fleet, Sophocles and Eurymedon. Unhappily political rancour in Sicily led to further appeals for Athenian interference, and in 416, when called upon by Segesta for aid

---

[1] This fleet had to return from Corcyra to Pylos, where it was detained for some time.

against Selinus, the Assembly, cajoled by the fascinating eloquence of Alcibiades, in spite of the warnings of Nicias, determined to send a large armament of some 140 triremes and 500 transports, under the command of Alcibiades, Nicias, and Lamachus, to support Segesta and other anti-Dorian cities in their revolt against the authority of Syracuse – the reduction of which city was the prime object of the expedition.

Just before the expedition sailed a strange event occurred – the mutilation of the busts of Hermes which stood in front of temples and many private houses. The excitement and alarm was such as might be caused in some Roman Catholic countries by a wholesale multilation of roadside crucifixes and Madonna images. Whether it was an act of drunken vandalism or of impiety or had political meaning was never discovered. Possibly it was perpetrated by paid agents of Sparta or Syracuse. Alcibiades was suspected, and evidence was forthcoming that he had indulged in profane mimicries of mystic Eleusinian rites. The fleet had already started, but orders were sent for his return. At Thurii he managed to get ashore and before long was at Sparta, where he revealed all the schemes of the Athenians, vented his disdain of democracy as 'acknowledged folly,' and induced the Spartans to fortify Deceleia, in North-western Attica – a stronghold which proved most troublesome to Athens.

The besieging of Syracuse both by land and sea by Nicias – who after the gallant Lamachus had fallen was the sole general – seemed at one time not unlikely to succeed. But Nicias was slow and unenterprising. Moreover, the Syracusans were fighting for their homes and their liberty, while he and many of his men, when they thought of Marathon and Salamis, must have felt but little enthusiasm for their task. Soon, however, they themselves had to fight for their lives, for, their blockade on the land side being ineffective, Syracuse was reinforced by the Spartan Gylippus (who with four ships had reached Himera and had collected 3000 men), and they therefore abandoned the higher ground and entrenched themselves on Plemmyrion, near the sea. Here they were closely surrounded by the Syracusans and finally driven to camp on the marshy western shores of the great harbour near the mouth of the river Anapus.[1]

---

[1] Ancient Syracuse lay on the island of Ortygia (joined to the mainland by a causeway) and extended up the heights of Achradina and Tyche, and later included the more westerly heights of Epipolae, which the Athenians at this time occupied at first with their circumvallation. The Great Harbour is formed by Ortygia and Plemmyrion, between which there is a narrow exit.

A fleet of seventy-three triremes under the command of Eurymedon and Demosthenes was sent from Athens for their relief and entered the harbour in triumph. But also the enemy had gained large reinforcements, and after some fruitless attempts to act on the offensive the newly arrived generals persuaded Nicias to embark the troops and withdraw by sea to some place of safety. This was still practicable, and the armament would have doubtless escaped had not an eclipse of the moon taken place (August 27, 413). The soothsayers insisted on the departure being deferred for a month, and Nicias yielded to the superstitious clamour of the soldiers. The Syracusans, learning the intention of the Athenians to escape, attacked with seventy-six vessels. Though five miles in circumference, the space afforded by the harbour did not allow the Athenians to take advantage of their superiority in manœuvring. They were worsted and Eurymedon was slain. Then the Syracusans blocked the exit of the harbour with vessels and chains, and a desperate conflict took place, the walls of Ortygia, the heights of the upper city, and the shores of the harbour being crowded with innumerable spectators as in a mighty amphitheatre, while the two fleets – about 200 vessels, carrying thousands of armed men – struggled for mastery. At last the Athenians were driven back to their camp, and in spite of the entreaties of Demosthenes refused to make another effort to break through the barrier. It was then decided to attempt a retreat by land. In a state of pitiable distress and despair they started – a host of about 40,000. The march was directed inland with the object of reaching friendly Sicel territory. After four days they reached a precipitous hill, the Ascraean cliff, where the road passed through a narrow ravine. This was strongly occupied by the enemy, and the fugitive army turned southward. The rear division, under Demosthenes, was surrounded and capitulated. Nicias, after pushing forward desperately under enormous losses for two days more, surrendered to Gylippus. The chief captives – Athenians and their allies – some eight thousand in number, were consigned for months to the stone quarries of Achradina and Epipolae, in which deep, unsheltered dungeons many perished miserably. The survivors were treated as convicts or sold as slaves – a fate that doubtless befell all the rest of the prisoners.[1]

---

[1] Browning's *Balaustion* should be read in this connection. In commemoration of their victory over the invader the Syracusans issued some very beautiful coins of the same type as the Demareteia (coin 6, Coin Plate IV) struck after the battle of Himera.

In spite of much that the true lover of Greece may well leave to chroniclers of the horrors and political insanities of which ordinary Greek history so largely consists, the intense human pathos of this Sicilian disaster as related by Thucydides makes it a most impressive and memorable episode. The remaining nine years of the war, two of which only are described by him, offer far less of interest. Athens had lost two-thirds of her ships and probably half her trained fighters. Incited by the renegade Alcibiades, almost all her allies now revolted. Sparta made an infamous treaty with the satrap Tissaphernes, giving over the Ionian Greek cities to Persia in return for financial aid against Athens. But Alcibiades, who had fallen into disfavour with the Spartans and had taken refuge with Tissaphernes, persuaded him to transfer his aid to the Athenians on condition that an oligarchy should be set up at Athens. This was effected (411). A council of Four Hundred with practically absolute powers was instituted, but the army and fleet assembled at Samos (which had remained faithful to Athens) declined to recognize it, and a counter-revolution took place re-establishing the democracy. In the midst of all these political dissensions the Spartan fleet more than once nearly took Athens by surprise, and succeeded in defeating a hastily raised Athenian squadron off Euboea and causing that island to revolt. The sea-power of the Spartans and their allies had become almost equal to that of the Athenians, but the latter gained several naval successes in the next few years (Cynossema, Cyzicus, Byzantium), some of them due to the strategic genius of Alcibiades, who made a triumphal entry into Athens and was given supreme command of all land and sea forces.[1] In 407, however, a slight defeat induced the mob to dismiss their hero, who retired in disgust to the Thracian Chersonese.[2] In 406 the sea-fight of Arginusae (near Lesbos) was won by the Athenians – a victory memorable chiefly for the fact that six of the victorious commanders (among them the son of Pericles) were accused of having abandoned the crews of certain disabled vessels, and without due hearing or legal process were condemned to drink hemlock. In passing it is interesting to note that the only man among the state-councillors (*prytaneis*) who, not overawed by the popular clamour, persisted in his protest against this illegality was Socrates.

---

[1] The leaden plate on which the curses of the priests against him (as profaner of Mysteries) had been inscribed was cast into the sea by the hysterical *dēmos*.

[2] Hence he tried to reach the court of Artaxerxes in Susa, but was prevented by Pharnabazus, and in 404 was murdered, probably through Spartan influence.

The final triumph of Sparta in the war was largely due to funds supplied by Persia, especially by Cyrus, the younger brother of King Artaxerxes. Cyrus had been sent as satrap to Sardis[1] by his father, Darius II, and was strongly attached to the Spartan interest and to Lysander, the Spartan commander, to whom he even entrusted his satrapy when he was called to the deathbed of his father in 405. In this same year, at Aegospotami ('Goat's Rivers'), on the coast of the Thracian Chersonese, Lysander captured almost the whole of the Athenian fleet (of about 170 vessels) while the crews were on land. Between 3000 and 4000 Athenians were made prisoners and were all put to death. The Athenian commander-in-chief, Conon, escaped, but, fearing to return to Athens, took refuge with Evagoras, king of Salamis, in Cyprus. Lysander then blockaded the Peiraeus, while the kings Agis and Pausanias with the Spartan army besieged Athens. A conference of the Peloponnesians was called, which voted that the city which for so long had enslaved Greece should be razed and her whole population sold into slavery. But, like Florence, Athens was saved by the magnanimity of her great rival. Sparta refused to destroy a city that had done such noble service against the barbarian invader. The conditions imposed (at first rejected by the influence of the demagogue Cleophon, a lamp-maker and a worthy successor of Cleon) were that Athens should become the ally and acknowledge the supremacy of Sparta; that she should give up all her possessions except Attica and Salamis, and all her ships; that the Long Walls and fortifications should be pulled down, and that all exiles should be recalled. After the terms were ratified, the Spartan fleet entered the Peiraeus (April 404) and the Athenians aided in demolishing the walls to the sound of flutes and the jubilant shouts of the Peloponnesians, who imagined that at last the day of freedom for Greece had dawned.

Even in this hour of humiliation the Athenians found it necessary to spend their remaining strength in the insane fury of political strife and bloodshed. A supreme council of thirty (known as the 'Thirty Tyrants') was instituted under the approval of Lysander, who occupied the Acropolis with his Spartans. To the Thirty belonged Theramenes, a former member of the Four Hundred, and Critias, a violent oligarch, who had been exiled

---

[1] Tissaphernes was ousted by Cyrus at Sardis and given the less important satrapy of Caria, which explains his hostility to Cyrus. Pharnabazus continued as satrap of Hellespontine Phrygia till about 387.

by the democrats.[1] These two quarrelled and Theramenes was put to death. But the exiled democrats under Thrasybulus fortified themselves in the stronghold of Phyle, on Mount Parnes, and seized the Peiraeus, where Critias was slain in a fight. The Thirty were deposed by the Athenian mob, and, to make matters worse, a Council of Ten was elected, strongly supported by Lysander. At last the Spartan king Pausanias intervened, and by his counsel and the influence of advisers from Sparta reconciliation and general amnesty were proclaimed, and the ferocious and turbulent Athenian *dēmos* had a season of enforced quiet under 'the laws of Solon and the institutions of Draco.'[2]

## SECTION A: THUCYDIDES

The *History* of Thucydides has been mentioned and quoted several times already, and his main characteristics as a writer have been noted. All that is known for certain about his life and that is of any importance has been already related except what may be gathered from the following quotations and except the facts, if they are such, that during his exile he lived for some time at the Macedonian court, and that he was also in Sicily and perhaps present at the fight in the Great Harbour, and that not long after his return from exile (*c.* 403) he was assassinated at Athens, or, according to others, by a robber in Thrace. From internal evidence it would seem that the first three or four books of the *History*, except two passages inserted later, were finally composed (from his notes) during his exile in the pause that occurred after the Peace of Nicias (421), and that he at that time considered the war as finished; but in Book V he protests against this view, and regards the subsequent (Deceleian) war as a continuation of the original

---

[1] It did not redound to the popularity of Socrates that both Alcibiades and Critias had been among his followers as young men. Socrates, however, again showed his character by refusing to obey an illegal command of the Thirty. The orator Lysias, afterwards a considerable power, barely escaped the Thirty by fleeing from Athens.

[2] It is strange how differently the acts of the Athenian *dēmos* affect some minds. Grote speaks of 'a generous exaltation of sentiment and an absence of ferocity such as nothing except democracy ever inspired in Grecian bosoms.' In so far as a democracy means self-rule it is ideally the highest form of government, but, even if it may not be indispensable (as in the case of Plato's ideal republic) that all self-rulers shall be philosophers, it is surely necessary that they shall be incapable of such insanities and atrocities as those perpetrated by the Athenian mob.

war, which he asserts (v. 26) to have lasted twenty-seven years. The work ends abruptly at the year 411. Probably he had collected material for the rest, which had not been put into literary form at the time of his death. Book VIII was perhaps 'written up' from such notes – some say by his daughter, or by Xenophon. Without the slightest intention of presuming to offer a critique of Thucydides, perhaps I may note once more his critical, analytical, sceptical (or, rather, agnostic) attitude, and his 'surly' reserve, as it has been called – qualities which are possibly admirable in an historian and which offer a striking contrast to the urbanity and humanity of Herodotus. Whether with all his descriptive powers, his analytic subtleties, his brilliant antitheses, and his polite scepticism he has the breadth of view and the deeper insight that are sometimes vouchsafed to more childlike and sympathetic natures may perhaps be doubted. He mentions Hesiod and Homer, makes Pericles say, 'We need no Homer to praise us,' and quotes Homer for historical purposes. But he gives no evidence of any sense for art or poetry or philosophy, such as is frequent in Herodotus. Such contemporaries as Aeschylus, Pindar, Sophocles, Anaxagoras, Socrates, Pheidias he does not deign to mention, and never alludes to art, I think, except on one occasion ('We love what is beautiful without extravagance'). There is, I think, in his book no sympathetic mention of any woman, such as of Artemisia, Atossa, Agarista, Gorgo, and others in Herodotus; indeed, hardly any woman is named but Brauro, who murdered her husband, King Pittacus. Perhaps Thucydides, like Euripides (whom he must have known at Athens and also at the court of Archelaus in Macedonia), was a confirmed misogynist. Anyhow, he was no admirer of female notorieties, and evidently agreed warmly with what he makes Pericles say: 'Great is her glory who is least talked of among men either for good or for evil.' Herodotus, being a colonial and having lived long in Ionia, was not hampered by old-fashioned Athenian proprieties and could allow range to his broader sympathies as regards women.

**Thucydides and his Book**

'Thucydides, an Athenian, wrote the history of the war between the Peloponnesians and the Athenians, how they warred against each other, having begun directly it broke out, with the expectation that it would prove important and more worthy of description than any that had preceded it. . . . As for what was said on either side, it was hard to remember the exact

369

words, both for me, in regard to what I myself heard, and for those who reported it to me from other quarters; but as I thought they would have most likely spoken on the subjects from time to time before them, while I held as closely as possible to the general sense of what was really said, so I have recorded it. But with regard to the facts and deeds of the war I did not think right to state what I heard from a chance informant, nor what seemed to me probable, but I have related only those events at which I was myself present and those which, after learning them from others, I have investigated with all possible care in every detail. . . . Now for recitation perhaps the unfabulous character of my work will appear not very attractive, but all who shall wish to study what really happened and what is bound by reason of human nature to happen again – in the same or similar forms – for such to judge it to be useful will be sufficient. The work is meant to be a possession forever rather than a prize composition to be listened to for a passing hour. . . . The same Thucydides, the Athenian, has also written of all these things in order as they severally happened, by summers and winters, until the Lacedaemonians and their allies put an end to the empire of the Athenians and captured the Long Walls and the Peiraeus. . . . I lived on through the whole of the war, being of an age to apprehend events and using my judgment in order to gain accurate knowledge. It was moreover my lot to be an exile from my country for twenty years after my command of the expedition to Amphipolis, and being, by reason of my banishment, present at the transactions of both sides, especially of the Peloponnesians, I was enabled to gain at my leisure a better acquaintance with them.' (i. 1 and 22; v. 26.)

**Character and Policy of Pericles**

'But not long after, as a mob is wont to do, they again elected him general and entrusted all public affairs to him . . . and as long as he was at the helm of the state in time of peace he governed it with moderation and kept it in safety, and during his rule it was at the height of its greatness; and when the war broke out he again seems to have foreseen the capabilities of Athens also in this respect. For he said that if they kept quiet and attended to their navy, and did not try to increase their empire during the war and thus imperil the safety of the state, they would prove successful – whereas they did exactly the contrary in all these matters, and in other matters too, which apparently had nothing to do with the war, their policy was actuated by selfish ambition and greed and proved fatal to themselves and to their allies. . . . And the reason [of his success] was that, wielding a powerful influence by means of his reputation and intellect and being manifestly and absolutely beyond the range of bribery, he controlled the populace with a free rein so that they followed his guidance, not he theirs, because he said nothing to please them for the sake of gaining power by improper means, but was able on the strength of his character to contradict them even at the risk of their displeasure. Whenever, for instance, he perceived them to be unseasonably and insolently self-reliant, by his words he dashed them down to alarm, and when, on the other hand, they were unreasonably terrified, he would restore them to self-confidence. It was in name a democracy, but in reality was absolute rule carried on by the foremost man of the state.' (ii. 65.)

### The Plague

'It is said to have first come from Aethiopia and to have spread over Egypt and Libya and most of the king's territory. On the city of Athens it fell suddenly, first attacking the people in the Peiraeus, so that it was reported that the Peloponnesians had thrown poison into the tanks. . . . Now, everyone, whether physician or private person, can say what he thinks as to its probable origin and the causes that he considers sufficiently powerful to have produced such a distemper. I shall simply describe it and state clearly its symptoms so that any one who notes them may not fail to recognize it if ever it should break out again; for I myself had the disease and I saw others who were attacked by it.

'The year, as was generally allowed, happened to be particularly healthy as regards all other disorders, and if any one did have any previous illness it always developed into this. In other cases persons who were quite well were suddenly and without any apparent reason seized at first with violent feverish headaches and their eyes became red and inflamed, and the internal parts, throat and tongue, at once assumed a bloody appearance and emitted a strange and noisome breath. Then sneezing and angina came on, and in a short time the pain descended to the chest, accompanied by violent coughing, and as soon as it settled in the stomach it produced vomiting . . . and in most cases the empty retching caused violent spasms. Externally the body was not excessively hot to the touch, nor was it pallid, but reddish, livid, and broken out in small pimples and sores; internally

Fig. 94  Herodotus

Fig. 95  Thucydides

Fig. 96  Pericles

Fig. 97  Alcibiades

there was such intense heat that they could not bear even the very lightest garments or fine linen to be laid upon them, nor to be anything else but naked, and most gladly would have thrown themselves into cold water; indeed, many among those who were not taken care of did throw themselves into tanks, overcome by their unquenchable thirst; and it made no difference however much or little they drank. . . . And the birds and quadrupeds that prey on human bodies either did not come near them, though there were many unburied corpses, or perished after tasting them. . . . And what added much to the distress was the crowding into the city from the country, especially in the case of the newcomers, for as there were no houses for them they lived in stifling cabins in the hot season of the year, and the mortality spread uncontrolled, the bodies of the dying lying one on the other or rolling about half dead in the streets and round all the fountains, in their craving for water. The sacred precincts also, in which they had camped, were full of the corpses of those who had died there, for the calamity was so overwhelming that men, not knowing what was to become of them, came to disregard everything both sacred and profane alike. . . . Such was the calamity which befell Athens and by which it was afflicted, the people dying within its walls and the land being devastated without.' (ii. 48 *ff.*)

## The Night Escape from Plataea

'They made ladders equal in height to the siege-wall of the enemy, calculating it by the layers of bricks where the wall looking towards them happened not to be plastered. Many counted the layers at the same time, and although some were bound to miss the correct number, most would hit it, especially as they counted often and were at no great distance. Thus they ascertained the right length of the ladders, guessing it from the thickness of the bricks. Now the rampart consisted of a double line of walls, which were about sixteen feet apart, and between these walls quarters had been built and assigned to the men on guard; and they were continuous, so that it seemed to be one thick wall with battlements on both sides. And at intervals of ten battlements there were large turrets of the same breadth as the rampart, extending across to its inner and to its outer front, so that there was no passage alongside the tower, but they passed through its middle. Now at night, whenever it was wet and stormy, they left the battlements and kept watch from the towers, as these were at short distances from each other and were roofed. . . . When all was ready, having watched for a stormy night with rain and wind and at the same time moonless, they sallied forth. First they crossed the moat that encircled the town, then they got up to the enemy's wall without being noticed by the sentinels, who could not see far through the darkness and could not hear them because the clatter of the wind drowned the noise of their approach; moreover, they kept far apart so that their weapons might not clash together and attract notice; also they were lightly equipped and were shod only on the left foot as security against the [slippery] mud. Thus they reached the battlemented rampart at a point between two towers, knowing that here it was unguarded. First those who carried scaling-ladders approached and planted them; then twelve light-armed men, with only daggers and breast-plates, mounted . . . then more with javelins, whose shields, to facilitate the advance, others carried in the rear, ready to hand them over as soon as they came upon the enemy. When now a considerable number had mounted, the sentinels in the towers discovered them, for one of the Plataeans in catching hold of the battlement dislodged a tile, which made a noise when it fell; and forthwith a shout was raised.' [The Plataeans nevertheless seized two towers and all got safely over the double wall; but outside the external wall, as a defence against any attack from Athens, the Peloponnesians had dug a second moat, on the inner edge of which the fugitives now found themselves, and in the meantime 300 of the enemy with torches were rapidly approaching 'outside the wall and in the direction of the shouting.'] 'Now the Plataeans from their dark position on the brink of the moat saw the enemy better and directed their arrows and javelins against the unprotected parts of their bodies, while they themselves were hidden and still less easily discerned on account of the torches, so even the last of them got safely across the moat, though with difficulty and after great efforts, for ice had formed upon it, not firm enough to walk upon but watery, as usual with a wind more easterly than north; and the night, being snowy and with a wind of this kind, had made the water in it deep, so that they crossed with heads barely above the surface; but all the same it was the violence of the storm to which they owed their escape.' (iii. 20 *ff.*)

## Corcyraean Atrocities

'They [*i.e.* the democrats] then began to massacre all of their political opponents whom they had happened to catch, and dispatched, while they were landing them, all those whom they had persuaded to go on board. They also went to the sanctuary of Hera and persuaded about fifty of the suppliants to take their trial, and then condemned them all to death. Most of them were not to be persuaded, and when they saw what was being done they slew one another there in the sacred precinct. Some hanged themselves on the trees, others killed themselves as they could. During the seven days that Eurymedon remained there with his sixty ships the Corcyraeans went on murdering those of their fellow-countrymen whom they believed to be hostile to them. They accused them of abolishing democracy; but some were killed for private enmity, and others were slain by their debtors for money owed them. Every kind of death was experienced, and all that is wont to happen at such times happened now, and still worse; for father slew son and men were dragged out of sanctuaries and slain near them, while some were walled up in the temple of Dionysus and thus perished. So bloody was the course of the revolution.' (iii. 81. See also remarks by Thucydides in 82, 83.)

'When the Corcyraean [democrats] had caught them, they confined them in a large building. Then they took them out by twenties and led them roped together through two ranks of heavy-armed men, who smote and stabbed any personal enemies they saw. And men with whips went by their side, hastening on their way those who were going too slowly. As many as sixty they had thus led forth and butchered without raising the suspicions of those in the building, who thought they were being removed to some other place. But when they learnt the truth (some one having informed them) they refused to leave the building. So the Corcyraeans, not being disposed to force their way in by the doors, climbed up on to the top of the building, and, having broken through the roof, began to hurl the tiles and shoot arrows down on them. And they defended themselves as best they could, while at the same time many tried to kill themselves by thrusting down their throats the arrows discharged by their assailants and by strangling themselves with the cords of certain bedsteads which happened to be in the building and by strips that they tore off their clothing, and thus in divers ways during the greater part of the night (for night came on during these atrocities), either by laying hands on themselves or by being struck by missiles from above, they perished. And when it was day the Corcyraeans piled them in cross layers on wagons and carried them out of the city; and all the women who had been captured in the fortress [Istone] they enslaved.' (iv. 47 *ff.*)

**Sea-fight in the Harbour of Syracuse**

'When the Athenians came near the bar [formed by vessels and chains stretched across the harbour mouth] they charged, and with their first onset they got the better of the ships posted near it and tried to loosen the fastenings. But soon afterwards the Syracusans and their allies bore down on them from all quarters, and the fight no longer went on only near the bar, but became general all over the harbour; and it was a severe engagement, such as no previous one had been. . . . And as a great number of vessels attacked each other in a small space (indeed, never had so many fought together in so small a space, for altogether they fell scarcely short of two hundred) ramming was little used, as to back water or to break through the enemy's line was impossible, but collisions were more frequent, just as one ship might chance to run into another while flying from or attacking its adversary. Now, as long as a vessel was bearing down on another those on the decks used javelins and arrows and stones in great quantities against it, but when they came to close quarters the seamen fought hand to hand and tried to board each other's ships, and on account of the narrow space it often happened that while they were charging others they themselves were being charged, and that two, or even sometimes several, vessels were forcibly entangled round one. . . . The foot-soldiers of both sides on shore, while the result of the sea-fight hung in the balance, experienced an intense anguish and conflict of feelings, the men of Sicily being eager for still greater honour and the invaders fearing to fare still worse than hitherto. For since with the Athenians all was staked on their ships their anxiety as to the result was like none they had ever felt before . . . and every kind of clamour was to be heard, lamentation and triumph, *They conquer! They are beaten!* and other such various exclamations as a great armament in great danger would be constrained to utter – until finally, after the fighting had lasted for a long time, the Syracusans and their allies routed the Athenians, and, following up their advantage brilliantly, with great shouting and cheering pursued them to the shore.' (vii. 70 *ff.*)

**The Retreat from Syracuse**

'It was pitiable, not only because of the fact that they were retreating after having lost all their ships and all their high hopes, and having brought themselves, and Athens too, into peril, but also because on leaving the encampment they all had to look upon things grievous to the sight and grievous to the mind; for the dead were unburied, and whenever any saw one of his friends lying there he was filled with grief and with fear; and the living who were being abandoned, the wounded and the sick, were to the living much more painful than were the dead, and more piteous than those who had perished, for, betaking themselves to entreaty and to wailing, they drove them into despair, begging to be taken, and calling upon each one individually, if they saw anywhere any friend or relation, and hanging on to their comrades as they were on the point of departure, and following as far as they could; and if strength or bodily power failed they were left behind not without many adjurations to the gods and many groans. So the whole army, filled with tears and distress of this kind, did not find departure easy, though it was from a hostile country and though they had already suffered woes too deep for tears, and were full of anxiety as to their sufferings in the unknown future. They resembled nothing so much as a city starved out and trying to escape by stealth – and no small city, for the whole multitude that started numbered not less than forty thousand.' (vii. 75.)

**The Surrender**

'The Athenians pressed on towards the river Assinarus, being urged to do this by the attacks of the enemy and also by weariness and the craving for water; and when they reached it they cast themselves into it with no further regard for order, every one wishing to get across first, while the enemy assailed them and made the crossing difficult. For, being compelled to advance in a dense mass, they fell on the top of one another and trod one another down, and some were killed by falling on the javelins and baggage, and others got entangled and were swept down-stream. On the further bank, which was precipitous, stood the Syracusans and launched their missiles down on the Athenians while most of them were drinking eagerly and crowding together confusedly in the hollow river-bed. Moreover, the Peloponnesians came down to attack them, and slaughtered those especially who were in the river. And the water was forthwith spoiled, but none the less it was drunk by them together with the mud, all bloody, and was even fought for by most of them. At last, when many dead bodies were already lying one upon the other in the river and the army had been cut to pieces, some of it in the river-bed and whatever part escaped thence by the cavalry, Nicias surrendered to Gylippus.' (vii. 84.)

SECTION B: SOPHOCLES, EURIPIDES AND ARISTOPHANES

In the tragedies of Aeschylus, Sophocles, and Euripides we can trace the same kind of development – or, as some would call it, degeneration – that is noticeable in the three principal stages of Greek sculpture. First we have the supernatural, the mysterious, the terrible, the sublime – forms of more than mortal grandeur and a spirit often majestically disdainful of ordinary humanity; then man's nature idealized and the perfect balance and exquisite symmetry of the human form divine – the mortal as he should be rather than as he is, such as we see him in the heroes and heroines of Sophocles and in the works of Polycleitus and the still more gracious forms of Praxiteles; then the attempt to portray in sculpture and in sculpturesque drama the diversity and passion and movement of actual life, with details which, however significant and interesting they may be in life itself, often become trivial or offensive when borrowed by the artist for purposes of sensation, pathos, or prettiness.

Few perhaps can admire equally things so different as the stern grandeur of Aeschylus, the perfect art, the sculpturesque strength, dignity, and beauty of Sophocles, and the vivid colouring, the living warmth, and varied movement of Euripides; but even though we may with Aristophanes place Aeschylus (or Sophocles in his absence) on the throne of tragedy, we must surely be insensate if we do not feel moved by much in the plays of Euripides, by his passionate, almost Wordsworthian love for our common humanity and for the beauty of Nature, and by his pathetic power, which has never, perhaps, been equalled except by Shakespeare – a power so supreme that Aristotle, the master of all critics, calls him 'the most tragic of the poets.' How deeply he aroused the admiration of the ancients is shown by the fact that eighteen of his plays (as against seven by Sophocles) have survived, besides a great number of fragments on papyri. Dante, the greatest of mediaeval poets, refers to him, though he mentions neither Aeschylus nor Sophocles. Browning's *Balaustion*, besides being a tribute of intense admiration from a great modern poet to

> Euripides, the Human
> With his droppings of warm tears,
> And his touches of things common
> Till they rose to touch the spheres,

378

is founded on an historical fact that proves how magical among the ancients was the influence of the last Athenian tragedian. 'Numbers of the Athenian captives in Sicily,' says Plutarch, 'were saved by Euripides, and when they had returned home they greeted him with gratitude and related how by singing his poems, as much as they could remember, they had been released from slavery, or how, when wandering about after the battle, they had by the same means procured food and drink.' Aelian, too, tells us that Socrates seldom went to the theatre except to see some new play of Euripides, and the philosopher is even suspected of having had a hand in some of these plays.

A few biographical facts and a brief account of some of the chief plays of Sophocles and Euripides may be of more use than comment.

## Sophocles

Sophocles was born about 495 at Colonus, near Athens. He is said to have led the chorus of boys at the rejoicings after Salamis, 'dancing and playing on the lyre around the trophy.' As already related, he conquered Aeschylus in 468, when Cimon and the other generals voted for his *Triptolemus*. About 440 he brought out his *Antigone*, which, probably against his wishes, procured him his election as a general in the expedition against Samos (see p. 320). 'I do my best,' he is said to have remarked, 'since Pericles will have it so; but I am no general.' In 413, after the Sicilian disaster, he was elected, doubtless unwillingly, as one of the 'Advisers' (*probouloi*) who counselled the establishment of the Four Hundred. He died in 406, in his ninetieth year. Of his 130 (or 113) dramas perhaps half were written in the last third of his life. Seven are extant.

The *Antigone* (c. 440) continues the story of the Aeschylean *Seven against Thebes*. In spite of the commands of her uncle Creon, who, after the sons of Oedipus had slain each other, has reinstated himself as king of Thebes, Antigone determines to bury her brother Polyneices – which she does by sprinkling dust on his dead body. She is condemned to be buried alive in a tomb. Haemon, Creon's son, who loves her, kills himself, and his mother, Eurydice, also commits suicide. The strong and impulsive character of Antigone forms a fine contrast to that of her timid younger sister Ismene.

The *Ajax*, which seems from its form and style to be of early date, has for its subject the overthrow of a noble mind by the consciousness of shame. As a so-called psychological study it is comparable with *King Lear*

*Fig. 98  Sophocles*

or *Hamlet*. In order to follow the internal action one must read the play. Its external action is simple. The arms of the dead Achilles have been adjudged to Odysseus. Ajax in his furious indignation determines to make an onslaught on the Achaean princes, but is afflicted by Athene with a sudden fit of insanity, during which he slaughters a number of sheep and cattle, believing them to be his foes. On his recovery his sense of shame drives him to suicide. After the catastrophe the play drags on rather wearily. Odysseus, though his great rival, persuades the Atridae to give Ajax burial.

The *Electra* treats the same subject as the *Choephoroe* of Aeschylus and the *Electra* of Euripides, with which I shall compare it later. The contrast between two sisters, Electra and Chrysothemis, is not unlike that depicted in the *Antigone*. One of the finest passages in the play is a description given to Electra by an old man of a chariot-race at the Pythian Games, in which, as he reports, Orestes was killed. The lament of Electra over the funeral urn in which she believes the ashes of her brother to be is as beautiful as anything in literature, and for dramatic effect the last scene, where Aegisthus, believing it to be the corpse of Orestes, unveils the dead body of Clytaemnestra, is probably unsurpassed.

The *Trachiniae* (so called from the chorus, consisting of maidens of Trachis, near Thermopylae) describes the fearful end of Heracles. The legend is that when Nessus the Centaur was killed by Heracles with an arrow that had been dipped in Hydra poison he bade Deianira, the wife of Heracles, preserve some of his blood as a love-charm. Being jealous of Iole, a princess captured by Heracles, Deianira steeps a robe in this poisoned blood and sends it to him for a sacrificial ceremony. The robe cleaves to his flesh and the venom enters his body. In his madness he seizes Lichas, his companion, by the feet and hurls him into the sea, and writhes in terrible anguish while trying to tear the clinging poisoned robe from off his limbs. He is borne in a litter, or ship, to Trachis, his home. Deianira hangs herself. Heracles bids his son Hyllus bear him to the peak of Mount Oeta and place him on a pyre of wood and set it aflame. Hyllus at last obeys, and the play ends as Heracles is being carried away. From other writers we learn that Hyllus refused to light the pyre, which was done by a shepherd, Poias, who was passing by. This Poias was father to Philoctetes, to whom he bequeathed the bow and arrows given him in gratitude by Heracles. Some say that Philoctetes himself lit the pyre and was given the weapons.

*Oedipus Tyrannus* was probably composed in the year (430–429) of the Great Plague, to which there is evident allusion in the well-known opening lines. Although written long after the *Antigone*, this drama and the *Oedipus at Colonus* (*c.* 420?) were doubtless intended to form together with it a Theban trilogy on somewhat the same lines as those of the Aeschylean trilogy to which, as is believed, the *Seven against Thebes* belonged. The story of Oedipus – how he, as was fated, slew his own father and was wedded to his own mother, and how he discovered the terrible truth and blinded himself – scarcely needs recounting. The art with which all is made to lead up to the awful catastrophe, and with which the contrast is depicted between the powerful and haughty monarch of the opening and the blinded and humiliated sufferer and outcast of the later scenes, is supremely great. In the second play the old blind king, led by his daughter Antigone, comes to the grove of the Eumenides at Colonus, a village near Athens (the birthplace of Sophocles). He feels conscious that his involuntary crimes have now been atoned for and that the Avenging but Kindly Goddesses[1] will receive him. His other daughter, Ismene, now joins him, and Creon of Thebes appears and tries to carry off the two girls. Theseus, the Athenian king, recovers them and protects the suppliants. Him the blind Oedipus, as guided by some inner light and by the calling of a voice, leads to the place (perhaps the sanctuary chasm of the Eumenides) where it is fated that he shall die; and here he passes away from sight.

In the *Philoctetes* is related how Odysseus and Neoptolemus (son of Achilles) intend to carry off from Lemnos the son of Poias, Philoctetes, who (see above) possessed the bow and arrows of Heracles, without which Troy could not be taken. Philoctetes had been stung by a viper, and the loathsome sore thus caused on his foot had induced the Greeks before Troy to banish him to Lemnos. He refuses to return, and at first Neoptolemus consents to aid Odysseus in using guile; but his nobler nature revolts, and he confesses all to Philoctetes. Heracles then appears from heaven and induces Philoctetes to change his mind.

It is interesting that in two at least of these plays the main action is founded on motives such as are not present, or not easily to be discovered, in any drama of Aeschylus – on the dictates of what we call conscience, or the moral sense – on those inviolable unwritten laws of the heart which are higher than all ordinances proclaimed by human authority in the name of justice or religion. Both Antigone and Neoptolemus obey that voice by

---

[1] The sanctuary itself was in a cleft of the Areopagus, near the Acropolis, two miles from the village of Colonus.

which, as Goethe says in his *Iphigenie*, the gods speak to us through our hearts. Antigone, 'daring a holy crime,' perishes, but, like Cordelia, proves herself a conqueror over death. Neoptolemus, like the heroine of Goethe's play, will dare or suffer anything rather than practise a mean deceit. Here, I think, is intimated a very essential difference between the ethical teaching of the two poets. As we have already seen, Aeschylus depicts man in his struggle against inexorable Fate – against the external and immutable laws of Necessity; but Sophocles points to a moral law within the heart, which to obey is to conquer destiny and death.[1] In Euripides we have indeed at times admirable courage and defiance of misfortune, but it is the courage and defiance of the Stoic. There is no deep sense of the eternal laws of the conscience, nor even a tragic battling against an overwhelming fate, for all is guided by Chance rather than by Necessity, and the gods themselves are little else but useful stage machinery.[2] He gives us a picture, often intensely real and moving, of human character amid the various accidents of life; but, as tragedy was still limited to the myths of gods and heroes, the purely human element often causes a descent from the sublime to the commonplace, and even to the ridiculous, so that the remark is not so unjust as it may seem that Euripides was the precursor of the New Comedy. Indeed, the writers of this later comedy of common life and character, such as Menander, acknowledged Euripides as their model, especially in dialogue, where clever repartee, smart epigram, and quotable apophthegm were in request.

### Euripides

Euripides was born, some say, in Salamis on the very day of the battle (*c.* September 20, 480). When twenty-five years of age he was 'granted a chorus' (officially allowed to compete), but did not win the prize till fourteen years later. Of his ninety-two plays, it is said, only four or five were

---

[1] 'The interest of a Sophoclean drama is always intensely personal, and is almost always centred in an individual destiny. In other words, it is not historical or mythical, but ethical. Single persons stand out magnificently in Aeschylus, but the action is always larger than any single life. . . . In Sophocles vast surroundings fall into the background and the feelings of the spectator are absorbed in sympathy with the chief figure on the stage, round whom the other characters (the chorus included) are grouped with the minutest care.' – Professor Lewis Campbell.

[2] In nine of the eighteen extant plays of Euripides the problem is solved by the appearance of a *deus ex machina*.

Fig. 99  Euripides

crowned, which seems to show that his popularity was very much greater than his appreciation by contemporary critics.

Late in life (about 408) he withdrew to Thessaly, and thence to the court of King Archelaus of Macedonia, possibly on account of the domestic troubles which embittered so much of his life, or because his philosophical and political sentiments exposed him to danger at Athens. He died in 406, a few months before Sophocles. The story that he was torn to pieces by dogs possibly arose from the fact that in his last play, the *Bacchae*, written probably in Macedonia, Pentheus is torn to pieces by infuriated Bacchanals.

Of the eighteen extant plays of Euripides (excluding the *Rhesus*, which is probably a later imitation, but including the *Cyclops*, the only complete extant Greek satyr play) perhaps the finest are the *Alcestis* (438), *Medea* (431), *Ion* (c. 420), and the two *Iphigeneias* (412–408), the stories of which are well known and need not here be recounted. But in order to illustrate some characteristics of the poet a few remarks may be made on one of his less known dramas, the *Electra*. All three of the great Athenian dramatists treated the subject of the *Electra*, and all three dramas are extant. The main action of the *Choephoroe* and of the Sophoclean *Electra* has already been briefly intimated. Euripides has chosen the same story, namely, the return of Orestes, his recognition by his sister and the slaying of Clytaemnestra and Aegisthus; but he has used a very different setting, his object doubtless having been to bring it all nearer to us – 'menschlich näher,' as Schiller expresses it. The scene opens, not before the palace of Argos or the tomb of Agamemnon at Mycenae, but before a cottage, out of which steps forth an old peasant. In a long prologue – an introductory device much used by Euripides – he explains for the benefit of the audience, though evidently talking to himself, that Electra had been forced by her mother to marry him, and that she lives with him, but as a daughter, not as a wife. Electra then enters, bearing on her close-shorn head a pitcher, and, in spite of the dear old man's entreaties, insists on performing the menial work of the household. With such a *mise-en-scène* we might have had a very pathetic and withal a dignified play; but, unfortunately, there is much that one might think more adapted to satisfy the taste of the tragical-comical players in *Hamlet* than that of an Athenian audience. After the catastrophe Electra puts a wreath on her brother's head, while he holds the head of Aegisthus suspended by its hair; she then pours vituperation and sarcasm on the dead man's head. When Orestes, in his alarm (though he sees no Furies, as in the *Choephoroe*), determines to flee, Electra exclaims, a little irrationally, 'Who will now marry me?' The play is wound up by the appearance *ex machina* of Castor and Pollux, who order Pylades to marry Electra and to give a liberal compensation to the peasant.

But perhaps nothing in the whole play 'lets us down' quite so much as the deliberate and sarcastic way in which Euripides expresses, through Electra (lines 524 *ff.*), his disapproval of the means used by Aeschylus to bring about the recognition, namely, a lock of hair and footprints. Certainly the scar that he uses for the purpose has Homeric precedent and is more satisfactory; but the attack on his great predecessor is surely in bad taste and much out of place in a work of art.

In the *Iphigeneia in Aulis* the *dea ex machina*, or rather the substitution of a fawn instead of the victim by the invisible Artemis, is in keeping with the old legend, but in the case of the *Iphigeneia in Tauris* the deadening effect on our sympathies of such contrivance is apparent when we think of the solution of the knot by Goethe, who in the place of a stage divinity makes the power of courage and truth on the part of Iphigeneia save her and her brother from the infuriated Scythian king. In some of his dramas, such as the *Phoenissae*, in which the Oedipus story is employed, Euripides alters the old legends very considerably or uses rare versions. He even gives contradictory versions in different plays. In the *Helena* the heroine (whom Homer and Herodotus state to have been in Egypt, evidently on her way back from Troy with Menelaus) never reaches Troy at all. What accompanied Paris to Troy was a wraith. The true Helen was all the time in Egypt, in charge of King Proteus. Schlegel calls it the 'merriest of tragedies.' But I prefer to end with Goethe's words, referring to Schlegel, rather than with Schlegel's disparagement. 'If a modern critic,' he said, 'must pick out faults in so great a master of drama, he should do it on his knees.'

### Comedy

The names are known of 104 Greek comic poets. About forty were writers of the *prisca Comoedia*, the Old Attic Comedy (*c.* 480–390), and produced something like 360 plays. Of these nothing worth mention has survived except eleven, out of perhaps forty, of the comedies of Aristophanes. How great our loss is we cannot tell. Aristophanes was a great poet as well as a comedian. 'The Graces,' said Plato, 'chose his mind for their dwelling.' But, excepting his work and several plays of Menander discovered on papyrus, we have no evidence that there was much of permanent value in all this immense output of comic verse, and for our purpose it will suffice if, after a few remarks on the rise of Greek comedy, we consider briefly some of these eleven plays that have been preserved by the admiration of Alexandrian critics.

Tragedy, as we have seen, originated at the rustic festivals, where the peasants, disguised as goat-eared satyrs, or dressed in goatskins, danced and sang their 'goat songs' and dithyrambs in honour of Dionysus, and in course of time introduced dialogue and representations of old legends, both tragical and satyric.[1] Comedy, the song of 'revelry' (*kōmos* – which is also the name of the god of revelry), originated, as Aristotle tells us, in festivals connected with the divinities of fertility, at which much licence was allowed (as at the Roman Saturnalia), much coarse jesting and abuse and repartee and pasquinade and comic dialogue (as with the old Latin Fescennine songs), accompanied by processions and dances of mummers and maskers in all kinds of quaint and indecent disguises. (On old Attic vases may be seen such maskers depicted – disguised as birds or other animals, and in one case as knights mounted on the back of slaves.) Ludicrous acting was then introduced – first mere improvised mummer-show. We hear of an early and rather mythical Attic comic poet, Susarion, but it was in Sicily that comic plays were first learnt for recitation, and it was Epicharmus, of Sicilian Megara (about 500, somewhat later than Thespis, the Attic founder of tragedy), who first composed parodies, or burlesques, of old legends. A few small fragments of his plays are extant. This old Sicilian comedy was transplanted to Athens in the age of the Persian invasions, and rapidly struck root. It was soon recognized by the state, and the comic poet was granted a chorus like the tragedian, and allowed to compete publicly for a prize. Among the first Athenian comic poets we hear of Chionides, Magnes, Crates, Cratinus, and Eupolis. The last two were early contemporaries and rivals of Aristophanes. Crates was perhaps the first to raise comedy above personal lampoon and to attack vice and folly in the abstract. Under

---

[1] Plutarch says that after the Thespian tragical performances had come into vogue the common people were discontented, missing the old humour of the original 'tragedy' – *i.e.* the 'goat' or 'satyr' song – and asked: 'What has this to do with Dionysus?' Therefore humorous 'satyr plays' were often acted in connection with the later 'tragedies,' which had become too serious for public taste. In the greatest of all tragedies, Shakespeare's, there is humour – unintelligible to minds like Voltaire's, but not to minds like that of Socrates, who affirmed that every tragic poet should also be a comic poet. Plato, too, calls jesting the 'sister of earnestness,' and Horace tells us that it often decides great things better and quicker than seriousness.

Pericles great licence was allowed to the comic poet, but he might be impeached for 'doing wrong to the people' by attacking unfairly their magistrates. During the trouble with Samos (440) comedy was suppressed, and again when democracy fell in 411, and although it revived with the democracy it was no longer allowed to satirize public characters.

## Aristophanes

Of the life of Aristophanes (c. 445–380) very little is known. He produced his first play, the *Banqueters*, in 427, when 'hardly more than a boy,' and two years later he won the first prize with the *Acharnians*, the earliest of his extant comedies. It was directed against the iniquity and folly of the war. A good old Attic farmer, angry at the constant rejection of peace, sends a private embassy to the Spartans and secures immunity for himself and his family. He rails off his property and invites his neighbours to an open market and all the blessings of peace, including a fine banquet. The play teems with political allusions. The consequent complications, social and political, are most ludicrous. The chief butts of the satire are the demagogues and Euripides.

In the *Knights* (424) a most audacious attack was made on Cleon, just then elated by his success at Sphacteria (see p. 359–61). It was the first play that Aristophanes exhibited in his own name, and as no one dared to play the part of Cleon, nor even to make a mask for the character (see line 232), the poet himself, it is said, undertook the role with his face stained, as in old times, with wine-lees. Cleon is represented as the drunken and crafty Paphlagonian slave and 'demagogue' of the old gentleman, Demos (the People), and is finally outwitted by a sausage-seller. After ridding himself of his pestilent 'demagogue' the old Demos appears rejuvenated, takes again into favour his honest servants Nicias and Demosthenes, and is enthusiastic for good old Marathonian times. It was probably on account of this play that Cleon brought an action against Aristophanes to prove that he was an alien and not entitled to exhibit plays. What grounds there were for the action is uncertain, though it is possible that the poet's father came from Aegina, or Rhodes. Anyhow, the suit failed, and Aristophanes prided himself later on his Herculean contest with the monster; but he never again ventured on any such violent personal attacks on public characters, unless we except Euripides, and perhaps Socrates.

The *Clouds* (423) is directed especially against the sophists and rhetoricians and the 'modern education.' An old gentleman, deep in debt, takes his son (evidently typical of Alcibiades) to Socrates to be educated in the new sophistry, so as to free himself from his creditors by forensic quibbles; but he suffers so much from his up-to-date offspring that he burns down the Socratic 'thinking shop' on the stage. The attack on Socrates is elsewhere described (see p. 398). It is evident that the humour was understood by even such an admirer of Socrates as Plato, for he sent the play to Dionysius, and in the *Symposion* he speaks with admiration of Aristophanes.

In the *Wasps* is satirized the mania for lawsuits and serving as jurymen, whereby all home life and professional duties are neglected, the whole male population swarming like wasps to the law-courts. In 421 Aristophanes exhibited his *Peace*, in which (in reference to the Peace of Nicias, concluded in that year) a peace-loving Athenian flies up to heaven, mounted on a dung-beetle, in search of the Goddess of Peace. In heaven, however, he finds only the Demon of War, pounding up the cities and races of men in a gigantic mortar. Peace has been hurled from heaven and lies buried in a deep pit, whence all the nations of Greece haul her forth with ropes. The *Birds* (414), in which the building of 'Cloud-cuckoo City' is described, probably alludes to the great air-castle that the Athenians were endeavouring to erect by extending their empire to Sicily. The play appeared shortly before the disastrous end of the Sicilian expedition. In the *Frogs* (405) the god Dionysus descends, like a second Heracles, to Hades – crossing the Styx amid loud croaking of the chorus of frogs – in order to bring back Euripides (who had lately died) to give the Athenians, now in great political trouble, his sage advice. Dionysus finds him disputing with Aeschylus the right to the throne of tragedy, and finally Aeschylus returns to earth with Dionysus, leaving Sophocles as his representative in Hades. In the remaining extant plays social questions are dealt with. In the *Plutus* we have the unjust distribution of wealth and the question of communism. In the coarse but exceedingly humorous *Lysistrata* and the *Women in Parliament* we have the rights and political influence of women (who institute a socialistic state with community of wives). In the *Thesmophoriazusae* the women assembled at the festival of the Thesmophoria, to which no men were admitted, swear to avenge themselves on Euripides for his misogyny, and finally amidst indescribable excitement detect the presence of his brother-in-law, whom he had persuaded to enter the assembly in female disguise.

Greek thought delineates or suggests in sculpturesque outline every philosophy worthy of the name, and especially distinct is the picture that it offers us of the gradual development of the conviction that the ordering force omnipresent in the universe cannot be accounted for by any supposed 'self-creation' and 'self-movement' of prime matter, but solely by the existence of an Intelligence and a Will that not only manifests itself in the sensible world, but is also recognizable by the mind as the one Reality. Theoretically, at any rate, Anaxagoras had reached this doctrine, and we shall see later how Socrates and Plato accepted it as the foundation for their philosophy. But here it is necessary to note a remarkable genius of the materialistic or 'mechanical' school, whose influence aided the development of those brilliant intellectualists and fashionable lecturers known as the Sophists.

## Democritus

Democritus of Abdera, in Thrace, was born in 460, and is said to have lived until 361. He was perhaps the son of that Damasippus who entertained Xerxes at Abdera. After some years of travel, of which he writes somewhat boastfully, he resided at Athens, and seems to have excited the dislike of Anaxagoras (his senior by forty years), probably on account of his self-conceit and mockery – which may have earned him the sobriquet 'the Laugher'. Plato, too, is said to have disliked his writings so much that he wished to collect and burn them. Lengthy fragments of these writings remain. His style is praised by Cicero as similar to that of Plato. His physical theories were derived from Leucippus, of whom nothing is known. They come to us mainly through Epicurus (*b.* 341) and the Roman poet Lucretius. He, or Leucippus, is regarded as the founder of the atomic theory, which has been largely held by modern science and which supposes matter to consist of minute solid particles (*not* infinitely divisible, as Anaxagoras believed) possessing weight and the power of coherence. These 'atoms' Democritus conceived as infinite in number; therefore it was necessary to assume a boundless space to accommodate them. Through this boundless, dark Inane streamed like everlasting rain the endless torrents of atoms, clashing together and by fortuitous concurrence forming 'another and another frame of things for ever,' as is described by Tennyson in his poem *Lucretius*. By giving his atoms weight Democritus assumed persistent gravity – which is absurd in the case of bodies moving endlessly through boundless space. Moreover, atoms acted upon by any such force would 'ruin along th' illimitable Inane' for ever in parallel lines without colliding. He, or perhaps Epicurus, saw this difficulty and tried to meet it by asserting that Necessity (self-created from all eternity), or else Chance, as a kind of side wind, caused the atom-streams to deviate, collide, and combine, thus forming all the objects of the natural world, and by the coherence of specially fine and durable particles forming also living organisms and even spiritual beings and the Deity himself. Thus is the materialist, if he is not content with agnosticism, ever forced to assume some immaterial first cause, even though he may not vouchsafe it intelligence or will. As ethical thinker Democritus preached (so did Epicurus later) moderation and virtue as the means of attaining cheerfulness – a comfortable state of mind (*euthymiē*) like the Stoic's *aequus animus*; and since no one is willingly unhappy, the one thing necessary for virtue he held to be knowledge. This seems very like what Socrates taught, but the 'knowledge' of Democritus (seeing that he believed in nothing but his atoms and his Inane) was something very different from that of Socrates, who, if we are to believe Plato rather than Aristophanes, regarded the investigation of physical causes as, at the best, an innocent form of recreation, and likened the erudite and fashionable intellectualists of the day to men eagerly scanning and discussing shadows cast on a cavern's wall, while the rhetoric by which they degraded the search for truth into a mere display of dialectic skill he disdainfully put on the same level as the art of cookery.

## The Sophists

And yet some of these Sophists – whom Aristotle describes as 'trading in false wisdom' – were men of great learning, exceedingly 'well educated' from our modern point of view.[1] Such was the Sicilian Gorgias, who was sent (427) as an ambassador to Athens and excited there by his eloquence intense enthusiasm. Such was Protagoras of Abdera, friend of Pericles and Euripides, whose philosophy was summed up in the assertion that 'man is

---

[1] Some regard the Sophists as valuable 'spreaders of enlightenment,' and assert not only that Socrates was called a *sophistēs* by contemporaries, but that there was no essential difference between his teaching and theirs.

the measure of all,' and who, according to Plato, made by his teaching more money than Pheidias and ten other sculptors, and was impeached at Athens for asserting that he was 'unable to know whether the gods exist,' and is said to have perished at sea while fleeing to Sicily. However, whatever their merits may have been, their ideal, which was that of the mere intellectualist, was entirely false, in the judgment of Socrates, who, when the Delphic oracle proclaimed him the wisest of men, interpreted it to mean that he alone was fully conscious of his own 'nothingness in regard to wisdom.' But perhaps I cannot use my limited space better than by giving two pictures, copied roughly from Plato, of some of these professional lecturers. The first is from the *Hippias Major*.

Hippias of Elis, the popular teacher and lecturer, has been bragging to Socrates how he had been sent on embassies of state and had also been going from city to city lecturing on science and literature and history and logic and ethics and the like, and winning huge renown and a large fortune by his discourses. 'Going to Sicily,' he says, 'in a very short time I made more than 150 minae [equivalent to about 15,000 days' pay for a skilled worker]. Indeed, I am inclined to think that no two other Sophists, name whom you will, ever acquired so much money. And even at Sparta, where the law prevents a foreigner from giving instruction to the young, everybody flocked to my lectures and lavished much praise upon me.

*Socr.* But in the name of the gods, of what kind were those lectures for which they gave you such rewards and praises? On what subjects do they so delight to hear you harangue? No doubt they were the subjects in which you have such surpassing knowledge – the stars and the celestial phenomena.

*Hipp.* Yes, sometimes. But the Spartans will hear no word on such subjects.

*Socr.* Then I suppose it was about geometry and mathematics.

*Hipp.* Not at all. Most of the Spartans are ignorant of the most elementary rules of arithmetic.

*Socr.* Then was it logic and the art of persuasion? Or perhaps that subject in which you of all men are so expert in accurately distinguishing and defining, I mean letters and syllables and the harmony of words and rhythms?

*Hipp.* The Spartans care nothing for such subjects.

*Socr.* Well, do tell me – since I cannot find it out by myself.

*Hipp.* It was about genealogies of heroes and distinguished men, and about the migrations of tribes and settling of colonies, and the antiquity and first founding of cities – in a word, everything concerning ancient history. And I have been obliged for their sakes to work up these subjects and perfect myself in that kind of knowledge.

*Socr.* By Zeus, Hippias, it was fortunate that they didn't want you to give a list of all the archons from the time of Solon!

*Hipp.* Why so, Socrates? Upon hearing fifty names repeated only once I will undertake to remember them.

Thus Socrates (or Plato) mocks the self-conceited intellectualism of the lecturing Sophist.

The other picture is from Plato's dialogue *Protagoras*, in which Socrates describes, with sly humour, a scene in which are introduced many of the more famous Sophists.[1]

'Entering, we found Protagoras walking up and down the portico, and with him, on one side, were Callias, Paralus, and Charmides, and on the other Xanthippus, the son of Pericles, and Antimaerus of Mende, who bears the highest reputation of all the disciples of Protagoras, and is studying with a view to hereafter being a Sophist himself. Others followed behind to catch what was said, seeming chiefly to be foreigners whom Protagoras brings about with him from every city through which he travels, charming them with his voice, as Orpheus of old, while they under the fascination follow the voice; some also of our countrymen were in the train. As I viewed the band I was delighted to observe with what caution they took care never to be in front of Protagoras, but whenever he turned, those who were behind, dividing on either side in a circle, fell back so as still to remain in the rear. "Him past, I saw" (to speak in Homeric phrase) Hippias of Elis enthroned beneath the opposite portico; around whom, on benches, sat Eryximachus, Phaedrus, and others. They seemed to question Hippias concerning the sublimities of nature and the revolutions of the stars, while he, reposing upon his throne, resolved each successive difficulty. Presently I came upon Prodicus of Ceos, who was not yet risen, but lay cushioned in a retired chamber among bedclothes, and around him were Pausanias, Adimantus, and others. The subjects of their discussion I could not gather from without, though extremely anxious to hear Prodicus; for I hold him to be a man of wisdom more than human; but the perpetual reverberation of his voice – an extremely deep one – confused the words in their echoes.'

---

[1] I have here borrowed from the version given by Archer Butler in his *Lectures on Ancient Philosophy*.

## Socrates

To give any full account of the teachings of Socrates, or even a bare outline of the great structure of Ideal philosophy built thereupon by Plato, lies far beyond the range of this volume. I shall only offer a few biographical facts and a few remarks and quotations for the purpose of intimating the nature of these teachings and this philosophy rather than of describing their exact form. For the life and personality of Socrates we are chiefly indebted to the *Dialogues* of Plato and the *Memoirs* of Xenophon; for his doctrines, although Aristotle tells us something, we have to investigate the fundamental principles of Platonic philosophy, endeavouring to distinguish them from the superstructure; for how far Socrates used the forms of thought and imagination (such as those of Ideas, and the allegories of Metamorphosis and Prenatal Existence) attributed to him by his great disciple is quite uncertain; nor can we feel quite sure that Plato has given us a perfectly trustworthy picture in all details even of such scenes as the trial and the last hours of his master. Still, it seems incredible that he should have misrepresented the essential tenets and the personality of Socrates, for it would have been at once detected and resented by those who had known him, and who, to use the words of one of them, had loved him as 'the wisest and justest and best man they had ever known.'

Of the external life of Socrates we know comparatively little, but we know enough to recognize a noble attempt to practise what he taught. 'In my life,' he said a few hours before his death, 'I have striven as much as I was able, and have left nothing undone, to become a true philosopher. Whether I have striven in the right way, or whether I have succeeded or not, I suppose I shall learn in a little while, when I reach the other world, if it be the will of God.'

The philosopher was born about 469 in the village of Alopeke ('The Place of Foxes'), not far from Athens. His father was a sculptor, or rather a 'stone-worker,' and he himself attained such proficiency that a group of three draped Graces made by him was to be seen on the Acropolis, Pausanias asserts, six centuries later.

He received the ordinary 'musical' and gymnastic education of an Athenian citizen – an education in the arts patronized by the Muses and in athletic exercises – the object of which was something very far removed from professional or mercantile success. His knowledge of Homer and other old poets was evidently extensive. From Xenophon we learn that he was 'fond of studying the treasures that wise men of old had left in their books,' such as the abstruse philosophy of Heracleitus, whose book, lent him by Euripides, he is said to have greatly admired, but to have found at times so difficult that 'it needed a Delian diver.' With the mathematical, astronomical, and philosophical works of Pythagoras he was acquainted, and in the *Phaedo* he tells us that when young he was passionately fond of physical science, but that he abandoned it later as dealing, not with realities, but appearances, and as useless except for merely practical purposes or as a recreation. He seems to have had an iron constitution and to have borne unflinchingly pain and fatigue and the extremes of heat and cold, so that the soldiers, says Alcibiades, 'looked angrily at him.' He went, at least in later years, always barefoot, and wore the same coarse, homely cloak in summer and winter alike. His features were not at all such as one associates with intellect or with Hellenism. Neither friends nor foes spared their jests on his satyr-like physiognomy, with its broad nose, its wide, thick-lipped mouth, and its prominent, glaring eyes. In the *Symposion* Alcibiades likens him to a figure of the satyr-god Silenus, which, when opened, discloses images of the Olympian gods. 'He thinks all such things as beauty and riches of no value and spends his life among us in irony and jest. But when he is serious and is opened, I know not if any of you have seen the images within. But I have seen them, and they appeared to me so divine, golden, all-beautiful, and wonderful that I was ready to do in an instant whatever Socrates might command.'

In 432, just before the outbreak of the Peloponnesian War, Socrates served as a hoplite in Thrace, at the siege of Potidaea, and here he saved the life of the wounded Alcibiades. At the battle of Delion, in 424, where the Athenians suffered a serious defeat, he behaved, as Alcibiades tells us in the *Symposion*, with great courage in covering the retreat, and perhaps saved the life of Xenophon, carrying him a long distance. Two years after Delion Socrates fought a third time for his country at the battle of Amphipolis, and once more distinguished himself by his courage and endurance. He was now forty-seven years old. Some time before this he had taken to frequenting the markets and colonnades and other public places and talking in a familiar way to any one, rich or poor, who cared to listen and answer his questions, 'babbling,' as Alcibiades puts it, 'about market-donkeys and coppersmiths and shoemakers and tanners' – testing those who thought they were wise and proving that they knew nothing truly, and didn't even know *that* – plaguing high-priests with some such elementary question as 'What is religion?' or the learned with 'What is knowledge?' and politicians with 'What is justice?' – refusing to accept cant definitions and current valuations but going back to primary, indisputable facts and simple, distinct conceptions, to the true nature and true value of everything – beginning discussion with some such tiresome, elementary question[1] as 'Do you allow that justice is anything? and if so, what is it?' – implanting thus in minds filled with the conceit of false knowledge the seed of self-knowledge and endeavouring to make men realize their own ignorance as the first step in the search for wisdom. As Bacon in science, so Socrates in a higher sphere set himself and others the task (as Bacon says of himself) of 'throwing entirely aside received theories and conceptions and applying the mind, thus cleansed, afresh to facts.' It is this inductive process, this search for a solid basis of fact on which to build up a general law, that Aristotle held to be the most important factor in the teachings of Socrates.

Socrates likens himself to a troublesome gadfly, and doubtless he did arouse great resentment among the fashionable and self-conceited intellectualists and the high-priests of Olympian orthodoxy, as any man is bound to do who goes about annoying respectable people with inconvenient questions on matters which should be left to the care of theologians and cabinet ministers. Doubtless, too, the fact that his example incited the young to disprove the wisdom of their elders by the application of the Socratic scrutiny must have winged a deadly shaft of accusation against him. 'I go about,' he says in his *Apology*, 'testing and examining every man who has the reputation of being wise, and if I find that he is not wise, I point out to him on the part of the God that he is not wise. And I am so busy in this pursuit that I never had leisure to take any part worth mention in public matters nor to look after my private affairs. I am in very great poverty by reason of my service to the God.' Twice, however, we hear of his taking part in public affairs (see pp. 366, 368), and on both occasions, unsupported and at the peril of his life, he refused to give his sanction to gross injustice.

That Socrates had gained notoriety and had aroused animosity even as early as the battle of Delion is proved by the celebrated scene in the *Clouds*

---

[1] The true subject of Plato's *Republic* is Justice, the ordinary conception of which is described by Socrates. He compares the high-priests of Justice in Athens to men who undertake to tame some savage animal. They learn its moods, learn what sounds provoke and soothe it and how to manage and coax it, and having thus discovered the temper and caprices of the many-headed beast, the public, they call that justice which it likes, and that injustice of which it disapproves.

*Fig. 100 Socrates*

*Fig. 101 Plato*

*Fig. 102 Aristophanes*

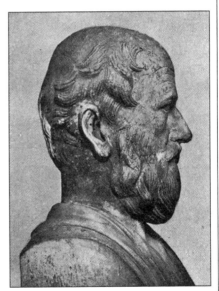

*Fig. 103 Lysias*

of Aristophanes (423) in which he is depicted as a believer in strange deities (such as Aether and King Vortex) and as a swindling Sophist and a corrupter of the young. But especially he is represented (of course quite falsely) as a scientist impiously prying into the secrets of Nature, suspended mid-air in a basket in order to examine the nature and motions of the heavenly bodies, and endeavouring to calculate the length of the leaps of a flea by dipping its feet in wax and using the impression as a measure. Aristophanes was not personally hostile to Socrates (at least in the *Symposion* the two seem on quite friendly terms), but he was a staunch conservative, a praiser of old Marathonian times, rigidly orthodox, strenuously imperialistic, and apparently quite incapable of distinguishing Socratic wisdom from the blatant intellectualism and the atheistic materialism of the day. Suspicion and resentment gathered year by year until at last the storm broke, and he who was among the Greeks the first to proclaim a God of perfect wisdom and goodness, whose will is the true cause of all things, and to assert that he 'held it more certain than anything else that the soul exists after death and that it will be better in that other life for the good than for the evil,' is condemned to die as a malefactor, on the charge of 'not believing in the gods of his country' and for 'corrupting the young,' exemplifying to no small extent in himself that 'truly just man' whom in Plato's *Republic* he thus describes: 'He will be misjudged, despised, and hated; he will be condemned as unjust and as an evil-doer; he will be scourged, tormented, fettered, have his eyes burnt out; and lastly, after having suffered all manner of evil, will be crucified.' The last scenes – those of his trial, imprisonment, and death – are well known, and to give any worthy picture of them is here impossible. I can only refer those who have not yet read it to the vivid and touching account given by Plato in the *Apology*, the *Crito*, and the *Phaedo*.

Doubtless many of the wisest and best were deeply shocked and grieved. The great Athenian rhetorician Lysias is said to have composed a speech for Socrates to use in his defence – but Socrates would not use it. Diodorus (who lived in the age of Julius Caesar) and other writers assert that even the Athenian rabble bitterly repented their act, and put to death the accusers of Socrates. It is said that certain verses of the *Palamedes* of Euripides ('Ye have killed, O Greeks, the all-wise, the nightingale of the Muses . . .') made the audience burst into tears. Such hysterical changes of public sentiment are common enough, but although there were many who, like Xenophon and Plato and Phaedo and Crito and Simmias, loved Socrates as the 'best and wisest man they had ever known,' it is not at all probable that the Athenian mob and its leaders were capable of repenting what they believed to have been a perfectly justifiable and wise extermination of a noisome and intolerable influence. Justifiable, from the point of view of the juryman, it may have been, and some historians, such as Grote, who regard with favour the Athenian juryman, speak of the 'marked and offensive self-exaltation' and the 'insulting tone' – such a tone as 'jurors had never heard before' – with which Socrates forced his judges to 'uphold the majesty of the court and the constitution.' To some of us the unwritten law which Socrates by his character and his teaching proclaimed was of a majesty inexpressibly more sacred than that of the Athenian juries, to which with such calm dignity he submitted himself.

Some of the intellectual and imaginative forms in which Socrates, perhaps, clothed his beliefs will be mentioned on a later occasion. Here I add only a few more words about the methods that he used – so entirely different from those employed by the fashionable lecturers and teachers of his day. His wisdom consisted, as he tells us, in the consciousness of his own ignorance. 'I never professed,' he says, 'to teach anyone any knowledge.' He did not profess to impart ready-made opinion, but by quiet discussion he tried gradually to bring about a certain attitude or frame of mind such as would prove receptive of truth. One of these methods was what is known as Socratic *irony*. In one way the 'irony' of Socrates was, of course, no pretence – for he was deeply conscious of his own ignorance – but he often pleaded ignorance in order to elicit the definitions of his opponents or hearers. 'Here is a specimen of your well-known irony,' exclaims some one in the *Republic*. 'I knew all the time that you would refuse to answer, and would pretend ignorance and do everything rather than answer a straightforward question.' How far the respect that Socrates often shows for the learned ignorance of his opponents was pretended or sincere it is not always easy to discover, but his 'irony' never has any tendency to sarcasm; it is always good-natured and modest; but nevertheless it must have often given great offence to self-conceit. Another Socratic method is what he calls the *maieutic*, or 'midwife' method. In playful allusion to the profession of his mother, Phaenarete, he says that he too merely helped at the birth of thought – helped the labouring mind to produce its offspring – something that shall be its own by the rights of nature, not merely a supposititious foundling picked up in the gutter of public opinion.

The word 'dialectic' (discussion) is used nowadays in rather a loose way to describe any of the artifices of disputation; but the dialectic of Socrates (or Plato) in its highest sense is the discourse of the mind on the beliefs of the soul – the manifestation in thought and words of that 'discussion of the soul with herself' which takes place without the voice.' But, as Dante tells us, 'form accords not always with the intention of art,' and even the serenest self-communion may seem sometimes to take the form, in Plato's dialogues, of rather exhausting and apparently quibbling disputation. To those of us who are impatient for conclusions the long-drawn discussion may at times seem tedious and unprofitable. In some cases no conclusion at all is arrived at, and one looks in vain for any dogmatic summing up, such as no modern writer on such subjects could afford to dispense with, if he had any respect for the critics. How entirely different the object of Socrates was from that of most who argue may be seen from what he says in the *Phaedo*: 'I am not in the least anxious that anyone present should believe in my theories, except just as may happen. . . . If this is not true, then something like it may be true.' He knew well that the highest truths were not to be thus attained and formulated – a fact that is well stated in a letter written probably by Plato himself.[1] 'About these things,' he says – he means the highest objects of philosophy – 'there never was and never will be any treatise of mine. For a matter of this kind cannot be expressed in words like other kinds of learning, but by long familiarity and living together with the thing itself a light, as it were of a flame leaping forth, will suddenly be kindled in the soul and will nourish itself there.'

Perhaps it may be asked: 'Of what nature, then, was this inexpressible object of the Socratic philosophy? And what is the use of this dialectic, or of any intellectual process, if it cannot hope to attain and formulate the highest kind of truth?'

What Socrates (or Plato) believed to be attainable by intellectual processes is explained in one of the most interesting and most difficult of the Platonic dialogues, the *Theaetetus*, where Socrates comes to the conclusion that the highest certainty attainable by the mind is what he calls 'a true opinion with reason' – that is, an observed fact which is confirmed by other facts and can be classed under a general law. Such inductive truths he accepted as 'rafts,' seaworthy enough to waft us over the waters of intellectual and practical life.

---

[1] The *Seventh Epistle*, which describes Plato's relations with Dion and Dionysius in Sicily, and seems, although sometimes questioned, to be genuine. (See *Selections from Plato*, edited by T.W. Rolleston.)

But there are truths beyond the reach of the unaided mind – truths of which the knowledge is identical with virtue (so that wrong-doing is only due to ignorance of such truths, and 'nobody is willingly – but only igno- rantly – wicked'). To gain a vision of such truths and realities is possible by means of some contemplative faculty, the 'reasoning part of the soul,' as it is called in the *Phaedrus*, and dialectic in its highest sense, as the 'voiceless discussion of the soul with herself,' induces these seasons of calm weather in which such visions are vouchsafed. And should we wish for some inti- mation of the nature of these truths, after which Socrates searched so earnestly, perhaps we cannot do better than turn to the definition that he has given of true philosophy (in the *Phaedo*): 'True philosophy is nothing else but the study of how to die and to be dead.'

But perhaps the following passage may still more clearly intimate of what kind was that knowledge of the true nature and cause of all things which was the aim of Socratic philosophy.

'When I was a young man,' says Socrates in the *Phaedo*, shortly before drinking the cup of hemlock, 'I was wondrously desirous of that kind of wisdom which they call natural science. It seemed to me a very grand accomplishment to know the causes of everything, and I tossed myself in speculating whether matter, when by alternations of cold and heat it has arrived at a certain state of putridity, generates life – and whether it was the blood or air or animal heat or the brain that generates intelligence and the senses, and thence memory and opinion. . . . However, I received no advan- tage from my inquiries. . . . But once I heard somebody reading out of a book which he said was by Anaxagoras, and when he came to that part in which he says that Intelligence [*Nous*] orders and is the cause of all, I was delighted and thought it an excellent idea that Intelligence orders every- thing and puts it where it is. But from this grand hope I was swept away when I read the book and found that the man made no use of this Intelligence in the ordering of the cosmos, but talked about airs and aethers and waters and all kinds of strange things. And he appeared to me like one who should first assert that all the actions of Socrates are due to intelli- gence, but should then declare that I am sitting here because my body is composed of bones and muscles, and that the muscles being elastic and the bones solid enable me to bend my limbs, and that this is the reason why in this crouching attitude I am sitting here, utterly ignoring the true reason, namely, that, since the Athenians thought it better to condemn me, on this account I also have thought it better to sit here, and more honourable to remain and endure whatever punishment they may have ordained. Otherwise, by the Dog, I think these muscles and bones would have long ago been somewhere in Megara or Boeotia.'[1]

SECTION D: SCULPTURE (*c.* 440 TO *c.* 400)

To divide anything of such vitality and continuous growth as Greek sculpture into distinct periods is perhaps unwise, but much of what was produced between the chief works of Pheidias (*c.* 450–432) and those of Scopas and Praxiteles (*c.* 390–360) seems to possess marked and interesting characteristics. Nothing is more striking in the wonderful development of Greek art and literature during the fifth century than the rise and preeminence of Athenian influence. We have already seen how in the earlier part of the century the influence of the 'athletic' Peloponnesian school found its way into Attica, especially through Ageladas, the master of both Pheidias and Myron, and how this vigorous, masculine style, wedded, as it were, to Attic grace and delicacy, produced the incomparable art that we still admire in the Parthenon frieze and pediments. In its turn the new and beautiful Athenian style influenced the sculpture of the Peloponnese and extended even to such distant regions as Lycia and Western Sicily.

(1) At Athens itself we find Lycius, son of the great sculptor Myron. Nothing of his has survived, but he is less of a mere name than many once famous Greek artists, for besides the numerous works mentioned by old writers, such as the celebrated group at Olympia representing the combat between Achilles and Memnon, he made one or more of the bronze equestrian statues that once decorated the Propylaea,[2] and on the basis of one of these his name may still be read. Another Athenian sculptor, a Cretan by birth and Cresilas by name, is of greater interest, for in the British Museum may be seen what is a fine copy (Fig. 96) of his bust of Pericles, the basis of which has been discovered during the excavations on the Acropolis. It is supposed to be an ideal rather than a realistic portrait – 'not so much an accurate presentment of the features of Pericles as an embodiment and expression of his personality.' It was probably one of the first

---

[1] *Phaedo*, xlv. *ff.*, abbreviated in parts.

[2] The great bronze four-horse chariots, one erected after the Chalcidian war in 506 and another probably by Pericles about 446, were probably placed on new bases when the new Propylaea of Mnesicles was built, *c.* 437, and perhaps the statues by Lycius were then erected.

states of public men erected at Athens. As in the case of coins, portraiture in Greek sculpture was rare till the fourth century. Even the statues erected to victorious athletes were usually, it is supposed, not realistic portraits, nor were, as a rule, in earlier times, the figures on tombstones. On the other hand, we have the statues of the Tyrannicides as early as about 500, and such portraits as that of Aristion, about 550 (Fig. 51). A figure of Miltiades, as we have already seen, stood in the Marathon trophy at Delphi, and Polygnotus introduced portraits into his pictures, and Pheidias did the same in the case of the notorious shield of Athene (Fig. 79); but until this bust of Pericles was set up, evidently to record the founder of the Parthenon and the Propylaea, no great Athenian seems to have been honoured by a public statue in his lifetime. Another Athenian sculptor of this period, Strongylion, has real interest for us, for one of his works, a colossal bronze figure of the wooden horse of Troy, is mentioned (*c.* 414) by Aristophanes, and its basis has been discovered on the Acropolis.

(2) Attic influence in the Peloponnese is well exemplified in the temple of Apollo at Phigaleia, in Arcadia (Fig. 84; Note A). It was built either after the Great Plague of 430 or about ten years later by the Athenian Ictinus, the architect of the Parthenon. The frieze, which is complete, is now in the British Museum. It represents combats between Centaurs and Lapithae and between Greeks and Amazons. Although the execution appears to be by local workmen and is defective, the design is undoubtedly by some great Athenian sculptor, and the figures and the grouping and the splendid, though roughly finished, drapery recall the Parthenon sculptures. An exceedingly finely balanced and vigorous group is that of which Heracles and the Amazon queen form the centre.

But perhaps the greatest triumph of Attic influence is to be noted in the celebrated Argive (or Sicyonian) sculptor Polycleitus, who is said to have been a fellow-pupil of Pheidias in the studio of Ageladas at Argos. Polycleitus continued the traditions of the Argive school, with its heavy-limbed, strongly muscular, and highly unintellectual athletes, but he combined with massive strength a certain amount of Pheidian grace and proportion, so that his statues were regarded as almost perfect representations of the highest ideal of the human form, and, although the numerous marble copies that we possess doubtless give a very poor idea of the bronze originals (which are said to have been of an exquisite finish), we can still recognize in the *Spear-bearer* and the *Diadoumenos* (an athlete binding a fillet round his head) something of what formerly excited such great

Fig. 104  Mourning Athene

Fig. 105  Stele with woman carrying vase

Fig. 106  Stele of Hegeso

Fig. 107  Figure from Greek tomb

admiration. The former (the *Doryphoros*) represents a nude athletic figure holding a spear sloped over his left shoulder, and was known as the 'Canon' – that is, the 'Rule' or standard of perfection in proportion – and served as an embodiment of the rules which Polycleitus published in a treatise of like name. But he did not limit himself to the athletic style. Influenced doubtless by the Athene Parthenos and the Olympian Zeus, he made a great chryselephantine statue of Hera for her temple near Argos; and this Hera is praised by some ancient writers as equalling or even surpassing the Pheidian statues. The goddess was enthroned and crowned and held a pomegranate in one hand, and in the other her sceptre, on which was perched a cuckoo. The head of this Hera given on Argive coins (Coins Plate V, 7) is certainly very much more beautiful than any relic of the Athene Parthenos. On the site of the Heraion near Argos have been found fragments of its sculptures, which both in the grace and variety of the figures and the floating or clinging drapery reveal a strong Attic influence; and many of them are in Attic (Pentelic) marble. An exceedingly beautiful female head in Parian marble, now at Athens, perhaps belonged to the pediment, or to a decorative statue. If these sculptures are by Polycleitus, as some believe and many hope, he must have been much more influenced by Attic grace than could be inferred from his *Spear-bearer* or from his heavily built and square-jowled Amazon (Fig. 108), and if more of his work were extant we should probably feel no surprise when ancient writers give the palm for 'art' to Polycleitus and for 'grandeur' to Pheidias.

(3) The Nereïd Monument, probably a regal tomb, was discovered by Sir Charles Fellows in Lycia. Its remains, lying scattered by earthquake, were brought to England in 1842 and are to be seen in the British Museum. On a square base, ornamented with two bands of frieze, rose an Ionic building, between whose columns stood female figures in floating drapery, probably representing ocean nymphs (Nereïdes) skimming over the surface of the sea. Some of these recall vividly the beautiful Victory of Paeonius (Fig. 93), and the subjects and style of the friezes show unmistakable resemblance to Attic work (such as the friezes of the Athene Nike temple at Athens) and to the Phigaleian sculptures. The date of the Nereïd Monument is probably about 420. Another, and perhaps older, Lycian monument which reveals similar influences has been found at Trysa, and is now at Vienna. It is, however, very weatherworn, being made of soft stone, and not, as the Nereïd tomb, of Parian marble.

(4) Greek tombstones (*stēlai*) are to be seen in many museums, and at

Athens especially there is a very large number of beautiful specimens of Attic work, found in the Cerameicus and in Athens (some built into the walls of Themistocles), and at the Peiraeus and elsewhere in Attica. Some of these, such as that of Aristion (Fig. 51), keep something of the form of the original *stelē* (*i.e.* column), which was anciently erected on the tumulus, and in older examples, the single figure is perhaps more often a portrait than it was in later times, when tombstones seem not seldom to have been bought ready made, it being enough if they represented fairly well the required age and sex. The single figure often represented the deceased occupied in some characteristic pursuit[1] – as an athlete with his strigil and oil-flask, or a child with a bird or a toy, or a hunter with his dog, or a lady (as in Fig. 106) with her jewels, or the warrior in battle (Fig. 109).

Many of the most beautiful and pathetic of these *stelai* date from the fourth century, but, as is natural in the case of funeral monuments, the designs are generally old and carry one back sometimes to Pheidian days. The original narrow pillar gave way considerably to broader tombstones, and the sculptured relief was often enclosed in an architectural framework. Frequently we find a family group represented, and a scene of farewell – a maiden perhaps having her sandals put on, as a sign of departure, or a man clasping affectionately the hand of his wife, or his child, or his aged father or mother. No relics of antiquity bring us nearer to past ages than these Athenian tombstones, nor do any surpass them in calm and delicate beauty.

---

[1] Thus in the *Odyssey* Elpenor begs that his oar

'Rowing with which when alive so often he toiled with his comrades'

shall be erected on his tumulus.

# Chapter 8

# The Spartan and the Theban Supremacy (404–362)

The story of the Persian invasions is associated with much that is great in Greek character and much that is interesting in the history of humanity, and the rise and fall of the Athenian Empire deserves study, in spite of many tedious and many revolting details, not only on account of the incomparable skill with which it is depicted by Thucydides, but also because it has many points of contact with the true history of Greece – with the history of that Greece which alone retains any importance for our age. But the period that intervened between the fall of Athens and the rise of the Macedonian power is not of this nature. It offers, indeed, some splendid examples of courage and self-devotion, which we must needs admire, however little we may sympathize with the causes that called them forth; but the endless quarrels and battles and political combinations, details of which, raked together from old authors, compose what is generally called the history of this rather dreary interval, no longer possess for us any appreciable value, except perhaps as an exercise for the memory. I shall, therefore, give only a short summary of the external events of these forty-five years, during which the baneful lust for 'supremacy' ever again reared its head, until a semi-barbaric empire arose against which ancient Hellas, drained of her life-blood by internecine strife, was powerless to stand.

### The Spartan Supremacy

At Aegospotami (405) Lysander had captured nearly the whole of the Athenian fleet, and shortly afterwards Athens was forced to renounce almost all her empire and to acknowledge the supremacy of Sparta both on sea and land. For thirty years Sparta had proclaimed herself as the liberator of Greece from the enslavement of the 'despot city.' At the beginning this claim had been sanctioned by the enthusiastic approval of the greater part of the Hellenic world, and at the end of the war the Long Walls of Athens had been pulled down to the music of flutes and amid jubilant shouts welcoming the dawn of the new liberty. But the enthusiasm was short-lived. It was soon apparent that Sparta had no intention of granting independence to the cities that acknowledged her supremacy. Athens was, like a wounded lioness, too dangerous to meddle with. For a year or so a Spartan harmost ('regulator,' or commandant) with his troops had occupied the Acropolis, and a decarchy (oligarchy of ten) managed the civil government, but the wisdom of the Spartan king Pausanias, doubtless influenced by the success of the political exiles under Thrasybulus, finally allowed the re-establishment of the democracy, while in the subject cities of the Confederacy, now under the control of Sparta, rapacious harmosts and subservient decarchies, from whom there was no appeal (as there had been under the Athenian Empire), for a long time continued to exercise the worst kind of tyranny. Sparta proved herself wholly incapable of founding any pan-Hellenic Empire. During her short-lived supremacy her one object was her own territorial extension, both in Greece and in Asia, and not only did greed and a brutal and stolid militarism render her incapable of any conception of pan-Hellenic federation or even any true imperial policy, but she also stooped to the meanest treachery against the Hellenic world. The descendants of the heroes of Thermopylae and Plataea, after overthrowing the Athenian Empire by Persian aid, purchased by the betrayal of the Ionic cities, and after proving faithless to their barbarian allies and attacking the western satrapies in the hope of Asiatic plunder, and after losing their naval supremacy at the battle of Cnidus (394), overpowered by the Persian fleet under the command of the fugitive Athenian admiral Conon (see p. 367), proved capable of once more abandoning the Ionians and of accepting the humiliating peace (that of Antalcidas, or the 'Peace of the Great King') by which Persia was recognized as the overlord and arbiter of the Hellenic states – and this merely in the hope of securing their own supremacy in their miserable quarrels with their neighbours in Greece. This hope was frustrated by the victory of Thebes at Leuctra in 371.

Such is the bare outline of the Spartan hegemony, and into this framework the following facts will easily fit themselves.

Of the first period the most important fact is probably the expedition of Cyrus, related by Xenophon in his *Anabasis* (see Section A of this chapter). It will be remembered that Cyrus had been sent by his father, Darius II, to supersede the satrap Tissaphernes at Sardis. He was the favourite of his mother, Queen Parysatis, and had been saved by her influence when his elder brother, Artaxerxes, who had succeeded Darius in 405, had endeavoured to put him to death on a charge of high treason, brought by Tissaphernes. He was intimate with the Spartan Lysander, whom he liberally supplied with money, and being a great admirer of Greek discipline and courage and fully aware of the powerlessness of Oriental forces against even a small body of trained hoplites, he determined to dethrone his brother, and set about enlisting Greek mercenaries; and in this he was helped by the Spartan government, who placed 700 men at his disposal. Soon he had collected about 100,000 native troops and a body of 10,600 Greek hoplites under the command of Clearchus, a Spartan harmost who had been banished for trying to make himself the tyrant of Byzantium.

Cyrus had led his army through Phrygia and Lycaonia and as far as Tarsus in Cilicia before the Greeks discovered that the object of the expedition was not, as had been given out, the punishment of the robber tribes of Pisidia, but a more distant goal, and it was not till they reached the Euphrates at Thapsacus that they learnt that they were marching against the Great King. By lavish promises of pay they were induced to proceed. The vast hosts of Artaxerxes barred their progress at Cunaxa, some sixty miles north of Babylon. Although the left wing of the barbarians fled in panic at the charge of the Greeks, their centre and right outflanked and surrounded the much smaller army of Cyrus, who in an ecstasy of fury led a band of horsemen against his brother and actually succeeded in wounding him with a javelin,[1] but was struck in the eye by the javelin of a Carian soldier, and, together with all of his faithful 'table-companions,' was overpowered and slain (401). Commanded to lay down their arms, the Greeks refused to obey, but they accepted the guidance of Tissaphernes, who misled them towards the north across the Tigris. Clearchus and Proxenus and three other generals and twenty captains were induced to visit the

---

[1] 'Wounded him through the corslet, as says Ctesias the physician, who also says that he himself healed him' (*Anabasis* i. 8). Ctesias was a Greek, a native of Cnidus, who for seventeen years was the physician of Artaxerxes and wrote a history of Persia, of which we possess abstracts given by the writer Photius.

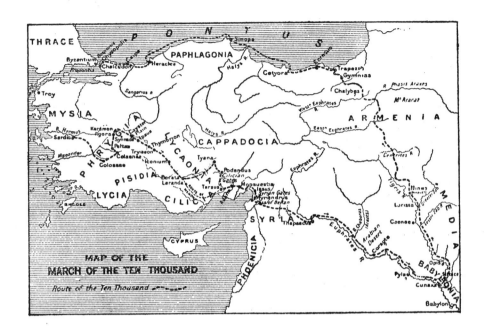

MAP OF THE
MARCH OF THE TEN THOUSAND

Route of the Ten Thousand ·—·—·—·

camp of Tissaphernes for a parley, and were massacred, together with their attendant soldiers. Then Xenophon the Athenian, though he had no rank, having joined the expedition as the guest of Proxenus, took the lead, and under his guidance and that of the Spartan Cheirisophus the Greeks, striking boldly northward through Kurdistan and Armenia, after many sufferings and losses succeeded in reaching the Euxine Sea at Trapezus (Trebizond), whence, partly by sea and partly by land, they made their way to Chalcedon, on the Bosporus. After serving for a time in Thrace they – the 6000 that still remained together – crossed over again to Asia Minor, where they found service against Persia under the Spartan general Dercyllidas and under King Agesilaus, with whom the remnant returned to Sparta. With these survivors of the Ten Thousand was Xenophon, who for a time had returned to Athens, reaching it a few weeks after the death of his much-loved master, Socrates (399). Of his subsequent life, as well as of his *Anabasis* and other works, more will be said later.

The death of Cyrus and the return of Tissaphernes to Sardis, intent on revenge, naturally alarmed the Greeks in Asia. They appealed to Sparta, and the Spartans, to whom the expedition had revealed the impotence of Oriental forces against Greek discipline, tempted by the hope of rich plunder and possibly the annexation of the Persian Empire, sent troops under Thimbron and then under Dercyllidas. But after some successes they made a truce with Tissaphernes and Pharnabazus and sent envoys to Susa to propose alliance and the betrayal of Greek Asia. The proposals were rejected. Artaxerxes had determined to prosecute the war by sea, and had set Conon, the exiled Athenian admiral, over 300 Phoenician and Cilician ships. Thereupon (in 396) the Spartans sent out with large reinforcements their king Agesilaus, who, lame and puny in stature but big with courage and ambition, regarding himself as a second Agamemnon,[1] dreamt of conquests such as some sixty-six years later Alexander realized. Having got rid of the troublesome and ambitious Lysander (who shortly after was killed at Haliartus, in Boeotia), he defeated Tissaphernes – who was consequently deposed and murdered by a successor sent from Susa by the influence of Parysatis – and occupied Phrygia, the satrapy of Pharnabazus; but affairs in Greece compelled the Spartans to recall him. Reluctantly renouncing his schemes of Oriental conquest, he left his brother-in-law, Peisander, in command of the Greek fleet and returned with his troops by the overland route – that of Xerxes – through Thrace and Macedonia.

The troubles in Greece that had recalled him were due to the insolent and overbearing conduct of the Spartans, who had alienated their allies, almost exterminated the Eleans, expelled the fugitive Messenians from Naupactus (see p. 361), and caused Athens, Corinth, Argos, and Thebes (incited by Persian emissaries) to form a hostile league. Fighting had taken place near Corinth[2] and at Haliartus, in Boeotia, and when Agesilaus arrived from the north a fierce and bloody battle took place at Coroneia (Western Boeotia), in which the Spartans were technically victorious; but their king, who was himself nearly trampled to death in the fight and was disheartened by the news of the defeat at Cnidus, retreated to the Peloponnese, crossing over from Delphi, as the confederates held the Isthmus. Only a week or two before Coroneia (August 394) there had been fought a naval battle near Cnidus, in which Peisander had been slain and his fleet utterly routed by

---

[1] He tried to sacrifice, like Agamemnon, at Aulis before starting, but was expelled by the Thebans – an insult he never forgave. His succession to his brother Agis, the fellow-king with Pausanias of Sparta, had been secured (in spite of an oracle that warned against a 'lame monarch') by Lysander, who, being foiled in a project to establish his own military dictatorship, and believing that he would easily rule such a cripple, voted for him against the son of Agis, Leotychidas, whom he accused of illegitimacy – as son of Alcibiades.

[2] See explanation of Fig. 109 in List of Illustrations.

411

Fig. 108  Amazon by Polycleitus

Fig. 109  Stele of Dexileos

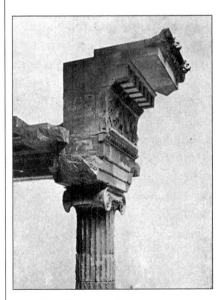

Fig. 110  From the Mausoleum

Fig. 111  Head of Cnidian Aphrodite

the Persian fleet under the command of Conon. The result of this defeat was that all the Greek cities of Asia expelled the Spartan harmosts and acknowledged Artaxerxes as their overlord. The satrap Pharnabazus then with his Persian fleet cruised round Greece, overawing the Spartans, and he allowed Conon with the crews of some of the Persian ships to land at the Peiraeus and help the Athenians to rebuild their Long Walls. Thus ended the naval supremacy of Sparta, which had lasted ten years (404–394).

Her land supremacy Sparta still upheld, though with ever-increasing difficulty. Even in Asia Minor she still warred against Persia, for the Great King had again disdainfully rejected her overtures for purchasing his alliance by the betrayal of the Greek Asiatic cities. At length, however, an impolitic and somewhat ungrateful act of Athens – the support of the Cypriot king Evagoras in his revolt against Persia – gained for Sparta the favour that she craved, and Artaxerxes listened graciously to the pleadings of her envoy, Antalcidas, and issued a decree claiming for himself Cyprus and all the Hellenic cities in Asia, and proclaiming himself the arbiter of Greece. 'If any,' he said, 'refuse to accept this peace, I shall make war on them with ships and with money.' This decree was engraved on tablets that were set up in all the chief sanctuaries of the Grecian states. To such a depth of humiliation by its insane fratricidal feuds had Greece demeaned herself before the barbarian. Nor did even such a foe of Persia as Agesilaus seem to feel the humiliation. He strongly favoured the 'King's Peace' (generally known as the 'Peace of Antalcidas'), and laughingly remarked that 'the Persians were Laconizing.'

On the strength of this understanding with Persia, and a similar understanding with the Sicilian tyrant Dionysius, the Spartans began again to act in a high-handed fashion. The city of Mantineia, in Arcadia, had at times given them trouble. They now razed it and dispersed the population into the five country villages of which it had originally (c. 470) been formed – an act worthy of Darius or Xerxes. Three years later (382) Lacedaemonian troops on their way towards Macedonia (where a confederation was beginning to cause Sparta suspicions) seized the citadel of Thebes – a violation of peace and an act of tyrannical insolence denounced by all right-minded men in Hellas, such as the venerable orators Lysias and Isocrates, and regarded sorrowfully by Xenophon, the lover of Sparta, as the fatal deed that brought down heaven's just retribution. This retribution came surely but somewhat slowly. The Cadmeian citadel was recaptured by Pelopidas with a band of Theban exiles, disguised as women, and under the new tactics and the discipline of his friend, the great Theban general Epameinondas, the military power of Thebes rapidly grew till she became the head of a Boeotian confederacy, and as the rival of Sparta won the alliance even of Athens, her hereditary enemy.

Moreover, Athens had already, since the crushing defeat of the Spartan fleet at Cnidus, regained her naval superiority and was again endeavouring to found another confederacy, if not another empire. In 376 she won a naval victory over the Spartans near the island of Naxos, and her new fleet, under Timotheus, the son of Conon, cruised triumphantly around the coasts of the Peloponnese, and an attack that the Spartans, aided by the Sicilian Dionysius, made on Corcyra was foiled by the Athenians. But Athens became jealous of the rising power of Thebes. She consented to an alliance with Sparta (the 'Peace of Callias,' 371). Thebes was to have been included in the peace, but refused to take the oath except as the head of the Boeotian confederacy. 'Will you leave the Boeotian cities independent?' asked the Spartan king Agesilaus. 'Will *you* leave the Peloponnesian cities independent?' replied Epameinondas. The name of Thebes was therefore struck out of the treaty.

Athens was now once more a 'great power,' and had Sparta been content to allow her the naval supremacy and to retain for herself the hegemony on land, this Peace of Callias might possibly have brought about some such pan-Hellenic federation as that which the Athenian orator Isocrates had so enthusiastically described in his *Panegyric*, delivered perhaps before the Greeks assembled at the Olympian festival (see p. 461). But two new forces had arisen to disturb the equilibrium – Thebes and Thessaly; for the military chief (*tagos*) of Thessaly, Jason, tyrant of Pherae, was aspiring to play a part similar to that borne so successfully a little later by Philip of Macedon. Relying on his powerful Thessalian cavalry, a large body of paid hoplites, and a rapidly increasing navy, he dreamed of uniting all Hellas under his command, and when in 371 the Spartans were routed and slaughtered by the Thebans at Leuctra, not far from Plataea, in Boeotia, it was Jason who, though he arrived too late to help the Thebans, dictated the terms. He behaved as the victor, and overawed all Northern Greece, threatening to usurp the rights of the Amphictionic Council and to elect himself president of the Pythian Games – possibly even to seize the treasury at Delphi. But after four years his career was cut short by assassination, and the power of Thessaly subsided as rapidly as it had arisen.

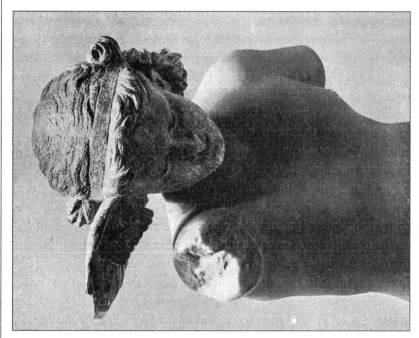

*Fig. 113 Hypnos (Sleep)*

*Fig. 112 The Hermes of Olympia by Praxiteles*

## The Theban Supremacy (371–362)

Leuctra was won by the tactics of Epameinondas. He adopted and improved a formation already used by the Thebans at Coroneia. He drew up his men in a wedge, fifty shields deep, which cut through the twelve-ranked Spartans, as Xenophon says, 'like the beak of a charging trireme.' A thousand Lacedaemonians, among them King Cleombrotus and four hundred Spartiats, were slain. During the next nine years the Thebans held the coveted 'supremacy,' and again and again invaded the Peloponnese under their 'Boeotarch' Epameinondas, while Pelopidas made frequent expeditions into Thessaly and Macedonia to support the cities against the despots and to extend the Theban hegemony.

Both in the Peloponnese and in Thessaly the Theban influence, guided by the wisdom of Epameinondas, was on the side of liberty, and in the midst of continual bloodshed we hear of certain acts that proved beneficial and of permanent value. Two great means of defence against tyranny, whether of a despot ruler or a despot city, are confederation and synoecism – that is, the centralization of a scattered population into fortified towns. This had induced Sparta to raze the Arcadian city of Mantineia and disperse its inhabitants, and no sooner was Sparta rendered powerless by the defeat at Leuctra than the Mantineians rebuilt their home and surrounded it with a double line of walls, in spite of the impotent remonstrances of old King Agesilaus. An Arcadian confederation was then formed, and by the advice of Epameinondas a new federal capital, Megalopolis ('Great City'), was founded not far from the Laconian border, on a tributary of the Alpheus. Thirty-eight village communities formed the bulk of its population. It was encircled by a strong double line of fortifications more than five miles long. The remains of its theatre and the great federal assembly-hall, the Thersilion, are still to be seen.

Epameinondas and his Thebans now invaded the Peloponnese. They crossed the Eurotas by Amyclae and (what no foe had ever done before) approached and threatened Sparta itself, and, had not prompt assistance arrived from allied Peloponnesian towns, the unwalled city would probably have been taken.[1] Epameinondas then crossed into Messenia, where on the slopes of Mount Ithome, using the site of the old stronghold for the

---

[1] The number of Spartans with full citizenship at this time is said to have been no more than 1500. To fill up the ranks of the fighters thousands of Helots had been emancipated.

new acropolis, he founded the city of Messene, to populate which the Messenian exiles, ejected in 399 from Naupactus by the Spartans and scattered through the whole of Hellas, came flocking. This new city – a Liberia in which the former thralls of Sparta were now free citizens of a hostile state planted on Spartan territory – held its own until (in 146) it was incorporated in the Roman Empire. The fortifications of Messene are described by the traveller Pausanias as the strongest he had ever seen, and the remains (Fig. 123) are still impressive.

In her distress Sparta now appeals to Athens and to Dionysius of Syracuse. Athens, jealous of Thebes, consents to an alliance. Dionysius sends troops – but soon withdraws them. Constant fightings take place, among them a 'tearless battle,' in which on the Spartan side not a man is killed. Vain attempts are made to patch up peace by a conference at Delphi. Then a general appeal is made to Persia to arbitrate in the insane fratricidal strife, and Artaxerxes (gained over by Pelopidas, who went as envoy to Susa) graciously issues a rescript dictating terms of peace favourable to Thebes and insisting on the recognition of Messenian independence. But even the will of the Great King proves powerless.

Also in Thessaly and Macedonia the Thebans were combating Spartan and Athenian influence and supporting liberty against despotism – the federated cities of Thessaly against the successors of Jason of Pherae, and the free cities of Chalcidice against the Macedonian kings (Alexander II, and afterwards the usurper Ptolemy Alorites). Pelopidas succeeded in making all the north of Thessaly a Theban protectorate and in forcing Macedonia to acknowledge Theban supremacy. From the usurper Ptolemy he took hostages, one of them being the boy-prince Philip (afterwards the famous Philip II of Macedon), who was sent to Thebes, where he was trained in Theban military science – soon to be used with such fatal consequences. But fortune deserted the gallant Pelopidas. He was caught and imprisoned by Alexander of Pherae, and it needed all the promptitude and diplomacy of his friend Epameinondas to rescue him. Some three years later he set forth for a third time from Thebes (against the warnings of an ominous solar eclipse, July 13, 364) in order to aid the Thessalian cities against the tyrant, and at the 'Dogs' Heads' (Cynoscephalae), crags that rise on the east of the Pharsalian plain, he fell in battle, having rushed into the ranks of the enemy at the sight of his hated adversary, as Cyrus did at Cunaxa. Athens meantime, aided by the skill of its generals Iphicrates and Timotheus (son of Conon), had been rapidly consolidating her new empire

417

in the Aegean and in Thrace. To check this a Boeotian fleet of 100 triremes was built, and Epameinondas, scouring the Aegean and the Propontis, succeeded in disaffecting several of the Athenian subject allies.

Thus the state of unstable equilibrium continued. For some years there was an interminable succession of fights and alliances and quarrels and endless political combinations and recombinations, fighting, between Pisans and Eleans, even going on in the sacred Altis of Olympia during the celebration of the games. The ridiculous folly of all these squabbles is evident from the fact that we find even Mantineia, which had been destroyed by Sparta and rebuilt by the aid of Thebes, now deserting Thebes and fighting on the side of Sparta.

To prevent further disaffection and to defend Messene and Arcadia the Thebans under Epameinondas now made their fourth descent on the Peloponnese. They once again nearly captured Sparta, the surprise planned by Epameinondas being foiled only by the swiftness of a Cretan runner. Then on the plain to the south of Mantineia, which city also he just failed to capture by surprise, Epameinondas (in the autumn of 362) outmanoeuvred the Spartans and their allies, and, as at Leuctra, the mighty wedge-formed column of the Thebans, like the ram of a trireme, came sweeping obliquely down on the right wing of the enemy, broke through the ranks of the Lacedaemonians, and put the whole army to flight. In the excitement of the pursuit Epameinondas fell mortally wounded, and with his dying breath he advised the Thebans to make peace. As at Lützen and at Quebec, the joy of victory was changed into mourning, and for Thebes the loss was irreparable. Her supremacy was doomed, for it had been sustained by the genius and the personality of her great general, and even he had been unable to combine Boeotia into a compact and permanent state. All that was great in the Theban supremacy – and there were elements of real greatness in it – was due to Epameinondas. The unanimous verdict of ancient writers, including even the Sparta-loving Xenophon, affirms him to have been not only a great military leader, but also in personal character one of the noblest of the Greeks – *princeps Graeciae*, as Cicero calls him.

Xenophon says that the battle of Mantineia (in a preliminary skirmish of which, by the way, his son Gryllus was slain) was expected to be a very decisive engagement, but that it left things in a 'ten times more unsettled' state; and this is probably true, except that it confirmed the independence of Messenia and Arcadia. Sparta had sunk low even before the battle. To what depths she descended is apparent from the fact that as early as 365 the white-haired King Agesilaus, perhaps partly actuated by his old hatred of Persia, but also, it seems, moved by the hope of high pay, had taken Spartan troops across to Asia to fight as mercenaries for Ariobarzanes in his revolt against the Great King; and now, after Mantineia, being eighty-four years of age, he took a thousand mercenaries to Egypt to aid in another rebellion against Persia. In Egypt the old warrior was at first treated scornfully on account of his lameness and insignificant person, but his military services brought him a fee of 230 talents. On his homeward journey he died, at the harbour of Menelaus in the territory of Cyrene.

## SECTION A: XENOPHON

Most of the facts that are known about Xenophon's life have been mentioned in connection with Socrates and with the expedition of Cyrus. He was born near Athens about 444, and he seems to have lived over ninety years. After his return to Athens in 399 (see p. 410) he was banished, probably on account of his relations with Cyrus. He rejoined the remnant of the Ten Thousand in Asia Minor, and, having returned overland with Agesilaus to Greece in 394, fought on the side of Sparta at Coroneia. The Spartans then gave him an estate in Triphyleia, near Olympia, where with his family he passed twenty years of quiet country life; but when Sparta, after the 'King's Peace,' began to stir up strife and had seized the Theban Cadmeia, Triphyleia became a bone of contention, and the Eleans succeeded in ejecting Xenophon. His sentence of banishment was repealed when Athens made alliance with Sparta (374), but whether he returned to his native city or spent the rest of his life at Corinth is unknown. Besides the *Anabasis* he wrote the *Cyropaedeia*, an imaginative account of the boyhood of Cyrus the Great and of the early Persian court and nation, and the *Memoirs* of Socrates, and the *Hellenica*, a chronicle of the Spartan and Theban supremacies. He also wrote a book about hunting, and although a soldier and a leader of men he was evidently happier amid natural surroundings, country scenes and wild animals, than amid the clash of arms and the turmoil of fratricidal wars. His keen observation and his picturesque descriptions of remote regions and of wild men and animals lend a charm to the *Anabasis* which is entirely wanting in the *Hellenica*. His piety, which recognized the will of heaven in every event and believed implicitly in the efficacy of vows and sacrifice, reminds one less, perhaps, of the childlike *naïveté* of Herodotus than of the manly, God-fearing character of such a soldier as Gordon. The following passages from the *Anabasis* are characteristic of his style.

'Now there was a certain Xenophon, an Athenian, accompanying the army neither as a general nor a captain nor a common soldier, whom Proxenus, an old family friend, had invited to come over from Greece, promising to obtain for him the friendship of Cyrus. When Xenophon had read the letter he informed Socrates about the expedition; and Socrates, fearing that friendship with Cyrus might inculpate Xenophon with the Athenians, seeing that Cyrus zealously supported the Spartans against Athens, advised him to go to Delphi and ask the god about the expedition. So Xenophon went and asked Apollo to which deities he should offer sacrifice and prayer so as best to undertake the journey that he contemplated and succeed and return in safety. And Apollo gave answer and told him to what gods to sacrifice. But Socrates blamed Xenophon because he had not first inquired whether it were better to go or not. "However," he said, "since you put the question in this manner, you must do all that the god commanded."' (iii. 1.)

'In this region the country was one great plain, as level as the sea, and covered with wormwood; and whatever other shrubs and reeds grew there were all fragrant, like aromatic pot-herbs; and not a tree was to be seen. And there were all kinds of wild animals, especially wild asses, and many ostriches, and also bustards and gazelles. When one chased the wild asses they would gallop off and then halt, for they were much swifter than the horses, and as soon as the horses approached they would do it again, and it was impossible to catch them except by posting hunters at intervals and taking up the chase with fresh horses. Nobody got an ostrich. Those who chased them on horseback soon gave it up, for the bird drew off at great speed, using the feet for running and lifting herself along with the wings, as with a sail. But the bustards [wild turkeys] can be caught if one follows them up quickly, for they fly only a short distance, like partridges, and soon tire; and they are very good eating.' (i. 5.)

'Thence they marched three stages, five parasangs [*i.e.* about nineteen miles in three days], over a plain, through deep snow. The third stage proved difficult, and a biting north wind opposed them, piercing through everything and freezing their very blood. One of the augurs

*Fig. 114  The Satyr (Faun) of Praxiteles*

suggested sacrificing to the wind. This was done, and every one remarked that the violence of the wind decreased perceptibly. The snow was six feet deep, so that many of the beasts of burden and of the menials perished, and about thirty soldiers. They got through the night by lighting fires, for they found a large store of wood where they encamped; and wherever a fire was lit the snow melted and great pits were formed right down to the ground, and one could thus measure the depth of the snow. . . . But those who had fallen behind on the march had to camp without food or fire, and some of them perished, and although dense masses of the enemy were pressing on the rear, frequently capturing broken-down pack-animals and fighting with each other over them, it was nevertheless necessary to leave behind those of the soldiers who had been blinded by the snow and those whose toes had been rotted off by the cold. . . . And they caught sight of a dark patch, where there was no snow, and thought it had melted; and so it had, on account of a stream which was steaming in a gully near by. And they left the line of march and sat down there and refused to move. And Xenophon, who was bringing up the rear, when he perceived it, used every art and means of persuasion to induce them not to give up, telling them that great masses of the enemy were close behind; and at last he grew angry. But they told him to kill them, for they simply could not go any further.' (iv. 5.)

'Their homesteads were underground, with openings like the mouth of a well, but below they were extensive. For beasts of burden there were entrances excavated, but the people descended by means of ladders. In the homesteads there were goats, sheep, cattle, fowls, and their young. All the beasts in the place were fed on hay. There was also wheat and barley and pulse and barley-wine in bowls; and the barley-corns themselves were there, level with the brims; and reeds without joints were lying in the bowls, some of them large, others small; and one was expected, whenever one was thirsty, to take a reed and suck.' (iv. 5.)

'When the vanguard had got to the top of the hill a great clamour arose. And Xenophon and the rearguard, when they heard it, thought that some other hostile bands were making an attack. But as the shouting became louder and nearer, and each company as it came up started running towards those who continued to shout, and the uproar became greater as the crowd increased, Xenophon felt that it must be something of importance. He therefore mounted his horse, and together with Lycius and the cavalry rode forward to the rescue; but soon they hear that the soldiers are shouting *The sea! The sea!* and are passing the word to their comrades. Thereupon all set off running, even the rearguard, and the beasts of burden were driven forward and the horses; and when all had reached the summit they began to embrace each other, generals and captains and everybody, shedding tears of joy.' (iv. 7.)

[*In explanation of the following passage it should be stated that a tithe from the ransom of certain prisoners had been entrusted to Xenophon for dedication to Artemis, and that he had for a time deposited this money in the great temple of Artemis at Ephesus.*]

'But when Xenophon was banished, and was already settled at Scillus, near Olympia, Megabyzus, the warden of the Ephesian temple, came over to attend the Olympic festival, and restored the deposit. So Xenophon, having received the money, purchased a precinct for the goddess in a place pointed out by the god [Apollo?]. A stream called Selinus ['Wild Celery River'] happened to flow through the place, just as a river Selinus flows past the temple of Artemis at Ephesus; and in both there are fish and shells; but in the precinct at Scillus there are chases [preserves] of all kinds of game. And he built an altar and a shrine from the same money, and henceforward he used to devote to the goddess the tithes of all the produce of the estate at a sacrificial festival in which all the townspeople and neighbours, both men and women, took part, camping in booths and being supplied by the goddess with meal, bread, wine, dried fruits, and a share of the consecrated portion of the sacrifice, and also a share of the game; for with a view to the festival a hunt was got up by the sons of Xenophon and of the other townspeople, and grown-up men joined in it, if they wished. The quarry consisted of wild pig, gazelles, and deer. Now the place lies on the road between Sparta and Olympia, about twenty stades [2½ miles] from Olympia. . . . And around the shrine was planted a grove of cultivated trees, the fruits of which grow ripe and edible. And the shrine was a small model of the great Ephesian temple, and the wooden image [*xoanon*] was like the image at Ephesus, as far as cypress wood can resemble gold.' (v. 3.)

SECTION B: SICILY AND THE CARTHAGINIANS

The struggle between the Hellenic and Semitic races in Sicily was probably more important for the future of humanity, and was certainly on a larger scale and of a more interesting nature, than the internecine strife that for a century exhausted Greece, and after humiliating her before the barbarian left her an easy prey to Macedonia. But the connection between Western and Eastern Hellas after the disastrous Sicilian expedition was slight. We hear of triremes and troops sent to the aid of Sparta by the elder Dionysius; Plato visits Syracuse in the vain hope of founding a model state; Corinth commissions Timoleon and a thousand mercenaries to eject from Syracuse the second Dionysius; Archidamus, son of the old warrior Agesilaus, takes Spartan troops across to help Tarentum (c. 338) against the Lucanians, and is slain on Italian soil; but, on the whole, the later history of the Sicilian and Italian Greeks has little to do with the history of Greece proper. They formed no part of the world-empire of Alexander and his successors, but continued to struggle for existence against Italian tribes and the Phoenician power until Rome swallowed up both them and their foes.

For my present purpose a very brief résumé of Sicilian history during this period will suffice.

After the crushing defeat of the Carthaginians at Himera in 480 they gradually re-established their power in Western Sicily, and when, about 410, Segesta appealed to Carthage for aid against its rival Selinus, the Carthaginian *shophet* (general) Hannibal, grandson of the Hamilcar who perished at Himera, was sent from Africa with 100,000 men. He sacked Selinus and then attacked Himera, which, although Syracusan ships rescued some of the inhabitants, was captured and utterly destroyed; and Hannibal sacrificed with torture 3000 captives on the spot where Hamilcar was said to have leapt into the flames (see p. 300). In 406 he blockaded Acragas. A pestilence broke out among his troops and he himself died. After eight months the besieged sallied forth at night, leaving sick and aged behind, and reached Gela in safety. Himilco, Hannibal's successor, massacred the abandoned Acragantines and sacked the place. (But the gigantic temples survived the sack, and the city was afterwards rebuilt by Timoleon, though the great Olympieion was never finished. Finally it was captured by the Romans (210), and, as Agrigentum, was one of the chief cities of the Roman province of Sicily.) In 405 Gela was taken by Himilco, in spite of

*Fig. 115  The Apollo Sauroctonos of Praxiteles*

the assistance of Syracuse, or possibly with the connivance of the tyrant of Syracuse, Dionysius.

This Dionysius, a man of obscure origin, who had risen to the position of sole military authority in Syracuse (profiting by political feuds between democrats led by Diocles and aristocrats led by Hermocrates – both of whom had been expelled), had persuaded the people to allow him a body-guard, and, in the same way as Periander and Peisistratus, had seized the chief power, which he retained for thirty-eight years. To assure his position he made peace with the Carthaginians and recognized their lordship over almost the whole of Sicily, but in 397, having extended his sway over Catane, Leontini, and other cities, he felt strong enough to renounce the compact. Thereupon Himilco blockaded Syracuse, and Dionysius was reduced to such straits that he tried to make his escape. Pestilence, however, once more attacked the Carthaginian troops, encamped in the marshes of the Anapus, and Himilco was glad to purchase safe retreat with a bribe of 300 talents, leaving all his allies behind to be massacred by the Syracusans.

The empire of Dionysius now extended rapidly. In 393 he defeated Mago, a Carthaginian, who came over with a great army from Africa, and by 384 we find him master not only of all Sicily except the western extremity, but also of a great part of Magna Graecia (Italian Hellas) and of Epirus, the Greek mainland opposite Corcyra. He even planted on the distant shores and islands of the Adriatic various colonies, such as Ancona, Issa, and Hadria, near the mouth of the Po. Syracuse was at this time the greatest and most powerful city of all Hellas. It had 500,000 inhabitants and was enclosed by a line of ramparts, which encircled not only the original stronghold on the island Ortygia and the higher ground of Achradina, Neapolis, and Tyche, but also the heights of Epipolae – a line about eighteen miles long, considerably longer than the Aurelian walls of Imperial Rome. (Massive ruins of the fort Euryalus, at the western angle of the ramparts, still exist, and beneath them a labyrinth of underground passages and chambers.)

Dionysius cultivated art and literature, and, after many failures that excited much ridicule at Athens, one of his tragedies is said to have won a prize; but he seems to have been jealous of real genius, to judge from his relations with Plato, who in 388 is said to have visited his court, and to have soon left it under a cloud – indeed, according to one report, he was sold as a slave to the Spartans by the despot! On the other hand, stories are told of the wisdom and generosity of Dionysius, one of which is well known through Schiller's ballad *Die Bürgschaft*.

When Dionysius the elder died in 367 (perhaps in consequence of a great banquet held after his tragic victory at Athens) he was succeeded by his son Dionysius II, a weak and self-opinionated young man. The new lord of Syracuse at first was under the influence of a wise adviser, Dion, the brother of one of the late tyrant's wives. Dion invited Plato to return to Syracuse, suggesting that he might attempt to realize the model state the outline of which he had sketched in his *Republic*. Plato gladly fell in with the suggestion, for it was his belief that such a model state was a possibility in case 'fortune should bring a wise lawgiver in the way of a young ruler who was intelligent, brave, and generous.' Unluckily the young ruler in this case proved a failure, or perhaps Plato, like Milton, was too exacting with the young. (In accordance with the rule of his academy, 'Let no one enter who is ignorant of geometry,' he insisted, it is said, on putting his royal pupil and the whole court of Syracuse through a preliminary course of this science, holding that, as Euclid remarked to King Ptolemy, 'there is no royal short cut to geometry.')

Dionysius soon afterwards (360) succeeded in expelling his mentor, Dion, and Plato was allowed to return, doubtless somewhat disillusioned, to his Academeia on the Cephisus. Once more, perhaps persuaded by Dion, who was at Athens, Plato acceded to the request of Dionysius and returned (357) to Syracuse, whence he seems to have escaped with his life only through the influence of the Pythagorean Archytas. About the same time, while Dionysius was absent on an expedition to Italy, Dion returned and was enthusiastically received as their ruler and lawgiver by the Syracusans. However, their hopes were disappointed. Dion developed tyrannical proclivities and was assassinated in 353, and a few years later (346) Dionysius returned and re-established himself in the stronghold of Ortygia. In 344, hearing that the Carthaginians were preparing a vast armament for the invasion of Sicily, the Syracusans appealed to their mother-city, Corinth, and ten ships with 1000 hoplites were sent under the command of Timoleon. This man had once saved his own brother's life in battle, but had afterwards killed him, or instigated his murder, to save the state from his treasonable plots. Abhorred by many as a fratricide and admired by others as a patriot, he had long lived in obscurity, but was now given the chance of proving his real character. He was welcomed as deliverer by many of the Sicilian cities, and before long Dionysius capitulated and was allowed to retire to Corinth, where he spent the rest of his life in fashionable diversions, and, it is said, in presiding over a school, or literary academy – perhaps in imitation of his old teacher!

Timoleon succeeded in ejecting the tyrants from many of the Sicilian cities and uniting the Hellenic power against the Carthaginians, who were planning another great invasion. In 339 they brought over an army of 70,000 men and 10,000 horses in a fleet of more than a thousand vessels. Timoleon's forces amounted to less than 10,000; but on the river Crimisus he gained a complete victory. Many thousands of the enemy were slain or drowned, 15,000 were made prisoners, and immense spoil was captured. Carthage was glad to make peace and to confine herself to the western end of the island. Timoleon now resigned his powers and retired to an estate near Syracuse. He had become totally blind. Plutarch tells us how at times he visited Syracuse and was drawn in a car into the middle of the great theatre amid the deafening applause of the immense multitude, who listened with reverence to his words. He died in 336, only two years after his great victory – in the year that Alexander the Great ascended the Macedonian throne.

The Syracusan democracy lasted till 317, when Agathocles, a potter, made himself tyrant. The Carthaginians had once more overrun all Sicily. They defeated Agathocles at Himera and blockaded Syracuse; but Agathocles boldly transported an army to Africa and for years laid waste the Carthaginian territory. Finally he established himself as the king of Sicily. In 270 Hiero II was elected king of Sicily. At first he sided with the Carthaginians against the Romans, but afterwards became the faithful ally of Rome. His grandson Hieronymus, reverted to the Carthaginians, and Syracuse was thereupon (212) besieged and captured by Marcellus and became the chief city of the Roman province of Sicily.

SECTION C: PLATO

Some of the facts of Plato's life have been given in connection with Socrates and with Dionysius.

It is only necessary here to add that he was born at Athens in 428, and became a follower of Socrates when about twenty years of age. After the death of his master he lived for a time at Megara, and seems to have visited Cyrene, Egypt, and possibly other Eastern lands, as well as Sicily and Magna Graecia, where he became intimate with Pythagorean and Eleatic

*Fig. 116  Demeter*

philosophy. When forty years of age (after his first visit to Dionysius) he acquired a small estate on the southern slope of Colonus, and for the next forty-two years, except during his two later visits to Syracuse, occupied himself by writing his dialogues and by teaching in his own house or in the gymnasium and avenues of the Academeia – a place of public resort, named after the old hero Academus, and laid out by Cimon – adjacent to his garden. All his chief works, thirty-six dialogues, have come down to us. Of these the *Republic* consists of ten and the *Laws* of twelve books.

In the case of Socrates it is the personality of the man and the fundamental principles of his teaching that are of interest; with Plato it is rather the superstructure of thought and imagination that is important, not only for the consummate grace and power of his style – which is perhaps the most perfect in all prose literature, reminding one of the movements of some strong and beautiful animal – nor only for the poetic faculty by which he bodies forth the forms of things unknown and intimates to us in parables what 'cannot be communicated directly by words like other kinds of learning,' but also for the illumination and insight that his intellectual conceptions bring us. No more can here be done than to indicate the more important of these intellectual conceptions, and give one or two specimens of his imaginative parables.

Aristotle tells us that Plato as a young man was much impressed by the doctrines of Heracleitus, as taught by the Athenian Cratylus, concerning the ceaseless movement (flux) and instability of all things and the impossibility of any certain knowledge founded on phenomena. These doctrines, which we find constantly in Plato (generally attributed by him to Socrates), were doubtless confirmed by his study of the Eleatic philosophy, such as that of Parmenides; but he, or Socrates (with whom we may henceforward identify him), was too wise to accept the paralysing Eleatic denial of the practical reality of the natural world. While holding the sole absolute reality of the One he accepted the Many as practically real, as 'rafts' useful for wafting us over the sea of earthly life. And for intellectual existence also he accepted such 'rafts.' In the *Phaedo* he says that he had given up gazing directly at absolute truth, lest he should be blinded as those who gaze too long at the sun, and had sought its reflected image – *i.e.* he had given up pure contemplation, as apt to paralyse thought and action, and had taken to forming intellectual conceptions, which he accepted as temporary rafts, to be abandoned at any time if they did not prove seaworthy.

When Socrates gave up the study of natural science, wondering how any one could be so blind as 'not to be able to distinguish between a true cause and that through which it operates,' he went back, like Descartes, to fundamental principles and the simplest possible conceptions. 'I began thus,' Plato makes him say. 'I assumed what I judged to be the strongest principle' – the strongest beam for his raft – 'and then accepted as true whatever was in agreement with it.' What one of these strongest principles was he tells us in the *Phaedo*. 'Nothing,' he says, 'has any reality except so far as it participates in the real Existence, or Idea, of which it is the manifestation. . . . If any one tells me that a thing is beautiful because it possesses a rich colour, or a certain shape, or so on, I bid farewell to such statements, for they only confuse me. I keep to the simple, uncritical, and perhaps foolish opinion that nothing else causes it to be beautiful but the presence, or operation, of ideal Beauty. How this takes place I cannot say, but I do assert that all beautiful things become such through ideal Beauty.'

In another passage he puts it thus: No two material things were ever perfectly equal. What then do we mean by saying that things are equal? We must mean that they more or less approach that perfect Equality which, as it exists nowhere on earth, we must have seen in some other life, before the sleep and forgetting of our birth; and just as we are reminded of a person by a portrait, so when we see two things nearly equal ('longing for Equality') we are reminded of that truly existing ideal Equality of which they are the imperfect manifestation. This is the Platonic doctrine of Reminiscence (*Anamnēsis*), which connects itself with the doctrine, or parable, of a conscious prenatal existence, and, as we shall see later, with that of Transmigration (Metempsychosis).

In order to gain any satisfactory view of Plato's doctrine of Ideas, it is necessary, I think, to regard it from various standpoints. Firstly, the parable of the One and the Many is useful. Secondly, an Idea has some analogy to what one calls an Archetype – and one may conceive, if one can, such Archetype as an independent objective existence, of which all the individuals of a genus, or species, are more or less imperfect copies; or, from the opposite standpoint, we may consider it (though Plato tried *not* to do so) as a mere generalization, or abstraction, existing only in our own minds. Again, an Idea may sometimes be regarded as the real Cause, or Life, of a thing. For instance, when the scientist analyses the protoplasm and finds nothing left in his pot but water, carbonic acid, and ammonia, and exclaims, 'Lo, here in my pot is the First Cause!' the intellectual conception or parable of an Idea of life – an ideal Reality, a true Cause, existing in all eternity quite independent of 'that through which it operates' – is helpful, just as a raft. And there is another way of regarding the Platonic Idea which is sometimes useful. In the case of both things and persons there are certain accidental qualities which seem to affect only the senses and the mind and to make no difference in our *feelings*, whereas there are other elements, both in things and in persons, which appeal straight to our affections, and it is these elements that compose the real person or the real thing. So we may, perhaps, say that the Idea is that real inner Self of a thing or of a person which appeals to our heart rather than to our mind. Thus Plato speaks of that ecstasy of 'divine madness' which we experience when we recognize in earthly forms the reflection of that divine Idea of beauty or of truth which our soul has seen and loved in a former existence.

As in every allegory, there are in this parable of Ideas various points against which our understanding stumbles. Firstly, it is not easy to understand how our mind is related to these Ideas, and how we apprehend them, or are certain of their existence as Realities. They seem to be mirrored darkly in our mind as Reminiscences, and to be contemplated by some special 'reasoning part of the soul.' Secondly, in regard to the presence or operation of the Idea in material things Plato himself says, 'How this takes place I cannot say.' It is the same kind of question as that of the connection between mind, or life, and matter. In such cases one has once more to take refuge in allegory, and Plato does so when he tells us that the material universe is an 'imitation' and that it 'participates in' and 'has community with' the Perfect and Eternal and Divine.

By allowing that all things participate in Perfection he endowed the natural world with a certain reflected reality and dignity, such as lends a value to earthly existence, but (as Socrates is made to confess to the old Parmenides in the dialogue of this name) he was also obliged to suppose an Archetype, or Ideal, of *everything*, even of ugliness, of filth, of evil. To such an 'unfathomable abyss of absurdity' was he led by his theory. And yet he retained his theory as the most seaworthy raft he could find, and on this 'strongest principle' he reared a structure that has proved for many a refuge against the blasts of materialism.

The following are specimens of Plato's imaginative allegories.

'Imagine,' says Socrates, 'people in a subterranean place like a cavern, with an entrance expanding to the light across the whole width of the cave. Suppose them to have been in this cavern from their childhood with chains on their legs and necks, so as only to be able to look towards the inner part of the cave, and unable to turn their heads round. And suppose behind, between these fettered men and the light, a low stage or parapet, like those on which mountebanks show their curious tricks. And imagine that along this parapet pass men bearing all kinds of things raised aloft – human statues and figures of animals and all kinds of utensils.'

'You mention,' says Glauco, 'a strange comparison and strange fettered men.'

'Yes,' answers Socrates, 'but such as resemble us human beings. Now I suppose you will allow that they can see nothing but only the shadows thrown by the light on the further wall of the cavern?'

'How can they,' says Glauco, 'if all their life they have had their heads thus fixed?'

'Such people as these, then, will believe that there is nothing truly existing except these shadows?'

'Necessarily.'

'Well, then, if one of them should be loosed and made suddenly to rise up and turn his head round and look towards the light, and in doing this should be so pained and blinded by the splendour as to be unable to behold the things of which he had formerly seen the shadows, do you not think he would turn away from the light and seek again the shadows and believe that they alone are real?'

'He certainly would do so.'

'Well, but if some one should drag him thence by force up the steep and rough ascent and never stop till he had drawn him right up to the sunlight, would he not be distressed and full of indignation? And when he had come up into the light and his eyes were filled with its splendour, would he be able to see any of the things that are there called real? Would he not require time so as to become accustomed to it? And first he would perceive shadows best, and then the images of things reflected in water, and after that the things themselves. . . . Last of all, he would be able, I think, to perceive and contemplate the sun itself.'

'Assuredly,' answers Glauco.

'Well, then, when he remembers his first habitation and the wisdom that was there, and those who were his companions in bonds, do you not think he will esteem himself happy by the change, and pity them?'

433

'He will, greatly.'

'And if there were any honours and renown and rewards among those fettered men for him who most acutely perceived the shadows that passed along the wall, and who best remembered which were wont to pass foremost and which last, and which of them went together, and from this knowledge were even able to foretell what was coming, does it appear to you that *he* would be desirous of such honours, or envy those who are thus honoured and rewarded? Or would he not wish, as Homer says, *To work as the hireling of some portionless man*, or to suffer anything, rather than to hold such opinions and live in such a fashion?'

'I think,' says Glauco, 'that he would rather suffer and endure anything.'

'Now consider this. If such an one should descend once more into the cave and resume his seat, would not his eyes be filled with darkness in consequence of coming back suddenly from the sunlight? And should he *now* be obliged to give his opinion about those shadows, and dispute about them with those men who are there, eternally chained, whilst still his eyes are dazed and before they have recovered their former state, would he not afford his companions laughter? And would it not be said of him that, having ascended, he had returned with his eyes damaged, and that it is wrong to attempt to go up to the light, and that should any one ever try to liberate *them* and lead *them* up to the light, if ever they should lay hands upon him, he should be put to death?'

'They would most certainly,' says Glauco, 'put him to death.' (*Rep.* vii.)

'Let us compare the soul to the combined energies of a winged chariot and a charioteer. The horses and charioteers of the gods are all noble and of noble descent, but those of other natures are very various. With us men the charioteer does indeed direct the chariot, but of the horses one is well proportioned and well bred and the other is quite the reverse; whence it results that the work of guiding the chariot is exceedingly difficult.' [These winged chariots are described as soaring up to the apse of heaven preceded by the host of the divine charioteers.] 'The sovereign ruler Zeus leads the van, guiding his winged chariot and disposing and controlling all. After him comes the host of

*Fig. 117  Eirene and Plutus bu Cephisodotus*

the gods and divine powers in eleven companies, Vesta (the Central Fire) alone remaining in the palace of the immortals. And as they ascend to the zenith of heaven's vault the chariots of the deities, always in perfect balance, advance with lightness and ease, while the others toil on with difficulty, for the evil courser drags down earthwards the car, unless he has been right well trained by his driver. Here comes the great and sore trial of the soul. The souls of the immortals, when they have reached the zenith, place themselves on the outer surface of the heavenly vault, and the revolution carries them round and they behold that region above the sky of which no earthly poet has ever sung nor ever shall sing worthily where true Existence (Reality) dwells, colourless, formless, impalpable, not to be contemplated except by the mind that guides the soul. . . . Such is the life of the gods. Among the others that soul which best follows and resembles the divine lifts the head of the charioteer into the upper region and is carried round by the revolution, but it is much troubled by its horses and with difficulty contemplates true Existences. Another is now lifted, now depressed. The plunging of its horses allows it to see some Existences and not others. The rest follow afar, eager to contemplate the higher region, but are powerless to do so and are carried round beneath the surface. They clash together and fall one over the other, each attempting to get to the front; they crowd, they battle, they toil, and by the awkwardness of their charioteers many are lamed and many lose the best part of the plumage of their wings, and after painful and unavailing efforts are foiled in gaining a view of Reality and are obliged to find their aliment in the fodder of opinion. Such a soul, becoming fattened on the gross food of vice and forgetfulness, gravitates, loses its wings, and falls to earth, and takes to itself a body; but the law protects it from animating the body of a beast in its first stage.'

The philosopher then describes the destinies of the undying soul passing through various forms of death – sinking perhaps even below the level of the beasts, until it is cast as incurable into Tartarus, or rising in the course of ten earthly lives and through ten millenniums of purgatory until it regains its wings and finally reaches heaven, where it 'dwells for ever with the gods.'

In one case only this period is abridged – in that of the lover of Wisdom, whose soul recovers its wings after the third millennium. During his earthly existence he prizes above all else the reminiscence of those Realities which in a former life he has beheld. 'The man who turns these precious recollections to good account,' says Plato, 'shares perpetually in the true and perfect Mysteries and himself becomes perfect. For withdrawn from earthly interests and attached to things divine, he is warned by the multitude to give up his folly. They treat him as an idiot. They see not that he is inspired.' (*Phaedrus*, 246.)

## SECTION D: SCULPTURE, ARCHITECTURE, PAINTING TILL THE ACCESSION OF ALEXANDER

There is a striking difference between the sculpture of the fourth century and that of the fifth. In the fifth almost all works of sculpture were public dedications. Even the statues of victorious athletes and charioteers, erected by cities or tyrants or other wealthy persons, were for the most part national monuments and seem to have been generally rather of a typical character than personal – as is seen also in the case of sculptured tombstones and in such idealized portrait busts as that of Pericles (Fig. 96). The gods, too, were represented as majestic and somewhat impersonal beings beyond the range of mortal affections. In the fourth century sculpture became (as in Homer poetry long before had been and as in the plays of Euripides even the drama had now become) more individual, personal, and emotional, and the artist began to inspire his statues of the divinities with human feelings, and to lend them the subtle distinctions of personal character, without, however, disturbing (as was done later by the more emotional Hellenistic and Graeco-Roman sculpture) the perfect balance of dignified self-restraint that is essential in all great plastic art. The great sculptors of this period are Praxiteles and Scopas (*c.* 390–340). In connection with Praxiteles should be mentioned his father (or maybe his elder brother), Cephisodotus, a copy of one of whose statues is at Munich. This work (Fig. 117) represents Eirene (Peace) as a benignant matron holding on her left arm the infant Plutus (Wealth). It very forcibly illustrates the new tendency, its touch of nature and human affection reminding one of the Madonna and Child of mediaeval art. Also it is interesting because the attitude and motive are almost identical with those of the one work that we possess by the hand of the son, or brother, of Cephisodotus – the famous Praxitelean Hermes with the infant Dionysus. This Hermes (Fig. 112) was found by German excavators, about the year 1877, in the Heraion at

437

Olympia (Fig. 47 and Note A). It is doubtless the very same statue that Pausanias saw there and described as 'a Hermes of marble, carrying the infant Dionysus, a work of Praxiteles.' Excepting the Nike of Paeonius, it is the only statue that we know to be the actual work of one of the great Greek sculptors – though perhaps we may not be wrong in believing parts of the Parthenon frieze and pediments to be the work of Pheidias, or in attributing the *Charioteer* to Calamis, or the Aeginetan marbles to Onatas. The Hermes has elicited much enthusiastic admiration from experts on account of its wondrous technical perfection, but to many it does not appeal strongly. There is a well-groomed, somewhat dandified air about the god, and the child, 'whose proportions are those of a much older boy,' seems far less attractive than the infant Plutus of Cephisodotus – indeed, more of a homunculus than a real child.

The masterpieces of Praxiteles, according to old writers, were the Aphrodite of Cnidus, the Eros of Thespiae, the *Satyr*, and the *Apollo Sauroctonos* ('the Lizard-killer'). It is said that the famous professional beauty Phryne, to whom Praxiteles had promised a statue, wished to discover which he considered the best, and told him that his house was on fire, whereupon he exclaimed that he was ruined if his *Satyr* and his Eros were burnt. The Cnidian Aphrodite, regarded by many old writers as the most beautiful of all statues, was, it is said, offered to the Coans, who, however, preferred a draped goddess.[1] The people of Cnidus thereupon bought it, and during many years it attracted multitudes of visitors to their town. The Bithynian king Nicomedes offered to pay off the public debt of Cnidus in exchange for it, but in vain. From Cnidian coins, on which it is represented, copies of the statue have been recognized. The best of these is in the Vatican (Fig. 118 is from a cast taken before the statue was clothed, by papal orders, in a tin skirt. See also Fig. 111). The face of the Vatican statue is very much more beautiful than that which we find on Cnidian coins, and may give us some idea of the original, which the Greek writer Lucian praises so highly for its loveliness. The goddess shows strong human feeling, a natural shrinking, as it were, from even her own unveiled presence, but it is combined with perfect self-command, dignity, and repose, whereas in the Graeco-Roman Venus dei Medici (which copies the motive) we see affectation and assumed embarrassment before human spectators.

---

[1] And yet 'Coan vestments' had a bad repute as almost invisible garments affected by fashionable women in Rome!

Of the Eros no copy is known. The god was, to judge from coins, probably represented as a full-grown youth and with long wings – more like the strong, manly Eros of antiquity than the chubby Cupid of later times. The so-called Cupid of the Vatican may be a reminiscence of it. The little Boeotian town of Thespiae, Phryne's birthplace, to which she gave the statue, became as celebrated by this means as Cnidus.

The *Satyr*, of which the 'Faun of the Capitol' is perhaps the best extant copy, needs no description (see Fig. 114). It is well known from Hawthorne's *Transformation*. A fine torso in the Louvre is thought by some to have belonged to the original statue.

Of the *Apollo Sauroctonos* (perhaps a bronze) marble copies exist, of which the best, though evidently a late and rather weak and emasculated imitation, is to be seen in the Tribuna at Florence (Fig. 115).

Praxiteles was the inheritor of the early Attic manner, in which beauty of form was pre-eminent, rather than a follower of Pheidias, whose style combined all the best qualities of Attic grace with the masculine vigour of the Argive school. He is credited with many great works of which no known relic is extant except small and vague reproductions on coins. Possibly many of the well-known but unauthenticated statues in our galleries may be derived from some Praxitelean type – though the general motive may be sometimes more ancient. The genius of Praxiteles probably created many types of grace and beauty which deeply influenced Hellenistic and Graeco-Roman art, but they were too often spoilt by the false sentiment and prettiness of the later sculptors.

Scopas of Paros excelled in dramatic expression of strong emotion, which in his open-eyed and strenuous faces and figures offered a striking contrast to the calm restraint and dreamy beauty of Praxiteles, and was a quality more Peloponnesian than Attic. Although he is sometimes described as the Greek Michelangelo, we have no certain proofs of this greatness. Two heads with traces of intense passion on their mutilated faces have been excavated at Tegea, the temple at which place he is said to have rebuilt, and also a decidedly fine figure and head that may perhaps belong to each other and represent Atalanta. These are sometimes attributed to him, as also the head[1] of a Demeter statue in the British Museum (Fig. 116), which was discovered at Cnidus. The Roman writer Pliny tells us that

---

[1] The head is of Parian marble and of far finer work than the body, which, although grandly designed, is of inferior execution and of inferior Cnidian marble.

*Fig. 118  The Cnidian Aphrodite of Praxiteles*

Scopas sculptured one of the columns of the new temple of Artemis at Ephesus (begun about 355; see Note A). Fragments of the drums of several of these columns are in the British Museum. One is fairly complete and of great beauty (Fig. 120). It probably represents the scene between Alcestis, Death, and Hermes the Guider of Souls. It is totally unlike what we should expect from Scopas. Its delicate beauty of form and sentiment is decidedly Attic – and far more like the work of Praxiteles than anything we know of Scopas. It is, however, probably by neither of these sculptors, for many artists were employed.

The influence of the passion-fraught style of Scopas on later art was evidently very strong, and as Praxitelean beauty degenerated into effeminacy and coquetry, so the dramatic vigour of Scopas led to such inartistic strenuosities as the Pergamon Altar, the Farnese Bull, and (*pace* Lessing!) the Laocoön. Probably numerous sculptures exist which are more or less close imitations of his works, such as of his celebrated raving Bacchante. The *Apollo Citharoedus* at Rome (a statue of the god singing to his harp) and the *Venus Victrix* of the Louvre may possibly be copies of his works. Of the Niobe group I shall speak later.

A subject of great interest in connection with Scopas is that of the Mausoleum of Halicarnassus, the magnificent monument erected by Artemisia (352–350) to her husband Mausolus, lord (dynast) of Caria. It was an oblong building with thirty-six Ionic columns (Fig. 110) on a high basement decorated with reliefs. Above the columns was probably a frieze, and this was surmounted by a roof in the form of a pyramid with twenty-four steps, on the top of which was a chariot. Pliny, who thus describes it, tells us that Scopas and four other famous Greek artists were employed on the sculptures. The Mausoleum stood till perhaps the tenth century of our era, and it was almost entirely demolished by the Knights of St. John, who used the material for building the castle of Budrum, and burnt most of the marble sculptures for lime. All that remained was excavated and brought to England about 1857, and is in the Mausoleum Room of the British Museum. Some of the fragments of the frieze reliefs (Greeks and Amazons and Centaurs) show a dramatic vigour such as one might expect in a work of Scopas, and in the relief depicting a chariot-race there is a fine figure of a charioteer leaning forward in a long *chitōn* (like the Delphi charioteer) which may well be by him. But by far the most interesting relic of the Mausoleum is the very striking and noble statue of Mausolus (Fig. 121), which probably stood inside the building, *not* on the roof beside the chariot, as is intimated

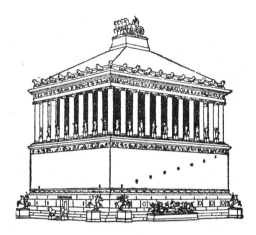

*Fig. 119  The Mausoleum of Halicarnassus, a reconstruction by Adler*

by its position in the Museum, for, although found near the remains of the chariot, the statue, as also that of Artemisia, seems too small in proportion to the chariot, and too well preserved to have stood in the open and to have sustained a fall from such a height. The statue is evidently a realistic portrait of the Carian prince, the features being decidedly non-Hellenic.

A word should be said here on the subject of painting,[1] which since the time of Mandrocles (see p. 215) and of Polygnotus (see p. 269) had attained great development. As, however, the works of the great Greek painters have entirely perished, the subject has little value except for the antiquarian. It will suffice to mention a few names. Apollodorus the Athenian is said to have first given attention to the effects of light and shade (*chiaroscuro*), or rather what Plutarch calls *apochrōsis – i.e.* tone, or the gradations not only of light into shade but of colour under the influence of light and shade. By such means, as Pliny says, he first painted men and natural objects realistically and so as to 'attract observation.' Zeuxis of Heraclea, who was patronized by King Archelaus and may have met Euripides and Thucydides at the Macedonian court, was a great master of colour, and especially excelled in depicting female beauty of the heroic type. The *Helen* that he painted for the people of Croton, using as models five of the most beautiful Crotoniat maidens, was one of his most famous pictures. (See Note A, the 'Temple of Hera Lacinia', and Fig. 40.)

---

[1] For vase-painting see Note D.

*Fig. 120 Drum of column from the later temple of Artemis, Ephesus*

Parrhasius of Ephesus, who lived mostly at Athens (*c.* 400), was somewhat younger than Zeuxis and rivalled him in splendour of colouring and grandeur of form. He called himself the 'prince of painters,' and according to Pliny was the most insolent and arrogant of artists, not even excepting Zeuxis.

Many other painters are named, and many of their pictures are described by old writers and many anecdotes are related about them, but the complete loss of all such works makes the subject almost valueless in comparison with that of Greek sculpture.

# Chapter 9

# The Rise of Macedonia: Philip and Alexander (to 334)

SECTIONS – A: ISOCRATES, AESCHINES, DEMOSTHENES, LATER
PHILOSOPHERS – B: LYSIPPUS, HELLENISTIC SCULPTURE

We have seen how after Mantineia the Theban supremacy rapidly declined, and how Athens once more began to build up an oversea empire. In this she might have been successful had it not been for the rise of two semi-Hellenic powers, Caria and Macedonia. Whether she would have held her own against the maritime expansion of Caria, which under Mausolus seems to have been very remarkable, it is idle to speculate, for both she and her rival were swallowed up by Macedonia, and it is a question of more practical import whether a united Greece (if such a thing is conceivable) might not have succeeded in resisting the Macedonian conqueror, against whom the miserable feuds that for seventy years had drained, and were still draining, her life-blood now left her powerless.[1]

When Thebes was at the height of her power Pelopidas had brought even Macedonia under Theban influence, if not under Theban dominion, and to assure the fidelity of the Macedonian ruler (at that time a usurper, Ptolemy Alorites) he had sent as a hostage to Thebes the young Macedonian prince, Philip, afterwards the victor at Chaeroneia and the father of Alexander the Great.

Until this time neither Macedonia nor Thessaly had really come within the range of Hellenic politics. We hear indeed of Thessalian cavalry under

---

[1] Of course another view can be taken. One may regard Macedonia as a Hellenic state and Philip and Alexander as the beneficent founders of a vast Hellenic Empire in which the petty squabbles of the Greek cities found peace as brawling streams when they reach the sea, to use a Dantesque simile.

*Fig. 121  Mausolus*

their king, Cineas, coming to help Hippias (*c.* 510) and defeating the Spartans, and of constant wars between Thessalians and Phocians (Hdt. vii. 176), and of the Thessalian Aleuadae, who sided with the Persians and fought for them at Plataea; and later we hear of a Spartan attempt to subjugate Thessaly (476) and the wild attempt of Jason of Pherae, after the battle of Leuctra (371), to seize the hegemony and place himself at the head of the Hellenic world (as did afterwards Alexander); but Thessaly was not regarded by the southern Greeks as a part of Hellas, and Macedonia, though its kings claimed to be of Hellenic blood, was looked upon as scarcely less a barbarian country than Scythia itself.

The race that in the early age of Greece inhabited Macedonia was probably related to the Thracians and the Phrygians. It was of Indo-Iranian stock (as the remains of the language prove), but not Hellenic – that is, neither Achaean nor Doric. Later the coast region and the more fertile inland plains were overrun by Hellenes from the south, who drove the natives to the hills. These Greeks, or semi-Greeks, of the lowlands regarded themselves as 'companions' of the king. They composed the royal bodyguard and, like the Norman nobility, formed a distinct class. It was long before the wild Macedonian hill tribes, as well as the Paeonians, Thracians, and Illyrians, were sufficiently subjugated and civilized to coalesce with their conquerors and to form a powerful nation.

The Macedonian kings, as has been said, claimed to be of Hellenic descent – a fact that Demosthenes fiercely denied, calling Philip II a 'pestilential Macedonian and in no way related to the Greeks.' But it was proved to the satisfaction of the judges when Alexander I, who had entered for the foot-race at Olympia, was challenged as a non-Hellene. 'He proved himself to be an Argive,' says Herodotus, who in another passage (viii. 137) gives us a very picturesque story about three Argive brothers, descendants of Temenus (and therefore of Heracles), who fled (*c.* 700?) to Illyria and thence crossed to Macedonia 'and took up their abode near a place called the Gardens of Midas, where there are roses of incomparable sweetness, many with sixty petals. And above the gardens rises a mountain called Bermius,[1] which is so cold that none can reach the top. . . . And from this place by degrees they conquered all Macedonia.'

---

[1] Now Verria, the range running north of Olympus and separated from it by the valley of the Haliacmon. Under the range lay Aegae (Edessa), the old capital and burying-place of the Macedonian kings. Archelaus made Pella the capital.

Such is the legend that intimates the reflux of Hellenes from the south. The youngest and cleverest of the brothers, Perdiccas, founded the dynasty of the Macedonian kings. The fifth of these, Amyntas I, was contemporary with Peisistratus and submitted to Megabazus, the general of Darius (see p. 215). His son and successor, Alexander I, about whose assassination of some Persian envoys Herodotus tells a weird story (v. 22), was obliged to side with the barbarians during the Persian invasion, and was sent by them as ambassador to Athens; but he is said to have been secretly in favour of the Greeks and to have clandestinely imparted to them at Plataea the plans of the Persians. He competed at the Olympian Games as above stated, and set up a golden statue at Delphi (Hdt. viii. 121). Perdiccas II lived during the Peloponnesian War and changed sides more than once. Then came Archelaus, who was a great admirer of Greek civilization and art, and entertained at his court many Greek notabilities, such as Euripides, Thucydides, Agathon, and Zeuxis. The relationships of the succeeding Macedonian monarchs will be best explained as follows:

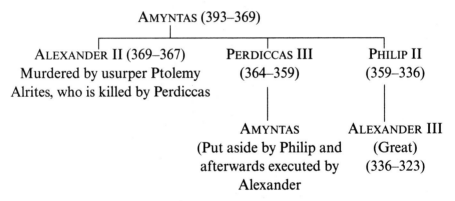

AMYNTAS (393–369)

ALEXANDER II (369–367)
Murdered by usurper Ptolemy
Alrites, who is killed by Perdiccas

PERDICCAS III
(364–359)

PHILIP II
(359–336)

AMYNTAS
(Put aside by Philip and
afterwards executed by
Alexander

ALEXANDER III
(Great)
(336–323)

When Perdiccas III fell fighting against the Illyrians his brother Philip was probably acting as ruler in his absence. After crushing the Illyrians, Philip, probably by the invitation of the nobles, put aside his young nephew Amyntas (to whom he afterwards married one of his daughters) and assumed the crown.

Philip's education in Thebes had given him a deep insight into Greek character and Greek politics. He possessed great intellectual gifts and a genius for diplomacy. Under a frank and attractive personality he concealed a subtle cunning and an ambition that was as unscrupulous as it was boundless. Conscious that the last appeal was to force, he gave the greatest attention to the formation and training of a powerful standing army, the efficiency of which was much increased by the use of newly invented engines of war (catapults, etc.), and also by the introduction of a new formation – that of the famous Macedonian phalanx, the idea of which Philip probably took from the deep wedge-like column invented by Epameinondas and used with such effect at Leuctra. The single phalanx (at least later) consisted of about 4000, and its ordinary depth varied from sixteen to thirty-two (that of the old Spartan phalanx having seldom exceeded eight). The men were heavily armoured and bore great shields. Their principal weapon was a very long spear (the *sarissa*), and the files were so arranged that the spears of even the fifth rank protruded three feet in front of the first rank. The greater phalanx sometimes consisted of four such bodies of about 4000 each; but even the single phalanx was unwieldy, and if once broken was useless. Otherwise its impact was almost irresistible.

But Philip did not trust only to his army. By the acquisition of Thracian mines and by getting Thasian miners to work the gold in the neighbourhood of his town, Philippi, newly founded on the site of the ancient Crenides, he obtained large revenues (see Note C on Coins), and it was by gold that he gained many of his successes.[1]

Philippi and its gold-mines brought Philip and the Athenians into collision. Amphipolis, at the mouth of the Strymon, cut him off from the sea and commanded the access to the gold-bearing range of Mount Pangaeus. This city, a colony of Athens, had been more or less independent ever since the time of Brasidas (see p. 362), and the Chalcidian Confederacy of Greek towns, headed by Olynthus, had tried in vain to gain it as an ally. By cunningly playing off Olynthus against Athens Philip duped both of them and captured Amphipolis, and soon afterwards Pydna and Potidaea fell into his hands. This happened in 356 – the year in which his son Alexander was born; and, as Plutarch remarks, the year brought Philip a third gift of fortune, namely, an Olympic victory.

It is not my purpose to follow closely the tortuous and perplexing course of events during the next twenty years. Some of the more important details will be given later in connection with Demosthenes. The following brief

---

[1] *Diffidit urbium Portas vir Macedo . . . muneribus* 'The man from Macedon burst through the gates of cities with bribes' (Hor. *Carmina* III, xvi.). Juvenal calls him the *callidus emptor Olynthi* 'the crafty buyer of Olynthus'. Cicero tells us that Philip used to say he could take any town into which an ass could climb laden with gold.

summary will suffice to show how the crafty Macedonian took advantage of the rivalries and dissensions of the Greek states, and how he deluded the hopes of those who, as Isocrates and Eubulus and Phocion, more or less openly and warmly hailed him as the healer of the feuds of the Greeks and their leader against the barbarian foe. We shall see how he extinguished the last possibilities of liberty and of nationality and of that self-government whereof the Hellenic world, by its never-ending fratricidal wars and its political animosities and atrocities, had proved itself to be unworthy.

Between 357 and 355 Athens has once more, as of old, serious troubles (sometimes called a 'Social War') with her allies. Byzantium, Rhodes, Chios, Cos, Lesbos, Corcyra, all revolt. Expeditions are sent, first under a young firebrand, Chares, and the old warrior Chabrias, the victor of Naxos, and when Chabrias is defeated and slain the veteran commanders Timotheus (son of Conon) and Iphicrates are dispatched to support Chares. This fiery and dissolute son of Ares accuses his more prudent colleagues of cowardice, and the Athenian mob, evidently influenced by bribed demagogues, actually condemns Timotheus and imposes a fine of 100 talents, so that the old admiral has to escape to Chalcis, where he dies. Chares then allies himself with the revolted satrap Artabazus and so incenses the Great King, Artaxerxes III (Ochus), that he threatens to aid the revolted allies of Athens. Mausolus, too, the dynast of Caria, who had acquired a large fleet and had annexed Lycia, actually affords them aid, so that finally the Athenians are obliged to recognize the independence of many of the subject states of their new empire, the whole revenues from which now amount to no more than forty-five talents yearly.

Meanwhile a disastrous quarrel had broken out between the Thebans and the Phocians. Phocis was accused of having cultivated a part of the sacred Crissaean, or Cirrhaean, plain near Delphi. Some ninety years before (448) the Phocians had with the aid of Athens seized Delphi, but had been ejected by the Spartans, who restored the Delphians.[1] On the present occasion the Athenians openly and the Spartans secretly sided with Phocis, which had of late become powerful enough to contest the 'supremacy' with Thebes and to occupy Thessaly, and had renewed her claim (founded on a line in Homer) to the possession of 'rocky Pytho.' Being fined heavily by the Amphictionic Council, the Phocians, led by Philomelus, seized Delphi. The Thebans, however, defeated them and

---

[1] The three 'Sacred Wars' of _c._ 590, 448, and 356 should be noted.

Philomelus perished, leaping over a precipice to save himself from capture. The Phocians were then led by Onomarchus, brother of Philomelus, who hired a large body of mercenaries with the treasures of the Delphic temple.

At this juncture (353) Philip of Macedon intervened. He had just captured Methone,[1] on the Thermaic Gulf, the last ally of Athens in that quarter, and pushing down into Thessaly, after two serious repulses, utterly routed the Phocians and killed Onomarchus; but, finding Thermopylae and Boeotia occupied by the Athenians, he returned to Macedonia, and turned his attention to the conquest of Thrace and the Chersonese.

It was now that Demosthenes, who for the last three or four years had been attracting notice by his public speeches, came forward to attack Philip. Public affairs at Athens were at this time under the guidance of a political party the chief leaders of which were Eubulus and Phocion. The former had proved himself a wise financier as president of the public Theoric Fund, and his policy, as well as that of the *stratēgos* (general) Phocion, was that of non-aggression, of peace and amity among the Greek states, and of friendliness and confidence towards Macedonia – without probably going so far as the old orator Isocrates, who seems almost to have hailed Philip of Macedon as the heaven-sent leader of Hellas. Whether was wisest the policy of this moderate party, the pro-Macedonian pan-Hellenism of Isocrates, or the fierce miso-Philippic, self-centred, and exclusively Athenian patriotism of Demosthenes, is not an easy question to answer satisfactorily. The programme of Isocrates was what was destined to be carried out – except that Greece was to become enslaved by the heaven-sent Macedonian leader – but it is impossible not to feel moved by the fiery indignation and the eloquent zeal of the great Athenian orator, however much one may deplore a state of things in which an irresponsible and excitable democracy is swayed by mere oratory.

Philip, as we have seen, had already possessed himself of Amphipolis, Potidaea, and other Athenian towns in Chalcidice and the neighbourhood. He now (351) threatens Olynthus, the chief of the Greek Chalcidian Confederacy. Demosthenes endeavours by his Olynthiac orations to rouse the Athenians, but the peace party is slow to move, and Philip, by means of his war-engines and his gold, gains possession of the town. He razed it to

---

[1] He is said to have lost an eye during the siege. As Demosthenes said, 'To gain empire and power Philip had an eye knocked out, a collar-bone broken, an arm maimed, and a leg lamed.'

the ground and enslaved the population. Then he attacked the Chersonese, and thus threatened to cut off the Euxine trade, on which Athens largely depended for supplies – a move by which at last public feeling was thoroughly excited and the influence of Demosthenes strengthened. Meanwhile the 'Sacred War' between the Phocians and Thebans had been continued from year to year with no decisive results, although both Athens and Sparta had sent large contingents to help the Phocians, whose leader, Phayllus, a brother of Philomelus and Onomarchus, freely plundered the Delphic treasury to pay his mercenary troops. At last Athens, weary and possibly somewhat ashamed of her Phocian allies, was meditating friendship with Thebes, when Philip, quick to see and seize his opportunity, made overtures to the Athenians. They forthwith dispatched to Pella an ambassador, Philocrates, with nine officials in his train, among whom were Demosthenes and his great rival, Aeschines; but the wily Macedonian seems to have been too clever for them all, and to have once more found his gold effective. He sent commissioners to Athens, and a second Athenian embassy visited Pella and was kept waiting for weeks till he returned from a Thracian expedition, and then had to dance attendance on him while he marched through Thessaly; and when at last they were allowed to return, with the humiliating treaty at length fully ratified, they were closely followed by Philip, who this time found Thermopylae unoccupied and the Phocians at his mercy.

Great was the indignation and the consternation at Athens when it was realized that, instead of crushing Thebes, Philip meant to annihilate Phocis. The partisans of Demosthenes were full of impotent fury, and he himself fiercely assailed Aeschines[1] and Philocrates on the charge of accepting bribes from Philip and playing a treasonable part as peace-commissioners; but the Athenian mob was paralysed with fear and sent congratulations to Philip, renouncing their support of the Phocians. Every town in Phocis, except Abae, was then razed to the ground and the inhabitants dispersed into small hamlets. For this act Philip had craftily obtained the sanction of the Amphictionic Council, which also decreed that Phocis should restore by yearly payments all that had been taken from the Delphic

---

[1] He was, however, cowed for the time by an attack made by Aeschines on Timarchus, one of his associates of evil repute, and did not renew the charge until 343, when Philocrates evaded trial by flight and Aeschines, who was supported by Eubulus and Phocion, made a plucky defence and was acquitted – though doubtless he had accepted Philip's gold.

treasury. The Macedonian king, as a Greek potentate, was then given the votes in the Amphictionic Council (see coin 9, Coins Plate V) which had been possessed by Phocis, and as champion of the Delphic god he was granted the presidency of the Pythian Games, which happened to be celebrated in this year (346). At Athens this was regarded as insufferable. No delegates were sent to the festival. Philip contemptuously ignored the insult, but sent a formal notification of his election, which was equivalent to an ultimatum; however, he deferred open hostility till a more convenient season.

Such was the sequel of the dishonourable Peace of Philocrates, in which Athens had been thoroughly outwitted by the craft and the rapidity of Philip. She was forced to conceal her shame and indignation under a show of servility. Even Demosthenes himself thought it advisable in his speech *On the Peace* to advocate a temporizing submission, while at the same time his fury against his personal enemy, Aeschines, was, as we shall see, intensified by the failure of his impeachment. More worthy of our respect, even if we cannot allow it our full sympathy, was the action of the 'old man eloquent,' Isocrates – now in his ninety-first year. By his written speeches and letters he had for a long time persistently and quietly asserted his belief in Macedonian hegemony, and he now addressed to Philip a letter full of dignity, urging him to assume the leadership against Persia and begging him to prove that he was not plotting against the liberties of Greece.

Between 346 and 341 this Peace of Philocrates, though a hollow affair, continued to remain formally unbroken, in spite of the vehement attacks made on the Macedonian king by Demosthenes, whose *Second Philippic* (344), by its outspoken accusations of perfidy, proved that the orator had recovered from his temporary mood of submission. Philip took but little notice. He was waiting for his opportunity. Meantime he ravaged Illyria, occupied Thessaly, and, having built a considerable fleet (ostensibly against Persia), began to menace the Athenian settlements on the Chersonese, whereby Athenian and Macedonian troops actually came into collision. Hereupon Philip, with crafty impudence, sent a letter of remonstrance to Athens, recounting his grievances and complaining that the Athenians had rejected his overtures and refused arbitration. A result of this was a speech by Demosthenes *In Answer to the Letter of Philip*, and another *Concerning Affairs in the Chersonese*, and these speeches were followed up by the still louder war-blast of the *Third Philippic*. Moreover, the orator actually tried to practise what he preached. He went to the Hellespont and persuaded Byzantium and Perinthus to secede from alliance with Philip. But the man

*Fig. 122  The Lion of Chaeroneia*

*Fig. 123  Arcadian Gate, Messene*

of deeds took little notice of the man of words. He forthwith captured various Greek towns on the Propontis and brought up his siege-engines against Perinthus, and tried to surprise Byzantium. In these undertakings, however, he was foiled by the advent of a large Athenian fleet under Chares and Phocion. For a few months he withdrew into the wilds of Thrace in order to punish rebellious Scythian tribes; but the open defiance of the Athenians had determined him to take his revenge at the first opportunity.

This opportunity soon came. The cultivation of the sacred ground near Delphi (anciently called the Crissaean or Cirrhaean plain) had once more excited the votaries of the god. This time it was the town of Amphissa that had perpetrated the sacrilege, and the Amphictionic Council called upon Philip, as the champion of the deity, to punish the offender.

In the spring of 338 he marched southward; but instead of attacking Amphissa he seized Elateia, a town of Northern Phocis, and began to entrench himself. At Athens the news caused an indescribable panic. On the advice of Demosthenes an embassy was sent to beg the Thebans for support, and a combined army of Thebans and Athenians, with a few auxiliaries from Corinth, Megara, and Euboea, marched to meet the Macedonians. A few miles before they reached the frontier of Phocis they were met, on the plain of Chaeroneia, by the army of Philip, and suffered a disastrous defeat (August 7, 338). The battle is said to have been decided by a brilliant charge of the Macedonian 'companions' (horse-guards), led by Alexander, then a youth of eighteen,[1] but the result was mainly due to the larger numbers of the Macedonians and their superiority in arms, training, and generalship – for the best of the Athenian commanders was Chares, and he was opposed to Philip himself. The Thebans who fell were buried on the field of battle, and beside the cemetery was erected a great stone lion, which was still in position in the days of Pausanias, but subsequently was overthrown and covered with earth. In the late nineteenth century the fragments were excavated, and were later reconstructed (see Fig. 122).

Demosthenes was present at the battle as hoplite, and saved himself by flight. It is said that Philip, after celebrating his victory at a banquet, came reeling drunk to the field of battle and jeered at his prisoners and the flight of the great orator, singing in triumph the words (that happened to make

---

[1] 'Alexander's oak,' under which, it is said, his tent was pitched, still stood some centuries later.

a comic iambic verse) *Dēmosthenēs Dēmosthenous Paianeus tad' eipen* –
'Demosthenes, the son of Demosthenes, of Paeania, thus spake.'

But among the captives was an Athenian orator named Demades, who,
though a bitter adversary of Demosthenes and an advocate of
Macedonian supremacy, was so moved by disgust as to tell Philip that
'though fortune had given him the part of Agamemnon he was playing the
part of Thersites.' This sobered the king, and instead of resenting the
remark of Demades he took him into his confidence and sent him as envoy
to Athens. Moreover, he had the magnanimity, or the diplomatic wisdom,
to treat the Athenians with surprising lenience, and to win their approba-
tion by his severity against the Thebans. He sent back all the Athenian prisoners unransomed and laden with gifts, while he occupied the Cadmeia of
Thebes with a Macedonian garrison. He then marched southwards, and
after accepting the submission of all the Peloponnese except Sparta, whose
territory he ravaged, he held a congress at Corinth and was appointed chief
commander of the Greek states against Persia.[1]

War was formally declared against the barbarian, and after consolidating his northern dominions, from Ambracia to Byzantium, the
Macedonian generalissimo of Hellas began to collect a great army for the
invasion of Asia.

But Philip's dream of Oriental conquest was not to be realized. He had
already sent across to Asia the vanguard of his army under the command
of his generals Parmenio and Attalus, and was intending soon to follow,
when his life was cut short. Olympias, the mother of his son Alexander, was
an Epirot princess, daughter of the king Neoptolemus, who traced his
descent from the son of Achilles. She had perhaps inherited the proud and
wrathful temperament of her great ancestor, and possessed the somewhat
savage characteristics of Epirot women, who were noted for their wild
excesses in the worship of Dionysus. Her uncanny habits (one of which was
the keeping of poisonous snakes) and her violent temper seem to have
repelled Philip and to have exposed her to the suspicion of insanity – a suspicion that seems justified by not a few acts of her son. Philip, who is said
to have possessed a considerable harem besides his queenly spouse, took to
himself as consort (perhaps after formally repudiating Olympias) the niece

---

[1] Artaxerxes III was poisoned by the eunuch Bagoas in 338, and his son Arses was also murdered by him (336), whereupon the all-powerful Bagoas set Darius III on the throne. In
338 Athens entreated Persia for help against Philip, but was 'haughtily and barbarously'
repelled.

of his general Attalus, Cleopatra by name. At the wedding feast the intox-
icated uncle of the bride called upon heaven to bless the marriage with a
'legitimate' heir to the throne of Macedonia, and Alexander, in furious
indignation at the insult, hurled a wine-goblet at Attalus. Philip seized his
sword, but reeled and fell as he rushed at Alexander, who left the banquet-
hall exclaiming, 'Lo, the man who wishes to cross from Europe to Asia, but
falls as he crosses from one couch to another!'

Olympias and her son fled – she to her brother Alexander, king of Epirus,
he to Illyria. Philip, however, offering the hand of a daughter to his brother-
in-law, and bringing his powers of persuasion to bear on the young
Alexander, succeeded, strange as it may seem, in effecting the return of the
fugitives.

In the spring of 336 the marriage of Philip's daughter and the Epirot
king was solemnized with great magnificence at Aegae, the ancient capital.
On the following day a public procession took place, during which a young
man suddenly rushed forth from the crowd and plunged a sword into
Philip's side, killing him on the spot. He was pursued and cut down by the
royal guards. It is said that his motive was to revenge an outrage of Attalus
which Philip had refused to punish; but doubtless he was also instigated to
the deed by Olympias. That Alexander knew and approved is not probable,
although one of the accomplices, Alexander of Lyncestis, who was foremost in acclaiming him as the new monarch, not only escaped the punishment that Alexander threatened against the conspirators, but later enjoyed
the friendship of the king and was loaded with honours.

The existence of ancient Greece as a free country (a nation she never had
been) is often said to have ended with the disaster of Chaeroneia. Her
history is henceforth, after a few vain attempts to regain liberty, for many
years merged in that of Macedonia, and is no longer of much interest
except in so far as by her art and literature and philosophy she 'took captive
her barbarian conqueror.'[1]

But perhaps we may regard the departure of Alexander for the East in
334 as the real beginning of the Hellenistic age, for before this took place
he had asserted the Macedonian supremacy and crushed out all hope of
resistance by a chastisement still more terrible than that of Chaeroneia.[2]

---

[1] *Graecia capta ferum victorem cepit* . . . 'Captured Greece took her wild victor captive' (Hor.
*Epistles* II, i. 156) applies equally well to Macedon and to the later conqueror, Rome.

[2] Once more, after Alexander's death, Athens persuaded other Greek cities to join her in
revolt, but was finally overwhelmed at Crannon, in 322.

Fig. 124  Alexander

Fig. 125  Isocrates

Fig. 126  Aeschines

Fig. 127  Epicurus

Demosthenes had proposed to celebrate Philip's death by a public thanksgiving and to pay honour to the memory of his assassin. The proposal had been indignantly opposed by the more noble-minded Phocion, who, in words that recall the rebuke administered by Odysseus to old Eurycleia, exclaimed that 'nothing shows a more dastardly nature than to rejoice over the death of an enemy.' But public jubilations took place in Athens, and Demosthenes poured his contempt on the young king, whom he likened to the Homeric 'Margites' – the well-known type of a blatant braggart. Other cities also began to show signs of disaffection, and embassies were being sent to Persia and to Attalus, who had declared for his niece's infant son. But with astounding rapidity Alexander swept down on Greece, suppressed an insurrection in Thessaly, strengthened the Macedonian garrison in Thebes, received a submissive embassy from Athens, called a congress at Corinth (where he was appointed generalissimo of Greece in the place of his father, and had his celebrated interview with the Cynic Diogenes), and then hastened back to chastise the Thracians and other northern tribes, whom he chased over the Danube, and finally turned his arms against the western tribes of Illyrians and Taulantians and reduced them to submission.

A rumour now reached Greece that Alexander had been slain in battle. Demosthenes produced a man who swore that he had witnessed it. The Thebans blockaded the Macedonian garrison in the Cadmeia, and called on Athens and other cities to rise. But suddenly, before any plan had been developed, a Macedonian army was reported in Boeotia, and scarce had the Thebans recovered from their delusion that he was dead when Alexander was before their walls, and soon after he was in possession of their city. A terrible massacre took place. Six thousand were butchered and thirty thousand enslaved. The Greek allies of Alexander, the Phocians, Plataeans, and Orchomenians (or perhaps the delegates of the Corinthian Congress), were commissioned to decide the fate of Thebes. The city was razed to the ground and her territory divided among other Greek states. Only one single house was left standing – the house of the great Theban poet. Perhaps the temples were spared, although Milton tells us that

> The great Emathian conqueror bid spare
> The house of Pindarus, when temple and tower
> Went to the ground.

Alexander, it is said, repented this destruction, and attributed his fits of uncontrollable fury (in one of which he killed Cleitus, who had saved his life) to the anger of the wine-god Dionysus, who specially favoured Thebes. The city, thus cruelly destroyed in 335, was rebuilt by Cassander in 316, but never again became of much importance.

The conduct of the Athenians on this occasion, although allowance may be made for panic, seems very contemptible. A few days after deciding to send troops to aid Thebes in her revolt they sent an embassy to Alexander congratulating him on the annihilation of the rebellious city. Alexander replied by demanding the surrender of Demosthenes and other anti-Macedonian demagogues, and Demosthenes owed his life to the interces-sion of Phocion.

The name of Phocion reminds us that we should not judge the Athenian people solely by the decrees of popular assemblies, the verdicts of jury courts, and the rancour and sophistries of orators. Although scorned by the militant imperialism and Demosthenic patriotism of the day as a pro-Macedonian and an advocate of peace at any price, Phocion, like doubtless many other wise and honest men in Athens, sincerely, if mistakenly, believed in what he held to be a higher form of patriotism, not merely Athenian, but Hellenic, and he was, what can be said of very few Greek political celebrities except Aristides and Timoleon (and certainly not of Demosthenes), as 'manifestly proof against bribery' as Pericles himself. It is pleasant to be able to end this brief chronicle of the external history of ancient Greece with an anecdote which is well invented, if not (though it possibly is) perfectly true. Alexander sent Phocion a present of a hundred talents. Phocion asked how he had deserved such a distinction. 'Because,' replied the envoy, 'the king regards you as the only just and honest man in Athens.' 'Then,' answered Phocion, 'I beg him to allow me to remain such.'

Alas! justice and honesty force one to add that some eighteen years later, amidst frenetic acclamation, this 'one just man' was condemned to death for treason by the Athenian Assembly – to the same death as that by which Socrates had died – and that not long afterwards they celebrated his funeral obsequies at public expense and erected a statue to his memory, thus hon-ouring him as a patriot and martyr.

## Isocrates

Isocrates (436–338) was an Athenian. Among his teachers were Socrates
(who in Plato's *Phaedrus* prophesies great things of him) and Gorgias. He
first taught rhetoric in Chios, and afterwards in Athens, where he acquired
great reputation and wealth. Of his twenty-two extant orations the best
known are the *Panegyricus* and the *Areopagiticus*. On account of his timid-
ity and weak voice, as he tells us, he renounced public speaking, and even
the *Panegyricus*, an early work and ostensibly addressed to a national
assembly (*panēgyris*), such as that at Olympia, may not have been delivered
in public. The one great idea that dominated Isocrates all through his long
life was the possibility of putting an end to the insane fratricidal strife of the
Greek cities for 'supremacy' and of uniting them against the common
enemy. It was shortly after the humiliating 'Peace of the Great King' (Peace
of Antalcidas) in 387 that he wrote his *Panegyric* – fifty years before
Chaeroneia, and some thirty years before Philip's accession. At this time he
had not yet given up the hope that Athens and Sparta might be reconciled
and might share the hegemony, Athens supreme on the sea and Sparta on
land. He begins by lamenting (as Solon did) that while honours are show-
ered on athletes no honour awaits the wise counsellor, for rhetoric with its
sounding brass and its sophistries fascinates public regard, 'depreciating
what is important and exalting trivialities, talking in a new-fangled way of
old things and in archaic fashion of new.' He next states his case for the ami-
cable division of the supremacy, and then launches out into eloquent and
enthusiastic praise (hence the later meaning of 'panegyric') of Athens,
showing how from the legendary age of the heroes down to the present she
had deserved well of Greece and had won, and lost, and yet once more was
winning, a supremacy as queen of the sea. He defends her (not very successfully) against the charge of despotism and inhumanity. Then he turns
to Sparta and speaks of Thermopylae and Plataea, and how she has won a
right to military supremacy on land. He then points out how, in spite of her
great size, Persia had never been able to hold her ground before Greek
courage, and he cites Marathon and Cunaxa. Then he returns to the burden
of his lamentations against the civil wars of Greece, and bids his imaginary
hearers think of the glorious and exhilarating poetry, such as that of Homer

461

and of Aeschylus, that describes the victories of Greeks over barbarians, and reminds them (forgetting the *Seven against Thebes*, but otherwise reminding them with justice) that no great Greek poetry described the quarrels of Hellenes with each other. And very justly, too, he inveighs against the shameful peace lately dictated by the Great King, and once more turns with rapture to the visions of a united Hellas and of the conquest of Asia Minor by the Greeks. One of these visions was indeed in a fashion realized, but under a hegemony of which he at that time did not dream.

The *Panegyric* was applauded as a triumph of literary oratory, but the visionary politics of Isocrates were not taken seriously by the Athenian public, and even by men like Phocion they were probably regarded as of such stuff as dreams are made of. Athens and Sparta could never share hegemony.

The *Areopagitic Oration* (after which Milton named his famous treatise on the liberty of the Press) was written *c.* 355, after the so-called Social War, in which Athens had lost some of her chief subject-allies. It was not spoken, but is addressed to the Athenian Ecclesia. After warning the Athenians against their love of money and display and their arrogant self-conceit, and urging a return to simplicity and manliness, he points out the perils that threaten them, and then states (what must have excited many a smile) that the only means of safety is to restore the old Solonian and Cleisthenic democracy and to revive the supreme authority of the ancient and aristocratic court of the Areopagus. In 346, when a peace (that of Philocrates) had been made with Philip, Isocrates, as we have seen, addressed him a letter. 'This is,' he says, 'no sudden and passing whim of an imbecile old man, but a belief that I have held all my life. The hour is now come. Under thy leadership Hellas shall conquer Persia.' But he entreats Philip to prove that he is *not* plotting against the liberties of Greece.

What Isocrates thought of Philip's rapid acquisition of Hellenic cities and of the fate of the Phocians it is not easy to discover. Whether the tidings of Chaeroneia did cause, as Milton asserts, the death of the 'old man eloquent,' and whether it was caused by grief or by a sudden access of hopeful enthusiasm, are questions that have received very diverse answers.

### Aeschines

Of Aeschines, the great rival of Demosthenes, we possess only three orations – that against Timarchus, that on the *Embassy*, and that against

462

*Fig. 128  Demosthenes*

Ctesiphon. All three are directed against Demosthenes. After the failure of his attack on Ctesiphon, who had proposed that Demosthenes should be presented with a golden crown in the great theatre at the festival of the Dionysia, Aeschines, not having gained a fifth of the votes, was heavily fined, and escaped to Rhodes, where he founded a school of rhetoric. He died at Samos in 314.

## Demosthenes

Many of the facts of the life of Demosthenes have already been related, for his rhetorical activity is intimately connected with the political events of the last period that we have considered. For some time after the departure of Alexander for the East in 334 we hear comparatively little of him. The *cause célèbre* of the Golden Crown was decided in 330. We possess the speeches of both orators, and can listen, as it were, to the very tones of the passionate denunciations that they thundered at each other. The speech of Aeschines, with its scathing review of the life of Demosthenes, is so irresistibly eloquent that, like his audience at Rhodes, to whom he recited it, we can hardly believe it possible that it should have failed – until we read the reply of Demosthenes, which, if it does not impress us so much with its sincerity and straightforwardness, is incomparably greater in eloquence.

In 324 the general Harpalus, whom Alexander had left to administer the satrapy of Babylon, having revolted, passed over to Greece with a fleet of thirty ships and much treasure and endeavoured to incite the Greek cities to join him. Harpalus was murdered, and 700 talents of his money were seized by the Athenians to be handed over to Alexander. Half of the money disappeared, and Demosthenes was condemned of theft or of gross negligence. He was imprisoned, but escaped, and lived in Troezen and Aegina till Alexander's death, when he was recalled. But Antipater, Alexander's proxy in Macedonia, crushed the Greeks at the battle of Crannon (322) and Demosthenes fled. He was overtaken by Antipater's emissaries on the islet of Calaureia, near Troezen, where he had taken sanctuary. When arrested he poisoned himself.

In the oratory of Demosthenes, as in that of Cicero, there is nothing of the sublime. Its characteristics are passionate intensity, dauntless courage in attack, unrivalled skill in defence, and an incomparable mastery over words. He used a language free, natural, personal, direct, perfectly plain and unaffected, entirely untainted by the rhetoric of the schools. He depended, not on an elegant and decorated diction, but on force, vigour, and dramatic emphasis – such as he meant when he said that the three things necessary for the orator were *Acting* (*hypokrisis*), *Acting* and *Acting*. A few lines from his *Third Philippic*, though they suffer much in translation, may illustrate this. How different his feeling about the fratricidal wars of the Greek states was from that of Isocrates is very evident from the opening words.

'Ay, and what is more, you know well that whatever wrongs were done to Greeks by the Spartans or by us were at any rate done by genuine sons of Greece, and one might regard it just in the same way as when a son who by birth is the genuine heir to a large property indulges in some pursuit not admirable or right. Such conduct in itself certainly deserves to be blamed and reprimanded; but one cannot regard it as if he did not belong to the family and were not the heir, whereas if a servant, or some supposititious child, were to destroy or spoil what was not his own, good heavens, how much more readily would every one declare that he was a scamp and deserved their anger! But concerning Philip and his doings they have no such feelings – and yet he is not only not a Greek and no connection of the Greeks, but not even a barbarian of any country of which one can speak with respect. He is just a pestilential Macedonian – of a country from which one never could buy even a decent slave.'

The following passage is, in the original, a good specimen of his vigour and his pugnacity – and perhaps also of his ingenuity, for in many of the manuscripts the word which I have translated by 'hireling' is in this passage accented on the first syllable, *místhōtos*, whereas the accent generally falls on the last, and this seems to confirm the truth of the story that Demosthenes purposely mispronounced the word, and that the audience, far more shocked at the false accent than at any iniquity of Aeschines, shouted out *misthōtós* – thus at the same time correcting the orator's mispronunciation and answering his question as he desired.

'As for what then took place, there is much more that I could say. But I think I have said enough – perhaps more than enough. And it is his fault if I have, for he so drenched me with the dregs of his own rascality and that of his rascally conduct that I was obliged to clear myself before those who are too young to remember the facts. But even before I said a word you yourselves were probably thoroughly disgusted – those of you who knew about his hireling servility. *He*, forsooth, calls it intimacy and friendship, and on some late occasion spoke about my 'insulting his *friendship* with Alexander.' Where did he get it from? How did he earn it? *I* wouldn't call him a 'friend' either of Philip or Alexander – I'm not such an idiot – unless one ought to call reapers, or others who do anything for hire, the 'friends' of those who hire them. No! I call you a hireling – formerly of Philip and now of Alexander; and so do all these gentlemen. If you don't believe me, ask them! – or, rather, I'll do it for you. . . . Which, O Athenians, do you think Aeschines to be – Alexander's *friend* or his *hireling*? . . . You hear what they say!' (*De Corona*, 242.)

### Later Philosophers

The greatest teachers, knowing that truth, as Plato says, 'cannot be communicated like other branches of learning,' have ever been more anxious to intimate, and to enforce by word and deed, deep-lying principles than to formulate doctrines and build up systems. Of such nature was the teaching of Socrates. He wrote nothing, and it is probable that the underlying principles that he enforced were intimated by him in a much less systematized form than that in which they are presented by Plato. It was therefore natural that his followers, when they began (as was inevitable) to formulate and systematize, should split up into various schools. The doctrines of these diverse schools of post-Socratic philosophy, being intimately connected with the later philosophy, that of the Romans and the early Christian ages, lie beyond the scope of this volume. I shall therefore only say a few words on the subject.

Besides Plato, Socrates' greatest disciple, who, as we have seen, founded the Academic school, should be mentioned Eucleides, Aristippus, and Antisthenes, who founded respectively the Megaric (Dialectic), the Cyrenaic, and the Cynic schools. To the Cynics belonged Diogenes, and the Cynic philosophy led towards Stoicism, which was founded by Zeno of Cyprus about the same time as Epicurus of Samos was proclaiming his philosophy (*c.* 300).

Far more famous (at least in mediaeval and modern times) than any of these philosophies was that of Aristotle and his followers, the so-called

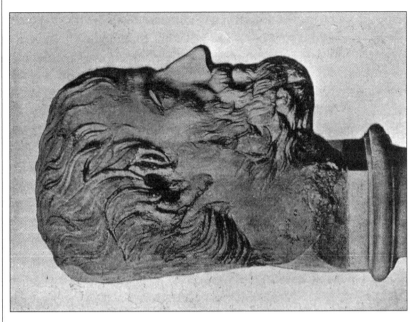

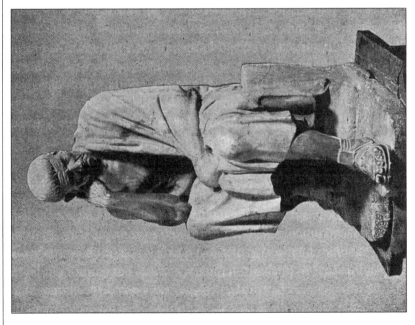

*Fig. 129 Aristotle*

467

Peripatetics. Aristotle was born at Stageiros (or Stageira), a town of Chalcidice, which was destroyed by Philip, but rebuilt, at the philosopher's request, by Alexander. In 342 Aristotle was invited by Philip to act as tutor to the young Alexander, and remained at Pella till 335, when he settled at Athens, and for thirteen years taught at the Lyceum. He died in Euboea in 322.

SECTION B: LYSIPPUS, HELLENISTIC SCULPTURE

Scopas and Praxiteles, as we have seen, flourished from about 390 to 350. Towards the end of this period we hear of Leochares, who together with Scopas was employed by Artemisia to supply sculpture for the Mausoleum. He is of interest also because he was the designer of the gold and ivory images of Philip II and his family which were erected in the Philippeion, a hall built at Olympia by the Macedonian king. Moreover, the bust of Isocrates (Fig. 125) may be founded on his statue of the orator which was erected at Eleusis, and the well-known group of Ganymede and an eagle, copies of which are to be seen in museums (the best of them in the Vatican), was probably his work. Considered as a realistic production, the latter offends by the evident impossibility that the bird could lift such a weight – though Professor Gardner tells us that 'boy and eagle strain upward in an aspiration like that which Goethe expresses in his poem of Ganymede' – and regarded as a work of art, it seems to fail entirely in satisfying one's imaginative faculty. It is doubtless clever, but surely rather too much of the *tableau vivant* type.

## Lysippus

Somewhat younger than Leochares was Lysippus, whose name one associates with Alexander, for it is said that the monarch allowed no sculptor but Lysippus and no painter but Apelles to portray him – that is, probably, other artists were denied a sitting after having once 'failed to render,' as Plutarch says, 'his manly and leonine aspect while trying to represent the bend in his neck and the emotional glance of his eyes.' Lysippus was of the school of Sicyon – the athletic school of Polycleitus – but his ideal of the manly form was more lithe and slender than that of his predecessor, with a smaller head (an eighth instead of a seventh of the total height). It is said that he put a coin in his money-box whenever he received payment for a commission, and at his death 1500 coins were found within it; and yet

*Fig. 130  Aphrodite of Melos*

until lately the only extant statue believed to be a copy of a work of his was the *Apoxyomenos* of the Vatican (an athlete scraping himself with a strigil), to which was sometimes added the bust of Alexander found at Alexandria and now in the British Museum (Fig. 124), the best of many such portraits. But the French excavations at Delphi brought to light an exceedingly fine statue of the athlete Agias, probably a marble replica of a bronze original – a much finer work of art than the *Apoxyomenos*. The face, though not highly intellectual, is of a far nobler type than that of any known statue by Polycleitus or Scopas, or than that of the Praxitelean Hermes, and the skill shown in the splendid nude figure displays the great artist, not merely the anatomical expert. Lysippus produced several works of enormous size, among them a colossal Zeus at Tarentum, sixty feet high, and a Sungod (Helios, or Baal) in a four-horse chariot at Rhodes – anticipating the Colossus of Rhodes, which was by his pupil, Chares – and a huge seated Heracles, of which he made a minute copy as a table ornament for Alexander – a statuette which, if we are to believe Martial, afterwards belonged to Hannibal and Sulla.

A statue of Alexander by Lysippus, described by Plutarch, represented him (somewhat as in the bust, Fig. 124) gazing upwards with the head a little bent to the left (in consequence of a wound), a defect, Plutarch tells us, imitated by some of his successors. The 'leonine' face with its over-hanging mane of hair and its 'swimming' eyes, in whose depths passion and madness seem to lurk, became a type which long pervaded sculpture, so that not a few extant works of the later period are either evidently meant for portraits of Alexander or contain reminiscences of the type created by Lysippus; and doubtless Apelles, whose famous picture of Alexander represented him wielding a thunderbolt, helped to confirm this type. A magnificent work of art which is doubtless a product of the school of Lysippus – possibly even a work of Lysippus himself, who is known to have made groups representing Alexander in battle and hunting with his companions – is the so-called Alexander Sarcophagus (Fig. 131). It was found, together with others,[1] at Sidon, and is now in the Istanbul Museum. On it 'we seem

---

[1] *E.g.* the 'Tomb of the Satrap,' and the 'Lycian Sarcophagus' (of about 420 perhaps), with Attic influence, such as we see in the Nereïd Monument (p. 405), and a sarcophagus with eighteen most beautiful female figures, 'the Mourners,' reminding one of Athenian tombstones. The Alexander Sarcophagus is of Pentelic (Attic) marble. It is not supposed to have contained his body. A sarcophagus in the British Museum (brought from Alexandria) was once thought, but is no longer thought, to have claims to this honour.

to recognize the features of more than one Macedonian warrior besides Alexander himself, and their peculiar helmets and arms are rendered with accuracy, as well as the swathings and drapery' – and the *braccae* or *anaxyrides* – 'of their Persian opponents.' It is probably the best preserved of all monuments of antiquity. The colours with which the marble was stained are still plainly visible. 'No one,' says Professor Gardner, 'who has not seen this sarcophagus can realize the effect produced by a correct and artistic application of colour to sculpture.'

Another product of this period, and one which illustrates the tendency towards bigness and theatrical pose, is the well-known and often much-admired group of Niobe and her children. The original was brought to Rome, probably from Cilicia, about 35 B.C. Pliny describes it and tells us that it is 'doubtful whether it was by Praxiteles or by Scopas.' It is most evidently by neither. Although free from the contortions of later Hellenistic art, it shows neither in its forms nor faces nor drapery nor attitudes the characteristics of the best Greek sculpture. The group probably stood, not in the pediment of a temple, but on some rocky elevation against a background, and possibly statues of the vengeful deities, Apollo and Artemis, were placed on some higher level. Good ancient copies of fourteen of these figures are to be seen in the Niobe Hall of the Uffizi at Florence. Some of them were dug up at Rome in 1583, and may possibly be the statues seen by Pliny.

## Hellenistic Sculpture

It may be useful to add a few words indicating the main features of later Greek sculpture. After the conquests of Alexander Greek art died down to the root, though it did not become entirely extinct, in the mother-country, but its scions, planted in Eastern soil, flourished exceedingly. The religious characteristic of old Greek statuary, the main function of which was to produce images of the gods and heroes, has been to a large extent lost. Sculpture is now used a great deal for portraiture, and for personifications such as of Wealth and Peace and Fortune and of countries and cities,[1] and

---

[1] Europe and Asia are figured on the little Arbela tablet (given in my *Quintus Curtius*), and a very beautiful seated female figure representing the 'City Antioch,' by a pupil of Lysippus, is given in Gardner's *Handbook*. In earlier art a river was often personified by a river-god (or bull), and a city by its tutelary deity; but that was an essentially different method.

Fig. 131  The 'Alexander Sarcophagus'

the tendency towards the colossal, already observed in Lysippus, becomes stronger. This is especially noticeable at the two great centres of Hellenistic art, Rhodes and Pergamon. In Rhodes, according to Pliny, more than a hundred huge statues existed, of which the greatest, the famous bronze Colossus, made by Chares, was 105 feet high. It represented the Sun-god (see coin 13, Coins Plate VI). The well-known groups of Laocoön and the Farnese Bull were brought to Rome from Rhodes, and are wonderful illustrations, though *comparatively* small, of later Rhodian work, with its Michelangelesque mastery over huge masses of material and its ostentatious display of anatomical knowledge. In connection with this taste for the gigantic may be mentioned the bronze equestrian statues of, perhaps, Castor and Pollux on Monte Cavallo at Rome, which are evidently a Greek work and of this period – although an inscription (of the age of Constantine) attributes them to Pheidias and Praxiteles!

The other great Hellenistic school of sculpture was the Pergamene. Attalus, the third king of Pergamon, the Troad city which was later the literary rival of Alexandria, erected many statues and groups to commemorate his victories, especially those over the Gauls (Galatians), whom he had forced to settle down in the province henceforth known as Galatia. Many of the bases of these sculptures have been discovered, and from the way in which the feet of the statues have been carefully cut out of the pedestal it is certain that the figures were carried away to Rome or Constantinople. One of these – or possibly only a copy of the original bronze – is the *Dying Gaul* (in the Capitoline Museum at Rome), formerly called the *Dying Gladiator*. Other sculptures of smaller size, representing battles of Greeks with Persians, Athenians with Amazons, and Greeks with Gauls, were placed by Attalus on the Athenian Acropolis. The son of Attalus, Eumenes, made Pergamon famous by means of the enormous base (100 feet square) on which, surrounded by a colonnade, stood the altar of Zeus. On this altar-base there were friezes whose huge contorted figures represented the battle of the Giants against Zeus and all the divinities, major and minor, of the Greek Pantheon, aided by numerous non-Hellenic deities and by various demi-gods, each of the great divinities attended by his or her sacred animal – a 'writhing mass of giants with whom their divine antagonists are inextricably entangled,' reminding one of the horribly impressive giant-frescoes by Giulio Romano in the Mantuan Palazzo del Te. The weather-worn remains of these Pergamene sculptures are now at Berlin.

Of the many other extant statues that are attributed to the earlier

Hellenistic age, or the preceding period, perhaps the finest are the Aphrodite of Melos, the Apollo Belvedere, and the Nike of Samothrace (Figs. 130, 132). The Aphrodite was discovered on the island of Melos in a grotto, in which also a fragment of a pedestal was found bearing a few words of an inscription that contained the last part of the artist's name, viz. 'sander' or 'xander,' and gave Antioch on the Maeander as his home. The sculptor is unknown, but from the character of the writing the inscription was believed to date from about 100. However, it is quite uncertain whether this fragment ever belonged to the pedestal of the statue, and it has now disappeared. To judge from the statue itself one cannot but believe that it dates from a much earlier period. 'For a conception of the female figure at once so dignified and so beautiful,' says Professor E. A. Gardner, 'we have to go back to the sculpture of the Parthenon, and we see the same breadth and simplicity of modelling in the drapery as in the nude. . . . The sculptor who made this Aphrodite must have lived in spirit in the age of Pheidias.'

The Apollo Belvedere is by some attributed to Leochares, merely by reason of some supposed similarity (perhaps in technique) to the Ganymede. This attribution I find quite impossible to accept. Modern criticism has rightly pointed out that the Apollo shows what might be called a degradation of Praxitelean grace and a loss of masculine vigour. The attitude is somewhat theatrical, and the modelling of the nude is smoothed away so much and the limbs are made so slender that we have an almost painful idealism and unreality. But in spite of all this it remains unquestionably one of the most magically beautiful of all Greek statues, although only a marble copy of a bronze original.

The Victory (Nike) was discovered on the island of Samothrace, and is now (headless, alas! and armless) in the Louvre. The trophy was erected by Demetrius Poliorcetes to commemorate a naval victory won in 306. The goddess – a magnificent figure with wind-swept draperies like the Nike of Paeonius, but more stately – stands on the marble prow of a warship with her wings outspread, reminding one of the vision of Dante on the shore of the Purgatorial Mount – the angel standing on the vessel with his snow-white wings outspread as sails,

*Trattando l'aere con l'eterne penne.*

*Fig. 132  The Nike of Samothrace*

## Note A

### Greek Temples

In order to avoid the distraction that would be caused by frequently interrupting the narrative, or by dealing with the subject in several widely separated Sections, I have relegated to this Note a few details concerning the chief Greek temples of different ages. The chronology is, of course, not always certain. The Index and List of Illustrations should be consulted. Pictures are given of thirteen of these temples.

(1) The Heraion (Temple of Hera), at Olympia, Doric: 6×16. Built perhaps *c.* 900. The stone foundations (probably the most ancient relic of a Greek temple extant) were originally surmounted by walls of sunburnt brick and wooden pillars. Stone columns were gradually substituted, which accounts for the fact that, to judge from the remains of thirty-six of the columns and of twenty capitals, they were almost all different. Pausanias saw one old wooden pillar still remaining. Nothing has been found of an entablature, frieze, etc. The Hermes of Praxiteles was found in this temple, buried in the clay of the sunburnt bricks.

(2) Temple of Apollo, Corinth. Doric: 6×15. Probably built by Periander, *c.* 600. Seven monolith columns of rough limestone, originally overlaid with yellowish stucco, still stand and bear a part of the architrave. They are finely profiled, with a noticeable entasis, but are shorter than usual in proportion to the thickness, the height (23½ feet) being only 7⅔ modules (semi-diameters), and the capitals are remarkably massive.

(3) Temple of Apollo, Delphi. Built to replace the ancient temple, burnt down in 548. The architect was Spintheros of Corinth. A fourth of the expense was to be borne by the Treasury of Delphi, and the rest was raised by subscription through all Hellas (even Amasis of Egypt contributed). But the Alcmaeonidae undertook the construction (thus probably saving the Treasury much expense), and carried it out in a more splendid manner than was stipulated in the contract, using Parian marble in many parts instead of poros or tufa. The remains show that the columns were of white tufa coated with stucco, and that the outer colonnades were Doric and the inner Ionic. The pediments contained figures of Apollo and other deities and the nine Muses. To the architrave were attached golden shields, offerings of the Athenians after the battle of Marathon. In the vestibule were engraved the sayings of the Seven Sages – *e.g.* 'Know thyself,' etc.

(4) Temple of Athene (or Aphaia), Aegina, in the northeastern corner of the island. Doric: 6×12. Built perhaps before 500. The pediment sculptures were erected probably soon after the battle of Salamis. Twenty-two columns are still standing, bearing the entablature. They are of yellow limestone covered with stucco. The sculptures of the pediments were discovered in 1811, and bought by the Crown Prince of Bavaria. They were restored and reconstructed by Thorwaldsen, the great Danish sculptor, and are preserved in the Glyptothek at Munich. An inscription excavated in 1901 seems to show that the temple was sacred to Aphaia, a 'local goddess with affinities to Artemis.'

(5) Temples at Selinus and Acragas (Sicily). The remains of seven ancient Doric colonnaded temples, some of great size, built probably soon after the foundation of the city, c. 628, are to be seen at Selinus, in South-western Sicily, where a wilderness of enormous ruins covers the acropolis and an adjacent hill. The greatest of these temples, called the Apollonion, was almost as large as the huge Olympieion at Acragas, and was, similarly, not finished when the city was taken by the Carthaginians in 409. Some of the still unfinished column drums are to be seen in a quarry three miles distant. The most ancient of the Selinus temples had the unusual proportions 6× 17. Many of its huge columns are lying in a row side by side, just as they fell when a great earthquake (it is not known when) overthrew all the temples of Selinus and some at Acragas. Some very ancient metopes from the frieze of this temple are preserved at Palermo.

At Acragas (Lat. Agrigentum, Ital. Girgenti) many splendid temples were erected by Thero after the victory over the Carthaginians at Himera in 480. A portion of the still older Athene temple is yet to be seen forming a part of a church inside the city, but the temples erected by Thero lined the south city wall, and from their lofty plateau overlooked the sea. Of these the unfinished Olympieion was the greatest Greek temple in existence, as its widespread ruins testify. The magnificent 'Concordia' temple (Doric: 6×13) is one of the finest and most perfect Greek temples extant (Fig. 76), and the so-called temple of Lacinian Hera (also 6×13), of which many columns still stand on an elevated site, is one of the most impressive of all ruins. The name 'Concordia' is due to a Latin inscription which has nothing to do with the temple, and the 'Lacinian' temple got its name from a mistake made by Pliny, who states that Zeuxis painted for Agrigentum a picture of Helen of Troy, whereas it was painted for the temple of Hera on the Lacinian promontory (see paragraph 11 of this Note).

(6) Temple of Apollo at Didyma (now Hieronda), near Miletus, called the Temple of the Branchidae, who were the priestly family in charge. It was famed for its antiquity and wealth and for its oracle. The original temple perhaps dated from the early days of Ionian migration (say about 1000). In 603, before the battle of Carchemish, Pharaoh Necho presented his cuirass to the temple. Also Croesus made costly golden offerings (Hdt. i. 92). The building was plundered and burnt by the Persians after the capture of Miletus in 494 (possibly without the consent of Darius, who, as a letter of his to the satrap of Ionia proves, felt great reverence for this oracle of Apollo). The Branchidae were accused of having surrendered the temple and treasure, and to save them from the vengeance of the Ionians Xerxes transplanted them to Sogdiana (Turkestan), not far from Lake Aral, where they founded a Greek town, some 2000 miles distant from Miletus. But about 170 years later Alexander, when greeted on his victorious campaign by this little Greek colony, revived the accusation and massacred every man, woman, and child – one of the foulest deeds that his insanity perpetrated. The Branchidae temple was rebuilt in the age of Alexander, and probably by his orders, and was said to be the greatest Greek temple in Asia Minor – so great that it could not be roofed![1]

But by far the most ancient relics of Didyma are some of the great seated figures which lined the 'sacred way' from the temple to the sea (about two miles). These date from about 550. Several are in the British Museum (see Fig. 58, and Hdt. i. 92, 157, v. 36, vi. 19).

(7) Temple of Artemis, Ephesus – about a mile north-east from the ancient city. The *first* (perhaps really the third) temple was burnt by the Cimmerians about 678. The *second*, which during the siege of Ephesus by Croesus was attached to the city by a rope (see p. 207), was finished during his reign and received many gifts from him, including the sculptured drums of some of the columns, one of which is in the British Museum (Fig. 52). The huge Ionic front columns rested, it is thought, on great square blocks which brought their shaft bases on a level with the floor of the temple, and these blocks, as well as the lowest drums of the columns, were decorated with bas-reliefs. This second temple – the only Greek temple spared by Xerxes – was burnt down (by Herostratus – merely, it is said, in order to perpetuate his name!) on the very night when Alexander the Great was born (356). The *third* was begun at once and finished about 300. Alexander

---

[1] *Editor's note.* The Temple at Didyma has been partially reconstructed.

offered (*c.* 334) to bear the whole expense if he were allowed to have the fact recorded by an inscription; but his offer was declined with the rather clever excuse that 'it was not meet for one deity to build a temple to another.' (No such scruples seem to have deterred Croesus!) This third Ephesian temple was a copy of the second (see sculptured drum, Fig. 120), but on a more magnificent scale, and was the largest temple of the Greek world. It was regarded as one of the Seven Wonders, and continued in use (see Acts xix.) till the abolition of paganism.

(8) Temple of Apollo at Phigaleia, or Bassae ('The Ravines,' a village near Phigaleia, in Arcadia), stands on a fine site among mountainous solitudes. It was probably built to enclose an ancient shrine of Apollo Epikouros ('the Helper'), and was, says Pausanias, erected in hope of averting the Great Plague of 430 – and seemingly not in vain, for Thucydides says the disease did not spread to the Peloponnese. The architect was Ictinus, who built the Parthenon. It is Doric, 6 × 15, but the inner temple had ten Ionic and *one* Corinthian column (now lost). What is unusual, it faces north and south; but the inmost shrine (probably the ancient sanctuary around which the temple was built) had its door to the east, so that the image of the god faced the rising sun. The great bronze statue of Apollo was taken by Megalopolis. It was replaced by a marble statue, of which fragments, as well as twenty-three tablets of the frieze, are in the British Museum. In spite of earthquakes about thirty of the thirty-eight external columns are standing.

(9) The Temple of Segesta. The Sicilian city of Segesta (Greek Egesta) was situated in the mountainous north-west coast of Sicily. It was originally the chief city of the Sicilian Elymi (see p. 147), who had a town and a great temple on Mount Eryx, a promontory some 2000 feet above the sea, dedicated to Aphrodite (or rather to Astarte, the Phoenician goddess). But Greek influence afterwards prevailed, as is testified by a magnificent Doric temple that now stands in majestic solitude among the hills, not far from the ancient site of Egesta. Its columns are of rough stone without flutings, and the fact that they were never finished gives us a clue to the date of the temple. The cessation of the work was probably due to the troubles caused (about 410) by the quarrel between Segesta and Selinus, which ended in Segesta calling on Carthage for aid and in the destruction of Selinus and the establishment of Carthaginian supremacy in Western Sicily.

(10) The Temples at Paestum, in Southern Italy. Poseidonia, called Paestum by the Romans, was a colony of Sybaris, founded *c.* 524. Of its

three Doric temples that of Poseidon ($6 \times 14$, built about 450) is by far the finest, rivalling the Parthenon and the 'Concordia' in its splendid proportions. The so-called 'Basilica' is unusually broad ($9 \times 18$). It is perhaps more ancient, but the architecture is not so perfect. It was divided down the middle by columns, the two portions having probably been sacred to different deities. The temple of Demeter, as it is called, is less massive than the Poseidon temple, and the columns have an exaggerated entasis, but it is a splendid ruin.

(11) Temple of Hera Lacinia, near Croton. One solitary column (Fig. 40) remains of this great Doric temple, built probably about 480–450 to replace the ancient temple which was for centuries the first landmark that greeted the Greek on his way to the far West. Here he generally landed and made sacrifice. The marble-roofed temple was surrounded by pine-groves where were erected statues of Olympic victors. It was the assembly-place of the Greeks of Greater Hellas, and festivals were celebrated here, with athletic games. It possessed great riches – amongst other things a pillar of gold and a picture of Helen by Zeuxis. Hannibal here slaughtered 2000 Italian mercenaries and put up a brass tablet (used by Polybius) to recount his victories. In A.D. 1600 the temple was still almost intact, but was demolished by a bishop, Lucifero by name. Two columns were left. One was overthrown by earthquake in 1638.

(12) Temple of Hera at Samos. Of this, the greatest Greek temple known to Herodotus, only one Ionic column remains. It stands not far from the sea-shore about four miles from the ancient city of Samos. The temple was finished by Polycrates and burnt by the Persians, but rebuilt in the time of Herodotus.

(13) The Parthenon is regarded as the ideal of Doric architecture. For details as to its proportions, its sculptures, etc., see Chapter 4, Section B, and Chapter 6, Section A.

(14) The Erechtheion is in a depression on the north side of the Acropolis plateau. It stood incomplete for many years and was finished (as proved by an inscription in the British Museum) *c.* 409. It is considered a model of Ionic style, but is of very unusual form, being as different from the ordinary Greek temple as San Vitale is from the ordinary Christian basilica. It is only about 66 feet long, and has two side porches, as well as the eastern portico. The southern of these porches is that of the 'Maidens' or Caryatides (one of these Maidens is of terracotta, the original being in the British Museum). The unusual form of the building was evidently

Fig. 133  Temple of Athene Nike

Fig. 134  Erechtheion

occasioned by the fact that it included several distinct old Ionian (Athenian) shrines – that of Erechtheus and that of Athene Polias and perhaps others. Erechtheus, the old Athenian snake-hero-god, was identified with Poseidon, and in early times shared with Athene the 'house of Erechtheus' (mentioned by Homer). The lair of his snake, and the hole made by Poseidon's trident in the rock, and the olive planted by Athene, were all shown in the old Erechtheion, which was burnt by the Persians in 480. Athene's olive thereupon put out a long new shoot within two days, and the new temple was promptly taken in hand. The question of the old site is puzzling, for between the Parthenon and the Erechtheion, and almost contiguous to it, have been discovered the foundations of the ancient temple of Athene Polias (the 'Hecatompedos,' the 'hundred-foot' temple, built, or more probably turned into a Doric temple, by Peisistratus). If, as some assert, this old temple was rebuilt on the same site after the Persian invasion the Caryatid porch could not have been erected without making a breach in the wall of the new building, and thus utterly ruining the view of the porch and forming a most ugly and ridiculous complex. It is easier to believe that the Erechtheion replaced this old temple (whose site was left unused), and that it also included the ancient shrines in the precinct.

(15) The Theseion, the best preserved of all ancient Greek temples, stands on an elevation north-west of the Acropolis. It is smaller than the Parthenon (*i.e.* 6×13), and the columns of Pentelic marble are somewhat slenderer. The sculptures of the pediments have entirely disappeared. Only the metopes on the east front, and four of the adjoining fields on each side, were sculptured. These eighteen reliefs represent the labours of Heracles and of Theseus, and the frieze of the sanctuary (which, as in the Parthenon, is continuous, like an Ionic frieze) depicts the contest of Centaurs and Lapithae, in which Theseus had a part. It seems, therefore, very probable that the temple is, as till lately has been universally believed, the building in which Cimon deposited the bones of Theseus. But because Pausanias seems to ignore it and speaks of a temple of Hephaestus, and because the architecture seems to be as late as that of the Parthenon, some writers have asserted that it cannot be Cimon's 'Theseion.'

(16) The Olympieion at Athens was begun (about 530) by Peisistratus (Thuc. ii. 15). This original temple was Doric. It was planned on such a vast scale that at the height of her power Athens never ventured to complete it. Aristotle mentions it as a 'work of despotic grandeur.' In the year 174

*Fig. 135 The Acropolis from near the Olympieion (See List of Illustrations)*

Antiochus Epiphanes, king of Syria, undertook to finish it. The fifteen huge Corinthian columns still standing (56½ feet high) may date from this period. Sulla (85 B.C.) when he plundered Athens carried off some of the smaller (Doric?) columns. Augustus forwarded the work (described by Livy as the 'only temple on earth worthy of the greatness of the god'), but it was not finished until the reign of Hadrian (A.D. 120). It had 100 columns and was 353½ feet in length.

(17) Temple of Zeus at Olympia. Built c. 470 by the people of Elis from the spoils of Pisa, which they had destroyed a century before (c. 572, when they finally won from the Pisatans the supremacy in the games). It was a Doric temple (6×13), 210 feet long, with a sanctuary, aisled by two rows of columns, containing the famous statue by Pheidias of Zeus Olympios. Many of the columns and some capitals are still to be seen, lying where they fell when overthrown by earthquake. For the sculptures of pediments and the statue of Zeus, etc., see Chapter VI, Section A.

(18) Temple of Athene on Sunion. Cape Sunion (Lat. Sunium), now Cape Colonna, is the steep promontory, about 200 feet high, in which Attica terminates. The earliest temple on 'sacred Sunion,' as Homer calls it, was dedicated to Poseidon (at least Aristophanes calls Poseidon 'the god invoked on Sunion'), but, as at Athens, the sea-god was forced to share his shrine with Athene (or possibly to allow his shrine to be overshadowed by her larger temple). Eleven Doric columns of Laurion marble still stand. The temple was like the Theseion, but somewhat smaller, and was built about the same time. Some very weather-worn sculptured metopes possibly once depicted the feats of Theseus.

(19) Temple of Athene Nike (i.e. Athene in her character as Victory), sometimes wrongly called the temple of 'Wingless Victory,' is a small early Ionic shrine (only 27×18 feet) of Pentelic marble, with a portico of four columns at each end. It was built on an elevated platform of rock to the right of the Propylaea, as one ascends, probably after the original great plan of the Propylaea had been given up (i.e. during the Peloponnesian War, c. 425). In 1684 it was entirely demolished by the Turks, who used the material to build a bastion. In 1835 the fragments were carefully collected and the shrine was reconstructed. Of the frieze (about 18 inches high) some blocks remain in the rebuilt edifice. Others were brought to England by Lord Elgin. The frieze-reliefs represent an assemblage of gods and contests between Greeks and Persians and between Greeks and Greeks (perhaps in allusion to Plataea). A balustrade surrounded the shrine. On it were sculptured

figures of Athene and of winged Victories (Nikai). Fragments of these reliefs are in the Museum at Athens. Some of them are of great beauty, especially one representing a Victory binding on her sandals. The delicate, almost transparent, drapery is much admired.

## Note B

### Dress

To follow with any certainty, after the lapse of millenniums, the ever-varying fashions of dress is impossible. The differences that prevail on the subject among antiquarians are mainly due to the fact that fashions are apt to change very rapidly, to revert to old types, to develop new combinations, and to exist simultaneously, even in close contact. But some well-marked characteristics are noticeable at certain periods of Greek history.

(1) In Minoan and 'Mycenaean' civilization, to judge from pictorial evidence (Figs. 5, 10, 16, etc.), the men when at war generally wore nothing at all, and at other times often only a sort of bathing-drawers garment, and footgear curiously like 'puttees.' Their hair was often built up into a high coiffure with long pigtails, and in many paintings they have extraordinarily slender waists, as if they laced tightly; or perhaps they gained their slimness by such gymnastic training as was necessary for the Cretan matadors (Fig. 17). The women had strangely modern-looking costumes – heavy, deeply flounced, embroidered skirts, and (when the bust was not nude) puff-sleeved jackets or blouses (often very *décolletées*). The hair was elaborately coiled and curled.

(2) In Homer we find quite a different dress, which we may call Achaean, evidently of northern origin. It differs essentially from the Minoan and Mycenaean composite sewn dress, and consists (with the possible exception of the linen undergarment) of a single piece of cloth, or lighter stuff, fastened by brooches, or safety-pins (*peronai*, Latin *fibulae*), which were not required, except for ornament, in the older sewn garments. Homer's men wear a *chitōn* (an under-garment, sometimes of thicker coloured stuff, sometimes 'soft and shiny as the skin of a dried onion') and either a kind of mantle called the *pharos* ('thin,' 'silver-white,' 'purple,' 'great') or a warmer cloak, the *chlaina* ('woollen,' 'shaggy,' 'purple'), which was also used at night as a blanket. The *chlaina* was fastened in front by a brooch, as we see from the celebrated passage in which the golden brooch of

Odysseus is described (*Od.* xix. 225). The women have the *chitōn* and the *pharos* ('light,' 'silver-white' – *Od.* v. 230), or else the warmer *peplos*, a long robe fastened with brooches. (A *peplos* with twelve brooches is mentioned in *Od.* xviii. 293.) The brooch, or safety-pin, was perhaps introduced by the northern (Achaean and Dorian) invaders, and was of course necessary for unsewn garments. On the head women in Homer sometimes wear the *krē-demnon*, a kind of scarf or short veil (but long enough to be tied round Odysseus' body – *Od.* v. 346), or a 'covering' (*kalyptrē*), a head-dress often richly ornamented (Hesiod calls it 'daedal').

(3) In the Asia Minor colonies the long linen *chitōn* and ample over-garment were retained by the 'chiton-trailing Ionians,' as Homer calls them, but the Dorians (say about 1100–1000) seem to have introduced into the Peloponnese and Doric colonies a simpler northern style of dress for both sexes, viz. a single square woollen raiment, which took the place of both the linen *chitōn* and the over-garment. This 'Doric chiton' was sleeve-less and simply wrapped round the body horizontally under the armpits and fastened, either with or without flaps, over both shoulders by long dagger-like pins. It was left open at one side (even in the case of women at Sparta), or sometimes fastened with brooches (safety-pins), or confined with a girdle. The Doric fashion does not seem to have found favour at Athens for some time, since the ancient Mycenaean cut-out and sewn dress is still depicted on Attic (Dipylon) pottery of the Dark Age; and also in Hesiod's Boeotia the female dress with protruding 'bustle' still prevailed (see p. 134). Doubtless the anti-Spartan sentiments of the Athenian women were more inclined to perpetuate the old Aegean or Ionian fashions or to introduce the luxurious style from the Ionian colonies – against which, it is said, Solon had to legislate – than to adopt the new and simpler Doric *chitōn*. But even before Solon's age, probably about 750 or 700, a Doric-like *chitōn* with shoulder-flaps and dagger-pins (or is it a cut-out and sewn bodice?), combined with a richly ornamented skirt of the Minoan style, seems to have been in vogue at Athens, as is proved by the very fashionably dressed ladies on the François Vase (Fig. 141).

(4) About 568 the tragic event took place (see p. 169) which forcibly and suddenly changed the fashion in Athens. The women were commanded to give up their long, dangerous stiletto-pins and to adopt the long, soft, and generally crimpled Ionian linen *chitōn*, stitched or buttoned, or fastened with quite small safety-pin brooches, over the shoulder and down the upper arm. Above this was worn a wrap or shawl (*himation*, Latin *pallium*), which

Fig. 136 *Caryatid from Erechtheion*

Fig. 137 *Monument of Lysicrates*

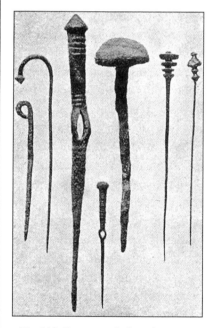

Fig. 138 *Bronze and silver dress-pins*

Fig. 139 *Ionic Chiton and Himation*

*Fig. 140  Doric chiton and dagger-like pins, from a toilet-box in the British Museum.*

at first was small and oblique, fastened over one shoulder and under the other armpit (as in Fig. 37). In course of time this outer garment becomes much larger and more elaborately folded and decorated (like the Roman *toga* or the *palla*). In 'classical' statuary we have generally the long Ionic *chitōn* in the case of women, and a shorter tunic for men, and for both sexes a voluminous outer garment, coarser and heavier in the case of men (see Figs. 98, 107, etc.), as well as the smaller *chlamys*, a scarf or cape that some-times takes the place of the heavier woollen *himation*, and sometimes is carried loosely on the arm or shoulder.

(5) It should, however, be noticed that after the Athenian women were thus forced to adopt the Ionian dress (*c.* 568) the new and more effeminate Eastern *chitōn* seems to have prevailed for a time also among the men, but *only for a time*. Thucydides tells us (i. 6) that 'the Athenians were the first who gave up wearing iron [military garb] and changed to greater luxury. And the elders among the rich classes *not long ago* ceased wearing linen chitons and binding up the coil of the hair on their heads with a fastening of golden cicalas.' Now 'not long ago' would mean about the time of the Persian wars, and it seems that then or a little later the Athenian men reverted to the simpler and (in war) more convenient woollen Doric *chitōn*, or to a short shirt-like linen *chitōn* with a square woollen *himation*, which was the male dress during the Peloponnesian War.

Lastly, it should be remembered that this change to simpler Doric, or

488

*Fig. 141  Early female dress, from the François vase.*

northern, habits which is mentioned by Thucydides meant also the rejection of the loin-cloth of the older Aegean and Ionian civilization, and the
adoption in athletics, as also to a great extent in war, of nudity (except for
armour and tunics), a matter in which, curiously enough, the Greek considered himself far in advance of the Oriental, who regarded nudity as
shameful.

**Note C**

**Coins**

Coins are believed to have been first made in Lydia, where the Mermnadae
kings began, *c.* 700, to punch ingots of *electron* (an alloy of gold and silver)
with official marks (see I, 1) as assurance of full weight. The Greek Asiatic
cities soon adopted the invention and used engraved dies, and the lower
side (obverse) of the coin was adorned with the badge of the state or city
(often an animal) or a tutelary deity or his symbol (see I, 2, 3, 4, where El.
= electron). Croesus probably first used gold and silver coins (staters)
instead of electron, and Darius adopted the practice in his gold *daric* and
silver *siglos* (shekel). Pheidon, the Argive king, is said to have first introduced standard weights and measures into Greece, and the first European

Coins Plate I (c. 700–500)

1. Lydia. El. c. 700. Earliest known coin.
2. Miletus. El. c. 630.
3. Samos. El. c. 525. Reign of Polycrates(?).
4. Old Smyrna (?). El. Phocaean stater. c. 600.
5. Tenedos.
6. Aeolian cyme (?). Before 600.
7. Delos. Before Persian wars.
8. Phocaea. Age of Croesus.
9. Cnidus.
10. Lycia. Before 480.
11. Thasos of Thrace. El.
12. Potidaea.
13. Corcyra.
14. Thebes.
15. Aegina. Age of Pheidon(?). c. 650.
16. Corinth. Age of Periander. c. 600.

*Coins Plate II (c. 600–500)*

1. Athens. About age of Solon. c. 570.
2. Crete. Minotaur and Labyrinth. c. 550.
3. Taras (Tarentum). c. 560.
4. Poseidonia (Paestum). c. 510.
5. Elea (Velia). c. 520.

6. Sybaris. c. 600.
7. Crotona. c. 600.
8. Acragas (Arrigentum).
9. Himera. Before 481.
10. Syracuse. Reign of Gelo. c. 480.

coins were probably struck in Aegina (see I, 15). Archaic coins are frequently bean-shaped. In the earliest specimens the reverse generally bears only an official mark, or incuse square (I, 6), but later both sides bore a type. Before about 500 the eye of the profiled human face is represented (as in some old reliefs) as if fronting one, and the hair consists of small dots and the mouth has the 'archaic smile' (I, 5, 9; II, 1).

In the period *c.* 500–400 very great advance was made in artistic engraving. The Syracusan coins are especially noticeable for their exquisite beauty (II, 10; IV, 6). The Athenian coinage had so great a circulation through Hellas and so high a reputation for weight and purity that it was thought inadvisable to alter the old type. Hence the Athenian coins do not show such technical perfection as one might expect (see III, 7, compared with II, 1).

In the age of Praxiteles and Scopas – that is, during the Spartan and Theban supremacies (400–338) – and in the early times of Alexander the Great numismatic art is considered to have reached its highest perfection. The electron staters of Cyzicus (III, 1) continued to have a large circulation in Asia Minor (especially as medium between Agesilaus and the Persian satraps), and in Greece proper the chief currencies were Theban, Athenian, and Corinthian (Sparta had probably till the third century only iron money, of which no specimen remains). After the victories of Epameinondas and the founding of Messene we find Arcadian and Messenian coinage (V, 11, 12). In Southern Italy and in Sicily during the Dionysian tyranny and under Timoleon many very beautiful coins were struck (VI, 1, 2, etc.). The fine coinage of Philip II of Macedonia is especially noticeable (V, 5, 6, 8). The working of his Thracian mines, and especially of those near his new-named city of Philippi, afforded him a great abundance of gold for his 'royal coinage,' as Horace calls his 'Philips,' and the means to 'break open the gates of cities and undermine rival kings by bribes' (Hor. *Carmina* III, xvi.). Until these golden 'Philips' attained currency the coinage of Greece itself had been mostly silver, gold being coined only on special occasions, when treasure had to be melted down to meet exceptional needs. (Gold staters of Croesus and golden Darics were, however, current in Greece in earlier times.)

The usual type of Alexander's coins (VI, 7, 8) shows a Heracles head with the lion-skin (the features bearing a distinct likeness to those of Alexander), and on the reverse the seated figure of the eagle-bearing Olympian Zeus of Pheidias. After his death and deification some of the states of the empire (*e.g.* Macedonia and Greece) continued for two centuries to issue coins in his name and with his portrait, as Heracles with the lion-skin, and also with the ram-horns of Zeus Ammon, whose son he had claimed to be. In Egypt, Syria, and other provinces the Diadochi (Successors), such as Ptolemy Soter, Seleucus, and Lysimachus, at first struck coins as the vicegerents of Philip III and of the young Alexander IV, the son of Alexander the Great and Roxana (*e.g.* VI, 11); but when they assumed the regal title they began to introduce (as had long been done by Persian kings and satraps) their own portraits – the first in Greek coinage with the exception of Alexander's (who was a god!) – at first timidly under the type of the Heraclean Alexander and then *in propria persona* and no longer under the guise of a deity (VI, 9, 10). For some time the reverse bore the seated Zeus, or some design of a similar motive. The following additional explanations of some of the reproduced coins may be useful.

I, 5. Janiform head, possibly Zeus and Hera. For the religious symbol of the double axe (*Labrys*) see Index; and for Zeus Labrandeus see V, 2.

I, 8. A 'type parlant,' for the Greek word *phokē* means a seal.

I, 9. The lion was symbol of the Asiatic sun-god. On the reverse is Astarte, the Asiatic Aphrodite.

I, 11. A centaur (Thessalian or Thracian?) carrying off a nymph (?).

I, 12. Poseidon Hippios (equestrian) with trident. The horse was sacred to Poseidon, who is said to have created it. The type is very possibly that of Poseidon's image that, according to Herodotus, stood 'in the suburb' of Potidaea (viii. 129).

I, 13. The floral pattern in the sinkings is by some thought to represent the 'Garden of Alcinous' described by Homer (*Od.* vii.). Corcyra (*Kerkyra*, Corfu) was believed to be the Homeric Scherie, the island of the Phaeacians.

I, 14. A Boeotian shield and an incuse at the centre of which is a cross in a circle – the archaic form of *thēta* (first letter of Thebes).

I, 15. Sea-tortoise. Perhaps the oldest extant Greek silver coin. See *Index*, 'Pheidon.'

I, 16. Pegasus and the old letter *koppa*, used anciently for K. Pegasus was captured by Bellerophon at the Corinthian fountain Peirene.

II, 3. The mythical Taras, son of Poseidon and founder of Tarentum, riding on a dolphin. On reverse a sea-horse and scallop-shell.

II, 4. Poseidon.

Coins Plate III (c. 480–400)

1. Cyzicus. El. c. 470.
2. Persia. Gold daric. c. 480.
3. Methymna. c. 480.
4. Ephesus. c. 450.
5. Chios. c. 450.
6. Olynthus. c. 475.
7. Athens. c. 460.
8. Elis. Nike.
9. Elis. Hera head.
10. Elis. Zeus head.
11. Byzantium.
12. Eretria (Euboea).
13. Terina.
14. Neapolis.
15. Thurii. c. 440.

*Coins Plate IV (c. 480–430)*

1. *Etruria (Fiesole?). c. 460.*
2. *Gela. c. 430.*
3. *Himera. c. 450.*
4. *Leontini. c. 475.*
5. *Selinus. c. 450.*
6. *Syracuse. Demareteion. c. 480.*

II, 5. Unknown archaic head; perhaps the river-nymph Hyele, Vele, or Elea (= the glassy stream?). *Cf.* II, 10.

II, 7. Notice the ϘPO instead of KPO.

II, 9. Before the seizure of Himera by Thero of Acragas in 481.

II, 10. The nymph Arethusa, about whose fountain on Ortygia see *Class. Dict.* under 'Alpheus.' An Olympic victory of Gelo is intimated by the Nike and the chariot. *Cf.* IV, 6.

III, 1. Cecrops, the mythical first king of Attica, half man, half serpent, holding olive-branch. The electron staters of Cyzicus had great circulation down to about 380. The usual mint-mark is a tunny-fish.

III, 2. Gold Daric: the Great King with bow and spear.

III, 3. Archaic head of Athene. Helmet ornamented with a Pegasus.

III, 4. The bee was the badge of Ephesus and a symbol connected with the worship of the Ephesian Artemis.

III, 5. Sphinx seated before an amphora. Chios was famous for its wine, and the Sphinx is a symbol of Dionysus, the wine-god.

III, 8. Copied on the medal commemorating Waterloo.

III, 9, 10. Heads of Hera and Zeus. See Note A for Heraion and temple of Zeus at Olympia.

III, 11, 12. The cow represents Io, who crossed by the Bosporus ('Cowford'), and according to one version recovered her human form and gave birth to Epaphus, not in Egypt, but in Euboea. The bird on the cow's back may be Zeus, who in this form guided Hermes to Io in order that the might slay the hundred-eyed monster, Argus.

III, 13. This most beautiful coin of Terina, in Southern Italy, probably represents Nike (Victory). The φ, scarcely visible behind the nape of the neck, is the artist's signature. It is also found on the obverse of III, 15. All the finest coins of Terina are by this artist.

III, 14. Athene. Naples was founded by Cyme (Cumae) possibly as early as 700. This coin may date from about 470. The naval battle off Cyme when Hiero beat back the Etruscans was in 474.

III, 15. Thurii was colonized by Athenians and cityless Sybarites in 443.

IV, 1. Winged Gorgon, said to be symbol of moon-goddess worship. Date about 470 probably. At Fiesole (Faesulae) there are ancient Etruscan ruins.

IV, 2. River Gelas in form of bull. For Gela see Index.

IV, 3. The river-nymph Himera sacrificing. Silenus bathing at a fountain.

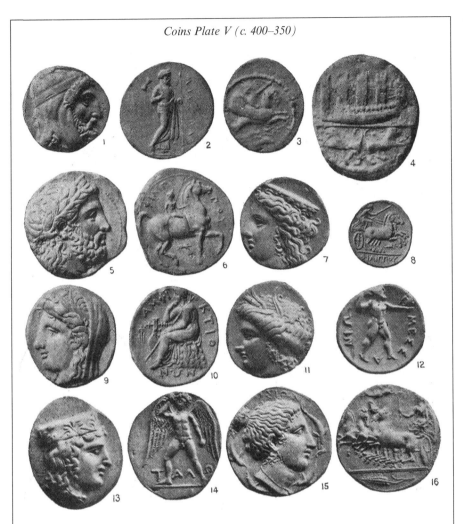

Coins Plate V (c. 400–350)

1. Colophon (?). Tissaphernes (?). c.
   400.
2. Coin of Mausolus. c. 370.
3. Tyre. c. 400.
4. Sidon. c. 375.
5 – 6. Philip II.
7. Argos. Hera head.
8. Philip II. c. 350.
9. 10. Delphi.

11 – 12. Messenia.
13. Cnossus. Hera head.
14. Phaestus. Talos.
15 – 16. Syracuse. Age of Dionysius I. c.
400.

Coins Plate VI (c. 380–300)

1 – 2. *Syracuse. El. Age of Timoleon.*
3 – 4. *Carthage. c. 380.*
5 – 6. *Cyrene. c. 380.*
7 – 8. *Coin of Alexander the Great.*
9. *Syria. Seleucus I. c. 306.*
10. *Sophytes (India).*

11. *Egypt. Alexander IV.*
12. *Ptolemy Soter. c. 306.*
13 – 14. *Rhodes. c. 304.*
15. *Tarsus. c. 323.*
16. *Sidon. c. 340.*

IV, 4. Head of Apollo and laurel-leaves. Probably by the artist of the Demareteia (IV, 6).

IV, 5. River-god Selinus sacrificing to Asclepios, whose symbol, a cock, is figured below the altar. Behind is figure of a bull (symbol of the river) and a leaf of *selinon* (wild celery). On reverse Apollo and Artemis in chariot, Apollo discharging arrows, a symbol of the plague which about 445 desolated Selinus and which Empedocles is said to have stayed – perhaps by draining a marsh.

IV, 6. A silver Demareteion, named after Gelo's wife Demarete and coined from the Carthaginian spoils (or indemnity) after the battle of Himera, 480. The head is that of Nike – possibly with a suggestion of the features of Demarete.

V, 1. A satrap, perhaps Pharnabazus or Tissaphernes. 'He wears the *tiara*, not the royal *Kidaris*' (Head). A fine example of an early non-Greek portrait-coin.

V, 2. A coin of the Carian king Mausolus, representing Zeus with sceptre and double axe (see Index under '*Labrys*').

V, 3. Melcarth, the Phoenician (especially Tyrian) sun-god and city-god (identified by the Greeks with Heracles), riding over the waves on a sea-horse and holding a bow.

V, 4. Galley before a fortified city. Below two lions (sun-god symbols).

V, 5, 6. A silver 'Philip.' Head of Zeus, perhaps from the Pheidian Zeus of Olympia. Jockey-boy on horse and holding palm-branch in commemoration of Philip's Olympic victories.

V, 7. The very fine Hera head copied from the celebrated Hera by Polycleitus at Argos (see p. 405).

V, 8. A gold 'Philip.'

V, 9, 10. Demeter and Apollo (seated on Delphic *omphalos*). Issued by Amphictionic Council after the Sacred War of 346.

V, 11, 12. Demeter and the eagle-bearing Zeus, probably copied from the statue made by Ageladas *c.* 455. But the coin must date *after* the founding of Messene in 369.

V, 14. Talos, or, as here spelt, Talon, was the bronzen giant who kept watch for Minos over the Cretan coasts, making the circuit of the island thrice daily and killing all strangers by embracing them in his red-hot arms – evidently a Moloch image.

VI, 1. Head of Zeus and legend 'Zeus Eleutherios [Liberator],' referring to the liberation of Syracuse by Timoleon.

VI, 3, 4. Female head in Phrygian-like tiara – possibly Dido, or the moon-goddess Astarte. Lion and date-palm. There are no Carthaginian coins till about 400.

VI, 5, 6. Zeus Ammon. The silphion plant (see p. 172).

VI, 7–12. See notes on Alexander's coins, see p. 492–30. Sophytes (or Sopithes) was an Indian king who submitted to Alexander and later issued coins of a Greek model. In VI, 11, the lion-skin is replaced by an elephant's scalp.

VI, 13, 14. Radiate head of Helios (sun-god), perhaps copied from the famous Colossus of Rhodes. On reverse a rose (five-petalled). Greek *rhodos* = 'a rose.'

VI, 15. Legend (in Aramaic characters), BAAL TARS (Zeus of Tarsus).

VI, 16. King (probably Artaxerxes III) in chariot. Attendant with sceptre and flask. Sidon was taken by Artaxerxes III *c.* 350.

VII. These portrait coins are mostly of late date, some of them struck in the age of the Roman emperors by Hellenic cities, which introduced portraits of their most celebrated citizens. These are sometimes imaginative, but sometimes they are doubtless taken from old types, or from old busts and statues, and on this account they are of great interest.

VII, 1. Silver coin of Ios (one of the Cyclades), where the supposed grave of Homer was shown. Some of these fine Ios coins go back to the fourth century B.C. Legend, OMHPOY (OMĒROU, of Homer).

VII, 2. Bronze coin of Priene. Legend, BIAC (BIAS).

VII, 3. Bronze coin of Mytilene. The only example; in Paris. Legend, ΠΙΤΤΑΚΟC (PITTAKOS).

VII, 4. The reverse of VII, 3. Legend, ΑΛΚΑΙΟC ΜΥΤΙΛΗΝΗ (ALKAIOS MYTILĒNĒ).

VII, 5. Coin of Teos, home of Anacreon. Legend, THIΩN (TĒIŌN, 'Of the Teans'). Probably from an early statue. On the Athenian Acropolis was one (see p. 222) side by side with that of Xanthippus, his friend, which Pericles is said to have erected. The description given of it is hardly credible, viz. that it represented him in a state of intoxication, with his clothes fallen to the ground and one sandal lost. There is a more decent picture of him on a vase in the British Museum.

VII, 6. Coin of Himera, perhaps of the second century B.C. After the destruction of Himera in 409 another town was built on the further side of the river and called Thermae. Hence the legend: ΘΕΡΜΙΤΑΝ

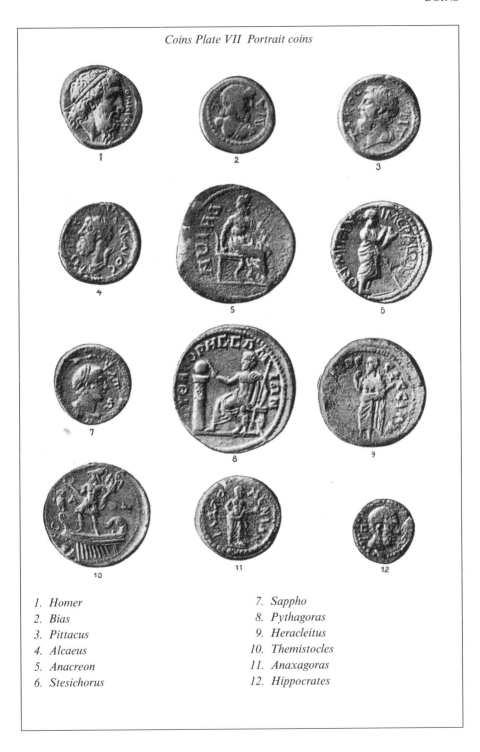

*Coins Plate VII  Portrait coins*

1.  Homer
2.  Bias
3.  Pittacus
4.  Alcaeus
5.  Anacreon
6.  Stesichorus

7.  Sappho
8.  Pythagoras
9.  Heracleitus
10. Themistocles
11. Anaxagoras
12. Hippocrates

IMEPAIΩN (THERMITAN IMERAIŌN, 'Of the Himeraean people of Thermae'). The figure of Stesichorus is evidently taken from the statue which Cicero says Verres wished to steal, and which represented Stesichorus 'leaning over a book.'

VII, 7. Coin of Mytilene. Legend, ΨΑΠ . . Ω. (PSAP . . Ō, 'Sappho'). There are numerous busts and vase-pictures of Sappho, but many very dissimilar and none trustworthy.

VII, 8. Coin of Samos. Legend, ΠΥΘΑΓΟΡΑC CAMIΩN (PYTHAGORAS SAMIŌN, 'Pythagoras of the Samians'). Column and globe.

VII, 9. Ephesian coin. Legend, . . . TOC EΦECIΩN ( . . . TOS EPHESIŌN, '. . .tos of the Ephesians') . The club in the left hand probably alludes to Heracles and the name Heracleitos.

VII, 10. Bronze Athenian coin of Roman Empire. Probably copy of some early representation of the Salamis monument. Themistocles standing on a galley and holding a wreath and a trophy.

VII, 11. Coin of Clazomenae with figure holding globe – probably Anaxagoras.

VII, 12. Coin of Cos. Legend, ΙΠ . . . (IP. . .). Numerous busts of the great physician Hippocrates exist, but none very trustworthy. This coin represents him as a very old man. He is said to have lived 104 years (460–356). Remains exist on the island of Cos of the baths, arena, temple, library, theatre, etc., connected with his famous school of medicine, which included open-air treatment and evidently also some kind of faith-healing, for fragments of prayers addressed to Asclepios have been found, and the god's 'familiars' in the shape of serpents were religiously tended by the patients. There is also to be seen a mighty plane-tree (2350 years old!) under which, it is said, Hippocrates used to sit. Dante speaks of 'supreme Hippocrates, whom nature produced for the animals that she holds most dear [*i.e.* human beings].'

## Note D

### Pottery and Vase-painting

In the List of Illustrations information will be found concerning the thirty-nine specimens of archaic pottery and Greek vases which are depicted in this volume. Here I shall add a few general remarks, and shall first note the fact that, while many of the vases of the classic era are of exquisite beauty

*Plate V An Apulian funeral amphora with volute handles*

and of inestimable value as works of art, also a fragment of common old pottery – the shard, maybe, of some ill-shaped, hand-made earthenware vessel, roughly decorated with scratches, or with artless and grotesque pictures of plants or animals or human beings, or incised perhaps with a few rudely scrawled letters – may be of very great interest, and that too not only for the antiquarian. It may have survived many a majestic work of art, many a splendid temple, many a famous city; it may have outlived the rise and fall of mighty empires; it may possess the power, as I said in reference to the inscription on little Tataia's oil-flask, to throw for us a fairy bridge across a vast abyss of time.

Of archaic pottery directly connected with Greek ceramics we have two important types – the Cretan and the Aegean, or 'Mycenaean.'

(1) Among the relics of the Neolithic Age (c. 6000–3000) are numerous fragments, excavated in Crete, of black, hand-made, unfired and undecorated pottery of the same character as the ancient Italian *bucchero*, the intensely black colour of which is supposed to have been obtained by laying charcoal and resin on the wet clay. Later relics of this age are hand-burnished and have linear incisions filled with white pigment. The 'Early Minoan' pottery (c. 3000–2000) is somewhat thick, but finely glazed and painted and often decorated with the so-called 'spiral' pattern. Many 'beaked' jugs belong to this period, towards the end of which wheel-made ware seems to appear.[1] The 'Middle Minoan' pottery (c. 2000–1500) is richly polychrome, beautiful in form and of wonderfully delicate consistency, like the finest porcelain. The decoration is both geometric and naturalistic – flowers, sea-plants, and marine animals, such as the polypus, being favourite designs. (For this and the beautiful Kamáres ware see Fig. 33 and List of Illustrations.) In the 'Late Minoan' era (c. 1500–1400), although fresco-painting, carving, metalwork, and plaster-moulding give evidence of a high degree of civilization, pottery shows manifest signs of decadence.

(2) Much archaic pottery of what is called the Mycenaean type (although it is very doubtful whether Mycenae itself was the chief, or even an important, centre of export) has been found in Rhodes and many other

---

[1] The date of the invention or introduction of the potter's wheel is much disputed. It is generally placed 'towards the end of the Bronze Age' (c. 1200?). In Cyprus and the Aegean islands all the pottery of c. 2500 to 1500 seems to be hand-made. The wheel is mentioned by Homer (*Il.* xviii. 600).

*Fig. 142  Red-figured vases and white lekythi c. 520–350*
*(See List of Illustrations and Note D)*

505

Aegean islands, in Cyprus, Egypt, and Sicily.[1] The earliest specimens resemble the Neolithic Cretan pottery, being black or monochrome, with incised lines filled with white pigment; then we find dull, lustreless colours, geometric or spiral patterns, and pot-bellied forms; then lustrous yellowish glaze, more graceful shapes, designs imitated from flowers, sea-plants, and marine animals, as in Middle and Late Minoan ware, and sometimes we have rude effigies of horses and men. (See Plate II on p.38 and Fig. 33 on p 127, and the Mycenaean 'Warrior Vase,' Fig. 8 on p. 47) A very characteristic example of the 'Mycenaean type' is the false-necked amphora shown in the plate on p. 38.

After the advent of the Dorians and the disappearance of Cretan and Mycenaean civilization there is a Dark Age in the history of Greek ceramics. Between the latest pottery of the Mycenaean type and the vases of the classic era we have little but 'Dipylon' vessels and 'Phaleron' jugs (see Chapter 2, Section A, and Fig. 35), rare specimens of exquisite pear-shaped 'proto-Corinthian' *lekythi*, of which fine examples may be seen in the British Museum, a few beautiful relics of 'Fikellura' (Samian) ware, numerous rather heavy but impressive Boeotian amphoras, some of them ornamented with carved or moulded figures, and the 'old Corinthian' ware, also rather heavy, but finely proportioned and richly decorated in a strikingly characteristic style (see Fig. 35).

Before passing on to the classic age of vase-painting it should be remarked that by far the greater number of the almost innumerable extant Greek vases of this era have been found, not in Greece, but in Italy, especially in Tuscany. From the latter half of the eighteenth century onwards many thousands have been unearthed at Vulci and Chiusi (Clusium, the city of Lars Porsena) and at Nola in Campania and on other sites of old Etruscan or South Italian cities. In 1767 great quantities of these so-called 'Etruscan vases' were brought to England by Sir W. Hamilton, and formed the nucleus of the splendid collection in the British Museum. It is not surprising that these magnificent vases were at first believed to be of Etruscan origin. The 'Etruscan theory' was stoutly maintained by most scholars of the day, and, although strongly opposed by the great German archaeologist Winckelmann, it was not finally disproved until about 1850, when the researches of Jahn and other Hellenists showed that these so-called Etruscan vases were indubitably of Greek (mostly of Attic) workmanship,

[1] The 'Hissarlik' (Trojan) type is again somewhat different. (See Fig. 33.)

and that the products of native Etruscan art were of a very different character.[1]

The question is how the presence in Etruria of such great quantities of Greek vases at such an early period is to be explained. In later times, doubtless, many imitations of Attic ceramic were produced in Italy, perhaps by Greek craftsmen, and in the third century there was a vast output of Italian vases – Apulian, Lucanian, and Campanian. But this does not explain why genuine Greek vases of the sixth and fifth centuries have been found in such great abundance in Etruscan cemeteries. The difficulty can only be solved by supposing that there was at this early age a large importation from Greece of such works of art. It will be remembered that even in the seventh century there was a very considerable emigration from Greece to the far West, and that Greek-Italian cities, such as Cyme, Sybaris, Croton, and Taras, as well as many Hellenic colonies in Sicily, rapidly became populous and wealthy, and liberally patronized the arts of the mother-country. It was doubtless through such settlements that Greek art became known to the great nation of the Tyrseni, or Etruscans, of whose powerful navy, allied to that of the Carthaginians, we have read, and who, in spite of their defeat by the Romans at Lake Regillus (498) and by Hiero at Cyme (474), continued for two centuries to be formidable for their military prowess and renowned for their riches and their luxury; and it seems unquestionable that the Tyrrhenian Lucumones (Princes) and other rich men of Etruria bought up large quantities of the finest obtainable works of Greek vase-makers. The facts, moreover, that these vases were much used for sepulchral purposes, and that the Etruscan cities were to a large extent depopulated, and their cemeteries forgotten, after the final subjugation of the country by the Romans (c. 280 B.C.), may be the reason why so many more Greek vases have been discovered in Tuscany than in Greece itself, where systematic pillage during several centuries accounts for their disappearance.

The age of classic Greek vase-painting may be divided into three

---

[1] The pottery of the ancient Etruscans (however interesting their terracotta plastique may be) seems surprisingly rude when compared with their work in gold and bronze, which is regarded as perhaps the most beautiful in existence and is eagerly copied by modern jewellers. Etruscan metalwork is said to have been largely imported into Greece in the classic era. (In *Od.* i. 184 Homer mentions Temesa, probably an Italian town, as an export-haven for bronze.) Egyptian influence is traceable in old Etrurian art, and cartouches of Psamtik I (660–610) have been found in Etruscan tombs.

periods, which, though not sharply definable chronologically, are strongly distinguished by their characteristic styles. These three periods are:

(1) That of the 'black-figure style' (*c.* 700–490).

(2) That of the 'red-figure style' (*c.* 490–350).

(3) That of the 'new' or 'beautiful' style, which degenerated into the richly ornate, florid, elaborate style of South Italian ceramic art.

In the Greek vases of the first classic period, of which the François Vase (Fig. 39) is one of the earliest extant specimens, male figures are black silhouettes on the red earthenware background. Details of the nude and the dress are given by lines incised in the black pigment. The nude of female figures is painted in a chalky white, as also are white horses, linen garments, and certain bright portions of armour. In order to represent heavy drapery the black pigment is sometimes laid on thickly and assumes a purplish or greenish tint. In other cases, where the pigment is thin, a reddish brown is produced. The black silhouette does not allow of the marvellous beauty and delicacy of outline and detail which we find in red-figure work; but these earlier vases with their naïve and realistic pictures are not seldom more valuable archaeologically and more interesting for the student of human nature than the more artistic and more idealized – sometimes more conventionalized – paintings of the later period. Fine specimens of the black-figure style are given in the plates on pp. 242 and 276, and in Figs. 55 and 56. The jar found at Daphnae, and the Greek amphora found, like the François Vase, in Etruria, are evidences of the wide influence of Attic skill in ceramics.

A fairly distinct line of demarcation between the first and second period seems to be supplied by the fact that all the vases except one found in the Marathon tomb are black-figured, whereas most of the fragments excavated on the Acropolis – relics of the sack of Athens by Xerxes – are of red-figured vases. This appears to prove that a sudden change of style took place between 490 and 480; but we must reckon here with the facts that for sepulchral purposes the old-fashioned black-figure vases were preferred long after the advent of the red-figure style, and that even in the fourth century, or later, antique black-figured vases continued to be given as prizes at the Panathenaic festivals (Fig. 55). It is likely that for a considerable time vases of both kinds were produced, and it seems certain that some celebrated craftsmen worked in both styles.[1]

---

[1] At Palermo a vase, signed by Andokides, shows on one side black and on the other red figures.

In these vases of the second classic period, the figures, which are of the natural red colour of the baked clay, are blocked out against a background of black pigment, the contours being softened by delicate incised lines, while details on the red surface are filled in with lighter shades of black. The best vases in this style are of incomparable dignity in composition and show exquisite skill in execution (see Figs. 92 and 142).

White Athenian *lekythi* (sepulchral oil-flasks) seem to have been in fashion contemporaneously with the red-figured vases. Many of them, especially earlier specimens, which present delicately outlined figures on a white ground, are exceedingly beautiful. (See Frontispiece and List of Illustrations under Fig. 142.)

Towards the end of the fourth century the simplicity, dignity, and classic repose of Greek vase-painting began to be seriously influenced by a taste for elaboration, prettiness, and dramatic affectation. In South Italy this 'new and beautiful' style struck root and flourished luxuriantly, while in the mother-country the art of vase-painting suffered a sudden decline, and by about 250 B.C. was practically extinct. Immense quantities of large and magnificently decorated vases, with elaborate paintings and with splendid mouldings and volute handles, were now manufactured in Apulia, Lucania, and Campania in order to adorn the palaces and villas of Roman nobles (see plateon p. 503 and Fig. 64). But in spite of their magnificence these vases are for the most part of no great value artistically, the paintings being weak and fantastic in composition, overcrowded with figures, and overloaded with architectural designs and trivial details.

## List of Important Dates

(See also pp. 102–3 and 177)
776. First year of first Olympiad.
743–668. First two Messenian Wars (traditional date).
*c.* 700 (750?). Pheidon of Argos.
683. List of annual Athenian archons begins.
664. Naval battle between Corinth and Corcyra.
648 (April 6). Solar eclipse mentioned by Archilochus.
*c.* 632. Cylon's attempt to seize power at Athens.
*c.* 620. Dracon's legislation.
*c.* 600. Periander tyrant of Corinth.

594. Solon's archonship.

c. 590. First 'Sacred War.'

585 (May 28). Solar eclipse during battle between Alyattes of Lydia and Astyages of Media.

560. Peisistratus seizes power.

556–540. Peisistratus is twice exiled.

540–528. Peisistratus rules Athens till his death; his sons succeed.

523. Polycrates crucified.

514. Hipparchus killed by Harmodius and Aristogeiton.

510. Hippias banished (Tarquins banished from Rome). Sybaris destroyed by Croton.

c. 510–505. Reforms of Cleisthenes.

499. The Ionic revolt.

497. Burning of Sardis.

494–3 (495–4?). Battle of Lade, and fall of Miletus.

493. Themistocles archon.

490. Battle of Marathon.

489. Death of Miltiades.

482. Ostracism of Aristides.

480. Battles of Artemisium, Thermopylae, Salamis, and Himera.

479. Battle of Plataea.

478. Capture of Sestos. Foundation of Confederacy of Delos (Athenian Empire).

474. Battle of Cyme (Italy).

472–471. Ostracism of Themistocles (d. 449).

470. Revolt of Naxos.

468. Battle of the Eurymedon.

464. Great earthquake at Sparta. Revolt of Helots.

462–460. Rise of Pericles. Cimon ostracized.

458–455. Building of the Long Walls. Athenian naval power at its height.

457–456. Aegina conquered by Athens.

446. Thirty Years' Peace between Athens and Peloponnesians.

440–439. Revolt and reduction of Samos.

438. Parthenon finished.

431–404. Peloponnesian War.

430. Outbreak of plague.

429. Pericles dies.

425. Capture of Spartans on Sphacteria.

424. Battle of Delion. Brasidas in Thrace. Thucydides banished.

421. Peace of Nicias.

418. Battle of Mantineia.

415. The Sicilian expedition.

413. The Sicilian disaster.

411–410. The Four Hundred at Athens and restoration of democracy.

406. Battle of Arginusae. Acragas destroyed by Carthaginians.

405–367. Dionysius I of Syracuse.

405. Battle of Aegospotami.

404. Athens surrenders. The Long Walls demolished. 'The Thirty.'

404–371. Spartan supremacy.

403. 'The Thirty' overthrown. Democracy restored.

401. Battle of Cunaxa.

399. Death of Socrates. Return of Xenophon.

398–360. King Agesilaus of Sparta.

395. Long Walls again begun.

394. Battles of Corinth, Cnidus, and Coroneia.

387. Peace of Antalcidas (the 'King's Peace').

386. Mantineia destroyed by Sparta.

382. Spartans seize the Theban Cadmeia.

379. Spartans expelled from Thebes by Pelopidas.

378. Second Athenian Confederacy (Empire) founded, exactly 100 years after the founding of the first.

371. Battle of Leuctra. Jason of Pherae.

371–362. Theban supremacy. Epameinondas rebuilds Mantineia and founds Messene. Pelopidas in Thessaly; he is killed at Cynoscephalae (364) and Epameinondas at Mantineia (362).

361–360. Agesilaus in Egypt; his death.

359–336. Philip II of Macedonia.

346. Peace of Philocrates. Phocians crushed. Philip president of Pythian Games.

339. Timoleon defeats the Carthaginians on the Crimisus.

338. Battle of Chaeroneia.

336. Philip assassinated.

336–323. Alexander the Great.

## Foundation of Early Greek Colonies

Cyprus has Mycenaean kings, *c.* 1400.
'Aeolian migration,' *c.* 1200.
'Ionian migration,' *c.* 1100.
Cyprus colonized by Hellenes, *c.* 1050.
Doris colonized, *c.* 900.
Cyme in Italy founded, *c.* 800 (or earlier).
Naxos, in Sicily, *c.* 735.
Catane, Himera, Syracuse, and Corcyra, *c.* 734.
Sybaris, *c.* 721.
Taras, *c.* 708.
Croton, *c.* 702.
Gela, *c.* 688.
Chalcedon, *c.* 685.
Byzantium, Sestos, Abydos, Cyzicus, *c.* 650.
Cyrene, *c.* 630.
Selinus, *c.* 610.
Massalia, *c.* 600.
Acragas, *c.* 580.

## List of the Persian Kings

Cyrus, 559 (549?)–529.
*Sardis taken*, 546. *Babylon taken*, 538.
Cambyses, 529–522.
*Egypt conquered*, 525.
The false Smerdis (usurper for seven months), 522–521.
Darius I (son of Hystaspes), 521–485.
*Thrace conquered, Scythia invaded*, 512. *Marathon*, 490.
Xerxes I, 485–465.
*Salamis*, 480.
Artabanus (usurper for seven months), 465–464.
Artaxerxes I (Longimanus), 464–425.
Xerxes II (two months), 425.
Sogdianus (seven months), 425–424.
Darius II (Ochus and Nothus), 424–405.
*Married Parysatis.*

Artaxerxes II (Mnemon), 405–359.
*Revolt of Cyrus the younger. 'Anabasis.' Cunaxa*, 401.
Artaxerxes III (Ochus), 359–338.
Arses, 338–336.
Darius III (Codomannus), 336–331.
*Conquered by Alexander at Arbela*, 331.

*Note*. Darius I was probably of the same family (Achaemenidae) as Cyrus, but was not the son of Cambyses. Sogdianus and Darius II were illegitimate brothers of Xerxes II. Darius III was a distant relative of Arses. With these exceptions and two brief-lived usurpations the crown descended from father to son.

## List of the Chief Greek Writers, Philosophers and Sculptors

*I. Poets, Historians, and Orators*
Homer.
Hesiod.
Archilochus, *fl. c.* 700.
Semonides, *fl. c.* 660.
Tyrtaeus, *c.* 660.
Stesichorus, *c.* 632–556.
Alcman, *fl. c.* 630.
Arion, *fl. c.* 625.
Alcaeus ⎱
Sappho ⎰ *fl. c.* 600.
Solon, *fl. c.* 600.
Theognis, *fl. c.* 550.
Ibycus, *fl. c.* 540.
Anacreon, *fl. c.* 530.
Simonides, *c.* 556–467.
Epicharmus, *c.* 540–450.
Aeschylus, 525–456.
Pindar, *c.* 522–442.
Sophocles, 495–406.
Herodotus, *c.* 484–426.
Euripides, 480–406.
Thucydides, 471–401.

Aristophanes, *c.* 445–380.
Xenophon, *c.* 444–350.
Isocrates, 436–338.
Demosthenes, *c.* 385–322.

*II. Philosophers*
Thales, *c.* 636–546.
Anaximander, *c.* 610–545.
Anaximenes, *fl. c.* 544.
Pythagoras, *fl. c.* 540–510.
Xenophanes, *fl. c.* 540–500.
Parmenides, *c.* 513–445.
Heracleitus, *fl. c.* 500.
Anaxagoras, *c.* 500–428.
Zeno, *c.* 488–420.
Empedocles, *c.* 480–425.
Protagoras, *c.* 480–410.
Socrates, 469–399.
Democritus, 460–361.
Plato, 428–347.
Aristotle, 384–322.

*III. Sculptors*
Ageladas, *c.* 540–455.
Antenor, *fl. c.* 500.
Calamis, *c.* 500–430.
Pheidias, *c.* 490–432.
Myron, *c.* 500–410.
Polycleitus, *c.* 480–412.
Paeonius, *fl. c.* 425 (450?).
Scopas, *fl. c.* 370.
Praxiteles, *fl. c.* 360.
Lysippus, *fl. c.* 330.

# *Index*

Page nos. in italics are illustrations. To save space, page ranges (e.g., 13–17) are used where discussion is broken by an illustration, as well as for a series of references. Concepts, mythical characters and later commentators are in general not indexed. Notes (e.g., 39n.2) are indexed only when they contain matter not signposted in the text. Dates are BC, unless specified.

515

Instead of life dates (525–456) or reign, year of birth (b.), death (d.) or activity (*fl.*) may be given.

b. = born          *c.* = *circa*          d. = died          *fl.* = *floruit*          *r.* = *regnat*

Instead of life dates (525–456) or reign, year of birth (b.), death (d.) or activity (*fl.*) may be given.

b. = born        c. = *circa*        d. = died        *fl.* = *floruit*        *r.* = *regnat*

Instead of life dates (525–456) or reign, year of birth (b.), death (d.) or activity (*fl.*) may be given.

b. = born     *c.* = *circa*     d. = died     *fl.* = *floruit*     *r.* = *regnat*

Instead of life dates (525–456) or reign, year of birth (b.), death (d.) or activity (*fl.*) may be given.

b. = born      *c.* = *circa*      d. = died      *fl.* = *floruit*      *r.* = *regnat*

Instead of life dates (525–456) or reign, year of birth (b.), death (d.) or activity (*fl.*) may be given.

b. = born    *c. = circa*    d. = died    *fl. = floruit*    *r. = regnat*

Instead of life dates (525–456) or reign, year of birth (b.), death (d.) or activity (*fl.*) may be given.

b. = born        *c.* = *circa*        d. = died        *fl.* = *floruit*        *r.* = *regnat*

Instead of life dates (525–456) or reign, year of birth (b.), death (d.) or activity (*fl.*) may be given.

b. = born      *c.* = *circa*      d. = died      *fl.* = *floruit*      *r.* = *regnat*

Instead of life dates (525–456) or reign, year of birth (b.), death (d.) or activity (*fl.*) may be given.

b. = born          c. = *circa*          d. = died          *fl.* = *floruit*          r. = *regnat*

Instead of life dates (525–456) or reign, year of birth (b.), death (d.) or activity (*fl.*) may be given.

b. = born          c. = circa          d. = died          *fl.* = *floruit*          *r.* = *regnat*

Instead of life dates (525–456) or reign, year of birth (b.), death (d.) or activity (*fl.*) may be given.

b. = born        *c.* = *circa*        d. = died        *fl.* = *floruit*        *r.* = *regnat*

Instead of life dates (525–456) or reign, year of birth (b.), death (d.) or activity (*fl.*) may be given.

b. = born    *c. = circa*    d. = died    *fl. = floruit*    *r. = regnat*

Instead of life dates (525–456) or reign, year of birth (b.), death (d.) or activity (*fl.*) may be given.

b. = born          c. = circa          d. = died          *fl.* = *floruit*          *r.* = *regnat*

Instead of life dates (525–456) or reign, year of birth (b.), death (d.) or activity (*fl.*) may be given.

Index written by
Gerard M–F Hill, 2003

b. = born          *c.* = *circa*          d. = died          *fl.* = *floruit*          *r.* = *regnat*